Norbert Pohlmann | Helmut Reimer | Wolfgang Schneider (Eds.)

ISSE 2008 Securing Electronic Business Processes

From Enterprise Architecture to IT Governance
by Klaus D. Niemann

Understanding MP3
by Martin Ruckert

Process Modeling with ARIS
by Heinrich Seidlmeier

Microsoft Dynamics NAV
by Paul M. Diffenderfer and Samir El-Assal

www.viewegteubner.de

Norbert Pohlmann | Helmut Reimer |
Wolfgang Schneider (Eds.)

ISSE 2008
Securing Electronic
Business Processes

Highlights of the Information Security Solutions
Europe 2008 Conference

With 128 illustrations

**VIEWEG+
TEUBNER**

Bibliographic information published by the Deutsche Nationalbibliothek
The Deutsche Nationalbibliothek lists this publication in the Deutsche Nationalbibliografie;
detailed bibliographic data are available in the Internet at http://dnb.d-nb.de.

Many of designations used by manufacturers and sellers to distinguish their products are claimed as trademarks.

The editors are grateful to Professor Dr. Patrick Horster for granting permission to use his layout for the following contributions.

1st Edition 2009

Editorial Office: Sybille Thelen | Walburga Himmel

Vieweg+Teubner is part of the specialist publishing group Springer Science+Business Media.
www.viewegteubner.de

Cover design: KünkelLopka Medienentwicklung, Heidelberg
Typesetting: Oliver Reimer, Ilmenau
Printing company: MercedesDruck, Berlin
Printed on acid-free paper
Printed in Germany

ISBN 978-3-8348-0660-4

Contents

Web 2.0 Security and Large Scale Public Applications ___ 195

Preface

Dear Readers,

ENISA is proud to be co-organising the Information Security Solutions Europe Conference 2008 (ISSE) together with eema, TeleTrusT
and INTECO. the Spanish National Institute of Communication
Technologies, in its tenth year..

The aim of the ISSE has always been to support the development of a
European information security culture and especially a cross-border
framework for trustworthy IT applications for citizens, industry and
administration. ISSE is renowned for its rich content perspective,
designed to inform ICT professionals, policy makers and industry
leaders on latest developments in technology and best practices. Also
ENISA is highly committed to these goals. For this reason we are
delighted to support the ISSE again this year. In our work we assist
and advise the European Commission, Member States, and business
community in the field of network and information security., The security of communication networks
and information systems is of increasing concern. In order to face today's complex information security challenges it is clear that working together is the key to generating new strategies to address these
problems. It has been an inspiring opportunity to facilitate this collaboration at the ISSE 2008, bringing
together the wealth of industry knowledge, information and research that we hold in Europe, as well as
across the globe.

The success of this event is based on the unparalled composition of, government, academia and other
stakeholders, generating ideas and participating in a frank, lively policy and technical debate in an non
commercial context. By sharing different perspectives, experiences and solutions around the complex
topics of IT security, the independent and varied nature of the programme guarantees interesting results.
This year, we are focusing on highly interesting, cutting edge security and related issues, like costs of
ownership, risk management and interoperability, which were all selected by worldwide specialists in
the field.

Some of the key topics explored at this year's conference have been chosen as the basis for this book,
which serves as an invaluable reference point for anyone involved in the IT security industry.

We hope that you will find it a out of the ordinary, fascinating and motivating read.

Andrea Pirotti, Executive Director, ENISA

About this Book

The Information Security Solutions Europe Conference (ISSE) was started in 1999 by eema and TeleTrusT with the support of the European Commission and the German Federal Ministry of Technology and Economics. Today the annual conference is a fixed event in every IT security professional's calendar.

The integration of security in IT applications was initially driven only by the actual security issues considered important by experts in the field; currently, however, the economic aspects of the corresponding solutions are the most important factor in deciding their success. ISSE offers a suitable podium for the discussion of the relationship between these considerations and for the presentation of the practical implementation of concepts with their technical, organisational and economic parameters.

From the beginning ISSE has been carefully prepared. The organisers succeeded in giving the conference a profile that combines a scientifically sophisticated and interdisciplinary discussion of IT security solutions while presenting pragmatic approaches for overcoming current IT security problems.

An enduring documentation of the presentations given at the conference which is available to every interested person thus became important. This year sees the publication of the sixth ISSE book – another mark of the event's success – and with about 40 carefully edited papers it bears witness to the quality of the conference.

An international programme committee is responsible for the selection of the conference contributions and the composition of the programme:

- **Ronny Bjones**, Microsoft (Belgium)
- **Gunter Bitz**, SAP (Germany)
- **Lucas Cardholm**, Ernst&Young (Sweden)
- **Roger Dean**, eema (United Kingdom)
- **Ronald De Bruin**, ENISA (Greece)
- **Jan De Clercq**, HP (Belgium)
- **Marijke De Soete**, NXP Semiconductors (Belgium)
- **Jos Dumortier**, KU Leuven (Belgium)
- **Walter Fumy**, Siemens (Germany)
- **Michael Hange**, BSI (Germany)
- **John Hermans**, KPMG (The Netherlands)
- **Marcos Gómez Hidalgo**, INTECO (Spain)
- **Jeremy Hilton**, Cardiff University (United Kingdom)
- **Francisco Jordan**, Safelayer (Spain)
- **Frank Jorissen**, SafeBoot (Belgium)

- **Matt Landrock**, Cryptomathic (Denmark)
- **Jorge Chinea López**, INTECO (Spain)
- **Madeleine McLaggan-van Roon**, Dutch Data Protection Authority (The Netherlands)
- **Tim Mertens**, ENISA (Greece)
- **Norbert Pohlmann**, University of Applied Sciences Gelsenkirchen, Chairman of the Programme Committee (Germany)
- **Bart Preneel**, KU Leuven (Belgium)
- **Helmut Reimer**, TeleTrusT (Germany)
- **Joachim Rieß**, Daimler (Germany)
- **Paolo Rossini**, TELSY, Telecom Italia Group (Italy)
- **Wolfgang Schneider**, Fraunhofer Institute SIT (Germany)
- **Jon Shamah**, CoreStreet (United Kingdom)
- **Robert Temple**, BT (United Kingdom)
- **Arie van Bellen**, ECP.NL (The Netherlands)

The editors have endeavoured to allocate the contributions in these proceedings – which differ from the structure of the conference programme – to topic areas which cover the interests of the readers.

Norbert Pohlmann   *Helmut Reimer*   *Wolfgang Schneider*

---

eema (www.eema.org):

For 21 years, eema has been Europe's leading independent, non-profit e-Identity & Security association, working with its European members, governmental bodies, standards organisations and interoperability initiatives throughout Europe to further e-Business and legislation.

eema's remit is to educate and inform around over 1,500 Member contacts on the latest developments and technologies, at the same time enabling Members of the association to compare and exchange views and ideas. The work produced by the association with its Members (projects, papers, seminars, tutorials and reports etc) is funded by both membership subscriptions and revenue generated through events. All of the information generated by eema and its members is available to other members free of charge.

Examples of papers produced recently are:- Towards Understanding Identity, Spam and e-mail Abuse Management, Role based Access Control – A User Guide, Password Synchronisation, Secure messaging within and between User Organisations. eema members, based on a requirement from the rest of the Membership, contributed all of these papers. Some are the result of many months' work, and form part of a larger project on the subject.

Any organisation involved in e-Identity or Security (usually of a global or European nature) can become a Member of eema, and any employee of that organisation is then able to participate in eema activities. Examples of organisations taking advantage of eema membership are Unilever, Volvo, Shell, Hoffman la Roche, KPMG, Magyar Telecom Rt, National Communications Authority, Hungary, Microsoft, HP, and the Norwegian Government Administration Services to name but a few.

Visit www.eema.org for more information or contact the association on +44 1386 793028 or at info@eema.org

TeleTrusT Deutschland e.V. (www.teletrust.de)

TeleTrusT Deutschland e.V. was founded in 1989 as a non profit association promoting the trustworthiness of information and communication technology in open systems environments. Today, TeleTrusT counts more than 80 institutional members. Within the last 19 years TeleTrusT evolved to a well known and highly regarded competence network for applied cryptography and biometrics.

In the various working groups of TeleTrusT ICT-security experts, users and interested parties meet each other in frequent workshops, round-tables and expert talks. The activities focus on reliable and trustworthy solutions complying with international standards, laws and statutory requirements. TeleTrusT is keen to promote the acceptance of solutions supporting identification, authentification and signature (IAS) schemes in the electronic business and its processes.

TeleTrusT facilitates the information and knowledge exchange between vendors, users and authorities. Subsequently, innovative ICT-security solutions can enter the market more quickly and effectively. TeleTrusT aims on standard compliant solutions in an interoperable scheme.

Keeping in mind the raising importance of the European security market, TeleTrusT seeks the co-operation with European organisations and authorities with similar objectives. Thus, the European Security Conference ISSE is being organised in collaboration with eema, ENISA and INTECO this year.

Contact:
Dr. Günther Welsch
Managing Director of TeleTrusT Deutschland e.V.
guenther.welsch@teletrust.de

Welcome

It is an honour for us to co-organise and host the ISSE 2008 Conference in Madrid (Spain).

INTECO

Since 2004, the Spanish government, through the Plan Avanza (www.planavanza.es) [an initiative for the development of the Information Society], has worked to promote and to foster the Information Society, the Knowledge Society and Information Technologies, paying special attention to e-government and in-formation security, increasing the security levels of companies,

Instituto Nacional
de Tecnologías
de la Comunicación

administrations and citizens, and promoting the safety culture and acceptable levels of awareness re-garding information security.

The penetration of information technologies and the Internet in Spain reaches levels significantly above the average of other similar countries, this year exceeding 22 million internauts and over 80% of companies connected to the Internet. Mechanisms, such as the creation of the digital identity through the Spanish National Electronic Identity Card (DNI-e) – which contains more than 500 services for e-government, e-commerce and e-banking –, or the reactive and preventive attention especially paid to information security incidents in all fields, act as a lever and support for an adequate development of the Information Society.

The inclusion of all sectors in the Information Society is vital to maintain a healthy and competitive economy. The introduction of such a necessary component of information security, allowing a reliable development and a sustainable maintenance, is vital.

ISSE 2008 will serve as an incomparable scenario to deal with the work of the organisations, industry and current and future trends in information security.

We hope that the topics discussed during the event will serve as a reference for the work of the organisa-tions, industry and countries involved and that they will provide a forward-looking perspective that will strengthen the efforts constantly being made in the field of Information Society.

Instituto Nacional de Tecnologías de la Comunicación
(National Institute of Communication Technologies)

Secretaría de Estado de Telecomunicaciones y para la Sociedad de la Información
(State Secretariat for Telecommunications and the Information Society)

Ministerio de Industria Turismo y Comercio
(Ministry of Industry, Tourism and Trade)

Security
Management
and Economics
of Security

The Information Security Framework for Daimler Financial Services and its Implementation

Lenka Fibikova · Roland Müller

Daimler Financial Services AG, ITF Information Security
Epplestraße 225, 70546 Stuttgart
{lenka.fibikova | roland.g.mueller}@daimler.com

Abstract

In 2003, the Board of Management of Daimler Financial Services initiated a 3-year project to establish an information security management system (ISMS) within its organization including all (at that time 43) subsidiaries worldwide. In this article, we describe the setup of the ISMS and demonstrate how this setup allowed extending the scope of the ISMS to entities outside of the financial services market.

1 Legal Requirements for Financial Services Providers

Daimler Financial Services provides financial services in the automotive area in 43 countries on five continents. The portfolio includes financing, leasing, fleet management, insurance brokerage services and structured finance services. These services have to comply with applicable law in all markets and countries. The applicable legal requirements can be structured as follows:

- Risk control legislation,
- Data protection legislation, and
- Legislation fighting organized crime and terrorism.

The following paragraphs will explain what implications each of these legal directives may cause for a corporation especially in the area of information security.

1.1 Risk Control Legislation

Risk Control legislation has always been important for financial institutions, for its primary goal is the protection of customers' money. Almost all countries have regulated the financial market in order to protect customers and avoid bankruptcies caused by poor business execution. However, it gained momentum in the last decade caused by criminal activities in major corporations outside of the financial market. Bankruptcies of large enterprises like Enron and WorldCom led to more rigid legislation to avoid similar misbehaviors. The U.S. Sarbanes-Oxley Act [SOA02] is the most known example resulting from these acts; Basel II [BAS04] is a world-wide accepted and more structured approach for the financial area.

Risk control legislation requires companies to sufficiently evaluate any risk it may face and develop adequate strategies to control the identified risks, may they be financial or non-financial. With respect to information security, integrity of financial information and business continuity are major areas to be taken into account.

1.2 Data Protection Legislation

Data protection plays an important role in Europe but becomes also more significant in the U.S. and Asia Pacific. Examples of this kind of legislation are the European directive on Data Protection 96/46/EC [EU96], the various national European privacy acts and the U.S. Gramm-Leach-Bliley Act [GLB99].

The intention of this legislation is the protection of personal information processed by companies. For financial services this targets on protecting customer information and avoiding any disclosure or other use without the customers' official consent.

With respect to information security, this legislation requires companies to protect customer data and to provide methods and processes that prohibit misuse and disclosure.

1.3 Legislation Fighting Organized Crime and Terrorism

This legislation, also known as money laundering legislation, can be seen as a contradiction to the data protection legislation for it requires companies to disclose those customers who are assumed to misuse financial transactions for laundering money gained by criminal acts. In light of terrorism, this legislation was amended to include money transfers with terrorist organizations. There are many countries addressing this topic in their legislation; an example of this on the national level is the German Anti-Money-Laundering Law [GWG93]. The United Nations addresses this topic by a program fighting money laundering and countering the financing of terrorism.

For information security, this requires processes to supervise money flow and customer clearance and rating procedures.

2 The Decision to Use an International Standard

Due to the fact that the various entities of Daimler Financial Services had no common understanding of information security nor had they followed any central initiative in the past, the IT management of Daimler Financial Services decided to make use of an internationally accepted approach. Various standards were taken into account:

- NIST Special Publication Series 800 [NIST800],
- German Information Security Agency's Baseline Security Handbook [BSI03],
- ISO/IEC 13335 Guidelines for the management of IT security [ISO13335], and
- ISO/IEC 27002 Code of practice for information security management, at that time known as ISO/IEC 17799 [ISO17799].

2.1 NIST Special Publication Series

The National Institute of Standards and Technology, an institute governed by the U.S. Department of Commerce, provides a lot of guidance material on how to establish information security. However, their primary target is the federal administration of the United States and this restricts the usability of their publications. On the other hand, the material provided is kept up-to date and offers valuable input for various areas of information security. The documents on business continuity, on the installation of an awareness program for employees and technical material on how to protect an infrastructure are a substantial help for any organization dealing with information security.

2.2 German Baseline Security Handbook

The German Baseline Security Handbook follows a similar approach in primarily targeting the German federal administration. Their stronghold is the technical guidance, but they lack management guidance. In addition, due to their concentration on technical issues, they bear the risk of becoming outdated.

2.3 ISO/IEC 13335 Guidelines for the Management of IT Security

The guidelines for the management of IT security published by ISO/IEC during the second half of the last decade are strongly focusing on managerial tasks with respect to information security. Topics like the implementation of an information security organization, responsibilities and awareness are sufficiently well specified to enable an organization in fulfilling its tasks. In addition, risk management is described in a way to establish it without strictly following only one methodology. Finally, guidance is provided how technical issues like those offered in the NIST series or by the German Information Security Agency can be used to complement the series of standards. On the other hand, this standard series becomes less important with the progressing development of the 27000 family of standards.

2.4 ISO/IEC 27002 Code of Practice for Information Security Management

The final candidate was the ISO/IEC 27002, at that time known as ISO/IEC 17799. It was originally derived of the British Standard BS 7799 and tries to cover the technical and the managerial aspects of information security within one document. Although it is not the perfect fit, it offers the best solution for international corporations by its broad orientation. Its areas of control range from policies as the fundament of information security management to compliance with internal regulations and applicable law. Its weaknesses come from excluding risk management from the standard, but it tries to overcome these weaknesses by postulating risk management as a prerequisite. Its specific advantage is that it allows an evaluation of the status of information security on a high level, which executive management prefers.

2.5 Summary

Table 1 summarizes features of the above mentioned information security guidance approaches. Daimler Financial Services decided to focus on ISO/IEC 17799 being aware of the fact that the version from 2000 was to be revised within a few years.

Table 1: Information Security Guidelines

	NIST Special Publications 800-x	BSI Baseline Security Handbook	ISO/IEC 13335 Security Guidelines	ISO/IEC 17799 Code of Practice
Audience	Technical and management	Primarily technical	Management	Management and technical
Content	Technical and management oriented	Primarily technical oriented	Management oriented	Primarily management oriented
Completeness	High	Technically high	Management aspects high	Management aspects high
Software Support	Only few	Quite good	Not	Good
Pros/Cons	Very good quality of information	Good quality, not always up to date	Too extensive and sometimes poor quality	Good quality but requires additional guidance on technical level

3 Initial Information Security Status Evaluation

In order to map the existing status of information security in the organization, the Corporate Information Security Officer initiated an initial information security assessment in all entities of Financial Services. Since it was impossible to visit all 43 entities within a short time, the evaluation was based on a self-assessment conducted at all entities, complemented by on-site assessments, remote penetration testing and on-site technical evaluations at selected entities that helped to verify the plausibility of the results from the self-assessments. The initial status evaluation was conducted within three months.

3.1 Self-assessment

The self-assessment was based on an Excel based questionnaire consisting of more than 200 questions derived out of the ISO/IEC 17799:2000 standard. All ten security control areas of the standard[1] were covered to obtain a comprehensive status of the corporation's information security. Due to the fact that the portfolio of the various entities of the group differed, not each question was relevant for each entity; therefore any question could be answered by one out of four different answers: yes, no, partial, not applicable. The filled-out questionnaires built the basis for the next step – the identification of the appropriate actions on the corporate level as well as locally.

3.2 On-site Assessment

The on-site assessments were intended to verify the results from the self-assessment questionnaire. During the on-site assessment all areas of the questionnaire – the ten security control areas of the ISO standard – were evaluated. This way, information security did not only focus on those topics where IT is mostly involved, but especially on the areas where other departments (e.g., legal department, human resources) were in the lead. During the on-site assessment, all relevant departments were interviewed and each answer was confirmed by evidence. The outcome showed that the entities conducted the self-assessments diligently; deviations were primarily caused by misinterpretations of specific questions. In summary, six entities on three continents were visited and had to undergo an on-site assessment.

---

1 ISO/IEC 17799 (2000) consisted of 10 control areas; the version of 2005 added incident management as an additional control area.

3.3 Remote Penetration Testing

The remote penetration testing served as an evidence to show with restricted efforts how secure an entity was doing its business via the Internet. Due to the fact that it only concentrated on technical issues, the results were used to either confirm the proper setup of Internet connection or request immediate actions in order to protect the entity. However, it provided a well accepted method to quickly verify information security weaknesses. The remote penetration testing was conducted at four locations on three continents.

3.4 On-site Technical Evaluation

The final component, the on-site technical evaluation, was intended to identify existing vulnerabilities within the infrastructure, independently on whether accessible via the Internet or internally. This evaluation helped in closing security gaps on the border gateway, on server configurations and on workstation set ups. The on-site technical evaluation was performed at four locations on two continents.

3.5 Summary

In summary, all four assessment types helped to get an accurate information security status, but also allowed to close eminent holes at once. The selected entities covered all five continents where Daimler Financial Services was conducting business. The on-site activities and the penetration testing were conducted by an external service provider to generate an unbiased result.

Results from the evaluation were compared to a best practice benchmark in the financial sector (a Swiss financial services corporation acting globally). It clearly showed that Daimler Financial Services had to increase its efforts in that area.

4 Setting up the Goals

Knowing the legislative environment, in which Daimler Financial Services existed, selecting the ISO/ IEC 17799 as the basis for the implementation of the ISMS, and having documented the current information security status of Daimler Financial Services, the SAFE (Secure Applications – Fortify the Enterprise) Project was approved by the Board of Management and started in spring of 2004. The main goals of the SAFE Project were to

- Set up an information security organization within Daimler Financial Services that would enable an efficient and effective implementation of the ISMS at the local entities.
- Provide a framework, processes, tools and guidance to achieve adequate and uniform information security at all entities.
- Achieve 90% compliance with the ISO standard.

5 Information Security Organization

As the first step of the SAFE Project, an information security organization was set up. At every entity a local information security officer (LISO) was appointed. Large entities were able to assign this role to one dedicated person, in smaller (most) companies the role of the LISO was assigned to an existing function, usually the CIO. The task of the LISO is to play the role of the point of contact for information security at the entity. This includes implementation of information security measures, supporting the local departments, and communication of problems to the Corporate Information Security Officer. Additionally, the LISO chairs the Local Information Security Forum consisting of representatives of local IT and business functions, and representatives from the HR, legal and facility management departments. This forum is the local communication platform for discussing information security problems of all participating entities and developing local initiatives to improve the situation.

Coordinating the local activities, we had to take into account that our LISOs were located in almost all time zones. Therefore, we grouped them in regions and to each region a Regional Information Security Officer (RISO) was assigned. The tasks of the RISOs varied in different regions – in some regions the RISO was just an interface to the regional IT management with respect to information security, in other regions the RISO was also supporting LISO in their information security tasks. The communication of global activities from Corporate Information Security to LISOs and local problems from LISOs to Corporate Information Security was direct.

6 Derivation of Activities

The results of the initial assessments were evaluated and offered a comprehensive picture of the information security status within Daimler Financial Services. These results were presented to the board of management. Figure 1 shows the original graphical representation covering the control clauses[2] of the ISO/IEC 17799:2000 standard.

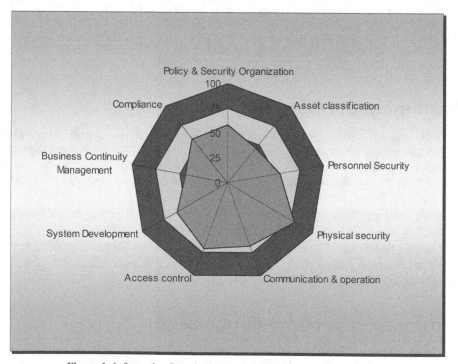

Figure 1: Information Security Status Graph aligned to ISO 17799:2000

---

2   In this representation, the first two control areas were combined into Policy & Security Organization covering the clauses on Information Security Policy and on Information Security Organization.

In general, almost all entities were actively supporting information security, but the outcome was not sufficient for an enterprise that considers itself as being a benchmark in its market. Those control clauses where technology plays a major role, were usually executed quite well, while other areas were lacking.

To achieve a fast improvement, the Corporate Information Security organized the results into two domains: weaknesses requiring local initiatives and those demanding a corporate-wide approach.

6.1 Corporate-wide Activities

The results clearly pointed out that some areas of information security crucial for practicing information security had not been sufficiently considered at the entities. These areas were identified and work steams were set up to improve the status.

6.1.1 Risk Management

Neither a common methodology nor processes and guidelines existed to conduct risk management with a focus on information security. Due to the fact that risk management was identified as a prerequisite for establishing an ISMS within an enterprise, this work stream had to provide a process, a methodology and tools for conducting risk management at Daimler Financial Services with a focus on practicability.

6.1.2 Information Security Policy Development and Adoption

Policies build the basis of the ISMS, for they define the goals and enforce appropriate measures to achieve those goals. As a start, a Corporate Information Security Policy was developed and signed by the board of management outlining the goals and principles how information security should be established within Daimler Financial Services. In addition, processes were required to guarantee that business and administration functions were involved in the policy development process. Finally, policies had to be developed in order to request appropriate requirements and increase information security at all entities.

6.1.3 Education and Awareness

This work stream was directed to address various groups involved in information security processes. The larger and most important group was the group of business users. Additionally, management, IT administration (user help desk, network, and system and application administration) and software developers were considered. The goal was to make them aware what threats the organization is facing and how they may counter them.

6.1.4 Asset Classification

An important prerequisite for directing information security initiatives is the classification of all assets. This work stream delivered a methodology and processes that helped business to classify its information assets properly enabling to derive appropriate measures for protecting them.

6.1.5 Tool Provision

In order to equip all entities with adequate tools, this work package concentrated on identifying information security tools for detecting vulnerabilities and improving the security status of the infrastructure. The identified tools were to be evaluated and properly configured to ease their use.

6.1.6 Business Continuity

This work stream was intended to provide a framework for developing business continuity plans. A process was developed and supported by various templates giving advice to management in taking the required steps to prepare for emergencies.

6.1.7 Incident Management

In order to deal with an incident – this may be a virus, a hacking attack or even computer theft – a process was required that allowed classifying the incident and initiating appropriate measures.

6.1.8 Monitoring and Reporting

Due to the fact that Daimler Financial Services consists of many entities distributed across five continents an important task was the recording of progress and the identification of areas for support. This task had to be supported by a monitoring and reporting process which is applicable to all entities and does not put too much burden on the respective management.

6.1.9 BS 7799 Certification:

The final proof for entities within Daimler Financial Services for achieving compliance with the ISO standard was certification according to the British Standard BS 7799-2 [BS7799b] whose part 1 was identical with ISO/IEC 17799:2000. This part was intended to be transferred into another ISO standard which would provide certification for organizations [ISO27001]. The certification was intended for those entities that were providing IT services to other Daimler Financial Services companies, since the certification would demonstrate its professional services.

6.1.10   Core Project Team

All the above-mentioned work streams were set up globally and were directed by work stream leaders from different entities of Daimler Financial Services. In addition, a core team of LISOs from the most important entities was established to support the project and promote it in their regions. The work stream leaders and the core LISO team were supposed to meet at least twice a year to ensure a common information basis.

In order to sufficiently integrate all entities, appropriate communication was established between all involved entities. This communication consisted of regular workshops where all major entities were participating and of regular telephone conferences. The workshops were intended to explain in detail all results and the telephone conferences should establish an ongoing communication between the workshops. In keeping the communication efforts successful and simple, the workshop participants were the core LISO team members, who should then carry the information to their neighbor entities.

6.2 Local Activities

In addition to the global activities, the assessment had identified a lot of other activities specific to the individual entities that needed to be taken care of locally. These activities were local for various reasons:
- they had to be aligned to the local infrastructure;
- they had to comply with regional and local law;
- they were aligned with local processes, or
- they required specific cultural refinement.

For such activities, each entity received an action plan containing the identified local deficiencies. Each IT manager was requested to provide information how and when he intended to work on these weaknesses and who would be responsible for executing the identified task.

With respect to budget, every entity was requested to plan for mitigating identified risks in fulfilling compliance with the ISO standard. In addition, information security was included into the target agreements of the IT managers for the upcoming years. This way it was assured that local management was strongly involved in information security.

7 First Results and Approach Optimization

By the end of the first year, an additional assessment was conducted with an identical setup as the initial evaluation, i.e. the four types of assessments introduced in Section 3 were performed. This time, different entities were evaluated to complement the picture of the first assessment.

In general, all entities had achieved progress, some only on a minor level, and some with remarkable results. Progress ranged from two percent to more than 140 percent. A few entities achieved slightly worse results, which was usually caused by misinterpretations of specific questions that we experienced also during the initial evaluation (see also Section 3.2).

Each country that was identified to be behind expected results was assessed by the Corporate Information Security Officer that conducted an additional gap analysis. This gap analysis concentrated on those topics that were reported to be not in compliance.

After evaluation of the first results, the project team decided to modify its approach: in order to prioritize the local tasks and increase general progress, annual information security goals were defined for each entity. In addition, a support process was initiated to help the various countries in achieving their annual goals. More tools and guidance support were necessary. Optimization of the evaluation and reporting was also unavoidable, since regular evaluation using a questionnaire consisting of more than 200 questions placed a significant burden on the LISOs.

8 The ISMS Portal

The first two self-assessments (in 2003 and 2004) had been supported by an Excel tool containing ten questionnaire sheets, each covering one chapter of the ISO/IEC 17799:2000 standard, and a summary sheet evaluating the provided input/answers and presenting them in a form easily understandable by management (see also Figure 1). As stated previously, the questionnaire consisted of 225 questions that could be answered by selecting one of four alternatives: 'yes', 'no', 'partial' and 'not applicable'. We soon experienced the disadvantages of the approach:

- The Excel Sheet tool was not able to signal questions that had not been answered (often since the LISOs needed to get some feedback from another department and forgot the question later) and questions where two or more alternatives were selected (e.g., 'yes' and 'partial'). This led to incorrectness in the results. Another problem with the same consequences was wrongly selecting the answer 'not applicable' where 'no' would have been the right answer. Spot checks showed that there was just a small fraction of such answers and those could not significantly influence the correctness of the overall result, but we wanted to avoid such cases as far as possible in order to get as good results as possible.

- Many questions were too complex to be answered by the LISOs with 'yes' or 'no' and therefore the 'partial' answer was necessary. However, there was no common understanding among LISOs what 'partial' actually means, thus the comparability of the results between entities was questionable. Anyway, every 'partial' indicated that there was some need for action, and therefore these results had considerable value for determining the necessary activities.

- One of the challenges of the project was to measure the improvement achieved to be able to present the effectiveness of the project to the management. However, to be able to repeatedly get plausible results, it was necessary that the LISOs fill out the questionnaire again and again. This would have meant a considerable work-load additionally to the existing tasks of the LISOs, running the local IT and improving the information security status at their entities. For small entities where the whole IT team consisted of a staff of two to three people, it was unbearable.

- For every measurement, one Excel sheet per entity had to be filled out. The Excel sheet was designed in such a way that the results for each entity could be presented in a nice and understandable way. However, consolidation of results from the individual entities to results for the whole company and identification of common deficiencies required inconsiderable manual work. Since we wanted to regularly measure our improvement, this meant a non-negligible work load.

Considering all the above-mentioned facts, it was clear that the Excel sheet was not the best tool for continuous assessment purposes. The challenge was to find a suitable solution that would fulfill at least the following conditions:

- It would be flexible enough to define new questionnaires – in the year 2005 the new ISO standard was about to be issued and we also considered defining different questionnaires covering some special topics and also different questionnaires for entities of different sizes.

- It would be easy to use and update the results, at best after implementation of every measure.

- It would allow for different roles, at least differentiating a role being able to update the results for assigned entity/entities (the LISO role) and a role having only a reading access (RISO, the SAFE team).

- It would enable us to consolidate the results on the regional basis and globally, and create various reports.

Unfortunately there was no commercial software on the market that was able to fulfill these minimum requirements. Therefore, in the middle of 2005 the decision was made to develop our own application, with the two pre-conditions that it must already be available for the assessment at the end of the year and it would be based on the new ISO 17799:2005 standard. Additionally, based on our previous experiences we wanted to establish and formalize a simple process that would encompass all activities for continuous improvement in an efficient and transparent way. Thus, within the Monitoring and Reporting work stream a new project was set up with the following goals:

- a tool that would allow for an easy definition and modification of questionnaires, easy handling for the LISOs, easy evaluation of results on different regional levels and easy tracking of the results;

- an exhaustive questionnaire that would cover all aspects of information security as defined in the ISO/IEC 17799:2005 (by now known as ISO/IEC 27002) standard – sufficiently detailed to be easily answered by the LISOs, but not too extensive to be transparent to everyone involved in the measurement; and

- processes that would clearly define how the information security goals should be achieved, evaluated, verified and communicated using one tool and (at the beginning) one common questionnaire for all entities of the organization.

8.1 Aspect 1: Tool

The tool was supposed to be our basis for all measuring and reporting activities concerning information security at Daimler Financial Services. Therefore the tool was supposed to fulfill two main requirements:

- To provide all levels of management (Daimler Financial Services management, Corporate Information Security, regional IT management, local IT management) with a measurement tool that would provide individual as well as consolidated results at any time
- To provide the LISOs with a tool that would guide them about what they need to do in order to achieve a reasonable information security status at their entity.

It was also supposed to model the hierarchical structure of the introduced information security organization by implementing five roles:

- SAFE Team being allowed to create and modify the questionnaires and see all entered results;
- LISOs: being able to complete the questionnaires that were assigned to their entities;
- RISOs: having just a supervising function being able to see all results within their regions, but not being able to intervene in the assessment process;
- Manager: an external function to the SAFE Project being able to download some pre-defined reports.;

Additionally to those four roles a role of an assessor has been defined. The reason was that we used external assessors for the on-site assessments and therefore we needed a role having restricted access rights to the answer sheets for the duration of on-site assessments.

8.1.1 The Questionnaire

After three months of rapid prototyping implementation we had a new tool available that we could use for the assessment although with some limitations. The tool was able to create any hierarchical structure of regions, sub-regions and entities and create any number of questionnaires with chapters, sections and controls containing questions of three possible types

- Simple yes-no questions where the 'yes' answer indicated implementation of a particular measure,
- Check-box questions where a positive answer to all the check-boxes was required to get the measure fully implemented (completeness of the implementation), and
- Radio-button questions where the individual answer items indicated a level of implementation (maturity of the implementation).

The questionnaire life-cycle within the application was mapped to our existing assessment process.

8.1.2 The Measurement Tool

Already the first version of the tool was able to provide the required reporting functionality. This was so simple and so powerful that we have never needed to extend or modify it. We used the idea from our original Excel sheet self-assessment tool and the great potential of data representation in MS Excel, and based the reporting on Excel sheet templates. The advantage of the approach was that we could modify, debug or completely change our reporting as many times as it was necessary without any change in the application.

We defined two templates:

- A quick feedback for LISOs and RISOs in the same form as it was designed within the old Excel tool
- A global feedback form for global evaluation of the information security status

The manager role with specifically defined reports was not yet set up, but available for controlling and other management functions within Daimler Financial Services interested in the information security status of the organization.

8.1.3 The Guidance for LISOs

The actual guidance is naturally provided by the content of the questionnaire; however, the tool contains a few small features that help LISOs in filling out the questionnaire and in identifying what should be done: The ISMS allows the questionnaire author to define help notes for each control, section and chapter of the questionnaire and the LISOs to

- Set a bookmark to a control or section, on which they currently concentrate. In such a way they can easily enter there new results whenever they have implemented a new measure without a long searching for the right place.
- Set question marks at the questions that they still need to clarify with other departments or with us and get back to the questions fast.
- See the status of every chapter, section and control to easily identify the weakest areas and prioritize the local activities.
- Delegate parts of the questionnaire to other departments for completion and also set up a deadline after which the delegated part is automatically released back to the LISO if it was not released by the completing party in time.
- Write explanations why they answered particular questions as they did and write internal notes that can be read only internally, i.e. by LISOs and the persons to which the questionnaire parts have been delegated.

8.2 Aspect 2: Questionnaire

Parallel to the development of the ISMS Portal, a new questionnaire based on the ISO/IEC 27002 (17799:2005) had been developed. To avoid the problems of the old Excel tool, we aimed for removing the 'partial' answer as far as possible. This implied a higher granularity of the questions implicitly increasing the number of questions. The tool enabled us also to restrict the 'not applicable' answer only to those questions where it was really relevant.

The first version of the new questionnaire covered all 133 controls of the ISO standard and included some other topics not covered by the standard (e.g., archiving, business aspects of disaster recovery). The questionnaire had altogether 380 questions (almost one and a half times the size of the old questionnaire). This seemingly large number turned out to be acceptable to the LISOs, since the simplicity of the questions without much space for interpretation allowed them to use the questionnaire as a kind of check list defining which controls they needed to implement. This simplified the LISOs' job, for most of them information security was yet another one of their duties.

8.3 Aspect 3: Process

The last, but very important part of the project was the establishment of processes for evaluation, reporting and continuous improvement of the information security status within Daimler Financial Services. Two processes, both based on the ISMS Portal self-assessment, helped us to accelerate the improvement of information security within the organization: the reporting processes and the information security assessment process.

8.3.1 Reporting Process

The reporting process covers evaluation of the global status, identification and mitigation of the global problems and reporting to the management. After the roll-out of the ISMS Portal, the LISOs were supposed to update the results in the ISMS Portal for their entities at least monthly, at best as soon as they implement a new measure. At the beginning of each month the local management as well as the executive management of Daimler Financial Services received a status report informing them about the current status of the entities (overall percentage of compliance), about the improvement within the last month, as well as about the ranking of the entity within the organization according to the results from the previous months. This caused a rocketing improvement at all entities in the last months of the project as shown in the Figure 2.

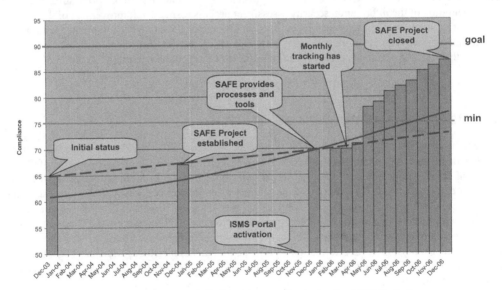

Figure 2: Improvement of information security during the SAFE Project

The dotted line in the Figure shows the expected improvement without the support by the ISMS Portal as the extrapolation from the previous results, the full line shows the expected results under the assumption that the results from the formerly used Excel questionnaire were less precise due to the fact that the method was based on the ISO standard of 2000 which was less comprehensive. This assumption was confirmed by the results of 2005 which delivered a lower perspective than expected, because the measuring method using the ISMS Portal was more precise.

8.3.2 Information Security Assessment Process

The information security assessment process concentrated on the verification of the status information and on the improvement at the individual entities. It consisted of four main activities:

- Self-assessment within the ISMS Portal
- On-site assessments where the results from the ISMS Portal were verified and additionally a technical vulnerability assessment was performed at selected entities
- Definition of local tasks (action plans) agreed with the LISO to improve the local status
- Providing local support, especially setup of task force for two critical areas: asset classification and business continuity.

There were 6-8 entities selected every year for an assessment. The selection process considered entities that reported results significantly below or significantly above average, and randomly selected entities with normal results in a way that almost all entities were visited during the SAFE Project.

9 The Show Must Go On

The SAFE Project was a success story. The deliverables from the individual work streams and the implementation of the information security assessment process resulted in improvement of the information security status of 22 percentage points, from an average of 65% to 87% compliance with the ISO standard. Forty-two percent of all subsidiaries met the goal of the SAFE Project to achieve compliance of more than 90%; ninety one percent of the subsidiaries achieved the requested minimum of 75%.

However, even after the SAFE Project, there was no time to rest.

9.1 New Management Model

In the final year of the SAFE Project (2006), the board of directors had decided to merge the central IT and HR departments of Daimler Financial Services and Daimler AG. The IT departments of Daimler Financial Services (including information security) have been integrated into the Sales and Marketing Division of Daimler AG (ITF). With that the number of entities in our responsibility almost doubled having one LISO per country. Almost every LISO took over the responsibility for two entities, one Financial Services (FS) and one Market Performance Center[3] (MPC), both having different IT infrastructures and, of course, completely different information security levels. Additionally, we temporarily took over the responsibility for information security at the Trucks and Busses Division (ITC), the former parent division of ITF, with its 13 plants worldwide. To be able to face the new task, we had to answer several fundamental questions:

- What is the appropriate level of information security for the new MPCs as long as the infrastructure and the processes of both the entities are separated? And after the merger?
- How much do the information security requirements of a plant differ from the requirements of an office environment of ITF entities?
- What outputs from the SAFE Project can be reused within the new entities?

---

3 An MPC usually is the national Daimler company which imports vehicles and parts and distributes them to the local dealers taking care of initial registration in the respective market.

Fortunately, the answers to these questions were optimistic for us.

- An improvement of MPCs could be achieved by including the MPCs in the information security assessment process. The initial assessments showed that the MPCs struggled with similar problems as FS entities, only the deficiencies had a greater extent.
- The ISO/IEC 27002 standard is written in a general way so that most measures are applicable for both, office environment and plants, e.g., the perimeter must be protected, the secure areas are similar for both environments, requirements on HR processes or business continuity are comparable. Of course, there are controls in the ISO standard that are not directly applicable to a factory (e.g., teleworking), but we must not forget that there is also an office complex belonging to every plant, thus the requirements applying to an office environment apply to these as well.

9.2 Global Adoption of the ISMS Portal

At the end of 2006 we received an official recognition for the achievements of the SAFE Project from the global Daimler Security Steering Committee (SSC), when it decided to roll out the ISMS Portal and the information security assessment process to all entities of Daimler AG (passenger car plants, sales and marketing organizations, the after-sales organizations, and the central centers of competence for software development).

This required adoption of the application to the new (even larger) organizational structure. We also took the opportunity and refined the questionnaire using our SAFE Project experience.

9.3 Separation from Chrysler

In 2007 the Corporate Information Security Team was tasked to support the business units during the separation between the Daimler and Chrysler entities. This may seem to be an easy task – from an outside perspective two vehicle companies existed. Internally, the Financial Services and Sales & Marketing organization were fully integrated, for the sales or financing of vehicles is primarily a commodity function and does not need brand specific features.

In order to achieve a smooth separation we defined rules which ensured that the existing information security regulations stayed in place as long as the future two entities – Daimler and Chrysler – were jointly sharing infrastructure and applications. Then we defined a transitions approach that ensured two important requirements:

- the legal requirements especially the data protection and privacy legislation were ensured and the customers and
- dealers of both entities were receiving a service as usual.

Under the surface, the setup of an international Chrysler sales organization was initiated and part of the workforce was transferred.

The separation of Financial Services and Sales & Marketing was finalized within one year and both companies – Daimler and Chrysler have now fully functional IT and service departments for these divisions. With respect to information security, the separation work was successful due to the good personal relations with our former colleagues and the common understanding of the enterprise's information security strategy. The general information security approach had new main goals during that period.

9.4 Custodianship

During the SAFE Project, the idea of using a core LISO team did not successfully work out; the core LISO team members concentrated on their local responsibilities and did not sufficiently involve other local entities. The role of the RISO was also quite weak and the most RISOs left due to the organizational changes. Therefore, Corporate Information Security had to align the communication process to ensure that all entities received all important information and the requirements of them were sufficiently communicated. As a result, the core LISO team and the RISOs were replaced by a regional custodian concept.

For each region, a team member of Corporate Information Security was appointed to be the caretaker and godfather for all entities of the region, we called it the custodian. The custodian serves as the interface to the local information security officer, collects requirements, initiates and supports information security activities that were centrally directed but had to be conducted locally. Finally and foremost, they provide the central know how to the local entities and are the communicating partner for all information security issues and problems.

10   The Message

Four years have passed since the SAFE Project was set up. The project and especially the post project events showed that:

1. It is a fundamental truth that information security improvement can be achieved only with management support. However, a good assessment and reporting process is as important as the management support. Without regular reporting (quarterly turned out to be an optimal period, monthly in specific cases) management does not pay attention to the importance of continuous improvements.

2. Legislative requirements differ in various countries and information security requirements are more stringent for financial institutions. However, even in a heterogeneous company like Daimler all entities are able to participate in the same assessment process using the same questionnaire, since the information security baseline is for the most companies similar. And ISO/IEC 27002 is a good basis for such an assessment.

3. Another fundamental truth is the importance of information security education and awareness. However, the LISO is the mediator for the local entity. A trust relationship with the LISOs is crucial for getting forward with information security. Especially at the entities where LISOs have no special training or skills in information security, it is very important for them to have a contact providing know how and guidance. This is particularly important in crisis situation like incidents. A trust relationship with the LISOs also enables better assessment of the information security status, since the LISOs do not feel like needing to hide their problems.

4. Guidance material, processes and tools are very important when a large organization wants to succeed in improving information security. When information security is just one of many functions of the LISOs, they need good cook books and good tool sets. It is a nice expectation that LISOs should think about what suits their entities best and what are the related risks. However, LISOs fully covered by operative tasks will neglect information security if it costs them too much time – the priority of their customers (the business) is and will always be the proper operation of their applications and information security, although important, will stay secondary; finally they are earning money by doing their business not by being secure.

References

[BAS04] International Convergence of Capital Measurement and Capital Standards, Basel Committee on Banking Supervision, 2004.

[BSI03] IT Baseline Protection Manual, Bundesamt für Sicherheit in der Informationsverarbeitung, 2003 (http://www.bsi.bund.de/gshb).

[BS7799b] BS 7799 Part 2: Information Security Management Systems – Specification with guidance for use, British Standards Institute, 2002.

[EU96] Directive 95/46/EC on the protection of individuals with regard to the processing of personal data and on the free movement of such data, European Commission, 1996.

[GLB99] Gramm-Leach-Bliley Financial Services Modernization Act, United States Congress, 1999.

[GWG93] Gesetz über das Aufspüren von Gewinnen aus schweren Straftaten (Act on Identifying Profits from Capital Crime), Bundestag 1993.

[ISO13335] ISO/IEC 13335: Guidelines for the management of IT Security (5 parts), International Organisation for Standardisation, 1996-2001.

[ISO17799] ISO/IEC 17799: Code of practice for information security management, International Organisation for Standardisation, 2005.

[ISO27001] ISO/IEC 27001: Information systems management system requirements, International Organisation for Standardisation, 2005.

[NIST800] Special Publications (800 Series) – Documents of general interest to the computer security community, National Institute of Standards and Technology, Information Technology Laboratory, 1995-2008 (http://csrc.nist.gov/publications/PubsSPs.html).

[SOA02] Public Company Accounting Reform and Investor Protection Act, United States Congress, 2002.

Information Security Status in Organisations 2008

Anas Tawileh · Jeremy Hilton · Stephen McIntosh

School of Computer Science, Cardiff University
5 The Parade, Cardiff CF24 3AA, UK
{m.a.tawileh, jeremy.hilton, s.b.mcintosh}@cs.cardiff.ac.uk

Abstract

This paper presents the results of the latest survey on information security management and pracitces in organisations. The study is based on a holistic approach to information security that does not confine itself to technical measures and technology implementations, but encompasses other equally important aspects such as human, social, motiviational and trust. In order to achieve this purpose, a comprehensive intellectual framework of the concepts of information security using Soft Systems Methodology (SSM) was utilised. The survey questions were drived from this conceptual model to ensure their coherence, completeness and relevance to the topic being addressed. The paper concludes with a discussion of the survey results and draws significant insight into the existing status of informaiton assurance in organisations that could be useful for security practitioners, researchers and managers.

1 Introduction

The Internet is offering unprecedented opportunities for businesses and organisations to create and access new markets and maximise their productivity and profitability. These opportunities come at a price. As more information is digitised, stored, transmitted and processed on electronic communication networks, these networks become attractive targets for people with malicious intents. Organisations counter these threats through the implementation of many countermeasures that aim to deter or detect any malicious activity against their information systems. The extent to which organisations have adopted sound and relevant information security practices varies considerably among organisations of different sizes, industries and location. Understanding the prevailing trends in information assurance practices is a critical starting point for setting the security research agenda, designing and implementing security awareness programmes and justifying the case for security investments in organisations. This paper reports the results of a recent survey conducted to assess the current status of information assurance in organisations.

The rest of the paper is structured as follows: a detailed description of the proposed methodology is provided, followed by an in-depth report and analysis of the survey results. The relevance of the developed survey is then evaluated. The paper concludes with a summary of brief discussion of the survey findings, along with an account of the trends observed.

2 Methodology and Approach

Surveys are designed and executed to ensure that all the needed information for the analysis for a specific purpose are available [Fowl02]. O'Muircheartaigh suggests that "every survey operation has

N. Pohlmann, H. Reimer, W. Schneider (Editors): Securing Electronic Business Processes, Vieweg (2008), 20-29

an objective, an outcome, and a description of that outcome" [O'Mui97]. This feature makes surveys a preferred method for data collection compared to other unstructured approaches. However, ensuring that the survey is designed in such a way as to guarantee that its questions actually contribute to the intended purpose and cover all of its aspects requires a methodological approach to survey design and development. The literature contains ample guidance on how to formulate survey questions [Tayl98] [WeKB96] [MoMo02], but very little of the published work gives a structured, methodological account for questionnaire design. Murray asserts that "the formation of a questionnaire requires a clear definition of the issue under consideration, and the related concepts involved." [Murr99] He suggests literature search, interviews, brainstorming sessions and Delphi studies to attain these aims. We argue that the Soft Systems Methodology (SSM) provides a comprehensive intellectual framework to define and represent purposeful human activity systems [Chec99]. The modelling tools offered by SSM could be utilised to design survey questions relevant to the main purpose of the research. Because every activity in the SSM conceptual model is logically derived (and could be defensibly traced back) to the Root Definitions capturing the system's purpose, formulating the survey questions based on these activities will ensure the relevance of every question to the purpose of the study.

An SSM conceptual model describes the activities that should be performed by any system to achieve its ideal state as captured in the formulated Root Definitions. Wilson [Wils84] suggests the use of activities in the conceptual model as the basis of a gap analysis exercise to analyse the extent to which activities undertaken in the real world deviate from those in the conceptual model. The outcomes of the analysis could be utilised to derive courses of action or redesign the business processes in the organisation to realign the real world system with the purpose it strives to achieve. Survey studies do not usually involve intervention with real world problematic situations. Most survey studies aim to analyse a particular problem or to answer a specific question. Questions in the survey are formulated in such a way as to elicit information that would facilitate the analysis of the problem or question being investigated. We claim that activities in SSM conceptual models provide an attractive basis for survey questions because they describe what the system should do to be the system described in the Root Definitions.

For the purposes of this research, we intend to exploit the conceptual model relevant to information assurance developed by Tawileh et al. to assess the status of information assurance in organisations. The activities in the conceptual model describe what an organisation should do to achieve an ideal state of information assurance. Hence, assessment of the information assurance posture of a particular organisation implies the analysis of the extent to which activities in the conceptual model are conducted by this organisation. Such analysis could be facilitated by the development of a set of questions to ask managers whether they currently undertake these activities within their organisations.

The process of the survey development entailed rephrasing the activities in the conceptual model relevant to information assurance into a question format. During this stage, we noticed that due to the comprehensive nature of the conceptual model, some activities may not be relevant to the target organisations. Some activities were combined together when the context of the questions permits. This has the added advantages of reducing the length of the survey and avoiding repetition. An optional, open ended question was added to collect feedback and comments from participants. The resulting questions (40 in total) were collated in an online survey and an invitation to participate was distributed by email. The next section presents the survey findings.

3 Survey Findings

In total, we collected 94 complete responses to our survey. Respondents came from organisations of all sizes, and represented quit a sparse geographic distribution. Table 1, Figure 1 and Figure 2 illustrate the demographics of the survey respondents. The distribution of respondents' organisations is represented in Figure 3.

Table 1: Geographical Distribution of Respondents

Organisation's Headquarters Located in	
US and Canada	37.2%
Europe	35.1%
Middle East	8.5%
Latin America	3.2%
Asia	12.8%
Africa	3.2%
Australia and New Zealand	0.0%

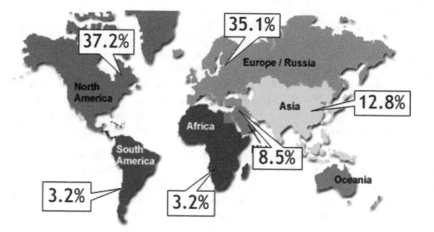

Figure 1: Geographical Distribution

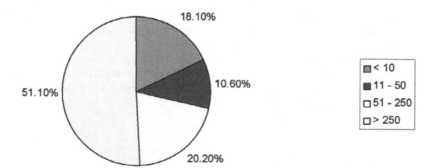

Figure 2: Organisation Size

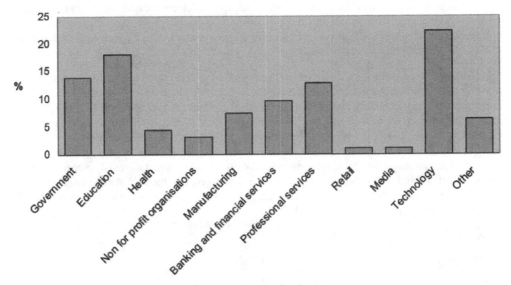

Figure 3: Organisation Sector

When asked about whether they have a documented inventory of business information stored or processed by the information systems in their organisation, 55.3% of respondents agreed while 29.8% said no and 14.9% were not sure. On the other hand, only 47.1% of small organisations reported the existence of documented information inventories. Large organisations seem to be more aware of the impact of information on business benefits, with 45.8% confirming that they have conducted a comprehensive assessment of the impact of information on business benefits for the organisation compared to only 23.5% of small and 31% of medium sized organisations.

The results also show a significant discrepancy between small and large organisations in implementing information classification schemes. Just over 17% of small organisations surveyed said that they actually have a documented and implemented information classification scheme, in contrast to 66.7% of large organisations. 34.5% of medium sized organisations acknowledged the existence of such schemes. Organisations of all sizes seem to suffer from a considerable lack of awareness of the impact of security incidents, such as information theft, manipulation and denial of service, on the business benefits to the organisation. Only 54.2% of large organisations have ever conducted a comprehensive assessment of such impact. The situation is even worse in small and medium sized organisations, where only around 30% have ever undertaken such an assessment.

Awareness of possible threats that may affect the organisation vary significantly, with more than 80% of large organisations claiming that they have identified potential malicious activities that could be undertaken on their information systems against 44.8% of the medium sized and 58.8% of small organisations. However, only 47.1% of small organisations reported that they have procedures and systems in place to detect suspicious activities on their organisation's information systems. The figure jumps to 69% in medium sized and 83.3% in larger organisations. Surprisingly, organisations appear to be less prepared in terms of capabilities against malicious activities. Large organisations come first with 72.9% claiming that the have documented procedures and mechanisms to react to suspicious activities on their information systems. 47.1% of small businesses have documented procedure and mechanisms compared to only 31% of medium sized organisations. The results also suggest that few organisations adopt a systematic approach to the evaluation and selection of detection capabilities. Less than half of the surveyed large organisations confirmed the existence of a specific procedure for evaluating and selecting the most appropriate detection capabilities for the organisation. About one in eight medium sized and a quarter of small organisations consented.

Organisations also seem to have different stances towards the different aspects of information assurance. When asked about the aspects of information assurance for which the organisation has documented requirements, confidentiality and authentication come first, for which 71.4% and 67% (respectively) of all organisations claimed that they have documented requirements. Availability and integrity come next, with 56% and 50.5%. Non-repudiation lags significantly behind, for which only 24.2% of respondents said that they have documented requirements. Interestingly, 16.5% of all organisations do not have documented requirements for any of these aspects. The results also suggest a great discrepancy between large organisations and SMEs (Small to Medium-sized Enterprises) in the area of security requirements. Over a quarter of SMEs do not have any documented information assurance requirements, compared to only 6.3% for large organisations (Figure 4).

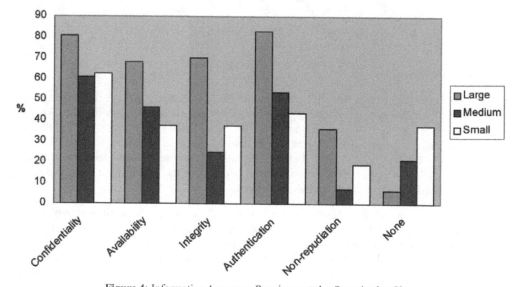

Figure 4: Information Assurance Requirements by Organisation Size

Despite the increased concern about the threats to the privacy and integrity of user information collected, stored and processed by information systems, less than two thirds of organisations said that they have clearly identified user information stored in their information systems. The situation is even worse in smaller organisations, where just about 63% of SME have done so. Moreover, not all organisations have identified the privacy and integrity requirements for their users' information. While 83.3% of large organisations claimed that they have identified these requirements, only 69% of medium and 52.9% of small organisations agreed. The survey results suggest that the adoption of appropriate protection mechanisms to ensure the integrity of private user information stored and processed by the organisation's information systems follows the same pattern. About three quarters of large organisations declared the existence of such mechanisms, compared to half of the medium sized and just over third of small organisations. When asked about the methods used to assess the integrity and privacy of private information stored in the organisation's information systems, in house capabilities come first for organisations from all sizes where 60.4% of large and 41% of SMEs attesting that they have developed such capability. However, one in every eight large organisations indicated that they do not assess the privacy and integrity of private information, in contrast to about a third of medium sized and a half of small organisations.

Responses collected indicate that risk assessment and analysis is still lagging in many organisations. Only 64.6% of all large organisations surveyed confirmed that they evaluate the negative consequences of potential information security incidents. The concern is even greater in smaller organisations, where just over 41% of medium sized and 47% of small organisations actually conduct such evaluation. The findings suggest that most of the organisations that conduct risk assessment actually implement measures and practices to prevent liability and negative consequences of information security incidents. The numbers stand at 62.5% of large, 41.4% of medium sized and 47.1% of small organisations. Moreover, responses indicate that the implementation of protection capabilities and the continuous assessment and improvement of these capabilities are different matters. Just over two thirds of large organisations do assess their protection capabilities on a regular basis, compared to about 40% of medium sized and a third of small organisations. Adoption of a systematic process approach to information assurance management varies considerably among organisations. Two thirds of large organisations reported that they conduct regular assessment of the information security status in the organisation. About 65% of large enterprises have also implemented appropriate mechanisms for the monitoring of information security within the organisation. The situation in medium sized organisations paints a completely different picture. Less than half of these organisations actually conduct regular assessment and about 45% do have monitoring mechanisms in place. Small organisations seem much less keen on adopting a systematic process approach to information security management, with only one third reporting that they perform regular assessment of information security. However, about 47% of these organisations said that they have implemented appropriate security monitoring mechanisms.

Incidents of theft, manipulation or denial of service may disrupt normal business operation of the organisation and cause substantial damages. However, not all organisations actually understand the potential impact of such incidents on their business operations. Around 90% of respondents in large organisations confirmed that they do understand the impact of information security incidents. Medium sized organisations follow closely with 86%, while small organisations lag behind with one in four not understanding the extent of the impact information security incidents on business operation.

The interconnected nature of today's marketplace mandates increased collaboration and partnership among organisations all over the globe. The emergence of concepts such as virtual organisations, co-innovation and collaborative development are but a few examples [MaTo07] [MoWa94] [BoBr03]. The survey findings confirm these trends and show that 87.5% of large organisations collaborate with external business partners, compared to 72.4% of the medium sized and around 70% of small organisations. The same figures apply to the understanding of the requirements for communication, information sharing and cooperation with business partners. However, the results reveal that despite the understanding of communication and collaboration requirements, fewer organisations are well prepared for enabling such collaboration securely. About two thirds of large organisations claimed that they have evaluated, selected and implemented appropriate mechanisms to enable secure communication, information sharing and cooperation with business partners. Only one in two medium sized organisations agreed to this question compared to one third of small organisations. From those who have implemented appropriate mechanisms to enable secure communication, information sharing and cooperation with business partners, only 70% said that they undertake regular review of the implemented mechanisms.

Surprisingly, although legislators in many countries around the world have been strengthening the regulatory requirements for information assurance, organisations may not be picking up the message. Just over half the large organisations surveyed do understand the applicable regulatory compliance requirements for information security. The figure falls to around 45% in medium sized and 47% in small organisations. Ethical requirements for information assurance seem to have higher priority, which 83% of large organisations claim to understand compared to 87% in small and medium sized firms. The results also suggest that organisations of different sizes have varying degrees of understanding of the information assurance requirements imposed by social responsibility. Large organisations pave the way with 58.3% stating that they understand social responsibility requirements, followed by 47% in small and 38% of medium sized organisations. The greatest discrepancy between organisations of different sizes appears in the action taken to ensure compliance with ethical, social responsibility and applicable regulatory requirements. About 56% of large organisations monitor all activities related to information security to ensure compliance. On the other hand, just about a quarter of medium sized and small organisations claimed to do so.

Interestingly, data backup appears to be widely spread among organisations. 9 out of every 10 large organisations reported that they have evaluated possible backup and restoration methods and implemented the most appropriate method for the organisation. The situation may not be as good in SMEs, but they are certainly catching up with about two thirds of survey respondents answering positively to the same question. Backup frequency tends to be higher in large organisations, with 73% of respondents conducting daily backups, 10% weekly and 12.5% monthly. Only 4.2% of large organisations do not perform backups at all. The frequency is much less in SMEs, where 43% perform daily backups, 26.1% weekly and 13% monthly. The proportion of those who do not perform backup at all is much larger at around 15% (Figure 5). The survey results suggest that despite the significant presence of disaster recovery plans and procedures in large organisations, only 45% of medium sized and a third of small organisations reported the existence of such plans and procedures. However, all organisations seem to pay less attention to the continuous testing and update of their disaster recovery procedures. Only 60% of the large organisations surveyed said that they test their disaster recovery procedures. The situation is much worse in medium sized and small organisations, where only 25% perform such testing. Among the organisations who claimed to have implemented backup and recovery solutions, only 56% actually evaluate the completeness and effectiveness of information systems restoration after each security incident.

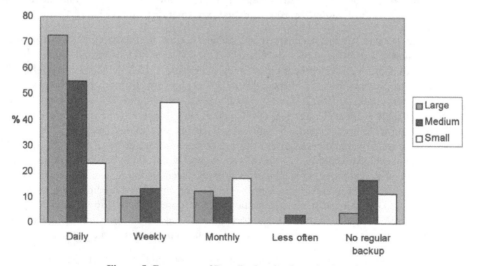

Figure 5: Frequency of Data Backup by Organisation Size

Most organisations are particularly vulnerable to internal misuse and security incidents. The results suggest a considerable gap in this area between organisations of different sizes. While 73% of large organisations have identified possible internal threats to their information systems, only 62.1% of medium sized and 52.9% of small organisations have followed suit. Organisations also differ in the approaches they adopt to tackle internal misuse of information systems. Large organisations, however, seem to be much more prepared to address internal incidents than their smaller counterparts (Figure 6).

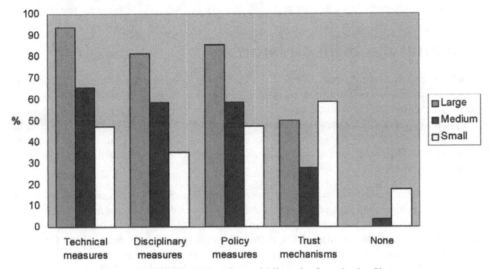

Figure 6: Measures Against Internal Misuse by Organisation Size

4 Respondents Feedback

In order to evaluate the relevance of the survey to its target audience, respondents were given the opportunity to send their comments and feedback about the survey in an open-ended question after they have completed all other questions of the survey. Willimack et al. [WLMJ04] suggest that respondents' feedback provides an appropriate tool to evaluate the quality and relevance of surveys and questionnaires. The following are few examples of the collected feedback:

"This research is a good checklist for organizations in terms of measuring their level of security provision in information systems."

"My goals as IT supervisor and management goals are not always the same, management is worried about sales/profits, and not security."

"It would be nice to know how many "no's" one selected out all questions to slam it in the face of those opposing any IT security."

"Interesting to be asked about the social/societal impact of information security, this rarely happens in surveys but is a very important piece overall – i.e. companies now tend to make investments in infosec on the basis of potential reputation damage IMHO as opposed to actual ROI or benefit."

"I am concerned. I am the one and only who is concerned. After hours, anyone who somehow got admitted into our offices could walk out with a laptop sitting on the reception desk containing practically all the confidential info we have. Refusal to invest in a steel cable."

The respondents' feedback indicates the achievement of a significant degree of success in assessing the holistic status of information assurance within organisations. It also supports our perspective of the need for future information assurance management systems that acknowledge the soft nature of the information security problem and adopt a holistic approach that extends beyond technical measures.

5 Summary and Discussion

The gap between large organisations and SMEs in the area of information assurance management portrays itself in several areas. A fundamental difference seems to exist in the level of awareness of the impact of information on the business benefits to the organisation. While larger organisations appear to have proactively pursued different measures to enhance their information assurance posture, SMEs lag significantly behind. Less SMEs reported the existence of documented information classification schemes, and they are twice less likely to understand the impact of information security incidents on their business operations.

The results also show a notable discrepancy between the adoption of detection capabilities against information security incidents and the reaction capabilities to these incidents. This places organisations of all sizes at a disadvantage, as what matters most when a security incident occurs is how well the organisation is prepared to tackle the incidence. The attitude towards the different dimensions of information assurance across organisations also varies, with confidentiality and authentication claiming the lion's share whilst non-repudiation features much lower on the organisations' priority lists.

Privacy of user information is another area of concern. Despite the increased awareness of the importance of protecting the privacy and integrity of user information collected and stored by information systems, many organisations have not clearly identified such information and derived specific requirements and implemented measures for the protection of its privacy and integrity. Adoption of risk assessment proved to be rather limited in organisations of all sizes. Nevertheless, smaller organisations are much less likely to embark on risk assessment exercises than their larger counterparts.

The institutionalisation of information assurance processes and the implementation of continuous assessment and improvement mechanisms seem to be significantly weaker than required to successfully tackle the plethora of contemporary security threats. The situation is worst in small organisations, and medium sized firms are not much better off.

Increasingly, organisations of all sizes are building collaborative relationships with external business partners in order to survive in today's highly complex business environment. These trends have major consequences for information sharing and protection. However, few organisations have implemented appropriate mechanisms to satisfy the security requirements mandated by these developments. Fewer organisations confirmed that they undertake regular review of the implemented mechanisms.

Organisations surveyed showed an alarming lack of understanding of applicable regulatory compliance requirements for information security. On the other hand, ethical obligations tend to attract more attention when information assurance systems are designed and implemented, followed closely by social responsibility requirements. Although organisations of all sizes rank closely in their level of understanding the regulatory, ethical and social responsibility security requirements, large organisations seem to respond better than their smaller counterparts. The survey results also depict a widespread neglect of the human factor in information assurance management in organisations. Analysis of the collected responses confirms the over-reliance on technical measures to identify and tackle information security incidents, along with little attention being paid to the human aspect.

References

[BoBr03] G. Booch and A. Brown (2003), Collaborative Development Environments. Advances in Computers, 2003. 59: p. 2–29.

[Chec99] P. Checkland (1999), Systems thinking, systems practice. Chichester: John Wiley.

[Fowl02] F. J. Fowler (2002), Survey Research Methods. Sage Publications Inc.

[MaTo07] S. P. MacGregor and T. Torres-Coronas (2007), Higher Creativity for Virtual Teams: Developing Platforms for Co-Creation. Information Science Reference.

[MoMo02] J. Moore and L. Moyer (2002), Questionnaire Design Effects on Interview Outcomes. Survey Methodology, p. 3.

[MoWa94] A. Mowshowitz and G. Walsham 1994), Virtual organization: a vision of management in the information age. An alternative view. Reply. The Information society, 10(4): p. 267-294.

[Murr99] P. Murray (1999), Fundamental issues in questionnaire design. Accident and Emergency Nursing, 7(3): p. 148-153.

[O'Mui97] C. O'Muircheartaigh (1997), Election 97: a triumph for the pollsters. MRS Res, p. 14-22.

[TaMa07] A. Tawileh and S. McIntosh (2007), Understanding Information Assurance: A Soft Systems Approach. Proceedings of the United Kingdom Systems Society 11th International Conference, September 3-5, Oxford University, UK.

[Tayl98] E. Taylor-Powell (1998), Questionnaire Design: Asking questions with a purpose.

[WeKB96] H. F. Weisberg, J.A. Krosnick and B.D. Bowen (1996), An Introduction to Survey Research, Polling, and Data Analysis. Sage..

[Wils84] B. Wilson (1984), Systems: Concepts, Methodologies, and Applications. New York, NY: John Wiley & Sons, Inc.

[WLMJ04] D. Willimack et al. (2004), Evolution and Adaptation of Questionnaire Development, Evaluation, and Testing Methods for Establishment Surveys. Methods for testing and evaluating survey questionnaires. New York: John Wiley & Sons.

Quantified Trust Levels for Authentication

Ivonne Thomas · Michael Menzel · Christoph Meinel

Hasso-Plattner-Institute, University of Potsdam
{ivonne.thomas | michael.menzel | meinel}@hpi.uni-potsdam.de

Abstract

Service-oriented Architectures (SOAs) facilitate applications to integrate seamlessly services from collaborating business partners regardless of organizational borders. In order to secure access to these services, mechanisms for authentication and authorisation must be deployed that control the access based on identity-related information. To enable a business partners' users to access the provided services, an identity federation is often established that enables the brokering of identity information across organisational borders. The establishment of such a federation requires complex agreements and contracts that define common policies, obligations and procedures. Generally, this includes obligations on the authentication process as well.

However in an SOA, requirements for authentication and authorisation should depend on the services themselves and might be subject to frequent changes. Moreover, different partners in the federation might have different regulations on the authentication process that even exceed the requirements of a service provider. Therefore the authentication method should not be stipulated in advance. For a flexible service access, different authentication methods should be allowed that comply with the service's requirements. However, more flexibility in the authentication step results into a complicated access control step. For this reason, approaches exist to subsume different properties of the authentication process into a level of trust and grant access to a resource if the requirements of the expected trust level are met. Typical approaches define levels of trust by grouping requirements into categories of similar impact, by considering the economic loss or by using a combination of impact and likelihood. Moreover, ideas exist to describe the strength of the authentication by a numerical value and to subsume them into a quantified trust level. However, the question of the semantic of such a "strength" level and its calculation is still open.

Therefore, in this paper we present a formal definition of a trust level to quantify the trust that is established by using a particular authentication method. As a mathematical foundation classical probability theory is used to describe the strength of an authentication method.

1 Introduction

One of the main advantages of the SOA paradigm is the easy integration and use of services from different service providers – even across trust domains. However, the seamless integration of services results in the need to secure service access. Service providers need identity information of service users to perform access control and to hold users liable for their actions. Therefore, the service must be able to verify the provided user information. Traditional approaches are based on the prior registration of users at the service provider.

However, especially in a Business-to-Business scenario, in which different organisations establish a long-term federation, the separate and multiple registration and administration of users in each organisation is inadequate. Therefore, the concept of identity federation emerged, which attempts to address these inefficiencies by extending the validity domain of an identity to the federation. A federation is a

N. Pohlmann, H. Reimer, W. Schneider (Editors): Securing Electronic Business Processes, Vieweg (2008), 30-38

group with a common agreement, in which each participant trusts its partners that the statements they make correspond with the truth. Users in a federation authenticate themselves at a federated identity provider and retrieve a security token if the authentication was successful. Service providers as the relying party accept this token as a proof of the user's identity. Such a federation of service providers allows web services to interact far more seamlessly, giving the user the illusion that he is operating within a single security domain, in which he just needs to authenticate once to benefit from the variety of services.

The essential pre-requisite to build up a federation and to share the user authentication across different security domains is the establishment of trust between the collaborating partners. Usually, this is achieved by setting up complex contracts that describe common policies, obligations and procedures to be followed by each federation member. These trust requirements assure that a common trust level is achieved within the federation. However, with regard to complex SOA – that might be based on the dynamic selection of services and service providers – defining and enforcing a common trust level based on pre-defined authentication and security mechanisms is disadvantageous: A common trust level between the federation partners would require an authentication mechanism which is sufficient for the service with the strongest authentication requirements. This, however, might not be necessary for all services within the federation and might change if this service is dynamically replaced. Consequently, users are forced to authenticate by a pre-defined strong authentication method, even though weak authentication would be sufficient for the service they want to access. Likewise, when users are fixed to a pre-defined authentication method according to the specified trust level, access will be denied even though the user might be able to verify his identity in an even more trusted way.

Therefore, it is not advisable to fix requirements characterized by a high variability – such as the required authentication procedures – in the federation contracts. Instead each service provider should be able to define the requirements for authentication independently according to the service's needs. To express authentication results, an interoperable language is needed which is understood by all federation partners. SAML [OASIS05] as such a language provides a standard security token to express assertions about a user's authentication, authorisation and attributes. In addition, futher information can be specified to describe how an authentication has been performed, encapsulated in a so called a *Authentication Context Class*. The relying party can use this information to assess the trust it can put in the authentication and to decide whether this authentication trust is sufficient to grant access. For example, the used authentication procedures, parameters such as the minimum password length or the used encryption algorithm are some of the aspects that can be considered.

However, enabling access control based on the quality of the authentication process results in a complex definition of access control rules. Each possible authentication method and its parameters must be defined in advance for each service leading to configurations that are not administrable due to its complexity. Therefore, we propose the introduction of an *Authentication Trust Level* that represents the trust that a user corresponds with the claimed identity.

The general idea of classifying authentication methods according to their level of trustworthiness is not new. Especially in the field of e-Government, various countries have launched e-authentication initiatives in order to secure access to critical e-Government services [OEE02, IDABC07, KWINT07, EAI04]. All of these initiatives have in common that they define authentication trust levels – mostly four different levels – in a way that covers the main use cases, reaching from 'no security needed' to 'critical application'. For each level, requirements for the authentication process are defined. This means, authentication methods are always assigned to predefined levels, but not the other way around. To provide authentication in a truly flexible manner, we present in this paper a formal definition for authentication trust levels to quantify the trust that is established by using a particular authentication method and an approach to determine the trust level based on an authentication context.

This paper is organized as follows. Section 2 introduces SAML as a specification to describe and convey meta information for authentication. Based on this information about an authentication context, Section 3 defines an Authentication Trust Level and describes how this value can be determined. Section 4 describes related work, while Section 5 concludes this paper and highlights some future work.

2 Meta Information for Authentication – SAML Authentication Context Classes

To exchange identity information between two trust domains, interoperable languages are necessary which describe the structure of the identity information itself and related meta information. The Security Assertion Markup Language (SAML) [OASIS05] has been approved as an OASIS standard to describe security assertions about the authentication, authorisation or attributes of a subject with the aim to share this information between different trust domains. The latest version, SAML 2.0, was ratified in March 2005. SAML 2.0 has been a major step towards federated identity management, since it provides formats and mechanisms to describe the attributes of a person as well as authentication and authorisation decisions in a standard XML format. For this reason, it is also the underlying standard of the specifications of the Liberty Alliance Project [Liberty08], a consortium of over 150 companies, which aims at providing standards and guidelines for federated identity management.

While SAML 1.1 only offered the possibility to state that an authentication process was performed using a specific authentication method as, for example, a password, Kerberos or hardware token, Authentication Context Classes [OASIS05b] are a concept introduced in SAML 2.0 which allows to specify how the authentication was performed in addition to the fact that it was performed. Authentication Context Classes address the fact, that the quality of an authentication depends highly on the way this authentication was performed: A password with a length of two characters is nearly useless, while a password with six characters, which was well-chosen and has a limit of three false attempts provides a strong protection. If the service provider who receives a message with an authentication assertion has to rely on the authentication process of the authentication authority, it requires to know whether the authentication process has been performed using a password with a length of two or six characters. This information is additional to the assertion, but it is essential, since the relying party needs to assess the level of confidence which it can place in this assertion and finally bases its decision whether to grant or deny access to the assertion's subject on this assessment. This additional information is referred to as "authentication context" in the SAML 2.0 specification. Listing 1 shows an example for a SAML assertion with context information.

An authentication context consists of two parts. The first part is the name of the authentication context class, which identifies a concrete authentication method. This class is equivalent to the level of detail which was possible in SAML 1.1. It describes the 'what', but not the 'how' of the authentication. In a simple scenario with, for example, two business partners, this might already be sufficient information. If both business partners know the details about the authentication process of their partner implicitly, this will work fine as long as there is no change from either side. However, in scenarios involving many service providers, the 'how' of the authentication needs to be transferred from one party to the other, as well. In this case, a second part is added to the authentication context called authentication context declaration. Inside the authentication context declaration the properties of the authentication are described by an XML schema which is assigned to the authentication context class. Here, it is also possible to define a custom schema to describe a mechanism or to extend an existing schema with additional attributes.

```
<saml:Assertion
  xmlns:saml="urn:oasis:names:tc:SAML:2.0:assertion">
  <saml:AuthnStatement>
    [...]
    <saml:Subject>
      <saml:NameID>MaxMustermann
      </saml:NameID>
    </saml:Subject>
    <saml:AuthnContext>
      <saml:AuthnContextClassRef>
        urn:oasis:names:tc:SAML:2.0:ac
        :classes:PasswordProtectedTransport </saml:AuthnContextClassRef>
      <saml:AuthenticationContextDecl
        xmlns="urn:oasis:names:tc:SAML:2.0:ac:classes:PasswordProtectedTransport">
        <AuthnMethod>
          <Authenticator>
            <AuthenticatorSequence>
              <RestrictedPassword>
                <Length min="5"/>
              </RestrictedPassword>
            </AuthenticatorSequence>
          </Authenticator>
        </AuthnMethod>
      </saml:AuthenticationContextDecl>
    </saml:AuthnContext>
  </saml:AuthnStatement>
</saml:Assertion>
```

Listing 1: An example SAML assertion with authentication context information.

3 Authentication Trust Levels

SAML and the SAML Authentication Context Classes facilitate the representation and exchange of trust-related authentication information across different trust domains. This enables the brokering of authentication information to a relying party, such as a service provider. The service can use the context information in the SAML assertion to assess the confidence into the authentication process performed by the user's identity provider and decide whether the performed authentication meets the authentication trust requirements of the service. Depending on the result of the assessment the service provider will, for example, provide less functionality or deny access to the service at all. Only if the service provider has sufficient evidence into the authentication of the subject of the assertion, access will be granted.

However, the more information is exchanged between an identity provider and a relying party, the more complicated the access control step gets, since the relying party has to analyse all the retrieved information and to compare it with its access control policy. This, however, is necessary if the service provider wants to support the authentication from different sources. If the service provider wants to adapt to each authentication method that might be used within the federation, then its access control policy will get quite large and difficult to maintain in a consistent state. For this reason, approaches exist to subsume different requirements into a level of trust. Access to a resource will be granted if the requirements of the expected trust level are met. Therefore, the required trust level can be fixed in the access control policy. Each time a request is received, the actuel trust level is determined by an adequate algorithm and compared to the required one. If the actuel level is equal or higher than the required one, access is granted.

This section introduces the notion of an authentication trust level and presents an approach to define a numerical value to describe authentication requirements in a consistent way. In our aproach, we propose a formal definition for a quantitative trust level using classical probability theory. We develop a mathematical model which can serve as a common base for further research in this area of quantifying trust in an authentication method. The aim is not to answer the question whether a password is more secure than a smart-card, but to provide a common model to which people can map authentication methods in order to compare their security.

3.1 Authentication Trust Level Definition

An authentication trust level refers to the trust or confidence that a service provider has into a single authentication method or the combination of different authentication methods. It reflects the strength of the authentication and how easy it is for an attacker to fool the authentication process: The stronger the authentication, the higher the confidence that a user corresponds with the claimed set of attributes. However, the strength of an authentication method depends on many criteria and these criteria differ tremendously between different categories of user authentication. While biometric authentication methods are mostly characterized by criteria like the false acceptance rate (FAR) and false rejection rate (FRR), it would be odd to use these criteria for knowledge-based authentication methods: A user who is accepted with a password which is close to the registered one is an unrealistic scenario. Instead, a far more dangerous threat for knowledge-based authentication methods are brute-force attacks and hence criteria like the theoretical or effective password space as well as whether passwords were auto-generated or chosen by humans decide about the provided security. These examples show, how different the criteria are which are used to assess the authentication trust level. This makes it hard to find a clear meaning for the metric of an authentication trust level: What does it mean, if an authentication method has a level of 1, what if the level is increased by 0.5? Our idea is to use a criterion, which is common to all current and future authentication methods and which arises from all the other criteria. The intention is that this criterion forms a base with a clear semantic meaning, so that all other criteria that differ from authentication method to authentication method can be mapped onto this base. As this criterion, we propose to use the *probability that an attacker can crack the authentication method* and personate as the right user. This probability is a value, which is much more tangible than trust and confidence. If someone tells us, that the probability that a certain authentication method is cracked is 0.1 percent, we know that this mechanism fails in one out of a thousand cases. Based on this idea, we define an authentication trust level in the following way:

Definition 3.1 Let A be the event that the authentication method A' is cracked by an attacker. P is the corresponding probability distribution. We define an authentication trust level as:

$$\text{level}_A = -\log(P(A))$$

Note, that we use a logarithmic scale with a base of ten in order to deal in a more human-readable way with small probability values.

Given this definition, we can assess all the criteria which characterize an authentication method with regard to their influence on the probability that the authentication method is cracked. The next section will go into detail about how the probability that a method is cracked can be derived from the given criteria.

Given Definition 3.1, we can derive directly some characteristic values:

- An authentication trust level of zero represents no trust at all.
- An authentication trust level of one means that this authentication method fails in 10 percent of all authentication attempts.

- An authentication trust level of two means that this authentication method fails in 1 percent of all authentication attempts.

Therefore, increasing the authentication trust level by one means that this authentication method is ten times more secure. If an authentication method is twice as secure as a method B' its authentication trust level is increased by approximately 0.3 or rather log(2). We summarize this relation in the following definition.

Definition 3.2 Given two methods A' and B', we define the security ratio of A' and B' as:

$$\frac{P(A)}{P(B)} = 10^{level_A - level_B}$$

This way, there is a clearly defined metric, which allows to compare authentication methods and to rate them according to their security.

3.2 Authentication Trust Level Determination

Given the authentication requirements in the authentication context classes and the authentication trust level definition, the task of determining the authentication trust level consists of deriving from the context information the probability that the authentication process has been cracked by an attacker. Recalling the information described by the authentication context classes, each authentication mechanism is described by class name and authentication context information consisting of several parameters as for a password, for example, its length, generation procedure or the enrolment process. Each parameter has a certain influence on the probability that this authentication mechanism is cracked. In order to calculate the probability, also classical probability theory can be used.

In classical probability theory, two approaches are used to identify probabilities: Either the theoretical probability is calculated or probabilities are determined empirically based on observations. Whenever possible, the first approach should be used, since it provides more exact results. However, there are certain preconditions: One has to be able to define all the possible outcomes and all possible events must be equally likely. In most cases, the world is not that easy and the only way is to determine the probabilities experimentally. Regarding authentication methods however, there are parameters which are qualified to be determined theoretically. One of these parameters is the theoretical password space.

If we have a PIN of n digits, the probability that someone can crack the PIN by guessing is $\frac{1}{10^n}$. However, this number is the probability that an attacker can guess the PIN in one attempt. If the attacker has an infinite amount of time and an infinite number of attempts, the probability increases up to one. Hence, if the password space is relatively small, a maximum number of attempts is used to keep the probability that the authentication method is cracked small. In order to include this criterion into the calculation, we can still use probability theory. We get the probability that a mechanism is not cracked after n attempts by multiplying the single probabilities for each attempt. This is for the first attempt $1-\frac{1}{10^n}$, for the second $1-\frac{1}{10^n-1}$, for the third $1-\frac{1}{10^n-2}$ and so on. Finally, we get the following formula for the probability $P(X)$ that a PIN of a length of n digits is cracked after k attempts:

$$P(X) = 1 - \prod_{i=0}^{k-1}\left(1 - \frac{1}{10^n - i}\right)$$

However, this calculation deals with the theoretical password space. Most often the actual password space is much smaller, which has the consequence that brute force attacks are much more effective. Many passwords can be guessed by doing a little research on the user or trying standard password lists. How hard it is to guess a password is described by a measure called entropy. While the theoretical password space can be computed easily, it is often hard to estimate the entropy of user-chosen passwords, since it is based upon the actual used password space. To evaluate the user's influence on the strength of a password, several studies have been conducted [Zvirian99, Nali04, Ge02, Jeff00].

Such or similar approaches can be used for text- and image-based authentication methods in order to describe the influence of the size of the password space. However, many parameters do not allow being evaluated using theoretical considerations. The only way here is to determine the probabilities empirically. Therefore experiments with a great number of iterations and a great number of test data are necessary, which are seldom available. However, the more an authentication method is established, the more benchmarks and test results already exist. This is, for example, the case for fingerprint-based authentication systems. In order to compare and evaluate the security of fingerprint readers of different vendors, the Fingerprint Vendor Technology Evaluation [NIST03] has been conducted by the National Institute of Standards & Technology (NIST) in the US in 2003. As a measure, which can be mapped to the probability, the false acceptance rate can be used. The false acceptance rate is the probability that a false claim will be accepted as being true: e.g., someone fools the system and access is granted to an unauthorized person. Several publications also evaluate the security of fingerprint systems and biometric authentication in general as for example [Pr03, Ga06, Burnes03]. Similar studies on the security of smart-cards, palm-print readers and many others are also available (cf. e.g. [Kim06, Kong08, Kong06]).

While such studies are a good starting point to determine the authentication trust level of an authentication method, one has to keep in mind that evaluating the security of an authentication mechanism is a challenging and critical task, which has to be done by experts and those results should be reviewed several times.

4 Related Work

Several approaches to define levels of trustworthiness for authentication mechanisms have been proposed in recent years indicating the importance of such a concept. In the area of e-Government, the *UK Office of the e-Envoy* has published a document called "Registration and Authentication – E-government Strategy Framework Policy and Guideline" [OEE02]. Depending on the severity of compromise, four authentication trust levels are defined, reaching from Level 0 for minimal damage up to Level 3 for substantial damage.

The IDABC [IDABC07] (Interoperable Delivery of European eGovernment Services to public Administrations, Businesses and Citizens) is a similar project managed by the European Commission. Its Authentication Policy Document defines four assurance levels as well, which are also associated with the potential damage that could be caused.

The government of the Netherlands has also started several initiatives in cooperation with industry, consumer organizations and experts. One relevant result for authentication trust levels is the KWINT project report [KWINT07] which proposes to use three levels, which should be chosen depending on the type of service, convenience and liability.

The e-Authentication Initiative is a major project of the e-Government program of the US. The core concept is a federated architecture with multiple e-Government applications and credential providers. In this context, the initiative has published a policy called "E-Authentication Guidance for Federal Agencies" [EAI04] to assist agencies in determining the appropriate level of identity assurance for electronic transactions. The document defines four assurance levels, which are based on the risks associated with an authentication error.

Similar approaches have also been proposed by New Zealand's e-Government unit [NZ08] and the Australian AGAF initiative [AGAF08]. Both approaches propose also four authentication trust levels, which are matched to the risk associated with a transaction.

Finally, the need for authentication trust levels is also a topic which has been discussed within ENISA. The agency aims at providing a common language for authentication mechanism metadata, which also comprises the idea of quantified authentication trust levels.

While all of the mentioned approaches concentrate on authentication concerns, there are also approaches that are aiming at rating the trust relationship as a whole between the interacting parties. Such approaches are based on the reputation of a user and the trust propagation along a path of involved parties. Wu et al. [WuWe07] define trust requirements in the scope of federated environments. They highlight that "federated trust management incorporates not only internal factors (definitions and regulations) but also external factors (reputations and recommendations) into the process of forming trust intentions and their resultant trust behaviours".

In [SaGo06], Sampath and Goel present an overview about trust definitions based on reputation systems. They argue that in most related work subjective trust measures are used without a meaningful categorization of these trust values (e.g. good or bad). Therefore, they define requirements for reasonable trust measures and propose a model that also considers the user's behaviour.

Also various patents[1] describe the idea of mapping a service's authentication requirements and the authentication mechanisms available to a level of trust. If the required level of trust is smaller or equal to the trust level of the user, access is permitted. While these patents also propose the usage of a numerical representation for a trust level, the semantic of such a level and its calculation is not described.

5 Conclusion

The benefit of our approach presented in this paper is an improved flexibility of the authentication process and a simplification of access control policies. The authentication trust level allows a description of the confidence in an authentication process on an abstract level and, hence, replaces the specification of concrete authentication mechanisms in authorisation policies.

We introduced the authentication trust level based on the probability that an attacker can crack the authentication method. In addition, we discussed approaches how probability theory can be used to determine the trust level based on the SAML context classes. A distinctive feature of this model is that the strength of an authentication method is reflected by a numerical value with a clear semantic meaning. Having such a clear semantic meaning of a trust level, such a model is applicable to all current and upcoming authentication mechanisms and can therefore serve as a base for further research in this area. Morover, this approach enables the calculation of the combined trust level of two authentication mechanisms based on basic probability theory. The combined trust level would represent the confidence into a multifactor authentication.

There is an ongoing effort to implement this approach based on WS-Federation and to evaluate its applicability in various scenarios. Further research investigates the trust requirements when having differ-

---

1 cf. United States Patent 6892307, 7086085 http://www.freepatentsonline.com/

ent models for identity management as well as the applicability of the model to trust requirements other than the authentication process.

References

[AGAF08] Australian Government Authentication Framework for Individuals. http://www.agimo.gov.au/ infrastructure/authentication/, 2008.

[Burnes03] J. Burnes and W.Chang: An intrinsic assessment and comparison of biometric systems through wavelet analysis. In: IEEE International Conference on Systems, Man and Cybernetics, Jan 2003.

[EAI04] e-Authentication Initiative, US: E-Authentication Guidance for Federal Agencies. http://www.white-house.gov/omb/memoranda/fy04/m04-04.pdf.

[Ga06] J. Galbally-Herrero and J. Fierrez-Aguilar: On the vulnerability of fingerprint verification systems to fake fingerprints attacks. In: Carnahan Conferences Security Technology, Jan 2006.

[Ge02] E. Gehringer: Choosing passwords: security and human factors. In: Technology and Society, Jan 2002.

[IDABC07] IDABC – Interoperable Delivery of European eGovernment Services to public Administrations, Businesses and Citizens. http://europa.eu.int/idabc/, 2007.

[Jeff00] J. Jeff, Y. Alan, B. Ross, and A. Alasdair: The Memorability and Security of Passwords: Some Empirical Results. In: Technical Report No. 500,Computer Laboratory, University of Cambridge, Jan 2000.

[Kim06] H. Kim, J. Oh, and J. Choi: Security Analysis of RFID Authentication for Pervasive Systems using Model Checking. In: Proceedings of the 30th Annual International Computer Software and Applications Conference, Jan 2006.

[Kong06] A. Kong, D. Zhang, and M. Kamel: Analysis of Brute-Force Break-Ins of a Palmprint Authentication System. In: IEEE Transactions on Systems, Man and Cybernetics, Jan 2006.

[Kong08] A. Kong, D. Zhang, and M. Kamel: Three measures for secure palmprint identification. In: Pattern Recognition, Jan 2008.

[KWINT07] KWINT Project. A safer internet for all. http://www.ecp.nl/downloads/id=43/ download.html, 2007.

[Liberty08] The Liberty Alliance Project. In: http://www.projectliberty.org, 2007.

[Nali04] D. Nali and J. Thorpe: Analyzing User Choice in Graphical Passwords. In: Technical Report, 2004.

[NIST03] National Institute of Standards (NIST): Fingerprint Vendor Technology Evaluation (FpVTE), 2003.

[NZ08] E-government in New Zealand. http://www.e.govt.nz, 2008.

[OASIS05b] OASIS: Authentication Context for the OASIS Security Assertion Markup Language (SAML) V2.02. In: OASIS Standard Specification, March 2005.

[OASIS05] OASIS: Security Assertion Markup Language (SAML) V2.0. In: OASIS Standard Specification, March 2005.

[OEE02] Office of the e-Envoy, UK. Registration and Authentication – e-Government Strategy Framework Policy and Guidelines. http://www.cabinetoffice.gov.uk/ csia/documents/pdf/RegAndAuthentn0209v3.pdf, 2002.

[Pr03] S. Prabhakar, S. Pankanti, and A. Jain: Biometric recognition: security and privacy concerns. In: Security and Privacy Magazine, Jan 2003.

[SaGo06] R. Sampath and D. Goel. RATING: Rigorous Assessment of Trust in Identity Management. RES 2006. The First International Conference on Availability, Reliability and Security, pages 14-23, 2006.

[WuWe07] Z. Wu and A. C. Weaver. Requirements of federated trust management for service-oriented architectures. International Journal of Information Security, Jan 2007.

[Zvirian99] M. Zviran and W. Haga: Password security: an empirical study. In: Journal of Management Information Systems, Jan 1999.

Identity Management in Open Environments

Manel Medina[1] · Estíbaliz Delgado[2] · Diego Fernández[3]

[1]UPC/ SeMarket
medina@ac.upc.edu

[2]ESI
estibaliz.delgado@esi.es

[3]ISDEFE
dfvazquez@isdefe.es

Abstract

The project SEGURIDAD2020 has been leaded by ISDEFE as R&D project during 2006 and 2007. The consortium was made of 22 partners including large and SME enterprises, technology centres and universities.

The citizen is the centre of reference in this project: How can the different digital environments be accommodated to the user? How can the different systems manage the numerous digital identifications for a single user?. How can the system ensure that it is achieved the appropriate trust level required by the user? The works were done within security and confidence framework.

The first approach is global and long-term, getting requirements from specific use cases in order to take a global solution in terms of architecture and confidence to be applied on specific case studies.

1 Security Requirements

It was taken into account the requirements from business, legal, user and technical perspective to get security provision of future scenarios.

Two crucial areas have been addressed to build trust communications in future scenarios, where the user can choose any trusted device with any digital identity, in order to demand services using different roles or environments:

- Identity management, through identity federation allows the multi-identification and role assignment.
- Trust environment. Both, user and service need a common recognition of each other, with a set of security mechanisms to establish a confidence relationship. The actual set of mechanisms will depend on the level of trust required by the application. We have integrated PKI, and different biometric identification methods in an Identity Provider Liberty Alliance (LAP) compliant.

We applied this flexible approach to relevant and specific environments: Financial, Transport and Government, in applications that required several levels of trust on user identity, and the migration of users between services.

N. Pohlmann, H. Reimer, W. Schneider (Editors): Securing Electronic Business Processes, Vieweg (2008), 39-44

We addressed also the identification of the main threats and security requirements from legal and standardisation viewpoints.

2 Security Architecture

The typical testing environment of two Circle of Trust of LAP with their Identity and Service Providers (IdP and SP), was complemented with Several Identification components, installed as "front end" of the IdP.

These components provided different levels of trust on the real user identity, and range from the traditions password to innovative multi-biometric identification, including PKI based Spanish national e-identity card.

The LAP functionality to allow SP to request re-identification of user, depending on the operations she requests was implemented, to ask the IdP to use a stronger identification method to validate the actual identity of the user.

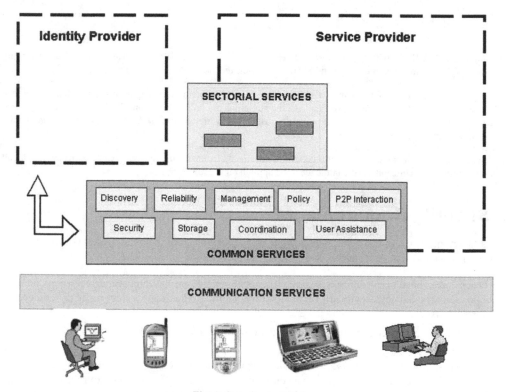

Fig. 1: Security Architecture

In addition to these fundamental architectural components we have identified the following ones:

- **Discovery**, to have a secure service to find trustable services.
- **Reliability**, to prevent Denial of Service

- **Management**, to provide continuity to the security policy stated requirements
- **Storage**, to preserve documents and electronic objects in long term scale.
- **Policy**, to define the adequate and suitable security policy for each of the environment components, such that provide trust to the whole circle.
- **Coordination or agreement**, to set up the security statements related to the behaviour of the components when they act on behalf of other component or provide a service to it (e.g. service providers or Attribute providers managing personal data)
- **P2P Interaction**, to ease the collaboration between a user and a set of SP providing a complex service.
- **User Assistance**. The "help desk" is the basic component to prevent social engineering threats and system incidents due to user lack of knowledge.

3 Identity Trustworthiness

3.1 The concept of Trust

The concept of "Trustworthiness" is related to the notion of "Trust". An entity is trustworthy (for a certain task) when we have an assurance that it will perform its promised service as expected [ALRL04]. Unfortunately, in many cases it is almost impossible to have an unquestionable assurance about the trustworthiness of an entity; therefore, the choice of considering an entity trustworthy for a certain task involves a decision to trust. In this paper, we utilise the following definition of Trust [KnCh96]:

The problem of trustworthiness evaluation is the extent to which one party (the Trustee) is willing to depend on another party (the Trusted) in a given situation with a feeling of relative security, even though negative consequences are possible.

Depending upon the specific scenario the Trusted and the Trustee roles can be fulfilled by different types of entities. From the perspective of dependability and security, in this paper we consider Trusted and Trustee entities to be software components.

3.2 Justification of Trust Management

Trust Management has recently attracted the attention of Computer Science research especial for the application areas of distributed access control and reputation networks management. (cf., [GrSl00, JøIB05]). The problem of trustworthiness evaluation that we address has many similarities with the task of selecting a trustworthy web service. Users generally favour web services that they expect will honour their agreements as described in the form of previously established a Service Level Agreement (SLA). For example in [ShLK06] it is suggested that a web-service can be ranked according to a trust value that is calculated by a trusted registry using a set of user reports on the service over time. In the case of the project Seguridad2020, the trustworthiness evaluation is addressed to select the most trustworthiness identity management technique, depending on the application domain context.

3.3 Objective of Trust Management within Seguridad2020

Therefore, Seguridad2020 project presents a Quantitative Framework for evaluating the threat vulnerability attack resistance of a system, that is, a Quantitative Framework that allows evaluating the trustworthiness level of a system both at design phase and at run-time phase. In particular, we have applied the trustworthiness. Even though this framework offers the mechanisms to evaluate different characteristics of a system, the purpose of Seguridad2020 is focused mainly on the evaluation of one specific characteristic of the system, that is, the identity management system trustworthiness level.

The project addresses the particular problem of the monitoring and enhancement of Trust, Security and Dependability (TSD) of a component-based system or web-services-based system, in the domain of SOA (Service-Oriented Architecture) approach. For this purpose, it is proposed a Quantitative Framework which, while acting on the behalf of the user (Trustors), supervises the system's existing Trusted-Trustee relationships and preserves the overall system level of Trust, Security and Dependability (TSD). This is achieved by monitoring quality metrics on the system (or services or components that compose a system) behaviour, by periodically evaluating their trustworthiness, and (when applicable) by controlling them.

The Quantitative Framework is also capable of looking after user satisfaction about the requirements and expected QoS (Quality of Service, including parameters as Trust, Security and Dependability) of all the active Trusted-Trustee relationships in the system, and afterwards, it is capable of making control decisions.

For example:

- A negative compliance of the required trust level may result in:
  - the replacement of a service against the component, e.g. deactivation of a component $c2$ that offers a security functionality of encryption with the encryption algorithm of Triple DES, and being substituted by a safer one.
  - the initialization of a component $c2$ that allows the encryption using another encryption algorithm as RSA.
- A decrease in measure $m1$ may trigger a re-estimation of the trust attributes and compliance re-evaluation.
- While a decrease in measure $m2$ may cause the component to be re-instantiated in a different mode of operation or in a controlled environment.

3.4 Seguridad2020 Quantitative Framework

The Quantitative Framework is composed by this scheme of elements:

- The *Trustworthiness Model* defines the scheme of trustworthiness attributes required for both Trustworthiness Evaluation and Trustee's decision-making. The Trustworthiness Model suggests that the Trusted's profile is defined and described in a Quality Profile Model, and that the way of reasoning of the Trustee, when it uses a certain component, is supplied in the Trustworthiness Profile.

- The *Trust Management Framework Model* describes the mechanisms and solutions used for monitoring the Trustee's quality attributes metrics. Monitoring includes a mechanism that can obtain measurements and for controlling certain Trustee quality attributes. Monitoring includes a mechanism that can obtain measurements e.g., type of encryption algorithm, type of identity management technique, CPU load, Process Memory footprint, network usage (number of sockets, bandwidth utilisation), containment level of a component, attempts to access unauthorised resources, component lock-up, component non-availability, etc. This model also provide a mechanism for the Trustworthiness Evaluation, that is, a functionality that is offered to the Trustee for evaluating a Trusted's trustworthiness level.

The main roles within Trustworthiness Management are:

- A Trusted entity: specifies has a Trustworthiness Profile, which it uses to specify its "requirements" with respect to Trustworthiness Evaluation, and that
- A Trustor has a Quality Profile which indicates what it uses to measure (metrics of) Quality Attributes that are asserted to hold for that service instance.

A *Quality Attribute* is a high-level characteristic of an entity that describes and quantifies an aspect of its quality. Quality has to do with the degree to which something possesses a combination of properties that are desirable to its stakeholders. In the context of Seguridad2020, we are mainly focussing on Dependability, Security and Performance.

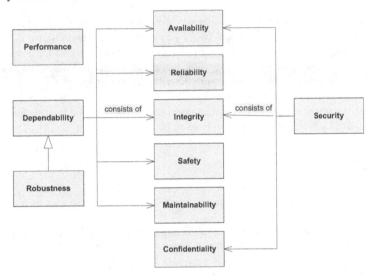

Fig. 2: Trust, Security, and Dependability attributes scheme

The trustworthiness model defines the attributes scheme for Trust, Security and Dependability (TSD), together with a set of trustworthiness metrics to be monitored for each attribute. Examples of metrics: CPU consumption, memory usage, presence of encryption mechanisms, type of encryption algorithm integrity data via checksums, mean time between failure, type of identity management mechanism, etc.

The decision to trust is taken in the next way. When the calculated trustworthiness value (Tr) exceeds the threshold supplied by the Trustee, (Th), then a positive decision to trust can be taken. Whereas if the threshold is not met, then the decision to trust would be negative. For making trust decisions it is needed to 'extract' the quality metrics of trusted entities. This can be achieved in two moments in time:

- **Development Time**: After developing a trustee some quality attributes can be measured and distributed with the trusted entity. To ensure that other parties have a higher trust on these metrics, it is possible to let a trusted party do the measurements, and certify these values.
- **Run Time**: A lot of quality attributes can be measured during run time.

It is left up to the trustee to decide which type of quality metrics it is interested in, and which 'weights' are put on these metrics.

Let us assume that "Availability" QA is modelled by the two metrics "response_time" (rt) and "uptime" (up), both measured in seconds. A predicate over availability can be the following:

$$Pavailability = (rt < 16) \text{ and } (up > 1000)$$

4 Conclusion

The tools to achieve the identity management in Open environments are available now, we just have to use them, and integrate security measurement tools to prevent abuse of confidence from other components of the environment.

Digital Identity requires "just" a trusted CA, Identity Management in Open environments requires the creation of chains of trust between users and (web) service providers, that require the application of multiple controls, ranging from business to ethics and personal data protection, through service level agreements. Identity attributes have to be shared by agents belonging to different legal and social environments, and even diverse cultures that require the achievement of specific agreements to raise the level of trustworthiness of all the agents in the chain of trust, so that users will be always confident that their personal attributes will not be lost, damaged or misused by any of the intermediaries involved in the provision of complex web services in open environments.

References

[ALRL04] Avizienis, A., J.-C. Laprie, B. Randell and C. Landwehr, Basic concepts and taxonomy of dependable and secure computing, IEEE, Transactions on Dependable And Secure Computing 1 (2004), pp. 11–34.

[KnCh96] McKnight, D. H. and N. L. Chervany, The meaning of trust, Technical Report MISRC 96-04, University of Minnesota, Management Information Systems Research Center (1996).

[GrSl00] Grandison, T. and M. Sloman, A survey of trust in internet applications, IEEE Communications and Survey, Forth Quarter 3 (2000), pp. 2–16.

[JøIB05] Jøsang, A., R. Ismail and C. Boyd, A survey of trust and reputation systems for online service provision, Decision Support Systems (2005), (available on line on ScienceDirect) in press.

[ShLK06] Sherchan, W., S. W. Loke and S. Krishnaswamy, A fuzzy model for reasoning about reputation in web services, in: H. Haddad, editor, Proc. of the 21st ACM Symposium on Applied Computing (ACM SAC 2006) – Trust, Recommendations, Evidence, and other Collaborative Know-how (TRECK), 23-27 April 2006, Lyon, France (2006), pp. 1886–1892.

Identity management and privacy languages technologies: Improving user control of data privacy

José Enrique López García · Carlos Alberto Gil García ·
Álvaro Armenteros Pacheco · Pedro Luis Muñoz Organero

Telefónica Investigación y Desarrollo S.A.U
Network and services security department
{jelg | cagg | aap | plm}@tid.es

Abstract

The identity management solutions have the capability to bring confidence to internet services, but this confidence could be improved if user has more control over the privacy policy of its attributes. Privacy languages could help to this task due to its capability to define privacy policies for data in a very flexible way. So, an integration problem arises: making work together both identity management and privacy languages. Despite several proposals for accomplishing this have already been defined, this paper suggests some topics and improvements that could be considered.

1 Introduction

Over the past few years, with the vertiginous development that is experimenting the Information Society, both individuals and organizations have been involved in a transformation process that has changed the way in which traditionally were interacting, so that now demand greater "digitalization" that expands the supply of services available through the Internet. A good illustration of this is the Web 2.0, the rise of electronic banking or e-administration.

However, this process of transformation has also led to the emergence of new risks and threats in the field of user's identity and privacy management, as it has prevented the creation of coordinated initiatives that establish a common and synergistic framework for digital identity. This, in turn, has led to the proliferation of particular niche solutions of identity repositories where sensitive information from users is being stored, but where, in many cases, user can make no control over it.

One of the main problems with this scenario is that it generates mistrust among the parties involved in a service (whether it is a business or a social network.) Whether the user, who does not know what is actually being done with his identity or the personal information he is providing, or the service provider, which can not be absolutely sure about the veracity of the identity or data the user is providing.

Identity management technologies, as those proposed by Liberty Alliance and WS-* in the field of the organizations, or OpenID and CardSpace more focused on the end user environment, are intended to fill this confidence gap in the use of services, and basically, they propose a framework where trust is provided by a third trusted party (identity provider) accepted by user and provider, which is the one that ensures the correct use of identity and its related attributes when they are requested.

However, what happens with user attributes once they are in possession of the service provider? And what about if the user does not want to share certain attributes which are being demanded by the service provider? How the user attributes are shared when he is not online in order to approve its use? These questions, presently, are issues of the highest order in the user's privacy area which, however, the identity management technologies are not always able to answer with satisfaction.

Thus, with these technologies, the control that a user can carry on using their attributes is reduced to grant or not the sending of them to the service provider that makes the request, and the "ad hoc" possibilities that, in this sense, the service provider logic which is going to receive those attributes or the identity provider give.

Technologies dealing with privacy languages, as Privacy Preference Expression Languages (i.e: CARML, AAPML, or P3P) or WS-Policy, could be used to cover this lack of control over the attribute sharing, because they provide much more richness and flexible capabilities to the process of defining attribute privacy policies. Privacy languages could allow the user to determine what type of use grant to each specific attribute to such an extent that defining who gave it, for how long, what kind of permission it approves for the assignment of the attribute to third parties, etc....

By this way, we could imagine the moment in which the system will ask to the user what kind of identity he wants to use for logging into a service (identity management functionality); it could be considered a feature to submit a screen (a "privacy policy form") where the user may determine this, through a "checkbox", and for each attribute requested (privacy languages functionality):

- Send attribute: yes/no
- Attribute lifetime: 1 hour/1 day/1 month…
- Number of uses allowed: 1use/10 uses…
- Data transfer to third parties: yes/no
- User data erasing in the system: yes/no

Alternatively this information could be entered in the identity provider by the user, in order to act according to user preferences whenever a service requests those atributes.

This type of functionality, coupled with the already provided by identity management technologies, could allow users to know with much more detail the use that is being done of the information provided, which in the end would result in greater confidence in the use of services that would allow this kind of control.

Now, the issue is to look for a way to make both work together: Identity management technologies and privacy languages. Along the first part of this paper we will describe some current approaches to solve this integration problem. In the second part, we will describe several suggestions and improvements to those approaches in order to make them more "user-centric" and easier to deploy.

2 Solving the integration problem

Before showing the different approaches, we will introduce the main concepts of the involved technologies.

2.1 Technologies Involved: Identity Management

Talking about identity management, there are three concepts that are usually present regardless the selected solution we were working with [Libe03]:

- Identity Provider (IdP): It is the entity which serves the user identity when it is needed. Also, it usually holds the attributes of this user and serves them when they are requested.
- Service Provider (SP): It is the entity which provides the services and, in order to do that, requests a set of user attributes (in addition to its identity) to the IdP.
- Circle of Trust (CoT): A virtual association of SP arround an IdP, which is considered to be trusted by all of them.

In an usual process, the user tries to access to a SP service. The SP then requests the user identity (together with some user attributes it may need) to the IdP. After that, the IdP autenticates the user and in the event of a success, sends to the SP the user identity and the requested attributes. Finally, the service access is granted to the user.

2.2 Technologies Involved: Privacy Languages

In the context of this paper, a privacy language (PPEL from Privacy Preferences Expression Languages) could be defined as a protocol (or set of them) which allows the communications among users, providers and third parties in order to set, consult, negotiate and evaluate a privacy policy about the user information. Conceptually, a privacy language defines three main entities: "User", which has its own attributes. "Custodian", which holds the user attributes. And the "Requestor", which requests them. In addition to this, a privacy language usually implements the following capabilities:

- To set privacy preferences to anyone of the involved entities: This will allow the user or the requestor to set its privacy policies.
- To define the proposed use for the requested information: This will allow the requestor to tell the custodian about the intended use for its attributes. This could also be considered as a privacy policy proposal (It will be considered that way in the rest of the paper).
- To accept or deny a privacy policy: This will allow the requestor and the custodian to accept or not the proposed privacy policy of the other part.
- To set the accepted privacy policy for served information: This will allow the custodian to add a privacy policy together with the served information.
- To decide if a proposed privacy policy fits or not another privacy policy: This will allow the custodian to decide if the requestor proposed use for an attribute should be allowed.

Usually, but not required, there is another privacy language element: The policy server. Its role is to hold the privacy policies, allowing the presence of references to them into the custodian-requestor dialogue. This helps to simplify implementations, to slim the size of the packets and, of course, standardizes the policies definition.

A typical privacy language protocol sets that the requestor demands some user attributes to the custodian, and in order to do so, it adds to the request a description of the intended use for those attributes. The custodian then checks the privacy policy which is applied to the requested attributes (whether it was defined by the user or directly by the custodian) against the privacy policy (the attribute use) proposed by the requestor. If either both match or the requestor's policy is more restricted that the one defined by the user, then the custodian sends the attributes to the requestor. Otherwise, the attributes are not sent.

Finally, it has to be noticed that XML could be considered as a good platform to build privacy languages. In fact, the most part of them are XML-based (P3P, CARML, AAPML, ODRL, WS-Policy, etc.) In addition to this, XML is in the core of the identity management solutions we are going to consider in this paper, so that, it seems a good idea to set XML based privacy language as the focus of this study. For next chapters, P3P has been selected. However, the suggested ideas are leashed to the concept of privacy languages, not to one of them.

2.2.1 A privacy language: Platform for Privacy Preferences (P3P)

2.2.1.1 Concept

P3P [W3c02] is a XML-based privacy language that describes the privacy and/or user preferred policies for a Web site. The P3P vocabulary allows describing what information is collected on a site and how it is used. So, sites implementing such policies make their practises explicit and thus open them to public scrutiny. Finally, P3P descriptions are machine readable, so that, intelligent interfaces could be built to act on behalf of the user or to help it to understand those privacy practises defined by sites (SP).

P3P usually manages the concept of "user agent". P3P user agent is the "intelligent interface" we were talking about. It typically allows users to specify their privacy preferences so that they can automatically compare a web site's policies to these preferences. P3P user agents can also provide tools that make it easier for users to quickly assess a site's privacy practices for themselves. Some user agents display symbols that summarize a site's privacy policy or indicate that it has a privacy seal (a certification that the site follows its stated privacy policy and/or complies with some set of privacy standards) or is bound by certain privacy laws. Some user agents also include buttons that load a site's human-readable privacy policy without the user's having to search for it on the site. Finally, the user agent is intended to be deployed in user side (that is, the user PC), but it is not mandatory, so it could be deployed anywhere. In fact, the idea of this paper is adding this user agent functionality to the user trusted IdP.

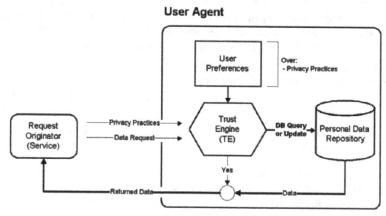

Figure 1: User agent concept

2.2.1.2 Policy description

P3P provides several elements in order to define a privacy policy. By this way, services providers can specify (i.e.) the data that should be required to user, and what will be the purpose of using this information. The user will be informed about this practise through the use agent and will make a decision according his preferences.

A sort example of these elements is shown as follows:

- Policies: Gathers one or more P3P policies together in a single file. This is provided as a performance optimization: many policies can be collected with a single request, improving network traffic and caching.
- Policy: Contains a complete P3P policy.
- Purpose: Describes the purposes of data collection or uses of data.
- Recipient: Describes all intended recipients of the collected data.
- Retention: Indicates the retention policy that applies to the data.
- Access: Indicates whether the SP provides access to the collected data.
- Disputes: Indicates dispute resolution procedures that may be followed for disputes about an SP's privacy practices.
- Remedies: Specifies the possible remedies in case a policy breach occurs.
- Data: Elements used to describe the type of data that a site collects.

With these elements, a SP can establish if user data will be storage in its server or will hand over to other enterprises, if the data is stored for administration purpose or for telemarketing, etc. References to current regulation could also be done in order to apply the law.

Example

This very simple example shows a privacy policy (a group of privacy sentences) that could be defined by an SP to request some user attributes. This privacy policy would allow to show to the user what attribute is defined as mandatory and what is marked as optional, in order to leave this decision in his hand.

```
<DATA-GROUP>
<DATA ref="#user.home-info.IDcard"/>
<DATA ref="#user.home-info.email"/>
<DATA ref="#user.home-info.bank-account" optional="yes"/>
</DATA-GROUP>
```

In this example, "user.home-info.Idcard" and "user.home-info.email" are "mandatory" requests for the SP, while "user.home-info.bank-account" is tagged as "optional". So, in the user side, User agent will act according user preferences. If user allows sending all the information, the three data will be sent to the SP, but if the User Agent is configured to avoid all the information tagged as "optional", only the "IDCard" and "email" will be sent and be accepted by the SP. If the User Agent is configured more restrictive and deny providing some of the "mandatory" information, SP will not allow user to access its service.

Now, it is easy to imagine some kind of interface which would translate the "optional" statements to "checkboxes" that can be selected by the user. So, there would not be automatic decisions accordingly to a previously defined user privacy policy, but user would take the decision "on line" instead.

2.3 Identity management and privacy language integration: Scenarios.

In an identity management context, the user will never hold its attributes by itself, but IdP will do instead. So, it is easy to match an IdP to the privacy language role of "custodian" and a SP to the privacy language role of "requestor". Therefore, the SP and the IdP will be in charge of the "privacy dialogue", so that they will be those that will use the privacy language mechanism.

According to this matching process, we could describe three main scenarios to integrate Identity management solutions and privacy languages. They are as follows:

- The SP proposes the privacy policy.
- The User proposes the privacy policy.
- SP and User negotiate the privacy policy.

The SP proposes the privacy policy
In this scenario, the user tries to access to the SP service. The SP then asks the user for authentication in the IdP and includes an user attribute request. In this request, the SP sends also the privacy policy it is going to apply to the user attributes. Then, the IdP authenticates the user and checks if the privacy policy of the request match or not the one defined for the user attributes (whether it was defined previously by the user or by the IdP itself) In the first case, the IdP sends the user identity and its attributes to the SP. In the second one, the authentication and attribute request are cancelled.

The main advantage of this scenario is that the privacy policy check is done before the SP knows the user identity. This is a good privacy point. On the SP side, there is the fact that only the SP's privacy policy is considered. So, the potential number of privacy policy to be considered is reduced to those defined, and accepted, by the SP. This is a good fact for the services providers.

The User or the IdP proposes the privacy policy
In this scenario, the SP doesn't send an intended privacy policy to be applied to the user attributes it is requesting. Once the user is authenticated by the IdP, the requested attributes are sent to the SP (together with the user identity), but also a privacy policy to be applied to them does. In this case, the SP has to decide if this privacy policy match or not its own intended use for those attributes. If it is not, the use of the attributes is not granted. So, the SP has to act consequently denying the user access to the service and discarding the received attributes.

In this case, the SP has to accept the received privacy policy and, due to the fact that this privacy policy could be defined by the user itself or, at least, by a trusted IdP, it could be considered a more "user-centric" scenario. However, it opens a wide range of potential privacy policies that the SP has to be able to match. It could be difficult and complex to implement and, from a business point of view, it may even be unacceptable. In addition to this, the user identity and attributes are sent before privacy policy was accepted. From a privacy point of view, this is not desirable.

SP and User negotiate the privacy policy
This scenario is complementary to the previous ones. Now, both, user and SP, send their privacy policy preferences (In the case of the SP the privacy policy is the intended use for the attributes), and eventually, a mixed privacy policy is agreed. Despite privacy languages should support this feature, the possibility to deploy this kind of scenario highly depends on the identity management solution capability to support this dialogue.

2.4 Identity management and privacy language integration: Initiatives

2.4.1 IGF Liberty Alliance project's Initiative

Liberty Alliance project [Libe03] has been developing several works about the possibility of deploying PPEL's functionality into its Identity management approach. Specifically, the paper "Liberty architecture framework for supporting Privacy Preference Expression Languages (PPELs)"[RMS+03] proposed a framework to introduce P3P policies into the SOAP messages exchange between a Service Provider (SP) and a Web Service Provider (WSP). Doing so, the SP could send its privacy policy to a WSP acting as a part of an Identity Provider (IdP). This IdP (in fact, the WSP) would store the user data join to the user's privacy policy (also defined with P3P) and would be able to automatically check the matching between both, SP's privacy policy and User's privacy policy, and act accordingly. Based on this idea, the Identity Governance Framework (IGF), a Liberty Alliance promoted initiative, is working on a more detailed framework.

The IGF is about the secure and appropriate exchange of identity-related information between users and applications and service providers in the basis of providing deeper and richer functionality for services oriented architecture. The goal is defining a framework to help enterprises easily determine and control how identity related information, including Personally Identifiable Information (PII), access entitlements; attributes, etc. are used, stored, and propagated between their systems.

IGF is designed for developers to build applications that access identity-related data from a wide range of sources and administrators/deployers to define, enforce, and audit policies concerning the use of identity-related data. Also, reporting and auditing support is considered. As proposed, IGF will have four components:

- Identity attribute service: A service that supports access to many different identity sources and enforces administrative policy.
- CARML [Hunt06], Client Attribute Requirements Markup Language: Declarative syntax using which clients may specify their attribute requirements, i.e. what identity information an application needs and how the application will use it.
- AAPML [Mish06], Attribute Authority Policy Markup Language: Declarative syntax which enables providers of identity-related data to express policy on the usage of information. AAPML is a XACML extension.
- Multi-language API (Java, .NET, Perl) for reading and writing identity-related attributes.

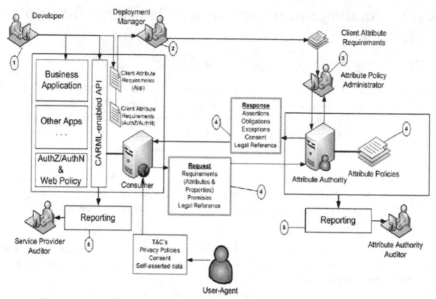

Figure 2: A full lifecycle for the IGF components (from Liberty Alliance project)

As seen in the image above, IGF tries to cover the issues related to all the key actors involved in the management and processing of identity data.

Summarizing, CARML would allow a SP to specify the user attributes it needs and the expected use for them. In the other hand, AAPML would be use to define the privacy policy to be enforced on the user attributes. IGF does not define whether the IdP or the user is in charge of defining this privacy policy enforcement. Doing so, all of the previously defined scenarios could be easily fitted by IGF.

Despite IGF is strongly designed from the point of view of enterprises as common attribute authority owners, in a way that reminds of an organization-centric focus, it is important to note that IGF is not bounded to any specific identity management system, so it may be considered as a Multi-protocol privacy solution that could be applied to different kinds of Identity management solutions.

2.4.2 SAML-XACML approach

Some approaches for privacy matters may use Extensible Access Control Markup Language, XACML [Oasi05], standardized by OASIS. Primary goal of XACML, as expressed in its charter, is defining a core schema and corresponding namespace for the expression of authorization policies in XML against objects that are themselves identified in XML. This expression includes some features as use of arbitrary attributes in policies, role-based access control, security labels, time/date-based policies, indexable policies, 'deny' policies, and dynamic policies. In other words, XACML is a full featured access control policy language.

From the point of view of privacy issues, XACML can address them because of we can consider privacy rules as a subset of general access control rules, i.e. one of the reasons of allowing or denying access to your personal data is your own privacy preference on them. In the same way, personal data is a subset of the target set covered by XACML (indeed, it covers anything meant to be protected). The best example is the previously mentioned AAPML language, which is an XACML profile focused on these subsets.

Combining XACML with other identity related protocols is an alternative for enhancing privacy in identity-based systems. For instance, XACML has been used along with SAML in federated scenarios, being the former in charge of providing access control policies for resource requests and the latter the Single Sign On and Federation features enabler. As stated before, privacy could be achieved in the same way, particularizing for privacy policies and personal private data.

3 Improvements proposal

3.1 Making easier the integration in Liberty based solutions

IGF already fits the previously defined scenarios, but due to the fact that this approach aims to integrate privacy languages through SOAP messages, it is needed to develop the required modules to add the privacy sentences. For that reason, it could be interesting to define integration through the planned mechanisms to extent Liberty specifications.

Authentication context extension.
The authentication context [Libe03] is part of the SAML specifications, and it is used by the SP to communicate authentication conditions to be observed, like the desired authentication method to be applied to the user. Previously, SP and IdP have exchanged their metadata where the details to interpret this authentication method are defined. The authentication context extension is a Liberty mechanism to define new authentication methods to be used. The details of the new method are defined into the metadata as a new authentication context class that will be stated in the authentication context request of the SP. So, we could consider defining a new authentication context class that would define both, the authentication method and a reference to a privacy policy in an external policy server. The metadata would hold the details to correctly interpret the context class and to access the policy reference.

Others proposals could be consider. For example, to define a new "Privacy-context" in addition to the common "authentication-context". Doing so, the full privacy policy information could be sent to the IdP in a more elegant and flexible way, but it would be needed to extent the Liberty specifications.

3.2 Improving the "user-centric" focus

3.2.1 The "privacy policy form"

In the beginning of this paper, we described the confidence problem that could arise when identity management systems take control of user attributes in order to distribute them among service providers. We also have described some scenarios and approaches that could be used to integrate privacy language capabilities into identity management solutions based on some kind of circles of trust, as a way to tackle this confidence problem. Now we will try to add a feature to improve the user-centric "flavour" of the involved scenarios and we will describe a means to implement it in some identity management solutions.

The problem
In an identity management context where users and organizations interact, the "user-centric" concept stands for the user is in the middle of a data transaction [Hard06]. Intuitively, it also can stand for the user is conscious about all the transaction process. So, the integration of privacy languages could be seen as a "user-centric" feature because it gives to the user the ability to control the use of its attributes which improves the confidence of the whole process. However, the described scenarios and approaches doesn't specify the user role, so an automatically solution with limited user interaction could be as-

sumed. That is, the IdP will automatically apply the previously user defined privacy policy and, eventually, send the attributes to the SP. But, Would the user really like to apply the same policy to any attribute request no matter which SP is requesting them? Indeed, Would it like to apply the same policy to the same SP request each time? May be, but, of course, the user would be more conscious about the use of its attributes if it can decide about these questions each time it makes a transaction. That is, this capability would improve the "user-centric" focus of the identity management solution.

The solution
In that context, it is not enough to offer a means to define privacy policies for the user attributes (like IGF does); it is also necessary to accomplish that user were absolutely conscious about the permits it is granting to the SP in the course of a transaction. That is, it should be allowed for the user to decide a new privacy policy for each transaction it does. Even if it is a repeated transaction for the same service. The final goal is to improve the perceived trust. This issue suggests avoiding automatic response excesses from the IdP. So, it should be provided a means to allow user to dynamically decide the privacy policy to be applied to the transaction (SP-service) it is currently developing. For instance, a "privacy policy form"

3.2.1.1 Improving scenarios

The already described scenarios could be converted to a more "user-centric" point of view by means of this "privacy policy form" (like the one described in the Introduction chapter) which would be shown to the user to decide the acceptance of an "offered" privacy policy or to define a new one to be sent to the SP.

The SP proposes the privacy policy
This scenario, as it was presented in previous chapters, could be solve by means of IGF proposal. However, if we want to add a "user-centric" point of view it is needed something more. Firstly, a conscious user interaction is needed, so the IdP has to show the SP privacy policy and allow the user to decide about it. Doing so, once the IdP authenticates user identity, it translates the received privacy policy into a "human-readable" form (the "privacy policy form") which is shown to the user. Then, the user accepts or denies the "offered" privacy policy. In the first case, the IdP sends the user identity and its attributes to the SP. In the second one, the authentication and attribute request are cancelled.

But this scenario is not much flexible, because, in the end, the user only has an "all-or-nothing" control over the privacy policy to be applied to its attributes. So, we could improve it by means of the inclusion of some kind of "optional process" to the user decision. Doing so, the SP's privacy policy would include optional sentences that the user could accept or not, without cancelling the whole request. So, when the IdP shows the received privacy policy to the user, the "privacy policy form" offers the capability to check or uncheck some of the premises (In a similar way that the one stated in the Introduction of this paper). Finally, the IdP sends the attributes to the SP with the user selected privacy sentences (by means of the privacy language). That sentences could be then stored by the SP as a kind of "proof of grant". For this scenario, it is needed a privacy languages with the "optional sentence" functionality available.

The User proposes the privacy policy
Once again, the "user-centric" focus will be added by means of the "privacy policy form". This time, instead of adding a previously defined privacy policy to the attributes, the IdP would show to the user a form which would allow the building of a privacy policy that will be translated to a privacy language again in order to be sent to the SP.

SP and User negotiate the privacy policy

Adding the "privacy policy form", this scenario would be a mix of the previous ones. The form would show to the user the SP privacy policy and the user would be able to change the privacy sentences or define new ones to be sent to the SP. Then, the process would start again.

3.2.1.2 The "privacy policy form" in Liberty based solutions

In a common Liberty dialogue between a SP which is requesting some user attributes and an IdP which holds those attributes, no user interaction is needed. The IdP serves the attributes to the SP. However, Liberty implements a feature that offers to the user the possibility to take some decision about the transaction. Typically, the user will be asked about whether continuing or not the transaction. This feature is accomplished by means of the "interaction service" [AMC+06].

The interaction service (IS) is an ID-WSF (Liberty Web Service Framework) service that provides a means for simple interactions between an ID-WSF implementation and a Principal (i.e. the user). It allows a client (typically a web service provider, also known as WSP, acting as a web service consumer, also known as WSC, towards the interaction service) to query a Principal for consent, authorization decisions, etc. An IS provider accepts requests to present information and requests to a principal. The IS provider is responsible for "rendering" a "form" to the Principal. It is expected that the IS provider knows about the capabilities of the Principal's device and about any preferences he or she may have regarding such interactions. The IS returns the answer(s) of the Principal in a response that contains values for the parameters of the request.

Through this mechanism, user privacy interaction could be enabled by setting up an ID-WSF interaction service, capable of asking the user any time its data is requested, presenting details of the interaction. That is, this IS would be in charge of showing the "privacy policy form" to the user.

Therefore, the IS should be able to interpret the privacy policy received by the SP and, after that, to translate it to a form with checkboxes or deployable lists where privacy options would be shown to the user. Once the user check its privacy preferences, IS would translate them to a privacy language message that would be sent back to the SP.

Regarding P3P issues, the IdP would be the "custodian" of the user attributes and the IS (as a part of the IdP) the one which would deploy the "user agent" functionality of the privacy language (Notice that "user agent" would not be deployed in the user side)

Finally, deploying such as "privacy interaction service" is completely standard, because Liberty specifies the role of the interaction services, but details about their functionality are not. In addition to this, this service would fit all of the three previously defined scenarios, because the IS is only a means to interact with the user and it does not add any requirement to those scenarios.

3.2.2 Privacy languages in OpenID

The current OpenID specification does not allow to implement any other scenario but the "The User proposes the privacy policy" one. It is due to the fact that the Relying Party (RP, the SP) is only allowed to send to the OpenID Provider (OP, the IdP) a list of requested attributes. And this list could not be modified to add privacy issues because the only accepted items are the standardized attribute names together with a variable which sets if the attribute is optional or not.

For the referred scenario, OpenID 2.0 [Open07] has to be used because it has the "OpenID attribute exchange extension" feature. This capability will allow us to define a new attribute: "openid.

myattributes.Privacy-policy", which would hold the user (or OP) defined privacy policy. That is, a XML file (or a reference to a policy server where the policy could be found). The policy length will not be a problem, because the new version of OpenID includes the possibility to send http POST messages (instead of http redirects). Finally, the RP would have always to request the defined privacy policy attribute as "mandatory", in order to be able to receive the user privacy policy.

Of course, the RP has to be able to interpret the received privacy policy, but this is not part of the OpenID mechanisms itself and, so that, it could be coded.

OpenID is a "user-centric" identity management solution which has already considered the need of a form to inform the user about the privacy issues of a transaction (like CardSpace does with its "identity selector"). Currently, this form only shows the mandatory requested attributes and allows to decide about sending or not the optional ones, but it seems a good starting point to deploy a full "privacy policy form" as the one stated in this paper.

4 Conclusion

The identity management solutions and privacy languages integration problem is not closed yet. Despite there are several proposals to solve it, there still are some suggestions that could be considered to facilitate the deployment of this integration and to improve the final confidence level of the whole solution.

Along the paper we have suggested a different way to tackle the integration task in Liberty Alliance based solutions, that could make it simpler in some cases than IGF approach. Also, we have suggested a means to introduce privacy languages in a user-centric solution: OpenID. Finally, we have described the concept of the "privacy policy form", as a way to make the user more conscious about the privacy policy decisions it takes about its attributes.

References

[AMC+06] Aarts, R and others: Liberty ID-WSF Interaction sercive specification. www.projectliberty.org/liberty/content/download/885/6231/file/liberty-idwsf-interaction-svc-v2.0.pdf. Aarts, Robert; Madsen, Paul, 2006.

[Hard06] Hardt, Dick: What is user-centric identity?. http://identity20.com/?p=61. Identity 2.0, 2006.

[Hunt06] Hunt, Phil: IGF-CARML specifications. http://www.oracle.com/technology/tech/standards/idm/igf/pdf/IGF-CARML-spec-03.pdf. Oracle, 2006.

[Libe03] The Liberty Alliance: Liberty Alliance Project. http://projectliberty.org, 2003.

[Mish06] Mishra, Prateek: IGF-AAPML specifications. http://www.oracle.com/technology/tech/standards/idm/igf/pdf/IGF-AAPML-spec-08.pdf. Oracle, 2006.

[Oasi05] OASIS: OASIS eXtensible Access Control Markup Language (XACML) TC. http://www.oasis-open.org/committees/tc_home.php?wg_abbrev=xacml. OASIS, 2005.

[Open07] OpenID Authentication 2.0 – Final. http://openid.net/specs/openid-authentication-2_0.html. OpenID.net, 2007

[RMS+03] Aarts, R and others: Liberty architecture framework for supporting Privacy Preference Expression Languages (PPELs). http://www.projectliberty.org/liberty/resource_center/papers/privacy_preference_expression_languages_whitepaper_pdf. Liberty Alliance project, 2003.

[W3c02] W3C: The Platform for Privacy Preferences 1.0 (P3P1.0) Specification. http://www.w3.org/TR/P3P. W3C, 2002.

Security Economics and European Policy[1]

Ross Anderson[1] · Rainer Böhme[2] · Richard Clayton[1] · Tyler Moore[1]

[1]Computer Laboratory
University of Cambridge, UK
{ross.anderson | richard.clayton | tyler.moore}@cl.cam.ac.uk

[2]Faculty of Computer Science
Technische Universität Dresden, DE
rainer.boehme@tu-dresden.de

Abstract

In September 2007, we were awarded a contract by the European Network and Information Security Agency (EN-ISA) to investigate failures in the market for secure electronic communications within the European Union, and come up with policy recommendations. In the process, we spoke to a large number of stakeholders, and held a consultative meeting in December 2007 in Brussels to present draft proposals, which established most had wide stakeholder support. The formal outcome of our work was a detailed report, "Security Economics and the Internal Market", published by ENISA in March 2008. This paper presents a much abridged version: in it, we present the recommendations we made, along with a summary of our reasoning.

1 Introduction

Until the 1970s, network and information security was the concern of national governments. Intelligence agencies used eavesdropping and traffic analysis techniques against rival countries, largely in the context of the Cold War, and attempted to limit the penetration of their own countries' networks by rival agencies. From the 1970s until about 2004, however, the centre of gravity in information security shifted from governments to companies. As firms became ever more dependent on networked computer systems, the prospect of frauds and failures has increasingly driven investment in research and development.

Since about 2004, volume crime has arrived on the Internet. All of a sudden, criminals who were carrying out card fraud and attacks on electronic banking got organised, thanks to a handful of criminal organisations and a number of chat-rooms and other electronic fora where criminals can trade stolen card and bank account data, hacking tools and other services. Hacking has turned from a sport into a business, and its tools are becoming increasingly commoditised. There has been an explosion of crime-ware – malicious software used to perpetrate a variety of online crimes. Keyloggers, data theft tools and even phishing sites can be constructed using toolkits complete with sophisticated graphical user interfaces. The 'quality' of these tools is improving rapidly, as their authors invest in proper research, development, quality control and customer service.

---

[1] This chapter originally appeared in Eric M. Johnson (ed.) "Managing Information Risk and the Economics of Security", (c) Springer 2008

N. Pohlmann, H. Reimer, W. Schneider (Editors): Securing Electronic Business Processes, Vieweg (2008), 57-76

Most commonly, crimeware is spread by tricking users into running code that they got in email attachments or downloaded from a malicious web site. However, its distribution is becoming more sophisticated as the criminal economy develops. For example, one so-called affiliate marketing web site offers to pay webmasters a commission ranging from US$0.08 to US$0.50 per infection to install iframes that point to an attacker's site which distributes crimeware [JR08]. Meanwhile, network and information security is of growing economic importance in Europe (as elsewhere): sales of anti-virus software, cryptographic products, and services ranging from spam filtering through phishing-site 'take-down' to brand protection and copyright enforcement are in the billions of euros per annum. The economic study of information security is thus of rapidly growing relevance to policy makers.

Since about 2000, researchers have realised that many security failures have economic causes [AM06]. Systems often fail because the organisations that defend them do not bear the full costs of failure. For example, in countries with lax banking regulation, banks can pass more of the cost of fraud to customers and merchants, and this undermines their own incentive to protect payment systems properly. In addition, so long as anti-virus software is left to individuals to purchase and install, there may be a less than optimal level of protection when infected machines cause trouble for other machines rather than their owners.

Our key message is that in order to solve the problems of growing vulnerability and increasing crime, policy and legislation must coherently allocate responsibilities and liabilities so that the parties in a position to fix problems have an incentive to do so. For a variety of reasons, the state will have a role to play, either as policeman, or regulator, or coordinator. In the specific case of the European Union, regulatory options range from direct legislation (previous examples being the Data Protection Directive and the Electronic Commerce Directive), sector-specific regulation (such as the recent Payment Services Directive), coordinating groups (such as the Article 29 Working Party on data protection law), the funding of research, public procurement, down to the collection and publication of information.

In our complete report[2], we provide a more complete regulatory context and weigh the different options in greater detail. In this short paper, we describe just the final recommendations we made, along with our reasoning. By way of disclaimer, we note that these recommendations are our own and do not necessarily reflect the policy of ENISA or any other European institution.

1.1 Economic Barriers to Network and Information Security

We used five general headings to classify and analyse the economic barriers to network and information security, which form the structure of our paper: information asymmetries, externalities, liability, diversity, and the fragmentation of legislation and law enforcement.

Information Asymmetries: Asymmetric information can be a strong impediment to effective security. Akerlof's model of the 'market for lemons' [Aker70] appears to apply to many security product markets. The tendency of bad security products to drive out good ones from the marketplace has long been known, and at present the main initiative to overcome asymmetric information supported by the Commission and Member State governments is the Common Criteria.

It has also long been known that we simply do not have good statistics on online crime, attacks and vulnerabilities. Companies are hesitant to discuss their weaknesses with competitors even though a coordinated view of attacks could allow faster mitigation to everyone's benefit. In the USA, this problem

---

2 „Security Economics and the Internal Market" (2008), available at http://www.enisa.europa.eu/doc/pdf/report_sec_econ_&_int_mark_20080131.pdf

has been tackled by information-sharing associations, security-breach disclosure laws and vulnerability markets.

Externalities: Many important security threats are characterised by negative externalities. For example, home computers are increasingly being compromised and loaded with malware used to harm others. As a result, a user who connects an unpatched computer to the Internet does not face the full economic consequences of her action. A further set of externalities affect Internet service providers (ISPs). Small-to-medium ISPs have an incentive to clean up user machines (as being a source of spam damages their peering relationships [SC05]) while large ISPs at present enjoy a certain impunity.

Network externalities also affect many protective measures. For example, encryption software needs to be present at both ends of a communication in order to protect it; the first company to buy encryption software can protect communications with its branches, but not with its customers or its suppliers. In other circumstances, investments can be strategic complements: an individual taking protective measures may also protect others, inviting them to free-ride.

Liability Dumping: Firms seeking to manage risk often dump it on less powerful suppliers or customers. Software and service suppliers impose licenses on customers disclaiming all liability, including for security failures, and may also take 'consent' to the installation of spyware. This may delay the emergence of a market for more secure languages and tools, and lessen demand for the employment of professional software engineering methods.

Another example is the problem of mobile phone security; mobile phones have a long and complex supply chain, starting from the intellectual property owners, the chipmaker, the software supplier, the handset vendor, the network operator and the service provider. Each of these players seeks to have others bear the costs of security as much as possible, while using security mechanisms to maximise its own power in the chain. One side effect has been the failure of the OMA DRM Architecture V2 to come into widespread use, which in turn may have depressed the market for music downloads to mobile phones.

A third example is in payment services. The recent Payment Services Directive [EU07] goes some way towards harmonisation of service rules across the EU but still leaves consumer protection significantly behind the USA. Banks are allowed to set dispute resolution procedures by their terms and conditions, and do so in their favour – as found for example in the recent report of the UK House of Lords Science and Technology Committee into Personal Internet Security [HoL07], which recommended that the traditional consumer protection enshrined in banking law since the nineteenth century should be extended to electronic transactions too.

Lack of Diversity: Lack of diversity is a common complaint against platform vendors, whether Microsoft or Cisco or even Symbian. This is not just a matter for the competition authorities; lack of diversity makes successful attacks more devastating and harder to insure against, as high loss correlation renders some market segments uninsurable. Thus the market structure of the IT industry is a significant factor in society's ability to manage and absorb cyber risks.

Communication service providers are also affected; smaller ISPs find it cheaper to use single peering points, with the result that only large ISPs offer their customers resilience against peering point outage. This not only places these smaller ISPs (which are mainly small-to-medium enterprises (SMEs) and providing services to SMEs) at a disadvantage but shades over into critical national infrastructure concerns.

Fragmentation of Legislation and Law Enforcement: The fragmentation of jurisdictions hinders rapid response. For example, the most important factor in deterring and frustrating phishing attacks is the speed of asset recovery. A bank learning of a customer account compromise needs to be able to trace and freeze any stolen assets quickly. The phishermen send hot money through the banks of Member States with a relaxed attitude to asset recovery. This issue spills over to money laundering.

A serious problem is that traditional mechanisms for international police cooperation are too slow and expensive for the Internet age. They evolved when international investigations were infrequent and dealt with matters that were either procedurally simple (such as the extradition of a fugitive) or a large investigation of mutual interest (such as drug smuggling). They do not cope well (or in some cases at all) with volume crime that crosses national boundaries.

2 Information Asymmetries

There has long been a shortage of hard data about information security failures, as many of the available statistics are not only poor but are collected by parties such as security vendors or law enforcement agencies with a vested interest in under- or over-reporting. These problems are now being tackled with some success in many US states with security-breach reporting laws, which we describe in Section 2.1. We also consider other opportunities for collecting relevant data in Section 2.2.

2.1 Security-Breach Notification

The first security-breach notification law to be enacted in the United States was California's A.B. 700 in September 2002 [CSS02]. It applies to public and private entities that conduct business in California and requires them to notify affected individuals when personal data under their control have been acquired by an unauthorised person. The law was intended to ensure that individuals are given the opportunity to take appropriate steps to protect their interests following data theft, such as putting a 'lock' on their file at credit agencies. It was also intended to motivate companies holding personal data to take steps to keep it secure. Indeed, Acquisti et al. [AFT06] found a statistically significant negative impact on stock prices following a breach. Breach disclosure laws have also had the positive effect of contributing valuable data on security incidents to the public domain.

The California law has been followed by further laws in at least 34 other states[3], although they differ somewhat in their details. The variations have led to calls for a federal statute, but although bills have been introduced in Congress, none have had much success so far. In Europe, a security breach notification law has been proposed that would require notification to be made where a network security breach was responsible for the disclosure of personal data [EC07]. This is a very narrow definition and will only deal with a small fraction of the cases that a California-style law would cover. Many incidents, such as criminals fitting an automatic teller machine (ATM) with a skimmer that steals card details [BBC07], would only be covered by a California-style law.

The US experience demonstrates the disadvantages of a patchwork of local laws, and the obvious recommendation is that a security breach notification law should be brought forward at the EU level, covering all sectors of economic activity rather than just telecomms companies. Indeed, the point of security breach notification is to avoid all the complexity of setting out in detail how data should be protected; instead it provides incentives for protection. It does not impose the burden of a strict liability regime across the whole economy, but relies on 'naming and shaming'. Competent firms should welcome a situation where incompetent firms who cut corners to save money will be exposed, incur costs, and

---

3   http://www.ncsl.org/programs/lis/cip/priv/breach.htm.

lose customers. This levels up the playing field and prevents the competent being penalised for taking protection seriously.

Recommendation 1: We recommend that the EU introduce a comprehensive security-breach notification law.

As well as informing the data subjects of a data breach, a central clearing house should be informed as well. This ensures that even the smallest of breaches can be located by the press, investors, researchers, and sector-specific regulators. The law should set out minimum standards of clarity for notifications – in the US some companies have hidden notices within screeds of irrelevant marketing information. Finally, notifications should include clear advice on what individuals should do to mitigate the risks they run as a result of the disclosure; in the US many notifications have just puzzled their recipients rather than giving them helpful advice.

2.2 Further Data Sources

While breach-disclosure notification laws also serve as a useful data source on information security, a wider selection of data needs to be collected in an unbiased manner. A number of sources already collect relevant data, which comes in many forms. For the past twelve years, the US-based Computer Security Institute has annually surveyed enterprises, asking respondents whether they have been attacked and, if so, what the resulting losses were [CSI07]. In 2003, Eurostat started collecting data on Internet security issues from both individuals and enterprises in its "Community Surveys on ICT Usage" [EC06]. Many security vendors also regularly publish reports on attack trends (e.g., [Syma07]). Industry groups also sometimes disclose useful statistics, including the Anti-Phishing Working Group and APACS, the UK payments association. Finally, some academics conduct useful data collection and analysis (e.g., analysing phishing website lifetimes [MC07] and tracking botnets [ZHH+07]).

While governments can specify requirements for data collection, it is up to the stakeholders to actually provide the data. Security vendors will feel it in their interest to provide inflated statistics; phishing statistics often seem particularly fishy. For example, the anti-phishing group PhishTank has boasted about the large number of sites it identifies [Open07], when in reality the number of duplicates reduces the overall number several fold. APACS provides another example by asserting a 726% increase in phishing attacks between 2005 and 2006 (with merely a 44% rise in losses) [APA07].

ISPs, by contrast, have an incentive to undercount the amount of wickedness emanating from their customers, particularly if they are held to account for it. But there is an even more pernicious problem with ISP reporting: ISPs hold important private information about the configuration of their own network that influences measurements. In particular, policies regarding dynamic IP address assignment can greatly skew an outside party's estimate of the number of compromised machines located at an ISP. ISPs also regard the size of their customer base as a company secret, which makes cross-ISP performance comparisons difficult.

In more mature sectors of the economy, we can see useful examples of statistical institutions collecting business data jointly with industry bodies. For example, safety and accident statistics for cars are collected by police and insurers, while media circulation figures are typically collected by private firms, some of them jointly owned and controlled by publishers and advertisers.

At the behest of the European Commission, ENISA recently investigated whether to establish a framework for sharing collected data on information security indicators between interested parties [Casp08]. They identified around 100 potential data sources, then surveyed a core of potential partners (CERTs,

MSSPs, security vendors, etc.) who were invited to a workshop to further gauge interest. Unfortunately, there was very little desire for sharing raw data, aggregated data, or indeed any information that doesn't already appear in the publicly-issued reports. Hence mandatory reporting of particular indicators may be required for sharing to happen.

We recommend that ENISA's information sharing efforts focus on industries with a clear benefit but where sharing is not already taking place in every Member State – and the two industries where more information should be made available are the financial industry and ISPs.

Individual banks are usually keen to keep data on fraud losses private. But one notable exception is the UK, where APACS has published aggregated figures for the annual amount lost to phishing attacks, as well as ATM crime and other financial fraud [APA07]. While the incentives are against individual financial institutions revealing losses publicly, a country-wide aggregation may still aid policymakers without inhibiting honest reporting very much. As far as we can tell, no other Member State publishes statistics of this kind. As banks collect such statistics for operational, internal control and audit purposes, and aggregating them nationally is straightforward, we believe this practice should become standard practice in the EU. The statistics are particularly critical to the formulation of policy on network and information security since the majority of the actual harm that accrues is financial. Without a good measure of this, other figures – whether of vulnerabilities, patches, botnets, or bad traffic – lack a properly grounded connection to the real economy.

Recommendation 2: We recommend that the Commission (or the European Central Bank) regulate to ensure the publication of robust loss statistics for electronic crime.

In many cases, fraud statistics are already collected by the police or banking associations, so regulatory action should aim at harmonisation of definitions, metrics and release cycles across Member States. A good first step would be to require figures broken down broadly as the APACS statistics are and show losses due to debit and credit card fraud (subdivided into the useful categories such as card cloning versus cardholder-not-present, national versus international, and so on).

As for the information that should be published by and about ISPs, it is well known at present within the industry that some ISPs are very much better than others at detecting abuse and responding to complaints of abuse by others. This is particularly noticeable in the case of spam. A small-to-medium sized ISPs may find its peering arrangements under threat if it becomes a high-volume source of spam, so such ISPs have an incentive to detect when their customers' machines are infected and recruited into botnets. Large ISPs don't face the same peering-arrangement pressures, so as a result some send significantly larger quantities of spam and other bad traffic than others. We feel it would be strongly in the public interest for quantitative data on ISPs' security performance to be made available to the public.

Recommendation 3: We recommend that ENISA collect and publish data about the quantity of spam and other bad traffic emitted by European ISPs.

As Europe has some 40,000 ISPs, a staged approach may be advisable – with initial reports collected using sampling, followed if need be by action through telecomms regulators to collect more detailed statistics. However, even rough sample data will be useful, as it is the actions of the largest ISPs that have the greatest effect on the level of pollution in the digital environment.

Anyway, we feel that ENISA should take the lead in establishing these security metrics by setting clear guidelines, collating data from ISPs and other third parties, and disseminating the reported information. To begin with, ENISA could make a positive contribution by collecting and disseminating data on the rate at which ISPs are emitting bad packets. Such data could serve as a useful input to existing interconnection markets between ISPs since high levels of bad traffic can be costly for a receiving ISP to deal with.

The types of digital pollution to be measured must be defined carefully. To track spam, useful metrics might include: the number of spam messages sent from an ISP's customers; the number of outgoing spam messages blocked by an ISP; the number and source of incoming spam messages received by an ISP; and the number of customer machines observed to be transmitting spam for a particular duration. To track other types of malware, the number of infected customer machines would be relevant, along with the duration of infection.

Once data are available on which ISPs are the largest polluters, the next question is what should be done about them. This moves us from the heading of 'information asymmetries' to our next heading, 'externalities'.

3 Externalities

Externalities are the side effects that economic transactions have on third parties. Just as a factory belching smoke into the environment creates a negative externality for people downwind, so also people who connect infected PCs to the Internet create negative externalities in that their machines may emit spam, host phishing sites and distribute illegal content such as crimeware. The options available are broadly similar to those with which governments fight environmental pollution (a tax on pollution, a cap-and-trade system, or private action). Rather than a heavyweight central scheme, we think that civil liability might be tried first. We first discuss the different stakeholders to whom pressure might usefully be applied before detailing our recommendation.

3.1 Who Should Internalise the Costs of Malware?

At present, malware used to harm others is the backbone of the underground economy in electronic crime. Such malware is installed using social engineering, by exploiting weaknesses in core platforms (operating systems, communications systems and server software) or via applications. Responsibility for correcting the externality might plausibly fall on several stakeholders.

One option is to assign responsibility to the software vendors for making software vulnerable in the first place. We consider what can be achieved using the stick of software liability in Section 4. However, we note here that the incentives are not as misaligned for core platforms – Microsoft has been improving its security for some time and suffers negative publicity when vulnerabilities are publicised. However, exploits at the application level require a different approach. Users readily install add-on features to web browsers, load web applications from untrustworthy firms, and run unpatched or out-of-date software. Users might also not install or update anti-virus software.

The machine owner is another important stakeholder. But there is a big difference between large and small owners. Large companies manage their machines by having a network perimeter where devices such as firewalls minimise exposure to compromise and restrict outbound communications from compromised machines; they also employ technicians to repair infected devices.

Individual end users and SMEs can do much less. They can and should maintain updated software, from the OS to applications and anti-virus tools; but they cannot protect themselves at the network perimeter as effectively as large businesses can, and can have tremendous difficulty repairing compromised devices.

The next influential stakeholder is the ISP. Compared to the others, ISPs are in a good position to improve the security of end-user and SME machines. ISPs control a machine's Internet connection, and therefore its ability to harm others. There are many steps an ISP can take to limit the impact of malware-infected customer devices onto others, from disconnection to traffic filtering. ISPs can also communicate with customers by telephone or post, not just by Internet channels.

ISPs are divided on whether they should actively isolate infected customer machines, let alone whether they should try to prevent infections. One survey found that 41% of ISP respondents believed that they should clean up infected hosts, with 30% disagreeing and 29% uncertain [MLH07]. Taking costly steps to repair customer machines, potentially including the unpopular move of temporarily cutting off service, is undesirable for ISPs when most of the negative effects are not borne by others.

3.2 Policy Options for Coping with Externalities

If ISPs should take action to raise the level of end-user security, then how can we best encourage them? A laissez-faire approach of encouraging best practice through self-regulation is tempting but likely to be insufficient. This is because the incentives on taking costly remedial action are weak at best [vEB08], and since the poor performance of even a minority of ISPs can overshadow the operations of the best. Assigning liability for infected customers to ISPs is undesirable in practice due to the potentially high transaction cost of lawsuits, and the difficulty of valuing the monetary loss associated with individual events.

An alternative is to introduce fixed penalty charges if ISPs do not take remedial action within a short time period of notification. Upon notice of malicious activity, ISPs should place the machine into quarantine, clean up the offending content and reconnect the user as soon as possible. At present, there is great variation in the response times for ISPs when notified that a customer's machine is infected – the best ISPs remove phishing sites in less than one hour, while others take many days or even weeks to respond. Introducing a fixed penalty for machines that continue to misbehave after a reasonable duration, say 3 hours, would drastically speed up remedial action.

Fixed penalties are useful because they avoid the problem of quantifying losses following every infringement. They have been used effectively in the airline industry, where the EU has introduced penalties for airlines that deny passengers boarding due to overbooking, cancellations or excessive delays. The goal of this regulation is provide an effective deterrent to the airlines. Fixed penalties are also routinely used for traffic violations. Again, the penalties deter violations while simplifying liability when violations occur. The threat of penalties should alter behaviour so that, in practice, fixed penalties are rarely issued.

For fixed penalties to work, a consistent reporting mechanism is important. Fortunately, existing channels can be leveraged. At present, several specialist security companies already track bad machines and notify ISPs to request cleanup. This process could be formalised into a quarantine notice. End users could also send notifications to *abuse@isp.com*, as is already possible for reporting spam.

One issue to consider is to whom the fixed penalty should be paid. To encourage reporting, the penalty could be paid to whoever sent the notice. What about duplicate payments? One compromised machine might send millions of spam emails. If a fixed penalty had to be paid for each received report, then the fine may grow unreasonably large. Instead, the penalty should be paid to the first person to report an infected machine, or perhaps to the first ten who file reports.

Given the threat of stiff penalties for slow responses, ISPs might become overzealous in removing reported sites without first confirming the accuracy of reports. This might lead to a denial-of-service-attack where a malicious user falsely accuses other customers of misdeeds. There is also the established problem that firms who want a machine taken down for other reasons – because they claim that it hosts copyright-infringing material, or material defamatory of their products – are often very aggressive and indiscriminate about issuing take-down notices. These notices may be generated by poorly-written automatic scripts, and result in risk-averse ISPs taking down innocuous content.

In theory, a user can tell her ISP to put back disputed content and assume liability for it, but often the ISP will then simply terminate her service, rather than risk getting embroiled in a legal dispute. In many countries, ISPs have got into the habit of writing their contracts so that they can terminate service on no notice and for no reason. So there has to be a 'put-back' mechanism that users can invoke to get their ISPs to reconnect an incorrectly classified machine quickly by assuming liability for any wicked emanations. Consumers only need assume liability if they skip the quarantine process. In practice, we anticipate most consumers will elect to participate in the ISP's cleanup service.

It is not the purpose of our report to provide a detailed design of a fixed-penalty system, as this would have to evolve over time in any case. We nonetheless feel that it is the single measure most likely to be effective in motivating the less well-managed ISPs to adopt the practices of the best.

Recommendation 4: We recommend that the European Union introduce a statutory scale of damages against ISPs that do not respond promptly to requests for the removal of compromised machines, coupled with a right for users to have disconnected machines reconnected by assuming full liability.

We learned from the stakeholders' meeting that this is the most controversial of our recommendations. We therefore say to the ISP industry: do you accept it is a problem that infected machines remain connected to the Internet, conducting attacks for extended periods of time? And if so, what alternative means do you propose for dealing with it? Do we need policemen in each ISP dealing with infected machines, or could the ISPs' own staff deal with them more efficiently and cheaply?

4 Liability Assignment

A contentious political issue is liability for defective software. The software industry has historically disclaimed liability for defects, as did the motor industry for the first sixty years of its existence. There have been many calls for governments to make software vendors liable for the harm done by shoddy products. As society depends more on software, we will have to tackle the 'culture of impunity' among its developers.

To illustrate the many complexities surrounding software liability, we now describe an example using a navigation system. Suppose that a citizen purchases a navigation system to use with a mobile home and, relying on it, is directed by a software error down a small country lane where his mobile home gets stuck, as a result of which he incurs significant towing and repair costs. This case is interesting because navigation can be supplied in a number of ways as a product, as a service, or as a combination of both, for example:

1. one could buy a self-contained GPS unit in a shop;
2. a driver can also get a navigation system in the form of software to run on his PDA or laptop computer;
3. navigation is also available as a service, for example from Google Maps;

4. many high-end mobile phones have built-in GPS, and can also provide route advice either through embedded software or an online service;

5. a GPS receiver in a driver's mobile phone might connect to route-finding software in his laptop;

6. a driver's proprietary system might run on an open platform such as Linux;

7. as well as proprietary route-finding systems, there is a project[4] to build a public-domain map of the whole world from GPS traces submitted by volunteers.

So which of the above suppliers could the mobile home owner sue? Certainly it is common for GPS equipment vendors to put up disclaimers that the driver has to click away on power-up, but the Product Liability Directive [EEC85] should aid consumers. This suggests that, at least at the consumer level, we should be able to deal with the liability issues relating to embedded systems – that is, the software inside cars, consumer electronics and other stand-alone devices – as a product-liability matter.

However, the Product Liability Directive does not apply to business property. Thus although our mobile-home driver can sue, a truck driver whose load of seafood got stuck and spoiled in exactly the same narrow lane has no recourse under the Product Liability Directive. The Unfair Contract Terms Directive, or other legal doctrines, might come to the rescue. To be fair, this complexity is a general problem for Community law and is not IT-specific. There is a further problem of jurisdiction: a business might rely on software downloaded from a website in California, which makes it clear that the contract is governed by the laws of California, and subject to the exclusive jurisdiction of that state. If the contract contains an exclusion that is valid under California law, then there may be little that the business can do if it is damaged by a software failure. Again, this is a general problem: there may be little the Community can do, as even if EU courts took jurisdiction their judgments would not be enforceable in California.

4.1 Software and Systems Liability Assignment

The above example should illustrate that software liability is both widely misunderstood and complex. But something may still need to be done. Our civilisation is becoming ever more dependent on software, and yet the liability for failure is largely disclaimed and certainly misallocated. We take the pragmatic view that software liability is too large an issue to be dealt with in a single Directive, because of the large and growing variety of goods and services in which software plays a critical role. We suggest that the Commission take a patient and staged approach. There are already some laws that impose liability regardless of contract terms (e.g., for personal injury), and it seems prudent for the time being to leave standalone embedded products to be dealt with by regulations on safety, product liability and consumer rights. Networked systems, however, can cause harm to others, and the Commission should begin to tackle this.

A good starting point would be to require vendors of PCs and other network-connected programmable devices to certify that their products are secure by default. It is illegal to sell a car without a seatbelt, so why should shops be allowed to sell a PC without an up-to-date operating system and a patching service that is switched on? This gives a more direct approach to the problem than assigning more specific rights to sue for damages. However, vendors who sell insecure systems should then be exposed to lawsuits from ISPs and other affected parties.

Recommendation 5: We recommend that the EU develop and enforce standards for network-connected equipment to be secure by default.

---

4   http://www.openstreetmap.org.

The precise nature of 'secure by default' will evolve over time. At present, the most important issue is whether the operating system is patched when the customer first gets it, and subsequently. The most likely solution would be to redesign the software so that the machine would not connect to any other online service until it had visited the patching service and successfully applied an update. Regulation should seek to enforce the principle of security by default rather than engineer the details, which should be left to market players and forces. Note that we are careful to specify 'all network-connected equipment', not just PCs; if we see more consumer electronic devices online, but lacking mechanisms to patch vulnerabilities, then in due course they will be exploited.

One of the stakeholders expressed concern at the likely costs if all consumer electronics required Common Criteria certification to EAL4; our view is that it would be quite sufficient for vendors to self-certify. However, the vendor should be liable if the certification later turns out to have been erroneous. Thus if a brand of TV set is widely compromised used to host phishing sites, the ISPs who paid penalty charges for providing network connectivity to these TV sets should be able to sue the TV vendor. It would then be a matter for the court to decide fault on the facts. (We expect that once one or two landmark cases have been decided, the industry will rapidly adapt.)

In this way the Commission can start to move to a more incentive-compatible regime, by relentlessly reallocating slices of liability in response to specific market failures. The next question is what other liability transfers should be made initially. The most important matters at the present time have to do with patching – at which we now look in greater detail.

4.2 Patching

Patching is an unfortunate but essential tool in managing the security of information systems. Patching suffers from two types of externality. First, it is up to the software developer to create patches, but the adverse effects of a slow release are felt by consumers and the online community generally, rather than the companies directly involved. Second, the deployment of patches is costly, especially for large organisations. The publication of a patch often reveals the vulnerability to attackers, and then the unpatched, compromised machines are used to harm others; so the local benefits of patching may be less than the local costs, even when the global benefits greatly exceed the costs.

The first key challenge is to speed up patch development. The lag between vulnerability discovery and patch deployment is critical. During this period, consumers are vulnerable to exploits and have no recourse to protect themselves. Software vendors are often slow in deploying patches, and there is great variation in the patch-development times exhibited by different vendors. Among 5 leading OSs, Microsoft and Red Hat are fastest, Sun and HP are slowest by far, and Apple is in the middle [Syma07]. Consumer-oriented OSs tend to patch faster, perhaps because there is greater consumer demand and awareness.

For a sample of vulnerabilities exploited by Chinese websites in 2007 [ZHS+08], nearly half were actively exploited in the wild before a patch was disclosed. Furthermore, the time lag between a vulnerability being disclosed and appearing in the wild is just two days, while patches took nearly two weeks to be published (if they were released at all). This suggests that there is scope for speeding up patch dissemination.

Vulnerability disclosure is often what triggers the development and deployment of patches. Yet the process by which the vulnerability is disclosed can affect the time vendors take to release patches. Some security researchers advocate full and immediate disclosure: publishing details (sometimes including exploit code) on the Bugtraq mailing list[5]. While undoubtedly prompting the vendors to publish a patch, full and immediate disclosure has the unfortunate side effect of leaving consumers immediately vulnerable. Vendors, for their part, typically prefer that vulnerabilities never be disclosed. However, some vulnerabilities might go undiscovered by the vendor even when they're being exploited by miscreants, and non-disclosure creates a culture in which vendors turn a blind eye.

A more balanced alternative is responsible disclosure as pioneered by CERT/CC in the US. CERT/CC notifies vendors to give them time to develop a patch before disclosing the vulnerability to the public. When the vulnerability is finally disclosed, no exploit code is provided. Empirical analysis comparing the patch-development times for vulnerabilities reported to Bugtraq and to CERT/CC revealed that CERT/CC's policy of responsible disclosure led to *faster* patch-development times than Bugtraq's full disclosure policy [AKT+05]. The researchers also found that early disclosure, via CERT/CC or Bugtraq, does speed up patch-development time.

Another option is to assign liability for vulnerabilities to the software vendor until a patch is made available and consumers have had a reasonable chance to update. Cavusoglu et al. [CCZ06] compare liability and cost-sharing as mechanisms for incentivising vendors to work harder at patching their software. It turns out that liability helps where vendors release less often than they should.

Recommendation 6: We recommend that the EU adopt a combination of early responsible vulnerability disclosure and vendor liability for unpatched software to speed the patch-development cycle.

While quantitative measurements are difficult to obtain, the view among security professionals is that patches are already available for the majority of exploits used by attackers. Over half of the exploits in the study by Zhuge et al. [ZHS+08] first appeared on Chinese websites only after a patch had already made available. Hence, a second key challenge is to increase the uptake of patches among users.

So why do some users remain unpatched? While most operating systems offer automatic patching, many third-party applications like web browser add-ons do not. Vendors who do not provide automated patches could be held liable as part of the 'secure default' approach discussed in Recommendation 5. Meanwhile, some perfectly rational users (especially at the enterprise level) choose not to patch immediately because of reliability and system stability concerns.

Vendors must make patching easier and less of a nuisance for consumers. One simple way of doing this is to decouple security patches from feature updates. Users may not want to add the latest features to a program for a variety of reasons. Feature updates could disrupt customisation, slow down performance, or add undesirable restrictions (e.g., DRM). Even though most feature updates are beneficial, the few exceptions can turn users off patching, even when it is in their interest to patch.

Recommendation 7: We recommend security patches be offered for free, and that patches be kept separate from feature updates.

4.3 Consumer Policy

Where consumers are involved one may need more protection. A particularly important context is the resolution of payment disputes. Many online frauds result in debits from bank accounts, whether via transactions for nonexistent goods or services, via fraudulent use of credit card data, or via direct attacks on online banking systems. The impact of fraud on the citizen thus depends critically on the ease of

---

5 http://www.securityfocus.com/archive/1.

obtaining restitution. However this varies rather widely across Member States. Where banks can dump liability for fraud on merchants, or where banks and merchants can dump it on the customer, there arises a further moral hazard; when the parties most able to reduce fraud are shielded from its effects, they may make less effort than they should to prevent it.

The question of varying fraud liability and dispute resolution procedures has been raised from time to time, and so far has been avoided by legislators – most recently when the Payment Services Directive was being negotiated from 2002 to 2005 [EU07]. It is time for the Commission to tackle this issue.

Recommendation 8: The European Union should harmonise procedures for the resolution of disputes between customers and payment service providers over electronic transactions.

Competition is relevant here too. Consumers are in a weak position vis-à-vis competing vendors of products where there is an 'industry position' of disclaiming liability for defects (as with cars two generations ago, or software and online services today), yet they are in an even weaker position facing a monopoly supplier. In both cases, they are faced with shrink-wrap or click-wrap licenses that impose contract terms on them on a take-it-or-leave-it basis.

Shrink-wrap licenses are thought by legal scholars to be defective. The main applicable law in the EU is the Unfair Contract Terms Directive [EU93], which makes a consumer contract term unfair "if, contrary to the requirement of good faith, it causes a significant imbalance in the parties' rights and obligations arising under the contract, to the detriment of the consumer". This is widely flouted by the software industry. For example, Article 5 requires that "terms must always be drafted in plain, intelligible language"; yet in practice, end-user license agreements (EULAs) are written in dense legalese and made difficult to access; a large amount of text may appear via a small window, so that the user has to scroll down dozens or even hundreds of times to read it. Some companies use deceptive marketing techniques that break various EU laws. Spyware programs "monitor user activities, and transmit user information to remote servers and/or show targeted advertisements" [Edel08]. Spyware's installation strategies violate the Unfair Contract Terms Directive. In almost all cases, the installation will be done without valid, free consent, so spyware also violates the Data Protection Directive and the E-Privacy Directive [EU02]. As if that were not enough, spyware programs are often made deliberately hard to uninstall.

Dealing with spyware through regulation is difficult, since most spyware companies are based outside the EU (typically in the US). While directly regulating the practices of spyware vendors is difficult, effective sanctions are still possible by punishing the companies that advertise using spyware. In the 1960's, a number of unlicensed 'pirate' radio stations aimed at UK consumers were launched from ships just outside the UK's jurisdiction. The Marine Broadcasting Offences Act of 1967 made it illegal for anyone subject to UK law to operate or assist the stations. This immediately dried up advertising revenues, and the unlicensed stations were forced to fold. A similar strategy could undermine spyware, since many of the advertisers are large international companies that do business in the EU [Edel04]. While advertisers might object that they could be framed by competitors, an examination of the resulting evidence should detect any false accusations.

Another abusive practice already the target of regulation is spam. The EU Directive on Privacy and Electronic Communications [EU02] attempts to protect consumers from spam. For the most part, it prohibits sending any unsolicited messages to individuals, requiring their prior consent. However, Article 13 paragraph 5, states that protections only apply to 'natural persons', and leaves it up to Member States to decide whether to allow unsolicited communications to business. Direct marketing lobbies argued that spamming businesses was essential to their trade. In practice, the business exemption has undermined the protections for consumers. It gives spammers a defence against all messages sent to 'work' domains. It also drives up costs for businesses, who must contend with spam sent from potentially millions of other businesses. Finally, it is difficult (in practice perhaps impossible) to draw clear lines between 'natural' and 'legal' persons in this context: some businesses (one-man firms, barristers, partners in some organisations) are legally 'natural' persons, while email addresses of identifiable individuals in companies relate to 'natural' persons. So there is a strong case to abandon the distinction. Therefore, we recommend repealing Article 13 paragraph 5, the business exemption for spam.

Putting all these together:

Recommendation 9: We recommend that the European Commission prepare a proposal for a Directive establishing a coherent regime of proportionate and effective sanctions against abusive online marketers.

The issues raised in this section on consumer policy are not limited to abusive marketing and unfair banking contracts. Perhaps the most important example concerns the foundation of the Single Market itself. It is a long-established principle that EU citizens can buy goods anywhere in the Union. The challenge now is that physical goods are increasingly bundled with online services, which may be priced differently in different Member States, or even unavailable in some of them. The bundling of goods and services is an area of significant complexity in EU law. Moreover, the segmentation of online service markets can affect information security. Sometimes market segmentation in B2B transactions impacts consumers; for example, citizens in one country can find it hard to open a bank account in another because of how credit-reference services are bundled and sold to banks. This in turn reduces consumers' ability to exert pressure on banks in countries where online banking service is less competitive by switching their business elsewhere.

The 2006 Services Directive takes some welcome first steps towards harmonising the market for services [EU06]. This Directive tries to remove many protectionist measures erected over the centuries by Member States to cosset domestic service providers. In our view another aspect warrants attention: the deliberate use of differential service provision as a tool by marketers, both as a means of discriminatory pricing and in order to undermine consumer rights.

Single-market service provision is very much broader than the scope of our report. Like the liability for defects in software – and in services – it is such a large topic that it will have to be tackled a slice at a time, and by many stakeholders in the Commission. We encourage ENISA to get involved in this policy process so that security aspects are properly considered in consumer-protection questions.

Finally, universal access to the Internet may also benefit from action under the heading of consumer rights. If all the ISPs in a country align their terms and conditions so that they can disconnect any customer for no reason, this should be contrary to public policy on a number of grounds, including free speech and the avoidance of discrimination. Even those citizens who are unpopular with some vocal lobby group must have the right to Internet connectivity.

Recommendation 10: ENISA should conduct research, coordinated with other affected stakeholders and the European Commission, to study what changes are needed to consumer-protection law as commerce moves online.

5 Dealing with the Lack of Diversity

Diversity can help security. Physical diversity deals with geographical distribution of redundant infrastructure components and network routes, whereas logical diversity means that distributed systems do not share common design or implementation flaws. A lack of diversity implies risk concentration, which negatively affects insurability and thus an economy's ability to deal with cyber risks.

5.1 Promoting Logical Diversity

For logical diversity to happen, alternatives must be widely available and adoption well-balanced. In information industries, this has rarely occurred: technical lock-in, positive network externalities and high switching costs tend to yield dominant-firm markets [SV99]. Nonetheless, there are steps governments can take to improve, or at least not hinder, the prospects for diversity.

A policy to foster diversity must first ensure the availability of viable alternatives. One option is to promote open standards to facilitate market entry. But even successful open standards do not always deliver diversity. Another option is to promote diversity in public procurement. Consumers and firms are short-sighted when selecting software; positive network externalities lead them to discount increases in correlated risk. Governments need not be so myopic, but there are limits to the impact governments can have through public procurement policies alone.

Regulatory responses may occasionally be required. However, regulation tends to work rather more slowly than the industry. Cisco used to have a very dominant market position in the routers deployed in the Internet backbone. A vulnerability in Cisco routers [Zett05] was disclosed that could have removed a significant portion of the Internet backbone if a flash worm had been disseminated. So the lack of diversity among routers used to be a critical concern. But the market for backbone routers has balanced recently, given competition from Juniper and others. The market for mobile-phone software similarly used to be dominated by Symbian, but that has also corrected itself somewhat thanks to challenges by Apple, Google, Microsoft and others. Finally, the market for web browsers is now more competitive following years of dominance by Internet Explorer. In general, we feel the authorities should maintain a watching brief for competition issues that persist and have security implications.

Recommendation 11: We recommend that ENISA should advise the competition authorities whenever diversity has security implications.

5.2 Promoting Physical Diversity in CNI

Pitcom, a UK parliamentary group, has published a useful overview of critical national infrastructure (CNI) vulnerability aimed at legislators [Pitc06]. They show how an Internet failure could damage other parts of the CNI such as finance, food and health. Telecomms and power are known to be closely coupled: if a high voltage power line fails the engineers who go to fix it will keep in touch by mobile phone. But the mobile phones depend on the power supply to keep base stations operating. This particular problem can be fixed using satellite phones; but what other problems should we anticipate?

In principle, network designers avoid single points of failure using redundant components. However, as systems scale, they may be introduced beyond an individual network's control. For example, a major concern about single points of failure for the Internet is the growth of Internet Exchange Points (IXPs) such as LINX in London, AMSIX in Amsterdam, DECIX in Frankfurt, etc., and how one IXP per country tends to grow much larger than its rivals. ISPs use IXPs to reduce the costs of providing their customers with connectivity to the rest of the Internet.

The value of joining an IXP can increase as more ISPs join, leading to winner-take-all dynamics where one IXP is much larger than its local rivals. 11 EU countries have just one IXP; in almost all the others the largest IXP is 4 or more times the size of the next largest – the exceptions being Estonia, Spain, Belgium, and Poland (in each of which there are 2 roughly equal size IXPs, not a stable equilibrium) and France which, for complex historical reasons, is much more fragmented with 5 similar sized exchanges. These pressures towards a dominant IXP lead to possible single points of failure at the IXP itself. Some leading IXPs have invested heavily in redundancy; others haven't, mainly because of the expense.

CNI is now understood to be a multi-national issue. One of the key difficulties in this area is that CNI companies do not wish to discuss how they might be vulnerable, while governments have limited understanding of the real world: for example the COCOMBINE project in Framework 6 examined IXPs but failed to understand why peering does or does not take place between particular ISPs, and merely attempted to find spatial patterns, with limited success [IG06a,IG06b]. Hence the most obvious policy option to adopt is that of encouraging information sharing – and more, better informed, research into the actual issues.

Recommendation 12: We recommend that ENISA sponsor research to better understand the effects of IXP failures. We also recommend they work with telecomms regulators to insist on best practice in IXP peering resilience.

6 Fragmentation of Legislation and Law Enforcement

As well as providing the right incentives for vendors and service providers, and protection for consumers, it is important to catch cyber-criminals, who at present act with near impunity thanks to the fragmentation of law enforcement efforts. In order for the police to prosecute the criminals they catch, cyber-crimes must be offences in all Member States. Furthermore, as nearly all cyber-crimes cross national borders, cooperation across jurisdictions must be improved.

To a first approximation, existing legal frameworks have had no difficulty in dealing with the Internet. However, the cross-jurisdictional nature of cyberspace has meant that many criminals commit their offences in another country (often many other countries) and this leads to difficulties in ensuring that they have committed an offence in the country in which they reside.

The practical approach that has been taken is to try and harmonise national laws within a consistent international framework. The relevant treaty for the specific harms that cannot be dealt with by existing 'offline' legislation is the 2001 Convention on Cybercrime [CoE01] which sets out the required offences, provides the requisite definitions and sets out a uniform level of punishments. All of the EU states have signed the convention, but some six years later only 12 have ratified, while 15 have failed to do so. If the harmonisation approach is to bear fruit, this process needs to be speeded up.

Recommendation 13: We recommend that the European Commission put immediate pressure on the 15 Member States that have yet to ratify the Cybercrime Convention.

Co-operation across law enforcement jurisdictions is essential for online crime, yet there are very serious impediments against police forces working together. Police forces must make tough choices in deciding which crimes to investigate. In the case of electronic crime, one of the first questions is how many local citizens are affected, and how many local computers are being used to launch attacks. Using these criteria, most attackers are not worth pursuing, even if in aggregate they are having a devastating effect. Even those cases that are deemed worth pursuing invariably lead to computers located in other countries. The current structures for international co-operation were designed for physical crimes, where cross-border activity is rare. They slow down investigations and drive up costs.

When a crime involves another country, law enforcement agencies may first attempt to establish a joint operation between police forces. In a typical joint operation, the country where the investigation began does most of the work while the co-operating country serves warrants and obtains evidence as requested by the originating force. Joint operations are largely unfunded and carried out on a quid pro quo basis, so they cannot be relied upon as the baseline response to all cyber-crimes. Co-operation may also be possible via a mutual legal assistance treaty (MLAT). MLATs require a political decision taken by the requested country's foreign ministry to determine whether co-operation can commence, and are very slow to process. So many investigators prefer to avoid using them where possible.

The problem of countries working together for a common cause while preserving national sovereignty has already been tackled by the military – whether it was SHAPE in World War II or NATO today. The model is that each country takes its own political decision as to what budget to set aside for fighting cyber-crime. Part of this budget funds liaison officers at a central command centre. That command centre decides what tasks to undertake, and the liaison officers relay requests to their own countries' forces. This is in effect a permanent 'joint operation' that avoids the glacial speed of MLATs. The key is that countries trust their liaison officers to assess which requests carry no political baggage and can be expedited.

Recommendation 14: We recommend the establishment of an EU-wide body charged with facilitating international co-operation on cyber-crime, using NATO as a model.

7 Security Research and Legislation

Security research is important, and occurs at a number of places in the value chain. First, blue-sky (typically academic) researchers think up new algorithms, protocols, operating-system access-control schemes and the like. Second, applied researchers investigate how particular types of systems fail, and devise specific proposals for submission to standards bodies. These researchers can be academic, industrial, or a mix. Third, research and development engineers produce prototypes and write code for specific products and services. Fourth, users of these products or services discover vulnerabilities. These are often design or implementation errors rather than flaws in the underlying security technology.

Public policy has got in the way of security research on a number of occasions. The debate on cryptography policy during the 1990s led to EC Regulation 1334/2000 on Dual Use Goods under which the export of cryptographic software in intangible form (e.g. researchers swapping source code) became subject to export control. Many small software developers are unaware of this control regime and may be technically in breach of its implementation provisions in some Member States. More recently, in some Member States, well-meant but poorly drafted legislation has impeded security research. In Germany, the criminal law code (Strafgesetzbuch) has been amended with a new section 202c that makes it an offence to produce, supply, sell, transmit, publish or otherwise make accessible any password, access code or software designed to perpetrate a computer crime, or in preparation for such a crime. This has been opposed as excessive by many researchers who see it as threatening those who possess system engineering tools for innocuous purposes [Ande07]. In the UK, the Government amended the Computer Misuse Act to make it an offence to "supply or offer to supply, believing that it is likely to be used to commit, or to assist in the commission of [a computer offence]" so that it is the meaning of 'likely' which will determine whether an offence has been committed. The government's response to concern about the circumstances in which an offence would be committed has been to promise to publish guidance for prosecutors as to when the law should be invoked.

In both cases the concern is that IT and security professionals who make network monitoring tools publicly available or disclose details of unpatched vulnerabilities could be prosecuted. Indeed, most of the tools on a professional's laptop, from nmap to perl, could be used for both good and bad purposes. The resulting legal uncertainty has a chilling effect on security research [Clay07].

The industry needs an advocate in Brussels to ensure that its interests are taken into account when directives and regulations are being formulated – and as they evolve over time. In the case of export control, we recommend that ENISA push for cryptography to be removed from the dual-use list. In the case of dual-use tools that can be used for hacking as well as for bona-fide research and administrative tasks, we recommend ENISA take the position that sanctions should only apply in the case of evil intent.

Recommendation 15: We recommend that ENISA champion the interests of the information security sector within the Commission to ensure that regulations introduced for other purposes do not inadvertently harm security researchers and firms.

8 Conclusions

As Europe moves online, information security is becoming increasingly important: first, because the direct and indirect losses are now economically significant; and second, because growing public concerns about information security hinder the development of both markets and public services. While information security touches on many subjects from mathematics through law to psychology, some of the most useful tools for both the policy analyst and the systems engineer come from economics.

In our report, of which this is an abridged version, we provided an analysis based on security economics of the practical problems in network and information security that the European Union faces at this time. We have come up with fifteen policy proposals that should make a good next step in tackling the problems. We therefore hope that they will provide the basis for constructive action by ENISA and the European Commission in the future.

Acknowledgements

The authors are grateful to acknowledge input from the attendees at the ENISA stakeholders' meeting on December 10th, 2007; from people in the security industry who talked to us, mostly off the record; from colleagues in the security groups at Cambridge and Dresden; from members of the Advisory Council of the Foundation for Information Policy Research, particularly Nick Bohm, Alan Cox, Douwe Korff, Jim Norton and Martyn Thomas; and from Alexander Korff of Clifford Chance. Responsibility for any errors and omissions of course remains with the authors alone.

References

[AFT06]   Acquisti, A., Friedman, A., and Telang, R. "Is There a Cost to Privacy Breaches? An Event Study", in *5th Workshop on the Economics of Information Security (WEIS)*, Cambridge, United Kingdom, June 2006.

[Aker70]   Akerlof, G. "The Market for 'Lemons': Quality Uncertainty and the Market Mechanism". *Quart. J. Economics (84)*, 1970, pp. 488-500.

[Ande07]   Anderson, N. "German 'Anti-Hacker' Law Forces Hacker Sites to Relocate". *Ars Technica*, 14 August 2007. http://arstechnica.com/news.ars/post/20070814-german-anti-hacker-law-forcing-hacker-sites-to-relocate.html

[AM06]   Anderson, R., and Moore, T. "The Economics of Information Security", *Science* (314:5799), October 2006, pp. 610-613.

[APA07]   APACS. "Card Fraud Losses Continue to Fall", Press Release, APACS, 14 March 2007. http://www.apacs.org.uk/media_centre/press/07_14_03.html

[AKT+05]   Arora, A., Krishnan, R., Telang, R., and Yang, Y. "An Empirical Analysis of Vendor Response to Disclosure Policy", in *4th WEIS*, Cambridge, Massachusetts, June 2005.

[BBC07]   BBC. "Devices Attached to Cash Machines", *BBC News*, 15 October 2007. http://news.bbc.co.uk/1/hi/england/cambridgeshire/7044894.stm

[CSS02]   California State Senate. *Assembly Bill 700*, 2002. http://info.sen.ca.gov/pub/01-02/bill/asm/ab_0651-0700/ab_700_bill_20020929_chaptered.pdf

[Casp08]   Casper, C. "Examining the Feasibility of a Data Collection Framework", *ENISA*, February 2008.

[CCZ06]   Cavusoglu, H., Cavusoglu, H., and Zhang, J. "Economics of Patch Management", in *5th WEIS*, Cambridge, United Kingdom, June 2006.

[Clay07]   Clayton, R. "Hacking Tools are Legal for a Little Longer", *Light Blue Touchpaper*, 19 June 2007. http://www.lightbluetouchpaper.org/2007/06/19/hacking-tools-are-legal-for-a-little-longer/

[CSI07]   Computer Security Institute. "The 12th Annual Computer Crime and Security Survey", October 2007. http://www.gocsi.com/

[CoE01]   Council of Europe. *Convention on Cybercrime*, CETS 185, November 2001. http://conventions.coe.int/Treaty/Commun/QueVoulezVous.asp?NT=185&CL=ENG

[Edel04]   Edelman, B. "Advertisers Using WhenU", July 2004. http://www.benedelman.org/spyware/whenu-advertisers/

[Edel08]   Edelman, B. "Spyware: Research, Testing, Legislation, and Suits", June 2008. http://www.benedelman.org/spyware/

[vEB08]   van Eeten, M., and Bauer, J. "The Economics of Malware: Security Decisions, Incentives and Externalities", *OECD*, May 2008. http://www.oecd.org/dataoecd/25/2/40679279.pdf

[EC06]   European Commission. "i2010 Benchmarking Framework", November 2006. http://ec.europa.eu/information_society/eeurope/i2010/docs/benchmarking/060220_i2010_Benchmarking_Framework_final_nov_2006.doc

[EC07]   European Commission. "Report on the Outcome of the Review of the EU Regulatory Framework for Electronic Communications Networks and Services in Accordance with Directive 2002/21/EC and Summary of the 2007 Reform Proposals", November 2007. http://ec.europa.eu/information_society/policy/ecomm/doc/library/proposals/com_review_en.pdf

[EEC85]   European Economic Community. "Council Directive of 25 July 1985 on the Approximation of the Laws, Regulations and Administrative Provisions of the Member States Concerning Liability for Defective Products (85/374/EEC)", July 1985.

[EU93]   European Union. "Directive 93/13/EEC of 5 April 1993 on Unfair Terms in Consumer Contracts", April 1993. http://eur-lex.europa.eu/smartapi/cgi/sga_doc?smatapi!celexapi!prod!CELEXnumdoc&lg=EN&numdoc=31993L0013&model=guichett

[EU02]   European Union. "Directive 2002/58/EC of the European Parliament and of the Council of 12 July 2002 Concerning the Processing of Personal Data and the Protection of Privacy in the Electronic Communications Sector (Directive on Privacy and Electronic Communications)", July 2002. http://eur-lex.europa.eu/LexUriServ/LexUriServ.do?uri=CELEX:32002L0058:EN:HTML

[EU06]   European Union. "Directive 2006/123/EC of the European Parliament and of the Council of of 12 December 2006 on Services in the Internal Market", December 2006. http://eur-lex.europa.eu/LexUriServ/LexUriServ.do?uri=OJ:L:2006:376:0036:0068:EN:PDF

[EU07]   European Union. "Directive 2007/64/EC of the European Parliament and of the Council of 13 November 2007 on Payment Services in the Internal Market Amending Directives 97/7/EC, 2002/65/EC, 2005/60/EC and 2006/48/EC and Repealing Directive 97/5/EC Text with EEA Relevance", November 2007. http://eurlex.europa.eu/LexUriServ/LexUriServ.do?uri=OJ:L:2007:319:0001:01:EN:HTML

[HoL07]   House of Lords Science and Technology Committee. *Personal Internet Security, 5th Report of 2006-07*, The Stationery Office, London, August 2007.

[IG06a]   D'Ignazio, A., and Giovannetti, E. "Spatial Dispersion of Peering Clusters in the European Internet", *Cambridge Working Papers in Economics 0601*, January 2006. http://econpapers.repec.org/paper/camcamdae/0601.htm

[IG06b]   D'Ignazio, A., and Giovannetti, E. "'Unfair' Discrimination in Two-sided Peering? Evidence from LINX", *Cambridge Working Papers in Economics 0621*, February 2006. http://econpapers.repec.org/paper/camcamdae/0621.htm

[JR08]   Jakobsson, M., and Ramzan Z. *Crimeware: Understanding New Attacks and Defenses*, Addison Wesley, Upper Saddle River, New Jersey, 2008.

[MLH07]   McPherson, D., Labovitz, C., and Hollyman, M. "Worldwide Infrastructure Security Report Volume III", *Arbor Networks*, 2007. http://www.arbornetworks.com/report

[MC07]   Moore, T., and Clayton, R. "Examining the Impact of Website Take-down on Phishing" in *2nd Anti-Phishing Working Group eCrime Researcher's Summit (APWG eCrime)*, Pittsburgh, Pennsylvania, October 2007, pp. 1-13.

[Open07]   OpenDNS. "OpenDNS Shares April 2007 PhishTank Statistics", Press Release, 1 May 2007. http://www.opendns.com/about/press_release.php?id=14

[Pitc06]   Pitcom. "Critical National Infrastructure, Briefings for Parliamentarians on the Politics of Information Technology", November 2006. http://www.pitcom.org.uk/briefings/PitComms1-CNI.doc

[SC05]   Serjantov, A., and Clayton, R. "Modelling Incentives for E-mail Blocking Strategies", in *4th WEIS*, Cambridge, Massachusetts, June 2005.

[SV99]   Shapiro, C., and Varian, H. *Information Rules. A Strategic Guide to the Network Economy*, Harvard Business School Press, Boston, Massachusetts, 1999.

[Syma07]   Symantec. "Internet Security Threat Report Volume XII", September 2007. http://www.symantec.com/business/theme.jsp?themeid=threatreport

[Zett05]   Zetter, K. "Router Flaw is a Ticking Bomb", *Wired*, 1 August 2005. http://www.wired.com/politics/security/news/2005/08/68365

[ZHH+07]   Zhuge, J., Holz, T., Han, X., Guo, J., and Zou, W. "Characterizing the IRC-based Botnet Phenomenon", *Reihe Informatik Technical Report TR-2007-010*, December 2007. http://honeyblog.org/junkyard/reports/botnet-china-TR.pdf

[ZHS+08]   Zhuge, J., Holz, T., Song, C., Guo, J., Han, X., and Zou, W. "Studying Malicious Websites and the Underground Economy on the Chinese Web", in *7th WEIS*, Hanover, New Hampshire, June 2008.

How Economy and Society affect Enterprise Security Management

Eberhard von Faber

T-Systems
Eberhard.Faber@t-systems.com
Brandenburg University of Applied Science
Eberhard.vonFaber@fh-brandenburg.de

Abstract

Enterprise security management and the related daily work of the security management is greatly determined by the information technology and the enterprise specific context in which it is used. These effects are subject of other publications. In this paper influences from economy and society are considered. It is shown that the security management must actively deal with such extrinsic developments. As a result, security managers may modify the way information security is treated in their institution. There are new topics dictated from outside the institution which need to be considered and integrated into security strategy and architecture.

1 Keep IT and Security in Perspective

Information technology (IT) is used for easier, better and faster execution of business and administration. IT is a means to an end. It's all about business and administration processes. Consequently, IT security shall be understood as security of business and administration processes. Moreover, institutions consider, organize and measure IT and all aspects related to information security under the following prime objectives:

- ensure governance,
- comply with legal and other requirements,
- ensure the organization's smooth and efficient function („culture"),
- identify and manage risks, and
- improve efficiency.

For security managers this means that they have to develop their competencies beyond technology. IT security is part of information security which in turn becomes an integral element of corporate management. Accordingly, the way in which the security managers work is changing. Their work is no longer technology-oriented or IT focused. But enterprises are just and sometimes little hesitantly starting to adapt their organization to allow security managers to act accordingly.

IT risks put business at risk. Though this message is not completely new, security responsibilities are mostly not organized in this way. As a first step the "information security" should be further disjoined from the "IT department". Security officers shall act as a broker or intermediator between "IT production" and "business unit" (refer to Fig. 1). In a simplified model they are informed about technology or IT related risks by the "IT department". The "IT security" translates these issues to business risks which are to be discussed with the "business unit". It's up to the latter and not to the security people to decide if those risks are accepted or to be mitigated. Based on that business decision the "IT security" will define detailed security requirements to be met by the "IT department". The security people are responsible to verify if the security measures are appropriate and effective.

Fig. 1: Role of "information security" or "security officers" (simplified model)

Organizational and structural security measures are as important as IT security measures are. Therefore, the security officers should cooperate more closely with other departments such as facility management, factory security services or the audit department. In a second step such activities may be merged under one new umbrella which can be the "Corporate Risk Management Office" headed by the "Chief Financial Officer (CFO)". So, "information security" is no longer organized by IT people and the "Chief Information Officer (CIO)". Such an approach is suitable since some risks may originate from IT but securing information is a discipline which goes beyond pure IT.

Information security challenges all employees and all units they belong to and concerns all tools, technologies and processes that are used. Consequently, the company's "Department for Information Security" should concentrate on setting up and managing the main structures and processes which form the skeleton of a so called Information Security Management System (ISMS) as described in [ISO27001]. A few people are sufficient to do this work. The security department may not try to look after all the security measures and programs. Instead more and more responsibilities, tasks and work will be delegated into business operations. The security organization becomes rather virtual. Simultaneously, a strategy must exist to ensure the required security expertise and to have the right experts at hand. Therefore, some functions or tasks such as risk analysis or quality management including penetration testing should be centralized, and third party expert services should be utilized in addition. If security is organized along this way, it will become an integral part of the company's activities and the means used thereby.

2 Measure and Pinpoint Progress

Security breaches and incidents are the talk of the town. But information security requires resources and costs money. No doubt, also security requires a business case since nowadays all activities that cost need to be justified. What is the best rationale?

Often security managers refer to the increasing complexity of the IT which need to be secured. Complexity in fact drives costs, but who wants to pay for problems? The management wants to pay for solutions. Then one may point to the increase of threats. The key question here is the following: How to reasonably estimate the probability or likelihood of anticipated sometimes fictive incidents and their affect including possible domino effects? Insurance mathematics is based upon having a multitude of similar frequently occurring events. Security incidents are, hopefully, just the opposite: They are seldom and specific. Otherwise the security management flopped.

Does information security pay? Most probably not. Nevertheless it is required and costs can be justified. There are three ways: Security
- is a duty to take care,
- is needed as provision for risks and to avoid possible future costs, and
- provides a return on invest.

But one different concluding advice will be given thereafter.

Investments in security can firstly be considered just as a part of any business activity. No one disputes the locks in the doors or the fences which surround the premises. Hence, security is a "duty to take care" and therefore a genuine part of any valuable activity. Security people should endeavour the use of this argument. Similarly, for example, reputation is important for any institution. As a matter of course much is undertaken or forbidden to preserve and develop the reputation. The gain is self-evident, even though loss of reputation can cause financial losses.

The second argument is "provision for risks and avoidance of possible future costs". Examples are the disclosure of intellectual properties to competitors and the aftermath, production downtimes, non-productive time, loss of performance, costs for recovery and replacement, failure to comply with contracts, warranties and others. Many aspects allow an objective, quantifiable appraisal. However, potential losses are estimated by considering an anticipated scenario. But reality often diverges. Especially secondary effects become more important in reality than originally assumed and complexity is not handled adequately. The problem is more serious the more unlikely the loss is. This leads to a second factor: probability. The probability of an incident is difficult to estimate. This especially holds for very rare incidents. And the "average loss", calculated by multiplying the absolute potential loss and the probability of the incident, is most likely meaningless. This financial calculation only holds if statistical analysis is adequate. But this is only the case if the incidents appear sufficiently frequent. Security managers just try to achieve the opposite. These facts also apply to the next argument, but there is more.

The third argument may be "return on invest". However, mostly it's the IT which generates the benefit. Though security often enables the use of this IT in the first place. But whom to assign the gain? Of course there are some other aspects which constitute a real return. But these direct effects like increase of reputation or strengthening of brand are difficult to calculate. More general, the problem to demonstrate a return on invest actually applies to some extent to any secondary process. A TCO[1] approach were costs for IT and security are aggregated is a way out. However, it traces back to the first argument which looked at information IT security as an integral part of IT and information security in general as a duty to take care. Genuine return on security invests can be shown for efficient identity management systems for example. But there are not much cases were return on security invest can both properly and directly be calculated in Euro and Cent.

This leads to an additional conclusion. Justification of costs is one thing. But it is almost more important to demonstrate status and progress concerning security. This actually shows that the money is given to the right people and spend reasonably. Consequently, information security has to be considered and conducted as a part of quality management and in the context of a continuous improvement process. Thereby one may underestimate the importance of documentation, data collection, analysis, and reporting. But documentation is key. Without such information any tactical realization will fail and reviews as well as improvements will miss to have a sound basis.

Nowadays the quality of communication is as important as accuracy. The security managers must also be experts in communication and promotion since security is essential but rather small business. The general management is used to play big games only. In order to direct the general management's attention to security issues and in order to involve them as required, security people need to explain their

---

1 TCO: total costs of ownership

methodology and metric in a descriptive way. Secondly, it is important to show the progress made together with remaining problems. Third, it is necessary to compress all the information in a couple of numbers along a couple of dimensions: An example format for the bottom line is shown in Fig. 2. Here a target-performance comparison, supplemented by an industry benchmark value, is done in some disciplines such as strategy and planning, policies and rules, organization, processes, communication and awareness, architecture, technology and auditing instruments. Fourth, format is almost as important as content is. If the format does not suit, the content may fail to be effective.

Fig. 2: To demonstrate status and progress is often more important
than conducting disputable return-on-invest calculations

Finally one shall see the status of implementation and the maturity of information security being achieved in the enterprise or public authority. There are standardized models such as CMMI (Capability Maturity Model Integration) which show the principle and the way forward. Maturity can also be determined for security [ISO21827] since organizations may start with an absolute insufficient level, then define requirements and initially implement security measures till a phase is reached in which corrections and improvements are made (refer to Fig. 3). Finally there is a phase of excellence where most of the implementation work is done and technology and processes are only adjusted due to new challenges or in order to increase effectiveness. This also means that the costs for security are much smaller than in the phase where many security measures are initially implemented.

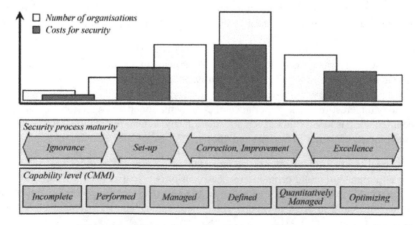

Fig. 3: Capability, status and maturity of enterprise security

Security will lose its special role with regard to discussions about costs and benefits on the one hand and about things like monitoring and maturity on the other. Security managers should review their relation to the management (as institution) as well as review their work and function. Try to quit a defending or excusing position and develop a proactive one showing value and progress.

3 IT becomes a Mass Product

The offering of IT services causes considerable costs. Hence optimization is required and done. The most successful way of increasing efficiency and to decrease costs is the "industrialization". Today most IT departments and also large computing centers are producing IT services in a different way. This becomes apparent if one considers the production of cars and the development inside the factories and in the value chains over the last 50 years. Much changed. And this will also happen to IT. IT is not too specific or individual to make industrialization impossible. The production will be standardized, whereas the product may remain specific or individual to some extent. Again one should consider the production of cars: There are not more than a few identical cars being manufactured each day in one factory. Pre-defined modules are used to produce an unique product. A look to the industrial value chain in automotive shows a decrease of vertical integration combined with an increase of outsourcing. Service providers with a very specialized offering are simultaneously able to extend there business and realize economies of scale. This leads in a cost reduction for customers.

IT will develop in this way. Security considerations will not stop that. Service providers will simply fulfill the requirements. Today an increasing part of security services are provided as ASP, SaaS[2] or In-the-Cloud-Services. Security services are produced on shared platforms. The use of shared or even public networks is taken for granted today. Systems and applications will follow. For security managers this means that their domain of direct control becomes smaller. Simultaneously, they must master a variety of cross-linked internal and external service providers with contracts and Service Level Agreements (SLA) which take security concerns into account. In addition, an overall standardization is required – since specialized service providers are used, but also to improve internal efficiency while reducing the complexity. In general, standardization can back up security. However, other influences are making this a hard job to do.

4 Consumer Solutions affect IT and Security

IT service providers are contracted where all the conditions also with respect to security are defined. Even more difficult if employees start to buy their own stuff and become their own "IT department". Enterprises as well as public authorities encourage employees to travel, work mobile or at home and to be flexible in sharing working time and spare time. As a result private life and working environment more and more overlap. For security managers this becomes a challenge (sometimes a nightmare). How to control all these satellites? Due to ever faster product development circles it becomes much more complicated to provide thousands of employees with a comprehensively tested standard equipment which is also up-to-date for the users. There is a tradeoff between security which requires time for testing, selection, standardization and rollout on the one hand and the variety of solutions, their short life-cycles and the user's whishes on the other. Security managers will probably not succeed in dominating the whole story. The employees' participation will be more important than ever.

---

2 ASP: Application Service Provisioning, SaaS: Software as a Service

Trained and cooperative users are essential with respect to security. But it's not for sure if this can straightforwardly be achieved. Not only technology is changing dramatically, the users' behavior and culture or ethos is changing too. The Internet is used differently than some years ago. The proliferation of wikis, web logs, social communities, and portals underlines this. Web 2.0 indicates the different use of internet services. Such service are becoming much more common. And again the boundary between private and business vanishes with stronger impact on security because people are exchanging information. A look into social community sites shows how these sites are used and that private and business related information is already mixed. Security managers can probably not control nor successfully ban the use of such internet platforms. Their use should actively be organized and maybe integrated in the long run.

5 Reputation and Regulation

In the early 1990ies the Internet was a pure showcase not a platform for real trading. However, even a showcase is not only relevant for business, often it's essential. A company needs to be well-known to make business. Trust and reputation are further requirements for success. Customers demand to expect quality and competence and they need to have reasons for this expectations. Otherwise they may buy from others. More and more information about companies and their offering is distributed over the Internet and customers use the Internet more and more as the primary source of information which influence or dominate their buying decision. Even more, customers share their experience and exchange other kind of information over the Internet using specific internet platforms just mentioned. And there are commercial information brokering and trading platforms which invite customers to rate products and services and to provide personal appraisals. So, the Internet is now an important e-business platform, but more important, the carrier of information about the market. Manipulations can obviously affect trading but also a company's reputation [Heis2007]. Reputation being constituted by all related information which exist somewhere is very hard to establish. But it can be lost quickly. Enterprises as well as public authorities need strategies to build up but also to defend their reputation in the Internet.

Standards provide comparability. They provide dependability as well if compliance is factually verified. Many standards contain security requirements, have an influence on security or describe best practices or even specific controls [BITK2007]. Users are interested to know if and to what extend service providers do comply to standardized requirements. In particular they want to know if security measures are actually in place. This information can be provided by a certification: A third independent party performs the assessment against the standard and based upon that evaluation or auditing compliance is attested with a certificate. Customers or users should demand such approvals and consider compliance issues when taking their buying decision.

Especially with respect to preventions, regulations are more effective than voluntary certifications. The goal might be similar but origin and effects are different. The reason why regulations such as KonTraG or SOX were put in place were crashes of enterprises and the globalization. Such standards stress the importance of risk management. However they are not very detailed concerning information security and related measures. Security experts tend to overestimate the practical impact of those regulations on security. But the important point is, that these standards directly address chartered accountants and the company's general management. Thereby they point at information security as a business requirement and therefore in a way in which information security should increasingly be understood.

6 Conclusion and Outlook

The above trends are only a part of a more complicated story. Other things that affect enterprise security management originate from information technology and the enterprise specific context in which it is used. These were not considered in this paper. This paper concentrated on influences from economy and society. Nevertheless there are further influences onto security which could have been considered here. Two examples are given:

Division of labor has considerably grown in the past due to development of industries and globalization. Linear value chains disappear. Instead vendors and consumers build are complex value grid. Consequently, the IT is changing in order to meet the new requirements. The IT loses clear perimeters, networks and applications change their structure. Service Oriented Architectures (SOA) and a crop of (mobile) devices are one answer on that. New challenges with respect to security appear.

In this context and for many reasons Identity and Access Management (IAM) becomes more and more important and is considered as a distinct discipline [Fab2007]. The challenge is to manage the creation, use, modification and retirement of digital identities and all related attributes including roles and rights in a way that business and administrative processes are being supported in an optimal but also secure way. Identity and Access Management developed to a pervasive field of work for the security management.

The trends described in this paper show that the security management must actively deal with developments in economy and society. They do affect IT as well as security. Security managers may modify the way information security is treated in the enterprise or public authority. There are new topics dictated from outside the institution which need to be considered and integrated into their security architecture.

References

[ISO27001] ISO/IEC 27001 – Information technology – Security techniques – Information security management systems – Requirements

[ISO21827] ISO/IEC 21827 – Information Technology – Systems Engineering – Capability Maturity Model (SSE-CMM)

[Heis2007] Heiser, Jay: Reputation: The Next Internet Revolution; Track Session, Gartner IT Security Summit 2007, Sept. 2007, London

[BITK2007] BITKOM and DIN: Kompass der IT-Sicherheitsstandards, Leitfaden und Nachschlagewerk (translation: Compass IT Security Standards, Compendium and Reference); www.bitkom.de or www.nia.din.de, December 2007

[Fab2007] von Faber, Eberhard: Identity and Access Management (IAM). Gain Agility through IAM – in Companies and Complex Supply Chains.; White Paper T-Systems Enterprise Services, 2007, www.t-systems.com/whitepapers and www.t-systems.com/ict-security

Information Security Industry: State of the Art

José de la Peña Muñoz

SIC
www.revistasic.com
jpm@codasic.com

Abstract

The processing of information by natural and legal persons by means of technologies and systems can generate risks. When these risks are linked to the availability, integrity, confidentiality and authenticity of information, we are dealing with security risks.

As defined by ENISA, ICT security is "the capacity of networks or information systems to resist unlawful or malicious accidents or actions that compromise the availability, authenticity, integrity and confidentiality of stored or transferred data with a certain level of confidence, as well as the services that are offered and made accessible by these networks".

The fast growth of the use of technological information systems has exponentially increased society's dependence on them, which means the level of exposure to security risks on the part of citizens, public and private organisations – large, medium or small – and critical information infrastructures that comply with their interaction is high.

The scenario of insecurity, which has been making its way into the use of the internet, – and which the great minds of the ICT sector were not able, or willing, to anticipate at the time by offering products and services with an appropriate level of quality in their characteristics and security, because they focused on basic provisions, such as speed and capacity – increased its criticality with people betting on distributed computing.

1 Introduction

At the end of the 90th, this scenario arrived to a turning point, as the world started betting on the use of the Internet for business purposes. This caused a big bang within the field of security, which was a field with little economic activity up till then. In time, though, it has gained its own personality in the ICT sector. In addition, it has been immersed in a process of expansion since then.

In this process of expansion, security has become stronger and has made its first achievements by involving leading security experts. This has led the general public to become aware of the fact that the market will not forgive them for ignoring the importance of the role security plays in its products and services. In order to minimize this business risk, experts consider it appropriate to acquire security tools and/or functionalities and integrate them into their catalogue of solutions.

There have been more than 400 purchases in these past four years. As mentioned before, some of them have been made by companies specialised in ICT security in order to offer a fuller range of products. Others have been made by key actors specialised in security and interested in providing global solutions with appropriate security levels to their clients.

N. Pohlmann, H. Reimer, W. Schneider (Editors): Securing Electronic Business Processes, Vieweg (2008), 84-89

2 The Spanish case

There are two main features that are applicable to the security sector in a country such as Spain, which is so poorly developed in the field of ICT R&D&I and production. The first feature affects the manufacturing industry, or rather, the developers of software tools, and the existence of pioneering companies in the field of protection against malicious code (in the beginning, anti-virus). Curiously, it also affects the development of hardware and software tools that are based on the application of cryptography to information security in the civil world, although in the latter case with truly modest economic results.

Of course, we may not forget the integrators specialised in security, two of which are great pioneers; one in the field of perimeter security and the other in the management of users and accesses, which is now rechristened to 'identity management'. In addition, we may not forget the wholesalers and distributors of tools who are committed to security (no more than three throughout history), who laid the foundation for collaboration between manufacturers and integrators.

Nor would it be acceptable to minimize the great and important role of auditing and consulting companies, which cleverly helped (and continue helping) large organisations to define policies on information security, analyse the information risks and to take measures encompassed in the so-called leading security plans. In this way, the need to have an annual investment and cost budget to acquire and manage security was formalised.

The second feature has to do with legislation. Not in vain, Spain has counted with a Personal Data Protection Act since 1992 (according to those responsible for private-owned files, this act is very severe in terms of penalties and fines), the famous Spanish Act on the Control of Automated Processing of Personal Data (or Ley Orgánica sobre el Tratamiento Automatizado de los Datos de Carácter Personal, LORTAD), which includes rules on safety measures for files containing personal data and which was repealed by the Personal Data Protection Act (or Ley Orgánica sobre Protección de Datos, LOPD, 1999, which is equally severe on companies and which modifies, extends and specifies the security measures of the original security regulation of LORTAD). The body that is responsible for enforcing compliance with the LORTAD is the Spanish Data Protection Agency. Furthermore, there are three operating autonomous agencies: Madrid, Catalonia and the Basque Country.

Thus, the compliance with laws – so in fashion today –, specifically in the field of personal data protection and development rules, has brought a significant impulse to the transformation of the security branch by promoting the creation of multidisciplinary structures in companies and public administrations that are aimed at personal data protection (almost all are).

At last, two important components were consolidated – although only in large organisations – to develop a market: internal expert teams entrusted with the management of security and investment plans in the area of ICT protection. It would be unfair not to mention the international standard ISO, which has been and which is an example for almost all organisations, as we should point out that, at that time, the management of information security began to appear (today included in ISO 27000) and the idea of creating some other standard on management and business continuity was born (today BS 25999).

However, our purpose is not to tell an exhaustive story and, as there would be many episodes left to treat until reaching the present time, let's take a leap to 2008, but not before recalling a significant detail, which affects the Spanish developing industry: the first "packetised" software tools, aimed at helping to comply with the personal data protection legislation, did not appear publicly practically until the arrival of the LOPD (1999) and the consequent repeal of the LORTAD.

That is too many years without a response. We must rebuke the industry, since the compliance in this area allowed for the creation of software tools without them being necessarily linked to projects. Was there a lack of informed businessmen in the ICT sector eager to take risks? Was it the professionals trained in the subject of laws who saw that this and others issues aimed at the protection of information had future?

3 Where are we?

Let's consider the current situation. Where are we? What awaits us?

Let's try to succinctly answer the first question: where are we? Well, we are in an exciting moment; we are on the verge of fulfilling a long-awaited goal: to carry out complete telematic procedures with enough technical security to support the necessary legal security with reasonable a guarantee, especially with regard to the identification and authentication of parties, as well as the intervention of trusted third parties that vouch for the transactions and participants.

The current Spanish Electronic Signature Act, which resulted in the emergence of numerous providers of certification services (some of them by government mandate, such as registrars and notaries), allows foreseeing an interesting growth in the fields of electronic invoicing and telematic commerce from fixed and mobile terminals. The positive development of the delivery of the electronic ID, which is an essential piece in the information society, opens the door to citizens who have now the possibility to massively use the telematic channel in their contacts with the administration and companies. In order to achieve this, it would be desirable to accelerate the development of applications used in the ID. (Let's hope that neither the ICT industry nor the organisations that are interested in telematically offering services and products will fail in their perception).

Other legal pieces have been added to this, such as the Spanish Act on the Electronic Access of Citizens to Public Services (or *Ley de Acceso Electrónico del Ciudadano a los Servicios Públicos*), filled with references to the 'pure ingredients' of security (availability, integrity, confidentiality and authenticity) and other 'mixed ones' (such as safekeeping and maintenance). According to this law, public administrations must make their services accessible from the network and they must coordinate their operations into one single structure. The date on which this will come into force is January 1, 2010. Whether or not there is a need for a pause, the course has been set.

There is also another law of vital importance: the law on the measures for the promotion of the information society (or *Ley de Medidas de Impulso a la Sociedad de la Información*), which obliges private companies from strategic sectors to provide specific "secure" services on the net (those companies that don't have them yet), and it obliges operators and service providers of the information society to take security measures and publish them.

Other laws, such as the law on data maintenance, together with the amendments in the Spanish Act on Information Society Services and e-Commerce (or *Ley de Servicios de la Sociedad de la Información y Comercio Electrónico)*, the Spanish Act on Electronic Signature (or *Ley de Firma Electrónica)* and the General Telecommunications Act (or *Ley General de Telecomunicaciones)*, brought about by its publication in the official Spanish state gazette (*BOE*), allow to forecast an increase in state controls (generally derived from UE procedures) to prevent the criminal use of ICT, repress the creation of ICT with criminal purposes and use ICT to prosecute crime.

The widespread use of the Internet as a medium in this scenario and the deepening into the mentioned different stages of its development (social networks and Web 2.0, Web 3.0), virtualisation (of infrastructures, applications and storage), the infrastructures aimed at SOA (service oriented architecture) services, web sites, the massive use of wireless devices (PDA, Blackberry, laptops and mobile phones) for the access to office applications and for personal use, communications integrated into the workplace, convergences, etc.... This is the world for which the industry is working and, especially, for security.

As stated above, the course has been set; in this world, providers who rather wait for users to demand first before satisfying that demand will not be able to survive. The speed of the market and the prevailing model will not allow this, as can be seen today.

Therefore, we have to find a way to detect new market niches. The one already known and somewhat predictable one corresponds to large companies. Nevertheless, the situation with the residential market and SMEs is quite different, as the information about them is fragmented. In this point, it is worth point-ing out that, in Spain, we have the National Institute of Communication Technologies (INTECO), which depends on the Ministry of Industry, Tourism and Trade and which has the objective of promoting and developing ICT security awareness among citizens and SMEs, as well as stimulating the establishment of an industry that creates technological tools with protection purposes.

According to the magazine *Information and Communication Security* (SIC), the Spanish corporate mar-ket of ICT security had a turnover of € 66.11 million in 1999; eight years later, in 2007, it reached the total of € 609.50 million. It is expected that the market will reach the amount of € 713 million at the end of this year.

These numbers are conservative and lower than in reality, because it has been impossible to individu-alise and extrapolate with a minimum accuracy the amount set aside by users for setting up activities aimed at the availability of systems, networks and services. Certainly, availability is a tremendous elu-sive part of security, which is melted and confused with other business and ICT areas. Nevertheless, it still continues to be a part of protection. (Furthermore, let's not forget that the technological security systems have to be available as well).

4 Global Panorama. What is awaiting us?

While the security needs of large organisations are reasonably known, as has been claimed, it is not so for SMEs and the housing market, whose systems, applications and computer networks are normally installed by providers that are illiterate and careless regarding information protection.

However, both groups (SMEs and households) have some things in common: they are heterogeneous and numerous, they deal with public administrations and are clients of large private companies (opera-tors, ISPs, banks and saving banks, payment means, energy, airlines, ICT providers, etc.). Apart from that, one can detect other less obvious similarities between them: they have no time to understand about technological security and to manage technology, they require solutions where usability takes priority and they don't have much budget.

The fact of taking these specific details into account may allow the industry to find out what SMEs, households and self-employed teleworkers will become, as well as helping to address their develop-ments and products to the needs of these actors and to understand that introducing SMEs and house-holds in the supply of security is best carried out by ISPs that integrate this security (or part of it) in their services.

The actors most interested in this to happen are public administrations and large private companies, as they have experience in securing their systems and networks and are willing to offer more and better telematic services to their users, clients and partners.

If the industry, as a whole, and, particularly, the Spanish industry is able to take distant future trends into account, it will probably have the possibility of finding new supply niches that are still unexplored or poorly explored regarding the development of packetised tools that serve as a base for operator and ISP services (whose clients are, in turn, public administrations and companies from the private sector), as well as for products related to specific projects or services, with the possibility of specialising in specific sectors (verticalisation). In this matter, universities should have an essential role in its relationship with the industry, however much we haven't been able – although fortunately there are exceptions, also in Spain – to detect talent and long-term business projects.

This seems difficult, but if minds are opened, ICT security doesn't stop being a part of the ICT sector, and, therefore, it is similar to others branches that make it up. However, ICT security has two interesting characteristics: on the one hand, security risks, unless otherwise proven, affect all ICT environments – including future ones – and, on the other hand, there will always be people trying to misuse this technology and they will accomplish it, even if security is incorporated into software development processes, however much the levels of confidence in technological products are certified and however much users are trained.

In short, although insecurity will change, it will not disappear.

5 Security trends

Consequently, there are two important factors to promote the development of strong security. The first one is related to law enforcement, i.e. the safeguard of personal and family privacy, the right to protect personal data and the protection of the processing of corporate information, particularly financial information (SOX and future EU regulations). It is an important factor, as it boosts the fight against the leak and loss of information, which does not only comply with the law, but also with the responsibility of organisations in the processing of valuable information for their business or activities.

Currently, the ICT security industry is devoted to the prevention of leaks, an area where there are also other established trends (e.g. perimeter defence) and conceptions (e.g. "deperimeterisation") more focused on information itself, documents, authors and recipients.

The other important factor is the prevention of and protection against fraud. Currently, techniques based on social engineering against clients of financial institutions and the financial institutions themselves are widely extended. However, all sectors are potential victims of this type of crime. For example, in Spain, there are cases of phishing against citizens that pay their taxes. In a relatively short time, criminals will find methods to go beyond financial institutions and auctions and practically any client of any institution conducting online transactions will become a target of criminal gangs.

This trend is related to spam, which is a carrier vector of phishing and has caused the emergence of an industry of malware and technological tools that are freely available to commit crime.

If drastic measures are not taken, the improvement of commercial operations by mobile phone will bring an increase in fraud.

In short, fraud is an important factor for the ICT security market, and, at the same time, it has stimulated the creation of multidisciplinary defence teams for financial institutions, in which, at least in this field, specialists in ICT protection and traditional security areas deal with the problem unitarily.

It is also important to remember that there is no global agreement in the adoption of common legislative and police measures in the fight against online fraud, not even in the field of privacy (although, in this area, there are interesting advancements). Apart from that, a formal, close and efficient collaboration among telecommunications operators, service providers, financial institutions and the police should be established.

Until now, citizens have not put pressure – though maybe they will in the future – due to the insecurity caused by the lack of privacy existing in social networks and by a possible drastic increase in distrusting the conduct of commercial operations over the Internet, which the rise in scams and persistent and changing fraud attempts has brought about.

There is also a last area worth mentioning: critical infrastructures. The United States and the EU have expressed their concern on the matter. However, there is the feeling that, at least in Europe (and particularly in Spain), authorities have not understood the importance of identifying and protecting critical infrastructures, as information infrastructures are never taken into account. This is probably due to the fact that it is more difficult to identify them than the traditional ones, as their limits do not necessarily coincide.

So, this is another large area that must also be tackled by ICT protection, as it is a strategic field that goes beyond each state, obliging all of them to act.

Privacy,
Data Protection
and Awareness

Freedom and Security – Responses to the Threat of International Terrorism

Marie-Theres Tinnefeld

University of Applied Sciences Munich
Germany
tinnefeld@cs.hm.edu

Abstract

The September 11 attacs have led to a number of changes in the legislative framework of the EU member states. Governments intended to react quickly, powerfully and with high public visibility reactions in public to justify the power of technology in the interests of national security. The new goal is to search terrorist activity in the ocean of telecommunications data retained by communications providers and accessed by intelligence authorities. EU member states have to put in place a national data retention law by March 2009. In Germany, the most recent problem is the question of the legality of the secret online-surveillance and search of IT-Sytems, especially concerning of individual's PCs. The German Federal Constitutional Court has held, that the area of governmental authority for intervention must be limited by the constitutional protection of human dignity and fundamental rights like information privacy, telecommunications secrecy and respect for the home. In February 2008 the highest German Court created a new human right of confidentially and integrity of IT-Systems. The decision has to be understood as a reaction to the widespread use of invisible information technology by legal authorities and their secret and comprehensive surveillance of the citizens.

This article highlights the critical question, whether civilization, human rights and democracy can survive at a time, when, after the rise of terrorism the security principle seems to be the primary arbiter of information society. In particular the German Court decisions will serve as convincing evidence on the real strength of balance between freedom and security, both of which are claimed to defend the open information society.

1 Introduction and Background

Since the Enlightenment in the 18th century, the constitutional states of Europe have justified their existence through the protection of fundamental civil and human rights. Their determination was not limited to the proclamation of individual freedoms, especially freedom of thought, conscience and religion, freedom of speech and expression and freedom of the media against power of the state. The greatest gift of the classical and contemporary idea of human rights is the insight, that the core values of the personality are inviolable.

In the most famous essay on privacy ever written, published in the Harvard Law Review in 1890, Samuel D. Warren and Louis D. Brandeis (WaBr 90) wrote that "the common law secures to each individual the right of determing, ordinarily, to what extent his thoughts, sentiments, and emotions shall be communicated to others." The legal principle that prevented prosecuters from scrutinizing diaries, letters books and private papers was the same principle that, in their view, should prevent gossip columnists from writing about the private lives of citizens. They called that principle the right to an "inviolate personality" as part of the more general "right to be let alone". Alan F, Westin defined in 1967 "information privacy" as "the claim of individuals, groups, or institutions to determine for themselves how, when,

N. Pohlmann, H. Reimer, W. Schneider (Editors): Securing Electronic Business Processes, Vieweg (2008), 93-98

and to what extent information about them is communicated to others (West67). Based on the arguments in the article "The Right to Privacy" written by Warren and Brandeis and the input by Westin the German Federal Constitutional Court postulated information privacy in connection with respect for human dignity in its pathbraking decision "Volkszählungsurteil" in 1983[1] as a "new" human right. It includes basically that:

- Personal data just shall be processed only for a certain purpose
- Individuals have a right to know to what extent their data is processed (requirement for transparency).

In 2004, in its decision on the „Great Eavesdropping Offensive" (*Großer Lauschangriff*)[2] concerning laws regulating wiretapping and visual surveillance, the German Court emphasized the fundamental nature of an individual´s right to be informed that he or she has been placed under (telecommunications) surveillance, even in times of terrorism. Part of this decision rests on the importance of:

- The role that one´s home and its physical space plays in insuring the "right to be let alone".
- Information privacy as a basic right is necessary for the free development of personality and for a liberal democracy.

The countries of the European Union confidently argued in the same way for the adoption of a general data protection directive in 1995 (Directive 95/46/EC). Accordingly, security technology has to support the understanding of information privacy, which views privacy as a right to control the use of one´s personal data.

As a result, security technology must guarantee:

- Transparency (the use of security technology has to be apparent to the data subject, Article 12 and Art. 17 Data Protection Directive.)
- Openness (Requirement for truthful information about the pros and cons of security technology in special contexts)
- Careful Treatment (In cases where the identification of a specific individual is not necessary for security purposes, it must be avoided.)
- Respect for legal requirement (Security technology has to comply with legal requirements. For example, security technology must support the person´s rights of recification, erasure or blokking of data, Article 12 lit. b and Article 17 Data Protection Directive.)

In response to the deadly attacks of 9/11 the situation has changed. The increasing use for security technologies jeopardizes the freedom of the citizen. Since the attacks, the U.S. have inacted more "predictive offense". Law enforcement authorities have moved towards preventive or "anticipatory" surveillance in the fight against terrorism. This development produced a number of counterterrorism laws and techniques – like, for instance, data mining searches (LeSch05), which have a significant negative impact on civil liberties. More specially, one could find leading examples of advanced technology control in George Orwell´s Telescreen from 1984, Jeremy Bentham´s Panopticon from 1791, in movies such as Minority Report from 2002 (Tinn08).

The following paper will first give a brief outline on the most significant changes in techniques and laws:

- Preventive Telecommunications Surveillance
- Data Mining Searches

---

1 BVerfGE 65, 1.
2 1 BvR 2378, 288-318, available at://www.bverg.de/entscheidungen/rs2004_1bvr237898.

- The Data Retention Directive 2006/24 EC.

Secondly, the developments will analysed in the light of the jurisdiction of the highest German Court, especially concerning the secret online-surveillance and search of IT-Sytems.

The final part identifies key issues of privacy principles and and other fundamental values of an open, democratic society, and might serve as a reponse to the threat of international terrorrism.

2 Terrorism Information Awareness

2.1 Preventive Telecommunications Surveillance

The U.S. and European Countries' law enforcement authorities are engaged in anticipatory strategies, especially in preventive telecommunications surveillance. Preventive wiretapping is different from the traditionel repressive surveillance (Abro3):

- Repressive wiretapping investigates a specific criminal offense, which requires proof that a crime has taken place or is likely to occur.
- Preventive wiretapping starts without a reasonable suspicion of a specific person or a specific offence. This means that there is a great danger of intruding into the privacy of innocent persons.

In its decision on the *"Große Lauschangriff"* in 2004, the German Constitutional Court emphasized that the constitutional protection of human dignity extends broadley to situation, in which an individual "communicates with others".

2.2 Data Mining Searches

Data mining refers to techniques which are used by intelligence authorities to extract intelligence from vaste stores of digital informations (LeSchw05). Based on the premise that the planning of terrorist leave their mark, they investigate "in the ocean of transaction data created in the course of daily life" (DeFl04). There is a big difference beween behavioural- and subject-based searches:

- Subject-based searches start from the basis of reasonable suspicion.
- Behaviour-based searches trust in the predictive power of behavioural patterns for the identification of terrorists.

The international well-known security specialist Bruce Schneier views data mining on behaviour-based searches as a sort of enlarging the proverbial haystack where you look for a needle, or a terrorist (Schn05). James X. Dempsey and Lara D. Flint point out, that the behaviour-based data mining is in conflict "with the constitutional presumption of innocence and the Fourth Amendment principle that the government must have individual suspicion before it can conduct a search" (DeFl05). This result corresponds with the preliminary judgement of the German Constitutional Court in March 2008 concerning the German Data Retention law adopted in January 2008. The judges held that under Art. 10′s explicit constitutional protection of telecommunications secrecy the use of telecommunications data is only permitted for the prosecution cases of serious crimes. The surveillance should capture evidence of the crime. An unlimited control of communications data strays into "communication behaviour" and damages the rights of an innocent person.

2.3 The Europeans Union Data Retention Directive

Initially, the supranational institutions of the EU were divided on the issue of retention of telecommunications data. But in 2006, problems with the "prevention, detection and investigation of crime and terrorism" led to the adoption of the Data Retention Directive 2006/24/EC (Watn07). By March 2009, all EU member states must provide for the retention of subscribe, traffic and location data generated through the sending of e-mails, and fax transmission, fixed-line and mobile phone calls and internet usage by communication service providers. Law enforcement agencies will have access to this data for public security purposes. Under German law implementing the directive which was adopted in January 2008, communications providers must save communications data for a period of six months. As described above, the Constitutional Court´s decision of March 2008 restricts the intelligence services´use of that data to the purpose of preventing, detecting and prosecuting serious crimes.

The European directive is limited to the surveillance of telecommunications data including, among other things, the telephone numbers dialed, e-mail address from which and to which a message is sent and subscriber details such as bank account numbers, that are transmitted with the use of the phone. The directive is not concerned with the content of those communications including the words spoken in a conversation or the words, pictures and sounds found in the message part of an e-mail or text message.

With the storage of communications data the state can track people´s online activities. Law enforcement agencies and intelligence services can develop comprehensive internet profiles of those persons.

In Germany, communications service providers may already store communications data for their own business purposes, for example billing purposes for as long as the data are required for those purposes. Under the EC´s Directive, Germany´s providers, like those of all member states, must now store those data for the purposes of the intelligent services. The 6-months retention period under the directive is likely to extend that which would have been permitted for billing purposes. Moreover, the directive actually permits the member states to adopt laws which allow the mandatory retention for up to 24 months. Many member states have indicated that they will require the retention for the maximum period.

This raises the spectre of the inconspicuous, if unlawful, use of those additional data by the communication service providers for their own purposes. This fear has been confirmed by the well-publicised "Telekom-Scandal" uncovered in Germany recently. Over a number of years the German Telecom AG systematically collected communications data relating to fixe-line and mobile telephone calls between employees of the company und journalists that were made via its network. The intention was to identify employees who may have disclosed confidential information about the company to journalists. Via which interfaces did the Telekom spies access the communications data? Did they access the data collected by the Telekom's billing and accounts department, or did they use the infrastructure put in place on behalf of German law enforcement authorities? Was there a logging of this accesses? According to new information the company is even said to have created individual profiles, collected banking data and cross-referenced location data relating to the peaple whose communications it monitored[3].

It becomes clear, therefore that adequate technological safeguards must be in place to ensure that access to such data is only possible only when it is necessary and where it is required by those with legal authority. Under the circumstances, the only „tidy" solution for data retention is likely to be the establishment of two separate databases:

---

3 http://www.heise.de/newsticker/Wissenschaftler-analysieren-individuelle-Bewegungsprofile-von-Handynutzern--/meldung/
109012

- One for data already being legally stored for billing purposes
- Another one for „communications data, intended to be accessed solely by law enforcement authorities.
- However, who is to implement security and logging functions? Can the industry be trusted to implement a government-only communications data database with no backdoors? Where access is reserved exclusively to law enforcement authorities?

3 The secret online-surveillance and search of IT-Systems

The Internet's technical qualities and the widespread use of information technology are linked to the secret online-surveillance and search of IT-Systems by intelligence agencies, especially of individuals' PC and portable devices. On these devices one can find diaries, love letters, health data, accounts data, mailing-lists and business reports: files that are a key to the privacy and intimate sphere of a person. On 27 February 2008, the German Constitutional Court has addressed this problem. The Court created a new human right of the "confidentiality and integrity of IT-Systems" as a constitutional safeguard under Article 2 (1) and Article 1 (2) of the German Constitution (*Grundgesetz*)[4].

In asserting this new human right that could protect citizens against the secret infiltration and search of IT-Systems the German Court says: "The right of informational self-determination does not sufficiently take account of the dangers of a violation of an individual's personality right resulting from the fact, that individuals depend on the use of information technology systems for the development of their personality and therefore entrust to those systems, are even forced to populate those systems, with personal data. A third party with access to such a system, is able to procure a substantial amount of crucial data and will no longer need to rely on further data retrieving or data processing measures. The impact of such access on the individual's personality exceeds by far that of specific data collection which the right to informational self-determination protects[5]."

The decision is part of the Court's evolving case law on personality rights. As noted above, the core of privacy information is the individual's right to determine " to what extent she or he will communicate his thoughts, sentiments, and emotions to others". This new fundamental right goes further. It protects the citizens against an invisible data access by the state, for example by "spyware". Protected are, for instance, recording processes in the background of an IT-System.

As Tomas Petri (Petr08) notes, the online search and surveillance intervention goes much further than a continuing telecommunication surveillance, from which the right to telecommunications secrecy provides protection. In its continuing case law, the Constitutional court has repeatedly pointed out that the state, when carrying out secret surveillance operations, must respect a core area within which the individual can make decisions about his private life[6]. In practice, it is of course not very easy for the law enforcement agencies to assess the limits of that core area before they start collecting the data. Consequently, security technolgy must be embedded in good privacy practice.

---

4 BvR 370/07 and 1 BvR 595/07, available under: http://www.bverfg.de/entscheidungen/rs20080227_1bvr037007.html
5 Id. Part 200
6 See BVerfGE 6, 32, 41; vgl. z. B. BVerfGE 109, 279, 313.

4 Conclusion

This article has posed the critical question, whether civilization, human rights and democracy can survive at a time when, after the rise of terrorism, the security principle seems to be the primary arbiter of human life. Security no longer means the certainty of legal freedom of a citizen against arbitrary state interference, but instead a never ending activity by the state in search of limitless risk prevention.

Democratic liberties cannot simply be pushed aside until the threat from terrorism abates. After all, it is necessary to evaluate the impact of preventative surveillance on the outcome of criminal prosecution and of terrorist acts. The German Constitutioal Court created a new human right of the confidentiality and integrity of IT-Systems. This new right arises from an adequate freedom in the information society. It will discourage the use of anti-terrorism techniques that threaten core values inherent in fundamental human rights. Security technology has to support the exercise of this right.

In a lecture titled "The purpose of a State is the protection of freedom", Hans-Jürgen Papier (president of the German Constitutional Court) quotes the Dutch philosopher Baruch de Spinoza (1670): "The final purpose of a state is not to rule nor to keep the people in fear nor to submit them to external violence but to free the individual from fear so that he can live as securely as possible and so that he can fully assert his natural right to be and to act without damage to himself or to others."

References

[Albr03]   Albrecht, Hans-Jörg et al.: Überwachung der Telekommunikation nach den §§ 100a, 100b StPO und anderer verdeckter Ermittlungsmaßnahmen (Legal Reality and Effiency of the Surveillance of Telecommunication under „" 100a, 100b of the Criminal Procedure Code and other Concealed Measures for Investigations), Max-Planck Studie (MPI Study), Institutsverlag.

[DeFl04]   Dempsey, James and Flint, Lara: Commercial Data and National Security, 72 Geo Wash L. Rev., 1459-1467.

[LeSc05]   Lee, Ronald D., Schwartz, Paul M. : Heymann: Terrorism, Freedom. And Security: Winning Without War, Michigan L. Rev. Vol. 103, No. 6, 1446-1482

[Petr08]   Petri, B. Thomas, Das Urteil des Bundesverfassungsgerichts zur „Online-Durchsuchung", 7 Datenschutz und Datensicherheit, is printing

[Papi08]   Papier, Hans-Jürgen: Der Zweck des Staates ist die Wahrung der Freiheit. Über das Spannungsverhältnis von Freiheit und Sicherheit aus verfassungsrechtlicher Sicht – Ein Vortrag auf der Tagung „Freiheit und Sicherheit – Verfassungspolitische Dimensionen der Akademie für Politische Bildung Tutzing am 30. Mai, available at http//www.welt.de/papier

[Schn06]   Schneier, Bruce, Why Data Mining Won′t Stop Terror, (Wired on March 9, 2006) avoided under: http://www.wired.com/politics/security/commentary/security matters/2006/03/70357

[Tinn08]   Tinnefeld, Marie-Theres: Freiheitsrechte vs. staatliche Trojaner. Anmerkungen zum „angstbasierten" präventiv-autoritären Sicherheitsstaat, 1 Datenschutz und Datensicherheit, 7-12

[WaBr90]   Warren, Samuel D. Brandeis, Louis D.: The Right to Privacy; 4 Harv. L. Rev. 193-197 (1890)

[Watn07]   Watney, Murdoch: The Legal Konflict between Security and Privacy in Adressing Crime and Terrorism on the Internet, Pohlmann, Norbert, Reimer, Helmut, Schneider, Wolfgang (ED.), ISSE/SECURE 2007, 26-37

[West67]   Westin, Alan F. , Privacy and Freedom, 1967

The Anonymity vs. Utility Dilemma

Michele Bezzi · Jean-Christophe Pazzaglia

SAP Research
805, Avenue du Docteur Maurice Donat
BP1216,-06254 Mougins, France
{michele.bezzi | jean-christophe.pazzaglia}@sap.com

Abstract

The number, the type of users and their usage of the internet, computers and phones have evolved considerably, due to the emergence of the *web 2.0*, the decreasing cost of portable devices, the expansion of wired and wireless internet access and the digitalization of the main entertainment media. Protecting the assets of service and software providers has been the main driver for the development of security solutions in the past ten years. However, the users/customers/citizen rights have been too often neglected since the risk related to the wrong usage of personal related information was not considered by the other stakeholders. Today, the Right to Privacy is appearing on everyone's radar and factors as regulations, increasing number of news stories on privacy breaches, brand damages, are forcing organizations to address user privacy as a priority. In this paper, we will briefly review the main business drivers behind the raising of privacy concerns, and outline some of the current technology solutions to address privacy requirements. Finally, we will describe some of the future challenges in the area of privacy.

1 Introduction

Privacy is appearing on everyone's radar: the regulations related to privacy, the increasing number of news stories on privacy breaches with a considerable economic and brand damage [PrivacyRights2008], the growing public attention on privacy issues, all these factors are forcing organizations to address user privacy as a priority. The straightforward solution -limiting the collection of personal data, or not collecting them at all- largely failed for several reasons:1) personal data are essential for businesses and government to provide personalized applications and services (e-government, e-health, etc..) 2) governments and polices perceive that personal data can be of great help for critical public security applications (protection against crime, terrorism, border-control) and 3) internet users are eager to share personal information in their communities, which is especially true since the emergence of blogging and social networking activities. In this context, it is crucial to find a balance between data availability and user privacy. To preserve user privacy, from this massive wave of data collections, governments have issued a number of different privacy regulations. These regulations establish the conditions for the collection, the processing and the exchange of personal data, they also give the rights of inspection, rectification and removal to each individual. In practice, the complexity of regulations, their different implementations across geographical areas, the different frameworks applicable depending on both user and server locations, and the incomplete enforcement render compliance with these regulations difficult to achieve. For these reasons, many organizations are now struggling to ensure that the personal data are protected and processed properly.

In the narrow space between citizens' desiderata, business needs, and national and transnational regulations, privacy technology may play a major role to guarantee the right to privacy. A number of technologies under the collective name of privacy enhanced technologies (PET), are focusing on reducing the

N. Pohlmann, H. Reimer, W. Schneider (Editors): Securing Electronic Business Processes, Vieweg (2008), 99-107

collection of personal information, or removing the most sensitive parts of information, while at the same time preserving the functionality of systems. In other words, the objective is to find the optimal trade-off between people privacy and data utility. The majority of PET is at early maturity level, and in many cases still in the realm of academic research. But, motivated by these driving factors, organizations and businesses are starting to consider them.

In this contribution, we will briefly review the main business drivers behind the raising of privacy concerns, and outline some of the current technology solutions to address privacy requirements. The last section is devoted describing some of the future challenges in the area of privacy.

2 Business drivers

Privacy, similarly to information security a few years ago, is often seen as a *disabling* technology, basically an additional technological and legal burden on business process as to deal with. But with the massive collections of personal data in the internet and the advent of pervasive technologies, people are becoming more and more concerned about the dissemination of their personal data, and the loss of control on. Therefore, privacy is becoming central for organizations to maintain user confidence. Furthermore, current data mining technologies and increased, cheap, computer power permit to analyse huge collections of personal information (census data, basket data, and social network relationships) with potential and considerable socio-economic advantages. Such analyses often run on personal data or may reveal sensitive personal information by inference from *not-supposed-to-be* sensitive data; accordingly to continue and expand the use of these analytical tools, organizations have to assure the protection of users' privacy and the compliance with existing regulations. In short, privacy compliance is becoming a necessary mean for data processing that would otherwise be impossible.

In Fig 1, we show the main drivers for privacy technologies, and the future challenges (discussed in the last section). In the following, we illustrate the most significant ones from the business point of view.

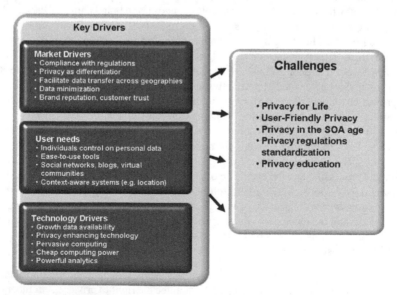

Figure 1. Privacy technology map: main drivers and challenges.

2.1 Compliance with regulations

Privacy regulations are based on main, broadly accepted, principles, such as right to access and to modify one's own information, data minimization, transparency in processing, explicit consent and security. Even if the basic principles are widely shared across different countries, the actual implementations of these principles can vary greatly across geographies. For example, European Union Data Protection directive [EUDir95] states the general privacy principles and specifies various mechanisms for their implementation. It also requires that each member state enacts legislation to fully address and implement the directive's principles. The United States does not have a single comprehensive privacy standard. They have issued a number of regulations specific to various sectors: HIPAA for health, Gramm-Leach-Bliley Act (GLBA) for finance, CFAA and ECPA for electronically transmitted or stored information, etc.

The adoption and implementation of these complex regulations are significant challenges for national and transnational organizations and for software vendors. However, organizations have to face these challenges, if they want to collect and process personal data and prevent costly liability and brand issues. Indeed, the cost and frequency of privacy breaches is constantly increasing, since 2005 more than 234 million records (for U.S. residents only) have been exposed to privacy breaches according to [PrivacyRights2008]. When a breach occurs, organizations must notify to all affected customers that their private data has been mishandled. In addition, they have to deal with the loss of user confidence, brand damage, and the implementation of new solutions to prevent a recurrence of the breach. Eventually the consequence of the breach can be the bankruptcy of the company. Although quantitative estimations are difficult, a number of studies [Ponemon2006] reported a cost between 90-305 per record lost. The implementation of effective and regulatory compliant privacy policies is the only viable strategy for organizations to minimize the risk of privacy, regulatory investigation, trials or class actions.

2.2 Privacy as differentiatior

Citizens are becoming more concerned about the dissemination of their personal information on the Internet: most European Internet users have little or no trust in personal data management over the Web [Eurobarometer2008]. As a result, the protection of personal data is essential for building confidence and sustaining the growth of the on-line environment: as customers' may recognize that some companies are more effective than others in protecting their private information, it can become a differentiator. On the other side, as discussed above, privacy breaches have a large negative impact on brands, and ultimately, on business.

2.3 Facilitate data transfer across different geographical locations

Privacy regulations and customers' perception about privacy vary greatly depending on the country and its culture. In addition, regulations impose strict constraints on data transfer across borders, and, even where regulations are not in place, organizations are often cautious about possible privacy breaches that might cause serious brand damage. However, and largely as a consequence of off-shoring, organizations have to move information around the world. This results in complex procedures on data handling, and a considerable effort from the technical, legal and administrative perspectives.

Privacy technology can provide more efficient way of automating the flow of information across systems located in different geographies, that increases the efficiency of processes. Let's take the example of a medical organization willing to outsource the development of an application processing patients' data to a software company located offshore. This software company will need some realistic data to test the application during the development lifecycle. However, since sensitive personal information are present, this company cannot access, neither copy, the totality or part of the production data from the medical company. Nevertheless, at the same time it needs data, *as close as possible*, to the real set for an effective testing phase. Typical solutions include creating *ad-hoc* synthetic data or, often, complex legal agreement between the two companies. Privacy technologies, such as anonymization, can help to increase the efficiency of the process, automatically removing and replacing sensitive information from production datasets, and producing, privacy-safe, testing datasets.

2.4 Data minimization

Privacy challenges (notably, data minimization and access right principles) force organizations to rationalize their approach on data management. Removing unnecessary data, enforcing policies for data collection, data access and their handling are critical steps towards implementing a privacy safe data management system. At the same time they result in significant benefits on the whole information infrastructure. For example, data minimization principle shifts the focus from data quantity to data quality, obliging organizations to collect the essential information for a defined business purpose, thus limiting data storage and the associated management and maintenance costs, and eventually being more effective, preventing the typical *"data rich, information poor"* syndrome. In this case, the implementation of privacy protection leads to potential cost savings for the organization.

3 Technology Solutions

Currently, data protection is centred on legal requirements; accordingly organizations are starting to invest a lot of resources on privacy policy development and management. On the other hand, user experience is rarely satisfactory. Typical user behaviour is just accepting the privacy policy of the service provider without even reading it. Still privacy concerns are constantly rising among users, as showed by a recent Eurobarometer poll reporting that 82% of European internet users believed that transmitting their personal data over the web is not secure enough. However, the same poll reported that only a minority (22%) used tools to increase data security and privacy on the web [Eurobarometer2008].

In this context, the development of technology tools to automate the management and the protection of personal information would be highly advantageous. Privacy-enhancing technology (PET) is a common name for a range of different technologies aimed at reducing the collection of private information and preventing unlawful or undesired processing of personal data. All of them limit the impact on the functionality of the data system.

They include, for example, privacy management systems, anonymization, privacy preserving data mining, privacy-preserving authentication. Their usage and effectiveness strongly depend on the application scenarios considered as well as on their implementation. In the following we will describe few of them, and the corresponding scenarios where they have been successfully applied.

3.1 Anonymization & Privacy metrics

Many organizations often have to release part of their data for research purposes, data analysis or application testing. For example, in network security research, sharing of network log data has proved to be a valuable approach to fight against coordinated attacks [Slagell2005] or statistical agencies often release their data with fine granularity for research purpose [Ciriani2007]. As these data may contain personal information, data are often altered to remove sensitive information before release to preserve individuals' privacy protection. This process, called anonymization, consists in applying various masking transformations to the original data to produce privacy-safe datasets. Anonymization techniques include: generalizing the data, i.e., recoding variables into broader classes (e.g., releasing only the first two digits of the zip code, or removing the least significant bits of an IP address) or rounding numerical data, suppressing part of or entire records, randomly swapping some fields among original data records or perturbative masking, i.e., adding random noise to numerical data values. Anonymization increases protection, lowering the disclosure risk, but, clearly, it also decreases the quality of the data and hence its utility [DuncanLambert1986]. Many research and commercial tools already provide anonymization capabilities, often under different names (data masking, data sanitazation, data scrabbling)

However, a naïve anonymization (such as removing names, social security number, street addresses) does not always preserve the privacy of individuals in the data. A study estimated that 87% of the population of the United States could be uniquely identified using the general attributes like gender, date of birth, and 5-digit zip code [Sweeney2000]. Indeed, current anonymization systems provide few, if any, guarantees on privacy, and are not able to quantify the privacy risk involved with data publishing. To achieve this goal, a number of privacy metrics have been proposed so far: *k-anonymity* [Samarati2001], *l-diversity* [Machanavajjhala2007], *t-closeness* [Li2007], *differential privacy* [Dwork2006]. Currently, privacy metrics are still in the realm of academic research, and suffer for scalability issues when applied to real-world problems, but these are important steps to implement a complete formal framework for guaranteeing the privacy of data collections and to provide evidences to the user or to the regulator that data are correctly handled.

3.2 Privacy-preserving authentications

Encryption is widely used technology to prevent malicious attacks during information transmission and to protect personal data against unlawful processing. Although, it is not considered as a specific PET by itself, it finds many applications to support privacy technologies. One promising direction is privacy-preserving authentication. Privacy-preserving authentication is a class of cryptographic mechanisms that allows users to authenticate, and, at the same time, protect their anonymity.

Consider the following scenario: Two entities want to cooperate in an unknown (possible hostile) environment, so they need to establish some initial trust. This initial trust can be then used to create secure channels, to establish integrity protected communications, to provide anonymity, non-revocation or any other high security requirements. However, the weak element of this seemingly strong chain is the initial assessment of trust: if during that phase, an individual gives its trust to a malicious entity; all the security measures taken thereafter are ineffective.

The initial establishment of trust typically involves an exchange of cryptographically certified data, attesting some information about the identity of the communicating party. This exchange is clearly necessary, but can also be seen as a violation of the privacy of the user, because it generally includes the sharing of personal information. Following Baldwin et al. [Baldwin1985], let us take an example: a company wants to hire a new employee with certain requirements (e.g., skills, experience, and reputation). The company does not want to publicly announce the open position, and, at the same time, potential applicants do not want to reveal their plans to leave current positions. They both want to do so only when they are sure when the job-seeker's wishes match the company job requirements. A similar example, taken from the work of Balfanz et al. [Balfanz2003], shows two secret intelligence agents that want to be able to authenticate themselves on field; they clearly want to reveal their affiliation only when they are sure to be talking with a fellow agent. These two examples show the need of a cryptographic primitive that helps two parties to authenticate each other, being sure that non-members are not able to either impersonate group members or to recognize legitimate group members. Besides, the communications between group members are designed so as to provide untraceability of any two protocol exchanges. Many protocols for *secret handshake* [Balfanz2003], [Ateniese2007] or *private matchmaking* [Meadows1986, Shin2008] address these issues and do offer such a cryptographic protocol, which is indispensable for preserving the privacy of any two communicating parties during the initial establishment of trust.

3.3 Privacy management systems

Privacy management software enables the user to express privacy preferences in a formal (machine-readable) language. Whenever a user accesses a service on a website, the system compares his privacy preferences to the privacy policies of the service provider automatically, and raises an alert in case of a mismatch. Privacy policy information includes: what data are collected and their purpose, whom the data are supplied to, how long the information will be stored, etc. . One operational example is the W3C standard: Platform for Privacy Preferences Project [P3P]. Some organizations have released user-tools that support P3P (e.g. user agents included in Microsoft Internet Explorer or Netscape web browsers, Privacy Bird plug-in, Privacy finder search engine). To give a glimpse of P3P functionality, let us describe how it works in one of these implementation. Microsoft Internet Explorer warns the user when the browser encounters a cookie that has not a P3P policy or has a P3P policy that does not match the browser privacy preferences, as set by the user in the privacy setting menu. The user can also ask the browser to show dynamically generated natural language privacy policy based on the P3P data. The P3P functionality in Internet Explorer is currently limited to cookie blocking, and it will not cover the entire website privacy policy. A more complete implementation in this sense is provided by the Privacy Bird plug-in.

Although P3P allows the user to be informed about privacy policies before releasing personal information, it does not implement any enforcement on privacy policies. In effect, the user is not sure that the site will act according to the presented policies. An additional limitation is the current limited penetration of P3P compliant websites in the internet, only 15% of the top 5,000 websites incorporate P3P as reported by a 2007 study of Carnegie Mellon University [CyLab2006]. The Enterprise Privacy Authorization Language (EPAL) [Ashley2002] was developed to include policy enforcement; so, it allows organisations to demonstrate the compliance with their stated privacy policy. EPAL policies are attached to the data (sticky policies) and they are enforced each time data is accessed (similarly as for access control policies), that can cause performance problems if data are frequently accessed. Finally, privacy management systems represent a valuable tool for end users to manage their private data, and, despite their current limitations, they are finding their way into commonly used applications.

4 Challenges

Technology trends, novel users and business needs result in the emergence of new challenges for privacy (see Fig. 1). In the following we illustrate the main ones, which require new technology solutions.

4.1 Privacy for life.

From the early days of the Internet, people have started to leave digital traces about their personal life, for example in personal webpages and comments on forums. Most of these data are still accessible almost two decades later, and many users have practically lost the control on that, or they are not even aware of their presence. Today, with the increasingly collaborative nature of the web, the emerging of social networks and virtual communities, the quantity and quality (e.g., list of friends, images, videos) of personal information in the web are rapidly increasing. Moreover, while in early 90's the large majority of internet users were technical people exchanging technical information, nowadays everybody including children and teenagers are exchanging information on a large spectrum of topics including their personal life. Users are starting to be concerned about the digital (often practically unerasable) traces they are leaving throughout their lifetime, and the possible unforeseen and uncontrolled usage of personal data. For example, an employer could access applicants' online community profiles or mine old forums before calling him for a job interview. Technical solutions in terms of anonymity or pseudo-anonymity, and more reliable data management tools are clearly needed to better manage personal data for a lifelong period.

4.2 User-friendly privacy

Privacy technologies may help users to better handle their privacy, but they also introduce concepts like anonymization, unlinkability, policy management, data minimization that are often hard to grasp for typical users. Usability could be increased making most of these technicalities automatic and transparent to the end user. However, the user should retain the whole control on privacy settings, limiting the number of features that can be handled automatically. This is exemplified by the opt-in/opt-out policy debate. Whenever an organization has to collect personal data, it has to ask for the consent to the user, and the opt-out approach is the consent system most commonly used. In the opt-out scheme, users receive a complete privacy policy, and accepting that (usually, clicking on a text expressing agreement to get the software or service being offered) they give the consent to collect and process personal information, at least until the user explicitly requests to remove the consent. In practice, many users do not read or fully understand privacy policies, often written in legal terms. Furthermore, even if the opt-out option is available, it is not used, because they require time and effort for the user. A more privacy safe approach is the opt-in scheme. In this approach, users explicitly have to decide which personal information they disclose, and the corresponding policies (time of retention, purpose limitation, etc...). However, empowering end users to define his policies is often unrealistic, because privacy settings are often difficult to define for the users, they also tend to change over time, and users often do not know their own privacy policies or are unable to express them. For this, and similar cases, there is still not a satisfactory solution, that finds the optimal equilibrium point between usability and user-control on data.

4.3 Privacy in the SOA age

System architecture is evolving towards service oriented architecture (SOA). Monolithic systems have being replaced by groups of services, loosely coupled, and, often, provided by different parties. Mashup technology permits the end user to easily build their own composed applications. In general, SOA offers greater flexibility, scalability and adaptability, but it also raises a number of privacy issues. Services may be provided by different providers, with different, sometimes conflicting, privacy policies. How to compose these policies and obtain a final policy for the composed service remains an open question.

5 Conclusion

Privacy protection is necessary for organizations to comply with national and international regulations and to preserve users and partners' confidence. Without that confidence, acceptance to efficient and individually tailored services will be at risk and services will be approached with suspicion. Accordingly, organizations have to put in place the right policies and allocate dedicated resources, including specific roles, and promote internal and external education on such issues. The emerging privacy preserving technologies can help in this scope, although at a early maturity level, they are becoming increasingly important in some processes, providing privacy protection with a limited impact on system functions.

An inclusive technology solution for privacy issues is not available yet, but there is a common understanding that privacy, in a similar way as information security a few years ago, must be addressed strategically: privacy cannot be seen as an additional feature on existing systems, but as a main requirement, *although non-functional*, in the design phase. In fact, organizations often see data protection as cumbersome. The main reason is that privacy protection is typically taken into consideration at a later stage. It then appears very inefficient, because privacy protection strongly impacts the whole process of data storage and management. Personal data protection has to be considered early in a business process and fully included in the system design. It goes together the functionality of the system without necessarily limiting it.

Acknowledgements

We thank A. Sorniotti for his contribution to "Privacy-preserving authentications" section, and M. Rahaman and S. Short for carefully reading the last version of the paper. This work was supported in part by the EU PrimeLife project, within the Seventh Framework Programme (FP7/2007-2013).

References

[Ashley2002] Ashley, P., Hada, S., Karjoth, G, Schunter, M.: E-P3P privacy policies and privacy authorization. In Proc. of the ACM workshop on Privacy in the Electronic Society (WPES 2002), Washington, DC, USA, November 2002.

[Ateniese2007] Ateniese, G., Blanton, M., Kirsch, J.: Secret Handshakes with Dynamic and Fuzzy Matching. In 14th Annual Network & Distributed System Security Symposium (NDSS'07), 2007.

[Baldwin1985] Baldwin, Gramlich, W.C. : Cryptographic Protocol for Trustable Match Making, Proc., IEEE Symposium on Security and Privacy, 1985.

[Balfanz,2003] Balfanz, Dirk, Durfee, Glenn, Shankar, Narendar, Smetters, Diana K., Staddon, Jessica, Wong, Hao-Chi: Secret Handshakes from Pairing-Based Key Agreements. IEEE Symposium on Security and Privacy 2003: 180-196

[Ciriani2007] Ciriani, V., De Capitani di Vimercati, S., Foresti, S., Samarati, P.: Microdata protection, (Advances in information security). – In: Secure data management in decentralized systems; Eds. by Ting Yu, Sushil Jajodia. – New York : Springer, 2007.

[CyLab2006] CyLab Privacy Interest Group, Carnegie Mellon University, 2006 Privacy Policy Trends Report http://www.chariotsfire.com/pub/cpig-jan2007.pdf

[DuncanLambert1986] Duncan, G. T., Lambert, D.: Disclosure-limited data dissemination, Journal of the American Statistical Association, vol. 81, no. 393, 1986.

[Dwork2006] Dwork, C.: Differential privacy, ICALP, 2006.

[Eurobarometer2008] Data Protection in the European Union Report, Citizens' perceptions, Flash Eurobarometer 225, 2008, http://ec.europa.eu/public_opinion/flash/fl_225_en.pdf

[EUDir95] Directive 95/46/EC on the protection of personal data, http://ec.europa.eu/justice_home/fsj/privacy/index_en.htm

[Li2007] Li, N., Li, T., Venkatasubramanian, S.: t-closeness: Privacy beyond k-anonymity and l-diversity, ICDE, 2007.

[Machanavajjhala2007] Machanavajjhala, A., Kifer, D., Gehrke, J., Venkitasubramaniam, M.: l-diversity: Privacy beyond k-anonymity, ACM Transactions on Knowledge Discovery from Data, vol. 1, no. 1, 2007.

[Meadows1986] Meadows, – Catherine: A More Efficient Cryptographic Matchmaking Protocol for Use in the Absence of a Continuously Available Third Party. IEEE Symposium on Security and Privacy 1986: 134-137.

[Ponemon2006] 2006 Annual Study: Cost of a Data Breach , Ponemon Institute, see also K. Kark, Calculating The Cost Of A Security Breach, Forrester, 2007.

[PrivacyRights2008] Privacy Rights Clearinghouse, A Chronology of Data Breaches, http://www.privacyrights.org/ar/ChronDataBreaches.htm

[Shin2008] Shin, Ji Sun, Gligor, Virgil D. , A New Privacy-Enhanced Matchmaking Protocol, NDSS Symposium 2008.

[Slagell2005] Slagell, A., and Yurcik, W., Sharing Computer Network Logs for Security and Privacy: A Motivation for New Methodologies of Anonymization, SECOVAL: The Workshop on the Value of Security through Collaboration, Athens, Greece, 2005

[Sweeney2000] Sweeney, L.,: Uniqueness of simple demographics in the u.s. population. Technical report, Carnegie Mellon University, 2000.

[Samarati2001] Samarati, P., Protecting Respondent's Privacy in Microdata Release, in IEEE Transactions on Knowledge and Data Engineering, vol. 13, n. 6, November/December 2001.

Governmental Control of the Internet in addressing Law Enforcement and National Security

Murdoch Watney

University of Johannesburg
South Africa
mwatney@uj.ac.za

Abstract

Some people contended that governmental regulation of the Internet would not be possible due to its inherent characteristics. This paper relates how governments, in addressing law enforcement and national security, have taken control of the Internet by means of legislation. Consideration is given to the influence and impact of powerful governments on the legal regulation of the Internet. It is pointed out that when addressing law enforcement and national security the borderless nature of the Internet is in reality bordered. It is concluded that in striving towards law enforcement and national security, enforcement of governmental control of the Internet is not easily achieved without the assistance of the Internet Service Provider (ISP) as well as international assistance and co-operation.

1 Exploring the dark side of Internet connectivity

All stories must have a beginning and an end. My story begins by looking briefly at the dark side of Internet connectivity as illustrated when the much publicized distributed denial of service (DDoS) attacks were launched in cyberspace against Estonia, a country in Eastern Europe, bordered by the Baltic Sea, Latvia and Russia and since 2004, a member of the European Union (EU).

A few years ago the Internet, cyberspace and criminal conduct in cyberspace would have been regarded as science fiction, but today these are the realities of the 21st century that challenge Internet connected governments, companies and users.

Denial of service (DoS) attacks are nothing new. Already in the 1980's DoS attacks threatened networked computers. DoS attacks attempt to overwhelm a computer or networking system by bombarding it with a high volume of information requests. If successful, the attack renders the targeted system unable to respond to legitimate requests, which could include providing access to a particular website. A DDoS attack operates on the same principle, but multiplies its impact by directing a "botnet" of networked computers that have been remotely hijacked to bombard the target system with many requests at the same time. Botnets can be controlled by a single individual. Some botnets in the attacks on Estonia included up to 100 000 machines, all making special requests for information from target websites at the same instant [Ryan08]. In 2000, a lot of publicity was given to online blackmailers that had launched DDoS attacks against the websites of CNN, Yahoo! and eBay with the consequence that these websites were paralyzed [Baum08].

What did the DDoS attacks against Estonia teach the international community? It placed Estonia on the world map, demonstrated once again the dangers of Internet connectivity and showed that the Internet can be used as a powerful instrument. In the instance of Estonia, it was used to commit a crime. What happened in Estonia is not a once off occurrence, but can be repeated against any target for various purposes. It is for these reasons relevant to look briefly at what happened in Estonia.

On approximately 27 April 2007 Estonia was hit by a blizzard of DDoS attacks launched against important Eustonian websites, such as the website of the president, parliament, leading ministries, political parties, major news outlets and Estonia's two dominant banks [Ryan08]. These attacks continued until at least as late as mid June 2007.

To understand the consequence and impact of the cyber-attacks, one has to understand that Estonia is a country that is highly dependant on the use of the Internet as a communication medium. It has whole-heartedly embraced the use of the Internet. It has a population of approximately 1,3 million people with almost 800 000 Internet banking clients and 95% of banking operations are conducted electronically [Ryan08]. In March 2007 Estonia became the first country in the world to allow Internet voting for parliamentary elections. Estonia's Internet usage is enviable. Worldwide most western countries are encouraging their citizens to make use of e-government services, such as e-filing of tax returns. Even a developing country such as South Africa invests considerably in promoting the usage of the Internet and is involved in upgrading its infrastructure to ensure more bandwidth for better communication. Countries have come to realize that the Internet has many advantages, but the down-side to the Internet is what happened in Estonia. The attacks brought the Internet in Estonia to a grinding halt and the country was severely affected, more so than a country less dependant on the Internet. However, computer technology and the Internet have become an integral part of most societies today with governments, companies and individuals all facing the challenges of cybercrime.

For purpose of this discussion, the motive and target of the DDoS attacks are relevant (par. 6). The attacks were presumably launched in protest against Estonian officials for moving a bronze statue of a Soviet soldier from a park in Tallinn, Estonia's capital, to a military cemetry. Ethnic Russians which makes up about a quarter of Estonia's population and Russia regarded this as an affront to the memory of soldiers who fought the Nazis during World War 2. In contrast most Estonians felt that the statue represented a symbol of almost five decades of Soviet occupation which ended when Estonia became independent from the Soviet Union in 1991.

Ryan (2008) predicts "(a) new age of anarchy and piracy that will both serve and undermine the interests of power is in prospect. The need both for security counter-measures and adequate legal frameworks to meet this threat is pressing." Does there exist any truth in this prediction or is it merely aimed at sensationalism?

This paper will explore the following questions: can governments control cyberspace within their territory, thereby ensuring protection to their citizens against various types of cybercrime (see par. 6.2 for a discussion of cybercrime). If affirmative, how do governments control the Internet (par. 4 and 5)? The latter question becomes even more perplexing. If a government can control the Internet in addressing law enforcement and national security, how effective is the enforcement of the governmental control, not only within but also outside its territorial borders (par. 7)?

2 Introducing the complexity of governmental control of the Internet

At the first Conference on Computers, Freedom and Privacy in 1991, Jim Warren warned that computing technology and the Internet was at a crossroad in respect of Internet control. He said "(f)or we are at a crossroad – as individuals, organizations and governments increasingly depend upon computerized information and digital communications…Customs, policies, regulations and statutes governing this new environment will be created. The question is: Who will create them and what will they be?" [Warre91]

Many opinions prevailed on who will create the legislation and what the content thereof would be. Most of these opinions proved either unfounded or were contradicted.

John Perry Barlow was of the unequivocal opinion that the government could not create statutes for the Internet and that Internet control will be in the hands of the Internet society. On 9 February 1996 he posted "A declaration of the Independence of Cyberspace" on the Internet. In the Declaration he stated that there exists no elected government in cyberspace, that the governments have no sovereignty in cyberspace and "nor do you possess any methods of enforcement we have true reason to fear" [Barl96]. In the Declaration of Independence, he stated that although government may indicate that there exist problems that should be addressed; these problems will be addressed by the internet society themselves. He stated in the Declaration "(w)e will create a civilization of the Mind in Cyberspace. May it be more humane and fair than the world your governments have made before" [Barl96].

Against this background, the question of whether a government can control the Internet in addressing law enforcement and national security will be investigated.

3 Understanding the concepts, Internet and cyberspace

Governmental control of the Internet in addressing law enforcement and national security concerns can only be fully appreciated by understanding the concepts of Internet and cyberspace. Cyberspace is sometimes used as an Internet metaphor, a *de facto* synonym for the Internet without clearly distinguishing the Internet from cyberspace and confusing the two concepts.

The Internet is an interconnected system of networks that connects computers worldwide. It relies on a physical infrastructure that connects networks to other networks using the Transmission Control Protocol (TCP) and Internet Protocol (IP). It does not comprise of a single physical entity. It comprises of an ever-growing network of networked computers that are networked to other computers.

The origin of the Internet is well known. It originates from the US in the 1960's when the US military wanted a communication system that could withstand a nuclear attack. The Internet design was unprecedented because it was designed as open, minimalist and neutral [GoWu06]. It was designed to be a decentralized, self-maintaining series of redundant links between computers and computer networks, capable of rapidly transmitting communications without direct human involvement or control and with the automatic ability to reroute communications if one or more individual links were damaged or otherwise unavailable.

When the US decided to commercialize the Internet in 1992, it could not have foreseen the impact the Internet would have on the rest of the world. The US must have been stunned by the enthusiasm with which other countries embraced the Internet. It is not an exaggeration that the use of computing technology and the Internet have become an integral part of society. What makes the Internet so unique, is that one can access the Internet from anywhere in the world.

Although no one owns the Internet, there are governments, organizations and institutions that own some of the computers and networks that comprise the Internet, in other words, pieces of the infrastructure.

Cyberspace denotes the "place" where communication on the Internet takes place. It is "a place without physical walls or even physical dimensions – where ordinary telephone conversations 'happen' where voice mail and email messages are stored and sent back and forth, and where computer-generated graphics are transmitted and transformed, all in the form of interactions, some real-time and some delayed among countless users, and between users and the computer itself" [Trib91]. Cyberspace exists everywhere that there are telephone wires, coaxial cables, fiber-optic lines or electromagnetic waves [Burn01].

William Gibson popularized the term, "cyberspace" in his 1984 novel, *Neuromancer*. *Neoromancer* was written about a future where information was worth more than money and where the global information infrastructure prevailed [Burn01]. What was merely science fiction in 1984, is proving to be the reality today. A large part of the book unfolded not in the physical world, but in a world that Gibson referred to as "cyberspace." In the 2000 documentary, *No maps for these territories*, Gibson commented on the origin of cyberspace by saying: "(a)ll I knew about the word "cyberspace" when I coined it, was that it seemed like an effective buzzword. It seemed evocative and essentially meaningless. It was suggestive of something, but had no real semantic meaning, even for me, as I saw it emerge on the page." Today the concept, cyberspace, denotes a world of its own.

Cyberspace must be contrasted with the physical space or real world. Gibson referred to the physical world as "meatspace." Barlow used the term, cyberspace in the "Declaration of Independence" (par. 2). He stated "(o)urs is a world that is both everywhere and nowhere, but it is not where the bodies live." It will be shown hereafter that cyberspace is very much bound to the location of the physical infrastructure, the Internet that makes the communication possible. People populate cyberspace. People cannot access cyberspace without engaging the Internet and the Internet exists in a physical space. Relevant for purposes of this discussion, is whether a government can control cyberspace within its territory.

4 Exploring the myth: death of governmental (nation states) in cyberspace

Cyberspace does not know any boundaries. As the Internet can be accessed from anywhere in the world, many argued that the nature and characteristics of the Internet would result in governments being unable to control the Internet [GoWu06].

Initially it appeared as if governments were not much interested in regulating the Internet (par. 5). The reason may have been that governments did not realize the power of the Internet and the impact it would have on society. Gradually governments came to understand the immense power of the Internet. Governments also realised that the power could be abused to commit crimes.

Although the Internet may be accessed from anywhere in the world, it does not imply access location cannot be established. Every time a user accesses the Internet, the Internet Service Provider (ISP) automatically records information such as the traffic data as the ISP needs this information to ensure that the communication is conveyed. Technology may enable an Internet user to hide his/her location, but cyberspace is still accessed in a physical world from within the territorial borders of a country.

When it comes to law enforcement and national security aimed at the prevention, detection, investigation and prosecution of crime which includes terrorism, cyberwar and iWar, governments have taken or are in the process of taking control of the Internet within their national borders. As shown hereafter, cyberspace did not bring an end to the nation state or differently put, territorial governmental control. Burlow who scathingly said that cyberspace should be free from governmental control would appreciate the reasons why governments took control of the Internet within their territories (see par. 5 hereafter).

5 Investigating the legal reality: governmental control of the Internet

5.1 Introduction

The legal regulation of the Internet can be divided into three phases, namely self-regulation, conduct regulation and expanding conduct regulation to include governmental control of information on the Internet by means of surveillance. The phases clearly show how governments have grappled with finding solutions in addressing national security and law enforcement while at the same time upholding a balance between security and human right protection.

5.2 Synopsis of the different phases of Internet legal regulation

5.2.1 First phase: no governmental regulation of the Internet

When the US commercialized the Internet in the early 1990's, it left the regulation of the Internet to the Internet community (consisting of Internet inventors and users). Initially the role of the law was perceived as irrelevant in respect of the Internet. It was felt that as the Internet was created by technology, it should therefore be regulated by technology.

The wake-up call for legal regulation came with the release of the 'I love you' virus in 2000 [HiCo02]. Although the Federal Bureau of Investigation (FBI) and the Central Intelligence Agency (CIA) traced the origin of the 'I love you' virus to the Philippines within 24 hours after its release, the conduct was not a crime in the Philippines at that stage. The perpetrator could therefore not be prosecuted or extradited to the US to stand trial [Carr03]. This illustrates the effect of globalization on crime, as crime is increasingly committed outside an effected country's borders. Furthermore, even if an effected country has legislation in place that criminalizes such conduct, the legislation is meaningless if the perpetrator resides in a country where such conduct is not also criminalized. Cybercrime can therefore only be effectively addressed if the various Internet-connected countries have harmonised legislation and provide assistance in the investigation of the crime and sharing of information (par. 7).

Countries realized that self-governance could not address law enforcement and national security on the Internet.

5.2.2 Second phase: Legal regulation of conduct

As Internet usage increased, the exploitation of the Internet by means of cyber crimes increased and governments realized that they had to take control.

Governments realised that they needed a solution to address Internet crime. Western governments also acknowledged that there should be an international treaty that provides guidelines in addressing cyber-crime and aims to establish harmonized legislation in the various Internet-connected countries. This would assist internationally with the combating and investigation of cybercrime.

In 2001 the Council of Europe Convention on Cybercrime introduced a treaty on cybercrime which was signed by all the Council of Europe member countries and four non-European member countries namely Japan, Canada, the US and South Africa [Watn07a]. This is currently the only international treaty on cybercrime. It is interesting to note that by 2008, 23 of the 43 signatory countries have ratified the Cybercrime Convention. Goldsmith and Wu (2006) are of the opinion that the treaty does not effec-tively address cross-border assistance and cooperation due to the time-factor in obtaining authorization for assistance. Mandatory traffic data retention may address this problem (see par. 7). The authors are of the opinion that the answer to international cooperation and assistance do not lie with a treaty but with informal unilateral cooperation and assistance. On an international level, countries are addressing cooperation. However, cooperation can only be effective if the information needed as evidence to prove a crime is available (see par. 7).

Countries implemented legislation aimed at prohibiting certain conduct in the cyberspace within their territory. The legal regulation of conduct on the Internet proved only partially successful. The applica-tion of the traditional law enforcement methods, tools and approach to crime within cyberspace (elec-tronic medium) hinders the effectiveness of conduct regulation. Traditionally a re-active approach was applicable to criminal investigations, in other words the crime is investigated after its commission and only then brought to the attention of the law enforcement agency.

A cybercrime such as 'identity theft' illustrates the shortcomings of a re-active approach. By the time the commission of the cybercrime is detected and reported, it is difficult to establish the identity of the perpetrator, since the information (evidence) identifying the perpetrator are in many instances not avail-able anymore. Information is vital in crime prevention and detection.

The police is traditionally responsible for the investigation of crime as well as ensuring compliance with, and enforcement of, laws. The Internet however, brings about challenges that necessitate the in-volvement of third parties, such as the ISP. For example, a government may place a statutory obligation on ISPs to prevent access to child pornography. If the ISP does not have such a statutory obligation, law enforcement becomes very difficult.

Due to the difficulties experienced with traditional law enforcement methods, governments were al-ready, prior to the terrorist attacks launched against the US on 11 September 2001 (referred to as 9/11), looking for a more effective solution to address criminal investigations on the Internet.

Effective investigation does not only rely on the prohibition of conduct as a crime but also on the col-lection of information on the Internet, because without collection of information that can be tendered as evidence, a criminal investigation and prosecution cannot be conducted successfully.

5.2.3 Third phase: the extension of conduct regulation to include laws aimed at governmental control of information available, accessed and distributed on the Internet.

The 9/11 US terrorist attacks served as a catalyst to move from conduct regulation to the third phase of Internet legal regulation, namely extending the laws regulating conduct to include laws aimed at gov-ernmental control of information available, accessed and distributed on the Internet.

Most western countries such as the EU member countries, the US and other countries such as South Africa apply surveillance technology or are in the process of enacting legislation regulating the use of surveillance technology (bearing in mind that different surveillance methods may be used).

The US was the first country to implement extensive surveillance legislation. In 2006 the EU implemented the compulsory traffic data retention Directive 2006/24/EC, making it compulsory for the 27 EU member countries to implement legislation providing for the compulsory traffic data storage of all users for a limited period of time, irrespective of whether the user is a suspect or not. By September 2009 all EU member countries must have such legislation in place. However, the EU has not escaped criticism. Some perceive the blanket traffic data retention as an unjustifiable violation of human rights. Others argue that this type of control comes from the security branch of the government and qualify as an exception to the guaranteed right to privacy in article 8 of the Council of Europe Convention on the Protection of Human Rights and Fundamental Freedoms of 1950. Although it emanates from the security branch, the manner of traffic data collection and storage must still comply with the consumer data protection as set out in the EU Data Protection Directives 1996/46/EC and 2002/58/EC [Watn07b].

Surveillance will not be discussed fully as the emphasis in this paper falls on whether a government can control the Internet in addressing law enforcement and national security as opposed to a discussion of the mechanisms used to control information on the Internet [Watn07b].

5.3 Conclusion in respect of governmental control legislation

The brief discussion of the different phases of Internet legal regulation gives credence to the following supposition: "(a)s viruses, online fraud, spam, and other abuses add up, the greatest dangers for the future of the Internet come not when governments overreact, but when they don't react alone. The old and primary role of preventing harm and protecting rights must be translated to the present for the network to continue to grow and prosper" [GoWu06]. The different phases also show how governments are tightening their control on the Internet.

It is also interesting that powers have emerged that shape the legal regulation of the Internet. A distinction can be drawn between the EU, US and China. Although the US was the first country to implement surveillance legislation aimed at gathering information on the Internet, the EU was the first to implement the surveillance method of traffic data retention. Other non-EU/US countries noted the legal regulation imposed by these powers and followed suit. It can safely be predicted that many other countries will follow in the EU footsteps as has been the case with consumer data protection.

It has been shown that governments can control the Internet within their territory by means of laws. The purpose of the laws is to address law enforcement and national security (par.6).

6 Negotiating an understanding of law enforcement and national security

6.1 Introduction

Understanding law enforcement and national security can be illustrated by again considering the DDoS attack launched against Estonian websites (par. 1). Were the attacks an example of iWar or cyber-war or cyber-terrorism? The starting point would be to establish whether the conduct is prohibited as a crime in the country. If a country does not provide for this type of conduct as a crime, then it cannot be investigated. In this instance a crime was committed, namely a DDoS attack. The target and the motivation for the attack become relevant to determine whether the investigation of the crime is in the interest of law enforcement or national security. It was alleged that Russia was involved, although Russia denied this allegation [Jone08]. Others were of the opinion that it was an orchestrated protest attack by a group of disgruntled Estonian citizens of Russian descent, an example of iWar [Ryan08] whereas some referred to the attack as cyber-terrorism [Heat08]. It is clear that a fine line exists between investigating crime in the interest of law enforcement and national security. Normally most crimes will clearly fall within the domain of law enforcement or national security.

6.2 Defining cybercrime, cyber-terrorism, cyber-war and information warfare (iWar)

Universal definitions for cybercrime, cyber-terrorism, iWar (information warfare) and cyber-war do not exist [TCL+06]. Some definitions may be too wide and others too narrow. However, for the purpose of this discussion, it is relevant to conceptualise the different terms.

Cybercrime is defined as any unlawful conduct involving a computer or computer system irrespective of whether it is the object of the crime or instrumental to the commission of the crime or incidental to the commission of the crime [TCL+06]. iWar or cyber-war and cyber-terrorism resort under the concept, cybercrime.

The term 'cyber-terrorism' was coined in 1996 by combining the terms 'cyberspace' and 'terrorism.' The term became widely accepted after being embraced by the US Armed Forces [JaCo05]. Much of the interest in cyber-terrorism and information warfare originates from the events of 9/11 and the subsequent discovery of information and communication technology tools used to plan and coordinate those attacks. After the events of 9/11 reports surfaced that Al Qaeda had been transmitting hidden data over the Internet. Data hiding refers to the act of taking a piece of information and hiding it within another piece of data. Hidden maps of terrorist targets and instructions were posted in sport chat rooms and pornographic sites that could be accessed by anyone with an Internet connection [TCL+06].

Cyber-war can be defined as the actions taken to infiltrate, corrupt, disrupt or destroy the information systems of an adversary, or to defend one's own information systems from such attacks. Information warfare by itself could be used as a means of mass disruption rather than mass destruction. However, if a nation is going to be physically attacked the attackers may well use any means at their disposal, including IW [JaCo05; TCL+06].

Ryan (2008) distinguishes iWar from cyber-war as follows: "iWar denotes attacks carried out over the internet that target the consumer internet infrastructure such as the website that provide access to online banking services. As a result, while nation states alone can engage in "cyber" warfare, iWar can be waged by individuals, corporations, and communities."

Cyber-terrorism can be defined as the unlawful attack or threat of attack on computers, networks and the information stored therein for the purpose of intimidation or coercion of a government or its people for the furtherance of a political or social goal [JaCo05; TCL+06]. At present the biggest threat lies with the use of the Internet for terrorist-related activities, such as secure communications between terrorists utilised for example for the exchange of ideas, information and plans related to the planning and targeting of terrorist attacks, canvassing of financial support, spreading of propaganda as well as recruitment. There are some who are of the opinion that cyber-terrorism will increase in frequency and that it will be a continuous threat during the 21st century [JaCo05; TCL+06; Ryan08]. Anil, head of the Nato Computer Incident Response Capability Co-ordination Centre, warned that a determined cyber-attack on a country's online infrastructure would be "practically impossible to stop" [Heat08]. Cyber crimes such as money-laundering and organised crime may also be used to finance terrorism.

The crime committed against Estonia, illustrates that it is not easy to draw a clear distinction between cyberterrorism or iWar or cyberwar. The fact remains however that a crime had been committed.

Other cyber crimes are website defacement (also referred to as web graffiti), the launch of malicious codes (malicious software or code refers to viruses, worms and Trojan horses, logic bombs and other uninvited software designed to disrupt a computer's operations or destroy files) and "identity theft" (fraud).

7 Facing the harsh reality: enforcing governmental control and obtaining international assistance and cooperation

Governments have implemented laws (statutes) that control (govern) the Internet within their territories. These laws indicate which conduct is prohibited as crimes within the cyberspace of their territory. Some countries are taking the control of the Internet even further and have or are in the process of implementing laws that control the information on the Internet and assist in the gathering of information (evidence). Most western countries impose surveillance legislation that provides for various surveillance methods in gathering information.

It is important to realize that conduct regulation alone does not assist in the investigation of a cybercrime. A crime can only be investigated if the law enforcement and national security agencies can collect information on the communication medium itself. Within the borders of a country, the ISPs assistance is of vital importance in the collection of information. In future, more emphasis will be placed on cooperation between ISPs and investigators, although some fear that the independence of ISPs will be threatened [Carv08].

If a perpetrator committed the crime outside the territory of a country but the effect was felt in that country, the law enforcement or national security needs the international co-operation and assistance of the country where the perpetrator is situated. Countries should have a legal structure in place to assist with the sharing of evidence amongst them. However, the investigation of cybercrime is not easy at the most of times, even with the perpetrator being present in the country that is investigating the crime.

Some may have argued that country's (nation state) laws will be replaced with international bodies who would draft international treaties that would embody global laws for different issues, such as copyright, consumer protection, child pornography and crime. It is conceded that such global laws would simplify the lives of the Internet user, since there would be no conflicting laws and no necessity to comply with the different laws of approximately 175 Internet connected countries. However, it is at this stage near impossible for the different countries and the different stakeholders who have different interests to agree on a global law applicable to all countries.

The biggest problem lies with the investigation of crimes. A country such as South Africa has the necessary legislation criminalizing conduct in cyberspace as well as legislation providing for the collection of information in cyberspace, similar to that of the EU traffic data retention directive 2006/24/EC. The biggest hurdle is the enforcement of these laws since the law enforcement and national security agencies do not have the necessary investigatory skills. The legislation providing for crimes and information gathering can easily amount to nothing but paper law, a law without any substance due to its unenforce-ability.

Most countries of the developed world is taking the investigation of cybercrime seriously and think-ing along the lines of setting up special investigatory agencies. It will be to the benefit of all Internet-connected countries if cyber-crime is globally addressed.

The differences between investigation in the physical world and in cyberspace cannot be overempha-sised, because it is the harsh reality that faces Internet-connected countries. Conducting a criminal in-vestigation in cyberspace as illustrated by the DDoS attack on Estonia poses many challenges [Ryan08]. Even if Estonia was able to prove that the attacks were orchestrated with the authorization of Russia, it is unclear how one state would respond to another in this regard. Does Barlow's statement "nor do you (government) possess any methods of enforcement we have true reason to fear" perhaps contain some grain of truth (par. 2)?

As a result of the cyberattacks on Estonia, NATO (North Atlantic Treaty Organization) has realized that cybercrime must be addressed. In 2008 it approved the setting up a cyber defence centre of excellence that will carry out research and training in how to combat cyber warfare. The centre will be based in Tal-linn in Estonia and will be used to train NATO's civilian and military staff in cyber defence techniques. Seven NATO member states haves signed documents for the formal establishment of the centre, namely Estonia, Germany, Italy, Latvia, Lithuania, Slovakia and Spain [Ferg08].

8 Reaching a conclusion

The story of governmental control in addressing law enforcement and national security is one of hope, but there is no conclusion as yet.

What have been established in this discussion is that the nation state (governments) did not, as initially predicted, lose control of the Internet within their respective territories. Governments have implemented laws aimed at controlling cyberspace within their own territory. Countries have realized that cybercrime can only be successfully addressed with the assistance of the ISP, international co-operation and harmo-nized cybercrime laws.

Governments are now moving onto enforcing the control. Enforcement of control refers to the inves-tigation of the cybercrimes and this is proving to be challenging. Goldsmith and Wu (2006) argue that governmental control does not have to be perfect to be effective. It is easier to achieve control within the national borders of a country, but it is debatable whether enforcement of control across borders is effective at present. Countries need access to across border information to investigate a crime.

Maybe one should go back to the beginning of the story, namely the dark side of Internet connectivity and what the Internet-connected world have come to realize, namely that cybercrime cannot be allowed to proliferate to such an extent that it amounts to anarchy and "kills" the Internet. When it comes to crime, all Internet-connected governments agree that the Internet is worth protecting, but at present gov-ernments grapple with how to implement the protection in the interest of law enforcement and national security, but at the same time maintaining some of Barlow's early vision for the Internet, namely respect for the right to privacy and freedom of expression.

References

[Barl96]   Barlow, John Perry: A declaration of the Independence of Cyberspace. In: http://www.islandone.org/ Politics/DeclarationOfIndependance.html (August 1, 2007).

[Baum08]   Baumann, Michael: Cyberattacks engulf Kremlin's critics, left and right. In: http://www.ioltechnology,co. za/article_print.php?iArticleID=5017802 January 24, 2008).

[Bowr05]   Bowrey, Kathy: Law and Internet Culture. Cambridge University Press, 2005, p. 8 – 9, 194 – 197.

[Burn01]   Burney, Brett: The Concept of Cybercrime – Is it right to analogize a physical crime to a cybercrime? The rise of the Internet. In: http://www.cybercrimes.net/Virtual/Burney/pages3.html (February 12, 2002)

[Carr03]   Carr, Indira: Anonymity, the Internet and Criminal Law Issues. In: C. Nicoll, J.E.J. Prins and M.J.M. van Dellen (Eds): Digital Anonymity and the Law. T M C Asser Press, The Hague, 2003, p. 161 – 188.

[Carv08]   Carvajal, Doreen: Europe poised to bolster web shield. In: http://yaleglobal.yale.edu/display. article?id=10598 (June 15, 2008).

[Ferg08]   Ferguson, Tim: Nato fires up cyber defences. In: http://software.silicon,com/se- curty/0,39024655,39223469,00.htm (June 15, 2008).

[GoWu06]   Goldsmith, Jack and Wu, Tim: Who controls the Internet. Oxford University Press, USA, 2006, p. 73, 81, 84, 103, 145, 163 – 167.

[Heat08]   Heath, Nick: Nato: Cyber terrorism "as dangerous s missile attack". In: http://www.crime-research.org/ news/10.03.2008/3241/ (March 19, 2008).

[HiCo02]   Hiller, Janine and Cohen, Ronnie: Internet Law and Policy. Pearson Education, Inc., New Jersey, 2002, p. 75 – 76, 95, 98 – 100, 169, 170 – 171.

[JaCo05]   Janczewski, Lech and Colarik, Andrew: Managerial Guide for Handling Cyber-terrorism and Informa- tion Warfare, Idea Group Publishing, USA, 2005, p. x, 43, 222 – 225.

[Jone08]   Jones, Huw: Estonia calls for EU law to ban cyber attacks. In: http://www.crime-research.org/ news/12/03.2008/3248/ (March 19, 2008).

[Ryan08]   Ryan, Johny: Outbreak of iWar imminent. In: Commercial Crime Journal, March 2008, p. 10 – 11.

[TCL+06]   Taylor, R.W., Caeti, T.J., Loper, T.J., Fritsch, E.J. and Liederbach, J: Digital Crime and Digital Terror- ism, Pearson Education, Inc, USA, 2006, p. 9 – 15, 27, 43, 378 – 379.

[Trib91]   Tribe, Laurence. H: The Constitution in Cyberspace: Law and Liberty Beyond the Electronic Frontier. Presented at the first Conference on Computers, Freedom and Privacy, held in 1991. In: http://www.fiu. edu/~mizrachs/CyberConst.html (March 22, 2008).

[Warre91]   Warren, Jim: Introduction. Presented at the first Conference on Computers, Freedom and Privacy, held in 1991. IEEE Computer Society. In: http://www.cpsr.org/conferences/cfp91/intro.html/view (March 21, 2008).

[Watn07a]   Watney, Murdoch: State Surveillance of the Internet: human rights infringement or e-security mecha- nism? International Journal of Electronic Security and Digital Forensics, Vol. 1, No.1, 2007, p. 42 – 54.

[Watn07b]   Watney, Murdoch: The Legal Conflict between Security and Privacy in Addressing Crime and Terror- ism on the Internet' In: N. Pohlmann, H. Reiner and W. Schneider ISSE/Secure 2007 Securing Elec- tronic Business Processes, Vieweg, Wiesbaden, p. 26 – 37.

Theft of Virtual Property – Towards Security Requirements for Virtual Worlds

Anja Beyer

Fachgebiet Virtuelle Welten/Digitale Spiele
IfMK, Technische Universität Ilmenau, Germany
anja.beyer@tu-ilmenau.de

Abstract

The article is focused to introduce the topic of information technology security for Virtual Worlds to a security experts' audience. Virtual Worlds are Web 2.0 applications where the users cruise through the world with their individually shaped avatars to find either amusement, challenges or the next best business deal. People do invest a lot of time but beyond they invest in buying virtual assets like fantasy witcheries, wepaons, armour, houses, clothes,...etc with the power of real world money. Although it is called "virtual" (which is often put on the same level as "not existent") there is a real value behind it. In November 2007 dutch police arrested a seventeen years old teenager who was suspicted to have stolen virtual items in a Virtual World called Habbo Hotel [Reuters07]. In order to successfully provide security mechanisms into Virtual Worlds it is necessarry to fully understand the domain for which the security mechansims are defined. As Virtual Worlds must be clasified into the domain of Social Software the article starts with an overview of how to understand Web 2.0 and gives a short introduction to Virtual Worlds. The article then provides a consideration of assets of Virtual Worlds participants, describes how these assets can be threatened and gives an overview of appopriate security requirements and completes with an outlook of possible countermeasures.

1 Introduction

1.1 Web 2.0 – a new comprehension of the Web

Although the term Web 2.0 is used controversial there is a good understanding of what the term means. In contrast to a widely misunderstanding Web 2.0 is not a new version of the Web. Instead we can describe it as a new understanding of using the web. The main difference to the (old) Web 1.0 is that of user participation. The users appear as prosumers of web applications instead of only being consumers. In older times the way of using the web was that someone created content, published it on a website and others who were interested could consume that content [cp. O'Reilly05].

But nowadays providers see an advantage in treating their users as co-developers (user-generated content). This means that at least some content is produced by the user. The provider only establishes a service which can be used. A very famous and successful example is that of Wikipedia. This online encyclopaedia is completely created by its users. This of course affords huge trust into users [cp. O'Reilly05].

Another principle of the Web 2.0 is that the more people use the service the better gets the content (like at Amazon customer reviews and Ebay feedback). Another commonly known development of Web 2.0

is the usage of blogs. So one could now ask where the difference to a personal web page is. The answer is simple: the entries are sorted chronologically. This is where the advantage of RSS feeds comes into play. With them one can easily get informed as soon as there is a change in a blog. So people stay informed and this in turn results in a good participation of interested people who can leave a comment or discuss about a certain topic [cp. O'Reilly05].

This is where it comes to the core: the new understanding of the Web 2.0 based on participation enables social interaction via the internet which is now better accepted and widespread [cp. O'Reilly05].

One kind of Web 2.0 applications are Virtual Worlds (see chapter 2). As users are so much involved into the creation of content they are somehow bound to it and they want to know their assets protected. But as there are a lot of threats (see chapter 3.2) some security measures are needed. With the increasing success Virtual Worlds also become the target of attackers just as other nowadays information and communication systems.

At last years ISSE 2007 conference in Warsaw Costin G. Raiu, Senior AV Expert at Kaspersky Lab, reveals that the theft of virtual property is an ongoing relevant topic [Raiu07].

2 Virtual Worlds

Virtual Worlds are computer-based simulated environments intended for its users to inhabit and interact via avatars. State-of-the-Art Virtual Worlds are three dimensional while Virtual Worlds of the past used to be textual or two dimensional.

To establish a common understanding of what is meant with Virtual Worlds in this paper the author wants to clarify the term. Above all, it seems to be necessary to distinguish between Virtual Worlds and Virtual Realitys (VR). Although both terms sound quite similar they mean quite different things. Both describe computer generated interactive environments. Interactivity refers to the exchange of messages (dialog) and therefore to mutual influence. The user's actions lead to a change of the world status and the reactions of the systems influence the user's behaviour.

While users of Virtual Worlds interact with the system via their avatars[1] on a screen, the users of Virtual Realities experience the display and perception of physical properties of the real world. For this, different kinds of input and output devices are needed for VR's like data gloves, shutter glasses and caves. The users of VR's are completely involved into the events. Nowadays VR's are mainly used for simulating real environments for training and design issues (like flight simulation, car development, etc.). Virtual Worlds nowadays use the keyboard and mouse or joysticks for input and a screen (monitor, canvas, etc.) for output. Various characteristics define Virtual Worlds:

- **Computer simulated**: The Virtual World needs a computer system (hardware and software) to exist.
- **Fiction**: The content creator is free in shaping the content; can be real or fictional (fantasy objects).
- **Visualisation** via output devices: Presentation on a screen.
- **Communication**: The users are able to communicate e.g. via chat.
- **Interactivity**: There is an action-reaction cycle of the user with the world (human computer interaction).
- **Interaction**: The users interact with the world via avatars.

---

1 The avatar is the virtual representation of the user in the system and is a three dimensional fantasy model.

- **Participation**: The user is involved in creating and developing the incidents in the Virtual World
- **Persistency**: The World is permanently available and develops at every state of time also when the user is not logged in.
- **Immersion**: Immersion is a state of experience of a user and means total involvement when he forgets the physical world around him and is fully involved with the happenings in the Virtual World
- **Multiplayer**: The World can be used by thousands of players at the same time

Why are Virtual Worlds so attractive? We receive amusement and entertainment in these worlds, handle our business transactions and do our teaching "out there" – just to name a few things possible.

There is the chance that these two applications might emerge in the future, so that Virtual Worlds can be entered through a Virtual Reality Environment (e.g. a CAVE). But for this paper the description of Virtual Worlds from above is applied.

2.1 What is going on 'out there'

The most successful Virtual World nowadays is the Massively Multiplayer Online Role Playing Game (MMORPG) World of Warcraft [WoW08]. Role Playing means that the player takes over a certain role (like warrior) and tries to improve the skills of that role. In the case of a warrior it is important to have good battle skills. In order to improve the skills this the player must:

- Explore the world (called "Azeroth")
- Solve quests (tasks given by Non Player Characters)
- Communicate and interact with other players, corporate in a guild
- Fight battles

For successful playing the game, the user receives experience points, a higher level, items and gold. The player can trade with the items and receive more gold. With the gold he can buy other valuable items like swords, armour, elixirs, etc. During the increasing success of the game, a successful black market emerged. Accounts are traded for real money on Ebay.

A second example of a Virtual World is Second Life [SecondLife08]. Although there are some aspects of role playing (as people can take over a certain role) it is more meant to be a platform to "express yourself". The provider requests the users to realize their dreams that might be impossible for them in the real world. One of the main differences to World of Warcraft is, that in the World of Second Life everything is user generated content. That means that the user can create objects with the help of a provided tool. So they create houses, cars, clothes, etc. There is no limitation to imagination or fantasy. Everything people can imagine can be built here. For the impression of vividness of the objects (e.g. trees that move in the wind) Second Live Provider LindenLab installed a scripting language. The users have the full copyright for the objects they created. Second Life also encourages Real Money Trade. The user can buy the ingame currency, the Linden Dollar, for US Dollars. There is a daily updated exchange rate comparable to real world stock exchange but without legal regularisation.

Accompanied by a huge media interest a lot of real world companies created their virtual counterpart, like IBM, Adidas, Reuters, etc. Also complete cities were built, like Frankfurt and Stockholm.

The german adult education centre in Goslar (VHS Goslar) provides teaching lessons in Second Life. Some universities teach their scholars in Second Life.

Fig. 1: A scene in Second Life   **Fig. 2:** Another scene in Second Life

Current Virtual Worlds show a trend in increasing integration into the real world. This shows in that the Virtual Worlds are used for real world business. Real Money Trade characterizes the feature of a Virtual World to trade with real world money. People are willing to pay real money in order to get virtual money. They pay for objects like clothing, houses, music, styles, etc.

2.2 Reasons for living in a Virtual World

People use Virtual Worlds for different reasons. On the one hand it offers a possibility to escape from the real world and to experience something new. Another aspect is that these worlds allow a good chance to communicate with other users and to get to know people. The worlds give the users a challenge and people like to compete in battles or contests. A further reason to use Virtual Worlds is to run a business. Second Life for example gives the people the opportunity to try out different professions and earn money.

While people do these things they perceive different feelings or emotions which must be taken into consideration as criteria for a good game design (beside others).

The motivation of the people spending their time in a Virtual World comes from positive perceptions of acting. The criteria for such positive experiences are Satisfaction of one's needs, Flow, Immersion, Fun, Gameplay, and Fairness which will be described in the following sections.

Following the theory of Maslow there is a hierarchy when people **satisfy** their **needs**. The absolute basic needs that must be satisfied before all others are physiological needs and therefore life sustaining needs like food, water, sex, sleep, etc. Further needs are safety and security, love and belonging, esteem and self-actualisation [cp. Maslow77]. In Virtual Worlds people are able to satisfy at least the last three by making friendships, achievements and the ability to be creative.

The term **"Flow"** was formed by psychologist Mihály Csíkszentmihályi and describes the state of involvement in an activity when a human being feels the balance between challenge and the own abilities. This means that the optimal motivation to follow an activity can be reached when the task is neither too easy nor too difficult. The people feel control over the situation [cp. Csíkszentmihályi00].

Immersion is a state of experience of a user and means total involvement when he forgets the physical world around him and is fully involved with the happenings in the Virtual World. Richard Bartle differentiates four steps to Immersion (Levels of Immersion), namely player, avatar, character and persona. These steps describe how deep the involvement of a player can be reaching from just influencing the world (player) to be a part of the world (persona) [Bartle01].

The game designer Raph Koster defines **Fun** as "the feedback of the brain when absorbing patterns for learning purposes" and "fun is primarily about practising and learning not about exercising mastery" [Koster05]. This definition makes clear that people experience fun while playing games when they try to find patterns for problem solving, e.g. during a quest. As soon as this pattern is found the task becomes boring and a new challenge must be posed.

Andrew Rollings und Ernest Adams describe **Gameplay** as "one or more causally linked series of challenges in a simulated environment" [Rollings03]. A good gameplay encourages the interaction of the user with the Virtual World by giving him a number of sequential events that give him interesting choices.

Fairness implies that all participants of a process (here the interaction with the Virtual World) have the same opportunities and that they comply with the defined rules. This requires the full awareness of all participants of what the rules are.

3 Chances & Risks

3.1 How I made millions trading virtual loot©

"How I made millions trading virtual loot" is the title of the book from Julian Dibbell [Dibbell06], a US Journalist, in which he published his diary from an experiment with the online game Ultima Online. In this experiment he tried to find out if one can make a living from trading in a Virtual World. Although the media reports about some success stories, like the one of Anshe Chung who succeeded in doing business in Second Life [BusinessWeek06], it is very unlikely that earning a living from a Virtual World is common for all inhabitants of the Virtual Worlds at the current time but imaginable for the future. Instead, thousand of players try out their sales talent in building some objects and selling them.

There the Web 2.0 characteristic of the Long Tail comes into play (see chapter 1). The main sales in volume come from a big amount of niche products instead of a few bestsellers. This in turn is important when it comes to threats. In the case of the lost of virtual property thousands of people are involved.

3.2 Threats

As Virtual Worlds are very complex systems with various actions that can be taken, a wide range of threats can be identified. In the following section these threats will be presented. In order to successfully analyse threats to a system, it is crucial to use a systematic approach. A commonly accepted way is to first analyse the assets in the system. The author decided to apply the criteria to secure systems with the assets. These criteria are defined by the protection goals confidentiality, integrity, availability, privacy and non-reputability.

Confidentiality means the protection against unauthorized access to data and information. **Integrity** refers to protection against unauthorized modification of data or information: the shown information has to be correct and presented unmodified. **Availability** indicates the protection against unauthorized interference of functionality. **Privacy** is the right of an individual person on informational self determination. It allows individual persons to decide about the usage of their personal data. **Non-Reputability** expresses the unauthorized non-commitment, meaning the loss of bindingness. Business partners have to be sure that both stay with their proposal to sell or buy.

Following assets can be identified for Virtual Worlds:

- Avatar: the virtual representative of the user in the Virtual World; 3D graphic
- Items: During gameplay the player receives various objects (e.g. house, clothing, elixirs, weapon, etc.)
- Payment instrument: like Gold, Platinum, Dollar, etc.
- Skills: During gameplay the avatar learns certain skills to improve the avatar (e.g. fishing, making credentials, repairing weapons)
- Level/ Experience Points (EP): For successful gameplay (e.g. solving a quest) the player receives experiences points and raises the level; this is an indicator for the experience of a user
- World: this is the space where the avatar lives. The world can consist of continents, islands, houses, rooms, etc.
- Games Rules: For fair interactions of the players the provider sets games rules (e.g. etiquette)
- Account Data: Account Data contains any additional information about the player's identity (like home address, email, playing behaviour, etc.)
- Contact Data: The contact data refers to the social contacts the player has within the Virtual World (Avatar name, group, mail and chat contact data)
- Communication Data: During communication process the participants exchange sensible information (e.g. the strategy for the next business deal)
- Login Data: the credentials the user needs to get access to the Virtual World

[cp. Beyer07]

Mapping the criteria to the assets leads to a long list of threats.

Table 1: Overview of Threats in Virtual Worlds

Asset	Loss/Breach of:				
	Confidentiality	Integrity	Availability	Privacy	Non-Reputability
Avatar	--	Unauthorized modification of the Avatar	Non-Availability of the Avatar	--	--
Items	--	Unauthorized modification of the Items	Non-Availability of the Items	--	--
Payment Instrument	--	Unauthorized modification of the Payment Instrument	Non-Availability of the Payment Instrument	--	Repudiation of having received a payment
Skills	--	Unauthorized modification of the Skills	Non-Availability of the Skills	--	--
Level/EP	--	Unauthorized modification of the Level/EP	--	--	--
World	--	Unauthorized modification of the World	Non-Availability of the World	--	--
Games Rules	--	Unauthorized modification of the Rules	Non-Availability of the Rules	--	Players do not comply with the rules (breach of Fairness)
Communication Data	Unauthorized access to Communication Data	Unauthorized modification of the Communication Data	--	Communication Data is used in a way the individual did not agree with	--
Login Data	Unauthorized access to Login Data	--	--	--	--
Contact Data	--	Unauthorized modification of the Contact Data	Non-Availability of the Contact Data	Personal Data is used in a way the individual did not agree with	--
Account Data	--	Unauthorized modification of the Account Data	--	Account Data is used in a way the individual did not agree with	--

4 Proposing Security Requirements

Before appropriate security measures can be designed a deep analysis of security requirements must be done. The following section will propose a list of security requirements which aim to face the threats defined above. The requirements are taken from the catalogue of part two of the Common Criteria for the Information Technology Security Evaluation [CC07].

- Class FAU: Security Audit:
- Audit Data Generation
- Profile Based Anomaly Protection
- Class FCO: Communication
- Selective Proof of Origin
- Selective Proof of Receipt
- Class FCS: Cryptographic Support
- Cryptographic support
- Class FDP: User Data Protection
- Access Control
- Data Authentication
- Internal Transfer Protection
- Stored Data Integrity Monitoring
- Class FIA: Identification and Authentication
- Identification and authentication of the users
- Class FPR: Privacy
- Compliance with privacy regulations (users act with a pseudonym)
- Class FPT: Protection of the TSF
- Failure Handling
- Class FTP: Trusted Path/Channels
- Confidential transport of data

The exact definition of the requirements for an evaluation process requires the compilation of a Protection Profile which will be the further work for the author.

5 Conclusion

Current Virtual Worlds like Second Life, World of Warcraft, etc. establish flourishing economies. Security experts postulate that security mechanisms for Virtual Worlds are essential [Koll07] as hackers try to attack the assets of the users to manipulate or destroy values. This in fact does not only affect the providers of Virtual Worlds who make them available but also players investments and communities fun of play. For the providers of Virtual Worlds it is crucial to have a security evaluation on an international accepted method, like the Common Criteria for the Information Technology Security Evaluation [CC07] to survive the competition.

For installing security measures it is necessary to respect the aims for positive perception of the users gaming experience (chapter 2.2). This means that these criteria (Flow, Immersion, satisfaction of one's needs, fun, gameplay, and fairness) must be taken into consideration while designing and programming appropriate security measures. Further research work is absolutely necessary in order to provide protection to the actor's assets without annoying them with obstacle through too difficult adoption of security mechanisms (e.g. accepting certificates) because this will interrupt game play.

References

[Bartle01]   Richard Bartle: Avatar, Character, Persona. Immerse yourself..., http://www.mud.co.uk/richard/acp. htm, published in 2001, last access: 11-07-2008

[Beyer07]   Beyer, Anja: Security in online games – Case study: Second Life. In Proc. Florida AI Research Symposium (FLAIRS-07), Key West, FL, USA, May 2007, Florida AI Research Society, 2007

[BusinessWeek06]   BusinessWeek Cover Story, My virtual life, http://www.businessweek.com/magazine/content/06_18/b3982001.htm, 01-05-2006, last access 11-07-2008.

[CC07]   Common Criteria for the Information Technology Security Evaluation, Version CC v3.1 (September 2007), Three Parts downloadable at www.commoncriteriaportal.org, last access 11-07-2008.

[Csíkszentmihályi00] Mihály Csíkszentmihályi: Beyond boredom and anxiety: experiencing flow in work and play. Jossey-Bass Inc., 2000.

[Dibbell06] Dibbell, Julian: Play Money: Or, How I Quit My Day Job and Made Millions Trading Virtual Loot, B&T, 2006

[Justia06]   MDY Industries, LLC v. Blizzard Entertainment, Inc. et al, Filing 39, http://docs.justia.com/cases/federal/district-courts/arizona/azdce/2:2006cv02555/322017/39/, last access 11-07-2008

[Koll07]   Koll, Virtuelle Welten warten noch auf Sicherheitsstandards, Computerzeitung, 2007, 38, 8

[Koster05]   Raph Koster: A theory of fun for game design. Paraglyph Press, Inc., Scottsdale, AZ, USA, 2005.

[Maslow77] Abraham H. Maslow. Motivation und Persönlichkeit. Walter-Olten Verlag Freiburg im Breisgau, 1977. The original title "Motivation and Personality" was published at Harper and Row, New York, in 1954

[Raiu07]   Raiu, Costin G: From viruses to malware; from malware to cybercrime, Information Security Solutions Europe, 25-27 September 2007 Warsaw, presentation slides.

[Reuters07]   "Police arrest teenage online furniture thief", news message at Reuters Website, http://www.reuters.com/article/oddlyEnoughNews/idUSN149845120071114, November 14th 2007

[Rollings03] Andrew Rollings and Ernest Adams: Game Design, New Riders, 2003

[SecondLife08] Website of the Virtual World Second Life by LindenLab, www.secondlife.com, last access 11-07-08

[O'Reilly05] Tim O'Reilly: What Is Web 2.0: Design Patterns and Business Models for the Next Generation of Software, article published at http://www.oreillynet.com/pub/a/oreilly/tim/news/2005/09/30/what-is-web-20.html on 30-09-2005, last access 11-07-2008

[WoW08]   Website of the MMORPG World of Warcraft, http://www.wow-europe.com/de/index.xml, last access 11-07-2008

Trusted Computing and Biometrics

Trusted Storage:
Putting Security and Data Together

Michael Willett · Dave Anderson

Seagate Technology and
the Trusted Computing Group
{michael.willett | david.b.anderson}@seagate.com

Abstract

State and Federal breach notification legislation mandates that the affected parties be notified in case of a breach of sensitive personal data, unless the data was provably encrypted. Self-encrypting hard drives provide the superior solution for encrypting data-at-rest when compared to software-based solutions. Self-encrypting hard drives, from the laptop to the data center, have been standardized across the hard drive industry by the Trusted Computing Group. Advantages include: simplified management (including keys), no performance impact, quick data erasure and drive re-purposing, no interference with end-to-end data integrity metrics, always encrypting, no cipher-text exposure, and scalability in large data centers.

1 Introduction

Is there no end to reports of data breaches? Every week headlines tell of yet more incidents. Data encryption has been recognized by law in 42 states and more widely as good practice by security experts to be an effective measure for protecting sensitive information against data breaches. Moreover, those laws state that the use of encryption eliminates the requirement for public notification of the breach.

Laptops and tapes are not the only potential risks. Every day, thousands of TB of data leak out of data centers as old systems are retired or replaced, often with little thought given to *properly* erasing the data they contain on their hard-drives. But what if those hard drives had all been quietly encrypting all of that data, transparently & automatically, such that only the true owner were able to access real data?

Until now, however, encryption has been hard to use, and in some cases discouraged users from incorporating it into their security strategy. Instead many users simply hope the data breach bug will not bite them. Embedding the encryption function within the storage device (often called Full Disk Encryption, or FDE) improves this, and makes it easier to choose protection over hoping. FDE offers several benefits over other approaches to encryption:

- Makes deploying and managing encryption easier, and doing so with no impact to system performance
- Makes the confidentiality that encryption affords even stronger
- Integrates better with other functions of enterprise storage architectures

N. Pohlmann, H. Reimer, W. Schneider (Editors): Securing Electronic Business Processes, Vieweg (2008), 131-138

This paper will explain these benefits in greater depth. It assumes a basic understanding of FDE operation. For information on FDE operations, see "Self-Encrypting Hard Disk Drives in the Data Center" on the Seagate web site: www.seagate.com or consult the Storage section of the Trusted Computing Group: www.trustedcomputinggroup.org) .

2 Definitions

- Array Controller: The hardware/software combination that abstracts and exposes for host access the logical blocks of the hard drives attached to it. For the purposes of Hard Drive-based security services, like FDE, the Array Controller is the only device that communicates directly with the Hard Drives. Consequently, it is responsible for directing how the security will be configured and arranging for the drives to be unlocked for use.

- FDE: Full disk encryption. A disk drive (see below) which includes within it the ability to encrypt all data stored on it.

- Hard Drive: A disk drive. In a data center the hard drive is usually attached to the Array Controller that will be responsible for managing it.

- IPSec. Internet Protocol Security. A method for providing confidentiality and authentication on Internet communications.

- Keys: Secrets used to protect the confidentiality of stored data and Hard Drives. This paper describes at least three types of keys:

  - Authentication Key. A credential used to lock and unlock an FDE drive.

  - Data Encryption Key, or Encryption Key: A symmetric key generated by the Hard Drive used to encrypt/decrypt data.

  - Session Key. An encryption key used to provide confidentiality of transmitted data. See IPSec and TLS.

- Entropy. A measure of randomness or unpredictability

- Storage System: See Array Controller.

- Re-encryption: The process whereby the data encrypted with one key is read from storage, decrypted, encrypted again with a new key and written back to storage.

- TLS. Transport Layer Security. A data transmission protocol designed to preserve the confidentiality of transmitted information.

3 Self-encrypting disk drives, simplifying management

3.1 FDE: Requires no changes to OS, applications, or networks

An advantage that first stands out when users learn of FDE is that it is isolated from most of the other system elements. The Operating Systems, applications, and network infrastructure do not have to change to accommodate FDE. Isolating the impact of introducing encryption to the storage system and its management minimizes who needs to be educated on FDE, and simplifies the adaptation of existing processes.

3.2 FDE: A model for completeness

Since FDE always encrypts everything written to the drive, there is no need to worry about data classification. Identifying all the instances of personally identifiable information can be a nightmare for an IT department, especially when such information can so easily be extracted from a protected database into an unprotected destination. An authorized user could paste social security numbers from a strictly controlled database into a spreadsheet, where tracking its existence is almost impossible. Since FDE makes it so simple to just encrypt everything, the entire problem of data classification (and the attendant management challenges that start once data is classified) is avoided.

3.3 One secret to manage

When managing encryption, there are typically two sets of secrets to keep track of and protect. The first are the data encryption keys. These are the values used to encrypt and decrypt the user data as it is written to or read from the drive. It is obvious that care must be taken to prevent the compromise of the encryption keys; the data is only as secure as these keys are safe. The other set of secrets are the authentication keys. These are the credentials that must be supplied to authorize the drive to commence operation. In some systems these are passwords, pass phrases, biometric scans or smartcard protected values. These often represent the authorization users have to make changes to the encryption function. For instance, an administrator may be authorized (know the authentication key necessary) to remove some storage from the data center for replacement. Should that administrator leave, security policy will likely call for that key to change. This would only be good practice.

The distinct advantage FDE brings to this situation is that the encryption key is in the drive, never leaves the drive, and never needs to be managed outside the drive. This lessens the problem of secrets management associated with the encryption function. As we will see later, in addition to simplifying key management, isolating the encryption key in the drive will make for a superior data destruction model. For key management, though, since no auditing, tracking, or external exposure of the encryption key is necessary with FDE, it is less likely that re-encryption will be called for than with any other encryption technology.

Although some approaches to encryption use only a single set of secrets, it should be pretty clear why there must be two sets of secrets, and why they must be kept separate. If the administrator who left knew the encryption key, it would have to change – and all the data protected by that key would have to be read and re-encrypted. In a large data center this could be traumatic. By separating the authentication keys from the encryption keys, a change in personnel would only require a change in authentication key and leave the encryption key unaffected. FDE embodies this, adding the benefit of eliminating the separate management of the encryption key.

3.4 An open interface and multiple sources

The FDE drive is intended to be a component in a larger security system. To this end, it exposes an interface, based on industry standards activity in the Trusted Computing Group (TCG) that enables exercising the various processes associated with key management. This makes it relatively straightforward for an array controller in a storage system to incorporate controlling the encryption function along with the other drive responsibilities it assumes.

Since every hard drive manufacturer in the world is actively participating in the definition of this TCG standard, we can expect that there will be multiple sources of FDE drives that could be used inter-changeably (with respect to encryption) in a storage system.

3.5 No performance impact to manage

Often the biggest management headache associated with encryption is managing the impact on perform-ance. Having to encrypt all data in a good-sized data center can represent a huge processing workload increment and impose considerable strain on both throughput and response time. FDE eliminates this problem completely by encrypting all data written to the drive at full interface speed, similarly decrypt-ing read data with no performance loss.

4 Self-encrypting disk drives equal higher security

4.1 Everything is encrypted, always

As users ponder the task of classifying each type of sensitive information, identifying all instances of each, and making sure every copy of every version of every derivation of each is protected, it can look pretty appealing to simply encrypt everything and be done with it. That is exactly what FDE offers – everything encrypted, always. Nothing else in a system can be as certain that all sectors on a drive are encrypted as can the drive itself. This is perhaps the greatest assurance FDE offers, encrypting every-thing, always. It's simple, complete, with no performance hit, making for a simple and attractive story in counterpoint to the prospect of a CEO having to explain why his company had a data breach.

4.2 No cipher text exposure

Encryption is simply a means to more effectively protect the confidentiality of information. No encryp-tion scheme is absolutely impervious to attack. However, some things can be done to make the chal-lenge of cracking it as difficult as possible. One of the benefits of FDE, and unique to FDE, is that the drive is not only storing the data, it is also controlling access to it. If the proper authentication is not provided, the drive will not allow access to the data, not even to the cryptographic text. This directly addresses one of the more common forms of attack, called traffic analysis, which involves inspecting the encrypted data for hints of patterns or predictable clear text values that might assist the attacker trying to crack the encryption.

Since the FDE drive is both the residence of the data and its security gatekeeper, it will prevent even ac-cess to the cryptographic text, making traffic analysis almost impossible. No other encryption approach can put up this same barrier to attack on the data. If encryption is done at any other place in the system, the drive can simply be pulled from that system, hooked up to a PC or analysis tool, the cryptographic text read and a traffic analysis begun.

4.3 A source for random numbers

Generating strong encryption keys is fundamental to getting the most security from an encryption function. This requires high quality random numbers. The physical operation of the drive produces random noise (entropy) that is used in turn by the FDE drive to produce random numbers. This gives the drive a method of generating keys that exhibits strong resistance to attack. Simple software generation of random numbers lacks such a source of entropy.

Moreover, because the encryption key is generated by the drive inside the drive and only used within the drive, the key is never exposed to capture by external threats.

4.4 Signed firmware prevents unauthorized code running on the drive

Although it does not relate directly to the problem of preventing a data breach, Seagate's FDE drives have implemented protection for the firmware running in the drive. This is intended to prevent unauthorized firmware being introduced into the drive, altering its operation. Only code that has been signed by a Seagate secret key can be loaded onto the drive.

4.5 Superior data destruction model

The primary purpose of FDE is to prevent a loss of data confidentiality should the drive on which the data is stored be lost or stolen. There are times when it is deemed appropriate to dispose of a drive: if it has failed, if it is too old, too slow or too low in capacity. (Higher capacity means greater storage per watt consumed; this has become more important recently.)

In fact, every drive in a data center will eventually leave the data center. Every one.

Having a secure method for preventing the data on departing drives from becoming a data breach headline is at least as important as preventing accidental or malicious events from causing a data breach. A side benefit of the FDE architecture is a data destruction model that is almost certainly easier than that of any other destruction approach.

Since for a given disk drive there is only one instance of the encryption key, the copy inside the disk drive, it is trivially easy to destroy the data by replacing that encryption key and be confident that there no longer exists an avenue of access to the data. This involves a straightforward storage system command – though the use of which is restricted by strong access control, of course – that in less than a second renders all data on a drive unreadable. Since the key has never left the drive and there is no other copy, the proof of data destruction is the execution of that single task. Of course, any other encryption approach can also destroy data by tracking down and destroying all copies of the encryption key, but will all copies – even those on the oldest and most obscure backup files – always be found? Only FDE can so easily identify and do away with all instances of the key.

5 Self-encrypting Hard Drives integrate better into server storage architectures

5.1 Compatibility with Protection Information (PI)

The desirability of encryption to prevent a data breach is understood. However, if incorporating encryption disrupts the storage processes and architectures needed for other aspects of storage management, it could make for difficult choices between equally desirable features or functions. FDE is perhaps the least intrusive. In at least a couple of specific cases, instead of conflicting, it enhances and takes advantage of those other storage management functions.

Data integrity is a long-standing problem that has only been made more of a challenge by the increasing complexity of storage equipment and infrastructures. The data integrity issue refers to the question of whether one can be certain, when a data block is read, that it is the same as was originally written. The industry has recently completed work on an important new standard to address this. The standard was originally called Data Integrity Feature, or DIF, but recently had its name simplified to Protection Information, or PI. This SCSI protocol standard specifies how each element in an I/O Path can read a special appendix on the data as it passes through that element to verify that the contents are correct. Both the storage community and industry leaders not normally associated with storage – such as Oracle – have endorsed this standard. Consider the prospect this suggests. At each processing element from the application (like an Oracle database) through the storage array controller down to the disk drive and back, the data can be inspected and verified that no corruption has occurred. This is an important improvement in the management of data, on the surface having nothing to do with encryption.

But it, in fact, does. If encryption is done anywhere above the disk drive, no element below the encryption can do the PI verification. Since the data below that point is encrypted there is no way to compare the protection information appendix to the data, because the appendix was created based on the unencrypted data. FDE is the only encryption solution that is designed to fully support PI through the entire data path. Encryption done anywhere other than in the disk drive means the user must choose between data confidentiality and the full data protection of PI. With FDE the user can enjoy the benefits of both.

5.2 FDE does not do the wrong (security) thing

FDE automatically restricts the scope of its protection to its intended domain. Since the encryption used to protect stored data will involve the use of an encryption key that will not change over extended periods of time, it is imperative to keep this key as safe as possible. FDE does this by using the key only within its parent hard drive, and never allowing either the key or any data encrypted with it outside the drive. It is a subtle temptation to let encryption protecting data at rest be used for the wrong security application. Specifically, if encryption is done on the other end of a transmission from the data residence, the hard drive, it may seem appealing that the transmission is also protected by the encryption for data at rest. In fact, this is exactly the wrong practice for both data in flight, the transmission to and from the storage device, and for the data at rest. It is important to understand why.

For data in flight, there are well-established practices that provide excellent confidentiality. Among these are IPSec and TLS. They are used to protect sensitive Internet transactions and add confidentiality to any network. It is instructive to note that even the Fibre Channel standard has added similar capability for protecting the transmission of SAN traffic.

One of the essential properties that makes these protocols so effective is the notion of a short session protected by an ephemeral session encryption key. That is, a given transmission can be encrypted by a session key that will be discarded immediately after the transmission. Any subsequent transmission will be protected by a new, different session key. These very short duration keys minimize the vulnerability of the data. Since so little data is exposed during a single transmission session, traffic analysis attacks have not been successful – when good quality keys are employed, of course.

By comparison, notice what goes wrong when data at rest encryption is applied to data in flight. The data in flight will be encrypted repeatedly with the same key; otherwise the stored data would have to be re-encrypted. This compromises both the in-flight and the at-rest data. Since the keys are long lived, key aging becomes an issue for the in-flight data. Since the at-rest key is being used constantly by the host, it not only exposes the encrypted data to traffic analysis, but also (and even worse) leaves the encryption key in memory essentially permanently, leaving it exposed to any number of malicious software attacks. This is typically the case whenever the encryption is being done in software by a general-purpose processor. The recent Princeton[1] attack on software-based encryption, while unlikely in practice, illustrates how the vulnerability of intermixing in-flight protection with at rest protection could be exploited. Both are compromised.

On the other hand, combining FDE with appropriate in-flight protection provides the right protection for both domains.

5.3 FDE makes use of existing redundancy features

Encryption is a sophisticated mathematical process. It might be asked: How can one be confident it is being done correctly? There are really two aspects to this question. The first is whether the encryption was designed correctly. Now, it is unlikely that any user organization is really competent to analyze this for itself. Federal agencies like NIST and the NSA are chartered to approve, among other security capabilities, encryption functions, the former for sensitive information, the latter for National Security Systems. Seagate has had its implementation of encryption approved by NIST.

The second and more important question though, is whether anything in a properly designed encryption function is not working as designed. There are no electronics components, no firmware or software modules that are absolutely guaranteed to never have a flaw. What if an encryption function goes bad? It could be a corrupted encryption key, firmware routine that uses the wrong key, an ASIC that malfunctions or any one of a myriad of other possible failure scenarios. It could result in the loss of data, could even cause the loss of all data below the failed encryption function. Such a failure at a high level could be disastrous.

Putting the encryption function in the disk drive incorporates encryption in such a way that should a given drive's encryption function fail, the existing storage redundancy capability of the array controller managing the drives can recover the data. This is another example of how FDE takes advantage of the protection mechanisms already in place in enterprise storage to not disrupt but rather enhance their benefit. It would be no different than if a drive failed for some other reason. The offending drive can be replaced with a spare and the parity architecture of the RAID array used to rebuild the data, RAID providing the same level of protection to the encryption function as it does to the traditional data storage function of the disk drive. Using the PI standard to ensure that the data is valid is a perfect complement to this.

---

1   (http://citp.princeton.edu.nyud.net/pub/coldboot.pdf),

On the other hand, if the encryption is above the redundancy management, it is not clear how the data is protected in the face of an encryption failure.

5.4 FDE supports storage efficiency, allowing data de-duplication and compression

As storage capacity requirements rapidly grow, so does the availability of effective data de-duplication schemes. The algorithms that scan discs looking for duplicate records are completely ineffective when presented with encrypted data, and are unable to provide more efficient use of expensive storage capacity. When encrypting multiple instances of exactly the same file, the encrypted results are all different.

When using FDE self-encrypting drives, the data appears as 'clear-text' to the system as it's automatically decrypted as it's being read. Therefore, data de-duplication schemes are completely unaffected allowing for more efficient use of valuable storage space.

The same principal applies to data compression. Encrypted data is not compressible, so by carrying out the encryption inside the hard drive, data may be compressed as the user wishes.

6 Conclusion

Encryption is recognized as an effective approach to preventing data breaches. Data Center encryption based on FDE drives can make the task of deploying easier, and make the resulting protection stronger. The fact that FDE integrates so well with other storage management functions further benefits the IT department.

Trust in Consumer Electronics

Klaus Kursawe[1] · Stefan Katzenbeisser[2]

[1]Information and System Security Group
Philips Research
klaus.kursawe@philips.com

[2]Security Engineering Group
Technische Universität Darmstadt
skatzenbeisser@acm.org

Abstract

While Trusted Computing is getting increasing attention in the PC world, consumer electronics devices have limited benefit from the Trusted Computing solutions currently under development. In this paper we outline the different requirements of consumer electronics devices, when compared to the PC world, and point out the technical consequences for standards like the Trusted Computing Group. In addition, we will touch on economic aspects that may inhibit or support Trusted Computing in this domain.

1 Consumer Electronics Security – Why Bother?

In the coming years, the consumer electronics (CE) industry can be expected to perform a similar transition the PC industry underwent with the advent of the Internet. Previously isolated (and thus, difficult to attack) devices increasingly communicate with each other and with the outside world. One reason for this development is the desire to come closer to the goal of "ambient intelligence", enabling full integration of all home devices, even in case they come from different vendors. Over the next months, we can expect a rapid development in this respect; in a recent announcement, a major consumer electronics company has announced plans to connect 90% of all their products by 2010 [Glasg08]. Another reason is that a single device implements several different functionalities, among them tasks that require network connectivity and were in the past only performed on personal computers.

There are several proof points that this technology shift can already be noticed in the market. Most noticeable is this trend in the field of entertainment devices, such as televisions and hi-fi systems. While they were in the past passive devices that only had an analogue input interface, modern systems get networked, can be personalized and are able to download content from the Internet. To enable new applications, traditional dedicated hardware in CE devices is replaced by general purpose computing equipment, which runs a tiny operating system and is fully programmable. This in turn also makes the production of high-end CE devices cheaper, as several models from one vendor can share the same hardware configuration; the functionality of a product is largely defined by the software that runs on the device.

While this allows a plethora of new applications, it also exposes consumer electronics devices to the same dangers that PCs are facing since years. Indeed, CE devices may form even more attractive targets for attackers than personal computers, due to their large number, their low level of protection and the general unawareness of their users of security threats. Even though the computational power of CE devices are limited, they may become an invaluable addition to bot-nets from an attacker's point of view: a hacked television or set-top box may be abused to send spam (this has already happened with an Internet connected DVD recorder), may act as a proxy or may be used to conceal an attack like any other computing system. Furthermore, CE systems may be easier to attack and an attack may remain unnoticed for a larger period of time due to infrequent software updates and limited user interfaces. If such systems share a connection with other devices, they may also serve as an entry point for an attacker to reach more worthwhile targets. Besides large-scale attacks, specific CE devices may be the target of an attacker in order to 'annoy' its owner or act as a new vehicle for unsolicited advertisement.

Besides external attacks through hackers, attacks of users (insiders) are of increasing concern. This is particularly important for entertainment devices that implement Digital Rights Management schemes and possess secret keys, which the owner of the device wants to obtain in order to remove the 'annoyances' of the protection scheme. Usually compliance rules mandate a certain level of protection of these secrets; protection of keys relied on the premise that dedicated (hardware) solutions cannot easily be reverse-engineered. Given the above-mentioned changes in the system architecture, an attack becomes much more feasible if a DRM client is implemented in software which runs on a general-purpose computing architecture and a standard operating system within the CE device.

In order to protect both against insider and outsider attacks, next-generation networked consumer electronics devices need a similar level of protection as PCs. While in principle security solutions developed for the PC world can be deployed in consumer electronics devices as well, the particular requirements of this domain limit their applicability.

2 Differences to the PC World

We can identify the following major differences between consumer electronics devices and traditional computers, for which classic security technologies have largely been designed.

2.1 Consumer Expectations

Consumer expectations for CE devices are substantially higher, while expectations on the security competence of users have to be lower than in the PC world; for example, a crashed PC is usually rebooted by its owner, a crashed CE device may be returned to the merchant for maintenance. Users of PCs have long been trained to accept security 'nuisances' such as frequent software updates or the use of virus scanners and firewalls. Users are trained to distrust incoming traffic and to having manually grant permission to perform security related actions. In the consumer electronics world, this kind of behaviour would be unacceptable – a TV that displays a popup window asking the user to grant permission to change the channel would probably be returned as defective.

2.2 Usage of Devices

Consumer electronics devices have different usage patterns than personal computers. CE devices usually run for an extended period of time. While a traditional PC may be rebooted once a day, a consumer electronics device may run (probably in stand-by mode) for weeks if not months. Security solutions only operating at boot time (such as attestation, provided by the Trusted Computing Group, which can be used to assure that a certain operating system was booted) are therefore largely ineffective, as they do not provide assurances that the system remains trustworthy afterwards.

In addition, the user interface of CE devices is very limited, in particular on low-cost hardware. While a traditional personal computer offers a decent user interface with a high-resolution monitor, keyboard and mouse, CE devices usually have only a few buttons and a limited (or even absent) display capability. Implementing security solutions that require user interaction is thus much more difficult.

2.3 Trust Models

Trust models vary widely depending on the concrete device. While in the past systems were designed, manufactured and sold by a single entity, modern systems are composed of standard components, produced by various manufacturers (even product assembly may be outsourced). These developments raises questions whether the whole production process is trustworthy; this is particularly problematic for devices that possess secret keys that need to be inserted into a device during the manufacturing process (examples can be found in various fields, from garage door openers to music entertainment devices). Secure operation of these devices crucially depend on the security of this step. Thus, in extreme cases the chain of trust must be further extended into the product lifecycle. This topic will be explored in more detail below.

2.4 Architectural Constraints and Production Costs

Protection goals have to be achieved on devices that are in many ways more restricted than traditional personal computers. Low-cost devices may have very limited computation power; as cost constraints are stringent, there is little room to invest in additional security mechanisms. Due to the low margins, security solutions that lower the gain are unacceptable, and adding new special hardware may be impossible.

3 Secure Manufacturing

In addition to the 'classical' security problems the consumer electronics industry will face in the near future, the trust model in CE security needs to be broadend to include attackers against the production process. While in the past the manufacturing process could be trusted (implying that hardware acts as it was supposed to do), the following new risks emerge from outsourced production:

- *Counterfeit devices.* Apart from a lost business for the brand owner, a counterfeit device may have a different functionallity than anticipated by the end user. This especially happens with functionallity that increases the manufacturing price of the device, but usually stays invisible to the end user – which does hold for security and safety measures. In a recent FBI investigation, counterfeitet routers have been found even within military installations [Krigs08]. While no reports of malicious backdoors have been published, the use of counterfeit devices poses a significant security risk.

- *Modified originals.* While current CE devices are usually not security critical, future uses of networked devices may motivate rouge production companies to deviate from the manufacturers' specification and modify the security architecture. One of the motivations for such producers is simply to save money – it already has happened in the past that safety aspects of a device got reduced by producers, to the point that massive recalls where necessary. In addition, future consumer devices may even allow for critical attacks: e.g., a coalition of smart electricity meters that interact with power-hungry devices can cause demand spikes that seriously damage the power grid, and devices that are part of a home automation system can abuse their control power.

- *Overproduction and key control.* While not a security risk to the end-user, overproduction can seriously hurt a manufacturer. Techniques are required to allow vendors to count the number of devices an external manufacturer produces. Furthermore, the use of critical keys needs to be controlled; this is usually done by device individualization where each device has a unique identity to which the critical data is bound to.

4 Towards Secure Consumer Electronics Devices

While some of the constraints of consumer electronics devices make deployment of security solutions even harder than in the PC, it is possible to avoid many of the problems we face today if the right design decisions are made in an early stage.

The primary advantage is that, as opposed to a personal computer, a CE device is very specialized. This does offer a number of opportunities for security. It is not necessary for arbitrary – or decades old – code to still run on the system; if third party code is needed to run, it does not require massive system resources. Finally, the system core does not need to accommodate for different hardware platforms – code can thus be specialized for particular hardware. This makes it relatively plausible to implement microkernel based solutions and virtual machines as described in [Kan06]. As most of the codebase is (relatively) static, it also is an option to reset the whole or a part of the platform to its default setting; if a CE device frequently restores the code to its factory default, it does become hard for an attacker to permanently infect a system. This relative stability of software running on a CE platform finally also allows the TCGs' remote attestation concept to work in end-user devices. As relatively few 'good' configurations exist for an individual platform, it is plausible to verify each CE device once it connects to the network (as mentioned above, though, this does require additional measures for runtime security, or a re-attestation even when the platform is not rebooted).

In addition, most CE devices have a very well known user behavior. While use cases for a PC exist that require massive data transfer without user interaction (e.g., a peer-to-peer client), it is safe to assume that an Internet connected TV has little requirement to connect to the Internet at all if set on standby; by simply turning off the connection in that case, it is thus possible to massively decrease the value a criminal can extract from a corrupted CE device.

5 Consequences for Trusted Computing

As for PCs, Trusted Computing can be an important building block in a larger security architecture. To this end, however, the corresponding standards will need to be adapted to the special constraints as described above. The Trusted Computing technology as originally defined by the TCG is a 'one-size-fits-it-all' approach: One hardware element (the TPM) carries the functionality to support numerous applications required by the different stakeholders. This has led to an enormous complexity, resulting in (relatively) high prices and implementation difficulties, which limit the applicability of Trusted Computing in CE devices that must meet stringent price and quality requirements. For mobile devices, a separate specification – the Mobile Trusted Module (MTM) [MTM08] – has already been developed as a low cost, specialised solution for handheld phones. However, to become truly versatile, the TPM needs to be changed in three ways:

Size. The trust boundary needs to be substantially smaller and separatable. Current TPMs support a lot of functionallity, leading to imense internal code size as well as required internal ressources. Furthermore, the requirement of non-volatile memory prevents intregration into larger chipsets, as memory requires additional, expensive production steps. Some of the TPM functionalities as well as resources could be implemented outside of the trusted hardware, or spread between several components, which would lead to a cheaper solution that can be integrated into existing platforms.

Modular design. The design should be modular; it should be possible to benefit from standardized and interoperable solutions without implementing the entire TCG functionality. The TCG currently has around 200 members with a wide range of target applications. Thus, most applications will not use the entire set of TPM instructions. While a one-size-fits-it-all TPM does have the advantage of the economy of scale, a moduar version that allows customers to choose only a subset of the functionality may result in better applicability of TPMs in the CE area.

Integration into existing hardware. The functionality must be more optimized to be integrated into existing hardware; ideally, this should be possible without endangering external certification. While it is realitvely easy to add additional functionality to the next generation of a microprocessor, an additional chip on a board is rather expensive. As already started with the MTM, more work is needed to allow a TPM to be integrated into the platforms in a secure way.

Finally, trusted consumer electronics devices require solutions to a wider scope of problems than currently taken into account by Trusted Computing technologies. This starts with a trusted production process – how does one prevent overproduction and protect cryptographic keys against an exernal manufacturer – and ends with a simple secure user interface that does not force users to make security decisions they are not qualified to make.

References

[Glasg08]   S. Glasgow, cited on Gizmodo Australia http://www.gizmodo.com.au/2008/07/sony_goal_90_of_all_ our_products_networked_by_2010.html

[Kan06]   T. Kan, T. Kerins, K. Kursawe, Security in Next Generation Consumer Electronics Devices, in Securing Electronic Business Processes, ISSE 2006 Proceedings, pp. 45-53

[Krigs08]   M. Krigsman, FBI: Counterfeit Cisco routers risk "IT subversion", http://blogs.zdnet.com/ projectfailures/?p=740

[MTM08]   Trusted Computing Group, Mobile Phone Specifications Version 1.0. Available at https://www.trusted-computinggroup.org/specs/mobilephone

NAC 2.0 – Unifying Network Security

Stephen Hanna

Juniper Networks
shanna@juniper.net

Abstract

As information technology becomes more strategic and essential, access to networks and applications must be pervasive yet secure and controlled. The purpose of Network Access Control (NAC) has evolved beyond simply managing network access and ensuring endpoint policy compliance. NAC systems today must integrate with other network security components and increase their built-in capabilities to include support for intrusion detection, role-based application access control, network and application visibility and monitoring, leakage detection, VPNs, and other network security technologies. In fact, we need a new unified vision and understanding of network security: one that involves multiple network security functions working together dynamically using open standards. This vision of unified network security has been called "NAC 2.0."

1 Introduction

Most modern computer networks include a wide variety of security technologies: firewalls, Virtual Private Networks (VPNs) for secure remote access and Wide Area Network (WAN) connectivity, identity management systems, key management systems such as PKI and Kerberos, access management systems, network intrusion detection systems (NIDS), email scanning and spam filtering systems, security incident management (SIM), vulnerability scanners, and sometimes Data Leakage Prevention (DLP) systems.

Endpoints (network-connected devices) generally include their own security systems: host-based firewalls, anti-virus, anti-spyware, and other anti-malware software, host-based intrusion detection and prevention systems, patch management, rootkit detection, security hardware, cryptographic libraries, host-based data leakage prevention, and of course more basic yet essential operating system or platform protections such as access controls.

Unfortunately, these many security systems have are generally not been well integrated with each other. This creates several kinds of problems:

1. If one security system detects a problem it cannot alert others. For example, a NIDS that detects an intrusion has no standard way to relay this alert to a firewall or other enforcement point that can respond to the alert. Instead, the NIDS generally issues a log message that may or may not be investigated later.

2. Security systems cannot share routine information to achieve better results. For example, a user that has authenticated to gain access through a VPN will often be forced to authenticate again to gain access to applications and services on the network because those services have no way to obtain the user's identity from the VPN gateway. Likewise, a NIDS cannot obtain user identity and role information to adjust its triggers. This results in many false alarms. Port scanning is normal for a penetration tester or vulnerability scanner but not for an ordinary user.

N. Pohlmann, H. Reimer, W. Schneider (Editors): Securing Electronic Business Processes, Vieweg (2008), 144-151

This paper describes how Network Access Control (NAC) is currently used to integrate some security systems and then describes a much more flexible integrated system called "NAC 2.0". It points out the strengths and weaknesses of each of these integration methodologies.

Many of the techniques described in this paper are not novel. They have been employed in NAC products from various vendors and in standards from the Trusted Computing Group [TRUS08]. However, this is the first conference paper to describe them.

2 NAC 1.0: Security Integration Today

2.1 Defining NAC

Many readers will be familiar with the term "Network Access Control". Many vendors and groups have used this term or similar terms but over time the phrase "Network Access Control" has become a standard generic term that means "controlling access to a network based on one or more of these factors: user identity and/or role, endpoint identity, endpoint configuration, and endpoint behaviour." Throughout this paper, this is the definition that we will use for the phrase "Network Access Control" or the equivalent acronym NAC.

Several clarifications of this definition are needed. First, "controlling access" can be more sophisticated than a simple "yes" or "no" decision. Many levels of access can be granted, depending on the factors listed above. For example, an unhealthy machine may only get access to repair servers. A user in the finance department may only get access to finance servers. Second, the list of factors above is not intended to be mandatory or exclusive. Some NAC systems support additional factors and many do not support all of the ones listed above. However, all NAC systems support at least one of the factors listed above.

By this definition, NAC has a long history dating back at least as far as early telephone networks that granted different access to operators and supervisors than to ordinary users. If one considers that foot messenger relays constitute networks that were only available to nobles, the history of NAC may even extend before the written word. However, this paper concentrates on present-day NAC as used in computer networking.

2.2 Today's NAC Architecture

As described in [TRUS08], today's NAC systems typically consist of three architectural entities, as illustrated in Figure 1: the Access Requester (AR), the Policy Enforcement Point (PEP), and the Policy Decision Point (PDP). These entities work together in a NAC decision process containing the following phases:

1. **Request:** The AR requests access to a network (implicitly by plugging into the wall or attempting to access a protected resource or explicitly by attempting to affiliate with a wireless access point)
2. **Assessment:** The PDP conducts an assessment of the endpoint and user to gather information
3. **Decision:** The PDP decides what access should be granted and sends its decision to the PEP
4. **Enforcement:** The PEP enforces the PDP's decision, granting or denying access as indicated in the decision

Present-day NAC systems include several refinements to this approach, such as allowing the PDP to modify its decision after the fact if things change but the essential approach remains the same. Different names may be used for the entities but the concepts are still the same.

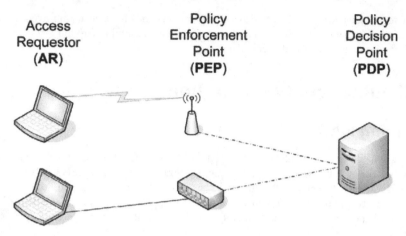

Figure 1: NAC Architecture Today

The factors considered by the PDP in making its decision vary. Businesses are generally most concerned with user identity, endpoint configuration, and endpoint behaviour. Universities generally have no interest in reviewing endpoint configuration and little interest in user identity except to provide accountability and support and perhaps to control access from non-affiliated users. Universities are more concerned with behaviour: detecting endpoints that are attacking others or violating acceptable use policies.

2.3 Benefits of Today's NAC

Current NAC systems provide several benefits and advantages to organizations that use them:

- Consistent access controls across all network access types
- Ability to exclude unauthorized users and endpoints from network
- Close management of endpoint health (leading to reduced downtime)
- Different access for different classes of users (if desired)

These benefits are especially compelling when considered against the backdrop of strict security regulations and requirements, user demands for access from any device at any time and place, and attackers' growing sophistication. Unrestricted network access is no longer an option.

2.4 Importance of NAC Standards and Interoperability

Building a successful NAC system requires integrating products from multiple vendors: software on the AR and the PDP that manages the assessment, endpoint security products whose health must be checked, identity management systems that must talk to the PDP, and PEPs of various sorts (VPN gateway, switch, wireless access point, etc.). To ensure interoperability between these components, the Trusted Computing Group (TCG) created the Trusted Network Connect (TNC) standards [TRUS08]

[TRUS07a] [TRUS07b] [TRUS07c] [TRUS07d] [TRUS07e]. These standards have been accepted by most major networking and security vendors and on track to approval in the IETF.

However, it should be noted that the original TNC architecture did not include standards for integrating behaviour monitoring systems (e.g. NIDS, DLP, and SIM), vulnerability scanners, and interior enforcement points such as firewalls. It also required endpoints to include or load TNC-compliant client software for authentication and health checking. These deficiencies have been remedied in the latest TNC standards, which extend the architecture to support many of the features described below as constituting NAC 2.0.

2.5 Deficiencies of Today's NAC

In spite of the benefits listed above, most current NAC systems have several disadvantages:

- Dependence on software-based endpoint health checks
- Lack of standards for behaviour monitoring and analysis
- Failure to integrate well with other network security components (DLP, IDS, etc.)
- Requirement for special endpoint software supporting NAC

The first of these deficiencies may be addressed by using hardware-based endpoint health checks, as described in [TRUS07]. The Trusted Platform Module (TPM) can be employed to detect rootkits and other stealthy infections that would otherwise go undetected. The other deficiencies require a different approach, described in the next section.

3 NAC 2.0: Unified Network Security

The previously unaddressed deficiencies of today's NAC are not inherent deficiencies in the NAC concept. They are simply the limitations that may be expected from the first version of a new technology. They can be addressed without needing to change the definition of NAC provided above. And by addressing them, many more benefits are received. This section describes how NAC 2.0 addresses these limitations by providing an open architecture and standards for sharing information among network security entities.

3.1 NAC 2.0 Architecture

Today's NAC successfully integrates several security systems: identity management, endpoint security systems, policy, network enforcement, and behaviour monitoring (albeit in a proprietary manner). But this integration is only half-hearted. The PDP obtains lots of information during the assessment phase but it does not share this information with any other entities. Also, there is no standard way for the PDP to receive more information at a later time (e.g. from behaviour monitoring system) and modify its decision.

To solve this problem, the previous NAC architecture can be extended by adding an information sharing database, a standard protocol for accessing that database, and standard schemas for information that is stored in the database. Figure 2 illustrates the architecture used for NAC 2.0, an extension of the existing NAC architecture. In addition to the AR, PEP, and PDP introduced in the preceding architecture, two new components have been added: a Metadata Access Point (MAP) and Sensors and Flow Controllers.

The MAP is a database server that stores security information shared between the PDP and the Sensors and Flow Controllers.

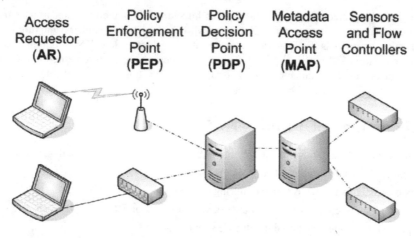

Figure 2: NAC 2.0 Architecture

Note that the terms Sensor and Flow Controller are not intended to be restrictive but rather connote broad categories that include any device or system capable of supplying information to or receiving information from the MAP.

Unlike the existing NAC architecture presented in slide 1, this architecture represents a break from current practice. Existing NAC systems do not provide a shared database for security information and a standard access protocol and schema for that database. Some of them include proprietary ways to integrate one vendor's NAC system with their sensors and flow controllers but, as we will see, there is considerable value in having a standard for this integration. No single vendor has all the sensors and flow controllers that a customer might want.

3.2 NAC 2.0 Examples

NAC 2.0 is all about sharing information via the MAP, using standard protocols and schemas. To illustrate the value of information sharing, this section gives a few examples.

The first example illustrates how the MAP enhances traditional NAC. The example starts with the Request, Assessment, Decision, and Enforcement phases described in section 2.2. After these phases are complete, the PDP publishes the information it used in the assessment and the decision it made into the MAP. A Flow Controller (such as an interior firewall or a server) can use this information to provide appropriate access, either using the decision from the PDP or using the information from the assessment phase along with a local policy. A Sensor can use this additional information to adjust its sensing, perhaps providing broader latitude for a network administrator. If the Sensor detects a problem such as impermissible behaviour by an endpoint, it can publish an alert to the MAP. The PDP will generally subscribe to any changes to endpoints that it is managing so the MAP will notify the PDP of the alert from the Sensor. The PDP can then reconsider its decision and perhaps inform the PEP and MAP of a revised decision, resulting in reduced access for that user. The PDP may also be able to send a message to the AR, resulting in a warning on the user's screen about the unacceptable behaviour.

The second example shows how the NAC 2.0 architecture handles endpoints with no NAC software or capabilities (a "clientless endpoint" like a printer). When the PDP recognizes a clientless endpoint, it can instruct the PEP to place the endpoint into an examination area of the network. Then the PDP publishes a notice on the MAP indicating that further analysis of this endpoint is required. Sensors such as device profilers and vulnerability scanners examine the endpoint using specialized tools that obtain as much information as is possible with the endpoint's software. They may perform a port scan, observe network traffic from the device, and characterize responses to stimuli, for example. They may also intercept web access and ask the user to authenticate or run scanning software. A web intercept like this is known as a "captive portal" and is well-established technology used in many hotel rooms and wireless hotspots. The Sensors then publish this information to the MAP and the PDP decides what access to grant to the endpoint. It may decide to grant no access, grant limited access with ongoing monitoring to ensure the device behaviour remains as expected, or grant full access. Clearly, this analysis will not be as secure as a hardware-based health check of the device but it is better than nothing and it can be perfectly adequate if the access given to the device is limited and the behaviour is carefully monitored. Certainly, it is better to give the PDP a way to analyze clientless endpoints than to force the PDP to decide without this information.

3.3 NAC 2.0 Benefits

NAC 2.0 systems provide the following additional benefits beyond those provided by existing NAC systems:

- Monitoring and analysis of endpoint behaviour (if desired)
- Fewer false alarms for Sensors (due to identity awareness)
- Simpler (identity-based) policy and reports for Sensors and Flow Controllers
- Automated response to Sensor alerts (if desired)
- Good support for clientless endpoints

Not only does NAC 2.0 address concerns with existing NAC systems, it also enhances the utility of existing Sensors and Flow Controllers while reducing the cost of managing them.

3.4 Standards for NAC 2.0

Standards are as important for NAC 2.0 as they are for existing NAC systems. A single-vendor system with NAC 2.0 functionality is less extensible and ultimately less capable than a system based on open standards, which can take advantage of new Sensor and Flow Controller products and technologies from any vendor as soon as they become available.

To build an open NAC 2.0 system, standard protocols for accessing the MAP must be defined and also standard formats for the data to be shared. The TCG has stepped into this gap with a new addition to the TNC standards: IF-MAP [TRUS08a]. The IF-MAP standard is new (released in May 2008) so no products support it yet. However, several major vendors of NAC systems, Sensors, and Flow Controllers have demonstrated prototype implementations.

3.5 Risks of NAC 2.0

Like every powerful technology, deployment of NAC 2.0 carries risks. This section enumerates and evaluates those risks.

First, the MAP is a nerve centre and therefore a target for attack. Compromise of the MAP could result in access policy violations so the MAP must be well protected and write access to the MAP must be limited and carefully monitored. Of course, this is no different from an identity management or key management system, whose compromise would have broad implications. In fact, those systems are more sensitive since they may contain long-term secrets. The MAP does not contain such secrets so the direct effects of a MAP compromise are limited to access policy violations.

Second, the MAP will generally contain security-sensitive and privacy-sensitive information such as user identity and role. Therefore, it should be carefully managed and read access should be carefully restricted.

Finally, IP traffic does not provide a strong identifier that Sensors and Flow Controllers can use to associate traffic with a particular user and endpoint in the MAP. They can use IP address for this association but this is subject to IP spoofing. To make this association secure, networks must employ IP spoofing prevention and/or detection technology. Of course, this is no worse than the existing state of the art for Sensors (like IDS) and Flow Controllers (like firewalls) but efforts to offer stronger associations continue.

3.6 Future Work with NAC 2.0

NAC 2.0 is not the end of the road for innovation in this area. In fact, it's probably the start of a new wave of innovation as Sensors and Flow Controllers can now gain access to critical information that will enable them to make substantial improvements to their technologies. Here are a few areas where innovation seems likely to occur.

1. A stronger way to identify IP traffic and associate it with a particular endpoint would be appreciated. Various ideas have been discussed but each one has its own downsides. Work continues in this area. For now, IP addresses are used and IP spoofing prevention is recommended.

2. Now that all security devices in the network can access user and role information and associate these with network traffic, they can move to policies based on identities and roles instead of IP addresses. This is much simpler and closer to what administrators want. However, the next step is to be able to define a single access control policy for the enterprise in business terms (something like "employees can access resources and services associated with projects to which they are assigned" but more complex). This policy could then be enforced and compliance checked by the NAC system, Sensors, Flow Controllers, etc. This will need a bit of work in policy languages and semantics but it may be doable.

3. NAC 2.0 does not yet extend to application or server security. This has several unfortunate effects. First, users must sign on at least twice: once for the network layers and again for the application layers. Second, applications can't yet benefit from all the information stored in the MAP. Work has begun to address these problems, perhaps using SAML assertions since they are the most widely-implemented Single Sign On system.

Innovators are encouraged to explore these areas and others. They are encouraged to contact the author with their thoughts to ensure coordination and avoid the development of incompatible solutions to the same problem.

4 Conclusion

While the value of today's NAC systems is considerable, this value is greatly enhanced by integrating these systems with a wide variety of Sensors and Flow Controllers. The advantages of performing this integration include stronger security through behaviour monitoring, reduced cost because of fewer false alarms, and improved ease of use with identity-based policies and reports. The potential for greater automation of security response is perhaps the greatest benefit.

Attack technology continues to improve. We must match this improvement with corresponding improvements in defensive technology. Defensive improvements will certainly come but without integration they will not be as effective as they should be. Complexity will increase and management costs along with it. To combat this increasing complexity, we must move to architectures that allow defenders to increase automation and move to higher-level policies and reports. NAC 2.0 is just such an architecture.

References

[TRUS07] Trusted Computing Group: Stopping Rootkits at the Network Edge. 2007.

[TRUS07a] Trusted Computing Group: IF-IMC 1.2. 2007.

[TRUS07b] Trusted Computing Group: IF-IMV 1.2. 2007.

[TRUS07c] Trusted Computing Group: IF-PEP 1.1. 2007.

[TRUS07d] Trusted Computing Group: IF-TNCCS 1.1. 2007.

[TRUS07e] Trusted Computing Group: IF-TNCCS-SOH 1.0. 2007.

[TRUS08] Trusted Computing Group: TNC Architecture for Interoperability 1.3. 2008.

[TRUS08a] Trusted Computing Group: IF-MAP 1.0. 2008.

Towards real Interoperable, real Trusted Network Access Control: Experiences from Implementation and Application of Trusted Network Connect

Josef von Helden · Ingo Bente

University of Applied Science and Arts, Hanover
{josef.vonhelden | ingo.bente}@fh-hannover.de

Abstract

Network Access Control (NAC) is the most promising approach to provide protection against sophisticated attacks that first compromise endpoints to subsequently continue their evil work in networks accessible via the compromised endpoint. Trusted Network Connect (TNC) is a NAC approach featuring interoperability and unforgeability due to its openness, broad vendor support and integration of Trusted Computing functions.

This paper presents experiences with TNC gained from the development of a TNC implementation, called TNC@ FHH and some analyses on how to adopt TNC in real world scenarios.

It comes to the conclusion that interoperability between basic TNC components of different vendors and developers is obviously actually good, unforgeability is well designed but hard to achieve, and the adoption of TNC in real world scenarios is on the one hand desired because of obvious security benefits, but on the other hand today there are several handicaps leading to high complexity and costs.

That's why further developments and enhancements concerning TNC and Trusted Computing are required to finally succeed in having a real interoperable and unforgeable NAC solution, being easily adoptable and manageable.

1 Introduction and Motivation

Due to global networking, especially the enormous growth of the Internet, the threat of network based attacks is generally very high. Due to changing network structures from static to heterogeneous dynamic networks new risks are raising, e.g. through guest devices joining the corporate network and thus being out of administrative control of the network provider. Common examples are consultants using their own notebooks connecting to the corporate network or students using their own notebooks in their university's network (directly or via VPN).

Today hackers have adapted their attacks to the new structure of today's networks (e.g. see [Syma08]). They often take a sophisticated and clever approach in first attacking the weakest IT component of a network they can find: endpoints like desktop PCs and notebooks. Typically operating systems and applications at endpoints are much more vulnerable than those on well secured servers behind firewalls. Once an endpoint has been compromised the malware is likely to stay hidden, waiting for crucial moments, e.g. to spy on passwords, eavesdrop on transactions, or even more: the malware waits until the user successfully authenticates himself to a service, before it does its evil work with the user's privileges.

N. Pohlmann, H. Reimer, W. Schneider (Editors): Securing Electronic Business Processes, Vieweg (2008), 152-162

Standard security measures like firewalls etc. do not protect against those kinds of sophisticated IT-based attacks. Hence new innovative security measures are needed to protect today's networks.

2 NAC and TNC

Network Access Control (NAC) is the most promising approach to provide protection against the kind of attacks described above. In short NAC solutions remotely check the integrity of network endpoints against a given policy before allowing them to join the network. To gain significant benefit from NAC solutions the following requirements are considered to be very important:

1. support for multi-vendor **interoperability** enabling customer's choice of security solutions and infrastructure,

2. unforgeability, i.e. the network (resp. a security server in the network) can really trust in the integrity information provided by the endpoint (countering the "lying endpoint problem")

Today no available NAC solution really meets the demands mentioned above. Cisco's NAC and Microsoft's NAP are both proprietary, thus breaching requirement (1). Requirement (2) is in general hard to achieve because it presumes having (a) a hardware based root of trust which (b) also is standardized to meet requirement (1).

Trusted Network Connect (TNC) appears to be the most promising approach.

The TNC architecture ([TNCA08]), defined by the Trusted Computing Group with more than 170 participating companies, is an open, non-proprietary standard that enables the application and enforcement of security requirements for endpoints connecting to the corporate network. The TNC architecture and specifications define the optionally use of the Trusted Platform Module (TPM) (see **Fig. 4**), a standardised secure cryptoprocessor. Thus, TNC is in general a NAC solution designed to achieve interoperability and unforgeability.

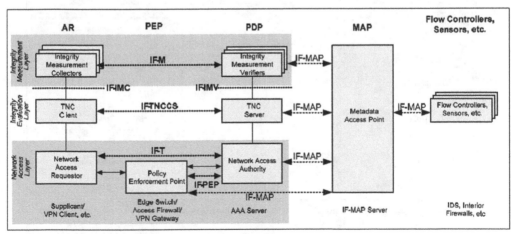

Fig. 1: The TNC Architecture ([TNCA08])

The TNC architecture consists of 5 entities (the columns in **Fig. 1**): the Access Requestor (AR, typically a notebook or desktop pc), the Policy Enforcement Point (PEP, typically an edge switch), the Policy Decision Point (PDP, typically Server, making the access decision), the Metadata Access Point (MAP, storing and providing state information), and Flow controllers, Sensors etc. (like IDS, Interior Firewalls). **Fig. 1** also shows three layers (Network Access, Integrity Evaluation, Integrity Measurement), different TNC components (depicted as rectangles) and interfaces between these components (depicted as dotted blue arrows).

At present, many of the most important TNC specifications are released and publicly available.

3 Experiences with TNC

In this section some experiences made with TNC are presented. These experiences basically derive from the following areas:

- from the development of a TNC implementation, called TNC@FHH and
- from some analyses on how to adopt TNC in real world scenarios.

This chapter is therefore organised as follows:

The next section summarizes the main components and features of TNC@FHH. Afterwards experiences gained during the development of TNC@FHH is described, subdivided in the aspects of interoperability and unforgeability. After that experiences from adopting TNC in real world scenarios are described. In the end, plans for the future development of TNC@FHH are mentioned.

3.1 TNC@FHH

TNC@FHH ([TNCFHH]) is an open source implementation from the University of Applied Sciences and Arts in Hanover, Germany (FHH). It was started to gain experience with TNC, particularly concerning functionality, interoperability and feasibility of the TNC approach.

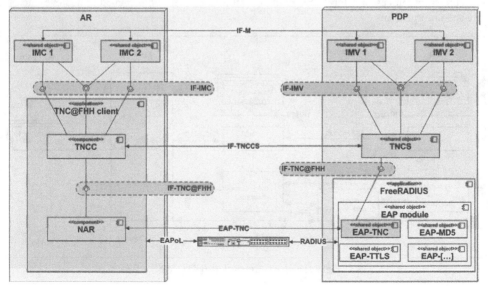

Fig. 2: Architecture of TNC@FHH

Today the main components of the TNC entities Access Requestor (AR) and Policy Decision Point (PDP) (see columns in **Fig. 1**) and interfaces between them are implemented in TNC@FHH.

Fig. 2 shows the architecture of TNC@FHH. Green boxes indicate components which were developed within the TNC@FHH project, forming also the interfaces depicted as blue ovals.

In more detail, at the Network Access Layer EAP is used as protocol for transporting the TNCCS messages. The Network Access Authority (NAA) is implemented via extending the FreeRADIUS ([FRE-ERA]) server with an EAP-TNC module. The Network Access Requestor (NAR) had originally been implemented from the scratch, assembling EAP-TNC packets and communicating them via 802.1x and EAPoL to and from the switch.

The components of the Integrity Evaluation Layer and Integrity Measurement Layer, i.e. TNCC, TNCS, exemplarily Integrity Measurement Collectors (IMCs) and Integrity Measurement Verifiers (IMVs), as well as the horizontal and vertical interfaces between them were all implemented from the scratch.

The PDP is running under Linux while on the AR side Linux and Windows are supported.

3.2 Experiences from the development of TNC@FHH

3.2.1 Interoperability

Interoperability is one of the most important aspects of networking in general and especially of NAC systems. Due to the openness of all specifications the interoperability potential of TNC is very high.

Actually several interoperability tests showed a high degree of interoperability between main TNC components of different TNC implementations, mainly from open source developments.

During the so called TNC plugfest in March 2008 the following components were interoperating without or with very little additional effort:
* XSupplicant ([XSUPPL]) or wpa_supplicant ([WPASUP]) as TNCC / NAR,
* sample IMC/IMV pair from libtnc ([LIBTNC]),
* TNC Server from TNC@FHH, integrated as part of FreeRADIUS running EAP-TNC inside of an EAP-TTLS tunnel.

Fig. 3 shows the TNC components interoperating during plugfest 2008.

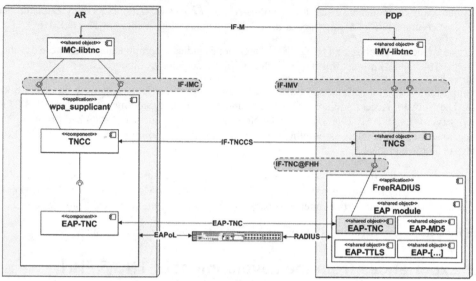

Fig. 3: Interoperating TNC components during plugfest 2008

One consequence of the high degree of interoperability was the decision of the TNC@FHH team to stop the development of their own TNCC / NAR. As both the TNCC and the NAR were written from scratch they were only supporting TNC, without any other EAP method. It seemed to be much more reasonable to contribute with further TNC developments to existing, fully arranged supplicants like XSupplicant and wpa_supplicant.

The tests described above confirm the high degree of interoperability between the following TNC components, due to the high quality of the specifications mentioned below (see also **Fig. 1**):
- IMCs and TNC Client, due to IF-IMC ([IFIMC07]),
- IMVs and TNC Server, due to IF-IMV ([IFIMV07]),
- TNC Client and TNC Server, due to IF-TNCCS ([IFTNCCS07]),
- NAR and NAA, due to IF-T ([IFT07]),
- NAA and PEP, due to IF-PEP ([IFPEP07]).

To complete the consideration of TNC components concerning interoperability, the following list takes a look at the remaining interfaces from **Fig. 1**:
- IF-M: This interface basically serves to exchange vendor specific information between IMC/IMV-pairs. Indeed, during plugfest different IMC-IMV-pairs were tested but only IMCs and IMVs of the same pair exchanged messages, according to their own specific protocol. IF-M may stay vendor specific without effecting the overall interoperability. Nevertheless, TCG is expected to standardize certain widely used messages as well as some security aspects to enable the use of a standardized secured channel between IMCs and IMVs.
- IF-MAP ([IFMAP08]): This interface allows the exchange of metadata about the current status of the network (including attached endpoints, connected users, used devices, VLAN, IP, MAC, ...). IF-MAP was introduced at Interop Las Vegas 2008, i.e. after plugfest.

The last interoperability remark concerns IF-TNCCS. In May 2007 TCG published SoH (Statement of Health) bindings for IF-TNCCS ([IFSOH07]) to achieve compatibility even with the Microsoft Network Access Protection (NAP) system. The specification states that "To be compliant with IF-TNCCS, TNC clients and servers MUST implement either protocol or both, depending on their requirements" ([IFSOH07], p.10). Thus the downside is, that it is possible to have fully compliant TNC Clients and Servers being not interoperable (e.g. a TNC Client supporting SoH binding only and a TNC Server supporting XML bindings only). It is expected that the next version of IF-TNCCS will integrate this bindings in one specification, hopefully ensuring full interoperability. At plugfest all TNC Clients and Servers supported XML bindings.

3.3 Unforgeability

The possibility of achieving unforgeability of integrity reports is one of the key features and advantages of TNC against other NAC solutions. The problem of "lying endpoints" was for example demonstrated on Cisco's NAC solution at the Blackhat Conference Europe 2007 ([RoTh07]).

The TNC architecture defines the optionally usage of the TPM during TNC handshake. The main idea is to use the TPM capabilities on the Access Requestor to verify the system integrity as well as to sign integrity reports generated by TNC components. The Policy Decision Point is then able to verify integrity reports in an unforgeable manner.

The general structure of the TNC architecture with TPM is shown in **Fig. 4**. The most relevant elements are PTS (Platform Trust Service) and the interface IF-PTS ([IFPTS06]). PTS is a system service that exposes trusted platform capabilities to TNC components. IF-PTS is the interface to access PTS services.

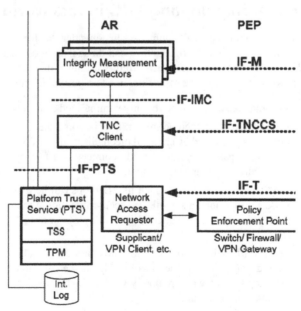

Fig. 4: TNC architecture with TPM ([TNCA08])

TNC@FHH has not yet implemented TPM support. Thus, it doesn't have any kind of unforgeability yet.

When implementing TPM support, two main aspects have to be regarded:

1. The TNC components have to use TPM functionalities e.g. to securely sign their integrity reports and

2. the TNC components themselves have to be measured.

Both points can basically be achieved using features of PTS. A crucial question is why one should trust the PTS. The answer is that the PTS itself has to be measured as part of a continuous chain of trust that has to be built starting from the root of trust for measurement (RTM) via bootloader, operating system and PTS to the TNC components. In other words a TrustedOS is needed.

Another question is how integrity reports are communicated between the AR and the PDP. According to the TCG specification ([IFPTS06], p.12) this should be done by a special IMC/IMV-pair, called PTS-IMC / PTS-IMV. While the PTS-IMC is basically responsible for creating the integrity reports and communicating them to PTS-IMV, the main task of PTS-IMV is to evaluate and verify the received reports. Exact functionality as well as the protocol for the communication between PTS-IMC and PTS-IMV aren't standardized yet. Generally this protocol can be seen as specialized version of IF-M. Conceivably it will be part of the IF-M specification where TCG is expected to standardize certain widely used messages.

To conclude: Unforgeability is an essential feature of a real trusted network access control system. Achieving the feature is a challenge.

3.4 Experiences from adopting TNC in real world scenarios

In theory, a TNC-based NAC solution provides numerous benefits that can lead to a significant enhancement of the overall security level of a network. But how can those theoretical benefits be realised in the real world scenarios? At FHH two master thesis are currently arranged that investigate the efficiency of TNC in companies real world scenarios. The results obtained so far will be presented in the following.

The status of today's corporate networks can be roughly summarized as follows:

- Most networks are well secured at their perimeter. That is, communication from and to a corporate network is controlled and secured by classical mechanisms like VPN-Gateways and Firewalls. But once this perimeter is passed (e.g. by directly connecting a Laptop to the corporate LAN), there are almost no security mechanisms existent.

- It is indispensable that mobile endpoints such like Laptops can be dynamically integrated into a corporate network. Furthermore, a smooth and secure integration must be possible, no matter if the connecting endpoint is known (e.g. employee's Laptop) or not (e.g. a guest device from a business partner).

- The current integration of such endpoints is normally based upon (1) the identification of the connecting device and/or (2) a user authentication. This is the common case when an employee wants to access the corporate network remotely via VPN. The integrity of the connecting devices is normally not taken into account.

Therefore, endpoint security is one crucial issue in today's networks. To decrease the threat that endpoints pose, most companies use tools like Anti Virus Software and Desktop or Personal Firewalls.

Furthermore, Patch Management Systems are used for keeping the endpoint's software up-to-date, and therefore more safe (or less vulnerable).

By using a TNC-based NAC solution, a company can enforce that only those endpoints are allowed to get access, that are regarded as being secure.

One crucial point is therefore, that one has to define what "secure" means. This is done by specifying a NAC policy. The TNC-based NAC solution measures the status of endpoints that want to access the network, compares the measurement results to the policy, and derives an access decision.

Unfortunately, there is no general NAC policy that fits everyone's needs. Each NAC policy has to be specifically developed, based upon the given mission scenario. But nevertheless, some core elements should be present:

1. Scope – This element defines to which entities the policy applies, e.g. all mobile devices, devices that try to get access by VPN or a group of users. Therefore, it will be common to have more than one NAC policy defined.

2. Authentication – Defines if an authentication of the endpoint and/or the user is required. If so, it further specifies which authentication mechanisms are allowed.

3. Assessment – Specifies the integrity information that are relevant for the access decision and therefore must be measured. Common examples are Anti Virus, Firewall and Patch Status of the operating system.

4. Evaluation – Once all the relevant aspects are measured, an access decision has to be derived. The evaluation model defines how this is done. A simple example is the "completeness" evaluation model. This means, that any property mentioned in the NAC policy has to be correctly fulfilled for getting access to the network. If not, access is denied.

5. Enforcement – The last element mentioned here defines how the derived access decision is enforced. Regarding TNC in a (W)LAN, enforcement is normally done by the edge switch the endpoint connected to, either by using VLANs or by setting up appropriate ACLs.

These core elements form a basic framework for a NAC policy. Depending on the requirements related to the mission scenario, this framework has to be filled with reasonable values – which produces another problem: In real world scenarios, it is not possible to measure any security relevant property of an endpoint. This would just take too much time (if feasible at all), disturbing the flow of work in an unreasonably way. Therefore, one must define an appropriate compromise between security and usability. Once defined, a TNC-based NAC solution is supposed to enforce the policy at the network's edge (VPN Gateways, Switches, Wireless Access Points).

Another important issue is the fact that new TNC mechanisms must be smoothly integrated in the existing IT infrastructure. This is not trivial, since TNC needs modifications (1) on the client side (2) on the server side and (3) concerning the physical and logical structure of the network itself. The task gets even more complicated, when existing security mechanisms should be integrated with the TNC-based NAC solution. As already mentioned, so called Patch Management Systems are widely adopted and assure that the software used on the endpoints is up-to-date. A powerful integration of such a Patch Management System with a TNC-based NAC solution could work as follows

- The TNC-based NAC solution measures endpoints and allows or denies access.
- In addition to this binary access decision, a third possibility is to isolate the accessing endpoint to a special segment of the corporate network. This makes sense when the endpoint fails to fulfil some properties of the defined NAC policy. In this isolation segment, the endpoint has only li-

mited access to services that support it in becoming compliant to the policy again. This process is called Remediation.

- An existing Patch Management System could be used as one of those "Remediation-Services" that can be used from the isolated network segment.

The benefit is, that one can use the established functions of the existing Patch Management System within the TNC-based NAC solution. Since those systems are normally proprietary, their vendors must render assistance to realise the described integration.

The last issue mentioned here refers to the "unforgeability" feature. TNC supports the use of TPMs to address the well known "lying endpoint" problem. But to achieve real unforgeability (1) every endpoint must have a TPM inside and (even worse) (2) the software running on the endpoint, especially the operating system, must support the secure use the TPM functionalities.

Those three issues described above (NAC policy, integration and TPM usage) are results taken from the master thesis. In the end, TNC seems to be able to implement the theoretical benefits in real world scenarios – but the process of integrating it in an existing environment is very complex.

3.5 Plans for the Future: tNAC

tNAC is a research project started on July, 1st 2008. It is scheduled for three years and sponsored by the Federal Ministry of Education in Germany. The project team is a consortium consisting of three universities and three companies:

- University of Applied Sciences and Arts Hanover
- University of Applied Sciences Gelsenkirchen
- University Bochum
- Datus AG
- Sirrix AG
- Steria Mummert Consulting AG

The overall goal is to develop an open source, TNC compatible NAC solution with full TPM support (referred to as tNAC).

One important issue is the strong involvement of the companies mentioned above. They will especially participate in the definition of requirements based upon real world scenarios and the fact, that tNAC must still be manageable in a convenient way despite its complex functionality.

tNAC will not be developed from scratch. The basic approach is to combine TNC@FHH with Turaya, an open source trusted platform resulting from the EMSCB-project ([EMSCB]). Turaya will be responsible for establishing a Chain of Trust that ideally includes all relevant components starting from the BIOS up to the PTS. After that, the PTS itself adds further TNC components to the Chain of Trust. This way, the integrity of the TNC subsystem located on the AR can be securely verified during the TNC handshake, which is a promising approach to counter the lying endpoint problem.

4 Conclusion and Outlook

TNC is in general a NAC solution where features like interoperability and unforgeability were being included in the design right from the start, basically due to its openness, broad vendor support and the integration of Trusted Computing functions.

From the experience gained from the implementation of TNC@FHH as well as from the adoption of TNC in real world scenarios the following conclusions are drawn:

- Interoperability between basic TNC components of different vendors and developers is obviously actually good. Some further standardisation is needed to support interoperability between application specific Integrity Measurement Collectors and Verifiers as well as to cope with the imminent loss of interoperability due to multiple optional choices on protocols to communicate between TNC Client and TNC Server.
- Unforgeability is well designed but hard to achieve because of the indispensable operating system support and the need of a verifiable chain of trust from the hardware based root of trust for measurement to TNC components and applications. Further research and development activities as well as further specifications and standardizations are needed.
- Concerning the adoption of TNC in real world scenarios on the one hand the security benefit of a TNC solution is evident and desired. On the other hand today there are several handicaps leading to high complexity and costs. The main handicaps are the high complexity of policy definition and enforcement, the efforts and investments required for integration of TNC into the existing IT infrastructure, and the today's impossibility to achieve unforgeability due to the lack of TPM support in standard operating systems.

Nevertheless, TNC seems to be the most hopeful approach towards a real interoperable, real trusted NAC solution. Furthermore the need for such a solution will grow according to (a) the increasing importance of endpoints for the overall network security and (b) to the strongly increasing security threats to such endpoints.

TCG and many others (like the tNAC consortium) are working on further developments and enhancements concerning TNC and Trusted Computing in general. Hopefully, tNAC and all the other combined efforts will contribute to finally succeed in performing a technology that will really enhance security, especially on endpoints and will be easily adoptable and manageable.

References

[EMSCB] Home of EMSCB project: http://www.emscb.com/

[FREERA] Home of FreeRADIUS: http://freeradius.org/

[IFIMC07] TCG Trusted Network Connect, TNC IF-IMC. In: https://www.trustedcomputinggroup.org/specs/ TNC/. Specification Version 1.2, Revision 8, 05 February 2007, Published

[IFIMV07] TCG Trusted Network Connect, TNC IF-IMV. In: https://www.trustedcomputinggroup.org/specs/ TNC/. Specification Version 1.2, Revision 8, 05 February 2007, Published

[IFMAP08]TCG Trusted Network Connect, TNC IF-MAP binding for SOAP. In: https://www.trustedcomputing-group.org/specs/TNC/. Specification Version 1.0, Revision 25, 28 April 2008, Published

[IFPEP07] TCG Trusted Network Connect, TNC IF-PEP: Protocol Bindings for RADIUS. In: https://www.trust-edcomputinggroup.org/specs/TNC/. Specification Version 1.1, Revision 0.7, 05 February 2007, Published

[IFPTS06]   TCG Infrastructure Working Group, Platform Trust Services Interface Specification (IF-PTS). In: https://www.trustedcomputinggroup.org/specs/IWG/. Specification Version 1.0, Revision 1.0, 17 November 2006, FINAL

[IFSOH07] TCG Trusted Network Connect, TNC IF-TNCCS: Protocol Bindings for SoH. In: https://www.trustedcomputinggroup.org/specs/TNC/. Specification Version 1.0, Revision 0.08, 21 May 2007, Published

[IFT07]   TCG Trusted Network Connect, TNC IF-T: Protocol Bindings for Tunneled EAP Methods. In: https://www.trustedcomputinggroup.org/specs/TNC/. Specification Version 1.1, Revision 10, 21 May 2007, Published

[IFTNCCS07]   TCG Trusted Network Connect, TNC IF-TNCCS. In: https://www.trustedcomputinggroup.org/specs/TNC/. Specification Version 1.1, Revision 1.00, 05 February 2007, Published

[LIBTNC]   Home of Project libtnc: http://sourceforge.net/projects/libtnc

[Pohl07]   Pohlmann Norbert, Integrity Check of Remote Computer Systems – Trusted Network Connect. In: ISSE 2007, http://www.internet-sicherheit.de/fileadmin/docs/publikationen/isse-2007-trusted-network-connect-pohlmann_21_09_07.pdf

[RoTh07]   Roecher Dror-John, Thumann Michael, NACATTACK. In: Black Hat Europe 2007, http://www.blackhat.com/html/bh-europe-07/bh-eu-07-speakers.html

[Syma08]   Symantec Global Internet Security Threat Report, Trends for July–December 07. In: http://www.symantec.com/business/theme.jsp?themeid=threatreport. Volume XII, Published April 2008

[TNCA08]   TCG Trusted Network Connect, TNC Architecture for Interoperability. In: https://www.trustedcomputinggroup.org/specs/TNC/. Specification Version 1.3, Revision 6, 28 April 2008, Published

[TNCFHH] Homepage of TNC@FHH: http://tnc.inform.fh-hannover.de

[WPASUP] Homepage of wpa_supplicant: http://hostap.epitest.fi/wpa_supplicant/

[XSUPPL] Homepage of XSupplicant: http://open1x.sourceforge.net/

Empirical research of IP blacklists

Christian J. Dietrich · Christian Rossow

Institute for Internet-Security
University of Gelsenkirchen, Germany
{dietrich | rossow}@internet-sicherheit.de

Abstract

IP blacklisting of spamming IP addresses is one of the oldest techniques to fight spam. However, while one of the oldest it is one of the most effective, too. Two analysis methods are described and results thereof are presented in this work. It is revealed that a lot of spam originates from short-lived IP addresses which are often not blocked by IP blacklists. This raises the need of highly dynamic blacklists. List properties of well-known blacklists are begin given as part of this paper. Furthermore, a glance of mail receiver distribution by country is included.

1 Introduction

IP blacklisting in the context of anti-spam describes collecting IP addresses in a list and prohibits any email communication initiated from these addresses. Usually IP blacklisting is the first level of spam protection at email servers. With the help of blacklisting in particular big Email Service Providers filter up to 95% of their incoming connections to mail systems ([Ross07], [Spam08], [MaRo07]).

Thus blacklists are the cornerstones of anti-spam appliances and a number of blacklists are offered by anti-spam providers. In order to choose which IP blacklists are to be used, IT leaders depend on hearsay and on their own experience or feeling. So far, only very few research results concerning IP blacklisting exist. This fact motivated our empirical analysis on IP blacklists.

In this paper we focus on two different analyses of blacklists. Starting with the contents analysis we give an overview about the current situation IP address reputations by reviewing the sizes of blacklists. In addition, we reveal that some blacklists have similar contents to a certain degree. Next, the behavior analysis reveals the usage behavior of blacklist users. In other words, we observe what requests are made to a given blacklist by mail servers receiving messages.

Following this section we motivate our research done for this paper. In Section 3, we present our analysis methods. Section 4 contains the evaluation results of applying the contents analysis method to 13 lists and the behavior analysis method to one blacklist. Section 5 provides a discussion of the results as well as possible future work before we conclude this paper in section 6 with a brief summary.

2 Motivation

To the best of our knowledge, key properties of well-known blacklists as well as the relationship such as intersections between different black-, white- and bogonlists have not yet been subject to research.

Furthermore, little is known about the behavior of blacklists. Only few research results concerning the behavior of IP blacklists exist ([RaFe06], [RaFV07], [RaFD06]). Ramachandran and Feamster analyze in [RaFe06] the network-level behavior of spammers by looking at a large spam sinkhole between August 2004 and December 2005 and correlating this with BGP routing information, blacklist lookups, traces from a known botnet and traces of legitimate email. DNS-based IP blacklists play a role in this study in that about 80% of the received spam was listed in at least one of eight blacklists. However, hardly any information is given concerning the eight blacklists that were used and their behavior or contents. Ramachandran et al. present in [RaFV07] so-called behavioral blacklisting, a technique used to classify email senders based on their sending behavior rather than on their IP address. The evaluation is based on email logs for over 115 domains. In this paper, the behavior of email from at least 1.3 million different senders to about 10,000 different receivers, corresponding to more than 10,000 target domains, has been analyzed.

Ramachandran et al. studied in [RaFD06] the behavior of a blacklist in order to detect botnet membership. They observed a mirror of a well-known blacklist for a 45-day period in November and December 2005. In this paper, we analyzed the behavior based on measurements of a total of 8 months during July 2007 and March 2008. Furthermore, we present for the first time an evaluation of blacklist usage statistics from the server's perspective as well as activity periods of email sources. Jung and Sit analyze DNS blacklist usage from the client's perspective ([JuSi04]) based on measurements in 2000 and 2004. Moreover, in this paper, key facts as well as the contents of 11 blacklists, one whitelist and a bogon list are analyzed for the first time.

Finally, in this paper, we present for the first time analysis methods and empirical results that reveal key properties of and intersections between 13 IP black-, white and bogon lists. These facts can be used by researchers, black- and whitelist operators and email operators.

3 Analyses

We developed and applied two analysis methods. Both contents analysis and behavior analysis will be explained in this section.

3.1 Contents analysis

Subject of the – as we define it – contents analysis is a full set of IP addresses at a given point in time, such as for example the contents of an IP blacklist. The contents analysis focuses on properties of one such set of IP addresses and the comparison of different sets of IP addresses. Moreover, it aims at monitoring the mutation of one or more sets over time.

- Properties of an IP list may be but are not limited to one of the following:
- Covered net range (the amount of IPv4 address space covered by the list)
- Number of entries (the number of entries of the list, single IPv4 addresses as well as IPv4 net ranges)
- Percentage of total IPv4 address space (percentage of the covered net range among the total theoretical IPv4 address space)
- Percentage of advertised IPv4 address space (percentage of the covered net range among the advertised IPv4 address space)

An overlapping entry of two sets means that a certain IP address or IP address range was listed in both of the two lists at a certain point in time.

Black-, white- and bogonlists change over time, i.e. new addresses get on the list, others may be removed.

3.2 Behavior analysis

Not only contents of blacklists are of interest. We define the term behavior analysis as looking into how clients request information of a list from a server. Most lists make use of the DNS protocol in order to query a black- or whitelist. Thus, our behavior analysis refers to DNS-based IP lists. A client can be any host that looks up a certain IP address in the list. Usually email servers lookup the source IP addresses of incoming SMTP connections (see figure 1). Apart from that, bots may look up their own addresses in order to find out whether they are listed or not as described in [RaFD06].

Two main sets of IP addresses result from the behavior analysis: The set of IP addresses that are requested, so-called requested IP addresses, and the set of source IP addresses of clients that perform the queries.

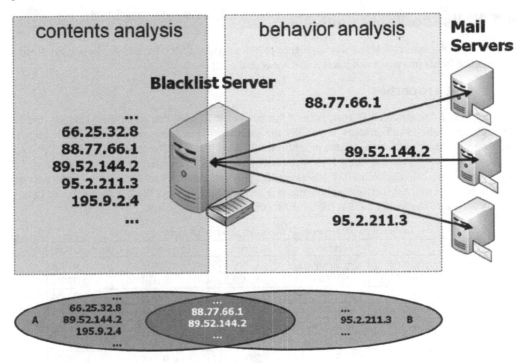

Figure 1: Contents and Behavior Analysis

For each request from a client to the blacklist server, the source IP address can be extracted. This leads to a set of source IP addresses of the users of the blacklist.

Figure 1 displays two different underlying sets between contents and behavior analysis. On the left side, set A represents the set of listed IP addresses, whereas on the right, set B is the set of requested IP addresses. The intersection of the two sets, A ∩ B, is the set of requested IP addresses that were on the list at the time they were queried. A \ B is the set of listed IP addresses that were never queried. B \ A is the set of requested IP addresses that were not listed at the time they were queried.

The behavior analysis reveals at least the following properties:

- Total number of requests to a list over a period of time
- Total number of positive and negative responses over a period of time
- The ratio between total requests and positive responses, so-called hit rate, over a period of time
- The number of distinct requested IP addresses over a period of time
- The number of distinct source IP addresses over a period of time

4 Evaluation

Both contents analysis and behavior analysis have been applied. We present the results in this section.

4.1 IP list contents analysis

In March 2008, contents analysis was applied to 11 blacklists, one whitelist and one bogon list. Results are grouped in list properties and intersection between the lists.

4.1.1 List properties

Very abstract information on IP lists, such as the number of entries, can reveal first insights into the concepts and policies of blacklists. Especially the amount of IP address space covered is of interest, since a single entry can be a net range of multiple IP addresses. Furthermore the amount of listed addresses among the whole theoretical IPv4 space can be computed. In practice, the amount of assigned IP addresses, the so-called advertised IP address space, plays an important role. Building a ratio between advertised space and list sizes shows how much is actually known about the IP address space. Table 1 displays this information for all lists taken into account during our research.

Table 1: List properties of 11 blacklists, 1 whitelist and bogon ranges

List	Net range	Entries	Coverage	Coverage adv.
all.dnsbl.sorbs.net	313,609,137	1,099,179	7.302%	16.979%
UCEPROTECT L1	1,300,216	1,300,216	0.030%	0.070%
NiX Spam	382,085	382,085	0.009%	0.021%
sbl.spamhaus.org	1,456,104	5,091	0.034%	0.079%
dnsbl.njabl.org	4,537,328	4,537,328	0.106%	0.246%
dul.sorbs.net	310,801,329	472,915	7.236%	16.827%
CBL	5,066,714	5,066,714	0.118%	0.274%
pbl.spamhaus.org	405,706,490	938,807	9.446%	21.965%
xbl.spamhaus.org	5,202,469	5,202,469	0.121%	0.282%
dsbl.org	13,755,714	13,755,714	0.320%	0.745%
ubl.lashback.com	1,199,454	1,199,454	0.028%	0.065%
dnswl.org	521,323	22,322	0.012%	0.028%
Bogus ranges	1,276,379,392	29	29.718%	-

Next to the plain number of entries, the covered net range of those lists is of interest. 7 out of those 13 lists list single IP addresses only, whereas the remaining 6 lists also list entire net ranges in a single entry. This design decision highly affects the eventual size of the set containing all IP addresses listed. An outlier is given with a list of bogus ranges, where only 29 entries cover more than 1.27 billion of single IP addresses. On the other hand, NiX Spam and others define in their policy to take into account single addresses only.

Another important aspect of the listing policies is the type of addresses that enter the list. As such, Spamhaus' PBL and SORBS' DUL both try to list addresses of home users, that should not run their own mailserver and are threatened to be used as spamming bots. Those listings usually cover big net ranges used by providers to assign to their dial-up customers. A union of all IP addresses of Spamhaus' PBL reveals that up to 22% of the advertised IP address space is listed in this list. On the other hand, for example CBL analyses email traffic and uses spamtraps to build up metrics based on single IP addresses. Building the biggest set of single IP addresses, dsbl.org lists ~0.7% of the advertised IP address space. However, a high coverage is certainly not per se an indicator for the quality of a list.

4.1.2 Intersections

Furthermore, a comparison matrix shows the amount of intersections between different lists. Figure 2 gives the percentages about which amount of IP addresses listed in list A (row) is covered by list B (column). The higher the value, the darker is the background of the table cell.

reference comparison	all.dnsbl.sorbs.net	UCEPROTECT L1	NiX Spam	sbl.spamhaus.org	dnsbl.njabl.org	dul.sorbs.net	CBL	pbl.spamhaus.org	xbl.spamhaus.org	dsbl.org	ubl.lashback.com	dnswl.org	Bogus ranges
all.dnsbl.sorbs.net	--	0.19	0.06	0.08	0.83	99.10	0.68	79.04	0.71	2.69	0.19	0.000	0.00
UCEPROTECT L1	46.21	--	14.54	0.16	2.56	42.84	75.32	83.42	75.38	13.24	23.68	0.001	0.00
NiX Spam	45.17	49.50	--	0.12	1.98	40.51	74.57	78.15	74.61	7.94	20.38	0.002	0.00
sbl.spamhaus.org	17.14	0.14	0.03	--	1.07	3.13	0.81	6.79	0.85	2.03	0.10	0.000	0.00
dnsbl.njabl.org	57.61	0.73	0.17	0.34	--	58.43	3.22	73.06	6.22	82.52	0.60	0.000	0.00
dul.sorbs.net	100.0	0.18	0.05	0.01	0.82	--	0.65	79.58	0.67	2.69	0.18	0.000	0.00
CBL	42.09	19.33	5.62	0.23	2.89	40.14	--	88.64	100.0	10.32	12.18	0.000	0.00
pbl.spamhaus.org	61.10	0.27	0.07	0.02	0.82	60.97	1.11	--	1.14	2.56	0.26	0.000	0.00
xbl.spamhaus.org	42.82	18.84	5.48	0.24	5.42	40.09	97.39	88.54	--	12.24	11.89	0.000	0.00
dsbl.org	61.31	1.25	0.22	0.22	27.22	60.76	3.80	75.43	4.63	--	0.87	0.000	0.00
ubl.lashback.com	49.76	25.64	6.49	0.13	2.28	45.89	51.47	86.61	51.58	9.97	--	0.021	0.00
dnswl.org	0.027	0.002	0.002	0.000	0.006	0.025	0.004	0.003	0.004	0.012	0.049	--	0.000
Bogus ranges	0.00	0.00	0.00	0.00	0.00	0.00	0.00	0.00	0.00	0.00	0.00	0.000	--

Figure 2: IP Address List Intersection Matrix

The red-coloured cells clearly reveal the relationship between blacklists of high intersection such as Spamhaus blacklists. It is obvious that Spamhaus' XBL covers CBL completely (100%). A huge part of the CBL is contained in Spamhaus' PBL (86%). On the contrary, the blacklist NiX Spam does not cover much of other blacklists due to its small size (~ 400,000 entries).

Combining two blacklists in order to fight spam is much more efficient if the two lists have a low intersection value. Thus, in our eyes, it does not make sense using the CBL in addition to Spamhaus' XBL. On the other hand, it is sensible to use NiX Spam in combination with dsbl.org, because they hardly overlap.

The last two columns and rows of the matrix play a special role. Being the only public whitelist considered in our research, dnwsl.org shows minor intersections with given blacklists. As one considers the goal of whitelists, namely preventing legitimate mails from getting blocked based on blacklist decisions, the values are reasonable. On average each blacklist is covered to ~0.001% by the whitelist, which in theory is one wrong entry out of 10,000. Practically one can neither assume the completeness of the whitelist, nor its correctness.

Finally considering bogus net ranges does not show any noteworthy intersection with blacklists. Only SORBS has little, but negligible intersections with not routable IP addresses. It can be considered to also block any SMTP or even IP traffic coming from those bogus net ranges. Other research deals with detecing spam based on further network-level properties ([RaFe06]).

4.2 Behavior analysis

The analysis of the blacklist behavior was performed between July 2007 and March 2008 on one DNS slave for the NiX Spam blacklist. The NiX Spam blacklist cluster consists of ten DNS servers. DNS requests to the blacklist are served in a round robin fashion. The NiX Spam has never been subject to any kind of empirical analysis before. NiX Spam was invented by Bert Ungerer, an editor of the German computer magazine iX.

4.2.1 Usage

4.2.1.1 Total requests

As part of the behavior analysis we measured the total number of requests as well as the total number of responses that were processed. In July 2007, our NiX Spam blacklist mirror analyzed on average 5.5 million requests per day. 5 months later, in December 2007 the number has increased to 9.5 million requests per day. Due to the immense increase in requests, our analysis setup had to be changed. Thus, the behavior analysis was interrupted between December 25th 2007 and February 14th 2008. Since February 2008 we analyze on average 16.6 million requests per day. Meanwhile the traffic to our blacklist slave has been measured without interruption. It shows a significant increase, as shown in Figure 3.

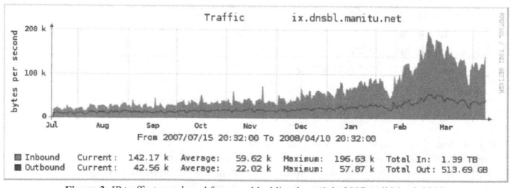

Figure 3: IP traffic towards and from our blacklist slave (July 2007 until March 2008)

4.2.1.2 Positive responses and hit rate

In the context of behavior analysis the number of positive responses can be compared to the total number of requests. The ratio of total requests to positive responses is called hit rate.

The hit rate of NiX Spam nearly doubled during the 8-month-period. In July 2007, it started at about 23% and finally reached 44% on average in February and March 2008.

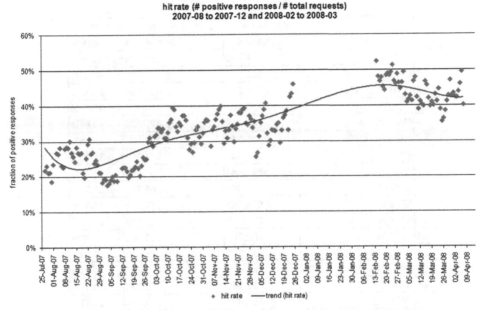

Figure 4: hit rate of NiX Spam blacklist between 2007-08 and 2008-04

A high hit rate means that many addresses requested from the list are actually listed and – in case of the NiX Spam blacklist – known as spam sources. This information is only reliable if the list provides a low false positive rate. In order to assess a blacklist, not only the hit rate, but also the false positive rate should be considered.

4.2.1.3 Interpreting source and requested IP addresses

Two further values for a blacklist are the number of requesting IP addresses (i.e. the source IP addresses of the query) as well as the number of requested IP addresses. The number of source IP addresses gives an impression of the number of users of a blacklist. In case of the NiX Spam, we detected on average about 11,000 different source IP addresses per day throughout the whole 8-month-period. It is important to note that this number is a lower bound due to DNS response caching. The number of different source IP addresses increases slightly towards the end of the analysis period. Surprisingly, however, it does not increase as much as the total number of requests or the traffic.

During February and March 2008, on average 1,529,054 distinct IP addresses have been requested on NiX Spam per day. Among these, 226,771 distinct addresses (14.83%) were on the list at the time they were queried. The NiX Spam blacklist had a total of 440,662 addresses listed on average. This shows that about 51.5% of the listed addresses were queried per day.

4.2.2 Mail receivers

When looking at regional characteristics of a blacklist, NiX Spam reveals that more than two thirds of all requests to the blacklist originate from Germany. More than a half of all requests issued from Germany have a positive response, which equals to a hit rate of 54% for German users. Only NiX Spam users from Sweden have the highest hit rate of about 55%. On the other side, the US also uses the NiX Spam list ranked 4th, but the hit rate for US American users is surprisingly low with 19%. Rows colored in grey show European countries (as will also be the case in the following tables).

	country	total requests	positive responses	hit rate
1	GERMANY	164,330,410	88,846,041	54.07%
2	(unknown)	21,423,462	10,338,175	48.26%
3	UNITED KINGDOM	13,963,515	6,190,899	44.34%
4	UNITED STATES	13,515,098	2,617,426	19.37%
5	AUSTRIA	7,220,563	2,724,336	37.73%
6	SWITZERLAND	5,540,029	2,475,036	44.68%
7	NETHERLANDS	5,336,509	1,198,597	22.46%
8	SWEDEN	2,262,446	1,243,369	54.96%
9	ITALY	1,138,883	209,495	18.39%
10	CANADA	1,079,405	266,755	24.71%
11	SPAIN	873,157	177,836	20.37%
12	SOUTH AFRICA	758,819	111,552	14.70%
13	AUSTRALIA	700,066	152,621	21.80%
14	RUSSIAN FEDERATION	695,938	128,739	18.50%
15	FRANCE	558,673	136,397	24.41%
16	BRAZIL	489,260	46,041	9.41%
17	INDONESIA	391,896	63,358	16.17%
18	DENMARK	385,435	78,028	20.24%
19	POLAND	351,719	67,058	19.07%
20	JAPAN	310,140	81,188	26.18%

Figure 5: countries of mail receivers

4.2.3 Activity periods of requested IP addresses

When looking at mail sources, the lifetime or better to say the activity period of a single IP address might be of interest. A long-lasting IP address could indicate a long-time legitimate mail sending host or a long-time spammer. Once reputation is known for a long-lasting IP address, decisions based on it have a significant effect. Short-lived IP addresses might indicate spammers from dialup IP addresses that "suffer" from DHCP churn.

The distribution of activity periods of requested IP addresses reveals that for NiX Spam only 8% of all requested IP addresses last longer than 3 days. In other words: 92% of all requested IP addresses are requested during a period of 3 days only. The numbers become even more obvious when looking at a single day: 3 of 4 requested IP addresses only last for one day.

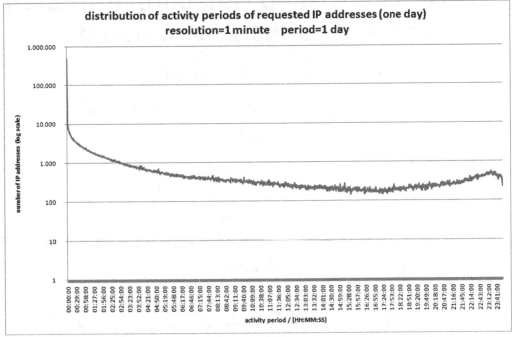

Figure 6: activity periods of IP addresses during one day

5 Conclusion

The results show important facts of blacklists such as the sizes and intersections among each other. The short activity periods of an IP address of less than or equal to one day prove that blacklists must react quickly and suggest that it might not be worth leaving addresses on the list forever. On the other hand the regional analysis reveals weaknesses such as low hit rates for users from certain countries. When applying blacklisting these results can help to optimize blacklisting as a means to protect from spam.

Literature

[Ross07]   C. Rossow (2007): Anti-spam measure of European ISPs/ESPs. http://www.internet-sicherheit.de/file-admin/docs/publikationen/anti-spam-measures-of-european-isps-esps.pdf

[Spam08]   Spamhaus (2008): Effective Spam Filtering. http://www.spamhaus.org/effective_filtering.html

[MaRo07]   P. Manzano, C. Rossow (2007): Provider Security Measures. Deliverable 2.1.6 of ENISA's Work Programme 2007. http://www.enisa.europa.eu/pages/spam/doc/enisa_spam_study_2007.pdf

[RaFe06]   A. Ramachandran, N. Feamster (2006): Understanding the network-level behavior of spammers. http://www.cc.gatech.edu/~feamster/papers/p396-ramachandran.pdf

[RaFV07]   A. Ramachandran, N. Feamster, S. Vempala (2007): Filtering spam with behavioral blacklisting. http://www.cc.gatech.edu/~feamster/papers/bb-ccs2007.pdf

[RaFD06]   A. Ramachandran, N. Feamster, D. Dagon (2006): Revealing botnet membership using DNSBL counter-intelligence. http://www.cc.gatech.edu/~feamster/publications/dnsbl.pdf

[JuSi04]   J. Jung, E. Sit (2004): An empirical study of spam traffic and the use of DNS black lists, http://www.imconf.net/imc-2004/papers/p370-jung.pdf

GIDRE: Grid-based Detection Intrusion and Response Environment

Olimpia Olguín[1, 2] · Manel Medina[1, 3]

[1]Catalonia Polytechnic University, Department of Computer Architecture,

[2]Indra Sistemas S,A,

[3]SeMarket S,A,

Barcelona Spain
{oolguin | medina}@ac.upc.edu

Abstract

This paper describes a new method to improve the efficiency and quickness of incidents detection by network protection systems. The principal element of this new method is the ADSH (Hybrid ADS, i.e. an ADS and IDS integrated solution, this is an upgrade of traditional IDS, ADS, NIDS, etc. This method is called GIDRE, and proposes an innovative mechanism for early detection and response to attacks, as well as distribution of information about its characteristics, allowing the optimization of resources and the response to them in their goal of protecting computer systems connected to the network.

To reach this goal, GIDRE has standardised mechanisms for exchanging information between clusters of intrusion and user anomalous behaviour (ADSH) detection systems, which will be distributed through the network using GRID architecture. These ADSH will realise a constant capture of the suspicious attack packets and anomalous packets, which circulate through the network. Thus, ADSH will share anomalies information detected in the network, having been able to discriminate almost immediately, if an attack of global form is taking place or if it is an accidental deviation of the behaviour of some particular user. When the ADSHs detects anomalous traffic it will trigger a Local Alarm (LA) about the protocols used in the attack, and this information analysis will be sent to the Console of the corresponding protocol (the ADSH assigned to that protocol) for further integration with potential LA,s coming from other sites. When the Console of the protocol analyzes the received LAs, it determines if it has taken place a GA (General Alarm) and if necessary, it will generate new configuration rules to apply in the perimeter protection systems of the affected local networks.

The GIDRE topology elements are as follows: there are several ADSHs distributed over different networks, several firewalls, and a Central Console in HD redundant architecture.

There have been some experiments in which we have demonstrated the advantage of having distributed ADSH compared to a single ADSH.

To demonstrate it, we analyze the SPAM behaviour, which is sent directly to the users' address book , who will have to be contaminated. It detects the nodes contamination processes, using ADSH distributed and a single ADSH.

N. Pohlmann, H. Reimer, W. Schneider (Editors): Securing Electronic Business Processes, Vieweg (2008), 172-180

1 Origin of the Project

The combination of firewalls + NIDS (Network Intrusion Detection System) [1] by signs and/or NIDS by anomalies we reached a high level of security in the network, but this turns into a system that reacts before an attack, virus or intrusions well-known and that have been detected through Data Base of virus well-known or a certain behaviour of the network and the firewall rules and it only reacts before well-known attacks, which entails to think to us about *What will happen with the intrusions that occur by means of vulnerabilities that have not been detected by the systems or by existing mechanisms security?*. the answer is very easy, the intruders will take advantage of vulnerabilities to propagate virus, to generate attacks, etc., is because of these reasons that we were decided to make an exhaustive investigation of *how to generate a mechanism that early detects and distributes alerts about potential intrusions to the computer science systems?*, we reached the conclusion that the best thing is to combine elements NIDS by signs (S-NIDS: Signature based NIDS) + NIDS by anomalies detection (A-NIDS: Abnormal behaviour based NIDS) in a new called element ADSH (Hybrid System of Anomalies Detection), this ADSH helps us to detect already well-known attacks as well as early detection of possible new ways of intrusions.

A single ADSH can only detect possible intrusions to a certain network if they have been reported and covered by the current version of the ADSH software installed, but what would happen if the same type of attack or other type of attack is happening in different networks and in different places at the same time? and if in addition, they are not protected by ADSHs?, The networks that do not contain the ADSH will be attacked and just a short time later they will contaminate other networks. In addition, if there are several ADSH installed but not connected among them, the discovery of possible new intruders will not be transmitted towards the other ADSHs. The discoveries of new intrusions would take in distributing itself toward other networks, it's for that reason that some virus propagation models have been analyzed and we have chosen in having a hybrid ADS of distributed way, this is obtained with the aid of the GRID technology (Distributed computing, see section 4). Applying this GRID technology we reached at the novel thing of this work and is the immediate diffusion of any anomalous traffic that is shortage in the ADSHs which they are had distributed towards all the elements of the GRID.

Later once the anomalous traffic (or possible intrusion) has been detected the system must react to protect the networks of the distributed system, this is achieved generating new rules that will be implemented (manually or automatically) in the Firewalls, taking in consideration the critic services.

2 Topology

The main topology that has been considered for its development is the following one (figure 1), the topology is constituted by several components, these are: firewalls, a central console, a backup console and several **ADSHs** located in different private networks or public networks, which could be universities, public companies, private companies, etc. The distribution and management of these components will be based on the use of the GRID computing to orchestrate the different platforms that constitute the GRID.

Next the operation of each one of the components of the system is described briefly.

The ADSH following the availability and capacity of their resources, will carry out the following functions:

- Capture of traffic by means of the ADSH [2].
- Analysis of the Local traffic that is being captured in order to detect one or several Local Alarms (LA). This analysis is realized passing the traffic through the S-NIDS where surely some known attacks will be detected, later the remaining traffic happens through A-NIDS where some possible intrusions are identified in an early way.
- Each ADSH will have to process their own work and in parallel to process information from other overworked ADSHs, reducing the workload of some other ADSHs.
- Each ADSH would be in charge to generate the LA of all the protocols. Each ADSH will conserve the Local Alarms of the protocol that manages and later the rest of the LAs will be sent to the corresponding ADSH. For example the ADSH (HTTP) will be the Console of protocol HTTP (Hypertext Transfer Protocol) and it will receive the LA,s related to the protocol HTTP from other ADSH,s. Later on, with these collected data, the ADSH(HTTP) generates the GA (General Alarm). Each ADSH plays also the role of Console of the protocol that was previously assigned to it from the Central Console.

The Central Console (and the backup console). The central Console coordinates the global operation of the system, generates the appropriate answers and provides the necessary mechanisms of supervision. Some of those tasks are the following ones:

- To assign to each ADSH the protocol that will manage.
- To supervise the operation and connectivity of ADSH platform.
- To characterize the networks and their weight to calculate a global weighted average.
- Alarm central log of all the protocols that are being analyzed.
- To contribute data for the generation of the new rules of firewall that will be implemented manually or automatically.
- List of ADSHs that shows the availability and technical characteristics by means of technology GRID.
- Work Distribution using GRID Computing.
- High availability of the distributed architecture.
- The ADSH send information of its state to the Central Console.

The Firewalls. The firewalls will mainly be in charge to protect the network deprived by means of the activation of rules that will be modified manually or automatically. The modifications in the rules will depend on the terms of the activated GA. The Firewalls will be the elements to which most of the reactive actions will go.

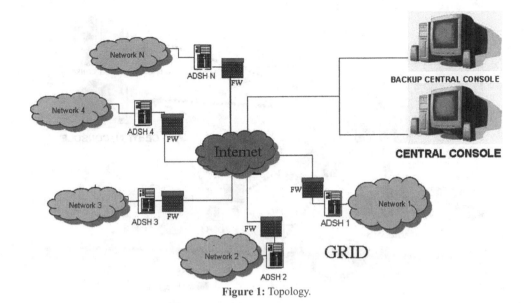

Figure 1: Topology.

3 Functional Analysis

In this work, we have developed an innovative mechanism of early detection, dissemination and fast response to possible attacks. The resources and the response itself have been optimized with the aim of protecting the computer systems connected to the network.

In order to achieve it, our proposal relies on standard mechanisms of information exchange between clusters of intrusions and abnormal behaviour of users detection systems (ADSH), which are distributed on the network using a GRID architecture. These ADSHs perform a constant capture of possible attacks and abnormal packets that circulate around the network. In this way, the ADSHs will share information on the abnormalities detected in the network, being able to discriminate almost immediately, if a global form of attack is taking place or if it is an accidental deviation of the behaviour of a particular user. When the ADSHs monitor anomalous traffic, they activate a LA on the affected protocol(s) and it is sent to the corresponding protocol Console (the ADSH assigned to that protocol). When the Console of the Protocol analyzes the received LAs, it determines if a GA has occurred and, if it is needed a specific policy to be applied in the perimeter protection systems of the affected local networks.

This policy is applied automatically if it does not affect critical services of a certain system. Otherwise, the authorization of the managers of the involved systems is required, who decide the most appropriate action.

The basic operation of the system is described in the following figure:

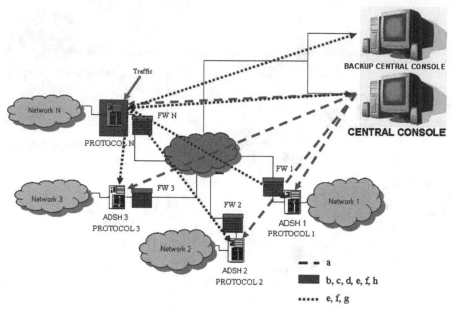

Figure 2: Functional analysis.

a. Assignment of Protocols to the corresponding ADSH.

The Central Console will assign a different protocol to each ADSH, starting from the first (ADSH 1) up to the nth (ADSH N).

b. Captures of traffic in the networks to protect.

Each ADSH will carry out captures of the network traffic as it has been established.

c. Analysis of the traffic inside the ADSH.

In each ADSH certain action patterns are stored together with the necessaries filters, which avoid the system to saturate on false alarms or old alarms. When a new attack is automatically disco-vered, it is added to the filter to avoid detecting it again as a new threat.

d. Phrase and Message Generation.

When an ADSH detects abnormal traffic it should generate a record called *phrase*, which stores the main characteristics of the traffic. The *phrase* is considered as a fluctuation of the normal network traffic and a *message* is considered as the phrase plus the percentage of that phrase. The percentage of a phrase is the percentage of appearance of that phrase on the traffic in a single ADSH on the associated protocol.

e. Registry of the message in the Protocol Console and Send the rest to the corresponding ADSH.

When the message arrives to the Protocol Console (ADSH), it verifies if other ADSHs have issu-ed the same message (LA) and recalculate the global frequency of this abnormality. Other LAs are sent to their corresponding Protocol Console (ADSH).

f. Global alarm detection in the Protocol Console.

The process calculates the number of local alarms from the Protocol Console, then determines a period of time from the last time mark detected, then generates a Lower and Upper limits and detect the elements found within these limits, then calculates the global frequency of each protocol phrase and determines if the percentage is greater that the phrase threshold, possibly there is a Global Alarm.

If there is a Global Alarm, then generated a general format of rule that will be implemented in each corresponding Firewall and send these GA to the Central Console and to the Backup Console.

g. Generation of the reactivates rule for Firewall.

Once sent the general format of rule from the Protocol Console to the rest of the ADSH in the system, each ADSH will adapt it to its firewalls. To do so, it is necessary a database for each network. The critical services must be previously defined, because if the reactivate rule includes critical service the rules will not be established automatically.

h. Generic Rule.

The generic rule [3] will be adapted to different Firewalls that we have in the network (Fig. 3).

These are the steps for implementing a generic rule in firewalls:

Steps:

1. The ADSH will send to the application-FW the GR (Generic Rule) that have found.

2. The application-FW finds the devices in which the GR will be apply depending of the service type (critical or not critical).

2a. No critical service: The rule will be applied directly.

2b. Critical service: The network manager is notified by means of email and SMS (Short Message Service) to his/her mobile telephone handset.

2b1. The manager should be connected to the application Web to accept or to deny the new rule.

2b2. If the manager accepts it, the rule can be applied to the firewall.

3a, 3b, 3c. The system creates the specific rule for each different firewall, to allow its addition to its configuration table. Each one of the rules will be adapted to the different firewalls.

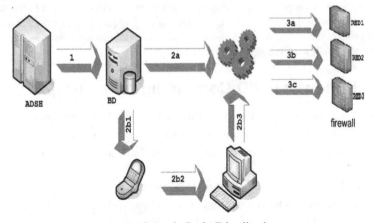

Figure 3: Generic Rule Distribution.

Insertion of critical rules.

When the rule has to be applied to critical services, the manager will receive an email and a message to his/her mobile telephone, notifying that s/he must visit the website because there are rules to be authorized for the Firewall.

Insertion of not critical rules.

In the Web the manager will be able to observe the rules that have been applied automatically and to control whether or not the automatically applied changes are needed.

4 Distributed Architecture

The distributed architecture arises mainly by the lack of resources to process and/or to store information. Many important projects require intensive computing process and in many cases the available calculation is not enough, is for this reason that distributed computing, using the spare CPU resources that are not used during the night or during the day, without disturbing the own processes being executed by the owner of the computer, this parties one of the principles of GRID Computing.

The Grid computing assumes a heterogeneous set of networks (farms), computers, storage devices, scientific visualization and instrument, that allows to manage and to distribute the available computing resources to all the computers connected to the GRID. The interconnection of computers is made through Internet, using communication protocols based on open standards, This allows turning a global network into a **"virtual supercomputer"**. **"One for all and all for one"** [4] [5].

The Grid is a platform, therefore, an interface with for the user is needed, so that the users can handle the resources and services in an easy to use way. This is achieved with the software called Globus Toolkit, that provides services, libraries and utilities; its documentation and the code are open source [6] [7].

We have implemented our system over Globus version 4.0. The GRID platform will allow us to use heterogeneous systems in our project, allowing us to instantiate ADSHs exactly into the strategic points of the net, to achieve the highest level of security in the management of our, work load data distribution in real time, to process the traffic data, suggest immediate response to the possible security threats, and update the firewalls configuration rules in a fast and effective way.

4.1 Contribution of GRID Computing to the project.

The specific objectives of our system that are enabled through this technology are:
- To distribute ADSHs overload, when the anomalous traffic is analyzed.
- Increase the security in the network, when information between the elements of the GRID is transmitted.
- To help the Central Console to process its information.
- To enrol the elements of the network and to assign them their rol in the whole system.
- To build a General Data Base of all the GRID members, in which their characteristics are stored (availability, service pay-load, etc).
- To assign service load to the free ADSHs.
- To manage and to synchronize the network nodes.

5 High availability

A great number of applications need to provide uninterrupted service 24 hours a day, 7 days a week, a very clear case is our system, which requires a continuously available system to provide a service that allows early intrusions detection, which is obtained by means of the capture and traffic analysis continuously.

The main objectives to get with the implantation of the high availability in our system are:

- High performance, so that if there is some failure, the system may be recovered in the shortest possible time and minimal disruption of the system service provision.
- 24x7 Availability, allows the effectiveness and availability of the early detection of attacks on computer systems to be available all the time.
- Redundancy of the service: real time backup of all the information that this circulating around our system.
- Information integrity means that there isn't loss of data, because the recovery of the services would be immediate and automatic.
- High system reliability.

5.1 Benefits that contribute to the project

The benefit that will provide cluster of high availability to our project is the capture and traffic analysis at any moment, allowing this way to early detect the possible attacks to the computer systems.

5.2 Operation

The main element of high availability cluster is the heartbeat. The heartbeat is a system that allows a service or set of services running into two servers to rise the level of service availability, providing failure tolerance in one of servers, without compromising the use of the service [8].

It is installed in the masters (Central Console) and in the slave system, which will be the backup server of the Central Console. The Heartbeat constantly sends requests (heartbeats) from backup server to the Central Console to check if the Central Console is active and working at any time, otherwise the backup server will take its place and the detection system will continue processing the information that is arriving from different ADSH, which constitute the Distributed System [9] [10].

6 Conclusions

This project is innovating to early detect and to prevent the possible attacks that can be generated in the computer networks, through the combination of security features and creating new mechanisms that allow the detection and reaction to such potential attacks.

- A set of innovative tools to detect anomalies produced by non well-known and very difficult to be detected effectively from other tools.
- A taking decisions tools is obtained based on data analysis (of captured traffic).
- The GRID network provides the highest response measures to this type of attacks, allowing the identification of agents through e-signature based mutual recognition mechanisms and validation of e-signature in real time.
- Contribution to the Internet security with early information about new attacks, based on the abnormal behaviour of the compromised nodes of the network.

- High availability in case a problems is presented in the center console or in any node of the network of ADSH,s.
- The advantage of scalability of our distributed system is the flexibility to incorporate new protocols to be analysed and new ADSH nodes to the system without service disruption.

As future work to be carried out, the most urgent are the validation of the system in a real environment, current experiments are being performed in virtual enviroments using the esCERT-UPC (Spanish Computer Emergency Response Team at Polytechnical University of Catalunya) Web server.

Acknowledgment

The development of this project was partially supported by the Spanish government through the Department of Education and Science in the National Plan of R+D + i (2005-2008). To the "National Polytechnical Institute" Mexico, for its support in the development of this project. And finally to the anonymous reviewers, for their comments, that have helped to improve the article.

References

[1]   Sistema de Detección de Intrusiones, http://www.rediris.es/cert/doc/unixsec/node26.html.

[2]   Una aproximación basada en Snort para el desarrollo e implantación de IDS híbridos, J. E. Díaz-Verdejo, Member IEEE, P. García-Teodoro, P. Muñoz, G. Maciá-Fernández y F. de Toro. IEEE Latin America Transactions, VOL, 5, No. 6, October 2007.

[3]   Implementación de regla genérica para cortafuegos (Firewalls) Proyecto Fin de carrera, Elena Galván, Manel Médina, Facultad de Informática de Barcelona, Universidad Politécnica de Cataluña, Barcelona España, 2006.

[4]   The Grid Today. Daily news and information for the global grid community, Sun Microsystems.

[5]   Grid computing, High Computing Performance, Dr. Simon See. Sun Microsystems.

[6]   Globus Toolkit 4.0, Documentation Overview. http://www.globus.org/toolkit/docs/4.0/doc_overview. html.

[7]   Draft. Everything you wanted to know about Globus but were afraid to ask. Describing Globus Toolkit Ver 4.0. Foster.

[8]   Heartbeat manual, http://www.linux-ha.org.

[9]   GIDRE: Entorno de detección y respuesta a intrusiones basado en GRID, Olimpia Olguín, Manel Médina, IGC 2006.

[10]   GIDRE: Environment of Detection and Answer of Intrusions based on GRID. Olimpia Olguín, Manel Médina, IJCSNS Internacional Journal of Computer Science and Network Security, April 2007.

[11]   "OCSP Requirements for Grids". Luna, J., Medina, M. et. al. Open Grid Forum, CA Operations Work Group. Working Document. May, 2005. https://forge.gridforum.org/projects/caops-wg

[12]   "Providing security to the Desktop Data Grid". Luna, J., Medina, M. et. al. Submitted to the CoreGRID PCGrid 2008 Workshop. November, 2007.

[13]   "An analysis of security services in grid storage systems". Luna, J. , Medina, M. et. al. In CoreGRID Workshop on Grid Middleware 2007, June 2007.

[14]   "Towards a Unified Authentication and Authorization Infrastructure for Grid Services: Implementing an enhanced OCSP Service Provider into GT4". Luna J., Manso O., Manel M. 2nd EuroPKI 2005 Workshop. Proceedings by Springer in Lecture Notes in Computer Science series. July 2005. http://sec. cs.kent.ac.uk/europki2005/

Biometrics and ID Cards – Enablers for Personal Security

Andreas Reisen

Head of Division Biometrics, Passports and Identity Documents; Registration
Federal Ministry of the Interior
Andreas.Reisen@bmi.bund.de

Abstract

The electronic ID card is a modernization and security project of the German Government. On the one hand, the multifunctional card is intended to boost security and the convenience of e-government and e-business applications. On the other hand, the new biometric ID card should allow citizens to use it as a travel document in the Schengen area and for specific destinations outside the European Union also in the future.

Whereas the solutions found for the electronic passport may be used also for the new ID card's biometric function, the "Internet function", i.e. electronic authentication and signature, is a completely new challenge. An important feature of these technical innovations is that they can only fully develop their potential if citizens trust in them and use them in everyday life. Data protection and data security have therefore always been central issues when preparing the amended ID card act and technical specifications.

The following paper explores the potential of the new ID card and discusses how its data can be appropriately protected. It focuses on technical, organizational and legal measures which ensure that citizens may actively exercise their right of privacy when using the authentication function.

1 The new ID card functions

1.1 Biometric data only for authorities

The biometric function of the future ID card will be based – like the already introduced passport – on a contactless chip including a digital photograph (full front view) and optionally two fingerprints (fingerprints are included only upon the citizen's request). Thus, the ID card would meet the security level required for travel documents by Regulation (EC) No 2252/2004.[1] As with the ePass[2], access to biometric data will be restricted to specific official control purposes. To implement this requirement not only legally but also technically, there are several instruments developed by the Federal Office for Security in Information Technology including Extended Access Control and the new PACE protocol (Password Authenticated Connection Establishment).

---

[1] Council Regulation (EC) No. 2252/2004 of 13 December 2004 on standards for security features and biometrics in passports and travel documents issued by Member States, published in the Official Journal of the European Union L 385/1, 29 December 2004.

[2] Cf. Section 16a of the German Passport Act (PassG).

N. Pohlmann, H. Reimer, W. Schneider (Editors): Securing Electronic Business Processes, Vieweg (2008), 181-185

1.2 Electronic authentication also for e-business

Contrary to the biometric function, the authentication function including name, address, age and validity of the document will be used for numerous e-business services. Thus, both the public and private sector will be able to provide services on the Internet which require secure identification for authentication or security reasons and therefore have not been provided online so far. In addition to completely new services, the electronic ID card will facilitate registration and login procedures because users will no longer have to remember dozens of PINs and passwords for different services but ideally will be able to use all services with their ID card and one single PIN.

With the ID card, fully electronic transactions will be possible also for those services which today require the written form and are not offered online for lack of nation-wide electronic signature schemes. The optional signature function of the new ID card may close this gap and finally end the era of PDF applications and contracts which can be downloaded but then usually have to be signed manually and sent by mail.

Against this background, the range of services for which the electronic ID card could be used in future seems to be unlimited. In e-government, the ID card could be used for mass procedures such as changing registration details for persons or vehicles or applying for government services online.

In e-business, it might be used for online banking, online shopping or online auctions. The private sector could benefit not only from the high reliability of identification procedures but also from the new function for the protection of young people: By transmitting the age, access of young people to harmful contents may be restricted, e.g. online forums or video-on-demand via the Internet. This option will also be useful outside the Internet, e.g. tobacco and slot machines. Outside the Internet, the electronic authentication with the ID card may be used also in areas where it is already being used for identification, e.g. checking in at a hotel and collecting registered mail or parcels at the post office.

2 Data protection precautions

2.1 Informed, targeted action

Regarding the ID card's electronic authentication function, data protection law requires that the card holder is able to decide on the use of identification, i.e. the transmission of personal data to third parties, in an informed and targeted manner. This was taken into account when developing the authentication function, so that the ID card must be physically available and a personal identification number (PIN) must be entered to transmit personal data to third parties. Hence, action by the card holder is always required.

However, card holders can reasonably decide on the transfer of personal data only if they are sufficiently informed about the contents and conditions of this transfer. This in particular includes valid information on *who* will receive the data, *which* personal data are to be transmitted and *for which purpose*.

2.2 Certificates for responsible bodies

So far it has not been clear who requested data of citizens (the body responsible for processing personal data). Although websites, for example, need to include the details of the one responsible for the website, it is still possible to (illegally) enter random data. In case of foreign websites – if there is such an obligation – these data often cannot be verified. How relevant this issue is in practice is also demonstrated by the phenomenon of phishing where citizens are misled about the entity requesting data.

The authentication function of the ID card is intended to prevent this by allowing access to valid personal data from the ID card only if the responsible body has an electronic certificate. This certificate shown to the card holder includes verified information about the certificate holder. The transmission of personal data to a body with a false identity will thus be much more difficult.

2.3 Data categories and purpose of the transfer

The access certificate will include information on the data categories (e.g. name, address, date of birth, etc.) requested by the responsible body and to be submitted by the ID card holder.

However, to be able to make a sound decision on the transfer of personal data, it is crucial that the holder is aware of the purpose of the data transmission. Therefore, the access certificate will include a short, concise explanation on how the data will be used.

On this basis the ID card holder can decide whether to transmit the requested data to the responsible body for the stated purpose. If so, the holder may authorize access to the data by entering a PIN. If the holder does not wish to transmit data, he/she may request further information (e.g. on data protection declarations) from the responsible body.

2.4 Data economy

In line with Section 3a of the Federal Data Protection Act the authentication function should be designed in such a way that access certificates are issued only for those data categories which can be used regularly, reasonably and legally in the intended e-government and e-business scenarios. This includes the following categories: name, first name, address and date of birth, and the expiry date of the ID card to verify its validity. The following categories are not included: digital photo, fingerprints, height and eye colour because these data only serve to clearly link the document to its holder. During online authentication, this link is established by producing the document and entering the PIN.

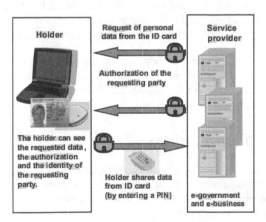

Figure 1: Opening a customer account with an electronic ID card

As described above, the electronic ID card should also be used to protect young people and prevent addiction. Especially in these contexts, however, a complete proof of identity is often not required or desired, but only proof of a certain minimum or maximum age. Therefore, it will not be necessary to request the entire birth date, but the access certificate will transmit a sufficiently current date which the ID card can use to verify whether the required age limit is met and send back a positive or negative value.

2.5 Data necessity

For many people there is no easy answer to the question whether certain data really need to be transmitted for a certain purpose since this would require knowledge about the further processing and business procedures. Whereas everyone understands that an address is necessary to ship goods, the verification of the age when entering a cigarette manufacturer's website might not be considered common sense that easily.

In such situations citizens should be supported by carrying out a plausibility check of the requested data categories and of the indicated purpose when issuing access certificates to the responsible bodies. This approach may give ID card holders the certainty that the transfer of verified ID card data really serves the indicated business purpose.

2.6 Key in line with data protection law

Numerous online services are based on a registration with the users' personal data. If the users return to the service, they usually log in using a name and a password. Such a login becomes more secure, and the misuse of user accounts can be reduced if the ID card is additionally used in its physical form.

However, a repeated login requires a unique identifying feature since account data are not to be disclosed to persons with the same name or address, for example. But it is neither permissible nor desirable that citizens use a uniform identifying feature for all sectors and transmit it via the authentication function to the responsible bodies.

When opening an online account, the ID card holder should therefore be able to use a key generated from a key of the responsible body and the ID card. On the one hand, this procedure allows for repeated logins to a specific service, on the other hand it prevents the identity of the ID card holder from being revealed through the key. The key can be used only by the ID card holder for an individual service.

Such a key in line with data protection law contributes to meeting existing demand without having to resort to unlawful solutions such as the use of serial numbers or key certificates. At the same time it can be ensured that the legal bans on serial numbers and the pending legal protection of the technically required key certificate are implemented in practice.

2.7 Control by ID card holders

In addition to the aforementioned technical and organizational solutions for the protection of privacy when using the authentication function, legal provisions will be needed to support these solutions. However, especially in international and online contexts legal provisions can only be effective if their implementation is controlled and enforced.

The comprehensive transparency functions described above allow citizens to actively control who uses which of their personal data and how. The aim is to take some burden from the authorities responsible for monitoring data protection so they have more possibilities to support the implementation of legal provisions.

2.8 Implementation by the responsible data protection authorities

The Federal Commissioner for Data Protection and Freedom of Information, the 16 *Land* Data Protection Commissioners and the 16 data protection supervisory authorities for the private sector are responsible for monitoring the processing of personal data and punishing violations of data protection provisions.

In the event that an ID card holder suspects a violation of privacy, it should be easy for him/her to contact the responsible data protection supervisory authority. Therefore, also the address and e-mail address of the supervisory authority are included in the aforementioned certificate.

2.9 Proof of identity in an international context

It may be expected that responsible bodies in Europe and in third countries will also be interested in using the electronic proof of identity via ID card.

For reasons of equal treatment, especially companies within the European Union will have to be authorized to use the authentication function. Due to the European data protection directive, it may be assumed that the level of data protection is the same as in Germany. The directive also includes provisions on data protection supervisory authorities which may assume a similar monitoring and implementing function.

The use of the authentication function outside the European Union should depend on the Art. 29 group's recognition instruments for adequate data protection standards in line with the European data protection directive in these non-European countries or companies (e.g. members of the Safe Harbour Agreement).

3 Conclusions

In the coming weeks and months, the presented plans on data protection precautions for the electronic ID card will be discussed at two levels: in the course of the parliament procedure for adopting the new ID card act and in a dialogue between data protection stakeholders, consumer associations and potential providers of online services, i.e. e-government and e-business. In addition to systematically evaluating the comments on the published concept for the introduction of the electronic ID card, the Federal Ministry of the Interior will organize various events to collect ideas from different groups in the fields of politics, administration, industry and society to include these ideas in the detailed planning of the project. If the law is successfully adopted, the first electronic ID cards will be issued on 1 November 2010.

Agatha: Multimodal Biometric Authentication Platform in Large-Scale Databases

David Hernando[1] · David Gómez[1] · Javier Rodríguez Saeta[1]
Pascual Ejarque[2] · Javier Hernando[2]

[1]Biometric Technologies S.L., Barcelona, Spain
{d.hernando | d.gomez | j.rodriguez}@biometco.com

[2]TALP Research Center
Universitat Politècnica de Catalunya, Spain
{pascual | javier}@gps.tsc.upc.edu

Abstract

Biometric technologies are each time more demanded for security applications. In this sense, systems for identifying people are gaining popularity, especially in governmental sectors, and forensic applications have climbed to the top of the list when talking about biometrics. However, some problems still remain as cornerstones in identification processes, all of them linked to the length of the databases in which the individual is supposed to be. The speed and the error are parameters that depend on the number of users in the database and measure the quality of the whole system.

In this paper, two different biometric technologies are used in order to increase speed and shorten error rates. Face recognition –normally faster than speaker recognition – is used to select a group of individuals and speaker recognition provides a finer adjustment. Multimodality plays an important role not only reducing the search time but also providing lower error rates.

1 Introduction

The number of biometric applications has increased a lot in the last few years, especially from the 11th of September of 2001. Concerns about security have been raising and each time more, biometric systems are playing an important role in order to protect networks or buildings. The automatic person recognition by some physical traits like fingerprints, face, voice or iris, has a very high demand around the world and the technology is already mature.

Speaker and face recognition technologies have increased their popularity in a market dominated by fingerprint technologies. Speaker recognition is not the most used technology but it is expected that will be much more important in the future, especially for voice portals in the Internet. In the case of face recognition, its use is growing every day because of low intrusiveness and the facility of capturing images.

There are other kind of biometric applications in where speaker recognition has experienced a high increase: forensic applications. In this type of applications, speaker recognition is used to prove if the evidence belongs to the suspect or not. Forensic speaker recognition is also used to identify speakers

N. Pohlmann, H. Reimer, W. Schneider (Editors): Securing Electronic Business Processes, Vieweg (2008), 186-193

looking for a certain voice in a database of suspects. Police forces in lots of European countries and also the FBI in the USA have speaker databases for this purpose.

Main characteristics –common to this type of applications- are the great amount of recorded data, because recordings are usually acquired without the consciousness of the person being recorded; the text-independence, although there is not any dependent text but also natural speaking; and finally the fact that data usually comes from the telephone lines because we are dealing basically with recorded conversations.

With regard to face recognition, its forensic view is very clear. The identification of suspects in a public place like an airport or a train station is an application every time more demanded. Police forces around the world have databases with photographs of criminals. When they get an image of an individual, they wish to identify as soon as possible if this person is in the database. They want to know who the unknown suspect is.

The aim of this paper is the implementation of an identification platform by means of speaker recognition, face recognition or the combination of both of them (multimodality). The system will be used in criminalistic or security environments. The present project intends to provide a solution to the problem of identifying an individual in large-scale databases from biometric characteristics by taking them individually or by using a combination of voice and face. The system will return the N most probable users ordered by probability. It is not necessary to make the identification in real time but it is important that results will be provided in a reasonable time depending on the technology available.

Speaker identification is a very complex task that it does not normally occur very fast with large databases. On the other hand, face identification can be much faster, although error identification rates strongly depend on the way of acquiring images.

This project wants to create a tool for speaker recognition, a technology in where much more investigation can be done, and face recognition to be used together. Both biometrics will be fused in the case that we have both kinds of data from the user. The high identification speed of face identification can be a perfect complementary technology to increase speed in speaker identification. Face identification system can provide, in an initial identification, the N most probable candidates. In this case, the combination of both biometric technologies is not only used to improve error rates but also to increase speed in speaker recognition, a biometric technology in where traditionally it had been impossible to identify speakers in real time.

Finally, it is worth noting that one of the main interesting points of the platform is that it gathers in a unique system both types of identification at the same time, giving the possibility of using one of them individually, speaker or face recognition, or in parallel.

2 Search strategies

The speed of biometric identification algorithms can be a big issue for large population applications which require a short delay. If no search strategy is used, a full search approach entails a linear increase of the identification delay with the number of clients registered in the system. Therefore, the goal of search strategies is to achieve reasonable identification delays for the target application while maintaining the system performance, with a minor degradation. In this section, we review some approaches that have been proposed in the literature and then we introduce a method to reduce the identification delay in a multimodal framework.

Based on a recognition algorithm using HMMs (typically for text-dependent recognition) or GMMs (text-independent recognition), usually adapted to an individual speaker using MAP from a reference universal background model (UBM) [Reynolds95], some methods have been proposed in speaker recognition to speed-up the identification process and to reduce the computational cost.

A simple strategy reported in [McLaughin99] studies the system degradation just by reducing the number of components in the speaker model as well as decimating the test sample. For instance, reducing from 2048 to 512 components leads to less than a 1% loss in EER. Regarding the decimation, the paper shows how discarding 90% of frames, i.e., with a decimation factor of 10, the EER only increases by 1%.

In [Reynolds95], for each speech frame, only the mixtures with the highest scores against the UBM are used to match the test feature vector with each speaker model in the identification process. Other methods build a hierarchical set of speaker models. In [Beigi99], the GMM models are merged in pairs in an iterative way, building a tree structure with two models on the top. Similarly, the ISODATA clustering algorithm is applied in [Sun03] to this task achieving speed-up factors from 3:1 to 6:1 with almost no degradation respect to the full-search strategy.

Another approaches [Auckenthaler01] compute a hash model from a large GMM model which consists of a reduced number of mixtures indexing a list of the best expected scoring components in the large model. For instance, given a model of 512 mixtures, a hash model of 32 mixtures indexing at least 16 components of the large model results in the scoring of just 48 mixtures per frame instead of the original 512. With a minor degradation, [Aunckenthaler01] reports a speed-up factor of 10:1.

A speaker pruning can be done with the model proposed in [Pellom98]. The input sequence is processed as usual but a reduced selection of nonadjacent frames is first scored against the speaker models. Speakers with lower scores are discarded before repeating the selection with a higher number of frames and updating the accumulated probability of each speaker model. This process is repeated until no speakers are pruned out or the complete input signal is evaluated. The authors presented a time reduction by a factor of 140 over the full search with this method.

In [Kinnunen06] an extensive summary of speed-up approaches is presented and some of them are applied to a vector quantization (VQ) based speaker identification system. In this work, the input frames are pre-quantized in order to reduce the number of feature vectors used to score the input signal against the set of speakers. Four different pre-quantization techniques are used: random subsampling, averaging, decimation and clustering. Together with a speaker pruning method they achieve a speed-up factor of 16:1 with minor degradation in the identification performance.

In general, face identification is faster than voice. The algorithm used in this work reaches delays as low as 0.5 seconds for a two hundred clients database. However, the speaker identification process with a full search needs about 19 seconds for an average speech signal duration of 6.7 seconds.

A multimodal identification platform that combines speech and face can exploit the high speed of face recognition to make a search in a reduced set of speakers. We explore in this work a simple method to reduce the total identification delay by a factor of 8:1 with a slight increase in error identification rates.

Our approach starts with a full search with the face recognition system followed by a selection of the N clients with the highest confidence scores. Then, with the speaker recognition system we search only among the reduced set of N clients. Finally, we fuse both modalities results and if the highest score is over a previously estimated threshold we determine that we have a positive identification.

We will discuss in section 4 how this method gives a higher weight to the modality where the first pruning is done. In this case, it is the face algorithm. Therefore, for small values of N, the performance of each algorithm can lead to an increase or to a decrease of the error rates.

3 Multimodal fusion

A multimodal biometric system involves the combination of two or more human characteristics (voice, face, fingerprints, iris, hand geometry, etc.) in order to achieve better results than using unimodal recognition systems [Bolle04]. Furthermore, the use of several biometrics makes the system more robust to noise or spoof attacks.

When several biometric traits are used in a multimodal recognition system, fusion is usually accomplished at three different levels: feature extraction level, matching score level or decision level.

Fusion at the matching score level is performed for the multimodal fusion of two unimodal experts: a speaker and a face recognition system. Matching score level fusion needs a previous score normalization step before the fusion itself [Fox03,Indovina03].

Since unimodal scores are usually non-homogeneous, the normalization process transforms the different scores of each unimodal system into a comparable range of values. The state-of-the-art Z-score technique, that normalizes the global mean and variance of the scores, has been used for the normalization of the unimodal biometrics. The normalized scores x_{ZS} are computed as

$$x_Z = \frac{a - mean(a)}{std(a)}$$

where $mean(a)$ is the statistical mean of the set of scores a, and $std(a)$ is its standard deviation.

After normalization, the converted scores are combined in the fusion process in order to obtain a single multimodal score. Matcher weighting, one of the most conventional fusion techniques for the arithmetic combination of the scores, has been used for the fusion process. For the application of this technique, each unimodal score is weighted according to its accuracy, so that the weights for more accurate matchers are higher than for those of less accurate matchers. The weighting factor for every biometric is proportional to the inverse of its EER. Denoting x^m, w^m and e^m the set of scores, the weigthing factor and the EER for the mth biometric, and M the number of biometrics, the fused score u is computed as:

$$u = \sum_{m=1}^{M} w^m x^m$$

,

where

$$w^m = \frac{\dfrac{1}{e^m}}{\displaystyle\sum_{m=1}^{M} \dfrac{1}{e^m}}.$$

4 Experiments

4.1 Experimental setup

The XM2VTS database and the Lausanne evaluation protocol (Configuration I) [Luettin98] have been used in this work. The database contains speech recordings and face images from 295 users, 200 clients and 95 impostors. It is organized in 4 sessions with 2 shots per session. Furthermore, each shot is formed by 1 front face image and two speaking sequences of 10 digits each, which yields a total number of 8 face images and 16 speech signals per user. For our experiments, scores from both speech signals in each shot are averaged.

In the speaker recognition system [Saeta06], speech utterances are processed in 25 ms frames, Hamming windowed and pre-emphasized. The feature set is formed by 12th order Mel-Frequency Cepstral Coefficients (MFCC) and the normalized log energy. Delta and delta-delta parameters are computed to form a 39-dimensional vector for each frame. Cepstral Mean Subtraction (CMS) is also applied.

Left-to-right HMM models with 2 states per phoneme and 4 mixture components per state are obtained for each digit. Client and world models have the same topology. Gaussian Mixture Models (GMM) of 32 mixture components are employed to model silence.

The identification platform uses Neurotechnology's VeriLook for face recognition. This engine is composed of five main modules. *Face detector* searches any number of faces in a grayscale image with different scales and head rotation. *Facial feature detector* estimates eyes position before that the *feature extractor* module computes discriminating facial features by means of Gabor wavelets. When several templates of the same face are available, a more precise recognition can be achieved by means of the *features generalization* technique which combines them to deal with intra-class variability. Finally, *feature matcher* module compares two templates.

4.2 Results

According to the Configuration I of the Lausanne protocol, client models are trained with the first shot of sessions 1, 2 and 3. In the evaluation phase the second shot of the same client sessions and all the data from a set of 25 impostors are used to obtain a user independent threshold that gives the Equal Error Rate (EER) in this dataset. Finally, in the test phase, both shots from the last client session and 70 impostors are used to measure the Half Total Error Rate (HTER) given by the threshold previously estimated. EER is also given for the test set to show the increase of error due to the database partition as it is explained below.

Table 1 illustrates the system performance in terms of identification error for each individual biometric modality, speech and face, and the fusion of both.

Table 1: Identification errors

	FACE	VOICE	FUSION
EER – eval	1.56%	1.20%	0.29%
HTER – test	4.60%	4.75%	1.00%
EER – test	2.22%	4.17%	0.97%

Table 2: FP and FN in test set for EER-eval threshold

	FACE	VOICE	FUSION
FPt	7.71%	2.00%	0.74%
FNt	1.50%	7.50%	1.25%

Voice performs better than face for the evaluation set, with an accuracy almost a 25 % higher. However, whereas identification delay is about 0.5s for face recognition, it takes an average of 19s for speaker identification in a 200 client database. In addition, the EER degradation in the test set with regard to the evaluation set is more remarkable for voice than for face, probably due to the use of speech sequences from the same sessions for training and evaluation and a different session for the test set.

Figure 1 shows fusion error curves for both, evaluation and test sets. Figure 2 shows in detail the intersection of these curves, where the values in table 1 can be observed.

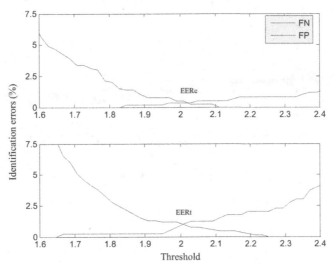

Figure 1: FP and FN for evaluation (top) and test (bottom) sets

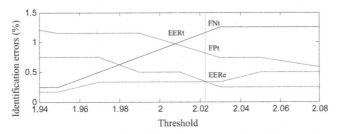

Figure 2: Evaluation and test identification errors from Tables 1 and 2

The search strategy described in section 2 is used in order to reduce recognition delay. Table 3 shows evaluation and test errors as the pre-selected number of faces, N, is reduced. Identification delay is also shown.

In Table 1 we observe that voice performs better than face. In contrast, for the test set face biometrics overcomes voice biometrics in terms of error rate. In our opinion, it can explain why the HTER increases in the evaluation set when a smaller number of faces is pre-selected, and a minor weight is given to the voice recognition system. However, in the test set, giving a higher weight to face recognition discards potential errors in voice recognition, and reduces the HTER when N decreases.

Table 3: HTER for different values of N

N	200	100	50	20	10	5	3	1
eval	0.29	0.50	0.56	0.65	0.71	0.79	1.00	1.00
test	0.97	0.85	0.46	0.28	0.23	0.51	0.51	0.74
delay (s)	19	10	5.2	2.4	1.5	1.1	0.9	0.7

Figures 3 and 4 show graphically results from Table 3. We can see that the HTER remains practically unalterable from N=60 faces because the true identity is in most cases within the pre-selected faces. In addition, we can see that for N<10 faces the system performance is similar to the unimodal case with face recognition.

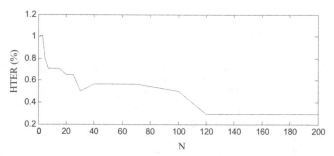

Figure 3: HTER in the evaluation set

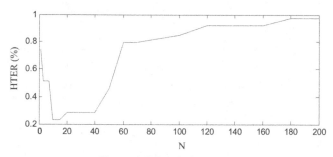

Figure 4: HTER in the test set

5 Conclusions

Biometric technologies are commonly used to enhance security and control the right to access to certain places. Forensic applications are not included in access control ones but they are becoming really important. They normally use large-scale databases and try to identify an individual among a group of previously enrolled users. Main challenges have to deal with the length of the databases, the identification delay and the performance in terms of EER. On the other hand, multimodal applications are also gaining popularity and can help to cope with the challenges mentioned before.

In this paper, we introduce a method to profit from the speed of face recognition with regard to speaker recognition to identify users in multimodal databases. Face recognition is used as the main engine to select a reduced number of speakers and speaker recognition provides an adjustment to improve speed as well as error rates. The final result can be seen as a trade-off between the identification delay and the error performance. The lower error is obtained for a selection of ten users through face recognition while lower delay is obviously provided for only one.

Acknowledgements

This work has been partially funded by the AGATHA project from the Spanish Ministry of Industry, Tourism and Trade.

References

[Auckenthaler01] Auckenthaler R., Mason J.S.: Gaussian selection applied to text-independent speaker verification. In Proc. Speaker Odyssey: The Speaker Recognition Workshop (Odyssey 2001), Crete, Greece, 2001, pp.83-88.

[Beigi99]   Beigi H.S.M., Maes S.H., Sorensen J.S., Chaudhari U.V.: A hierarchical approach to large-scale speaker recognition. In Proc. 6th European Conf. Speech Communication and Technology (Eurospeech 1999). Budapest, 1999.

[Bolle04]   Bolle R. M., Connell J. H., Pankanti S., Ratha N. K., and Senior A. W.: Guide to Biometrics. Editor: Springer, New York. 2004.

[Fox03]   Fox N. A., Gross R., Chazal P., Cohn J. F., and Reilly R. B.: Person identification using automatic integration of speech, lip and face experts. In ACM SIGMM 2003 Multimedia Biometrics Methods and Applications Workshop, Berkeley, CA, 2003.

[Kinnunen06] Kinnunen T., Karpov E., Fränti P.: Real-Time Speaker Identification and Verification. In IEEE Transactions on Audio, Speech, and Language Processing, vol. 14, no. 1, January 2006.

[Indovina03] Indovina M., Uludag U., Snelik R., Mink A., and Jain A.: Multimodal Biometric Authentication Methods: A COTS Approach. In MMUA, Workshop on Multimodal User Authentication, Santa Barbara, CA, 2003.

[Luettin98] Luettin J., Maitre G.: Evaluation protocol for the XM2FDB database (Lausanne protocol). In Communication 98-05, IDIAP, Martigny, Switzerland, 1998

[McLaughlin99] McLaughlin J., Reynolds D.A., Gleason T.: A study of computation speed-ups of the GMM-UBM speaker recognition system. In Proc. 6th European Conf. Speech Communication and Technology (Eurospeech 1999). Budapest, 1999.

[Pellom98]   Pellom B.L., Hansen J.H.L.: An efficient scoring algorithm for gaussian mixture model based speaker identification. In IEEE Signal Process. Lett. vol. 5, no 11, pp. 281-284, 1998

[Reynolds95] Reynolds D.A., Rose R.C.: Robust text-independent speaker identification using gaussian mixture speaker models. In IEEE Trans. Speech Audio Process., vol. 3, no. 1, pp. 72-83. 1995.

[Saeta06]   Saeta J.R., Hernando J.: Weighting scores to improve speaker-dependent threshold estimation in text-dependent speaker verification. In Lecture Notes in Computer Science. Editor: Springer-Verlag, vol. 3817, 2006, pp. 81-91.

[Sun03]   Sun B., Liu W., Zhong Q.: Hierarchical speaker identification using speaker clustering. In Proc. Int. Conf. Natural Language Processing and Knowledge Engineering 2003, Beijin, China, 2003, pp. 299-304.

Web 2.0 Security and Large Scale Public Applications

Development and Implementation of an Encryption Strategy for a global Enterprise

Guido von der Heidt

Siemens AG
Corporate Information Technology, CIT G ISEC
guido.von_der_heidt@siemens.com

Abstract

Encryption is a main instrument of Information Security Management to ensure confidentiality of electronic information and communications.

Following an information centric security approach based on risk management and information classification we develop an encryption strategy for a global enterprise and describe the implementation of this strategy in a case study on Siemens Corporation.

1 Introduction

Encryption controls are main elements of an Information Security Management Program to ensure confidentiality and with restrictions integrity of data and communications. Industrial espionage, (targeted) attacks against IT-enabled business processes, data privacy protection requirements, etc. increase the need for deploying encryption technologies and a variety of encryption products and solutions are available on the market. However, encryption technologies often are still not widely adopted or used in isolated scenarios only.

In this presentation we describe the development and implementation of an encryption strategy for a global enterprise based on a case study on Siemens Corporation.

Following an universal information centric security approach based on risk management, information classification and specific influencing factors – in particular the technical environment the dare processed in – we derive at first a generic Encryption Framework defining and prioritizing the demand for encryption.

In the second part of the presentation we discuss encryption technologies and business/IT-related requirements for encryption solutions. The identified encryption solutions are mapped to the Encryption Framework and a general Encryption Technology Deployment Strategy is developed.

In the last section we present the implementation of the described encryption strategy at Siemens, measure the current implementation degree and discuss open issues. As specific aspect for global enterprises we allude to the deployment of encryption technology in face of international regulations for import, export and use of encryption products.

N. Pohlmann, H. Reimer, W. Schneider (Editors): Securing Electronic Business Processes, Vieweg (2008), 197-207

2 Definition of an Encryption Framework

Confidentiality, Integrity, Availability and Liability are considered as core principles of Information Security. Thereby, confidentiality is defined as "preventing disclosure of information to unauthorized individuals or systems".

In order to determine appropriate confidentiality protection measures for a certain information asset an information centric security approach based on the classification of the information and an individual risk management is pursued, cf. the NIST Risk Management Framework [NIST02].

From Risk to Measures ...

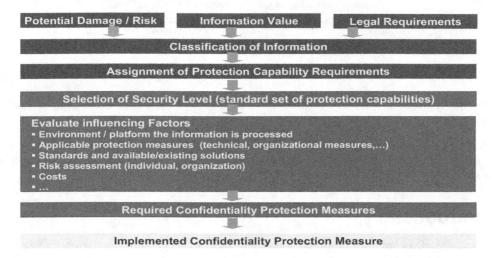

Figure 1: Information centric Security Approach to determine Confidentiality Protection Measures

2.1 Classification and Assignment of Security Levels

Information classification is a well-established practice in many companies and organizations. Classification means the categorization of (proprietary) information in classes with similar damage potential in case of unwanted disclosure of the information. Main factors for the classification of an information asset are:

- Damage / business impact of unwanted disclosure of the information
- Value of the information
- Legal and regulatory requirements (e. g. data protection laws)
- For this paper we assume a classification scheme consisting of 4 information classes:
- "Public"
- "Internal"
- "Confidential"
- "Strictly Confidential"

For each of these classes we define basic conditions for accessing information of the respective class and an required quality level for controlling the access. The access control and it's enforcement must comply with the confidentiality requirements of the respective class, i.e. the higher the confidentiality class the higher the required quality of the access control. In order to determine the quality levels we define a standard set of protection capabilities which must be met for each class:

- Access control enforcement capabilities
- Capabilities for proof of identity
- Authorization capabilities

These sets of protection capabilities form default security levels which are assigned to the information class. The following Tables give a generic definition of the 4 information classes and the assigned security levels.

Table 1: Information Classes

Classification	Definition	Access Conditions
Public	Public information	No requirements
Internal	Proprietary information with potential damaging consequences in case of unwanted disclosure	All employees / members of an organization can have access to the information.
		The information is not intended for outsiders but defined external partners can have access (e. g. in course of a contractual relationship).
		No further specification of authorization rules by the information owner
Confidential	Proprietary information with high business impact.	Only a defined group of users (.e . g. based on roles) is authorized to have access.
	Unwanted disclosure can bring substantial (financial) damage.	The group of authorized users is defined by the information owner.
Strictly Confidential	Proprietary information with very high business impact.	Only a explicitly named group of users is authorized to have access.
	Unwanted disclosure can bring severe (financial) damage.	The group of authorized users is defined by the information owner.

Table 2: Security Levels

Classification	Security Level	
	Access Control Enforcement	Proof of Identity / Authorization
Public	No requirements	No requirements
Internal	Authorization rules (if available) are applied to "standard" users	Simple proof of identity required, e. g. by possession of a device
	Privileged users (e. g. IT administrators) exist, authorization rules are not under control of the information owner	All users with sufficient access rights can define authorizations
Confidential	Authorization rules are applied to all users (if possible)	Explicit proof of identity required, the digital identity must be explicitly assignable to a person, team, etc.
	Privileged users may exist, access by privileged users is restricted and controllable	
	Fail-secure access	Explicit authorization rules required
	Negative access decisions and access by privileged users are traceable	Only a group of users defined by the information owner can define authorization rules
Strictly Confidential	Authorization rules are applied consequently to all users	Non-repudiation of proof of identity required, the digital identity must be explicitly assignable to a person
	No privileged users	
	Fail-secure access	Explicit authorization rules required
	All access control decisions are traceable	Only the information owner defines authorization rules

2.2 Scenarios and Risk Assessment

The definition of protection measures to realize a selected security level is significantly impacted by influencing factors such as:

- Environment and technical platform the information is processed or stored
- Applicable protection measures
  - Technical measures
  - Organization measures
  - Process measures
- Standards
- Available/existing products and solutions
- Specific business risks
- Individual risk assessment
- Costs

In particular the environment and the technical platform electronic information are processed is essential.

Finding appropriate protection measures for an individual information asset which comply with the selected security class is a complex process. In order to manage this process we define standard scenarios for the environment data are processed, perform a risk assessment for this scenarios and define an encryption framework based upon this scenarios.

We differentiate the following environments/platforms:

Networks

- Internal Networks – Networks exclusively managed for the company/organization by an internal service provider or IT department, e. g. LANs
- Outsourced Networks – Networks operated by an external service provider and leased or managed for the company/organization, e. g. WANs
- Public Networks – Public available/accessible networks, e. g. Internet, public telecommunication networks or wireless networks

Exposure to unwanted Disclosure

Systems

- Internal systems – Systems or applications in the intranet managed exclusively for the company/organization by an internal service provider or IT department
- Outsourced systems – Systems or applications in the Intranet managed for the company/organization by an external service provider, e. g. application service providing
- Extranet Systems – Systems accessible from external/public networks
- Mobile Systems – Mobile devices and removable media, e. g. notebooks, PDAs, USB sticks etc.

Exposure to unwanted Disclosure

The networks and systems are listed with increasing exposure to unwanted disclosure of information. Public systems are not considered since we assume here that storage/processing of classified data on public system is not allowed at all.

By mapping this characteristic with the confidentiality level of the information classes we obtain the basic risk assessment described in Figure 2.

The Y-axis lists the environments according to the exposure to unwanted information disclosure and the X-axis lists the information classes according to the confidentiality level and its averaged share in the total information volume.

Obviously, the business risk increases with the confidentiality of an information and the exposure to unwanted information disclosure of the network/system the information is processed. The greyscales in the diagram indicate a high, medium and low business risk.

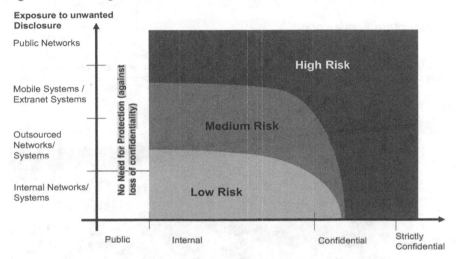

Figure 2: Scenarios and Basic Risk Assessment

2.3 Encryption Framework

Encryption and authentication technologies provide recognized, effective and efficient protection measures to meet the security levels and the corresponding access control requirements as defined in section 2.1:

- For electronic transmission of information there is basically no alternative to encryption available to ensure a reliable protection against unwanted disclosure.
- Authentication methods based on passwords, smart cards, tokens, biometrics etc. are standards and well-established practice realizing different levels of quality for proof of identity of authorized users accessing an information asset.
- Encryption of data at rest complements access control implementations in certain scenarios (e.g. protection against theft of notebooks or unauthorized access by privileged users)

From the protection capabilities required for the information classes and the risk assessment developed in section 2.2 we now derive an Encryption Framework.

The Encryption Framework described in Figure 3 defines the need for encryption and authentication for an information asset determined by the information class and the environment the information is processed. We differentiate between a "mandatory" use of encryption and the stated (minimum) authentication strength, a "recommended" use and use "on (individual) demand".

Authentication methods are covered by the Encryption Framework since encryption and authentication technologies complement one another. "Weak Authentication" refers to a one-factor authentication, e.g. password or a possession of a device. "Strong Authentication" refers to two-factor authentication such as smart card and PIN.

Encryption Framework

Mandatory
Recommended
On demand
- Not required

Classification / Security Level	Data in Motion: Public Network	Data in Motion: Outsourced Network	Data in Motion: Internal Networks	Data at Rest / Data Processed: Outsourced Systems	Data at Rest / Data Processed: Internal Systems	Data at Rest / Data Processed: Extranet Systems	Data at Rest / Data Processed: Mobile Devices
Public	-	-	-	-	-	-	-
Internal	Encryption	Encryption	-	Encryption Weak Auth.	- Weak Auth.	Encryption Strong Auth	Encryption Weak Auth.
Confidential	Encryption	Encryption	Encryption	Encryption Strong Auth.	Encryption Strong Auth.	Encryption Strong Auth.	Encryption Strong Auth.
Strictly Confidential	Encryption	Encryption	Encryption	Encryption Strong Auth.	Encryption Strong Auth.	Encryption Strong Auth.	Encryption Strong Auth.

Figure 3: Encryption Framework

3 Development of an Encryption Technology Deployment Strategy

3.1 Encryption Technologies

Looking at various encryption technologies we can distinguish encryption on network layer versus encryption on application layer, transport encryption of data in motion versus encryption of data at rest and gateway-to-gateway encryption versus end-to-end encryption.

In general, encryption on network layer (i.e. protocol layer 1 – 3) is independent from the data transported and thus suitable for a broad range of use. However, it provides transport encryption only and does not protect data at rest. Usually, the encryption is a gateway-to-gateway encryption and it does not provide end-to-end security and protection against internal attackers or unauthorized access by privileged users.

Encryption on application layer applies for a specific application or (communication) system only. On the other hand application/system specific encryption technologies can be used to encrypt data in motion and data at rest. Furthermore, they support scenarios where an end-to-end encryption between users or user and application system is required. Thus, application/system specific encryption solutions can protect against internal attackers and prevent unauthorized access by privileged users.

Network and application / system specific encryption complement one another and the encryption properties discussed above lead to the following basic approach for using encryption technologies.

Application specific encryption solutions should be used for an information centric protection of confidential and strictly confidential information where according to the defined classification scheme only a defined user group is authorized to have access and reliable protection capabilities are required.

Network encryption should be used as a basic protection for all classified information when sent over public or outsourced networks in order to protect against most simple eavesdropping by (professional) external attackers. Furthermore, network encryption can provide a fall-back solution for applications which do not allow a suitable encryption on application layer.

When selecting encryption solutions business and IT related requirements such as usability, interoperability, manageability, key management capabilities, and cryptographic strength need to be considered.

It is needless to mention that usability and transparency are prerequisites for the user acceptance and that encryption algorithms and strengths of cryptographic keys must comply with international recognized standards. Manageability and scalability are key factors for the deployment of encryption solutions in large scale organizations and a weakness of many current encryption solutions.

For encrypting data at rest the key management must support reliable and efficient processes for emergency data recovery and recovery of encryption keys. In particular, centralized key recovery processes become crucial to meet regulatory e-discovery requirements.

3.2 Encryption Technology Deployment Strategy

In order to develop a concrete strategy for the deployment of encryption technologies we examine common enterprise networks, systems and applications and prioritize them with respect to their significance, their spreading in the company/organization, the data processed and the risks according to the risk assessment described in Figure 2. By applying the Encryption Framework and mapping the encryption technologies discussed in the previous section to these networks, systems and applications we obtain the Encryption Technology Deployment Strategy shown in Figure 4.

Black boxes in the diagram mean a "mandatory" deployment, grey boxes a deployment "on demand" with high priority (urgency) and white boxes a deployment "on demand" (with a lower priority).

The deployment on demand should comply with the guidelines of the Encryption Framework. Deviations are possible based on an individual business risk assessment and whether alternative protection measures can be applied.

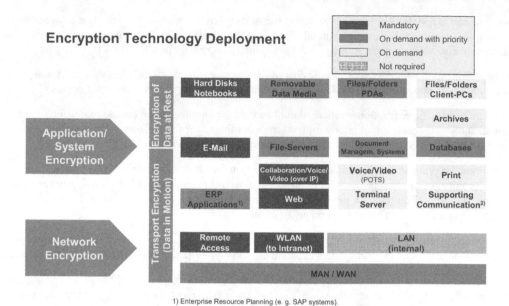

Figure 4: Encryption Technology Deployment Strategy

Remote Intranet Access and Wireless LAN connections are publicly accessible and must be encrypted in any case. E-Mail, Web and IP-based collaboration systems are the primary communication platforms and a major part of classified information is processed via this platforms. Information stored on local hard disks of notebooks are highly exposed to loss and theft and hard disk encryption is a widely recognized protection measure. Built-in encryption functions and numerous encryption products allow a cost efficient deployment of encryption for this field of application.

ERP applications, file-servers, document management systems and databases as well as MAN/WAN networks fall in the same class of risk and importance. However, encryption solutions are usually more complex and cost-intensive. Thus, a general deployment seems to be not reasonable and a usage on demand following the Encryption Framework is appropriate. An assessment of the demand on encryption for these areas should be performed with high priority.

Removable data media and PDAs are also highly exposed to theft and loss and a mandatory encryption should be considered.

When adopting this approach for developing an encryption strategy it is necessary to look at

- the specific classification scheme,
- to develop or verify the corresponding access conditions and protection capability requirements and
- to make an individual risk assessment and prioritization for the networks, systems and applications

of the respective organization.

4 Case Study Siemens

In the following we would like to discuss the implementation of the described encryption strategy at Siemens.

Siemens has implemented an information security policy with an information classification scheme consisting of 4 information classes

- "Public",
- "For internal Use only"
- "Confidential" and
- "Strictly Confidential".

For these information classes the Siemens information security policy defines access conditions and required protection capabilities similar to those defined in section 2.1. Furthermore, the policy defines explicit requirements for using encryption and (strong) authentication technologies.

The encryption and authentication requirements defined in the Siemens information security policies basically comply with the Encryption Framework developed in this paper.

Encryption solutions have been widely adopted within Siemens and Figure 5 shows the current deployment status compared with the Encryption Technology Deployment Strategy of Figure 4.

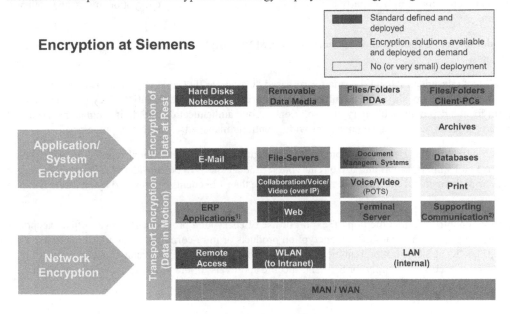

1) Enterprise Resource Planning (e. g. SAP systems).
2) Supporting communication (e. g. domain login, server-server,....).

Figure 5: Deployment of Encryption Solutions at Siemens

For E-Mail, Web, Remote Access and Wireless LAN encryption has been deployed company-wide based on corresponding standards and built-in encryption functions using digital certificates provided by a corporate Public Key Infrastructure (PKI). For e-mail S/MIME end-to-end encryption is used internally and with business partners (if possible). Using HTTPS encryption by default ensures transport encryption for all web-based applications including collaboration and document management systems.

For SharePoint document management systems and file-servers "native" built-in functions for the encryption of data at rest are missing what requires alternative measures for preventing or restricting the access by privileged users.

For file-servers a 3rd-party encryption solution is currently being introduced on demand for confidential and strictly confidential data. However, the manageability, the complex separation of IT and security management and costs are current issues for a broad use.

Hard disk encryption for notebooks (with sensitive data) based on a 3rd-party product is currently being rolled out and a significant coverage has been achieved.

Additional (file) encryption solutions for locally stored data depending on the device, data medium and use case have been introduced. Data encryption on PDAs is not widely used yet due to technical shortcomings of existing solutions.

For ERP applications transport encryption is used by default HTTPS encryption for web-based applications and on demand by a 3rd-party product for SAP systems providing encryption and strong authentication.

In addition to the encryption on application layer MAN / WAN encryption is used on demand for critical sites.

The corporate-wide PKI and the smart card based "Corporate ID Card" with more than 320.000 users are core elements of the Siemens Information Security Program, see [vdH07]. They provide the platform for the deployment of encryption solutions, strong authentication and digital signatures. The PKI ensures a secure key management and provides centrally managed key recovery processes.

When deploying encryption solutions in a global enterprise the international regulations and specific controls for import, export and use of encryption products need to be considered. Siemens runs a data base with the national encryption regulations of more than 125 countries provided by an external expert law firm.

Several countries restrict the import, export or use of encryption products. However, often exceptions for business travelers, mass market encryption products or intra-corporate communications can be applied. The local Siemens representations are responsible to clarify the particular situation in those countries and if necessary to apply for Siemens-specific approvals for the in-house use of encryption.

5 Conclusion

Encryption is a powerful and well-recognized measure to ensure confidentiality of proprietary information.

The paper describes a systematic and generally applicable method to develop an encryption strategy for enterprises based on classification of information, risk management and an evaluation and prioritization of the networks, applications and systems used.

Siemens is an example for the implementation of this method and the reasonable deployment of encryption solutions balancing risks and costs.

Main problems for deploying encryption solutions in a large scale enterprise like Siemens are manageability of existing encryption solutions, costs caused by purchasing and managing 3rd-party encryption products and the lack of suitable methods and tools for automated classification of information. Automated classification would avoid missing and reduce wrong classifications, and thus allow a more tightly focused use of encryption.

References

[NIST02] National Institute of Standards and Technologies: Risk Management Framework, http://csrc.nist.gov/groups/SMA/fisma/framework.html.

[vdH07] von der Heidt, Guido: PKI and Entitlement – Key Information Security Management Solutions for Business and IT Compliance, ISSE/SECURE 2007 Securing Electronic Business Processes, Highlights of the Information Security Solutions Europe / SECURE 2007 Conference, Vieweg, 2007, S. 376 – 385.

Transforming Mobile Platform with PKI-SIM Card into an Open Mobile Identity Tool

Konstantin Hyppönen[1] · Marko Hassinen[1] · Elena Trichina[2]

[1] University of Kuopio, Department of Computer Science
P.O.B. 1627, FI-70211 Kuopio, Finland
{Konstantin.Hypponen | Marko.Hassinen}@uku.fi

[2] Spansion International Inc.
Willi-Brandt-Allee 4, D-81829 Munich, Germany
Elena.Trichina@spansion.com

Abstract

Recent introduction of Near Field Communication (NFC) in mobile phones has stimulated the development of new proximity payment and identification services. We present an architecture that facilitates the use of the mobile phone as a personalised electronic identity tool. The tool can work as a replacement for numerous ID cards and licenses. Design for privacy principles have been applied, such as minimisation of data collection and informed consent of the user. We describe an implementation of a lightweight version of the of the mobile identity tool using currently available handset technology and off-the-shelf development tools.

1 Introduction

The identity of a person is composed of a number of partial identities, or profiles, which are used in different social and business scenarios. Even within the same organisation a person can have several different identity profiles, or roles. For example, in a hospital a doctor can use the role "employee" for opening the front door, and the role "neurophysiologist in charge" for signing an electroencephalography analysis. In computer networks, roles have been successfully used for many years for access control (role-based access control). Another representation of the human identity in the electronic world can be seen in the multitude of user accounts in different services. The problem of abundant registrations and, ultimately, remembering numerous passwords, has been addressed by federated identity management solutions [Chap06, Inte08, Libe07, Open07]. Nonetheless, their applicability is mostly limited to various on-line scenarios, whereby a service provider can trust a third party (identity provider) to securely authenticate the user.

In everyday life, the diversity of identity profiles can be seen in numerous cards and certificates that a normal person has, from a simple paper business card to a magnetic-stripe access control card to the most sophisticated bank and national electronic identification cards whose plastic bodies contain engraved biometric photo, holograms and hidden security markings and where information is stored and processed on a tamper-resistant chip enriched with cryptographic functionality (so called smart cards). It is reasonable to expect that we should be able to conduct various "identity transactions" electronically

N. Pohlmann, H. Reimer, W. Schneider (Editors): Securing Electronic Business Processes, Vieweg (2008), 208-217

with the same ease as we conduct them in various face-to-face situations, such as exchanging business cards at the conference, but with more convenience, better security and with a reasonable degree of privacy. In particular, we should be able to identify ourselves in trivial situations like proving our right to a concession ticket on a bus, without revealing other personal and non-relevant in these circumstances information such as name or address.

However, none of the currently available electronic identity tokens can tackle this identity management problem appropriately. A usual electronic identity document, such as an e-ID card or a biometric passport, contains normally only a single identity profile where an amount of personal information which is stored in a machine-readable form, and thus can be accessed instantaneously and indiscriminatingly, is significant. Although a card may be multifunctional (for example, Malaysian identity card includes 8 applications), uploading new applications or identity profiles in the post-issuance phase is generally not allowed.

The reasons for this are many. The main technological issue has for long time been the lack of on-card bytecode verification, the basic check that newly downloaded applications have to undergo for ensuring security of other applications on the same card. Currently, though, many cards feature on-board bytecode verification. Another technological problem has been the shortage of standard smart card terminals in common business places. The global introduction of chip-based payment cards has now fixed this issue. One more problem is the lack of trust between service providers. They are often competing with each other, and therefore do not allow downloading other applications on their cards. Furthermore, the card itself usually bears the issuer's logo and hence works as a valuable marketing tool. To summarise, user-centric identity management using multi-application smart cards is currently all but non-existent, and there is no clear solution to the problem of trust between service providers.

But it does not mean that there is no bright future for the idea. We argue in this paper that all components of technology necessary for ubiquitous mobile identity management already exist, and most of them are "free" to use. These components comprise already mentioned smart cards, nation-wide public key infrastructure, mobile phones and biometrics.

2 Using mobile phones for identity proofs

The emergence of GSM-type mobile phones enriched with Near Field Communication (NFC) technology is instrumental for the development of a multifunctional mobile identity management and mobile payment tool which can be used in proximity transactions.

Due to the personal nature of mobile phones, they are seen as a suitable medium for storing personal information and credentials for access to various services. Indeed, almost all mobile phone users store their personal phone books in the memory of their devices. In addition, the devices are often used for storing personal notes, calendar items, images and even credit card information. As a result, the mobile device becomes the owner's identity-on-the-move, which we refer to as a *mobile identity*. Psychologically, the mobile phone has therefore already become a suitable device for facilitating identity proofs and mobile payments.

Also technologically, the mobile phone is a reasonable tool for securely storing its user's identity profiles and communicating with identity verifiers (service providers). Indeed, any GSM mobile phone contains a *tamper-resistant secure element*, the SIM card. Many SIM cards are certified according to the Common Criteria (ISO/IEC 15408) standard, to Evaluation Assurance Level EAL4+, and therefore can be used for applications requiring a high level of security. Examples of such applications are officially recognised identity proofs and digital signatures. Existing mobile identity solutions, such as Mobil-ID in Estonia and similar systems in Finland and Turkey, show that storing officially recognised credentials on the SIM card is accepted both by the authorities and people and has a potentially bright future. In addition to the SIM card, many hand-held devices include, or will include soon, secure execution environments (such as TI M-Shield [SrAz08] or ARM TrustZone [AlFe04]) and embedded smart cards, which can also be used for storing keys and identity-related information.

One of the most important benefits of hand-held devices is that they incorporate both the secure element and a *terminal* for operating it. When it comes to monetary transactions, the users are more likely to trust their own mobile phones rather than a PIN-entry device of an uncommon model in a new place. Indeed, newer attacks on chip-and-pin cards are essentially man-in-the-middle attacks that are based on tampering with payment terminals. The problem here is the lack of a trusted path from the payment card to the user: it is easy to change payment details using malicious terminals. The same type of attack is harder to mount with the user's own terminal. Moreover, improved trust is also supported by better usability: when the user learns to operate only one interface on her own device, this suffices in every situation.

Recently, ETSI accepted a set of standards (namely, Host Controller Interface [ETSI08a] on a higher level, and Single Wire Protocol [ETSI08b] on the lower level) defining an interface between the SIM card and contactless front-ends (essentially, NFC). The standards describe procedures for contactless access to applications residing on the SIM, enabling development of new types of proximity applications. From the user's perspective, this turns the mobile phone into a new form of a contactless multi-application smart card.

Standard EMV payments are expected to be easily portable to this new architecture. Indeed, MasterCard and Visa have already operated contactless payments based on using mobile phones in a contactless smart card emulation mode. However, not all benefits of using the mobile phone as a trustworthy terminal are exploited yet: in the existing payment model, the customer still uses the potentially insecure merchant's terminal for confirming the payment.

Although the mobile phone has been projected to become a tool for mobile identity management [MüWo05], existing solutions concentrate only on on-line identity proofs, involving data exchange with the mobile network operator (MNO). In fact, all officially recognised mobile identity solutions are based on user authentication through the use of the MNO services. This increases communication delays, and raises the cost of transactions. In addition, depending on the use case, it might have a negative impact on privacy. To the best of our knowledge, there are currently no standards or specifications for privacy-enhancing identity management on mobile phones for proximity scenarios.

3 An Open Mobile Identity

We present an identity management scheme designed for implementation on mobile phones. The scheme supports multiple partial identities issued by different authorities. It supports biometric authentication of users, and can be used in various on-line and proximity scenarios, in official, business, and personal contexts. More detailed description of protocols is provided in [Hypp08]; here we concentrate on the general architecture of the tool and its use scenarios.

3.1 Architecture

As building blocks for the architecture of our system, we use currently available handset technology and open standards. Openness is the main requirement for the system: we demand that *any* identity provider can load an identity profile to the user's device. For enabling appropriate privacy protection, we demand the use of *informed user's consent:* the person must be informed about what information and to who is communicated. No identity information is sent unless the user's consent is acquired for this.

Our identity tool is comprised of two parts: an applet on a tamper-resistant security element (a SIM card), and an *identity proxy* (an application on a mobile phone) that is used for managing the security element. The latter is called a proxy because it provides an interface between the identity verifier's terminal and the SIM card of the prover's mobile phone. The main tasks of the identity proxy is to check identity verification requests, provide a user interface, and construct identity proofs in cooperation with the SIM-based applet. In particular, it checks identity verifier's credentials, shows a description of requested data, and acquires user's consent prior to constructing an identity proof. Furthermore, because SIM cards do not have their own clock, the identity proxy is the source of timestamps in identity proofs.

Both parts can be implemented in Java: the SIM card applet – with Java Card technology, and the identity proxy with Java 2 Mobile Edition (J2ME). Security and Trust Services (SATSA) API [Java04] is used as a channel for communication between them. The overall architecture is depicted in Fig. 1.

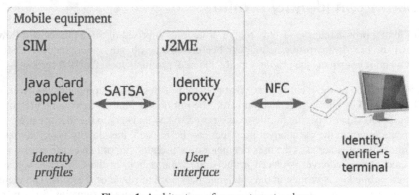

Figure 1: Architecture of our system at a glance

Often the same biometric (e.g., photo) or a pseudonym of the person can be used in different contexts, and therefore in different identity profiles. Therefore, identity profiles are issued to pseudonyms stored in an open *pseudonym pool*. The semantic meanings of pseudonyms in the pool could be, e.g., "User's photo" or "Customer ID of ShopChain Ltd.". Their content can thus be, for example, a biometric template, a number sequence, or a string. For improved privacy protection, identity profiles are issued to cryptographic hashes of pseudonym values. This means that biometric templates are not by default communicated to identity verifiers.

An identity profile is based on a private key generated on-card. The corresponding public key is signed by the identity issuer (working as a certification authority), in a public-key certificate issued to a pseudonym. Identity-related information, in a form of identity *attributes*, is stored separately from the certificate. Typical attributes in many "official" profiles are, e.g., "Date of birth", "Social Security Number (SSN)" or "Type of residence permit"; in self-created profiles these can be, e.g., "PGP Key", "Personal web page address" or "Mobile phone number". Attribute certificates (AC) associate attributes with the public key of the person. Values of attributes in the attribute certificates are masked: certificates contain only hashes of the form $H(A, M)$, where H is a cryptographic hash function, A is the value of the attribute and M is its randomly generated mask. Attribute certificates are signed by the identity issuer. Attribute values and masks are stored separately from the AC, in the same identity profile. An identity verifier can verify an attribute value only if it has received the value together with the corresponding mask (in addition to the attribute certificate).

In addition to the private-public key pair, an identity profile can contain also secret keys for symmetric encryption. This facilitates using the mobile phone as a secure authentication token for online banking, and as an electronic turnkey.

The mobile identity tool is issued to the person on a SIM card by her MNO. The identity applet on the card is initially empty: it contains no identity profiles except, maybe, a profile supplied by the MNO. As a root of trust, however, the applet includes a private key and a corresponding public-key certificate called *profile-loading certificate*. The subject name in this certificate is the same as the card number. The certificate is used later on for authenticating the card prior to loading any identity profiles to it.

The user must also install the identity proxy application on the phone. Alternatively, the application may be pushed over-the-air by the MNO.

3.2 Loading an identity profile

In order to load a profile into the identity tool, a protocol comprised of three phases is followed. First, the SIM card and the identity proxy, acting together, create a certificate signing request (CSR). Second, the identity vendor constructs the profile. Finally, the new profile is loaded on the card.

The process is started by the identity proxy that generates a fresh timestamp and submits it to the SIM card applet. A new key pair is generated on card. The public key and the timestamp are concatenated, signed using the SIM card specific profile-loading private key and sent to the identity proxy. If there is a suitable pseudonym in the pseudonym pool that can be re-used, the identity proxy retrieves it from the card. Otherwise, it either asks the user to enter a new pseudonym, or leaves the creation of it to the identity issuer. The pseudonym is placed in the subject name field of the CSR. The signature of the newly created public key is written in the challenge password attribute of the CSR. The identity proxy constructs the CertificationRequestInfo block of the CSR and acquires a signature for it from the card (the newly created profile-specific private key is used for signing). Finally, the CSR is submitted to the identity vendor, together with the profile-loading certificate.

Having received the CSR, the identity issuer verifies its signatures and checks the profile-loading certificate. Whenever needed, a normal user authentication procedure with regard to the presented pseudonym is performed. Namely, the user has to prove her connection to that pseudonym by either performing a biometric authentication or presenting a public key certificate (PKC) issued to that pseudonym and proving the possession of the corresponding private key. Alternatively, the identity vendor can provide a new pseudonym or accept the one suggested by the user. The identity vendor finally creates a new public key certificate and submits it to the identity proxy along with information and certificates related to identity attributes. In addition, the identity vendor can supply a number of secret keys encrypted using the user's public key. If a new pseudonym is created, its description is attached to it. The pseudonym will be stored in the pseudonym pool.

The identity proxy loads the new profile on the card. The card stores the certificates and identity attribute information without performing any checks on them. If a new pseudonym is supplied, it is stored in the pseudonym pool. Also secret keys are decrypted and stored in the profile.

3.3 Using identity profiles

An open mobile identity tool implemented on the mobile phone can be used in the following scenarios:

- *Identity checks.* The check is performed with regard to a certain identity profile, and a certain pseudonym. The user is notified about what information and by who is requested, and can either comply with or reject the identity check request. Only the minimally required set of identity attributes is opened to the verifier. Furthermore, certain profiles can be PIN-protected: the user has to enter her PIN code before the SIM card applet will provide an identity proof.
- *Digital signatures.* In addition to an identity check, the verifier can request a digital signature from the person. The text of the signed document is shown on the mobile phone screen. For digital signatures, a longer (e.g., 6-digit) PIN code could be used, whereas for standard identity proofs a standard 4-digit PIN is sufficient, if required at all.
- *Entity authentication.* While similar to identification, this is often related to, e. g., a device or an application, rather than an individual, and constitutes an act of establishing or confirming something (or someone) as authentic, that is that claims made by or about the thing are true. Typically, it could be done by:
  - *Challenge responses.* A service provider can request encryption of a challenge with a secret key included in a profile. With NFC communication, electronic keys and other access tokens are standard use cases for this scenario.
  - *One-time passwords.* This scenario is similar to the previous one; the only difference is that the current time is used as a challenge. The mobile phone can therefore be used as a secure authentication token which shows a new one-time password every minute or half a minute.

In proximity scenarios, *biometric authentication* of the user can also be easily performed. If a biometric identifier is used as the user pseudonym, a corresponding biometric pattern becomes available to the identity verifier, and can be used in normal biometric authentication. For example, if facial biometrics is used, the person's photo can be shown on a screen to the identity verifier representative, who can thereon compare it with the person's face.

An authentication token implemented using a mobile phone has certain benefits over usual security tokens. In particular, it is easier to provide time synchronisation with the service provider, because both the identity proxy and the service provider's authentication server can easily synchronise their clocks with the MNO. In many subscriptions this feature is enabled by default. Using mobile phones removes the need for separate hardware tokens, reducing expenditures on devices and logistical costs.

4 Implementation

The presented open mobile identity tool can be implemented with current handset technology using off-the-shelf tools. To test this, we implemented a lightweight version of the architecture supporting a limited number of its features. The proof-of-concept implementation works in the Sun Wireless Toolkit with a Nokia phone emulator. Here we describe APIs and tools used in the development process.

The identity proxy can be implemented most easily in J2ME, as the API for application protocol data unit (APDU) messages exchange with the SIM card, Security and Trust Services (SATSA), is available in many newer phone models. Examples of those are e.g., those based on Nokia Series 60 platform since its 3rd edition. For implementation, we used Nokia 6131 NFC SDK v. 1.1, integrated with Eclipse IDE. To facilitate exchange of messages between the identity proxy and the verifier's terminal, we used NFC (or actually its emulation in the SDK). The connection was implemented using Contactless Communi-cation API (JSR-257) [Java06]. In the emulator, messages were forwarded to an "external security ele-ment", which was in fact a Java program running the user interface of the identity verifier. Sun Wireless Toolkit was used for running the Nokia 6131 phone emulator.

Routines in the identity proxy that require cryptographic processing were implemented using Bouncy Castle API [Boun08]. Ant and Antenna [PlYa08] were used for building and packaging the identity proxy applet. The SIM card applet was implemented using JCOP tools running in Eclipse [IBMZ03].

To be able to connect to the SIM card applet, the identity proxy (J2ME applet) must be signed using the operator or the Trusted Third Party (TTP) domain certificate. An access control entry with a hash of this certificate is stored on the SIM card. The implementation of SATSA on the mobile phone compares this hash with that of the certificate used for signing the J2ME applet. The J2ME applet is allowed to exchange messages with the applet on the SIM only if the hashes match. This provides additional pro-tection against potential malware that might try to steal identity information or illicitly acquire digital signatures on user's behalf. No such misuse is permitted, unless the malware is signed by the operator or TTP, which must be hard to achieve in practise.

No operations with private keys are performed in the identity proxy. Signatures for identity proofs are generated on the SIM card; newer smart cards with cryptographic coprocessors are capable of comput-ing 1024-bit RSA signatures in less than 200 ms. Verification of the credentials used in identity proofs is performed by the applet running on a mobile phone. Because mobile chipsets do not normally have optimised cryptographic coprocessors, signature verification can take about 800 ms. We note, however, that in identity verification scenarios the user normally needs a few seconds to study the verifier's re-quest, and most cryptographic operations in the identity proxy can be performed during this time.

EEPROM or Flash memory can be used for storing profiles on the SIM card. Currently available high density SIM cards [HaTr07] which provide tens to hundreds of megabytes of non-volatile Flash memory have plethora of space for certificates, attributes, and other data. Cryptographic keys, however, must be stored in protected memory of the SIM. Requirements on random-access memory (RAM) for the SIM card applet are moderate: most operations can be performed within APDU buffer only.

5 Privacy-preserving biometric authentication

When identity documents are read by electronic means, a lot of information is not only revealed, but can be copied, stored and processed without our consent. With biometric patterns revealed to identity veri-fiers, this becomes a serious privacy problem. Usual paper or plastic based documents do not have this problem: the photo of the document holder is simply shown to the verifier, and is not stored anywhere electronically. We argue that similar privacy-preserving biometric authentication (where a facial photo is used as the least intrusive and the most common and widely accepted biometrics) can be performed with the mobile phone used as an electronic identity document.

Indeed, as mobile phones have screens with resolution sufficient for showing a face photograph, the only problem is ensuring the trusted path between the store place of the certified photo and the screen. We describe here how this can be achieved; details of the proof-of-concept implementation can be found in [HyHT08].

In fact, only a small modification of our open mobile identity scheme is needed. As described in Sect. 3.1, the person's photo is just another pseudonym stored in the pseudonym pool. Remember also that identity profiles are issued to cryptographic hashes of biometric patterns. From the identity proof, the identity verifier can check the integrity and authenticity of the hash of the photo, but cannot see the photo itself.

Now assume that both the identity verifier and the identity proxy compute a cryptographic hash of all messages exchanged between them during the identity proof protocol. We call this hash (perhaps, trimmed to only a few hexadecimal digits) an *identity proof fingerprint*. The identity proxy can then superimpose the fingerprint on the user's photo and show the result on the screen of the mobile phone. The identity verifier can then compare the fingerprints and check whether the photo matches the user standing in front of him. In this way we can ensure that the photo comes from the identity proxy, and not from a malicious program running on the same mobile phone. This scenario is depicted in Fig. 2.

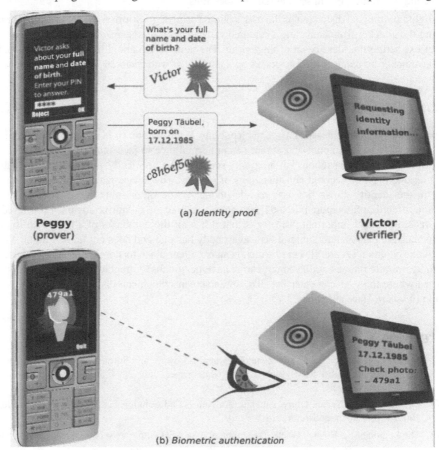

Figure 2: An example of an identity proof scenario

Because mobile phones are built on relatively open platforms, we must also consider potential attacks on this scheme. The identity proof fingerprint prevents an attacker from impersonating the user: if the attacker quickly switches from the identity proxy to another application for showing the attacker's photo instead of the proper one, he has to also show the correct fingerprint. The security architecture of J2ME uses the sandbox model, preventing applications from accessing memory space of other applications; therefore, the attacker's program cannot intercept data sent by the identity proxy. The fingerprint calculation includes two digital signatures made with the private keys unknown to the attacker; this essentially cuts the chances of guessing the fingerprint to 1 in 1048576, if five hexadecimal digits are used in the fingerprint.

Malware with screen capture capabilities could potentially be used to make a screenshot of the identity proxy terminal at the time when it displays the user's photo (a "fraudulent" user may wait for a second or two before showing the phone to a verifier without the latter becoming suspicious), extract the identity proof fingerprint and place it on another photo, to impersonate the legitimate user. To prevent these "screenshot attacks", the following techniques can be used:

- Visual distortion of the identity proof fingerprint (using e.g., CAPTCHA-like techniques).
- Placing the fingerprint in several random locations.
- Slight randomised distortion of the user's photo (using e.g., Stirmark). This is useful for preventing the attacker from analysing a captured watermarked image against a non-watermarked one, for extracting the identity proof fingerprint. The non-watermarked image could be obtained by the attacker by using collusion attacks on a number of watermarked images.

6 Conclusion

In this paper we propose a basis of a scheme enabling identification to occur in the electronic world with the same ease and modicum of assurance as in normal face to face situations. The scheme allows us to conduct "identity transactions" in proximity scenarios electronically, providing security and convenience and taking into account considerations of privacy. The device which a person is using when engaged in the identity transaction is a mobile phone. While other solutions, such as a nationwide smart token offered in Singapore [GrNa07], are possible, there are definitive advantages offered by our scheme. Its single most important property is that it has all the hallmarks of a public utility. Indeed, mobile phones are personal and ubiquitous—everybody has one and does not leave a home without it. Mobile phones contain secure SIM card which is an excellent place to store credentials and user's profiles. Finally, mobile phones, unlike smart cards, have personalised graphical user interface, including a keyboard where the user can enter her PIN, and a screen, which can display information for visual inspection in face-to-face situations.

References

[AlFe04]   Alves, Tiago; Felton, Don: TrustZone: Integrated Hardware and Software Security. Enabling Trusted Computing in Embedded Systems. ARM white paper, July 2004. http://www.arm.com/pdfs/TZ_Whitepaper.pdf

[PlYa08]   Pleumann, Jörg; Yadan, Omry: Antenna. An Ant-to-End Solution For Wireless Java. Version 1.0.1, 2008. http://antenna.sourceforge.net/

[Boun08]   The Legion of the Bouncy Castle: Java cryptography APIs. http://www.bouncycastle.org/java.html

[Chap06]   Chappell, David: Introducing Windows CardSpace. April 2006. http://msdn2.microsoft.com/en-us/library/aa480189.aspx

[ETSI08a]   ETSI: TS 102 622 V7.0.0. Smart Cards; UICC – Contactless Front-end (CLF) interface; Host Controller Interface (HCI) (Release 7). Technical specification, February 2008.

[ETSI08b]   ETSI: TS 102 613 V7.1.0. Smart Cards; UICC – Contactless Front-end (CLF) interface; Part 1: Physical and data link layer characteristics (Release 7). Technical specification, February 2008.

[GrNa07]   Gratzer, Vanessa; Naccache, David: Trust on a Nationwide Scale. In: Gutmann, P., Naccache, D., Palmer Ch. (Eds): IEEE Security and Privacy, 2007, p. 64-66.

[Hypp08]   Hyppönen, Konstantin: An Open Mobile Identity Tool: An Architecture for Mobile Identity Management. In: S.F. Mjølsnes, S. Mauw, and S.K. Katsikas (Eds.): EuroPKI 2008, LNCS 5057, Springer-Verlag Berlin Heidelberg, 2008, p. 207–222.

[HyHT08] Hyppönen, Konstantin; Hassinen, Marko; Trichina, Elena: Combining Biometric Authentication with Privacy-Enhancing Technologies. In: P. Lipp, A.-R. Sadeghi, and K.M. Koch (Eds.): TRUST'2008, LNCS 4968, Springer-Verlag Berlin Heidelberg, 2008, p. 107–118.

[HaTr07]   Handschuh, Helena; Trichina, Elena: High Density Smart Cards: New Security Challenges and Applications. In: Pohlmann, N., Reimer, H., Schneider, W. (Eds.): ISSE/SECURE 2007 Securing Electronic Business Processes, Vieweg, 2007, p. 251–259.

[Inte08]   Internet2: Shibboleth 2 Documentation. March, 2008. https://spaces.internet2.edu/display/SHIB2/Home

[IBMZ03] IBM Zurich Research Laboratory: JCOP Tools 3.0 (Eclipse plugin). Technical brief, revision 1.0, 2003. ftp://ftp.software.ibm.com/software/pervasive/info/JCOPTools3Brief.pdf.

[Java04]   Java Community Process: Security and Trust Services API (SATSA) for Java™ 2 Platform, Micro Edition, v. 1.0. Sun Microsystems, Inc., 2004. http://www.jcp.org/en/jsr/detail?id=177

[Java06]   Java Community Process: Contactless Communication API, JSR 257, v. 1.0. Nokia Corporation, 2006. http://www.jcp.org/en/jsr/detail?id=257

[Libe07]   Liberty Alliance Project: Liberty Alliance ID-FF 1.2 Specifications. December 2007. http://www.projectliberty.org/liberty/specifications_1

[MüWo05] Müller, Günter; Wohlgemuth, Sven: Study on Mobile Identity Management. FIDIS – Future of Identity in the Information Society, deliverable 3.3. May, 2005.

[Open07]   OpenID Foundation: OpenID Authentication 2.0 – Final. December 5, 2007. http://openid.net/specs/openid-authentication-2_0.html

[SrAz08]   Srage, Jay; Azema, Jerome: M-Shield Mobile Security Technology: making wireless secure. Texas Instruments white paper, February 2008. http://focus.ti.com/pdfs/wtbu/ti_mshield_whitepaper.pdf

Symmetric Key Services Markup Language (SKSML)

Arshad Noor

CTO, StrongAuth, Inc.
arshad.noor@strongauth.com

Abstract

Symmetric Key Services Markup Language (SKSML) is the eXtensible Markup Language (XML) being standardized by the OASIS Enterprise Key Management Infrastructure Technical Committee for requesting and receiving symmetric encryption cryptographic keys within a Symmetric Key Management System (SKMS). This protocol is designed to be used between clients and servers within an Enterprise Key Management Infrastructure (EKMI) to secure data, independent of the application and platform. Building on many security standards such as XML Signature, XML Encryption, Web Services Security and PKI, SKSML provides standards-based capability to allow any application to use symmetric encryption keys, while maintaining centralized control. This article describes the SKSML protocol and its capabilities.

1 Introduction

With the introduction of the Data Encryption Standard (DES) in generalized computing, many companies dealing with sensitive data have become used to dealing with encryption and cryptographic keys to protect data from unauthorized disclosure. In the intervening decades since then, while many advances have taken place in the field of cryptography, one feature has remained unchanged during this period: cryptographic key-management is still tightly-coupled with the applications using the cryptographic modules, thus making the key-management process non-standard and non-portable across applications and platforms.

Cryptographic key-management (KM) is defined to mean the discipline of managing the life-cycle of cryptographic keys: the generation, use, escrow, recovery and destruction of keys. While seemingly simple enough, the degree of technical and procedural security surrounding these activities determines the strength of the overall system in withstanding attacks.

Hardware and software vendors who have built encryption into their products, have – for lack of standards – implemented KM capability into their applications to make it easier for the application administrators to manage the process. This has led to the proliferation of many KM schemes despite the use of industry-standard application programming interfaces (API) such as Public Key Cryptography Standards (PKCS), Microsoft's Cryptographic API (CAPI), Sun Microsystems' Java Cryptography Extensions (JCE), and testing standards such as the US Federal Information Procurement Standards (FIPS), the Information Technology Security Evaluation Criteria (ITSEC) and/or Common Criteria (CC).

This has resulted in IT departments having to deal with numerous ways of implementing encryption in their applications. Even with just three major cryptography APIs – PKCS, CAPI and JCE – every single implementation performs key-management differently.

N. Pohlmann, H. Reimer, W. Schneider (Editors): Securing Electronic Business Processes, Vieweg (2008), 218-230

While Public Key Infrastructure (PKI) has brought signficant consistency to the management of asymmetric cryptographic keys through the protocol standards created by the International Standards Organization (ISO) and the Internet Engineering Task Force's (IETF) PKI X.509 (PKIX) Working Group, similar standards for the management of symmetric keys are sorely lacking.

2 OASIS Enterprise Key Management Infrastructure

To address this deficiency, members of the Organization for the Advancement of Structured Information Systems (OASIS) formed the Enterprise Key Management Infrastructure (EKMI) Technical Committee (TC) in early 2007, with four goals:

1. Create an XML-based protocol – called the Symmetric Key Services Markup Language (SKSML) for requesting and receiving symmetric key services;

2. Create implementation guidelines for building infrastructures that manage symmetric encryption keys;

3. Create guidelines that serve IT Auditors when auditing key-management infrastructures; and

4. Create a tool for testing implementations of SKSML for conformance with the standard.

5. The OASIS members on this TC believed that with the formation of standards that could be used by application developers and operations staff of IT environments, large-scale encryption of data and the management of those symmetric keys across applications and platforms would become practical and affordable.

6. At the time of writing this paper, the EKMI TC has completed DRAFT 6 of the SKSML protocol and has voted on releasing it to the internet community for public-review. It is anticipated that the protocol will be standardized by December 2008 after completing the remaining parts of the standardization process.

2.1 Symmetric Key Services Markup Language

SKSML is an XML-based request-response protocol for use by client applications and key-management servers. The implementation of SKSML on the client side is designated the **Symmetric Key Client Library (SKCL)**, while on the server side, it is designated the **Symmetric Key Services (SKS)** server. The collection of all SKCL clients and SKS servers within an enterprise is designated as a **Symmetric Key Management System (SKMS)**, and the SKMS in conjunction with a PKI, is designated an EKMI.

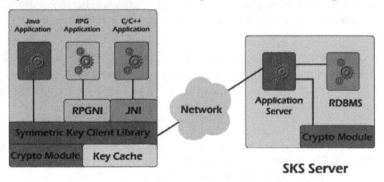

Figure 1: Typical SKCL-SKS implementation in an SKMS

SKSML defines the following types of requests:

1. A request for a single new symmetric key;
2. A request for a single used (previously escrowed) symmetric key;
3. A request for a single new symmetric key of a specific key-class;
4. A request for multiple new symmetric keys;
5. A request for multiple used symmetric keys;
6. A request for a key-caching policy;
7. and the following types of responses:
8. A response with a single new or used symmetric key;
9. A response with multiple symmetric keys;
10. A response with an error;
11. A response with a combination of key(s) and/or error(s);
12. A response with a key-cache policy;

2.1.1 A request for a single new symmetric key

When a client application has been linked to the SKCL and needs to encrypt sensitive data, it will call an API function within the SKCL for a new symmetric key. After the SKCL has determined that the application is authorized to make such a request, the SKCL sends the following SKSML request:

```
<ekmi:SymkeyRequest
        xmlns:ekmi="http://docs.oasis-open.org/ekmi/2008/01">
        <ekmi:GlobalKeyID>10514-0-0</ekmi:GlobalKeyID>
</ekmi:SymkeyRequest>
```

While the request looks extremely simple, it is secured by a Web Services Security (WSS) header that includes an XML Signature of the request. The signature must be generated from an X.509 digital certificate issued by a Certificate Authority known and trusted to the SKS server to be valid. The WSS header is not shown here to keep the paper readable.

In this request, the proposed XML Schema namespace for qualifying SKMS elements and attributes is http://docs.oasis-open.org/ekmi/2008/01.

The **GlobalKeyID (GKID)** is the unique identifier of a symmetric key being requested by the client application. The GKID is a concatenation of three distinct identifiers in the following order: the unique Domain Identifier, the unique Server Identifier within the domain and the unique Key Identifier generated on a server.

The Domain Identifier (DID) is the unique Private Enterprise Number (PEN) as assigned by the Internet Assigned Numbers Authority (IANA) to any enterprise requesting it. The DID ranges from 1 to 18446744073709551615 ($2^{64} - 1$). An enterprise setting up an SKMS for the first time is expected to use their unique PEN for the DID.

The Server Identifier (SID) is a simple sequential number ranging from 1 to ($2^{64} - 1$) which identifyies unique SKS servers within an SKMS for a specific domain. Just as an enterprise may have a few Domain Name Service (DNS) servers to serve its needs, it is expected that an enterprise will have only a few SKS servers. Companies may choose any fixed numeral from the permitted range to uniquely identify their SKS servers.

The Key Identifier (KID) is also a simple sequential number ranging from 1 to $(2^{64} - 1)$, and uniquely identifies every symmetric key generated on a specific SKS server. The concatenation of the DID, SID and KID make up the unique GKID for the enterprise. Assuming that every company implementing an SKMS is diligent about using only a PEN that belongs to them, the GKID of a given symmetric key becomes unique on the internet.

Using a "zero" value for the Server ID and the Key ID within a request for a symmetric key indicates a request for a new symmetric key.

2.1.2 A request for a single used symmetric key

When a client application needs to decrypt encrypted data (ciphertext), it needs the same symmetric key that was used during the encryption phase. Since applications within this architecture are required to store the GKID of keys used by them with the associated ciphertext, to decrypt data, applications must request the specific key from an SKS server (if they do not have the key cached on the client machine). To request a used symmetric key, the application will, typically, send the following request to the SKS server:

```
<ekmi:SymkeyRequest
        xmlns:ekmi="http://docs.oasis-open.org/ekmi/2008/01">
        <ekmi:GlobalKeyID>10514-1-37</ekmi:GlobalKeyID>
</ekmi:SymkeyRequest>
```

In this example, the application is requesting for GKID **10514-1-37**, indicating that this is the 37th key generated on the SKS server with an SID of 1, within the domain identified by the DID 10514.

As one can see, the difference between requesting a new or used symmetric key is very little: only the SID and KID are different in the request.

2.1.3 A request for a new symmetric key of a specific key-class

Applications may have a need for encrypting different objects with keys of different strengths and which may be governed by different company policies. To ensure that the SKS server returns a symmetric key with the correct type of key and policy, and assuming that the client is authorized to do so, the SKCL may request a new symmetric key of a specific key-class that encapsulates the policies and parameters required by the application:

The SKSML request would resemble the following:

```
<ekmi:SymkeyRequest
        xmlns:ekmi="http://docs.oasis-open.org/ekmi/2008/01">
        <ekmi:GlobalKeyID>10514-0-0</ekmi:GlobalKeyID>
        <ekmi:KeyClasses>
                <ekmi:KeyClass>HR-Class</ekmi:KeyClass>
        </ekmi:KeyClasses>
</ekmi:SymkeyRequest>
```

The only addition the SKCL needs to make, as shown in this example, is to include the element for the requested KeyClass. In this example, the client application is requesting a key that corresponds to the **HR-Class** key-class. If the application is authorized to receive keys of this class, the SKS server will return a new symmetric key with a policy associated with the HR-Class key-class.

Note that there is no point in requesting a *used* symmetric key of a specific key-class. All symmetric keys when generated and escrowed on an SKS server, are assigned to a key-class based on the policy under which the key is generated. Once a key is assigned a specific key-class, it is immutable. Thus,

requesting a key with a specific GKID always returns the key with whatever key-class that was originally assigned to the key.

2.1.4 A request for multiple new symmetric keys

Certain applications may have a requirement to encrypt different parts of a logical record with different
symmetric keys to isolate segments of the logical record from people unauthorized to view them. An
example is a Medical Record where a single logical record must be viewed by Doctors, Nurses, Phar-
macists, Insurance companies, Laboratory Diagnosticians, etc. However, not all of them need to see the
entire medical record – just the details that are necessary to do their part of the job.

SKSML provides the ability to request as many symmetric keys as the client application needs, limited
only by the bounds of XML, Simple Object Access Protocol (SOAP), Hypertext Transfer Protocol (HTTP)
and/or the client and server capabilities in handling SOAP and HTTP-based requests/responses.

A request for multiple new symmetric keys would resemble the following:

```
<ekmi:SymkeyRequest
        xmlns:ekmi="http://docs.oasis-open.org/ekmi/2008/01">
        <ekmi:GlobalKeyID>10514-0-0</ekmi:GlobalKeyID>
        <ekmi:KeyClasses>
                <ekmi:KeyClass>EHR-CDC</ekmi:KeyClass>
                <ekmi:KeyClass>EHR-CRO</ekmi:KeyClass>
                <ekmi:KeyClass>EHR-DEF</ekmi:KeyClass>
                <ekmi:KeyClass>EHR-EMT</ekmi:KeyClass>
                <ekmi:KeyClass>EHR-HOS</ekmi:KeyClass>
                <ekmi:KeyClass>EHR-INS</ekmi:KeyClass>
                <ekmi:KeyClass>EHR-NUR</ekmi:KeyClass>
                <ekmi:KeyClass>EHR-PAT</ekmi:KeyClass>
                <ekmi:KeyClass>EHR-PHY</ekmi:KeyClass>
        </ekmi:KeyClasses>
</ekmi:SymkeyRequest>
```

In this example, the client application – ostensibly an application in the health-care sector – is requesting nine (9) symmetric keys, where each key would correspond to a different key-class. Assuming the
client was authorized to receive keys of these key-class types, the SKS server will return nine (9) new
symmetric keys, each corresponding to the requested key-class.

If an application needed multiple keys of the same key-class, such as for five (5) new keys of the **EHR-
HOS** key-class, it would send out a request resembling the following:

```
<ekmi:SymkeyRequest
        xmlns:ekmi="http://docs.oasis-open.org/ekmi/2008/01">
        <ekmi:GlobalKeyID>10514-0-0</ekmi:GlobalKeyID>
        <ekmi:GlobalKeyID>10514-0-0</ekmi:GlobalKeyID>
        <ekmi:GlobalKeyID>10514-0-0</ekmi:GlobalKeyID>
        <ekmi:GlobalKeyID>10514-0-0</ekmi:GlobalKeyID>
        <ekmi:GlobalKeyID>10514-0-0</ekmi:GlobalKeyID>
        <ekmi:KeyClasses>
                <ekmi:KeyClass>EHR-HOS</ekmi:KeyClass>
        </ekmi:KeyClasses>
</ekmi:SymkeyRequest>
```

A request such as the following is also valid, since it requests four (4) new symmetric keys of a *default*
key-class, typically, configured on the SKS server as a default standard for the SKMS. The default key-
class may be site-specific, group-specific or client-specific:

```
<ekmi:SymkeyRequest
       xmlns:ekmi="http://docs.oasis-open.org/ekmi/2008/01">
       <ekmi:GlobalKeyID>10514-0-0</ekmi:GlobalKeyID>
       <ekmi:GlobalKeyID>10514-0-0</ekmi:GlobalKeyID>
       <ekmi:GlobalKeyID>10514-0-0</ekmi:GlobalKeyID>
       <ekmi:GlobalKeyID>10514-0-0</ekmi:GlobalKeyID>
</ekmi:SymkeyRequest>
```

2.1.5 A request for multiple used symmetric keys

Just as an application may request multiple new symmetric keys, it may also request multiple used symmetric keys in a single SKSML request, as follows:

```
<ekmi:SymkeyRequest
       xmlns:ekmi="http://docs.oasis-open.org/ekmi/2008/01">
       <ekmi:GlobalKeyID>10514-1-23</ekmi:GlobalKeyID>
       <ekmi:GlobalKeyID>10514-1-35</ekmi:GlobalKeyID>
       <ekmi:GlobalKeyID>10514-3-143</ekmi:GlobalKeyID>
       <ekmi:GlobalKeyID>10514-3-77</ekmi:GlobalKeyID>
</ekmi:SymkeyRequest>
```

In the above request, the client application has requested four (4) specific symmetric keys from the SKS server. Two of the keys were originally generated on an SKS server with an SID of 1, while two were generated on a server with an SID of 3. While the client does not have to care about where the keys were generated or where they are currently located, it is the SKS server's responsibility to locate the keys and return them to the client application (if the client is authorized to receive them).

2.1.6 A request for a key-caching policy

An SKMS supports the caching of symmetric encryption keys on the client for disconnected operations.; i.e. if the client is disconnected from the SKS server, as long as the client has the key(s) cached, it can continue performing cryptographic operations with the key(s) in accordance with the policies associated with them.

However, before a client can cache symmetric keys, it must know the current key-caching policy that applies to the client. It requests this policy from the SKS server with the following request:

```
<ekmi:KeyCachePolicyRequest
       xmlns:ekmi="http://docs.oasis-open.org/ekmi/2008/01"/>
```

This is it! The client needs to include nothing else, since the WSS header (with the XML Signature) gives the SKS server all the information it needs to determine the policy that applies to this specific client and return it to the client. If there is no specific key-cache policy for this client, the SKS server attempts to locate a group policy which applies to the client. If none exists, it returns the *default* key-caching policy that applies to the site. Every site will have a default key-cache policy defined when an SKMS is installed and configured, *even if the policy indicates that key-caching is disallowed!*

2.1.7 A response with a single new or used symmetric key

When a client application requests a new symmetric key, the SKS server processes the request by doing the following:

- Verifying the authenticity of the request through the digital signature in the request;
- Determining the clients' authorization to receive keys through access control policies defined on the SKS server;

- Identifying the key-use policy that applies to the client (or a *default* key-use policy if a specific one doesn't exist for the requesting client);
- Generating a key under the selected policy;
- Encrypting the symmetric key with the SKS server's own public-key and the site's Global SKS server's public-key;
- Escrowing the key in the database and digitally signing the key and its associated meta-data for message-integrity;
- Encrypting the symmetric key with the public-key of the requesting client;
- Digitally signing the response with the SKS server's Signing key
- and then sends the following response to the client:

```
[b01]    <ekmi:SymkeyResponse
[b02]                xmlns:ekmi='http://docs.oasis-open.org/ekmi/2008/01'
[b03]                xmlns:xenc='http://www.w3.org/2001/04/xmlenc#'>
[b04]        <ekmi:Symkey>
[b05]           <ekmi:GlobalKeyID>10514-1-235</ekmi:GlobalKeyID>
[b06]           <ekmi:KeyUsePolicy>
[b07]        <ekmi:KeyUsePolicyID>10514-4</ekmi:KeyUsePolicyID>
[b08]        <ekmi:PolicyName>DES-EDE KeyUsePolicy</ekmi:PolicyName>
[b09]                <ekmi:KeyClass>HR-Class</ekmi:KeyClass>
[b10]                <ekmi:KeyAlgorithm>
[b11]                     http://www.w3.org/2001/04/xmlenc#tripledes-cbc
[b12]                </ekmi:KeyAlgorithm>
[b13]                <ekmi:KeySize>192</ekmi:KeySize>
[b14]                <ekmi:Status>Active</ekmi:Status>
[b15]                <ekmi:Permissions>
[b16]                  <ekmi:PermittedApplications ekmi:any="false">
[b17]                      <ekmi:PermittedApplication>
[b18]                      <ekmi:ApplicationID>10514-23</ekmi:ApplicationID>
[b19]                        <ekmi:ApplicationName>
[b20]                               Payroll Application
[b21]                        </ekmi:ApplicationName>
[b22]                        <ekmi:ApplicationVersion>1.0</ekmi:ApplicationVersion>
[b23]                        <ekmi:ApplicationDigestAlgorithm>
[b24]                           http://www.w3.org/2000/09/xmldsig#sha1
[b25]                        </ekmi:ApplicationDigestAlgorithm>
[b26]                        <ekmi:ApplicationDigestValue>
[b27]                               NIG4bKkt4cziEqFFuOoBTM81efU=
[b28]                        </ekmi:ApplicationDigestValue>
[b29]                      </ekmi:PermittedApplication>
[b30]                  </ekmi:PermittedApplications>
[b31]                     <ekmi:PermittedDates ekmi:any="false">
[b32]                        <ekmi:PermittedDate>
[b33]                     <ekmi:StartDate>2008-01-01</ekmi:StartDate>
[b34]                        <ekmi:EndDate>2008-12-31</ekmi:EndDate>
[b35]                     </ekmi:PermittedDate>
[b36]                     </ekmi:PermittedDates>
[b37]                     <ekmi:PermittedDays ekmi:any="true" xsi:nil="true"/>
[b38]                     <ekmi:PermittedDuration ekmi:any="true" xsi:nil="true"/>
[b39]                     <ekmi:PermittedLevels ekmi:any="true" xsi:nil="true"/>
[b40]                     <ekmi:PermittedLocations ekmi:any="true" xsi:nil="true"/>
[b41]                     <ekmi:PermittedNumberOfTransactions ekmi:any="true"
                                       xsi:nil="true"/>
[b42]                     <ekmi:PermittedTimes ekmi:any="false">
[b43]                        <ekmi:PermittedTime>
[b44]                     <ekmi:StartTime>07:00:00</ekmi:StartTime>
[b45]                     <ekmi:EndTime>19:00:00</ekmi:EndTime>
[b46]                     </ekmi:PermittedTime>
[b47]                     </ekmi:PermittedTimes>
[b48]                     <ekmi:PermittedUses ekmi:any="true" xsi:nil="true"/>
```

```
[b49]                        </ekmi:Permissions>
[b50]                      </ekmi:KeyUsePolicy>
[b51]                      <ekmi:EncryptionMethod
[b52]                            Algorithm="http://www.w3.org/2001/04/xmlenc#rsa-1_5"/>
[b53]                      <xenc:CipherData>
[b54]                       <xenc:CipherValue>
[b55]                              E9zWB/y93hVSzeTLiDcQoDxmlNxTuxSffMNwCJmt1dIqzQHBn
[b56]                              hQhywCx9sfYjv9h5FDqUiQXGOca8EU871zBoXBjDxjfg1pU8t
[b57]                              UJow/qimxi8+huUYJMtaGHtXuL1Wtx27STRcRpIsY=
[b58]                       </xenc:CipherValue>
[b59]                      </xenc:CipherData>
[b60]                    </ekmi:Symkey>
[b61]         </ekmi:SymkeyResponse>
```

While the response may look daunting (perhaps, more so with the WSS header that isn't displayed here), it is fairly simple.

The key has a unique GKID assigned by the SKS server – in this case 10514-1-235, and a **KeyUsePolicy (KUP)** that applies to this symmetric key. The KUP identifies the type of symmetric key (3DES), key-length (192-bits), key-class assigned to this key (HR-Class) and whether the key is currently active. This meta-data is defined between lines [b07] and [b14].

The most powerful part of the KUP is the **Permissions** element between lines [b15] and [b49]. It allows policy-makers at a site to define exactly who may use the key, when, where, at what time of day, for what purposes, for how long and/or for how many encryption transactions. If the site is using Multi-Level Security (MLS)-based applications, the policy can even specify the security-classification level(s) at which the key may be used.

The actual symmetric key is shown between lines [b51] and [b59]. It is encrypted with the public-key of the requesting client, and therefore requires decryption with the client's private-key before it can be used by the SKCL.

When a client application requests a used symmetric key, the SKS server processes the request by doing the following:

- Verifying the authenticity of the request through the digital signature in the request;
- Determining the clients' authorization to receive the requested key(s) through access control policies defined on the SKS server;
- Decrypting the symmetric key with the SKS server's own private-key;
- Encrypting the symmetric key with the public-key of the client;
- Digitally signing the response with the SKS server's Signing key
- and then sends the response to the client. The response is identical to that shown for a new symmetric key in this section.
- Note that every object that is read from the SKMS database is verified for message-integrity before it is used by the SKS server. Any object whose digital signature fails in the database read-process, is **not** used by the SKS server.

2.1.8 A response with a multiple new or used symmetric keys

When a client application requests mulitple symmetric keys, the SKS server processes the request and sends the following response:

```
[h01]      <ekmi:SymkeyResponse
[h02]                     xmlns:ekmi='http://docs.oasis-open.org/ekmi/2008/01'
[h03]                          xmlns:xenc='http://www.w3.org/2001/04/xmlenc#'>
[h04]          <ekmi:Symkey>
[h05]          <ekmi:GlobalKeyID>10514-4-3792</ekmi:GlobalKeyID>
[h06]          <ekmi:KeyUsePolicy>
[h07]          <ekmi:KeyUsePolicyID>10514-9</ekmi:KeyUsePolicyID>
[h08]            <ekmi:PolicyName>EHR-CDC KeyUsePolicy</ekmi:PolicyName>
[h09]            <ekmi:KeyClass>EHR-CDC</ekmi:KeyClass>
[h10]            <ekmi:KeyAlgorithm>
[h11]                     http://www.w3.org/2001/04/xmlenc#tripledes-cbc
[h12]                 </ekmi:KeyAlgorithm>
[h13]                 <ekmi:KeySize>192</ekmi:KeySize>
[h14]                 <ekmi:Status>Active</ekmi:Status>
[h15]                 <ekmi:Permissions>
[h16]                  <ekmi:PermittedApplications ekmi:any="true" xsi:nil="true"/>
[h17]                  <ekmi:PermittedDates ekmi:any="true" xsi:nil="true"/>
[h18]                  <ekmi:PermittedDays ekmi:any="true" xsi:nil="true"/>
[h19]                  <ekmi:PermittedDuration ekmi:any="true" xsi:nil="true"/>
[h20]                  <ekmi:PermittedLevels ekmi:any="true" xsi:nil="true"/>
[h21]                      <ekmi:PermittedLocations ekmi:any="true" xsi:nil="true"/>
[h22]                      <ekmi:PermittedNumberOfTransactions
[h23]                                         ekmi:any="true" xsi:nil="true"/>
[h24]                      <ekmi:PermittedTimes ekmi:any="true" xsi:nil="true"/>
[h25]                      <ekmi:PermittedUses ekmi:any="true" xsi:nil="true"/>
[h26]                 </ekmi:Permissions>
[h27]          </ekmi:KeyUsePolicy>
[h28]          <ekmi:EncryptionMethod
[h29]                     Algorithm="http://www.w3.org/2001/04/xmlenc#rsa-1_5"/>
[h30]          <xenc:CipherData>
[h31]                      <xenc:CipherValue>
[h32]                          E9zWB/y93hVSzeTLiDcQoDxmlNxTuxSffMNwCJmt1dIqzQHBn
[h33]                          hQhywCx9sfYjv9h5FDqUiQXGOca8EU871zBoXBjDxjfg1pU8t
[h34]                      UlWtx27STRcRJMtaGHtXuLlWtx27STRcRpIsY=
[h35]                      </xenc:CipherValue>
[h36]              </xenc:CipherData>
[h37]          </ekmi:Symkey>
[h38]          <ekmi:Symkey>
[h39]          <ekmi:GlobalKeyID>10514-4-3793</ekmi:GlobalKeyID>
[h40]          <ekmi:KeyUsePolicy>
[h41]          <ekmi:KeyUsePolicyID>10514-12</ekmi:KeyUsePolicyID>
[h42]            <ekmi:PolicyName>EHR-CRO KeyUsePolicy</ekmi:PolicyName>
[h43]            <ekmi:KeyClass>EHR-CRO</ekmi:KeyClass>
[h44]            <ekmi:KeyAlgorithm>
[h45]                     http://www.w3.org/2001/04/xmlenc#tripledes-cbc
[h46]                 </ekmi:KeyAlgorithm>
[h47]                 <ekmi:KeySize>192</ekmi:KeySize>
[h48]                 <ekmi:Status>Active</ekmi:Status>
[h49]                 <ekmi:Permissions>
[h50]                  <ekmi:PermittedApplications ekmi:any="true" xsi:nil="true"/>
[h51]                  <ekmi:PermittedDates ekmi:any="true" xsi:nil="true"/>
[h52]                      <ekmi:PermittedDate>
[h53]                          <ekmi:StartDate>2008-01-01</ekmi:StartDate>
[h54]                          <ekmi:EndDate>2009-12-31</ekmi:EndDate>
[h55]                      </ekmi:PermittedDate>
[h56]                  </ekmi:PermittedDates>
[h57]                  <ekmi:PermittedDays ekmi:any="true" xsi:nil="true"/>
[h58]                  <ekmi:PermittedDuration ekmi:any="true" xsi:nil="true"/>
[h59]                  <ekmi:PermittedLevels ekmi:any="true" xsi:nil="true"/>
[h60]                   <ekmi:PermittedLocations ekmi:any="true" xsi:nil="true"/>
[h61]                   <ekmi:PermittedNumberOfTransactions
[h62]                                     ekmi:any="true" xsi:nil="true"/>
[h63]                   <ekmi:PermittedTimes ekmi:any="true" xsi:nil="true"/>
[h64]                   <ekmi:PermittedUses ekmi:any="true" xsi:nil="true"/>
[h65]                 </ekmi:Permissions>
```

```
[h66]                    </ekmi:KeyUsePolicy>
[h67]                    <ekmi:EncryptionMethod
[h68]                        Algorithm="http://www.w3.org/2001/04/xmlenc#rsa-1_5"/>
[h69]                    <xenc:CipherData>
[h70]                        <xenc:CipherValue>
[h71]                            qUiQXGOca8EU871zBoXBjDoDxmlNxTuxSffMNwCJmt1dIqzQHBn
[h72]                            hQhywCx9sfYjv9h5FDqUiQXGOca8EU871zBoXBjDxjfg1pU8tGF
[h73]                    UJow/qimxi8+ huUYJMtaGHtXuLlWtx27STRcRpIsY=
[h74]                        </xenc:CipherValue>
[h75]                    </xenc:CipherData>
[h76]                </ekmi:Symkey>
[h77]                <ekmi:Symkey>
[h78]                    <ekmi:GlobalKeyID>10514-4-3795</ekmi:GlobalKeyID>
                                    ...
[h79]                    <ekmi:KeyClass>EHR-DEF</ekmi:KeyClass>
                                    ...
[h80]                </ekmi:Symkey>
[h81]                <ekmi:Symkey>
[h82]                    <ekmi:GlobalKeyID>10514-4-3797</ekmi:GlobalKeyID>
                                    ...
[h83]                    <ekmi:KeyClass>EHR-EMT</ekmi:KeyClass>
                                    ...
[h84]                </ekmi:Symkey>
[h85]                <ekmi:Symkey>
[h86]                    <ekmi:GlobalKeyID>10514-4-3798</ekmi:GlobalKeyID>
                                    ...
[h87]                    <ekmi:KeyClass>EHR-HOS</ekmi:KeyClass>
                                    ...
[h88]                </ekmi:Symkey>
[h89]                <ekmi:Symkey>
[h90]                    <ekmi:GlobalKeyID>10514-4-3799</ekmi:GlobalKeyID>
                                    ...
[h91]                    <ekmi:KeyClass>EHR-INS</ekmi:KeyClass>
                                    ...
[h92]                </ekmi:Symkey>
[h93]                <ekmi:Symkey>
[h94]                    <ekmi:GlobalKeyID>10514-4-3801</ekmi:GlobalKeyID>
                                    ...
[h95]                    <ekmi:KeyClass>EHR-NUR</ekmi:KeyClass>
                                    ...
[h96]                </ekmi:Symkey>
[h97]                <ekmi:Symkey>
[h98]                    <ekmi:GlobalKeyID>10514-4-3803</ekmi:GlobalKeyID>
                                    ...
[h99]                    <ekmi:KeyClass>EHR-PAT</ekmi:KeyClass>
                                    ...
[h100]               </ekmi:Symkey>
[h101]               <ekmi:Symkey>
[h102]                   <ekmi:GlobalKeyID>10514-4-3805</ekmi:GlobalKeyID>
                                    ...
[h103]                   <ekmi:KeyClass>EHR-PHY</ekmi:KeyClass>
                                    ...
[h104]               </ekmi:Symkey>
[h105]           </ekmi:SymkeyResponse>
```

In this response, the first symmetric key is between lines [h04] and [h37], the second is between [h38] and [h76], the third between [h77] and [h80] (with intervening elements not displayed for brevity) and so on, until the last symmetric key in the response terminates at line [h104]. Each key has its own KUP, thus allowing the SKCL to use the appropriate policy with the corresponding key.

2.1.9 A response with an error

In the event the SKS server's processing leads to an error and a key cannot be returned to the client, the following response is sent to the client:

```
<ekmi:SymkeyResponse
              xmlns:ekmi='http://docs.oasis-open.org/ekmi/2008/01'
              xmlns:xenc='http://www.w3.org/2001/04/xmlenc#'>
       <ekmi:SymkeyError>
          <ekmi:RequestedGlobalKeyID>10514-0-0</ekmi:RequestedGlobalKeyID>
                <ekmi:RequestedKeyClass>EHR-PHY</ekmi:RequestedKeyClass>
          <ekmi:ErrorCode>SKS-100004</ekmi:ErrorCode>
          <ekmi:ErrorMessage>
                 Unauthorized request for key
             </ekmi:ErrorMessage>
       </ekmi:SymkeyError>
   </ekmi:SymkeyResponse>
```

The client application is expected to respond appropriately to the user of the application.

2.1.10 A response with key(s) and/or error(s)

When an SKCL requests multiple symmetric key, in the event the SKS server's processing leads to one or more errors, the following response is typically sent to the client:

```
<ekmi:SymkeyResponse
              xmlns:ekmi='http://docs.oasis-open.org/ekmi/2008/01'
              xmlns:xenc='http://www.w3.org/2001/04/xmlenc#'>
       <ekmi:Symkey>
              <ekmi:GlobalKeyID>10514-4-3795</ekmi:GlobalKeyID>
                            ...
          <ekmi:KeyClass>EHR-DEF</ekmi:KeyClass>
                            ...
       </ekmi:Symkey>
       <ekmi:Symkey>
              <ekmi:GlobalKeyID>10514-4-3797</ekmi:GlobalKeyID>
                            ...
              <ekmi:KeyClass>EHR-EMT</ekmi:KeyClass>
                            ...
       </ekmi:Symkey>
       <ekmi:SymkeyError>
       <ekmi:RequestedGlobalKeyID>10514-0-0</ekmi:RequestedGlobalKeyID>
                <ekmi:RequestedKeyClass>EHR-PHY</ekmi:RequestedKeyClass>
          <ekmi:ErrorCode>SKS-100004</ekmi:ErrorCode>
          <ekmi:ErrorMessage>
                 Unauthorized request for key
             </ekmi:ErrorMessage>
       </ekmi:SymkeyError>
   </ekmi:SymkeyResponse>
```

The response includes symmetric keys and errors. The client application is expected to respond appropriately to the user of the application.

2.1.11 A response with a key-caching policy

When an SKCL requests a key-caching policy from the SKS server, the following response is sent:

```
<ekmi:KeyCachePolicyResponse
                xmlns:ekmi='http://docs.oasis-open.org/ekmi/2008/01'
                xmlns:xenc='http://www.w3.org/2001/04/xmlenc#'>
        <ekmi:KeyCachePolicy>
            <ekmi:KeyCachePolicyID>10514-1</ekmi:KeyCachePolicyID>
            <ekmi:PolicyName>No Caching Policy</ekmi:PolicyName>
            <ekmi:Description>
                    This policy is for high-risk, always-connected machines on
                    the network, which will never cache symmetric keys locally.
                    This policy never expires (but checks monthly for any
                    updates).
                        </ekmi:Description>
                <ekmi:KeyClass>NoCachingClass</ekmi:KeyClass>
                <ekmi:StartDate>2008-01-01T00:00:01.0</ekmi:StartDate>
                        <ekmi:EndDate>1969-01-01T00:00:00.0</ekmi:EndDate>
                        <ekmi:PolicyCheckInterval>2592000</
ekmi:PolicyCheckInterval>
                    <ekmi:Status>Active</ekmi:Status>
            </ekmi:KeyCachePolicy>
        </ekmi:KeyCachePolicyResponse>
```

In this particular key-caching policy, caching is disallowed (since there are no references to how many keys are allowed to be cached). The policy is active forever (given the UNIX time-zero date) and the client is expected to check with the SKS servers once a month (2592000 seconds) for updates of the policy.

A key-cache policy that *does* permit caching might be as follows:

```
<ekmi:KeyCachePolicyResponse
                xmlns:ekmi='http://docs.oasis-open.org/ekmi/2008/01'
                xmlns:xenc='http://www.w3.org/2001/04/xmlenc#'>
        <ekmi:KeyCachePolicy>
           <ekmi:KeyCachePolicyID>10514-17</ekmi:KeyCachePolicyID>
           <ekmi:PolicyName>Laptop Key Caching Policy</ekmi:PolicyName>
           <ekmi:Description>
                    This policy defines how company-issued laptops will
                    manage keys used for file/disk encryption in their lo
                    cal cache. This policy expires on Dec 31, 2008 and
                    checks monthly for updates.
                        </ekmi:Description>
                <ekmi:KeyClass>LaptopKeyClass</ekmi:KeyClass>
                <ekmi:StartDate>2008-01-01T00:00:01.0</ekmi:StartDate>
        <ekmi:EndDate>2008-12-31T00:00:01.0</ekmi:EndDate>
        <ekmi:PolicyCheckInterval>2592000</ekmi:PolicyCheckInterval>
                    <ekmi:Status>Active</ekmi:Status>
                <ekmi:NewKeysCacheDetail>
                        <ekmi:MaximumKeys>3</ekmi:MaximumKeys>
                        <ekmi:MaximumDuration>7776000</ekmi:MaximumDuration>
                    </ekmi:NewKeysCacheDetail>
                <ekmi:UsedKeysCacheDetail>
                        <ekmi:MaximumKeys>3</ekmi:MaximumKeys>
                        <ekmi:MaximumDuration>7776000</ekmi:MaximumDuration>
                    </ekmi:UsedKeysCacheDetail>
            </ekmi:KeyCachePolicy>
        </ekmi:KeyCachePolicyResponse>
```

In this policy, up to a maximum of three (3) new (unused for any encryption transaction) keys may be cached for a maximum duration of ninety (90) days. It also allows for a maximum of three (3) used symmetric keys for a maximum of ninety (90) days from the time they are first used by the client application.

It is worthy mentioning that because a KeyCachePolicy (KCP) is associated with a specific key-class, a KCP response may contain multiple policies in the response, each policy applying to a specific key-class.

3 Conclusion

Application developers and Security Officers will never have to deal with SKSML directly, since the supplier of the SKCL and/or the SKS server software bears the responsibility of implementing the SKSML. However, an understanding of the semantics of SKSML provides deep insight into the capability of the architecture and the protocol, and how enterprises may use an SKMS for protecting data.

References

[SKSML] OASIS EKMI Technical Committee: Symmetric Key Services Markup Language Normative Specification 1.0 (DRAFT 6), http://www.oasis-open.org/committees/download.php/28655/SKSML-1.0-Specification-Normative-DRAFT6.0.pdf

[EKMI]   OASIS EKMI Technical Committee: http://www.oasis-open.org/committees/tc_home.php?wg_abbrev=ekmi

Managing business compliance using model-driven security management

Ulrich Lang · Rudolf Schreiner

ObjectSecurity Ltd,
St. John's Innovation Centre
Cowley Road, Cambridge, UK
{ulrich.lang | rudolf.schreiner}@objectsecurity.com

Abstract

Compliance with regulatory and governance standards is rapidly becoming one of the hot topics of information security today. This is because, especially with regulatory compliance, both business and government have to expect large financial and reputational losses if compliance cannot be ensured and demonstrated. One major difficulty of implementing such regulations is caused the fact that they are captured at a high level of abstraction that is business-centric and not IT centric. This means that the abstract intent needs to be translated in a trustworthy, traceable way into compliance and security policies that the IT security infrastructure can enforce. Carrying out this mapping process manually is time consuming, maintenance-intensive, costly, and error-prone. Compliance monitoring is also critical in order to be able to demonstrate compliance at any given point in time. The problem is further complicated because of the need for business-driven IT agility, where IT policies and enforcement can change frequently, e.g. Business Process Modelling (BPM) driven Service Oriented Architecture (SOA). Model Driven Security (MDS) is an innovative technology approach that can solve these problems as an extension of identity and access management (IAM) and authorization management (also called entitlement management). In this paper we will illustrate the theory behind Model Driven Security for compliance, provide an improved and extended architecture, as well as a case study in the healthcare industry using our OpenPMF 2.0 technology.

1 Introduction

Compliance with regulatory and governance standards is rapidly becoming one of the hot topics of information security today. This is because, especially with regulatory compliance, both business and government have to expect large financial and reputational losses if compliance cannot be ensured and demonstrated. Compliance is relevant to many types of organisations. Examples include Sarbanes-Oxley [SOX02] for publicly listed companies, HIPAA [HIP96] for healthcare organisations, and many other non-regulatory governance standards such as COBIT [ITG07] and HL7 [HL7].

In this paper we will illustrate the approach and architecture behind model-driven security for compliance, and provide a healthcare regulatory compliance case study using our OpenPMF 2.0 [Obje08a] technology.

N. Pohlmann, H. Reimer, W. Schneider (Editors): Securing Electronic Business Processes, Vieweg (2008), 231-241

2 Compliance implementation complexities

2.1 Bridging the business/IT requirements gap

One major difficulty of implementing such regulations is caused the fact that they are expressed at a high level of abstraction that is organisation-centric, business-centric, information-centric, legal aspects centric and human-centric. Regulations are not IT centric, nor expressed in IT terms. This means that the abstract and high level policy requirements defined by the regulations need to be translated into compliance and security policies that the IT security infrastructure can enforce. Carrying out this mapping process manually is time consuming, maintenance-intensive, costly, and error-prone. An automated, reliable technology approach is required to solve these issues.

2.2 Demonstrating compliance

Another major difficulty is related to compliance monitoring. How can an organisation demonstrate sufficiently that it complies with these organisation-centric, information-centric and human-centric and legal regulations and governance standards? And how can attempted compliance violations be detected early on and prevented before damage is caused? Doing this manually, as suggested by many survey-based compliance tools is too slow, costly, and error-prone. How can this be done in an automated way that is cost effective, timely, reliable, and automatic? Again, a suitable technology approach is required.

2.3 Agility

These two difficulties are particularly hard to deal with in distributed IT environments that are "agile", i.e. get reconfigured regularly. The current architectural style for agile distributed software applications is Service Oriented Architecture (SOA). One concept behind SOA is to specify and manage application interactions in an abstract model that bridges the gap between the business (business processes, workflows, BPM etc.) and IT (platforms like web services, databases etc.). In such model driven SOA environments, enterprise architects specify workflows in Business Process Modelling (BPM) suites, which are used to orchestrate underlying modular IT services. One of the main benefits is that the IT environment can be reconfigured easily to reflect changes in the business.

For compliance enforcement and monitoring, SOA agility poses a major complexity because security policies (both for compliance enforcement and monitoring) will have to be updated each time the IT environment gets reconfigured. Carrying out such policy updates manually each time the SOA gets reconfigured is clearly unworkable because this would be too costly, too slow, and too error-prone. So again, a suitable technology approach is required to automatically update compliance enforcement and monitoring whenever the SOA changes.

2.4 Traceability

Another interesting related aspect is how trustworthy the link between the regulation or governance standard on the high layer of abstraction, and its IT enforcement and monitoring on the low layer of abstraction is. This trustworthiness is relevant for defence accreditation (e.g. Common Criteria [CC08]) and many other safety and assurance standards. This is an especially important factor for agile systems, because accreditation of a static system (the normal way to achieve accreditation) is not possible.

3 Model-driven security

3.1 Definition

Model Driven Security (MDS) [MDS08] is an innovative technology approach that can solve these problems. MDS can be defined as the tool supported process of modelling security requirements at a high level of abstraction, and using other information sources available about the functional aspects of the system (produced by other stakeholders). These inputs, which are expressed in Domain Specific Languages (DSL), are then transformed into enforceable security rules with as little human intervention as possible. MDS explicitly also includes the run-time security management (e.g. entitlements/authorisations), i.e. run-time enforcement of the policy on the protected IT systems, dynamic policy updates and the integrated monitoring of policy violations.

In the first step of MDS, regulations and governance standards are modelled as a high-level security policy in a model-driven security tool (such as ObjectSecurity's OpenPMF 2.0). These models are then translated into low-level security policies that are enforced across the entire SOA environment (e.g. through local plug-ins integrated into the middleware or at a domain boundary). The local plug-ins also deal with the monitoring of compliance/security-relevant events. If tied into the SOA BPM suite and the SOA middleware (e.g. web application server), Model Driven Security can automatically update the compliance enforcement and monitoring whenever the SOA application changes.

3.2 Benefits

Model-driven security management (in the form implemented in OpenPMF 2.0 by ObjectSecurity) has the following benefits:

Model driven security regulates information flows and resource access between different systems (or software services/components) and users in a fine-grained, policy-driven way across a potentially large, heterogeneous IT environment. Furthermore, it ensures that security policy updates caused by IT agility, i.e. changes to the IT environment, can be managed without a maintenance cost explosion. All this helps reduce the security management effort.

Another core benefit is that model-driven security management helps align business security requirements (including regulatory and best-practice security requirements) and policy-driven technical IT security enforcement. This means that security requirements, which can be captured in an undistorted, abstract way close to human/business thinking, can be automatically transformed into technology-centric IT security enforcement. This reduces the cost and effort of security policy definition and maintenance. The automated technology approach also improves the traceability from requirements to enforcement and improves assurance, because human administration errors are minimised.

In addition, the model-driven security approach can tie security requirements into the overall business enterprise architecture, which ensures that the needs of the business are reflected.

4 Model-driven security – vision or reality?

MDS is an emerging hot topic. ObjectSecurity has been identified as the leading model-driven security vendor by Gartner, and ObjectSecurity's OpenPMF is mentioned as one of a handful of sample vendors on the emerging slope of various "hype cycles" and as "Cool Vendor 2008" [Gart07a-d, Gart08a-c]. Furthermore, a number of significant end users and vendors have worked with the authors because of the significance of model-driven security for their projects, including US Navy, US Air Force, UK Ministry of Defence, and BAA Heathrow Airport [Obje08b]. It also was used in the development of a prototype of secure air traffic management systems (ATM) in preparation of SESAR, the European Single European Sky ATM Research programme coordinated by Eurocontrol [Sch2006].

5 OpenPMF 2.0 – regulatory healthcare example

This section illustrates how one exemplary security-related high-level regulatory requirement is translated into enforceable authorisation rules. The example is chosen from the US Health Insurance Portability and Accountability Act (HIPAA), which was enacted by the U.S. Congress in 1996. According to the Centres for Medicare and Medicaid Services (CMS) website, Title II of HIPAA, known as the Administrative Simplification (AS) provisions, requires the establishment of national standards for electronic health care transactions and national identifiers for providers, health insurance plans, and employers. The Administration Simplification provisions also address the security and privacy of health data. The standards are meant to improve the efficiency and effectiveness of the nation's health care system by encouraging the widespread use of electronic data interchange in the US health care system.

The OASIS eXtensible Access Control Markup Language (XACML) [OASI08] is a standard architecture and XML based syntax for transferring authorisation rules called within the web services world. XACML includes Policy Administration Points (PAPs), Policy Decision Points (PDPs), Policy Information Points (PIPs), and Policy Enforcement Points (PEPs).

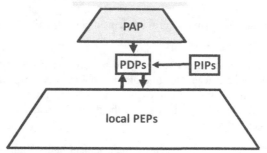

Figure 1: Conceptual XACML architecture

ObjectSecurity's OpenPMF 2.0 [Obje08a] security management technology has an extended and improved architecture also includes model-driven policy management points and runtime central monitoring points, two critical features to make security policy management manageable:

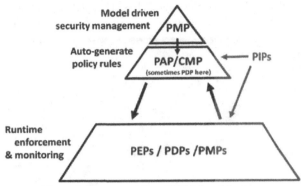

Figure 2: Conceptual OpenPMF 2.0 architecture

5.1 Security requirements capture

A particularly intuitive basic healthcare security/privacy requirement is:

Every doctor is only allowed to access the patient record of the patient they are currently treating (unless the patient is treated in a crisis context, or the patient consents etc.).

This requirement is stated in an abstract way, independent of the particular IT environment, patient identity, doctor identity, doctor-patient relationship, IT environment etc. In line with the OMG Model Driven Architecture (MDA) [OMG08] framework, we call these requirements "undistorted" by the particular deployment. This requirement can be captured in a modelling tool in a customised, customer-specific way:

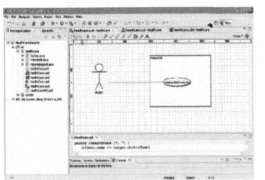 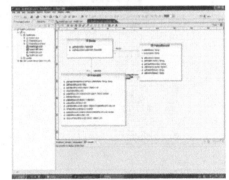

Figure 3: OpenPMF 2.0 security requirements capture in models model

5.2 System model usage

A crucial dimension of model-driven security is that other system models are reused in order to infer the authorisation rules for the particular deployment. For example, an application model can be taken from ObjectSecurity's SecureMiddleware Model Driven Architecture (MDA) tool chain. In order to be able to understand these functional system models, they need to be properly meta-modelled. In the case of OpenPMF 2.0 and ObjectSecurity's SecureMiddleware MDA tool chain [SMW08], both models are based on meta-models that are based on the same Eclipse [Ecl08a] de-facto standard meta-meta-model Ecore [Ecl08b], which simplifies model reuse.

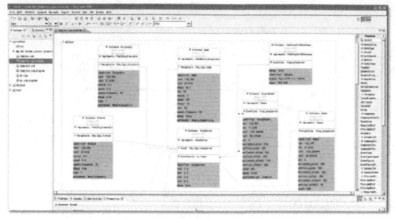

Figure 4: part of the functional model of a complex ATM system
(SecureMiddleware CCM MDA)

There are potentially many other sources for system models, such as Business Process Management System (BPMS) tools which are for example used by enterprise architects to capture the processes of a business and map them to the IT environment (e.g. SOA BPEL [OASI07] /web services). OpenPMF 2.0 has been designed to co-exist with modelling tools (both BPM and MDA) inside the same Eclipse IDE installation. For example, OpenPMF 2.0 can be used as a security add-on for Intalio's [INT08] open source BPMS:

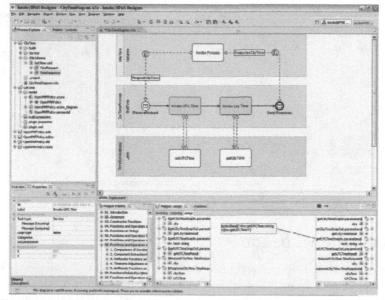

Figure 5: OpenPMF 2.0 as a security add-on for Business Process Management (BPM)

5.3 Identity management systems reuse

Model-driven security also needs to have access to the information about which particular participants exist, such as doctors and patients (the "who" in authorization rules). In many organisations, this information has been collected in a centralised identity management solution (IdM), e.g. IBM Tivoli, HP SelectIdentity, Microsoft ActiveDirectory. The XACML standard calls such directory or any other identity provider systems Policy Information Points (PIPs).

While IdM solutions are often called Identity and Access Management (IAM), they typically do not provide a means of specifying and managing (potentially many) fine-grained access rules (the "what" and "how" in authorization rules). Model-driven security can be seen as an extension for such already-deployed IdM solutions.

To reuse identity information, OpenPMF 2.0 supports identity (and role) import via LDAP, the standard protocol for directory access, and can be integrated with Public Key Infrastructures (PKI), e.g. based on X.509.

5.4 Authorization management rule generation

Using ObjectSecurity's patent-pending methods and algorithms, this high level regulatory requirement can then be transformed into potentially very many deployment-specific IT-centric message protection and authorisation rules at different layers. In order to automate this, the security model needs to be meta-modelled properly. Depending on the customers environment and concrete requirements, the model transformations may need to be customised in order to do the transformations, for example to support specific security policy features, middleware platforms or security mechanisms. ObjectSecurity provides this as a service the OpenPMF 2.0 deployment so that customers do not have to deal with this complexity. It is also possible to "slot in" generic, well-defined security requirements (such as multi-level security). With the model transformations and the models in place, many (potentially hundreds of thousands) of fine-grained authorization rules can be generated from a single high level rule, with the push of a button. These rules are stored in a repository, which is related to XACML PAPs.

The output of the patent-pending algorithm is a set of fine-grained, IT deployment specific authorization rules for each particular IT system, patient identity, doctor identity, doctor-patient relationship, IT environment etc

Such rules include specific technology attributes such as (without any specific syntax): *allow information flow if "caller X.509 cert. id doctor1" via "firewall IP..." calling "file patient1" on "database IP ..." and from "hospital IP ..." and "doctor1 is treating patient1" and/or "patient1 crisis"*. Two simple, concrete OpenPMF 2.0 PDL rules could for example be:

```
(client.name ==JaneMillerMD )&(target.name == PatientRecord.
JohnBrown)&(operation.name == {read, write}):allow;

(client.name == BackupProcess)&(TargetName ==
PatientRecord.*)&(operation.name == read):allow;
```

Such rules can be viewed and managed using OpenPMF 2.0's Policy Definition Language (PDL) [LaSc05] which is highly compact and readable. It is also possible – although not recommended – to fine-tune the rules using the OpenPMF 2.0 policy editor inside Eclipse, which supports auto-complete functionality to simplify this process:

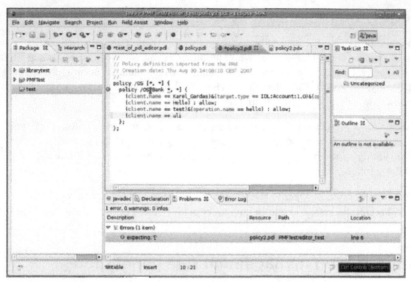

Figure 6: OpenPMF 2.0 Policy Definition Language (PDL) editor

5.5 Enforcement across a heterogeneous, distributed IT landscape

The next step is to distribute the generated authorization rules across the distributed, heterogeneous IT environment to enable runtime security enforcement of information flows. This is typically achieved by installing local Policy Enforcement Points (PEPs) on the systems that need to be protected. In the web services world, XACML is a standard architecture and XML based syntax for transferring authorisation rules . While XACML has been hyped up as the solution for fine-grained authorisation management (also called entitlement management), it is clear that XACML (and authorisation management) solves more the security policy interchange challenge than the security policy definition and management challenge. This is because the XACML architecture assumes that the (typically many) fine-grained technical enforcement rules are defined and managed at the low level of abstraction of IT enforcement. Specifying and maintaining thousands (or more) rules manually in an agile, ever-changing IT environment is clearly impossible.

Model-driven security solves this problem by generating these low-level rules from abstract requirements.

OpenPMF 2.0 can distribute authorization rules either to its own OpenPMF 2.0 plug-ins (which co-locate runtime decision making and enforcement) via its own secure, standards-based transport mechanism. Externalising security enforcement from the application logic is a sound design decision because it enables reuse and application development decoupled from security enforcement code.

Pre-developed plug-ins are available for a growing number of technologies, such as SOA web app servers (Oracle WebLogic, Glassfish), Authorization/entitlement management (XACML based, including Cisco Securent, Oracle Acqualogic, IBM Tivoli Security Policy Manager), Data Distribution Service (RTI DDS), CORBA Components (Qedo CCM), CORBA (MICO C++ JacORB Java), message-oriented middleware (XMLBlaster), firewall (ObjectWall IIOP Proxy, IPFilter). Additional customer-specific plug-ins are purpose-built by ObjectSecurity.

Alternatively, OpenPMF 2.0 can distribute XACML based authorisation rules to third party products that support XACML. A number of vendors are offering XACML based authorisation management and enforcement products today.

XACML calls the component that makes the decision to authorise access the Policy Decision Point (PDP). PDPs use the policies from the PAP as well as additional information it can get from PIPs. Policy Enforcement Points (PEPs) are the component where the request for authorization arrives. In XACML, the PEP sends a XAXML request to a PDP and then acts according to the PDP's decision. In OpenPMF 2.0, PEPs and PDPs are typically collocated in the OpenPMF 2.0 plug-ins to improve the reliability of security enforcement (e.g. if network connectivity is interrupted, for example by denial-of-service attacks). Non-collocated PDPs can be supported optionally.

Model-driven security can be seen as the missing piece at the top of the architecture that makes security authorisation management manageable. This was demonstrated in the so far biggest application of model-driven security, an experimental secure ATM system. In this system, with over a dozen service types, about 50 service instances running on 10 hosts on three sites, MDS automatically generated a security policy of more than 1000 rules from the systems' functional model. Whenever the system was modified, e.g. by changing the services, their interactions or the deployment of services on hosts, the security policy was automatically adapted accordingly. This ensured that the system was always protected according the high level security intent. The policy maintenance effort during these modifications was reduced to almost zero.

5.6 Runtime compliance monitoring

To close the security management loop, it is crucial to monitor security-relevant activities across the distributed IT environment. This is important to detect suspicious activities (e.g. blocked access requests), but also to be able to demonstrate regulatory compliance at any point in time.

The central policy manager in authorisation management solutions is an ideal place to display collected alerts and the security state of the system:

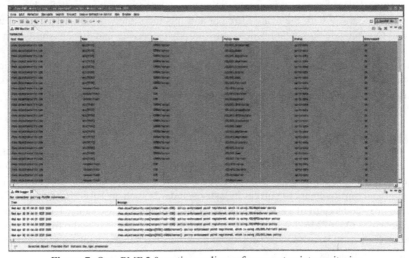

Figure 7: OpenPMF 2.0 runtime policy enforcement point monitoring

As an optional, additional, deeper level of defence, OpenPMF 2.0 pushes its policy-based alerts into an intrusion detection system (Promia Raven), which collects alerts from the network layer and uses the information from both sources to mine for attack patterns.

The XACML architecture does not specifically cover monitoring, but the OpenPMF 2.0 architecture includes Compliance Monitoring Points (CMPs) as a critical, integral part of the architecture.

6 Roadmap towards model-driven security

There is no doubt that model-driven approaches in general will become mainstream over the coming years (in whatever form). This is because IT complexity in today's complex, interconnected, ever-changing, ever-faster world has become unmanageable, and it has always been human nature to try to find an abstraction in order to be able to easier deal with that complexity.

On the other hand, pervasive changes to IT and business staff behaviour and technology has always posed a formidable adoption hurdle. However, industry analysts such as Gartner [Gart08] forecast model-driven approaches to become mainstream within five years, based on high-profile, big-vendor pushes (e.g. Microsoft "Oslo" initiative). Model-driven security will then be a feature with obvious benefits in the overall architecture.

Irrespective of that, the adoption of model-driven security does not have to wait for model-driven approaches to become mainstream. Instead, a non-intrusive gradual adoption roadmap is possible, starting with authorisation management as a policy-driven add-on to today's identity management (IdM) deployments. While not model-driven, such authorization management (integrated with IdM) can help bridge the time until full model-driven security gets adopted. While a number of authorization management solutions (mostly XACML based) are available today, only OpenPMF 2.0 provides the upgrade roadmap towards model-driven security.

The authors see the most complete deployment of model-driven security as a scenario where a model-driven security tool is used as an enterprise-wide security management tool that ties in with enterprise architecture (incl. BPM) , model-driven integration, model-driven engineering. Such a pervasive deployment would do away with the many different and incompatible ways of managing security infrastructure, and thus provide significant benefits, including cost-saving and manageability. An additional benefit of such a deployment is that the end customer "owns" the security policy model, and is therefore in a position to outsource most of the IT and IT security infrastructure "plumbing" to vendors and integrators without losing control and in-house security expertise. OpenPMF 2.0 has been designed to support this highly innovative enterprise-wide security ecosystem management thanks to its flexibility.

7 Conclusion

In this paper we illustrated the approach, architecture, benefits, and adoption roadmap for model-driven security in the context of compliance. We described a policy management architecture that is a significant extension and improvement to current industry standards such as XACML. Details of our implementation are provided as part of a healthcare regulatory compliance case study. The case study is based on ObjectSecurity's OpenPMF 2.0 security management product, which is the first full model-driven security technology in the market. The paper also discusses the general industry direction with respect to model-driven approaches.

References

[CC08]   Common Criteria Portal website, www.commoncriteriaportal.org, 2008

[Ecl08a]   Eclipse project web site, www.eclipse.org

[Ecli08b] Eclipse Modeling Framework website, www.eclipse.org/modeling/emf

[Gart07a] Gartner: Tear Down Application Authorization Silos With Authorization Management Solutions (G00147801), 31 May 2007

[Gart07b] Gartner: Model-Driven Security: Enabling a Real-Time, Adaptive Security Infrastructure (G00151498), 21 September 2007

[Gart07c] Gartner: Hype Cycle for Information Security, 2007 (G00150728), 4 September 2007

[Gart07d] Gartner: Cisco Buys Securent for Policy Management, and Relevance (G00153181), 5 November 2007

[Gart08]   Gartner website, www.gartner.com, 2008

[Gart08a] Gartner: Cool Vendors in Application Security and Authentication, 2008 (G00156005), 4 April 2008

[Gart08b] Gartner: Hype Cycle for Identity and Access Management Technologies, 2008 (G00158499), 30 June 2008

[Gart08c] Gartner: Hype Cycle for Context-Aware Computing, 2008 (G00158162), 1 July 2008

[ITG07]   IT Governance Institute: COBIT 4.1 Excerpt, Executive Summary, 2007

[HIP96]   Public Law 104-191: Health Insurance Portability and Accountability Act of 1996, 21. Aug 1996

[HL7]   Health Level Seven web site, www.hl7.org

[INT08]   Intalio product web site, www.intalio.com, 2008

[LaSc05]   Lang, Ulrich and Schreiner, Rudolf: Integrated IT Security: Air-Traffic Management Case Study. ISSE 2005 Conference Budapest, Springer, 2005

[MDS08]   Model Driven Security web site, www. modeldrivensecurity.org, 2008

[OASI07]   OASIS Consortium: Web Services Business Process Execution Language, 11 Apr 2007

[OASI08]   OASIS Consortium: XACML 2.0 Core: eXtensible Access Control Markup Language (XACML) Version 2.0, 1 Feb 2005

[OMG08]   Object Management Group, MDA web site, www.omg.org/mda

[Obje08a] ObjectSecurity: OpenPMF 2.0 Model Driven Security Management product website, www.openpmf.com, 2008

[Obje08b] ObjectSecurity website: Customer list with case studies and endorsements, www.objectsecurity.com, 2008

[Sch2006] Schreiner, R, Lang, U, Ritter, T, Reznik, J, Building Secure and Interoperable ATC Systems, Eurocontrol INO Workshop 2006

[SMW08]   ObjectSecurity: SecureMiddleware website, www.securemiddleware.org, 2008

[SOX02]   House of Representatives, Sarbanes-Oxley Act of 2002, 24 Jul 2002

Secure E-Business applications based on the European Citizen Card

Christian Zipfel · Henning Daum · Gisela Meister

Giesecke & Devrient GmbH
{christian.zipfel | henning.daum | gisela.meister}@gi-de.com

Abstract

The introduction of ID cards enhanced with electronic authentication services opens up the possibility to use these for identification and authentication in e-business applications. To avoid incompatible national solutions, the specification of the European Citizen Card aims at defining interoperable services for such use cases. Especially the given device authentication methods can help to eliminate security problems with current e-business and online banking applications.

Recently Giesecke & Devrient (G&D) and Wirecard Bank AG showcased the first e-business application that utilizes an electronic ID card based on the European Citizen Card standards together with a new online banking application that allows consumers to authenticate using an official personal identity document. Thus users and online service providers of this application can benefit from added security in their internet transactions, thanks to secure mutual authentication based on an official electronic document.

1 Motivation

With the increasing use of e-commerce and e-business applications the risk and number of fraud cases rises also. Most attacks target at the knowledge-based authentication and transaction authorization that uses an easily transferable secret only.

Criminal hackers therefore imitate well-known banking or e-commerce websites to lure online customers into entering credit card information or the authentication secrets like PINs or TANs. Sometimes a weakness or security hole of the user's browser is used to disguise these phishing websites further, so that the fake can only be detected by a thorough inspection of the websites certificates by an experienced user. Other attacks use malicious software like viruses or trojan horses to search the victim's computer for stored authentication information and log the keystrokes to sniff passwords and PINs while they are entered.

On the merchants or banks side it is hard to reliably identify and authenticate the valid online customer, as the authentication secrets may have been compromised through attacks.

The increasing number of countries issuing electronic ID documents lead to citizen- wide availability on secure e-business transaction, protected by ownership based authentication based on evaluated security of smartcards. In contrast to past attempts to use smartcard based authentication (e.g. HBCI smartcards), these ID documents can be expected to have a widespread availability with the customers even before registration or enrolment at the bank or e-business. Furthermore these ID cards are issued by the government and therefore are not tied to one provider but can be used in other industry sectors as well for cross border applications as well.

N. Pohlmann, H. Reimer, W. Schneider (Editors): Securing Electronic Business Processes, Vieweg (2008), 242-250

To solve incompatibilities between different national solutions on the different levels of physical transmission, logical data structures, security features and application interfaces (API) the simplest way would be to make use of a common standard or specification, if available.

2 The European Citizen Card (ECC)

Therefore the European standardization body CEN has published the technical specification 15480 [CEN TS 15480], the European Citizen Card (ECC) as an offer to be used for governmental purpose. The European Citizen Card is neither a physical card nor a specific card application or set of applications by itself, but a definition of logical data groups and services that can be provided by any governmental card issued for their own application context, e.g. ID cards or health cards.

Figure 1: Example for a European Citizen Card

The specification of the European Citizen Card envelopes four parts, so far: part 1 and 2 have been published in 2007, part 3 and 4 are currently under development in CEN TC 224 WG 15:

- Part 1: Physical, electrical properties and transport protocols (Physical Card Interface);
- Part 2: Logical data structures and card services (Logical Card Interface);
- Part 3 (preliminary): Interoperability using and application interface (Middleware);
- Part 4 (preliminary): Recommendations for issuance, operation and use (Card Profiles)

2.1 IAS services of the ECC

Many states are moving towards offering their cardholders card services combined with extra IT functions for electronic business transactions that go beyond basic personal identification used as a machine readable travel document or for proof of residence. The intention in supporting electronic services for identification, authentication and signature creation (IAS services) is to extend the possibility of transactions that citizens can perform electronically.

Therefore the European Citizen Card specification describes in part 3 in addition to the card itself a generic middleware that enables the ECC to be used securely in online transactions. New products to the benefit of citizens, business and government can be offered, for example through e-government applications.

The IAS services are mainly based on public key procedures, essentially, on RSA operations, as used by the German electronic health card eGK and the French identity card INES. However, offering equivalent security elliptic curve cryptography is gaining ground. Consequently, the European CEN prEN 14890 standard for secure signature creation [CEN prEN 14890] was expanded in the middle of 2005. This development paid particular attention to compatibility with ECC specification CEN prTS 15480 in order to enable IAS services to be based upon elliptic curves. The main IAS services for the ECC are presented in the following sections.

2.2 Passive Authentication

For the purposes of passive authentication, when issuing the ECC, the document issuer creates a digital signature from parts of the document data. Usually, this uses the less sensitive data in small amounts e.g. personal details, but no biometric features, as the basis. The signature is stored in the data object on the card inside the file EF.SOD. The integrity of this data can now be verified at any time by checking the signature with the public key of the document signer. At the same time, positive signature verification implicitly assures that the document was actually created by the document issuer and thereby passively authenticates it.

However, passive authentication is only useful for static data, i.e., data that does not change over time. Otherwise every change to name or address would require the signature to be updated at considerable cost.

2.3 Basic Access Control (BAC)

When using a contactless interface, it is necessary to ensure that the card can only be used with consent of the card holder. Theoretically the data of a contactless card can be read unnoticed (e.g. while still in a pocket), if no protection is in place.

For performing Basic Access Control, the machine-readable data on the card's surface is captured optically and used as input data for a key derivation. The derived symmetric key is already known to the card, as an equivalent value is stored in the card's secure memory location at personalization time. This key is used to establish a symmetric encryption key and a message authentication key. Since an attacker cannot acquire the optical data unnoticed, he cannot derive the encryption key to decipher the card for reading.

The disadvantage of this approach is the limited entropy of the data used for the key derivation.

2.4 Modular Extended Access Control (mEAC)

As its name implies, the *Modular Extended Access Control (*mEAC) protocol is based on the EAC protocol developed for e-passports. The same chip and terminal authentication modules have been adopted, although they are used in a modified sequence. The mEAC includes a new module for checking user consent, which can be executed before EAC. In an application that uses cards with contacts this can be accomplished via the traditional PIN-based user verification method, while for contactless communication the PACE protocol can be used (see next section) to secure the communication between the card terminal and the ECC locally.

In an online use (see Figure 2), the remote e-service for e-business or e-government performs the Terminal Authentication with the card to prove its authenticity. Now, that the card (and therefore the customer also) can be sure not to reveal information to an attacker, the card shows its authenticity to the e-service by the execution of the chip authentication module. At the same, a Diffie-Hellman key agreement is used to establish strong session keys, which are used afterwards to set up a secure channel with secure messaging directly between the e-service and the card.

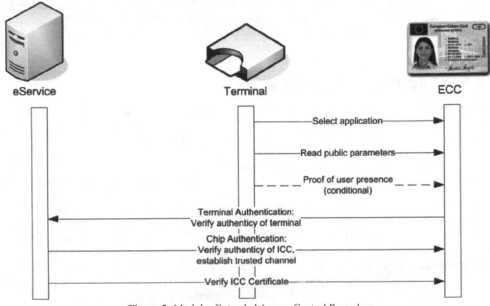

Figure 2: Modular Extended Access Control Procedure

2.5 Password Authenticated Connection Establishment (PACE)

PACE is a new protocol offered as a future replacement for the aforementioned BAC protocol. Same as in BAC, PACE ensures that only authorized terminals can communicate with the card. For this purpose it uses a short password or PIN to ensure the user's consent to perform PACE which is an entry parameter to a chain of Diffie-Hellman protocols between card and terminal on a local base.

PACE establishes strong session keys on base of Diffie-Hellman. The derived symmetric encryption key and message authentication key are used to protect the message, which cannot be retrieved even by knowing the password and after logging the whole communication protocol. To avoid forcing the users to memorize one or more passwords due to several applications, for certain use cases the password could also be printed on the card body e.g. with border control.

2.6 Signature service

An important basic service is the signature service, which can be integrated in the ECC for creation of qualified electronic signatures. A possible option is also to conditionally include the signature service itself on the card without installing the necessary certificates or keys at time of issuance. This can then be done subsequently at a later point in time upon request by the user.

2.7 Encryption

An Encryption Key Decipherment service is planned for encrypted e-mail communication or encrypted document transfer. Thereby the e-mail message or the document is encrypted with a symmetric procedure. The symmetric key itself is encrypted using an asymmetric procedure with the recipient's public key. The associated private key is stored in the card. It encrypts the symmetric document encipherment key after appropriate authentication, which can then be used outside the card to decrypt the e-mail message.

2.8 ECC application profiles

Part 2 of the ECC specification defines the services that are mandatory for a European Citizen Card as well as optional extensions. Since a card used as ECC can have many different primary applications (e.g. as an ID card or a health card), various instantiations of an ECC are imaginable.

Specific application profiles are contained in part 4, on one hand to present use cases which can act as a reference and on the other hand to exemplify use cases which are based on actual implementations,.

Each of these profiles contain one or more applications which use interfaces and transport protocols described in part 1 of the specification and services described in part 2. Each profile thereby is linked to a distinct object identifier (OID) to be used as interoperable reference, e.g. to ease the discovery of the card's and / or application's capabilities. In any other case the middleware according ECC part 3 has to detect the services on the card. For this purpose one so called global profile is integrated in Part 4, to retrieve the card capabilities as well as application capabilities. This profile can be used complementary to the application profiles, in case the card / application contains additional information, which is not covered by the specific profile in use.

Two application profiles have been developed in the past drafts, with the expectation, that others will be added by the time, the specification is adopted. These profiles are presented in the following sections.

2.9 Profile 1: ID card

ECC Profile 1 describes a card which is used as an identity document. One single mandatory contactless interface conforming to ISO/IEC 14443 is specified for all applications. The following three applications are envisioned:

- eID: This application implements electronic identity card services and data structure. The cardholder's data (corresponding to the data on conventional identity documents) are stored in distinct data groups. Access to these data groups is controlled in fine granulated layers by the rights defined in the terminal's certificate. Several roles can be defined to enforce different access conditions for different roles. For example, write access to individual data groups can be allowed for certain roles: after appropriate authentication a registration office could update the address data, so the card does not have to be replaced in case a person has moved.

- ICAO: Since ID cards are accepted as travel documents within Schengen States, this profile contains an MRTD application (Machine Readable Travel Document) in conformance to ICAO specifications, comparable to the e-passport. The mandatory card services are passive authentication, BAC, EAC chip authentication and EAC terminal authentication referenced by the specific OIDs, plus Secure Messaging for the ICAO application.

- SIG: The card includes a signature application in accordance with CEN prEN 14890 [CEN prEN 14890] which contains the signature service itself on the card with the added possibility of installing the necessary certificates or keys at time of issuance or alternatively having them already installed during the personalization process.

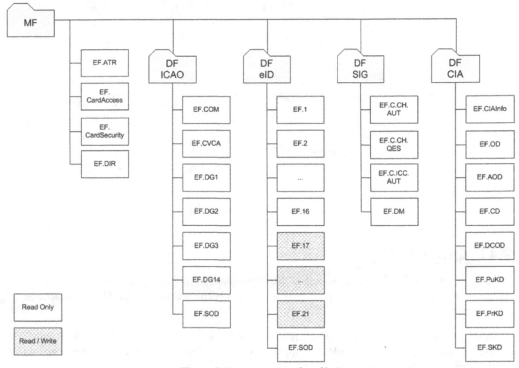

Figure 3: Data structure of profile 1

Profile 1 has been developed by the German Industry Forum (DIF AG 1, Deutsches Industrieforum) in collaboration with the German Federal Office for Information Security (BSI). The main focus is to ensure compatibility with the upcoming German national identity card.

The eID application is designed to be used for e-commerce and e-business purposes as well. The data fields, accessible from a merchants or banks terminal, are defined in the corresponding terminal certificate. Therefore the availability e.g. of the age or the address can be controlled for each application separately.

2.10 Profile 2: ESIGN

Profile 2 describes a card with an ESIGN application and the option for an additional functionality for digital signatures. It supports a contact-based interface according to ISO/IEC 7816-3 and the T=1 transport protocol. The profile is based on the specification for the German electronic health card (eGK). The protocols, services, and formats used in profile 2 are largely based on the prEN 14890 [CEN prEN 14890] standards.

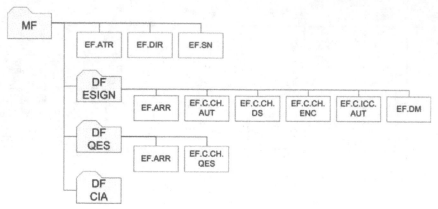

Figure 4: Data structure of profile 2

2.11 Other profiles

More profiles can be included and existing profiles are subject to further development and improvement before the specification is finally adopted. Even after it has been released, new profiles can still be added to the specification through the CEN TC224 WG 15 working group.

Therefore the standard provides a profile template to design new profiles in a comparable manner. The template contains guidelines in order to support anyone developing a profile; it clearly states which information has to be included in a profile.

3 Online-Bank Web Service with the ECC

Recently Giesecke & Devrient (G&D) and Wirecard Bank AG showcased the first e-business applica-tion that utilizes an electronic ID card, based on a subset of the profile 1 of the European Citizen Card specification. To use the application, consumers have to install a middleware software and a simple contactless card reader on their home PCs. This new application allows banks and consumers to authen-ticate each other using an official personal identity document and a personal identification number (PIN) for the first time ever. Giesecke & Devrient's new launch additional represents the first implementation of the standards for microchip-equipped European Citizen Cards along with the middleware in accord-ance to ECC Part 3 to support commercial applications.

The online banking application supports the following use cases:

1. Registration with the European Citizen Card
2. Log-In for Registered Users
3. Transaction Security

With the first use case "Registration" the new customer enrolls for the first time at the online-portal of the bank. After putting the card on the installed reader system, the server of the service provider is requesting the Card PIN of the holder's ID card. After confirming the Card PIN the access certificate in card verifiable format (CV certificate) itself (e.g. stating "issuing authority" and "validity date") and the selective access rights to data containers is displayed to the user. At this time the user is able to abort the transaction, e.g. if he does not want to reveal the requested data (see Figure 5). If he wants to continue, a simple click on the "OK" button initializes the communication protocol. Thereby the new EAC 2.0 protocol (see [TR-03110 V2]) is used, which can be interpreted as a specific tree of the mEAC protocol (see Profile 1 of the ECC) to provide a secure channel between the chip of the card and the server of the bank as service provider. In case that the service provider has got the obligatory access certificate with the respective access rights (see Figure 6) during the EAC 2.0 authentication protocol, now all data, can be read out of the card, which are to be used for the first time enrolment.

Figure 5: Card access during registration with user confirmation of the data to be read

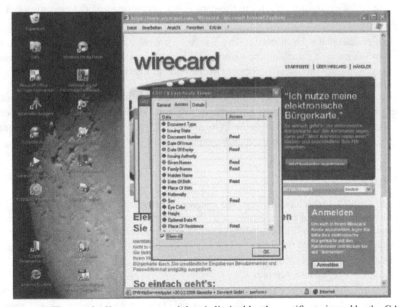

Figure 6: The terminal's access to card data is limited by the certificate issued by the CA

The user doesn't have to fill in any personal information, which is provided by the chip in the ECC. This method guarantees that wrong or incomplete addresses, filled in consciously by an attacker or even unintended by the user, are prevented. Only supplementary data, which are not stored in the card, e.g. email address or mobile number, are to be typed in manually.

After first time registration the user can log into the system conveniently by using the authentication application of his ECC. He does not have to use service provider specific "user name" and "password" but simply confirming the Card PIN of his card as asked for by the service provider server request. After PIN confirmation, the EAC 2.0 protocol again establishes a secure channel so that the user can access his account conveniently.

The transaction security provided by the ECC can replace the usage of PIN / TAN procedure which is common at most of the online-banking applications of today.

Thereby this method provides a higher security level as well as a higher convenience factor for the sake of the user.

4 Conclusions

By using an ID card based authentication many typical security problems of today's e-business, e-commerce and online banking applications can be solved:

- Registration and enrolment using the card data eliminates typing or other data entry errors and also protects against fraud by registration with wrong or stolen identities
- Phishing attacks can be ruled out, since the access to the card, that is necessary for authentication, is bound to certificates that are checked by the card instead leaving this up to the user
- Protection against malware attacks: Even if the PIN has been spied out e.g. during entry, the security protocols (e.g. PACE, EAC) make sure, that a secure, encrypted channel is established from the service provider directly to the card itself, protecting against eavesdroppers on the terminal, home PC or the internet transmissions
- Proof of Authenticity: Both parties, the e-service provider as well as the customer, can be sure to talk to the authentic partner. Imitations or fakes, whether fake websites or fake cards, are not able to authenticate themselves because of missing authentic certificates

Since a widespread availability of electronic ID documents this new method of secure authentication qualifies for a common, general purpose, interoperable solution instead of a provider-specific implementation, especially in conjunction with the ECC middleware component enabling different card types (e.g. ID cards and health cards) to be used at the same time.

References

[CEN TS 15480] CEN/TS 15480 Identification card systems – European Citizen Card, Part 1: Physical, electrical and transport protocol characteristics, Part 2: Logical data structures and card services, Part 3 (preliminary): Interoperability using and application interface, Part 4 (preliminary): Recommendations for issuance, operation and use

[CEN prEN 14890] CEN prEN 14890 Application Interface for smart cards used as Secure Signature Creation Devices — Part 1: Basic services

[TR-03110 V2] German Federal Office for Information Security (BSI): Technical Guideline TR-03110 Advanced Security Mechanisms for Machine Readable Travel Documents – Extended Access Control (EAC) and Password Authenticated Connection Establishment (PACE). Version 2.0 – Release Candidate.

Electronic Signatures for Public Procurement across Europe

Jon Ølnes[1] · Anette Andresen[1] · Stefano Arbia[3] · Markus Ernst[2]
Martin Hagen[4] · Stephan Klein[2] · Giovanni Manca[3] · Adriano Rossi[3]
Frank Schipplick[2] · Daniele Tatti[3] · Gesa Wessolowski[4] · Jan Windheuser[2]

[1]DNV, Veritasveien 1, N-1322 Høvik, Norway
{jon.olnes | anette.andresen}@dnv.com

[2]Bremen Online Services GmbH, Am Fallturm 9, D-28359 Bremen, Germany
{me | sk | fs | jwi}@bos-bremen.de

[3]CNIPA, via Isonzo 21/B, I-00189 Rome, Italy
{arbia | manca | tatti | rossi}@cnipa.it

[4]Freie Hansestadt Bremen, Finanzen, Rudolf Hilferding Platz 1, D-28195 Bremen, Germany
{martin.hagen | gesa.wessolowski}@finanzen.bremen.de

Abstract

The PEPPOL (Pan-European Public Procurement On-Line) project is a large scale pilot under the CIP programme of the EU, exploring electronic public procurement in a unified European market. An important element is interoperability of electronic signatures across borders, identified today as a major obstacle to cross-border procurement. PEPPOL will address use of signatures in procurement processes, in particular tendering but also post-award processes like orders and invoices. Signature policies, i.e. quality requirements and requirements on information captured in the signing process, will be developed. This as well as technical interoperability of e-signatures across Europe will finally be piloted in demonstrators starting late 2009 or early 2010.

1 Introduction

Public agencies in the EU Member States procure goods and services amounting to 1.500-2.000 billion Euro per year, or 15-20 % of the EU's GDP (Gross Domestic Product) [ICT-PSP]. It is estimated [COMM01] that use of electronic procurement can save up to 5 % on expenditure and 50-80 % of transaction costs. Following the principle of the internal market, electronic public procurement must be open across the entire EU or even wider, such as inclusion of the EEA area and states having trading agreements with the EU.

The EU Directives on public procurement [EU02] and [EU03] put electronic procurement processes on par with traditional means of communication. The directives focus mainly on tendering (pre-award) processes. Electronic exchange of business documents according to existing contracts (post-award) is another area that should be focussed, e.g. orders and invoices.

N. Pohlmann, H. Reimer, W. Schneider (Editors): Securing Electronic Business Processes, Vieweg (2008), 251-261

Signatures play an important role in traditional procurement processes and electronic signatures are in many cases deemed necessary for the corresponding electronic processes. Thus, electronic public procurement must rely on cross-border interoperability of signatures. This is identified by the EU Commission as a major obstacle [COMM01] and even mentioned as "the single most important blocking factor to cross-border e-procurement" [ICT-PSP].

This paper presents the signature interoperability challenges from the viewpoint of the PEPPOL (Pan-European Public Procurement On-Line) project: Status, issues identified, and directions for solving these issues.

2 The PEPPOL Project

PEPPOL[1] (Pan-European Public Procurement On-Line) is a three-year (mid-2008 to mid-2011), large-scale pilot project under the EU's Competitiveness and Innovation Framework Programme (CIP). The project covers the following aspects of public procurement:

- Virtual company dossier (VCD) covers interoperable solutions for utilisation of company information that is already registered, in order to reuse this information in electronic tendering processes across Europe.
- E-catalogues for use in both tendering processes and for orders.
- E-ordering – order and order confirmation.
- E-invoicing – claims for payment for goods and services.
- E-signatures in tendering processes as well as other procurement processes.

Following a specification phase and a development phase, PEPPOL will run real life pilots involving at least the countries that are partners of the project but possibly also other countries.

A VCD may be used to convey information in business registers as well as other information about the status of companies and their employees, such as roles and authorisations. Interactive, on-line solutions to business registers exist[2] and automated services (system to system) may be an extension. Results from the BRITE[3] project will be utilised by PEPPOL.

E-catalogues may be intended for human use, representing products, their specifications, and associated information such as price. Catalogues for system to system communication may also be envisaged, in this case based on standard product codes and standard message formats. PEPPOL will build on existing work in the area [EDYN].

Order, order confirmation (which may be optional), and invoice can also be intended for human use or system to system structured messages.

Catalogue, order, order confirmation, and invoice will in PEPPOL be based on the NES[4] profiles of UBL (Universal Business Language). PEPPOL will contribute to the ongoing standardisation work in these areas.

Signatures are primarily relevant for tendering processes and for invoicing (both covered by EU Directives, see below) but may be used for other aspects as well; e.g. one may sign a catalogue or order docu-

---

1 http://www.peppol.eu
2 As demonstrated by the European Business Register, http://www.ebr.org
3 Business Register Interoperability Throughout Europe, http://www.briteproject.net
4 Northern European Subset of UBL, http://www.nesubl.eu

ments, and the issuer of a VCD may sign the dossier if it is represented as a document. Further signed certificates and attestations may accompany an offer [Siemens].

3 The Public Procurement Directives, Signatures

According to a the EU Directives on public procurement [EU02] [EU03] and the accompanying requirements document [COMM02], contracting authorities[5] may decide that communication and exchange of information with economic operators shall be performed exclusively by electronic means or by a combination of electronic means and paper. Electronic communication must guarantee data integrity and confidentiality. Secure communication channels (such as provided by TLS/SSL) and/or advanced electronic signatures may be used to this effect. Traceability of processes must be guaranteed by storing the original version of all documents along with records of all exchanges carried out. Signatures may play a role in the traceability. Time stamping is required, by an independent time stamping authority or by other means that are considered sufficiently reliable.

Contracting authorities are free (subject to national regulations) to choose the appropriate means of communication and to require a specific format and structure for tenders. Economic operators shall comply with these specifications (which must be readily available to all interested parties) in order to present a valid tender or request to participate.

The directives state that neither signatures nor encryption shall be used by economic operators unless they are invited to do so by the contracting authority. National legislation may establish mandatory requirements for use of signatures, which all contracting authorities in this country must adhere to. In the absence of such legislation, the contracting authority can independently choose the level of signatures required for the particular case at hand.

Use of signatures shall be in accordance with the EU Directive on electronic signatures [EU01]. This directive explicitly states that a qualified signature shall be granted legal effect in the same manner as a handwritten signature, and that other electronic signatures shall not unduly be denied legal effect. The interpretation is that contracting authorities are required to accept any qualified signature that has been legally produced in any EU Member State, and any other signature that fulfil the required level.

In repetitive procedures, e.g. tendering among economic operators that already have entered framework agreements, the public procurement directives allow signature requirements to be lowered since the actors are known a priori to one another.

The public procurement directives focus on the tendering (pre-award) phase of public procurement. Obviously, there is a focus in many countries on efficiency in post-award processes as well and in particular on e-invoicing. According to [EU04] e-invoices shall either be signed or protected by other means according to the so-called "EDI clause" of [EU04]. The EDI clause limits open exchange of e-invoices but it still seems like the prevailing practice in most countries is to refer to this clause and to not sign e-invoices. Lack of interoperability of e-signatures is one explicit reason for this situation.

Other post-award procedures, e.g. an order process, are not covered by EU Directives and neither are other business documents like catalogues and VCD.

---

5 Terminology in this paper is aligned with [COM02], where "contracting authority" is the buying side (i.e. a public agency) whereas "economic operator" is the actor (usually private enterprise) offering goods or services.

4 Status for E-signatures in Public Procurement

The IDABC *Preliminary Study on Mutual Recognition of eSignatures for eGovernment Applications* [IDABC01] consists of separate reports giving national profiles for 29 European countries (the 27 EU Member States, Turkey, Croatia) and a final study report that sums up analysis, assessment, conclusions and recommendations. In addition to the general situation, key applications are surveyed with respect to eSignatures: public procurement (i.e. tendering in this case), VAT declaration, income tax declaration.

The survey shows that only 15 of the 29 countries[6] have procurement applications available, some of them with very limited functionality. This situation may change rapidly as there is work in progress in most countries. Note that as the study focuses on a national level, there may be additional, regional applications that are not completely covered by the study.

Of the 15 countries, 6 require qualified signatures while 7 require advanced signatures (some of them with the additional requirement of qualified certificate). Two countries (Finland, Estonia) require only authentication (can be interpreted in this context as a simple electronic signature). The survey gives limited information on how signatures are applied in the tendering processes (at what steps of the process and for which documents) and there is very limited information on use of signatures in other procurement processes, such as e-invoicing.

All tendering solutions surveyed support domestic eID issuers only, with some very limited cross-border interoperability being piloted in some cases (e.g. between Austria and Germany). Solutions typically require use of eIDs from one or a few specific issuers, possibly covering all domestic eID issuers. International interoperability is limited to acceptance of eIDs from specific, individually identified issuers in other countries.

The PEPPOL project is in the process of conducting a detailed survey of existing and planned use of e-signatures for public procurement in selected countries (at least Denmark, Finland, France, Germany, Italy, Norway) focussing on both pre-award and post-award processes and covering all interoperability aspects discussed below. The information will be used as an aid in specification of policies and technical solutions for the pilots in PEPPOL.

5 Interoperability Requirements

5.1 Overall E-signature Interoperability

As stated by the [ICT-PSP], interoperability of electronic signatures is a major challenge to cross-border e-procurement. Earlier documents, like [COMM01] refer to interoperability of qualified signatures only. Status in 2007 is that products offering qualified signature are available in only some European countries [Sealed], leaving in many cases the pragmatic (and for some countries desired) choice of accepting even non-qualified signatures for public procurement. This adds to the interoperability challenge.

For cross-border interoperability, the overall assumption shall be that the parties are independent and must be allowed to choose technical solutions and service providers independently [Ølnes]. The ultimate interoperability requirements are:

---

6   Of other relevant countries, notably Norway and Iceland have electronic public procurement solutions.

- An eID7 holder shall be able to use the eID to sign documents towards any counterpart. The eID holder independently selects the eID to use.
- The receiver of a signed document shall be able to accept signatures from all counterparts, regardless of the eID used by the counterpart, but provided that signature policy requirements are met. In an open market, the receiver cannot dictate the counterpart's selection of eID.
- A third party, receiving a document signed by other parties, shall be able to verify the signatures no matter the eIDs used by the other parties. One does not know at the time of signing who may need to verify signatures.

The interoperability issues are mainly faced by the contracting authority, as receiver of tenders and other signed documents originating in the entire EU area. The situation is symmetric in that an economic operator also needs to accept signatures from the contracting authority; however this part is less complex. The main issue faced by the economic operator is to obtain information about the policies and practices required by the contracting authority, and then to be able to comply with these requirements.

Below, issues and directions at solutions are outlined, referring to the interoperability layers (organisational, semantic, technical interoperability) from the IDABC Interoperability Framework [IDABC02].

5.2 Organisational Interoperability

5.2.1 Signatures in the Procurement Processes

Which documents must be signed (if advanced signatures are required at all), and what is required in terms of commitment and authorization?

As stated by [IDABC02], the main difficulties in the adoption of e-signature solutions for cross-border submission and acceptance of tendering documents are related to different internal structures and processes of the administrations of the Member States. The main issue is in the PEPPOL consortium's opinion not that requirements must be equal but that they must be transparent and non-discriminatory.

A requirement for public procurement solutions, at least in the long term, is the ability to deal with complex tenders [COMM02]. A complex tender may be delivered by a consortium of multiple parties in different roles, providing documents that potentially should be signed separately or jointly by members of the consortium. Additional documents may accompany a tender, such as certificates and attestations [Siemens], which may in turn be signed by the entities issuing the documents. Examples of other actors that may apply signatures related to a tender are time stamping authorities, notaries, and operators of e-procurement platforms.

PEPPOL will describe a few alternative strategies for signatures in tendering processes. Examples are: All documents signed, cover letter signed, summary document signed (e.g. document containing identification and hash values of all other documents). Strategies will also provide guidelines on how to specify the commitment implied by signatures. Signatures for e-invoices, orders etc. are more straightforward but will need to be specified to some extent.

---

7 A PKI-based (public key infrastructure) eID usually consists of two or three X.509 certificates and corresponding key pairs, separating out the encryption (key negotiation) function and possibly the electronic signature (content commitment) function to separate key pairs/certificates. To a user, this separation is normally not visible.

5.2.2 Binding to Organisation, Role and Authorizations

A signature binds to the name in the accompanying eID. In general, this is a person name only (eIDs containing additional organisational naming attributes and organisational eIDs with no person name may occasionally be encountered). There is a need to link this name to the organisation (typically the economic operator) and further to defined roles and authorizations, alternatively to verify that a set of signatures together represent the necessary authorizations. The issue is relevant also for certificates and attestations issued by other public or private parties to an economic operator. It is generally not recommended to include authorization attributes in eID certificates, as such attributes are frequently changed and thus their inclusion will lead to cumbersome eID management. Solutions exist where long-lived authorizations (such as being a medical practitioner) are represented in eIDs but it is not assumed that this will influence public procurement.

PEPPOL will outline a few strategies for establishing such bindings. The easiest one is to simply accept the signatures without any further question. In case of later disputes, there is a strong proof from the signatures, and if authorizations have been violated, this can be detected. This approach is built on the assumption that mistakes are rare.

A reasonable intermediate solution is a registration procedure to establish and verify the link between a person with a given eID and roles within companies as a step of the procurement process. While registration may be done for each contracting authority, a better solution may be to assign this to one or more trusted identity service providers. Thus, registration may be reused, and a service to provide log-on and mapping between identities is made available. While a European-wide network of identity providers may be a future vision, the scope of such a provider for the PEPPOL pilot will be determined by legal and trust issues.

The long-term goal may be automated discovery of links to organisation, roles and authorizations. This is achievable today within some countries by use of national identifiers. Cross-border use of different national person identifiers must be regarded as a too ambitious goal in the time frame of PEPPOL. PEPPOL shall however investigate the feasibility of including some key roles and the persons taking these roles as information in VCDs and business registries. It is also possible to publish such information in a directory. This requires specification of syntax and semantics for representation of roles and authorizations.

Use of employee eIDs[8] that bind a person name to a company will be investigated, as well as use of corporate eIDs without any person name. A corporate eID will contain the name of the company (as registered in a business register, commonly used name, or both) and the unique identifier (VAT number or equivalent) from the business register. An example of use is signing of e-invoices where the receiver should be concerned about the company issuing the invoice, not about the name of any person in this company[9]. Another example usage is signing of certificates from a public or private (e.g. ISO 9001 certificate) agency. One possible use is an inner signature from a person and an outer signature by a corporate eID of the economic operator. The legal situation with respect to use of corporate eIDs will need to be investigated.

---

8 Today, few corporate eIDs are able to fulfil even modest quality requirements for public procurement. There are exceptions, such as the qualified eIDs to be issued by (the Norwegian oil company) Statoil-Hydro's internal, corporate CA.

9 Note however that this may conflict with signature laws in some countries, where a person's name is required for all signatures (e.g. Italy).

5.2.3 Signature Policies

A signature policy[10] defines a set of rules for the creation and validation of electronic signatures, under which a signature can be determined to be valid (signature acceptance). The main purpose of a signature policy is to define quality requirements (cryptographic requirements, certificate policy requirements, requirements for use of smart cards etc.). A signature policy may also list trusted eID issuers. Additionally, the policy may set requirements for the signature format[11] to be used and information to be included in the SDO (signed data object), such as time-stamps, eID information, revocation information and policy identifiers. A signature policy according to ETSI must always be stated in a humanly readable form and parts of the policy may also be described in a form suitable for automated processing.

IDABC [IDABC01] finds 15 countries with e-procurement services in operation, where 6 require qualified signatures, 7 require advanced signatures (sometimes with the additional requirement of a qualified eID), while two countries require only authentication. The services furthermore either list one or a few eID issuers or are able to accept all domestic issuers and perhaps a few foreign issuers.

I PEPPOL's view, differences in national legislation as well as different requirements for different e-procurement processes necessitate development of a set of signature policies as common specifications. The number of policies should be small. The specification must provide non-discriminatory rules for acceptance of eIDs to replace present policies for national solutions, which refer to domestic issuers or national accreditation schemes (see below).

Signature policies from PEPPOL will be made available in humanly readable form. Computer readable representation for some policies, e.g. for e-invoices, will be investigated.

There are two main topics for the signature policies specification:

1. Quality requirements for eIDs and signatures, including a common definition of the concept "advanced electronic signature".
2. SDO requirements; which information to include in signed data objects.

As a part of the quality requirements, quality profiles for eID issuers and their certificate policies shall be developed. To determine if an eID fulfils quality requirements, the issuer and its policy must be assessed towards the corresponding quality profile.

For complex tenders one will usually measure all signatures from all parties towards the same signature policy; however signatures from time stamping authorities and issuers of certificates and attestations may need to be addressed separately.

Signature policies shall be described in general terms, not merely as a list of approved eID issuers. A trust list distribution service such as described by [ETSI01] may however be part of a solution.

There are two major issues that cannot be solved by PEPPOL alone: requirements for qualified signatures and use of national accreditation schemes.

Qualified signature is a requirement that is imposed by some national authorities and contracting authorities. This is actually compliant with the intentions of the e-signature directive [EU01]. But products and services that offer qualified signature are available in only about half the European countries. Thus, this is not a non-discriminatory requirement today.

---

10 Defined in ETSI TS 101 733 Annex C, see also ETSI TR 102 038, ETSI TR 102 272, ETSI TR 102 045.
11 Examples are XAdES (ETSI TS 101 903), CAdES (ETSI TS 101 733), PKCS#7 (RFC2315), CMS (RFC2630), XML DSIG (RFC3275), and PDF signatures.

The e-signature directive [EU01] is explicitly intended to enable cross-border use of e-signatures; however both the e-signature directive and the directives on public procurement have clauses that allow national authorities to introduce voluntary, national accreditation schemes for eID issuers, potentially recognizing only issuers that have obtained a national accreditation. The eID issuers then must declare conformance with national requirements that are additional to requirements for qualified eIDs (accreditation may be used for non-qualified eIDs as well). Since it will be practically infeasible for an eID issuer to declare conformance with national requirements in a lot of countries, and there may in fact be legal requirements on the contracting authority to accept only nationally accredited CAs, such accreditation systems may effectively block cross-border interoperability. This is identified by IDABC [IDABC01] as a major obstacle to cross-border use of e-signatures.

5.2.4 Risk and Legal Situation Related to Signature Acceptance

An eID issuer operates according to a certificate policy, which regulates use and acceptance of eIDs. A certificate policy will refer to the issuer's national legislation and may furthermore be written in the issuer's local language. This leaves the receiver of a signed document with a rather unpredictable risk picture in particular concerning liability and possibilities for claiming recourse in case of mistakes on the issuer's side. IDABC [IDABC01] cites this fact as another reason why national e-government services are reluctant to accept anything but eIDs from a few selected, and preferably domestic, issuers.

PEPPOL will explore use of a signature and eID validation platform to simplify the tasks of signature acceptance (adherence to signature policies), technical verification and risk management. The validation platform can be implemented by local software, possibly including use of a trust list distribution service [ETSI01], or by use of a trusted VA (Validation Authority) service [Ølnes].

The legal situation can only be improved by explicit agreements, i.e. transferring the situation from national law to contract law. It is clearly not feasible for the receiver of a signed document to have explicit agreements with all relevant eID issuers. The goal is to provide the receiver with a single (or at least only a few) trust anchor to make the situation symmetric with respect to the signer's relationship with his selected (one) eID issuer. This goal will be approached by the design of the validation platform to be piloted by PEPPOL. One alternative is outsourcing of signature verification and eID validation to a Validation Authority (VA) where the agreement with the VA covers all eID issuers supported [Ølnes]. Another alternative is a trusted list of accepted eID issuers, with a similar agreement as for a VA. In both cases, the actor running the service (VA or trust list distribution) needs agreements with the eID issuers.

5.3 Semantic Interoperability – Names in eIDs

The semantics of names in eIDs vary considerably across Europe. For a person, either full name or commonly used name or both will be included[12], and a unique identifier is normally also included as an attribute of the name. The unique identifier may be linked to a national personal identification scheme in countries where such a scheme exists, or it may be defined locally to the CA. The receiver of a signed document (or an eID used for any other purpose) must be able to make use of the name or translate it into a name that can be used in the receiver's systems. IDABC [IDABC01] finds that, where national person identifiers exist, e-government services tend to rely heavily on them, thus excluding foreign citizens from using the service. While national person identifiers are highly useful, a strict requirement implies an obstacle to cross-border operation.

---

12 It is assumed that pseudonymous eIDs will not be used in public procurement, although this need not be completely ruled out.

To some extent the same problem exists for corporate identifiers, although there are initiatives like the BRITE-project[13] to make such identifiers work across Europe. Corporate identifiers are not subject to any privacy concerns and are thus more easily used.

Interpretation of names in eIDs is not a core topic of PEPPOL but to some extent this is addressed along with the issues discussed in 5.2.1 above.

5.4 Technical Interoperability

5.4.1 Reliable Verification of Signatures

For signature verification[14], the receiver must be able to process the signature format, including fields like time-stamps signed by some trusted TSP (time stamp provider), the necessary hash and cryptographic algorithms, and the eIDs, including verification of key usage and other extensions. The public keys of all relevant eID issuers must be reliably available, and it must be possible to check revocation status of eIDs. Estimates indicate that in the order of 200 eID issuers must be handled to cover relevant eIDs in the EU. Current state in technical standards [Sealed] is that there are still some open issues. This is not the main interoperability problem but it must be addressed.

It is assumed that standard signature formats and signed data objects can be used for public procurement and that useful profiles exist that define e.g. how to sign an e-invoice.

PEPPOL will explore both local software solutions for signature verification and verification as a service from a trusted VA (validation authority).

5.4.2 Signing

One focus area for eID interoperability is mobility from the user perspective: How can I use my smart-card (or whatever I have) wherever I am? While this is an important issue in general, the importance is less in the public procurement case. Signers represent organisations (contracting authorities or economic operators) and will usually sign inside their corporate infrastructure. Signing as a part of the service interface from a portal-like procurement solution is however a challenge.

PEPPOL does not intend to do much work on this issue but rather utilize results from the parallel STORK pilot[15], which is assumed to do extensive work on this topic.

5.4.3 How can signatures be verified in retrospect?

Documents exchanged e.g. in a tendering process must be logged and retained for a period of time. The directives on public procurement and e-invoicing [EU02] [EU03] [EU04] all state that the original documents must be retained. The definition of "original" may however vary from country to country. With respect to signatures, strategies may be:

- Archive documents with signatures intact;
- Remove signatures and record their traces as metadata;
- Remove and forget signatures, storing only plain documents.

---

13 Business Register Interoperability Throughout Europe – http://www.briteproject.net
14 Note that this refers to technical verification of the signature. To accept the signature, one additionally has to verify compliance with the signature policy in force for quality and other requirements.
15 http://www.eid-stork.eu

The two latter enables re-formatting of documents to archival formats and may be valid approaches in some countries; however as an example [Dek05] shows that according to Belgium law the signatures must be kept.

In case of a dispute, it may thus be necessary to verify signatures years after the signatures were created; at a time when the eIDs may have expired. There are two approaches at historical verification of signed documents:

- Capture enough context information in the SDO (signed data object) at time of signing, e.g. revocation information and time-stamps, and ensure that the SDO can later reliably be validated. Verification of the outer signature of the SDO is taken as evidence that the content is correct – although in theory the content can also be checked.
- Ensure that enough context information is available in order to reconstruct state at the time of signing. A reliable time stamp is particularly important.

Requirements for content of SDOs will be addressed in the context of signature policies. A VA may be able to answer requests for verification relatively to a given time in the past [Ølnes]. Note also that the approach specified by [RFC4998] for archival of signed documents can be of relevance. Anyway, there are limitations to the lifetime of a signed object [Ølnes2], determined by lifetime of keys and certificates, lifetime of cryptographic algorithms, lifetime of trusted actors, and practical lifetime of formats (document formats, signature formats, certificate formats).

PEPPOL will not particularly address the long term challenges apart from work on signature policies and the validation platform.

6 Conclusion

The PEPPOL project will develop specifications and solutions for cross border interoperability of e-signatures for public procurement in Europe. PEPPOL will address all aspects of interoperability: organisational, semantic, and technical. Public procurement is an area where there is a real need for this interoperability. In practice, this is a B2B scenario with public agencies in a procurement role. If practical solutions are found to this case, the PEPPOL team believes that the solutions will be applicable also to other e-government applications as well as to other B2B scenarios.

References

[COMM01] Commission of the European Communities: Action Plan for the Implementation of the Legal Framework for Electronic Public Procurement. Communication from the Commission to the Council, the European Parliament, the European Economic and Social Committee and the European Committee of the Regions, 2004.

[COMM02] Commission of the European Communities: Requirements for Conducting Public Procurement Using Electronic Means under the New Public Procurement Directives 2004/18/EC and 2004/17/EC. Commission staff working document, 2005.

[Dek05] Dekeyser, Hannelore: Preservation of Signed Electronic Records. DLM Conference, Budapest, 2005.

[ETSI01] ETSI: Electronic Signatures and Infrastructures; Provision of Harmonized Trust Service Provider Information. ETSI TS 102 231 v2.1.1, 2006.

[EU01] EU: Community Framework for Electronic Signatures. Directive 1999/93/EC of the European Parliament and of the Council, 1999.

[EU02]   EU: Coordination of Procedures for the Award of Public Works Contracts, Public Supply Contracts and Public Service Contracts. Directive 2004/18/EC of the European Parliament and of the Council, 2004.

[EU03]   EU: Coordinating the Procurement Procedures of Entities Operating in the Water, Energy, Transport and Postal Services Sectors. Directive 2004/17/EC of the European Parliament and of the Council, 2004.

[EU04]   EU: Amending Directive 77/388/EEC with a View to Simplifying, Modernising and Harmonising the Conditions Laid down for Invoicing in Respect to Value Added Tax. Counil Directive 2001/115/EC, 2001.

[EDYN]   European Dynamics. Electronic Catalogues in Electronic Public Procurement. DG Internal Markets report, 2007.

[ICT-PSP] ICT Policy Support Programme (PSP): Guidelines to Common Specifications for Cross-border Use of Public Procurement. ICT PSP Programme note, 2007.

[IDABC01] Siemens, Time.lex: Preliminary Study on Mutual Recognition of eSignatures for eGovernment Applications (Final Study and 29 Country Profiles). IDABC, 2007.

[IDABC02] IDABC: European Interoperability Framework for pan-European eGovernment Services. IDABC Report, 2004.

[RFC4998] Gondrom, T., Brandner, R. Pordesch, U: Evidence Record Syntax (ERS). RFC 4998, 2007.

[Sealed]   Sealed, DLA Piper, Across: Study on the Standardisation Aspects of Esignature. IDABC Report, 2007.

[Siemens] Siemens: Preliminary Study on the Electronic Provision of Certificates and Attestations Usually Required in Public Procurement Procedures. DG Internal Market report, 2007.

[Ølnes]   Ølnes, J., Andresen, A., Buene, L., Cerrato, O. and Grindheim, H.: Making: Making Digital Signatures Work across National Borders. ISSE Conference, Warszawa, 2007.

[Ølnes2]   Ølnes, Jon and Seip, Anne Karen: On Long Term Storage of Digitally Signed Documents. Second IFIP Conference on e-Commerce, e-Business, e-Government (I3E), Lisboa, 2002.

Progress through uniformity

Detlef Houdeau

Silicon Trust
C/O Krowne Communications
Windsor House, Cornwall Road, Harrogate – HG1 2PW
North Yorkshire, UK
Detlef.Houdeau@infineon.com
operations.secretariat@silicon-trust.com

Abstract

Individuality plays a vital role in life and in business. It's what helps firms to mark themselves out from their competitors. It makes people easier to remember – and it keeps life interesting. After all, who wants the same experience in Berlin and in Bordeaux? Or in Salzburg and in Southampton? But this individualistic take on life and business has its limitations. Imagine a world where an identity document you were issued in Vienna would not work in Venice. So, to ensure smart cards and other ID documents operate within a specified area, work is taking place behind the scenes to ensure that both the documents and the devices are truly interoperable.

1 Achieving interoperability

To achieve technical interoperability, secure technologies firms need to develop technologies that adhere to application specifications that have already been established. For example, there are published specifications for the smartcard-based technology used in the European Union (EU) tachograph, which has been in operation since September 2006. Likewise, firms have to abide by the ePassport specifications set out in ICAO 9303 and by the EU for second generation passports, as well as the new generation of travel documents.

At this point, it is worth examining the difference between a standard and a specification. A standard can be thought of as a tool box, with some/many options and/or combination of options. A specification focuses on certain topics of a standard or describes a particular framework. In other words, standards allow many different kinds of implementation. For example, in the ePassport world, four security levels are set out in the standard. Meanwhile, specifications can stand alone from a standard.

An essential feature of establishing standards and specifications is evaluation. Test suites and reference implementations based on application standards are created from many relevant providers to a market. For example, with the EU tachograph, there are four providers of the application operating system (OS) on various micro-controllers worldwide and more than 20 providers of application OS exist for the latest generation of high-speed contactless microcontrollers.

Test specifications also have to be established for components such as smart cards, passports and readers. These must be based on application standards and application specifications. Such tests include so-called conformity tests for ePassports and reader/terminals, and are published under ISO 10373 part 6.

N. Pohlmann, H. Reimer, W. Schneider (Editors): Securing Electronic Business Processes, Vieweg (2008), 262-267

Testing, such as the five global interoperability tests of ePassports and border control terminals between 2004 and 2006, is organized by neutral, industry-independent bodies.

Interoperability tests for ePassports and border control terminals
- 1st Canberra, Australia   February 2004
- 2nd West Virginia, USA   July 2004
- 3rd Sydney, Australia   August 2004
- 4th Tokyo, Japan   March 2005
- 5th Singapore,   November 2005
- 6th Berlin, Germany   May 2006

Certified components tests must be carried out by neutral bodies, such as the **Central Information Systems Security Division** (DCSSI) in France, the Bundesamt für Sicherheit in der Informationstechnik (BSI) in Germany, the New Media Development Association (NMDA) in Japan or the National Institute of Standards and Technologies (NIST) in the US. Such bodies can carry out security certification, such as Common Criteria Evaluation Assurance Levels. They can also carry out application certification for particular components, such as the BSI Technical Guideline (TR ePass) tests for ePassports.

Interoperability influences every aspect of the secure technologies world, from the application standards which govern how a particular technology can be used for a certain function worldwide, such as travel, online authentication and card payment, to the technical standards covering issues such as protocols and coding. It requires a systematic approach that applies strategy, procedural and systems expertise to ensure that technical and infrastructure standards are maintained, and policies and laws governing a technology's use are adhered to (see box 1).

2 From technology...

At the international level, many standards are overseen by the International Organization for Standardization (ISO) and the International Electrotechnical Commission (IEC). These organizations establish and regulate many of the technical standards that apply to secure technologies. ISO 7816, for example, is the best-known standard for smart cards and applies to contact cards. Another standard that is increasingly being used commercially is ISO 14443. First used mainly in the mass transit market, it is now additionally applied to many other contactless uses such as eGovernment.

The ISO and the IEC also host a number of technical committees which develop standards for specific technologies. ISO/IEC Joint Committee 1 (JTC1), for example, establishes IT standards and has a number of sub-committees (SCs) that do work relevant to the secure technologies world. JTC1/SC17 is responsible for the international standardization of cards and personal ID, while JTC1/SC37 is responsible for biometric standards.

SC37 was established in 2002 and comprises six working groups (WGs):
- WG1 – Harmonized biometric vocabulary;
- WG2 – Biometric technical interfaces;
- WG3 – Biometric data interface formats;
- WG4 – Profiles for biometric applications;
- WG5 – Biometric testing and reporting;
- WG6 – Cross-jurisdictional and societal aspects.

These WGs have defined a number of standards, including the BioAPI specification, ISO 19784; ISO 19785, which covers the Common Biometric Exchange Framework Format (CBEFF); ISO 19794, which sets out the Biometric Data Interchange Format; ISO 19795, covering biometric testing and reporting; and ISO 24708, a protocol for communication between a system supporting a biometric device and a central repository of biometric data.

A number of standards also apply to Public Key Infrastructure (PKI) when used in the eID world. For example, ISO/IEC 18014 describes mechanisms producing independent tokens, and ISO/TS 17090-2 specifies the certificate profiles required to interchange healthcare information within a single organization, between different organizations and across jurisdictional boundaries. It details the use made of PKI digital certificates in the health industry and focuses on specific healthcare issues relating to certificate profiles.

3 To application…

In the applications world, work is taking place both internationally and throughout the European Union (EU) to ensure interoperability between devices and documents in specific sectors. For example, many of SC17's WGs are involved in producing eID document standards:

- WG1 – Physical characteristics and test methods for ID cards;
- WG3 – Identification cards – machine-readable travel documents;
- WG4 – Integrated circuit cards with contacts;
- WG8 – Integrated circuit cards without contacts;
- WG9 – Optical memory cards and devices;
- WG10 – Motor vehicle driver license and related documents;
- WG11 – Application of biometrics to cards and personal identification;
- WG15 – European Citizen Card.

ISO WG10 has been developing an international driver license standard since 1999, a project which has involved input from 13 member countries. It has established ISO 18013, which is now being used in countries such as Japan to combat counterfeiting, streamline license administration, improve driver convenience and protect driver privacy.

At the same time, SC7 WG3 has been working with the International Civil Aviation Organization (ICAO) to develop the global standard for ePassports. These specifications are set out in ICAO Document No 9303 (Doc9303).

4 EU perspective

The European Commission (EC) has also been heavily involved in developing standards and addressing the challenges of deploying documents across the EU. Its Joint Research Centre (JRC) has been supporting biometrics and acting as a moderator between developers and politicians looking at ways of carrying out large-scale deployments.

The EC has now passed a number of security-related regulations, including 2252/2004. This defines the standards for the security features and biometrics in passports and travel documents, and also sets out the rules governing the introduction of ePassports in all member states. In December 2004, it decided to introduce technical specifications to enable biometric markers to be included on travel documents under regulation 2252/2004. And by February 2005, it had adopted the first phase of the ePassport technical specifications. Member states were set an August 8 2006 deadline, by which date they had to include facial biometric images on all new ePassports. The image on each ePassport – which is stored on the chip along with personal information such as name and date of birth– must be protected by Basic Access Control (BAC) and Passive Authentication (PA) security protocols. On June 28 2006, the EC adopted the second phase of the technical specifications by calling for the use of fingerprints as a second biometric marker in ePassports. It also specified that information stored in the second generation of ePassports must be protected by Extended Access Control (EAC). Member states must comply with this by June 28 2009.

5 National ID and residence permits

The EC has also defined standards for the national ID cards that many EU citizens use for travelling to neighboring countries. These are set out in regulation 14351/2001 and specify chip-based ID1 format cards (credit card-sized) containing ID data.

Other regulations include 0269/2006, which covers the Schengen visa for foreigners who stay in Europe for a maximum of 90 days. This specifies a chip-less document with security printed biometric data that has a machine-readable zone line.

Regulation 1030/2002 provides standards for residence permit cards for foreigners who stay in the EU for extended periods of more than 90 days. This specifies a chip-based card with biometric data.

6 eHealth

International standards for eHealth cards have already been finalized in ISO TC 715. In the EU, work is continuing on turning the E111 card – which is used by EU citizens to obtain emergency medical treatment when traveling cross-border within member states – into an 8KB contact-based card. This could be rolled out as early as 2010.

7 RTP

ePassport technology is also being applied to Registered Traveler Programs (RTPs). However, development of standards in this area is lagging behind other applications. As a result, the use of biometrics in RTPs is not yet compatible with the ICAO 9303 scheme for ePassports, EU regulation 2252/2004 or the US VISIT framework (the scheme established in the US to protect its borders). Biometric matching in RTPs may be 'one-to-one' or 'one-to-many'. And, although most programs run a biometric in combination with a smart card, both contact-based (as is the case in the US) and contactless (as in France) technologies are being deployed.

However, progress is slowly being made. For example, in the US, the Registered Traveler Interoperability Consortium (RTIC) has been established to develop common business rules and technical standards to create a permanent interoperable and vendor-neutral RTP. And in Europe, the EC's Directorate-General (DG) for Justice, Freedom and Security (JLS) and DG Transport and Energy (TREN) are promoting a series of studies aimed at developing a means by which travelers can cross the EU's external borders using automated or semi-automated procedures.

8 CEN

The European Committee for Standardization (Comité Européen de Normalisation   CEN) supports the aims of the EU and European Economic Area (EEA) with voluntary technical standards, and contributes to work on smart card standards through Technical Committee 224 (TC224). This covers personal identification, electronic signature and cards and their related systems and operations (bank, transport, telecoms and eGovernment).

Status of CEN standards being developed

Project reference	Title	Status
prEN 1332-3	Identification card systems – Man-machine interface – Part 3: Key pads	Under approval
prEN 14890-1	Application Interface for smart cards used as secure signature creation devices – Part 1: Basic services	Under approval
prEN 14890-2	Application Interface for smart cards used as secure signature creation devices – Part 2: Additional services	Under approval
prCEN/TS 13987-1	Identification card systems – Interoperable Citizen Services – User Related Information – Part 1: Definition of User Related Information and Implementation	Under development
prEN 1332-1	Identification card systems – Human-machine interface – Part 1: Design principles for the user interface	Under approval

A number of CEN WGs are of particular interest to those involved in the secure technologies industries. CEN/TC244/WG15 focuses on European citizen cards; CEN/TC224/WG16 concentrates on application interfaces for smart cards used as Secure Signature Creation Devices (SSCDs); and CEN/TC224/WG17 covers SSCD protection profiles.

CEN Technical Specification 15480, 'Identification card systems – European Citizen Card, physical, electrical and transport protocol characteristics', was published in May 2007. Covering ID cards, smart cards, identification methods, travel and administrative documents, data processing, data security, and cryptography for eID cards issued in Europe, it contains four parts:

- Part 1: Physical, electrical properties and transport protocols;
- Part 2: Logical data structures and card services;
- Part 3: Middleware and interoperability;
- Part 4: Application profiles.

The specification describes the ID card as a chip card conforming to ISO/IEC 7186-1 and -2 standards for the contact interface and ISO/IEC 14443 for the contactless interface. The usual T=0 or T=1 transport protocols can be used, meaning that connection via USB is already supported.

9 Testing

Stringent testing procedures are a key factor in achieving interoperability. Numerous bodies established by governments and industry groups carry out testing based on either the technologies themselves or their applications.

Currently, ePassports are one of the key focuses of testing. Evaluation is most advanced in the area of BAC, where 90% of ePassports have now been tested. EAC assessment – which was started by the Essen Group (the organization behind ePassport document conformity testing) and is now being taken forward by the Brussels Interoperability Group (BIG) – has increased from 15% of current ePassport designs being tested at the beginning of 2007 to 50% being tested through BIG in Paris in October 2007. The eventual aim is to test 90% of current ePassport designs or EAC. Meanwhile, tests on ePassport readers are starting, while those on biometry and border controls have yet to commence.

Elsewhere, organizations such as the US National Institute of Standards and Technology (NIST) have been evaluating biometric technologies. Assessments include the Face Recognition Vendor Test (FRVT) and the Iris Challenge Evaluation (ICE). While these are not real-world evaluations, they do provide an insight into how the technology is developing. The NIST Information Technology Laboratory (ITL) is also working with government and industry on interoperability specifications and guidelines to provide organizations with an open and standard method for using smart cards.

In Europe, the Minutiae Template Interoperability Testing (MTIT) project aims to improve the interoperability of fingerprint biometrics for use in visa, residence permits and travel documents. Co-founded by the EC within the Sixth Framework Program (STREP), its starting point is the existing work on fingerprint minutiae data interchange standards and the current NIST benchmark of minutiae interoperability. It will build on these to improve the standards, the test methods and the interoperability of fingerprint minutiae systems.

10   Conclusion

With the secure technologies industry maturing rapidly, ongoing work to ensure compliance is essential. However, while progress has been made with applications such as tachographs and ePassports, there are others where interoperability will not be achieved. For example, there are now five different eHealth programs running in EU member states, and it is not possible to make these interoperable, with the German eHealth card (eGK) not working in France and the French eHealth card Sesam Vitale 2, not working in Spain.

As testing moves up a gear, the industry is learning the importance of developing both technologies and policies to ensure that documents and readers are interoperable worldwide. The BIG will take EAC forward to become an agreed standard with the necessary specifications, probably via the ISO. But there are still challenges, such as the need to achieve many goals within tight time constraints. This year could be a pivotal one for standards in Europe. With technical meetings being hosted by the BIG half way through 2008 and interoperability tests slated for September, the EU may be on course to take another step towards becoming a more unified region for eID. And with the EU putting its weight behind establishing greater interoperability, we – as a security community – must also work together to achieve the same goal in areas such as eHealth, RTPs, eDriving licenses, eResidence permits and eEntitlement cards.

PPs for applications with the Spanish National Electronic Identity Card

Elisa Vivancos

INTECO
Avda./ José Aguado, n. ° 41
24005 León (Spain)
elisa.vivancos@inteco.es

Abstract

The Spanish National Electronic Identity Card (DNIe) is currently being issued by the Spanish government, allowing citizens to use the electronic signature and authentication certificates incorporated in it. In this document, the situation of four sets of requirements (Protection Profiles) for signature-creation and verification applications with the DNIe will be shown. These requirements have been developed by INTECO with the collaboration of a technology partner and the industry and are based on the Common Criteria for Information Technology Security Evaluation (CC). These four Protection Profiles will be the way for developers to adjust their products to the functional and security assurance requirements specified in them, allowing the certification of their developments.

1 Introduction

Since 2005, the Spanish government has been issuing the National Identity Card in an electronic format (known as the DNIe) with SmartCard support. Currently, more than four and half million citizens have this card, allowing them to use the electronic signature and authentication certificates that are electronically integrated in the card's chip.

These certificates are the instruments that prove the identity of those participating in electronic communications and guarantee the origin and integrity of the exchanged messages. The applications that will be developed using these certificates will be essential to create trust in the relationship between citizens and the Information Society services.

In order to strengthen the trust that the use of certificates creates, it is necessary to have tools that allow us to certify the developed applications. To this end, the Spanish Ministry of Industry, Tourism and Trade, through the National Institute of Communication Technologies (INTECO), has drafted four documents, called Protection Profiles, which include normalized security requirements specifications based on the Common Criteria. These specifications are applicable to those products and developments that use the DNIe as a secure-signature-creation and verification device.

In this document, the content and the current situation of Protection Profiles for electronic-signature-creation and verification applications in home computers, DTT and mobile devices will be analysed.

N. Pohlmann, H. Reimer, W. Schneider (Editors): Securing Electronic Business Processes, Vieweg (2008), 268-277

2 Background

The arrival of the new DNIe involves an important advance in the traditional use associated to these cards, as it introduces new forms to prove our identity as citizens and to perform administrative and commercial transactions. The new DNIe contains two digital certificates: one to authenticate the citizens' identity in virtual environments and the other one to digitally sign documents with the same legal validity as if it were handwritten signed.

The Spanish law describes the DNIe as [ESPA03] "the national identity card that electronically prove the holder's personal identity and allows the electronic signature of documents".

2.1 Legislation

The current legislation includes the Spanish *Ley 59/2003, de Firma Electrónica* (Electronic Signature Act), which regulates its legal effectiveness and, along with other Acts, puts a date on the obligatory commitments for the administration and companies regarding its use.

Indeed, apart from amending some provisions of the Electronic Signature Act, the Spanish *Ley 56/2007, del 28 de diciembre, de Medidas de Impulso de la Sociedad de la Información* (Act 56/2007 of 28 December on Measures to Promote the Information Society) includes a new obligation for certain companies which entails the use of qualified certificates in their relationships with clients. This act forces utilities companies (electricity, gas, etc.) to provide a systematic means of electronic communication for those users with qualified certificates, such as the ones included in the DNIe.

On the other hand, the Spanish *Ley 11/2007 de Acceso Electrónico de los Ciudadanos a los Servicios Públicos* (Act 11/2007 on Electronic Access of Citizens to Public Services), considers communication with public administrations by electronic means a right of citizens and a duty for the administration. It is in this relationship by electronic means where the DNIe certificates have found another major field of application.

2.2 Comparison with the handwritten signature

Apart from verifying the citizens' identity, the importance of the DNIe lies in the fact that its signature has the same legal validity as the handwritten one.

As established in Royal Decree 1553/2005[1], an electronic signature with the DNIe will have the same legal validity as the handwritten signature, with respect to the data electronically assigned to the card and the data provided on paper.

In compliance with the Electronic Signature Act, its legal effectiveness and the provision of certification services is defined as follows:

- *Electronic signature*: set of data in electronic form attached to or associated with other electronic data that can be used as a means to identify the signatory.
- *Advanced electronic signature*: electronic signature that is uniquely linked to the signatory, is capable of identifying him/her, is created using means that are under the signatory's sole control and is capable to detect any subsequent change to the signed data.

---

1 *Real Decreto 1553/2005, de 23 de diciembre por el que se regula la expedición del documento nacional de identidad y sus certificados de firma electrónica* (Royal Decree 1553/2005 of 23 December regulating the issuance of the Spanish national identity card and its digital certificates).

- *Qualified electronic signature*: an advanced electronic signature based on a qualified certificate and created by a secure-signature-creation device.

Technically, the electronic signature uses a PKI (Public Key Infrastructure) key pair. The user's private key is used to encrypt the message digest (hash) of the document, which is unique for each document and allows us to verify that the document has not been altered.

The public key is used to decrypt it. The certificate associates the data to the user's public key and, is *signed*, itself, by a Certification Authority.

The verification process consists of using a public key to decrypt the hash associated to the document and verifying both the identity of the signatory and the integrity of the data.

2.3 The DNIe is a secure-signature-creation device

A secure-signature-creation device is configured software or hardware used to implement the signature-creation data (i.e. unique data, such as codes or private cryptographic keys, which are used by the signatory to create an electronic signature (Certificados del DNIe)), which complies with the requirements of Directive 1999/93/EC of the European Parliament and the Council of 13 December 1999 (DNIe).

RESOLUTION 1A0/38123/2007, of 16 May, of the Spanish National Cryptologic Centre, certifies the security of the Spanish National Electronic Identity Card, version 1.13, with the two DNIe configurations 1.13 A11 H4C34 EXP1-1 and 1.13 B11 H4C34 EXP1-1, developed by the Royal Spanish Mint in compliance with the protection profile CWA 14169 "Secure-signature-creation devices (EAL4+)" v1.05 Type 3-March2002.

2.3.1 DNIe certificates

According to the DNIe web portal[2], the DNIe contains X509v3 citizen certificates (authentication and signature) and their associated private keys, which are generated and inserted during the process of issuance of the electronic identity card. These certificates are:

- *Authentication certificate*: citizens can certify their identity vis-à-vis third parties through an Authentication Certificate, proving the possession of and access to the private key associated to that certificate, which verifies their identity.
- *Qualified signature certificate*: it allows citizens to conduct and sign actions and electronically take on obligations, as well as verifying the integrity of the signed documents by making use of the signing instruments included in it.
- *Digital certificate from the issuing authority*.

2.4 Qualified signature certificates

The DNIe permits to electronically verify the identity of the holder, the identity of the signatory and the integrity of the documents signed with the electronic-signature devices, allowing citizens to establish trust relationships with third parties using new technologies.

To this end, the Spanish Police Department, the authority responsible for issuing and managing the Spanish National Identity Card (DNI), has a Public Key Infrastructure (PKI), which provides the DNI with the digital certificates necessary to adequately meet the requirements laid down in Annex of Direc-

---

2 DNIe web portal of the Spanish Police Department http://www.dnielectronico.es/

tive 1999/93/EC of the European Parliament and of the Council of 13 December 1999 on a Community framework for electronic signatures, as well as the established in the Electronic Signature Act.

The certification-service-provider is the Spanish Police Department (Ministry of the Interior), which meets the requirements laid down in Annex II of the aforementioned Directive and set forth in the Electronic Signature Act. In addition, the certificates meet the standards regarding qualified signature certificates, specifically:

- ETSI TS 101 862: Qualified Certificate Profile.
- RFC 3739 Internet X.509 Public Key Infrastructure: Qualified Certificates Profile

On the other hand, in order to verify the validity of digital certificates, the PKI of the Spanish Police Department assigns functions of Validation Authority to external-validation-service-providers to strengthen the system's transparency. Currently and according to the mentioned DNIe web portal, these providers are the Spanish Royal Mint and the Spanish Ministry for Public Administration.

2.5 INTECO and the DNIe

INTECO is a platform for the development of projects in the field of innovation and technology that carries out tasks entrusted by the Spanish State Secretariat for Telecommunications and the Information Society (SETSI) and the Spanish Ministry of Industry, Tourism and Trade that are aimed at promoting the Information Society. One of these tasks, initiated at the end of 2007, is specially aimed at promoting the development of DNIe applications that foster its use in the private sector and in the relationship between users and the administration.

INTECO has already participated in DNIe projects on previous occasions. In particular, the laboratory of the Security Technologies Show-Room of INTECO has conducted the testing of devices for the use of the DNIe. Furthermore, different Awareness-Raising Seminars are organised across Spain, which describe and deal with the use of the DNIe. Finally, in the catalogue of the Show-Room, which can be accessed on the Internet, there is a category for products and applications with the SmartCard and DNIe.

On the other hand, INTECO has collaborated with the pilot veterinary prescription project using the DNIe, which will be the topic for another conference at this forum. The Veterinary Prescription project is an initiative of INTECO, in collaboration with the Vodafone Spain Foundation, the Spanish Police Department, the meat company Valles del Esla (Eulen group) and the technology partner PROCONSI. This initiative has developed an application which uses mobile technology to solve the current problems of livestock farmers and allows the signature of prescriptions with the electronic identity card.

In addition INTECO's web portal allows user registration and validation through the electronic DNI. The message "Click on the following button to use the DNIe for your user registration and validation process *(Some of your data will be automatically completed with the information obtained from the DNIe)*" informs users about how to use the DNIe for this function.

Finally, and the key issue of this document, INTECO has developed protection profiles according to the Common Criteria evaluation standards for electronic-signature-creation and verification applications with the DNIe, in collaboration with a specialised technology partner.

Other projects regarding the DNIe will focus on the launch of a DNIe web portal. This portal will include different tools and activities: online training, search engine of URLs using the DNIe, a signing tool called 'INTECO-firma', mailbox for queries, list and search engine of FAQ, etc.

2.5.1 Recent actions regarding Protection Profiles

After the creation of protection profiles, INTECO intends to initiate the necessary actions to achieve their adequate implementation among the industry actors and the administration.

Therefore, actions are aimed at:

- Disseminating and promoting the correct implementation of protection profiles in the development of signature-creation and verification applications.
- Promoting the certification of the applications developed according to these profiles.

In order to achieve the described objectives, the Certification of the Protection Profiles created is essential. With the certified profiles, the industry will be able to evaluate and certify the products that have been developed or manufactured according to them. In addition, this certification will favour the possibility of including compliance with profiles as a technical requirement in public or private biddings.

With regard to the actions targeted at the industry for the use of these profiles in the development and certification of applications that meet them, different user guides will be developed.

At the moment this document is being developed, the launch of the evaluation and certification project of the Protection Profiles created and the drafting of user guides are still in their initial phase.

3 Protection profiles according to the CC

Protection profiles are normalized security requirements that must be followed and met by signature-creation and verification applications with the DNIe that intend to be certified.

The security requirements specifications of IT products and applications must meet the Common Criteria validation standard (CC). In Spain, the National Cryptologic Centre-National Centre for Intelligence (CCN-CNI) is the national institution that issues certificates for products according to this standard.

The requirements that these documents contain adopt criteria from the Spanish and European legislations and specify the assurance level offered by a product that meets this profile.

CC[3] is a regulatory framework, adopted by ISO as an international standard in 1999 and implemented in many countries, to evaluate security and to allow:

- Users to specify their needs.
- Manufacturers and integrators to implement and define the security attributes of their products.
- Laboratories to evaluate products and determine if they really contain the specified attributes.

The CC standard ensures that the process of specification, implementation and evaluation of computer security products has been conducted in a standardised and rigurous way.

3.1 Creation of Protection Profiles

Protection profiles for signature-creation and verification applications with the DNIe have been developed with the support of the technology partner Epoche&Espri, the collaboration of the industry and the cooperation of the administration.

---

3 http://www.commoncriteriaportal.org/

They have been drafted according to the Common Criteria for Information Technology Security Evaluation (CC) and are the way for developers to adjust their products to the requirements specified in them, allowing the certification of their developments.

In order to develop the Protection Profiles (PPs), a mailing list, maintained by INTECO, has been created to serve as a tool to collect the opinions of the experts of the industry and the administration. The collection of opinions has been developed in three cycles, with the aim of taking into account the points of view of all actors involved and reaching an agreement that serves as an incentive for the industry to implement them.

Given that PPs are the means for the industry to develop products and applications that meet the mentioned specifications to be evaluated and certified, in this way offering the market the security assurance announced, the role of the industry in the development of profiles has been considered very important. Therefore, the group of experts is formed by a large number of representatives of the main associations of the sector.

On the other hand, in order to protect users when using the DNIe, the group of experts that discussed the preparation of these protection profiles is formed by the Spanish Police Department, the Spanish Data Protection Agency, the CCN-CNI and the SETSI.

The development of these profiles has coincided with the republication and maintenance by the CEN *(Comité Européen de Normalisation)* of the European regulations for electronic signature applications (CEN Workshop Agreement). The profiles under development have circulated in the group that undertakes these tasks under the European framework.

As a result, four protection profiles have been developed for electronic-signature-creation and verification applications with the DNIe as a secure-signature-creation device. These profiles correspond to two types (Type 1 and Type 2) depending on the characteristics of the platform where the created applications are used. In addition, for each type, two profiles (EAL1 and EAL3) are developed, each of them with an assurance level, as explained below.

3.2 Structure of PPs

The DNIe Protection Profiles are documents based on the CC standard. They use a standardised language [ISO 07] ensuring that the text of the document is not ambiguous, sufficiently abstract to propose different solutions to the same security problem, complete (with implicit requirements) and with the possibility of being evaluated.

According to the Common Criteria (ISO/IEC 15408_1) [CC 06], protection profiles must contain:
- A TOE summary, in this case the signature-creation and verification application, including a section for its use and the definition of the type of application.
- A definition of the security problem that the product must solve. This definition includes: a description of the use environment, the assumptions necessary for the secure operation of the product, the organisational policies to be met in its use, the assets that the product must protect and the possible attacks on these assets.
- A list of security objectives that the product must meet to solve the security problem and the correspondence with the security problem to avoid any vulnerability after the evaluation or the possibility of launching the identified attacks.

- The functional security requirement that the product must implement to meet the specified security objectives and the correspondence between them.
- The lowest evaluation level that must be implemented to evaluate a product designed to meet the protection profile.

The following figure shows the protection profile content:

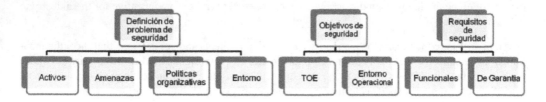

Fig. 1: Esquema del contenido de los Perfiles de Protección

• Definición de problema de seguridad: definition of the security problem	• Objetivos de seguridad: security objectives
	• TOE: TOE, target of evaluation
• Activos: assets	• Entorno operacional: operational environment
• Amenazas: threats	• Requisitos de seguridad: security requirements
• Políticas organizativas: organisational policies	• Funcionales: functional
• Entorno: environment	• De garantía: assurance
Fig. 1: Esquema del contenido de los Perfiles de Protección: Fig. 1: Diagram of the Protection Profile content	

3.2.1 Description of the security problem

The description of the security problem, in a standardised way, includes:

- The assets to be protected. For signature-creation and verification applications, these assets are: integrity and unambiguous representation of the signatory's document, integrity of the user data, integrity of the functionality of the application and PIN or biometric data confidentiality.
- The threats against which assets must be protected, in the case of signature-creation and verification application, these assets are: modification of user data, the obtaining of unauthorised signatures and the commitment of PIN or biometric data confidentiality.
- The environment specifications, in this case signatory and DNIe interfaces.
- The implemented organisational policies, in this case the DNIe as a secure-signature-creation device, data protection law, cryptographic algorithms and selected certificates.

The four profiles created share assets and threats. There are only slight differences in the description of the security problem between the profiles defined in the organisational policy, the profiles of the evaluation levels EAL1 and EAL3 and the environment specifications (hypothesis), and the profiles of the two types of applications (Type 1 and Type 2).

3.2.2 Functionality of signature applications

According to the developed profiles [INTE08a, b, c and d], signature-creation and verification applications have the following common functionality for each profile:

The signature-creation functionality allows us to:

- Select the document to be signed.
- Select signature attributes, certificates and policies.
- Show unambiguously the data to be signed for a certain number of formats.
- Request the PIN in an explicit way and check it.
- Send the data to be signed to the DNIe.
- Associate the created signature to the signed document or facilitate the signature as separate data.
- Delete the PIN and user data from the application's scope, if they are not necessary.

The signature-verification functionality allows us to:

- Select the signed document.
- Select the certification policy to be implemented.
- Show unambiguously the data linked to the signature and the signature attributes for a certain number of formats.
- Verify the signature according to the selected policy.
- Show the verification result (valid/invalid).

Two additional elements, common to all profiles, have been added:

- Secure viewer of the document to be signed (not allowing an ambiguous or misleading interpretation) and a warning to the signatory, according to the Data Protection Act, before introducing his/her PIN.
- Unambiguous list of the electronic formats allowed.

3.2.3 Differences between the two types of profiles created

Protection profiles [ISO 07] serve to define the security environment and requirements that are relevant to the users of a product used for a particular purpose. In the case of the protection profiles created for the DNIe, this purpose is the electronic-signature creation and verification. The main characteristics of this type of profiles are described below.

1. Protection profiles for signature-creation and verification applications (Type 1):
   - The applications that meet these profiles will have sole control over the hardware, firmware and software necessary to create and verify the electronic signature, including the signatory interface.
   - These profiles will serve to certify applications associated to DTT platforms, portable devices, such as PDA, or mobile phones.
2. Protection profiles for signature-creation and verification applications (Type 2):
   - The applications that meet these profiles will use a general-purpose and reliable platform for the signatory's interface, DNIe communications and the access to general resources (CPU or memory).
   - These profiles will serve to certify applications associated to personal computers with general-purpose operating systems.

Given that, according to the previous point, both Types share the signature-creation and verification functionality, the two types of applications identified are actually the same application for two different platforms. Furthermore, two profiles with different evaluation levels have been created for each type of application.

In the documents, the differences between the two types of profiles (Type 1 and Type 2) are focused on the TOE summary: their use and the exclusion of hardware and software.

Profiles of Type 2 contain one more environment hypothesis than Type 1, expressed in an additional objective to protect the assets of the signature-creation and verification application:

- Environment hypothesis (Type 2) [INTE08c y d]: *The general-purpose platform (...) provides the adequate protection and security mechanisms to protect the application assets through an efficient combination of technical measures, procedures and securisation of their environment.*

This shows that the configuration of the general-purpose platform, to avoid attacks on the application's assets, is not covered by these profiles.

3.2.4 Differences between the two security assurance levels

According to the CC, the Evaluation Security Levels (EAL) serve as an indicator of the importance and rigor necessary for the evaluation. The CC [CC 06] defines 7 assurance levels, ranging from 1 to 7, the last one being the most demanding. The levels used by these profiles are EAL1 and EAL3.

- EAL 1: "functionally tested". It analyses security functions by using functional specifications and the application interface to understand the security behaviour. The analysis is based on independent security tests.
- EAL 3: "methodically tested and checked". The analysis is based on a grey-box test with an independent confirmation of the result of the development tests and the search for obvious vulnerabilities. The control of the development environment and the management of the application configuration are also necessary.

By analysing the correspondence between objectives, threats and policies shared by both types of profiles (EAL1 and EAL 3), it is observed that the EAL3 profiles, for both types of applications, have an objective (O.ARC) referred to the secure design and construction of the application.

- O.ARC [INTE08b y d]: *The application will be designed and developed, so that it will implement sufficient self-protection features, domain separation and protection against defined threats and will protect the defined assets in combination with the applicable functional security requirements.*

With regard to the documents, the main difference between the two security assurance levels lies in the assurance requirements, which are more numerous at the EAL3 level than at the EAL1 assurance level. This requires a greater effort for the manufacturer and a higher level of depth in tests related to design.

The four profiles are documents that have many aspects in common. They share assets, threats and almost all the organisational policies and environment specifications, these two last points and the assurance requirements being the aspects in which the main differences among them are found.

4 Conclusion

INTECO has drafted four documents containing security requirements based on the Common Criteria (i.e. Protection Profiles), which are applicable to the products and developments that use the DNIe as a secure-signature-creation and verification device. The requirements included in these documents adopt criteria from the Spanish and European legislations.

The use of profiles will provide a clear benefit to both the industry and the citizens that use the DNIe.

Protection profiles have been defined as one of the tools for dynamising the security industry, as they promote the production of secure applications in the DNIe environment. They also serve as catalysts of the sector, as they promote the creation of quality developments that can obtain certification assurance according to an internationally recognised standard, as well as fostering the development and integration of new services that use these certified applications.

These profiles will also serve to provide final users with the necessary trust in the use of different DNIe services and applications that will help them access the Information Society services. Therefore, it is likely that they will act as engines to promote the services associated to electronic signature and digital identity.

To conclude, the sociologist Manuel Castells [CAST03] uses the metaphor of the Internet as the "tissue of our lives". Thus, it is expected that these signature-creation and verification applications, certified according to protection profiles that meet internationally recognised standards, will make this "tissue" a bit more robust.

References

[CAST03] Castells, M.: La galaxia Internet. Reflexiones sobre Internet empresa y sociedad. Barcelona, De Bolsillo, 2003, Colección Ensayo-Actualidad, n. ° 5.

[ESPA03] España, Jefatura del Estado LEY 59/2003, de 19 de diciembre, de firma electrónica. BOE, 2003, n. 304 de 20/12/2003, Art. 15

[ISO07] ISO/IEC JTC 1/SC27 N5792 Text for ISO/IEC 3rd WD 15446. Information Technologies – Security Techniques. Guide for the production of protection profiles and security targets.

[CC06] Common Criteria. Common Criteria for Information Security Evaluation. Part 1 Introduction and general model. V. 3.1, [en línea] 2006. CCMB-2006-09-003 http://www.commoncriteriaportal.org/files/ccfiles/CCPART1V3.1R1.pdf [consulta: 08/06/2008]

[INTE08a] PP1-EAL1. Perfil de Protección para el control exclusivo de los medios de firma con nivel de evaluación de los requisitos de seguridad del tipo EAL1.

[INTE08b] PP2-EAL3. Perfil de Protección para el control exclusivo de los medios de firma con nivel de evaluación de los requisitos de seguridad del tipo EAL3.

[INTE08c] PP3-EAL1. Perfil de Protección para la aplicación de creación y verificación de firma electrónica con nivel de evaluación de los requisitos de seguridad del tipo EAL1.

[INTE08d] PP4-EAL3. Perfil de Protección para la aplicación de creación y verificación de firma electrónica con nivel de evaluación de los requisitos de seguridad del tipo EAL3.

Fraud Detection, Prevention and Critical Infrastructures

OTP and Challenge/Response algorithms for financial and e-government identity assurance: current landscape and trends

Philip Hoyer

Senior Architect – Office of CTO, ActivIdentity (UK)
117 Waterloo Road, London SE1 8UL
Philip.Hoyer@actividentity.com

Abstract

This paper will analyse the current landscape of One Time Password (OTP) and Challenge-Response algorithms. It will detail the technical and security differences between algorithms such as the OATH algorithms (HOTP, OCRA, HOTP time based), EMV CAP and the proprietary algorithms from ActivIdentity. The paper describes the most common use cases and applicability as important tools for identity assurance in the financial and e-government industry sectors. It also outlines observed trends in current usage and future trends providing the audience with the valuable information to make a more informed choice in their identity assurance challenges.

1 Anatomy of OTP algorithms

Before delving into the history and differences between the various OTP algorithms lets start with the basics. This will allow the understanding of where the differences lie between algorithms and how they impact security and usability.

1.1 What is a one time password (OTP)

A code that changes after every use, can only be used once, hence is a one-time-password, or OTP.

An OTP is based on a cryptographic algorithm using a key K a cryptogram is generated

$$Cryptogram = f(K)$$

Computing the cryptogram with other, moving factors makes the output random and one time:
- Counter – increased with each usage (also called event) and/or
- Time – number of time intervals (e.g. seconds)

$$Cryptogram = f(K,C,T)$$

A truncation function makes it short and human readable:

$$OTP = Truncate (f(K,C,T))$$

N. Pohlmann, H. Reimer, W. Schneider (Editors): Securing Electronic Business Processes, Vieweg (2008), 281-290

1.1.1 OTP moving factor analysis

The moving factors used to make the password one-time have implications both for the usage and the security of the overall OTP algorithm:

1.1.1.1 Time only based algorithms

- the OTP changes based on time-interval (e.g. every 30 seconds)
- the OTP has a time to live (e.g. can be used within next 2 minutes)
- the OTP is harder to phish because it must be used within the time to live
- it is not possible to generate a new OTP within the same time interval (e.g. user needs to wait for next interval -> up to 30 seconds)
- needs replay protection on the server since a simple algorithm would successfully validate attempts with the same OTP within the same time interval

1.1.1.2 Event only based algorithms

- the OTP can be requested at any time (no need to wait for time interval to pass)
- the OTP can be used at any time after being produced = no time to live
- easier to phish since phisher does not need to use the OTP within a time to live but can harvest the passwords and use them later
- Replay protection is simply based on forward moving counter only

1.1.1.3 Time and Event algorithms (combines best of above)

- the OTP has a time to live (e.g. can be used within next 2 minutes)
- the OTP can be requested at any time (no need to wait for time interval to pass)
- the OTP is harder to phish because it must be used within the time to live
- Replay protection is simply based on forward moving counter only
- Needs more complex auto-resync (2 moving factors instead of 1 that could go out of sync between the server and the device)

1.1.2 OTP algorithm analysis

Let's look more closely at what cryptographic algorithms can be used to generate OTPs:

1.1.2.1 OTP algorithms using asymmetric cryptography

Because of the nature of asymmetric keys the verifier will need the complete signature to be able to validate it. The length of PKI signatures depend on the length of the key used so for example:

$$RSA\ 1024 = 1024\ bits\ long = 128\ bytes\ long = not\ easy\ to\ type$$

This makes the use of asymmetric algorithms less suitable for OTP algorithms, they could be used in situations where there is no human involved when transcribing the OTP for transmission to the validation server, for example in an OTP device that is connected via the USB port to a laptop.

1.1.2.2 OTP algorithms using symmetric cryptography

The nature of symmetric key cryptography means that the same Cryptogram can be regenerated by the verifying party and only part of the cryptogram (the truncated bit) can be compared. This means that an arbitrary length of the cryptogram can be used as the OTP making it short and easy to type.

Historically all well known OTP algorithms are based on symmetric key cryptography.

1.1.3 OTP authenticaion – how it works

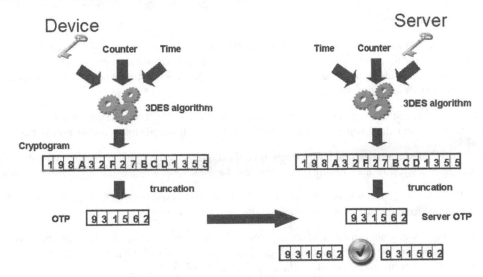

Figure 1: OTP algorithm in action

2 History and evolution of OTP algorithms

2.1.1 Traditionally – proprietary

Traditionally strong authentication algorithms using OTP were invented by private companies and their use immediately protected via patents.

One of the best known such algorithms is SecurID, invented in the U.S.A. by the company Security Dynamics, then acquired by RSA, now part of EMC. Initially these technologies were used to protect the network as part of authenticating a user strongly for access to the enterprise.

The same problem was solved independently on the old continent by companies such as ActivCard (now re-branded to ActivIdentity) out of France, now headquartered in Fremont California and later by Vasco (Belgium) now headquartered in Zurich.

With the emergence of internet based financial services, the need to protect those services became crucial and the same algorithms and technologies were used. Furthermore the requirement to protect specific transaction brought the emergence of challenge/response and Symmetric Key Signature (MAC over several parameter) algorithms.

2.1.2 Emerging – based on Industry standard (Financial Services)

The Europay MasterCard Visa Chip Authentication Program (EMV/CAP) is a set of specifications that detail the use of existing device technology [Mas04] (EMV compliant smartcard with unattached reader) for the use of consumer authentication for cardholder not present services e.g. internet based.

The specifications detail:
- A one time password algorithm
- A handheld reader
- A validation service

In 2003 MasterCard CAP was harmonized with an equivalent standard from the UK's Association of Payment and Clearing Services (APACS). APACS is currently developing a new specification which refines the user interface model for a handheld reader. This specification makes no proposed changes to the algorithm or validation service.

The EMV CAP specification seeks to leverage the extensive deployments of EMV chip based debit and credit cards, by expanding their use to include strong authentication and simple transaction signatures.

MasterCard CAP can also be used for transaction verification, either through forcing a re-authentication or more effectively through a Challenge/Response mechanism.

To use EMV for authentication requires the use of a Hand Held Device (HHD) that generates a One Time Password from the EMV card application (after correct PIN entry);

The resulting Cryptogram can be used for authentication to access and manage accounts held by the cardholder or during "cardholder not present" payments. As with other OTP technologies the model is suitable for use over the internet or other channels such as a call-centre.

Another benefit of the EMV CAP model is that the PIN used to activate the card is typically the same as the PIN that is already used with the card, for example to access ATM based services. This has the advantage that the customer is not required to remember an additional secret, and the infrastructure for PIN issuance and reset is already in place.

Visa, aside from a few minor changes to the standard, have adopted the MasterCard CAP specification, thus enabling re-use of CAP readers for Visa members. In Visa terminology, CAP is referred to as Dynamic Passcode Authentication – DPA.

The focus of this paper will hence treat the two as common under EMV CAP.

Currently EMV CAP is being deployed by major financial services institutions in the UK, Netherlands and France as an authentication mechanism for their retail customer base.

2.1.3 Recently – Open and Royalty free (OATH)

The Initiative for open authentication [OATH] is an industry consortium launched in 2004 and now grown to almost 100 members. OATH was formed after analysis of the existing algorithms for one time passwords suitable for a strong authentication ecosystem showed that they were all proprietary and from competing companies. OATH therefore endeavoured to create a royalty and patent free algorithm based on HMAC. This algorithm was submitted as a draft to IETF and has now become an RFC [RFC4226].

Based on the work done for RFC4226, OATH realised that some applications require an algorithm that is based on a challenge response mechanism, hence a new draft has been submitted to the IETF as OATH Challenge Response Algorithm [OCRA].

Additionally the interest in a royalty free, time based OTP algorithm was growing and the community asked OATH to produce one. In 2008 the first version of the time based OTP, TOTP, specification [TOTP], based on RFC4226 was submitted to IETF.

All OATH algorithms, being royalty free and easily embeddable bode well for a very wide adoption.

2.1 Evolution of use case and form factor

Together with the evolution of the algorithms themselves there has been an evolution of the use cases and applications of the technology. Especially since the launch of the royalty free algorithms the number of implementations has flourished in diverse form factors. The following is an attempt to show a time-line combining both use case and form factor evolution:

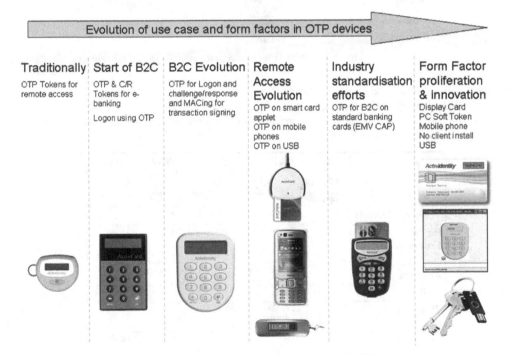

Figure 2: Evolution of use case and form factors in OTP devices

2.2 Why is OTP still relevant?

2.2.1 There are other interaction channels than the internet

When considering phishing and online fraud attacks it is important to consider all interaction channels a user has, some of these channels are often overlooked in phishing analysis that focuses only on the internet channel:

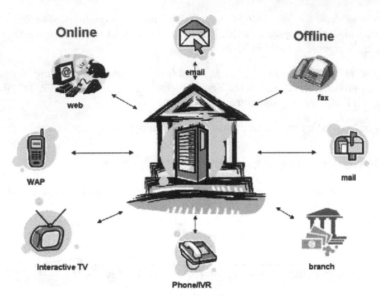

Figure 3: Possible user interaction channels

Additionally from a user and support perspective it is highly desirable to have the same mechanism to protect all channels, but not all strong authentication mechanisms can be used across all interaction channels. The following matrix provides an analysis of commonly used strong authentication mechanisms and how applicable they are for each channel:

	WEB	IVR	Phone	WAP	iTV
Static credentials	Y	Insecure	Insecure	Y	Y
Partial Credentials	Y	Y	Y	Y	Y
Question & Answers	Y	Complex / Impractical	Y	Complex / Impractical	Y
OTP	Y	Y	Y	Y	Y
Challenge Response	Y	Requires numeric	Y	Y	Y
Certificates (PKI)	Y	N	N	Partial	Complex
Biometric (voice)	Complex	Y	Y	Complex	N

Figure 4: Strong authentication mechanisms applicability by interaction channel

As one can see OTP still is one of the most applicable strong authentication mechanisms across all potential interaction channels

2.2.2 Advantages of OTP

- Can be used on existing non PKI enabled network access devices (VPN)
- Can be implemented in a tamper evident non hackable device (e.g. Token or smart card)
- No client install needed
- Often does not require change of access interface
- Username/Password – > Username/OTP
- Simple to use (user interaction)
- Long life devices (up to 6-9 years)
- Tried and tested
- Modest infrastructure requirements
- Truly multi-channel
- Can be used over phone/IVR

3 Algorithm comparison

This section will go into the technical detail of the algorithms and give the audience the information to compare them from an application and security angle.

The type defines the type of algorithm:

- OTP – One time Password
- C/R – Challenge Response
- MAC – Symmetric Signature of more then one parameter

3.1 ActivIdentity algorithm family

Table 1: Analysis of the ActivIdentity algorithm family.

Type	Characteristics	Analysis
OTP	- Algorithm 3DES - Time AND Event Based or Event only based - Auto-synchronisation digits within OTP (almost no synchronisation issues)	- the OTP has a time to live (e.g. can be used within next 2 minutes) - the OTP can be requested at any time (no need to wait for time interval to pass) - the OTP is harder to phish because it must be used within the time to live - Replay protection is simply based on forward moving counter only - Auto sync mitigates the issue of resync (2 moving factors instead of 1 that could go out of sync)
C/R	- Algorithm ANSI X9.8 - Fixed response for any give challenge	- The response has no time to live. The validation server needs to provide a timing mechanism between the issuance of a challenge and return of the response - The response is the same for the same challenge, susceptible to attacks where a previous challenge/response pair is known, on the other hand a fixed response for a specific challenge aids in non – repudiation cases
MAC	- 3DES - Time AND Event Based - Up to 10 parameters	- the MAC has a time to live (e.g. can be used within next 2 minutes) - the MAC can be requested at any time (no need to wait for time interval to pass) - the MAC is harder to phish because it must be used within the time to live - Replay protection is simply based on forward moving counter only - Auto sync mitigates the issue of resync (2 moving factors instead of 1 that could go out of sync)

Form factors: Tokens and Smart Card Applet

Industry: Enterprise – Business to Employees (B2E), Financial Services – Business to Employees and Business to Consumer (B2C)

3.2 EMV CAP algorithm family

Table 2: Analysis of the EMV CAP algorithm family.

Type	Characteristics	Analysis
OTP	• Algorithm 3DES – specified in CAP functional spec • Only Event Based • Auto-synchronisation digits within OTP (less synchronisation issues)	• the OTP can be requested at any time (no need to wait for time interval to pass) • the OTP can be used at any time after being produced = no time to live • easier to phish since phisher does not need to use the OTP within a time to live but can harvest the passwords and use them later • Replay protection is simply based on forward moving counter only • Auto sync mitigates the issue of resync (2 moving factors instead of 1 that could go out of sync)
C/R	• Algorithm 3DES • Event based (different response for same challenge)	• The response has no time to live. It is the validation server that needs to provide a timing mechanism between the issuance of a challenge and when the response returns • The response changes even with the same challenge which prevents previous known challenge/response pair attacks but could create issues during non-repudiation
MAC	• 3DES • Event Based • Challenge, Amount and Currency or up to 10 parameters	• the MAC has a time to live (e.g. can be used within next 2 minutes) • the MAC can be requested at any time (no need to wait for time interval to pass) • the MAC is harder to phish because it must be used within the time to live • Replay protection is simply based on forward moving counter only • Auto sync mitigates the issue of resync (2 moving factors instead of 1 that could go out of sync)

Form factor: Smart card applet with unconnected reader, mobile applet coming

Industry: Financial Services (B2C – Business to Consumer), Emerging in Government for G2E and G2C

3.3 OATH algorithm family

Table 3: Analysis of the OATH algorithm family.

Type	Characteristics	Analysis
OTP	• HOTP RFC 4226 • Algorithm HMAC-SHA1 • Event only • No synchronisation digits within OTP	• the OTP can be requested at any time (no need to wait for time interval to pass) • the OTP can be used at any time after being produced = no time to live • easier to phish since phisher does not need to use the OTP within a time to live but can harvest the passwords and use them later • Replay protection is simply based on forward moving counter only
OTP	• Time based HOTP • Algorithm HMAC-SHA1 • Time only • No synchronisation digits within OTP	• the OTP changes based on time-interval (e.g. every 30 seconds) • the OTP has a time to live (e.g. can be used within next 2 minutes) • the OTP is harder to phish because it must be used within the time to live • it is not possible to generate a new OTP within the same time interval (e.g. user needs to wait for next interval -> up to 30 seconds) • needs replay protection on the server since a simple algorithm would successfully validate attempts with the same OTP within the same time interval

C/R	• OATH Challenge Response algorithm (OCRA) • Algorithm HMAC-SHA1, HMAC-SHA256, HMAC-SHA512 • Event OR Time	• The response changes even with the same challenge which prevents previous known challenge/response pair attacks but could create issues during non-repudiation • The response has a time to live when time is used • Very flexible via algorithm suite and optional input like time or event
MAC	• Handled by OCRA (see above)	• Same as OCRA (see above)

Form factors: Tokens , Smart Card Applet, Display Card, Soft Tokens (mobile)

Industry: Financial Services B2C (Business to Consumer), Enterprise B2E ,(Business to Employee)

3.4 Algorithm comparison matrix

	OATH HOTP RFC4226	OATH Challenge/ Response OCRA	OATH Time based TOTP	EMV CAP/ DPA	AI	Vasco	RSA
Algorithm	HMAC-SHA1	HMAC-SHA1 HMAC-SHA256 HMAC-SHA512	HMAC-SHA1	3DES	3DES	3DES	AES
Moving Factors	Counter	Counter (optional) Time (optional)	Time	Counter	Counter and Time	Counter and Time	Time
Truncation	Dynamic based on last digit of cryptogram	Dynamic based on last digit of cryptogram	Dynamic based on last digit of cryptogram	Based on mask on the card	Fixed	Fixed	
Auto-Sync	N	N	N	Y	Y	Y	N
OTP	Y	Y	Y	Y	Y	Y	Y
C/R	N	Y	N	Y	Y	Y	Y
Sign (MAC)	N	Y	N	Y	Y	Y	Y

Figure 5: Algorithm comparison matrix

4 Trends

Currently it is possible to observe the following trends in the use of OTP:

- OTP authentication being rolled out by financial institutions to retail customer base is prevalently tokens, with EMV CAP cards gaining market presence.
- Economies of scale are starting to make a difference for EMV CAP
- Government looking at EMV CAP as means for large scale B2E and G2C authentication to ride on issuance of card readers from financial institutions
- Government looking at online EMV CAP authentication to provide proof of consent for access to centralised government database repositories

- OATH tokens starting to become a viable alternative especially now that time based algorithm has been published
- Proprietary algorithms such as ActivIdentity and Vasco still have a slight edge in security and usability (e.g. Time AND Event based and sophisticated re-sync digits within OTP)
- Mobile tokens re-gaining market interest but still not breaking into mass mainstream deployment
- New application and form factors such as DisplayCard and client less USB make use of this technology easier and more economical to deploy
- Emergence of managed service offerings in the OTP authentication (BT, VeriSign)

5 Conclusion

OTP authentication has come a long way from the proprietary offerings of its infancy. Especially the OATH algorithms have made implementation easier, more cost effective and in more form factors as before.

Although other forms of stronger authentication have gathered pace and the era of functionally working PKI authentication without complex client install is upon us, there is still a strong argument for OTP especially where access to resources over non internet channels is required (e.g. retail banking).

As demonstrated above there are some differences both in security and usability between the different algorithm offerings. Although proprietary offerings have still an advantage, the OATH time based algorithm brings a royalty free option with levels of security previously reserved to the proprietary ones.

More vertical markets are leveraging the technology experience of other verticals, such as the emergence of OTP in the Government to Citizen market, leveraging the financial services Business to Consumer experience.

Additionally new form factors such as the DisplayCard are finally bringing the usability difference that made a pure token offering undesirable in certain deployments.

This makes OTP, far from an 'old' technology, one of the best choices to strengthen the authentication beyond the password, especially in a multi-channel environment.

References

[OATH]   OATH, "Initiative for Open Authentication", http://www.openauthentication.org/

[RFC4226] IETF, "HOTP: An HMAC-Based One-Time Password Algorithm", http://www.rfc-archive.org/getrfc. php?rfc=4226

[OCRA]   IETF, "OCRA: OATH Challenge-Response Algorithms", http://www.ietf.org/internet-drafts/draft-mraihi-mutual-oath-hotp-variants-07.txt

[TOTP]   IETF, "TOTP: Time-based One-time Password Algorithm", http://www.ietf.org/internet-drafts/draft-mraihi-totp-timebased-00.txt

[Mas04]   MasterCard International Incorporated, "Chip Authentication Program – Functional Architecture", September 2004

NSA Suite B and its significance for non-USA organisations

Klaus Schmeh

cv cryptovision
klaus.schmeh@cryptovision.com

Abstract

In 2005 the US security authority NSA published a catalog of cryptographic methods to serve as the basis for the modernisation of the national cryptographic technology in the USA. The catalog is known by the name "Suite B" and has also generated great interest far beyond the borders of the USA. Suite B could exert appreciable influence on the application of cryptography for years to come. This paper covers the significance of Suite B for European organisations.

1 Introduction

The US National Security Agency has an almost mystical reputation for cryptographers. There are probably more encryption experts working in the heavily guarded offices of this gigantic organisation than in all the universities of the world combined. We can safely assume the NSA is always some years ahead of public cryptography. If the NSA suggests or prescribes some kind of cryptographic method, then it is important for two reasons: Firstly, the US authorities must keep to the NSA guidelines, and secondly, it can be assumed that it sets forth sensible provisions, due to the extensive knowledge of NSA specialists.

Suite B from 2005 is thus of significant interest. Within the scope of the Cryptographic Modernisation Program, its intention is to make US encryption technology fit for the 21st century. The list of supported methods is surprisingly short – it contains only four entries, whereas most methods are supported in differing variants. Some of the methods specified come as no surprise. To begin with we find the encryption method AES and the cryptographic hash function SHA (in the implementations SHA-256 and SHA-384). Both methods are in general use. Like all four Suite B methods, they are already specified in official US standards, all of which predate Suite B. In the case of AES it is FIPS 197 and in the case of SHA it is FIPS 180-2.

2 Elliptic curves

The two remaining Suite B algorithms are significantly more interesting. These deal with asymmetric methods based on elliptic curves (ECC). Cryptographers have known about these for a long time. ECC methods were first developed at the end of the 80s and were regarded from the mid-90s as the technology of the future. However, ECC methods have not penetrated the market as quickly as they were expected to, despite a gradually increasing trend that has been noticeable for years. One of the declared aims of the NSA is to promote the prevalence of ECC methods, in order to move forward from the lower performance of RSA, Diffie-Hellman and DSA.

N. Pohlmann, H. Reimer, W. Schneider (Editors): Securing Electronic Business Processes, Vieweg (2008), 291-295

The first of the ECC methods specified in Suite B is the Elliptic Curve DSA. This will be employed for digital signatures. It is described in FIPS 186-2, which in turn refers to ANS 9.62. Different elliptic curves are specified in FIPS 186-2 and the usage of any of these conforms to the standard. It differentiates between curves based on prime number fields, binary fields and Koblitz curves. The supported curves based on prime number fields are designated P-192, P-224, P-256, P-384 and P-521, where the number within each title relates to the bit length that the prime number is based on. Suite B only provides for the support of P-256 and P-384, while binary fields and Koblitz curves do not comply with the standard.

As a fourth method, Suite B supports Elliptic Curve Diffie-Hellman (ECDH) and, also derived from this, the Elliptic Curve MQV (ECMQV). These methods are used for key exchange. They are described in the NIST Special Publication 800-56, which in turn is based on ANS 9.42 and ANS 9.63. ECDH and ECMQV are also only supported in Suite B with P-256 and P-384.

If a supplier wishes to label his product as "Suite B compliant", he must support all methods in a standardized way. However, he can restrict the scope by parameters. In this way AES need only be implemented with 128-bit keys and SHA with only a 256-bit hash value length. The ECC method need only support the default curve P-256.

3 Evaluation programs

The NSA and the standards institute NIST offer three evaluation programs in total:

- CMVP (Cryptographic Module Validation Program): This is based on the FIPS 140-2 criteria for evaluation of cryptographic solutions. FIPS 140-2 is a proven standard for this purpose. The NIST is responsible for a CMVP evaluation. CMVP has been in existence since 1995. Primarily it has nothing to do with Suite B, but it is also applicable. CMVP is intended for Suite B products that fulfill purely cryptographic purposes.

- CCEVS (Common Criteria Evaluation and Validation Scheme): This is based on the Common Criteria (CC). The CC have likewise been employed within an evaluation framework that is not only relevant to cryptography, but also in general for IT security solutions. More is involved in a CC evaluation than a FIPS 140-2 evaluation. The CCEVS program is managed by the NSA. EAL 4 is the lowest defined grade. CCEVS is intended for Suite B products that fulfill other purposes in addition to the cryptographic. Such an evaluation is necessary in addition to CMVP.

- NSA evaluation: A third possibility is an evaluation that is carried out by the NSA, and that is not based on already existing standards. This evaluation is the highest of the three set out here. If a product is to be used for secret (classified) information, then an NSA evaluation is mandatory. A supplier must apply for an NSA evaluation. An inquiry by the author determined that such an evaluation is provisionally reserved for US suppliers. There are four variants of NSA evaluation:

- Commercial COMSEC Evaluation Program (CCEP): This evaluation is most relevant in the majority of cases. A CCEP evaluation means a contractual relationship between the supplier and the NSA. Due to the limited resources of the IAD this evaluation is only carried out when the intended usage of the respective product is transparent. The request for such an evaluation involves a questionnaire.

- User Partnership Program (UPP): This is only relevant for US official agencies, who wish to use Suite B products.

- Commercial Satellite Protection Program. This is only relevant to the suppliers of satellite products.
- Certified Product Sales and Support: This is only relevant to suppliers who already have a certified product.

In all cases, bottlenecks in carrying out evaluations at the NSA or the NIST need be reckoned with.

4 Standards

One of the first implementations of Suite B in a standard is an extension of the IPsec protocol. It was defined RFC 4869 [RFC4869]. There are four modes ("suites") by which the Suite B methods can be made use of in IPsec. These modes are labeled according to the AES key lengths and the type of AES operation defined in the ESP part of the protocol:

- Suite-B GCM-128: In this case the AES key length is 128 bits and AES operates in Galois-Counter Mode (GCM). Die ECDH key length is 256 bits. The Suite B GCM-128 mode provides integrity protection as well as encryption.
- Suite B GCM-256: Die AES key length is 256 bits and AES operates in the Galois-Counter Mode (GCM). The ECDH key length is 384 bits. The Suite B GCM-128 mode also provides integrity protection as well as encryption.
- Suite B GMAC-128: In this case AES is not used for encryption, instead only as a key-dependent hash function. The key length is 128 bits, the ECDH key length 256 bits. This mode serves only integrity protection, without applying encryption.
- Suite B GMAC-256: This mode is similar to Suite B GMAC-128, but where longer keys are used. Specifically a 256-bit AES key and a 384-bit ECDH key.

The RFC was compiled by two NSA employees. As it has only informational status, it is not an official Internet standard and it doesn't require the existence of implementations. RFC 4869 can therefore be regarded as a document created by the NSA in order to advertise Suite B.

Along with IPsec the protocol TLS (or SSL) lends itself to be operated with Suite B methods. However, the standards in this area are not so advanced as with IPsec. To date there is no RFC, but instead the second version of a draft with the name "Suite B Cipher Suites for TLS" [Draft]. This draft is only briefly set out and refers in many places to RFC 4492, where the usage of ECC methods for TLS is standardized. An NSA employee was also involved in this specification. The purpose of the draft is again to generate an informational RFC.

The email encryption standard S/MIME is also already usable with Suite B methods. The respective standard is RFC 5008 (Suite B in Secure/Multipurpose Internet Mail Extensions) [RFC5008]. The standard specifies two modes, known as Security Level 1 (SHA-256, ECDSA with P-256) and Security Level 2 (SHA-384, ECDSA with P-384). ECMQV is not supported. RFC 5008 has informational status. All authors are NSA employees.

There is so far no Suite B support for the XML Signature and XML Encryption standards. This could result from the fact that all the former standards of the NSA were developed as informational, while this form at the W3C was lacking. In 2007, the NSA announced that [NSA]: "The National Security Agency would like to see appropriate Suite B algorithms incorporated into XML Signature and XML Encryption." This request to the W3C to develop these standards resulted in the response that an extension of XML Signature and XML Encryption was at the time in planning.„Standard".

5 Products

Alongside the standards mentioned there are already the first products to support Suite B. The most important is without doubt Windows Vista, whose IPsec implementation was brought into conformance with Suite B in March 2008 with Service Pack 1 [MS]. The recently released Windows Server 2008 supports Suite B in any case. Other companies who support Suite B with their products include the following:

- Certicom: supports Suite B with the Security Builder NSE toolkit.
- cryptovision: supports Suite B in its PKI solution cv act PKIntegrated
- Entrust: supports Suite B with the solutions by their partner Spyrus (see below), which are certified as "Entrust ready".
- IdentiPHI: via Certicom
- RSA Security: supports Suite B with their toolkit BSAFE.
- Spyrus: supports Suite B with its product Talisman/DS suite.
- SUN: supports Suite B with its product Java Card 3.0.

In order to promote the deployment of Suite B, the NSA has bought 26 ECC patents from the Canadian cryptographic supplier Certicom. The NSA issues free licenses for the implementation of Suite B products by official US agencies. So far there it has not been clarified whether and what patent fees are due if such a product is used by another type of customer.

6 Suite B for European organisations

Most companies that support Suite B in their products are located in the USA (or Canada). This shows that Suite B plays a more important role for North American companies than for the European. The development of the standards confirms this, while the standards dominated by US companies IPsec, TLS and S/MIME are already conformant to Suite B, thanks to the collaboration of the NSA, whereas the World Wide Web Consortium, which is more influential in Europe, has yet to publish any equivalent standard. This development appears to be quite normal, since the interest in NSA standards in Europe is naturally less than it is in the USA.

For a prospective of the near future, the following aspects can be summarized:

- Suite B is expected to play an important role within the official US agencies. However, because the conversion period is really long (probably more than a decade), it tends to lead to a gradual development, primarily when new acquisitions are planned. However, to substitute these with Suite B products that solely target conformity on Suite B are not expected.
- The partners and suppliers of official US agencies will also convert to Suite B. Again it will also be a gradual process. As a part of this migration, companies outside the USA are also sure to implement Suite B technology.
- In addition, Suite B conformance can lead to a quality criterion and thus become a marketing instrument. Similar to FIPS-140, AES and SHA-1, which also play an important role beyond the borders of the USA, through this Suite B could become regarded as a de-facto standard worldwide. Even so, there are other countries who have their own standards and whose compliance makes sense. In Germany, for example, there are recommended algorithms by the BSI, while in Eastern Europe the GOST standards series is relevant to a certain degree.

With these considerations the importance of Suite B for European companies is quite easy to deduce. It mainly pays European companies to have support for Suite B if they have public sector customers in the USA. For US customers outside the public sector, support for Suite B also makes sense, but it is not imperative. For companies with customers outside the USA, Suite B support could also pay in the medium-term.

In this the question of an evaluation is interesting. Since an NSA-evaluation is only possible for US-based suppliers, the only choice is an evaluation by the NIST (CMVP for pure cryptographic solutions, CCEVS also for products that are otherwise deployable). Such an evaluation involves either a FIPS-140 or Common-Criteria-evaluation. A procedure of this kind is generally known to be expensive. Since its marketing value is limited, for many suppliers the attribute "Suite B compliant" will have to suffice.

References

[Draft]   Suite B Cipher Suites for TLS. Internet-Draft (2008)

[MS]   Description of the support for Suite B cryptographic algorithms that was added in Windows Vista Service Pack 1 and in Windows Server 2008. Microsoft 2008

[NSA]   XML Cryptographic Security and Suite B. National Security Agency 2007

[RFC5008] Suite B in Secure/Multipurpose Internet Mail Extensions. RFC 5008 (2007)

[RFC4869] Suite B Cryptographic Suites for IPsec. RFC 4869 (2007)

Managing vulnerabilities and achieving compliance for Oracle databases in a modern ERP environment

Stefan Hölzner · Jan Kästle

KPMG Deutsche Treuhand-Gesellschaft
Aktiengesellschaft Wirtschaftsprüfungsgesellschaft
Alfredstr. 277, D-45133 Essen
{shoelzner | jkaestle}@kpmg.com

Abstract

In this paper we summarize good practices on how to achieve compliance for an Oracle database in combination with an ERP system. We use an integrated approach to cover both the management of vulnerabilities (preventive measures) and the use of logging and auditing features (detective controls). This concise overview focusses on the combination Oracle and SAP and it's dependencies, but also outlines security issues that arise with other ERP systems. Using practical examples, we demonstrate common vulnerabilities and coutermeasures as well as guidelines for the use of auditing features.

1 Compliance requirements

Oracle databases are amongst the most used databases for modern ERP systems. They provide the storage for an organisation's most valuable data. This data has to be secured from violations of confidentiality, integrity and availability. Whereas most organisations have implemented an authorization concept on the ERP application layer, our experience and our surveys show that database security is often still neglected – mostly due to ignorance about the available security features and their limitations in current ERP application environments.

Local legislation and regulatory requirements have always stressed the need to enforce the integrity of data relevant for financial reporting. However, with recent developments like the Sarbanes-Oxley Act of 2002 and the upcoming 8. EU directive, database security moves even more into the focus of both business and auditors.

Information security standards and IT management frameworks already adress database security and the use of auditing and logging features directly or indirectly. E.g., the ISO/IEC 2701:2005 standard describing the requirements for an information security management system (ISMS) requires organisations to establish and maintain a technical vulnerability management (Annex A, A.12.6). This implies a vulnerability management for the databases in scope of the ISMS. The Payment Card Industry Data Security Standard (PCI DSS) in Version 1.1 explicitly requires the implementation of automated audit trails for all system components to monitor and track events like all individual user accesses to cardholder data, all actions taken by any individual with root or administrative privileges, invalid logical access attempts and even the use of identification and authentication mechanisms (PCI DSS Requirement 10). Similar requirements can be found in other standards and frameworks (e.g. CobiT).

N. Pohlmann, H. Reimer, W. Schneider (Editors): Securing Electronic Business Processes, Vieweg (2008), 296-306

Therefore, it is necessary to cover data security in an integrated holistic approach: considering both unauthorized access and controlled legitimate access to the database in combination with a given network infrastructure, operating system and application layer. But many security issues arise from unforeseen dependencies between the different software packages used on the different layers. In this paper, we focus on the scenario of an Oracle-based ERP application in general and on SAP specifically, as Oracle databases and SAP is one of the most commonly found combinations in many companies and organisations.

In the first part of this paper we focus on the management of vulnerabilities and security weaknesses of Oracle databases – also considering dependencies of possible security measures on the application in use – as preventive actions. In the second part we then analyse the use of logging and auditing features as the detective complement in this integrated approach.

2 Protection of the Oracle database

2.1 Protection of the TNS listener

To get a better understanding of the vulnerabilities associated with Oracle databases used for SAP systems it is best to approach this topic like a hacker would. A hacker with access to the internal network – possibly a malicious insider or an external person, who was able to hack into the network or to use an unprotected WLAN access point – will gather the necessary information to connect to the database as a first step. For a connection, the IP address of the database, the port of the TNS[1] listener and the System Identifier of the database instance (SID) is needed. Since the SAP application server will provide the hostname and the SID it is a good start to scan for the application server first. The so-called "dispatcher" of a SAP application listens on a port between 3200-3299 TCP, depending on the the system number, e.g. 3203 if the system number is 03. Note that SAP uses a couple of other ports too [1]. However, the dispatcher is used for access by the SAP GUI and is most commonly found. From the dispatcher some basic information about the SAP system can already be retrieved (see Listing 1), e.g. the hostname of the database server and the SID of the SAP System and the Oracle database. In general, the SIDs of the SAP System and the Oracle database instance are identical.

```
# sapinfo ashost=testdb07 sysnr=00
SAP System Information
-------------------------------------------------------
Destination                testdb07_Z00_00

Host                       dedevdb07
System ID                  Z00
Database                   Z00
DB host                    TESTDB07
DB system                  ORACLE

SAP release                620
SAP kernel release         620

RFC Protokoll              011
Characters                 1100 (NON UNICODE PCS=1)
Integers                   LIT
Floating P.                IE3
SAP machine id             560

Timezone                   3600 (Daylight saving time)
```

Listing 1: output of sapinfo

---

1 TNS: Transparent Network Substrate, the network service of an Oracle database

The default port for the TNS listener is TCP port 1527 [1]. Other ports in between 1520 and 1530 are also commonly found. To locate an Oracle database in a given subnet, a portscanner like nmap [2] can be used (see Listing 2).

```
nmap -sS -P0 -p 1520-1530 10.0.0.1-255
```

Listing 2: nmap scan for oracle databases

For Oracle release 9i and older, the SID can also be extracted from the TNS listener if it is in default configuration. This can be done with a query using the listener commands "status" or "services" (see Figure 1).

Note that an unprotected TNS listener already poses a high risk in releases 9i and older since misuse is possible: it provides access to the operating system (with the privileges of the user account that runs the TNS listener) and to the database. If remote administration of the TNS listener is enabled, among other things a new logfile can be set to an arbitrary file on the operating system. By sending "commands" to the listener it is possible to write to this very file. The write operation is executed with the privileges of the user account that runs the TNS listener – in general this is the oracle user itself – the files .rhosts, .bashrc, or glogin.sql would be suitable to gain access to the database or the operating system.

If the TNS listener is protected by the following configuration in the listener.ora file

- setting ADMIN_RESTRICTIONS_<LISTENER_NAME> = ON
- setting a password with the tool *lsnrctl*

the SID cannot be retrieved directly anymore. This is also the case with Oracle release 10g where the listener is already protected in its default configuration. In these cases it is still possible to do a brute-force attack on the SID. This is feasible since it is only a three letter combination and alphanumeric in the case of SAP. However, as demonstrated above, the SID can usually be learned from the application itself easily.

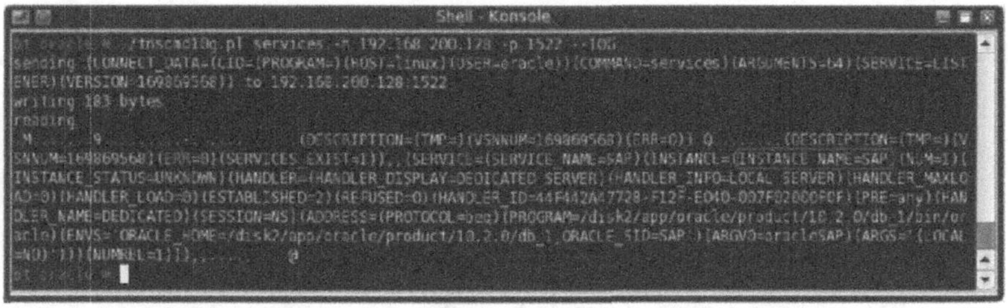

Figure 1: Listener query for available services (Oracle 9i and older)

2.2 Protection of default user accounts

The most common attack against Oracle databases aims at the large number of default users that are created upon installation of the database and that come with a default password assigned. The installed default users depend on the release and on the installed modules. Typical default users whose passwords remain often unchanged are DBSNMP and OUTLN. For SAP there is one additional database user that is used by the SAP application to connect to the database. In older SAP releases this user is called SAPR3. From SAP release 4.6C on the username depends on the SID and is called SAP<SID>.

A demonstration for this attack on the user accounts OUTLN and SYSTEM using the tool opwg from the oat-suite [3] is shown in Figure 2.

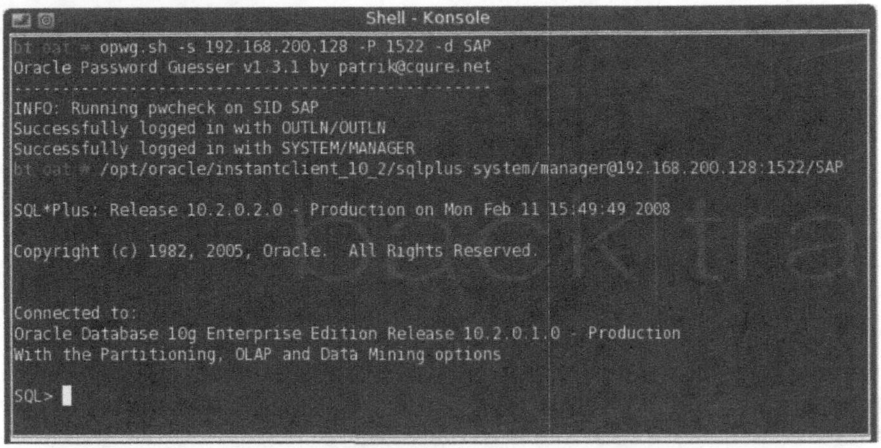

Figure 2: Attacking the default user accounts

If access is gained with a less privileged user account there are several possibilities to get administrative rights (database administrator, DBA). For example by exploiting one of the many privilege escalation vulnerabilites or by retrieving the hashes of the administrative users and using a password cracker. The user DBSNMP can read these hashes from the view dba_users[2].

The counter measures for this attack are obvious: all unnecessary default users should be locked and the password should be set to "expired". All user accounts that are actually needed should be protected with a strong password.

Since version 10g Oracle improved the handling of the default user accounts. Most of these accounts are now locked upon installation. Furthermore, the Oracle Universal Installer requires setting a new password for the active database users. However, the problem still exists, e.g. if the manual installation is chosen or if previously secure settings have been modified manually.

To further protect the user accounts from password attacks, they should be locked after a small number of failed logins. For Oracle in version 10g release 2 the default is to automatically lock user accounts after ten failed logins. For version 9i and older this configuration has to be set manually.

However, note that a login with the user SYS as SYSDBA is possible even after ten failed logins as this user is excluded from the rule.

2.3 Vulnerabilities caused by SAP specific configurations

Besides vulnerabilities which apply to all Oracle databases – as the attack on default passwords demonstrated above – there are vulnerabilities which arise from special configuration requirements of an application. In the following we will demonstrate such a SAP specific configuration.

A SAP system uses the following operating system accounts:

---

2 This view accesses the table USER$ where the actual user information is stored.

- <sid>adm and ora<sid> on Unix/Linux
- <SID>ADM and SAPSERVICE<SID> on Windows

In the Oracle database those accounts are also created using operating system authentication, i.e. the database trusts the operating system that those users have already been authenticated and does not perform its' own authentication. The corresponding entries in the view *dba_users* are shown in Listing 3 for the SID P01. Since operating system authentication is used, the usernames have the prefix OPS$.

```
USERNAME        USER_ID        PASSWORD
---------       --------       ---------

OPS$P01ADM   23               EXTERNAL
OPS$ORAP01   24               EXTERNAL
```

Listing 3: Extract from view dba_users

This authentication mechanism also has to work from the application servers that are usually installed on separate machines, since it is used for the authentication of the application server at the database. So it is required to set the init.ora parameter *remote_os_authent* to *TRUE* [4]. Thus the database trusts *every* machine that has previously authenticated these operating system users. This might as well be the attackers' machine, where the mentioned user accounts have just been installed.

From the application server the SAP application connects to the databases using the account <SID>ADM and retrieves the encrypted password for the user SAP<SID>, decrypts the password and connects to the database with the user SAP<SID>. The user SAP<SID> is subsequently used for the application connection to the database.

The users SAPSERVICE<SID> and <sid>adm have the role SAPDBA assigned. Often the privileges assigned are too extensive and direct access to the SAP tables is possible. If privileges are assigned correctly, a privilege escalation vulnerability can be exploited to get additional access to data.

In summary, an attacker just has to create one of the users mentioned above on her system and can then authenticate to the database without providing a password (see Figure 3).

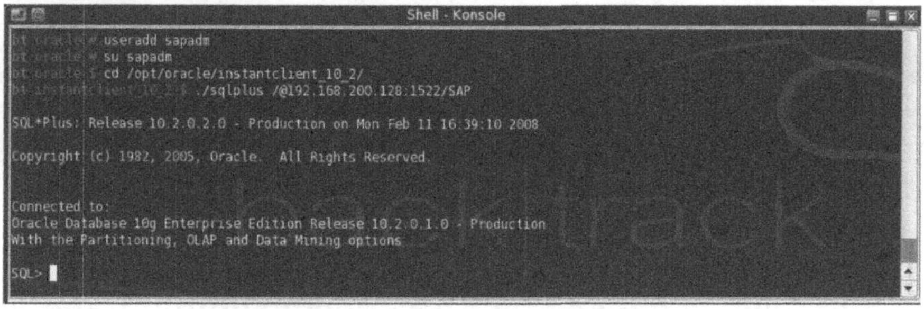

Figure 3: Authentication using OS authentication

For this attack to be successful, only network communication with the TNS listener is required. The only way to protect from the attack is to restrict network access. This can be done by Oracles built-in feature *valid node checking* in the listener configuration file sqlnet.ora (see Listing 4).

```
TCP.VALIDNODE_CHECKING = YES
TCP.INVITED_NODES = (IPs of application servers)
```

Listing 4: valid node checking

This feature works like a TCP wrapper by only allowing access from the application servers.

Note that this configuration is susceptible to IP spoofing. For a higher security level the database and the application server need to be placed in a separate network segment protected by a firewall. Only the ports needed by the front end systems (e.g. the SAP GUI) should be allowed to connect to the application server. This installation can be complemented by a SAP router.

2.4 Protection of unpatched databases

SAP does not only require specific configurations in the database but also interferes with applying security patches. These vendor supplied security patches fix known vulnerabilities, some of which result in local privilege escalation. Oracle publishes the so-called *Critical Patch Updates* (CPUs) quarterly. Conflicts with patches provided SAP are possible, thus SAP recommends to install CPUs only *"if you have important reasons for doing so"*. *"If you decide to install the patch, you may not be able to install many patches recommended by SAP or you may have to uninstall the CPU "*. [5]

For the current Oracle release 10.2.0.2 the CPUs from October 2006 to July 2007 were not approved. Only the CPU from October 2007 could be applied, which means that an affected database had to stay unpatched for almost one year.

An update to the current release, which contains the CPUs published until its release date, is also not always possible. The current release of Oracle 10g is 10.2.0.3, the current release approved by SAP is 10.2.0.2.

Our experiences from the audits we performed confirm that Oracle databases used for SAP are usually unpatched.

As long as access to the database is properly restricted, the risk for local privilege escalation is rather low. Only the administrative users as well as SAP's database user should have an active account in the database. However vulnerabilities that can be exploited remotely pose a high risk. As a compensating control all unneeded services should be deactivated to minimize the attack surface, e.g. the *XML database* or the *extproc* service of the TNS listener. In the past, both were affected by vulnerabilities that could be exploited remotely.

If a database cannot be patched, it is indeed necessary to restrict network access to the TNS listener and to the database server in general by the use of firewalls as described above. Furthermore, an update to the current Oracle release should be considered as soon as possible after approval by SAP.

2.5 Common security issues with non SAP systems

As a matter of course, challenges for database security also arise from the dependencies with other ERP software packages.

One common issue is a security design flaw in the application architecture. Some applications require that the client software on every user's workstation establishes a direct database connection with the

TNS listener[3]. A server side presentation layer (e.g. a web application server) is not used. In this case, a firewall that protects the database from all front end system connections will disrupt the application. For most small and mid-sized companies we found that defining "allowed" connection groups in the firewall ruleset is manageable only if the number of systems is low and not subject to regular change. In a multi-user environment this approach is not feasible. Possible solution scenarios for these types of applications include the use of terminal servers or – in case of custom applications – a redesign of the application architecture. The costs for both solutions can be significant.

A second security issue arises from applications that use database user accounts to authenticate application users, i.e. the application users and their respective passwords are stored in the Oracle table USER$. If the application does not support password policies, then weak application passwords automatically result in weak passwords for database users. Considering the multitude of privilege escalation vulnerabilities in Oracle this can result in unlimited access to all data stored in the database. Then again configuring password policies (regular change of password, minimum password length, password complexity etc.) on the database level might leave the application unusable because of the inability to handle user input and database error messages. In our audits weak passwords were commonly found for over 80% of all user accounts.

3 Defining and Setting up an auditing concept

Compliance with international regulations and standards as well as with local laws usually requires the implementation of logging and auditing of access to certain types of data. The auditing should enable a company to detect attacks against the database, to monitor access to certain type of data and to get a complete and comprehensible audit trail of administrative actions (traceability).

Oracle offers different types of logging functionalities, but basically the actual logging requirements for certain types of tables and data has to be derived from a business perspective and from compliance requirements. E.g. access to personal data (payroll records) might be subject to logging according to local law, access to cardholder data has to be tracked and monitored according to the PCI DSS.

An audit concept should cover the following elements:
- define what transactions (read, write, update, delete, etc.) on what data elements (tables, rows or columns) to be audited
- monitoring of administrative accounts and shared user accounts
- logging of security relevant events (logon / logoff, detecting malicious activities)
- logging of database schema structure changes
- adequate monitoring of log files
- ensure the integrity of the logfiles (logfiles cannot be modified or deleted, the auditing cannot be turned off)

Logging every access to every data element will inevitably result in unmanageable large amounts of log files and most likely in a decrease in system performance. Thus it is crucial to restrict logging to critical events. This will usually result in relatively small amounts of log data that can be processed automatically or manually.

---

3 E.g. IDL KONSIS and many custom applications

3.1 Mandatory Auditing

By default only *Mandatory Auditing* is active. Mandatory Auditing cannot be turned off. This type of auditing logs the start-up and shutdown of the Oracle database as well as connections initiated by the user SYS and by every user with DBA roles SYSDBA and SYSOPER. But as powerful administrative users without SYSDBA and SYSOPER roles are frequently granted special database privileges such as SELECT ALL TABLE and UPDATE ALL TABLE, they should also be targets of database monitoring. This cannot be achieved with the Mandatory Auditing functionality.

3.2 SYS Auditing

The auditing of all SQL statements submitted by the user SYS and of all users with SYSDBA or SYS-OPER privileges can be achieved with *SYS Auditing*. SYS Auditing can be activated by setting the init. ora parameter *audit_sys_operations* to *true*. A user connecting with SYSDBA privileges ("as SYS-DBA") authenticated through the operating system group dba always appears as the user "SYS" in the database. Likewise a user connecting with SYSOPER privileges appears as the user "PUBLIC" in the database. Therefore, traceability can only be achieved by using personalized operating system accounts. Personalized operating system accounts should be used anyway to achieve traceability at the operating system level. Note that the current operating system user is part of a log entry.

With remote administration there is no full control over the operation system accounts. Therefore the remote administration with SYSDBA and SYSOPER privileges should be turned off by setting the init. ora parameter *remote_login_passwordfile = none*.

In default configuration, the audit trail of the SYS auditing is written directly to operating system files. Since a user with SYSDBA privileges is able to delete log entries from the database table, the file permissions of the log files should be set appropriately. Considering that many database administrators have administrative access rights on the OS level as well, it is advised to use remote logging that allows for a better protection of logfiles. Even though it requires setting up a separate log host system, a segregation of duties for system administrators can be established. Syslog functionality is available since Oracle 10g.

Because no criteria or filters can be set, SYS auditing is not an ideal solution. However, it should to be activated to trace the use of SYSOPER and SYSDBA privileges.

3.3 Standard Auditing

Standard Auditing allows for auditing of specific privileges, statements or specific objects. The goal is to audit any unusual event that is not expected to occur in a live system and to detect malicious activities.

First of all access attempts to the database should be logged. This can be done by auditing the privilege „CREATE SESSION", which is necessary for a connection to the database:

```
audit create session;
```

Attempted logins for non-existent user accounts or large numbers of failed logins are a strong indication of an attack.

Furthermore it is necessary to detect changes to the audit configuration itself. This allows detecting an attacker that tries to cover her tracks:

```
audit audit system by access;
```

Activities worth auditing are the creation of user accounts and the granting of system rights. In an Oracle database for SAP only a handful of users are needed, so every change to user accounts or even new users in the database are also indications of an attack. Furthermore activities like creating database links or modifying database profiles would not happen during normal operation; they should only be done in maintenance slots and are worth being audited.

These statements can be audited as follows:

```
audit user by access;
audit system grant by access;
audit public database link by access;
audit database link by access;
audit profile by access;
```

Other statements that can be considered for auditing are alter system or alter database.

To apply standard auditing to the successful execution of any read or modify transaction on the HR payroll tables (e.g. PA0008) in SAP, the following statement can be used:

```
audit select, insert, update, delete on SAPR3.PA0008 by access whenever successful;
```

3.4 Fine-Grained-Auditing

The so-called *Fine-Grained-Auditing* allows the monitoring of data access based on content and therefore a more fine grained definition of audit conditions. These conditions are described in a *FGA policy*. It is useful e.g. if the auditing of read access to certain columns of a table is needed. This is relevant e.g. for PCI DSS that requires logging all individual user accesses to cardholder data.

If access to the payroll data in table PA0008 of an SAP system is to be audited, the according policy could be constructed as follows:

```
begin
   dbms_fga.add_policy (
       object_schema=>'SAPR3',
       object_name=>'PA0008',
       policy_name=>'PAYROLL_ACCESS'
   );
end;
```

If a user queries the table PA0008 by issuing

```
select * from SAPR3.PA0008;
```

the audit trail records this action. The audit trail includes, but is not limited to timestamp, database user account, operating system user account and the complete SQL query. Each organisation has to assess the data (tables) to be audited according to applicable legislation and regulatory requirements.

3.5 Integrity of the Audit Logs

When implementing the auditing concept the integrity of the audit logs should be ensured and an attacker should not be able to manipulate or delete audit logs. Therefore audit logs should not be stored within the database. Writing the audit logs into operating systems files allows for protection of the audit logs as long as file permissions are set appropriately. However, a strong protection of the audit logs can only be realized by sending the logs to a separate loghost.

Syslog functionality is available since Oracle 10g on Linux/Unix systems. On Windows-based systems the logs are written to the central event log and thus can also be sent to a loghost.

Oracle now offers a dedicated product for central logging, the *Oracle Audit Vault*. However, this product is not yet approved by SAP AG for use with a SAP system [7].

The *Oracle Database Vault* goes even one step further. It allows the segregation of duties in an Oracle database. For example the SYSDBA privilege that grants all privileges within the database, can be split up so that the security administration (e.g. audit configuration) is separated from regular administration tasks. This tool is also not yet approved by SAP.

4 Embedding database security into an ISMS

Security is a process that has to be established within a company. To achieve and maintain a good security level – including but not limited to database systems – it is good practice to follow the established Plan-Do-Check-Act (PDCA) model and to integrate it into a corporate-wide ISMS [6]:

- Plan: establish ISMS policies, objectives, processes and procedures relevant to managing risk and improving information security to deliver results in accordance with an organization's overall policies and objectives
- Do: Implement and operate the ISMS policy, controls, processes and procedures.
- Check: Assess and, where applicable, measure process performance against ISMS policy, objectives and practical experience and report the results to management for review.
- Act: Take corrective and preventive actions, based on the results of the internal ISMS audit and management review or other relevant information, to achieve continual improvement of the ISMS.

For a database system, an organisation might define the following approach as appropriate:

- Plan: define a secure database architecture; define a policy for security relevant database settings (password policies, auditing settings etc.); define a patch process; define an auditing procedure (regular monitoring of audit logs); assign roles and responsibilities; define notification/incident management and escalation processes (not necessarily database-specific)
- Do: implement the specifications in all databases in scope
- Check: perform regular self-checks; perform regular security audits for compliance with internal policies and guidelines and with external best practices (by an independent function, e.g. internal audit, external security auditor); define security key performance indicators / benchmarks to track developments
- Act: If deviations are found, determine the root cause and take action (e.g. modify the policies, objectives, processes or procedures); establish management reporting of corrective actions

The given examples have to be modified and checked for applicability for each actual corporate environment.

5 Conclusions

Trying to meet compliance requirements on the database level, organisations face several pitfalls and technical challenges. Although an Oracle database basically offers all security techniques needed to establish a secure environment, application requirements sometimes render database security techniques unusable. From a security perspective, in practice quite a number of questionable application architectures and design concepts are still around to challenge the security concepts of organisations.

In the foreseeable future, these challenges will persist. They will still need to be treated with adequate individual preventive measures and detective controls. There is no "one size fits all" solution for database security.

References

[1] SAP AG, TCP/IP Ports Used by SAP Applications: https://www.sdn.sap.com/irj/sdn/go/portal/prtroot/docs/library/uuid/4e515a43-0e01-0010-2da1-9bcc452c280b

[2] Portscanner nmap: http://nmap.org

[3] Oracle Auditing Tools: http://www.cqure.net/

[4] SAP AG, SAP Security Guide: http://help.sap.com/saphelp_nw04/helpdata/en/ed/18cc38e6df4741a26 4bddcd4f98ae2/frameset.htm

[5] SAP AG, SAP Note 1140644: http://service.sap.com/notes

[6] ISO/IEC 27001:2005(E)

[7] SAP AG, SAP Note 105047: http://service.sap.com/notes

Identity Theft in Electronic Financial Transactions
The experience of the Central Bank of Spain

María Luisa García Tallón

Head of the Complaints Department at the Central Bank of Spain
mluisa.garcia@bde.es

Abstract

Financial fraud usually goes hand in hand with the complex problem of identity theft in financial transactions. The experience gained in the Complaints Department through the presented cases and queries includes:

- Traditional falsifications in traditional financial transactions.
- The most innovative forms of digital identity theft, which covers numerous cases of credit card fraud and the increasingly worrying cases of online fraud, which are troublesome because of the impunity with which, in most cases, criminals operate on the Net and because of the high sums that can be defrauded.
- Cases of identity theft in the process of contracting financial transactions, with harmful consequences for those impersonated, as they are unjustly ordered to pay back debts and put on different defaulter's lists, such as the CIRBE (or the 'Risk Information Centre' of the Central Bank of Spain).

This work aims to illustrate the main problems presented by clients of financial organisations that have been the object of some type of online fraud and which have gone to the Complaints Department after failing to obtain a positive response from their organisation, and the solutions offered by the Complaints Department.

I am going to concentrate on the different cases resulting from the use of the e-Banking Services, as they have been causing most of the problems in the last years.

1 The implementation of e-banking (or online banking)

It is a fact that information and communication technologies are having more and more influence on the development of the economic activity and financial markets. The widespread use of the Internet is favourable to the growth of e-commerce and, on the other hand, the existence of an online financial services market is indispensable in the markets' current globalization framework.

Thirty years ago, people paid their purchases with money or cheques; they didn't have any other alternatives until the appearance of credit cards (which date back to 1958), without which we can't imagine carrying out most of our usual transactions.

N. Pohlmann, H. Reimer, W. Schneider (Editors): Securing Electronic Business Processes, Vieweg (2008), 307-312

In Spain, the first precedent of the release of credit cards dates back to 1971, when Banco Bilbao launched "BankAmericard". Since that year, the development of the technology applied to electronic transactions has been exponential.

Since e-banking appeared in the 90's (whose boom in Spain can be dated back to the year 2000), Spanish organisations have done an excellent job adapting and innovating and they have positioned themselves at the top of their sector in the field of technological banking systems, but now there's a challenge in security.

Financial organisations, which have gradually entered this market, have done it well by creating virtual banks, combining traditional face-to-face banking services with e-banking.

The development of online banking has been slow and uneven in the first years, because of various reasons: in the first place, it requires a process of adaptation and assimilation on the part of the users of this new channel and the financial organisations that offer the channel. Secondly, it poses problems that derive from the security and privacy of transactions and, finally, problems of accessibility and functionality.

In the last years, the offer of products and the provision of services through this channel has been increasing on the part of most of the financial organisations of the market, to such an extent that, nowadays, we can carry out practically any type of financial transaction through online banking: contraction of loans and credits, mortgage loans, e-mortgages, opening current accounts, contraction of time deposits, value purchase orders, investment funds, use of credit cards and even other types of less-known contracts, such as the so-called 'deposit, mortgage and pension fund auctioneer' and the financial aggregator.

Despite the fact the number of security measures of organisations has increased, security is still the biggest challenge we are facing. The biggest problems for the users of e-banking services have come with the appearance of financial cybercrime in the last years, which currently operates in an organised manner through international networks, carrying out massive attacks through the Net.

2 Problems of users

Now, I am going to analyse what the main problems are users of Electronic Banking encounter.

1. In the first place, NET THREATS, which comprises the installation of viruses, trojans, spyware, spam, etc. on the computer of users, and so-called social engineering techniques, such as the well-known scam known as PHISHING, through which users are tricked into revealing their passwords.

2. In the second place, there is a lack of inbred knowledge about computer security issues: most clients start using this channel without any knowledge on how it really works and without knowing the existing net threats and the most efficient way to protect themselves against them. In addition, users use the tools offered by their e-banking providers.

3. As a logical consequence of this problem, we find the theft of digital identities from those clients that are the object of fraud.

The theft of identities brings together multiple factors that should be analysed when it comes to determining whether the way the client has acted has been correct or whether (s)he has failed to comply with the commitment to safeguard personal information, as established in the e-banking agreement signed by the organisation. Factors such as the use of highly sophisticated techniques for the capture of passwords and personal data (which are practically impossible to be detected), social engineering techniques and identity theft to host websites from financial organisations (which are in most cases identical to the genuine websites) have to be taken into account when it comes to assessing the diligent behaviour of clients.

4. Difficulty in retrieving funds. Clients that are the object of fraud are made defenseless by the speed and the anonymity with which criminals act on the net and when organisations wash their hands of this problem by referring them to court, in order for them to report the incident and try obtaining a successful result.

5. Lastly, the inexistence of regulations applicable to this matter, which makes the contract terms signed by the clients and their organisations especially relevant. These contracts are in fact contracts of adhesion, in which organisations absolve themselves from all responsibility. The current positive law does not offer appropriate solutions to the problems caused by identity theft on the net and, even though the legal responsibility belongs to the clients, there is a moral responsibility that belongs to the financial organisation.

6. In the field of the European Union, there is a set of rules that are directly or indirectly applicable to the cross-border commerce of financial services: directives relating to banking and insurances, consumer protection and data and digital signature protection. But, above all, we should highlight the Directive 2000/31 on e-commerce, which, together with the Directive 2002/65, which was transposed into the Spanish legal system by Act 22/2007 of 11 July on distance marketing of consumer financial services, constitutes the true legal framework that regulates the development of electronic financial services, but they mainly refer to the warm up period and the right of withdrawal of contracts, without dealing with specific rules that are applicable to fraudulent transactions and e-banking transactions carried out through identity theft (except for cases of fraudulent credit card use).

3 Presented cases

In the last years, financial transactions carried out through e-banking in which identity theft has taken place are starting to gain importance. These transactions are normally characterized by money transfers from one person's account to an intermediary's account from which the same amount is drawn almost simultaneously in cash or through an overseas transaction, through an establishment that manages transfers, at which moment recovering the money is very difficult.

Fraud can cover drawing money from a holder's credit card up to the limit, in order to proceed as in the previous case. There have been even cases in which securities sell orders have been carried out by third parties impersonating the holder, in order for the securities to be paid on the said holder's account, from which they are afterwards illegally transferred to the account of a third party, at the very same time that they are withdrawn from this account.

4 Result of the analysis of the presented cases

There is a lack of specific regulations regarding transactions carried out through the Internet. It is clear that the biggest problem we encounter regarding long-distance business relationships through electronic ways is the correct identification of clients.

How is personal data obtained from a defrauded person?

The most used techniques for stealing passwords from users of this service are social engineering techniques, which are based on fraud and are used to direct the behaviour of a person (clicking on links, inserting passwords, visiting websites), in this way obtaining sensitive information. The most known technique is spam (unsolicited messages that are sent in bulk), which is one of the cheapest and most effective fraudulent dissemination methods and is increasingly used. In some cases, clients acknowledge that they have received a spam message or replied to a phishing e-mail. In other cases, the method used for obtaining passwords is not inferred.

In these cases, there is not a contract clause of limited responsibility for the holder (such as in the contracts for credit cards and other electronic paying methods) and, therefore, the defrauded sums can reach as high a limit as the total of the funds a client keeps in his/her account. In fact, the contract clauses for e-banking services, drawn up by the financial organisations, make the responsibility regarding the incorrect use of the digital signature always fall on clients, attributing the said wrong use to their carelessness in safekeeping their digital signature, for which they cannot take responsibility.

This problem is difficult to combat, which inevitably entails a considerable cost, which, up to now, was usually taken up by the financial organisations. Lately, though, it is also the clients who take up the cost, as some organisations wash their hands of the consequences of these types of fraud.

The numbers provided by the Antiphishing Service of Telefónica show a very rapid growth, as in 2004 there were already 33 recorded cases; in 2005, they were multiplied by more than eight, reaching 291 cases; in 2006, there were 1,040 and, in 2007, the number of cases that were treated and solved by Telefónica doubled those of 2006, with a total of 2,151 attacks. In 2007, therefore, more than two times the incidents were processed. The data of the Antiphishing Working Group show that the average duration of the attacks worldwide is more than 36 hours.

According to the report, the amount of received e-mails during the last year was also 2.25 times the amount of 2006 and the nearly 4 billion e-mails of 2007 are practically six times the number of e-mails received in 2004.

Viruses keep following a descending trend, whereas spam continues an opposite trend and, in 2007, they were multiplied by 4.5 with respect to 2006, with a large increase in the last part of the year, as 94 per cent of the total of processed e-mails was spam. This is due to the fact spam is normally aimed at generating illegal purchases, imitations and forgeries or fraud. In the pre-christmas and Christmas period, the phenomenon increases.

The continuing decrease of the number of viruses sent by e-mail, year after year, is largely due to a change in the modus operandi, such as the sending of links to URLs that have viruses, instead of sending them directly. This change of behaviour has changed browsers into the main entrance doors through which viruses enter.

Naturally, this situation causes concern and worry and the need to adopt measures that will increase security on the net. This concern is shared by the Complaints Department of the Central Bank of Spain, who has received numerous complaints from clients of financial organisations who have been victims of these frauds.

The defrauded amounts the Complaints Department has known about have varied from a minimum of € 600 to a maximum of € 40,000.

The organisations attribute the security of the channel and lack of diligence of clients to the safekeeping of passwords. The use of the SSL protocol of 128 bits based on asymmetric encryption techniques or public keys is widespread and, according to experts, it is the securest one known nowadays for the transmission of data.

The previously described points show that the biggest problem is the correct authentication of clients.

The authentication systems first used were one-time passwords, which use a symmetric or private encryption system. This system presents important vulnerabilities from the point of view of security, as the mere capture of passwords authorises intruders to carry out all types of financial transactions through e-banking.

The last observed trends tend to reinforce the authentication methods: some financial organisations admit the e-ID card, which includes a double authentication system with asymmetric encryption of information, which offers better security. Furthermore, many entities increasingly use a system which consists in sending an SMS to clients' mobile phone asking a random key from them, which is taken from their digital signature and which has to be inserted in order to carry out transactions.

We can conclude from all this that the problem of security in the correct identification of clients increasingly worries organisations due to the development and growth of online financial fraud, but we may not forget that it is in the hands of organisations to carry out appropriate improvements so that their clients can operate with maximum security, given that the use of this channel is massively and indiscriminately offered to all customers, without entering into any consideration about the necessary financial training and education for its correct use.

5 Development of the Criterion of the Complaints Department

In face of the results of this analysis, what has been the development of the followed criterion in our resolutions?

1. In the first place, an attitude of prudence was adopted, referring the delimitation of responsibilities with respect to the assumption of the costs resulting from the fraud committed to the resolution of the courts. This is due to the fact practically no incidents occurred until the end of 2006, due to the complexity in determining how they had occurred and the possible non-fulfillment by those involved and, in short, because what had happened was the commission of a fraud offence.

2. In the second place, the flow of cases that came up in a short period of time gave rise to worries about the adaption of the security systems some organisations were offering to their clients and about whether an absence of responsibility on the part of the organisations could be systematically claimed, because of the mere fact of proving the capture of passwords had occurred outside their systems and had been caused by the lack of diligence of the client in safeguarding the passwords.

It is true that it is difficult for organisations to prove their client has acted with lack of diligence with respect to safeguarding a password (for example, the client might have inserted his/her digital signature on a fake website impersonating the one from the organisation), but it is also difficult – or even more difficult – for the client to prove the opposite. In addition, we should not forget that, in the last case, fraud has been possible because the client has used a channel that was offered to him/her by the bank. This is the weakest part in the contraction of a service, whose functioning widely exceeds its comprehension, in most cases.

Therefore, even though it is true that inserting an electronic signature as a response to phishing may be considered not very diligent, in no case can it be called blamable. Neither can it be said that the level of negligence involves a 100% increase in the defrauded cost, without carrying out any probative action. This would be disproportionate to say the least and we cannot assess it according to good banking practices.

5.1 Demandable interventions from the organisations

Consequently, what interventions do we demand from the organisations in order to assess they operate in accordance with financial good practices?

1. Implementation of security measures that include a control of possible attacks to the corporation, implementation of better systems for the protection and use of certificates or strong authentication mechanisms for their clients.

2. Information for clients; in the first place, it is necessary to accredit the previously offered information about the knowledge on the agreement and assumed risk in the contraction. In the second place, the necessary training and advice, in order to appropriately use the channel, and the safekeep of passwords. For this, it is advisable for banks to include the following aspects on their website: the bank's identity and exact address (it is important to make the URL clear, as there have been cases in which URLs were practically identical, which is done to subtract data). With respect to contracts, it should be highlighted that they have to be accessible by the public before hiring the service, so that clients can analyze the contract terms and verify that the safety of their data is guaranteed. This applies as long as we are dealing with contracts of adhesion that cannot be modified by the clients, so that it is important for them to check their content before signing them.

3. Diligence in the management of recovering funds, in which collaboration agreements come into play which organisations execute to this effect (letter from the Spanish Banking Association (or AEB) giving procedure instructions).

4. Responsibility for the implementation of the system. Generally, we consider it is unfair for organisations who have offered their clients a system for the use of e-banking services that included vulnerabilities (in which vulnerabilities is to be understood as the easy way in which some websites have been impersonated or the use of weak authentication systems), which have been improving with the implementation of new and safer systems, to make the consequences of the committed fraud entirely fall on the clients who were the object of this online fraud and who were not able to get benefits from the main guarantees of security that are now offered by the organisation.

5. Probative activity. It is true that it is very complicated to carry out probative activities in order to show a clearly negligent act on the part of a client, as the organisations have claimed, but it is also true that is even more difficult for the clients to prove their diligence, in case we put the burden on them and demand them to prove their innocence, as some organisations pretend to do.

Finally, some type of self-regulation that delimits the responsibility assumed by each party, similar to the one that has been used in the case of credit cards, would be advisable, even though there is no legal obligation in this respect.

The need for the Protection of Critical National Infrastructures

Fernando J. Sánchez Gómez · Miguel Ángel Abad Arranz

Spanish National Centre for the Protection of Critical Infrastructures (CNPIC)
cnpic@ses.mir.es

Abstract

Currently, the concept of "protection of critical infrastructures" is one of the most important aspects that should be taken into account by all countries. In Spain, the National Centre for the Protection of Critical Infrastructures (CNPIC) has been recently created, which is responsible of all tasks related to this type of protection. It was established in accordance with all national and international laws and regulations that recommend the assessment of critical infrastructures, with the aim of improving the security of national infrastructures and the interests of Spain abroad by establishing the existing interdependencies between different infrastructures.

The protection of this type of infrastructures must be addressed not only from the point of view of physical security, but also from the logic framed within the ICT sector. In this way, the CNPIC permanently performs risk analyses at a sectorial level, taking into account each type of threat that can affect the infrastructures in process. This analysis provides the assessment of the criticality of each infrastructure, as well as its logical prioritisation from the national point of view.

The level of protection required by each infrastructure demands a smooth communication with other agencies or bodies, both at a national and international level, in order to be able to process a coordinated response in view of any potential attack that may affect one or various national strategic infrastructures. However, the CNPIC must act within its responsibilities regarding the support and coordination of basic security, applied by those responsible for the infrastructures. The existence of national or international alert networks contributes towards the development of these tasks and is in line with different European projects, whose purpose lies in this type of communication.

1 Strategic Sectors

After the approval of the European Programme for Critical Infrastructure Protection (EPCIP) by the European Council in December 2004 and the implementation of the Critical Infrastructure Warning Information Network (CIWIN), the Spanish government launched the *Plan Nacional de Protección de Infraestructuras Críticas* (or 'National Plan for Critical Infrastructure Protection') [SES07]. Afterwards, the Spanish National Centre for the Protection of Critical Infrastructures was created as a body responsible for the management, coordination and supervision of the protection of critical national infrastructures and depending on the State Department for Security of the Spanish Ministry of Interior.

The National Plan for Critical Infrastructure Protection [SES07] defines Strategic Infrastructures as:

> *"Facilities, networks, services and physical and information technology equipments, whose disruption or destruction would have serious consequences for citizens' health, security or economic well-being, as well as for the effective functioning of state institutions and public administrations".*

N. Pohlmann, H. Reimer, W. Schneider (Editors): Securing Electronic Business Processes, Vieweg (2008), 313-318

The said infrastructures are listed in the National Catalogue of Strategic Infrastructures, which was started to be drawn up in 2004. This catalogue includes 12 strategic sectors, which are subdivided into sub-sectors, areas and segments. The aforementioned sectors can be included in those that are related to national and citizens' security, as well as those whose primary value lies in the services provided to citizens. Specifically, the classification is as follows:

1. Related to security:
   - Chemical industry
   - Nuclear industry
   - Research facilities
   - Administration
   - Space
2. Related to Primary Public Services:
   - Energy
   - Telecommunications
   - Transport
   - Water
   - Food
   - Finance
   - Health

2 Political Initiatives

The European Council of June 2004 urged the Commission to develop a global strategy on the protection of critical infrastructures. On October 20, 2004, the Commission approved the Communication on Critical Infrastructure Protection in the fight against terrorism [COM04], which contains proposals to enhance the prevention, preparation and response of Europe against terrorist attacks that affect critical infrastructures (CI).

The Council's conclusions on the prevention, preparation and response against terrorist attacks, as well as the EU Solidarity Program on the consequences of threats and terrorist attacks, adopted by the Council in December 2004, support the intention of the Commission to launch a European Programme for Critical Infrastructure Protection and approve the Commission's creation of the Critical Infrastructure Warning Information Network.

In November 2005, the Commission approved a Green Paper on the European Programme for Critical Infrastructure Protection [COM05], which outlines the possibilities of the Commission to create the EPCIP and CIWIN. In December 2005, the Council of Justice and Home Affairs (or JAI) urged the Commission to present a proposal on the EPCIP, based on a global approach that would give preference to combating terrorist threats.

Finally, last June 5, 2008, the Council of Justice and Home Affairs approved the Directive on the identification and designation of European Critical Infrastructures. Although the contents of the Directive lacks specificity and relative applicability at the present time, its purpose is to improve the levels of protection of cross-border critical infrastructures by establishing a procedure for identification and designation, as well as to encourage each cross-border European infrastructure to have a security plan and an officer responsible for it.

However, these steps taken in the EU have served to encourage the development of the planning and organisation of the national system for the protection of our critical infrastructures, adapting itself to the European provisions as far as possible, although these develop significantly slower than the existing ones at the Spanish domestic level.

The main political initiatives are aimed at the integral security of the infrastructures of most strategic sectors. This security does not only involve the physical protection of the facilities, but also increasingly depends on Information and Communication Systems (ICT sector), whose security requires not only physical but also cyber protection.

So far, the initiatives set up by the Spanish Ministry of Interior and the State Secretariat for Security are the following:

- Terrorism Prevention and Protection Plan [SES05], approved on March 9, 2005, by the State Secretariat for Security. This plan outlines a series of strategic objectives by establishing a number of sectors or areas, depending on the damage that can be caused to citizens.
- The National Plan for Critical Infrastructure Protection [SES07], approved by the State Secretariat for Security on May 7, 2007, which:
  - Defines which type of facility should be considered a "strategic infrastructure" and which are the affected sectors.
  - Proposes the design of a catalogue of national infrastructures in which these infrastructures appear classified on the basis of a set of parameters, after conducting a proper risk assessment.
  - Designates the State Secretariat for Security as the superior authority for the management and control of all the measures foreseen in the Plan.
- Agreement of the Spanish Council of Ministers, dated November 2, 2007 [ACM07], whereby:
  - The State Secretariat for Security is designated as the responsible body for the management, coordination and supervision of the protection of the national critical infrastructures;
  - The development of the National Plan for Critical Infrastructure Protection is established [SES07];
  - The Spanish National Centre for the Protection of Critical Infrastructures is created.

3 Public Organisations

The extent of the concept 'critical infrastructure' and the multiplicity of affected sectors requires the need to approach its protection from a multidisciplinary point of view, with the involvement of numerous public and private organisations under one leadership and in charge of the promotion, coordination and supervision of all the activities related to the protection of critical infrastructures in a national field.

The coordination and management in the subject of Critical Infrastructure Protection devolves upon the Spanish Ministry of Interior, which, in its turn, has appointed the State Secretariat for Security as the one in charge of the management, coordination and supervision of the protection of critical national infrastructures.

Consequently, the State Secretariat for Security of the Spanish Ministry of Interior is the organisation responsible for the security policy of the national critical infrastructures, assuming the following specific competences:

- To design and lead the national strategy concerning the protection of critical infrastructures.
- To promote and coordinate the activities related to the protection of critical infrastructures that the rest of involved organisations depending on other ministry departments are developing and inform about the regulations that are being developed in this field by the mentioned organisations.
- To lead the implementation of the National Plan for Critical Infrastructure Protection [SES07].
- To act as a National Contact Point in matters of critical infrastructure protection together with the European Commission, other States and companies and organisations and managers of critical infrastructures.
- To be linked to the Critical Infrastructure Warning Information Network (CIWIN) of the European Union.
- To identify the different fields of responsibility in the protection of critical infrastructures, analyse the prevention and response mechanisms foreseen by each of the involved actors and disseminate and promote the adoption of measures and procedures that are considered ´best practices´.
- To establish permanent mechanisms for communication, collaboration, coordination and information with the managers and public and private owners of critical national infrastructures under the general principles of trust and confidentiality.
- To adopt the decision by which a certain infrastructure is considered as critical and, as such, is included in the National Catalogue of Strategic Infrastructures ('Catálogo Nacional de Infraestructuras Estratégicas').
- To study and evaluate the existing interdependencies between specific sectors of critical infrastructures.

3.1 Spanish National Centre for the Protection of Critical Infrastructures

Within the structure of the Spanish State Secretariat for Security, a body has been created that manages and coordinates the activities related to this subject that are entrusted to the Department: the Spanish National Centre for the Protection of Critical Infrastructures.

Its main tasks are:

- The safekeeping, maintenance and updating of the Security Plan for Critical Infrastructures and the National Catalogue of Strategic Infrastructures.
- The collection, analysis, integration and evaluation of the information coming from public institutions, the police services, strategic sectors and the cooperating international members.
- The assessment and analysis of the risks in strategic facilities.
- The design and establishment of information, communication and alert mechanisms.
- Command and Control Support in a Room for Operations; its activation is due in situations in which the level, as fixed by the Plan for Critical Infrastructure Protection, is activated.
- To create the National Contact Point within the framework of the Critical Infrastructure Protection of the European Union (European Programme for Critical Infrastructure Protection and the Critical Infrastructure Warning Information Network) and other similar organisations from third countries.
- To coordinate the work and participation of the different workgroups and meetings in the field of the European Commission.
- To supervise the development process of the intervention plans regarding critical infrastructures and participate in carrying out tests and simulations.

- To supervise and coordinate the sectorial and regional plans of prevention and protection that have to be activated in the different alleged risks and established security levels, both by the Law Enforcement Units and the people in charge of the operators.
- To draw up the corresponding Collaboration Protocols with personnel and organisations outside the Spanish Ministry of Interior and with companies that own and manage strategic infrastructures.
- To supervise projects and studies of interest in the protection of critical infrastructures and coordinate participation in financial programs and subventions coming from the European Union.

3.2 ES-CERT-CC

As one of the duties of the CNPIC is the design and creation of mechanisms for information, communication and alerts and as it is necessary to evaluate the infrastructures at a physical and cybernetic level, the CNPIC must provide the necessary coordination for a coordinated response against wide-scale attacks. Given the fact that CERTs and CSIRTs give a response to attacks that can affect the clients they give support to, a more complete vision that will include all these organisations within the national territory is necessary.

Apart from providing specific knowledge about the organisations specialised in giving a response to ICT attacks, the purpose of this has been to create a body that will allow for the management of a coordinated response in case of various affected structures, as this body knows the attacks and threats that can affect the critical infrastructures. In addition, the response carried out by the corresponding CERTs and CSIRTs will always be announced, whenever necessary, by the State Security Forces and Bodies, who are in charge of research in the fight against crime and terrorism, so that they can carry out the corresponding inquiries.

Therefore, these coordination duties of national CERTs and CSIRTs that are related to the critical infrastructures fall back on the CNPIC by legal mandate, for which the ES-CERT-CC is established. However, it is necessary to highlight the importance of the different national CERTs and CSIRTs, given the fact their work is the origin of any type of subsequent coordination. The basic missions of CERTs and CSIRTs are:

- The provision of information services, such as alert services on new threats and vulnerabilities.
- Carrying out research, training and dissemination jobs regarding information security.
- The provision of support and coordination services to solve incidents.

From these basic duties of prevention and reaction, the CNPIC will extend the last one from a national perspective, involving also the State Law Enforcement Units, as well as any other national body that may be affected or of which information can be obtained, with the purpose of guaranteeing the security of national strategic infrastructures.

However, the coordination carried out by ES-CERT-CC can be of an international nature as well, in case of a wide-scale attack by which critical infrastructures from different countries are affected. In this case, the CNPIC will also act as a coordinator for the response against these attacks and as an exclusive contact point in the subject of the protection of critical infrastructures.

In addition, apart from the collaboration of the national and international CERTs and CSIRTs, the implication, cooperation and participation of the owners of the companies and their managing bodies are vitally important in updating the Catalogue of critical infrastructures and in the communication of security contributions, response, etc.

4 Conclusion

With the creation of CNPIC, Spain is giving a great boost to national security, applying the criteria needed for the identification of critical infrastructures, in order to consequently apply protection and security measures that correspond to each infrastructure. In addition, considering this body depends on the Spanish Ministry of Interior, it provides an overview of the national security scene, which allows involving the various bodies that are somehow related to the infrastructures that have to be protected (persons in charge, owners, operators, etc.).

Despite the short period of time that has passed since its creation in November 2007, the CNPIC already has a catalogue that allows identifying and prioritising the critical national infrastructures, including their details. The aim of CNPIC is to reach a synergy between physical and cyber protection, identifying in the same way the ICT infrastructures, which, in case of an attack, may present a major impact on society, economy or the service provided.

Apart from identifying the critical national infrastructures, the CNPIC must provide mechanisms to ensure its activities are properly managed and coordinated. For this reason, and bearing in mind the existing threats and vulnerabilities of the infrastructures, the CNPIC will have to conduct both prevention and response tasks in case of attacks against strategic facilities. In the cyber area, the CNPIC provides a strategic framework through which all the bodies and agencies that are needed for a coordinated response in case of wide-scale attacks are integrated, in order to report the incidents to the corresponding agencies of intelligence and research in its turn.

All the tasks undertaken by CNPIC at a national level have an international scope, given that this centre acts as an international contact point in this matter.

References

[COM04]   European Commission: Critical Infrastructure Protection in the fight against terrorism, Brussels, 20.10.2004

[SES05]   The Spanish State Secretariat for Security: Terrorism Prevention and Protection Plan, 9.3.2005

[COM05]   European Commission: Green Paper on the European Programme for Critical Infrastructure Protection, Brussels, 17.11.2005

[SES07]   Spanish State Secretariat for Security: The National Plan for Critical Infrastructure Protection, 7.5.2007

[ACM07]   Agreement of the Spanish Council of Ministers: Creation of the Spanish National Centre for the Protection of Critical Infrastructures (CNPIC), 2.11.2007

Glossary

CERT	Computer Equipment Response Team
CI	Critical Infrastructure
CIWIN	Critical Infrastructures Warning Information Network
CNPIC	Centro Nacional de Protección de Infraestructuras Críticas
CSIRT	Computer Security Incident Response Team
EPCIP	European Programme for Critical Infrastructure Protection
ICT	Information and Communication Technologies
JAI	Consejo de Justicia y Asuntos de Interior

Challenges for the Protection of Critical ICT-Based Financial Infrastructures

Bernhard M. Hämmerli[1] · Henning H. Arendt[2]

[1]Acris GmbH & HSLU, Bodenhofstrasse 29
CH-6005 Lucerne
bmhaemmerli@acris.ch

[2]@bc® – Arendt Business Consulting, Malbachweg 3
D-65510 Idstein
bio@atbc.de

Abstract

A workshop was held in Frankfurt during September 24-25, 2007, in order to initiate a dialogue between financial industry (FI) stakeholders and Europe's top-level research community. The workshop focused on identifying research and development challenges for the protection of critical ICT-based financial infrastructures for the next 5 years: "Protection of Massively Distributed Critical Financial Services" and "Trust in New Value Added Business Chains". The outcome of the workshop contributed to the development of the research agenda from the perspectives of three working groups. A number of project ideas were spawned based on the workshop, including a coordination actions project entitled PARSIFAL, which this paper will focus on.

1 Introduction

1.1 General Overview

The rapid growth and deployment of information and communication technologies (ICT) that we are experiencing today are having profound impacts on the financial service industry. The ICT infrastructures through which critical financial services are being delivered, are becoming ever more interconnected, open and ubiquitous, but at the same time, more fragile and vulnerable to failure and cyber-attacks. The level of self-service will become significantly higher than today, using ubiquitous and mobile banking. Industrialisation, business process outsourcing and number of intervening actors in the service value creation chain will further increase, changing the way financial services will be composed and delivered, while continuing to guarantee their very high-level of trustworthiness. This, in turn, requires defining trustworthiness and new levels of trust in the ever-increasing supply chain, and improving reliability of highly distributed infrastructures while dealing at the same time with severe constraints over business continuity management. Security and privacy in both the clients and the client advisors' behaviour will be a key success factor for banking, and broadly, for the financial industry.

Considering the facts mentioned above, in early 2007 an organization committee started to prepare a workshop event on challenges for the protection of critical ICT-based financial infrastructures for the next 5 years. With intense preparation, financial stakeholders were persuaded to discuss their needs and leaks in a closed workshop. The workshop was held on the 24-25 of September 2007 in Frankfurt, Germany, and attracted nearly 40 attendees, of which half were from major EU and global financial industry players and key members from the ICT trust, security and dependability (TSD) and half were from critical information infrastructure protection (CIIP) research communities (academia and industry). The workshop served as an excellent platform for a structured strategic dialogue between these stakeholders and focused on:

- How the situation in the European financial sector would evolve over the next 5 years in the two main themes of the workshop: protection of massively distributed critical financial infrastructures and trust in new added value business chains

- Developing joint scenarios and consequent strategic plans and research directions on how future trustworthy financial services could be constructed and delivered over critical ICT-based service infrastructures and how these could be protected from any kind of cyber-threat

The workshop addressed issues beyond a single financial institution or national market. It specifically addressed global, cross border and multi-member state issues and correlations, which may affect critical ICT-based financial infrastructures of the European economy and possibly destabilize it.

The workshop outcomes were twofold:

- Bringing together the relevant stakeholder types (financial industry, ICT TSD and CIIP researchers) to engage in dialogue and stimulate collaborative research actions in view of the EU's FP7 call for R&D proposals in the area of critical infrastructure protection, including the protection of ICT-based critical financial infrastructures

- Provide input to future strategic research directions that the European Commission will support in its next work programme for ICT security research, for the period 2009-2010

In the workshop, a number of themes were identified as areas for further mutual research and development between the financial industry and researchers in ICT TSD and CIIP, which are summarised within this paper.

1.2 Result of the Workshop

During the workshop, a number of themes were identified as areas for further mutual research and development between the financial industry and researchers in ICT TSD and CIIP. Three dedicated working sessions were entitled (1) trust in new value-added business chains, (2) protection of the critical base infrastructure and (3) protection of massively distributed critical financial services. Each session was broken in two parts: firstly, scenario definition and second, based on the scenarios the discussion, definition and agreement of research topics considered beneficial and necessary for continued mutual collaboration between all the stakeholders. An outline of the result is given below, and more details will follow in the next chapter.

1.2.1 Trust in New Value-Added Business Chains

Challenges associated with optimised and new business processes, which are secure and critical in larger, faster and more complex (mobile) environments are as important as business ratings and its regulation. "Empowering the end-users" requires examination of the expectations, roles and awareness of the customers from the very start. This means providing the users with enhanced capabilities and giving them more control over their security aspects e.g. by allowing them to control who can access their data, when and why.

The need for two-side authentication (of users and clients at the same time) and anonymity aspects raised the question: "who will carry out the management role?" Options mentioned include the EU or a trusted third party association.

The security of systems including internet-based, mobile-based, bank communication and other financial infrastructure systems need to be studied, as well as cyber crime, which is developing with mobility and speed. Further research is needed urgently regarding the modelling of attacks, phishing (identification and avoidance and elimination of phishing), and developing a concept of a minimal tolerance to attacks and faults.

1.2.2 Protection of the Critical Base Infrastructure

Two key research topics are considered beneficial and necessary:
- How to protect massively distributed critical financial infrastructures; and, trust in new added value business chains
- Developing joint scenarios and consequent strategic plans and research directions on how future trustworthy financial services could be constructed and delivered over critical ICT-based service infrastructures and how these latter could be protected from any kind of cyber-threat

1.2.3 Protection of Massively Distributed critical Financial Services

The recognized challenges of protecting distributed and complex financial service systems include both technical and humanistic barriers, e.g. creating a federated, interoperable identification system linked directly to the resources within the critical financial infrastructure (CFI). Security policies, led by identity, can be used to control resources in terms of access and usage. The duality of resource protection – in terms of individual privacy versus collective or commercial data security – needs to be mutually assured within the system.

1.3 The EU Approved Project e.g. PARCIFAL

The workshop's outcome is much more than what is briefly summarized above. It was the first time in history that a reasonable number of high-level financial industry ambassadors addressed security challenges to the research community. It was a breakthrough in this respect. Some EU research projects were generated, but it seems that additionally there are huge industrial projects in the pipeline as well.

Protection And tRuSt In FinanciAL infrastructures (PARSIFAL) is just one of them, which will be explained below.

1.4 Co-Operation with COMIFIN EU Approved Project

Another project idea was born from some of the challenges presented in the Frankfurt workshop. This project is a small or medium-scale focused research project (STREP) entitled Communication Middleware for Monitoring Financial Critical Infrastructure (CoMiFin). From the beginning, PARSIFAL will have a mutually close relationship with the CoMiFiN project, whose main area of research and development is the communications middleware for financial critical infrastructures. The most prominent liaison between the two projects will be the organisation and participation towards joint workshops. PARSIFAL will plan their workshops to coincide with the CoMiFin workshops and vice versa in order to capitalise on the dual momentum each project will bring to the events. The two projects will jointly be involved in the organisational aspects of the workshops in a mutually beneficial way towards common goals and objectives.

2 Scenarios and Challenges as Defined in the Initial Workshop

The workshop addressed issues beyond a single financial institution or national market. It specifically addressed global, cross border and multi-member state issues and correlations, which may affect or destabilize critical ICT-based financial infrastructures of the European economy.

2.1 Trust in New Value-Added Business Chains

The scenario resulting suggested high level research topics as follows.

- Addressing the quantification / scale issues – information overload, dynamicity and complexity of systems: It was considered worthwhile to analyse what mechanisms could be used by interested parties, to manage the large amounts of available data and more easily and timely quantify/ adjudge the risks or levels of crime increase/decrease affecting the critical infrastructures.
- Widening and different areas of players / counterparts – e.g. foreign/non foreign users, banks / non-bank service providers, broadened user base with access to an extended range of functionality, combined with a desire to be in control of their data: It was considered to be worthwhile to analyse the implications of the increased complexity of the landscape of actors on the security of critical and complex infrastructures
- Consideration of the global dimension: It was considered worthwhile to analyse the impacts of location independent authorized and unauthorized access to critical infrastructures, which may hamper the legal protection of critical infrastructures against in particular unauthorized access.
- Definition and design of trust elements (models, authority, metrics to enable measurement and rating of CIP layers of protection, etc.): It was considered worthwhile to provide users and those responsible for critical infrastructures more guidance with regards to what they should focus on to protect themselves and ensure a high level of user confidence in the infrastructures.

From the given scenario, three of the deducted challenges are reproduced.

- Trust, specifically in the financial systems infrastructure: This global challenge, identifying institutions that build up trust – which we can trust and which earns trust. Empirical question of who builds up trust and how? Trust authority model: trusted authorities need definition of accountability and liability for them to play a constructive role. Are these trusted authorities to be driven by banks, by governments or another body?

- Business ratings and regulation clearing, observation of ratings and ranking industries build up: Need to think about new areas of observation and regulation (both soft regulation and gentleman's agreements). Need for structuring of information for selection and rating structures. Credit ratings parameters need to be researched and built – semantic, grid systems to simulate the ratings that are being provided. The need for processes and means for quicker response times in emergency cases.
- Cyber crime is developing based on mobility and speed: There is a need for further research on modelling of attacks, on phishing (identification and avoidance and eliminating phishing), and on developing a concept of a minimal tolerance to attacks and faults.

2.2 Protection of the Critical Base Infrastructure

Issues beyond a single financial institution or national market, specifically global, cross border and multi-member state issues and correlations are summarized in the scenarios, below:

- **End-user protection in a highly distributed environment** (mobility): Mobility is becoming one of the main differentiators within the financial services, providing the end user to access to the financial services anytime, anywhere. This situation creates some security deficiencies, related mainly with user terminals, privacy, malware detection and reaction, etc.
- **Secure communication channels** (internet): Was one of the most controversial scenarios, taking into account that secure communication channel is in principle part of the supposed internet security infrastructure and its protocols. Some group members thought this not a R&D topic.
- In a catastrophic disaster, **critical infrastructure recovery methods**: Concerns is related with the critical single points of failure and the questions, what could happen in case one of the main European infrastructure nodes would be down and how could the rest of the infrastructure recover?
- **Regulatory issues**, collaboration environments: Define a collaborative framework, managed and controlled by automatic processes that keep up-to-date every individual European entity (banks, government, police, etc.) with the possible threats environment.

With these scenarios, the team identified the main challenges.

- Personal data protection (privacy): To define a way for an identity and authentication management that guaranties the security within the user access, taking into account the mobile environment. Main concerns include the real time proactive and trusted data-sharing environment, the possibility to define a federation system where the financial entities could share threats, risks and some other important information. In order to go ahead with the previous topic, one important goal is the standardization, within the different interfaces.
- Risk assessment and risk modelling: Both require attack simulation and the possibility to identify cascading effects.
- Other important topics discussed included the following:
- European regulatory and laws enforcements
- Resiliency, redundancy, reliability of highly distributed financial environments
- Advanced behaviour detection, prevention and reaction mechanisms (i.e. heuristic analysis)
- Robust segmentation (of services and applications)
- Managing the organization of business aspects following merging of companies

2.3 Protection of Massively Distributed critical Financial Services

In the focus are the following issues:
- Socio economic trends drive towards
- Online accessible real-time services
- Further industrialization and commoditization of financial service supply chain
- Privacy and protection of data for customers (consumers and organisations)
- Exposure to online organized crime requires new approach to security modelling into business logic (misuse cases).
- Catastrophic events transiently change risk appetite, meaning that trust (to devices and individuals) increases during recovery phase without trustworthiness having changed
- The importance of identity in securing and controlling information
- The generation of trust as the key enabler for sharing information

From the impact discussion of these observations on the financial infrastructure only one of the outcomes is given due to the limited available space:

The trust will increase by combining 2-3 identities, which are semi-trusted. In such a scenario, the compromising of a single identity will not be sufficient to access secured data. Interoperability with bank identities introduces issues for financial institutions of accepting corresponding liabilities. A mixture of identities that could be used, include mobile phones, credit cards, government eID cards, EU passports, biometrics, company identity smartcards etc...

Challenges:
- Creating the ability to assign multiple identities to information
- Interoperability of identities
- Adding dynamic policies to control the security, privacy and access of data

The group believes that globally Europe is currently at the forefront in identity and privacy which offers a unique opportunity for innovation in these areas and the potential to set the global standard. The challenge is to maintain and capitalise on this lead and use it to scale up European innovation and to achieve pan-European and global acceptance.

3 The EU Project PARSIFAL

While attempting to achieve the second workshop objective (bringing together the relevant stakeholders and engage them in dialogue) it has been recognised that the workshop needs some form of continuation, in order to extend the initial research challenges in width and depth, as well as to coordinate actions and projects related to this area. The Protection And tRuSt In FinanciAL infrastructures (PARSIFAL) project is targeting this ambitious objective and is also adding new topics on stakeholders' agenda, how to better protect information infrastructure that link CFI with other sector critical infrastructures (CI) in Europe. The PARSIFAL, FP7 ICT, coordination actions that start in September 2008, work towards the achievement of these overall objectives by setting short-term project objectives, to be fulfilled during the project lifetime (18 months). PARSIFAL differentiates itself from other related CIIP initiatives as it focuses on CFI and involvement of stakeholders from the financial sector with special attention to the relation between protection of CII (and CFI) and trust.

PARSIFAL methodology of work will lead to a representative and well-balanced constitution of working groups with appropriate coverage of relevant stakeholders. Towards the end of the project, these working groups are expected to match technological challenges for the future financial service scenarios (e.g. international services that run on critical financial infrastructures). The results of these activities will feed into the EU policy process and research agenda.

PARSIFAL starts with a description of financial services, provided by financial institutions (e.g. banks, savings and loan associations, insurance companies mutual and pension funds) and financial infrastructure providers (e.g. stock exchanges, payment, clearing and settlement providers) and observes them as two separate categories: "retail services" and "wholesale services". In retail services, the financial institution or infrastructure providers are dealing directly with the consumer, whereas in the wholesale services, the financial institutions or infrastructure providers are dealing with other financial institutions or infrastructure providers and not with the consumer. While many protection and trust challenges are similar for both categories, it has been recognized that on the wholesale side, improvements have to be achieved by considerably shortening transaction cycles (e.g. in completing a payment or stock exchange order within 2 hours). This however, imposes new requirements on CFI protection that are expected to evolve in the near future.

4 Conclusion

The workshop held on the 24-25 of September 2007 brought together the stakeholders in the financial industry and the European research and technologies development community members from "ICT trust, security and dependability", and "critical information infrastructure protection". The event made it abundantly clear that a significant amount of R&D must take place in a coordinated fashion in order to protect massively distributed critical financial services and provide trust in new value added business chains.

The outcomes of this workshop included the following:
- In each of the scenarios, new technologies and associated risks were identified
- Exposure to online organized crime requires new approaches to be addressed
- Secure communication channels are required (current and future Internet)
- Regulatory issues in collaboration environments need to be addressed
- Significant joint efforts of academia, stakeholders and regulators are needed

Throughout the workshop, the European Commission presented a number of realistic cooperation mechanisms. The bringing together of the financial industry stakeholders with the communities of security and CIIP researchers would benefit each other and assist building up stronger and more productive collaborations in the future. In order to capitalise on the successful workshop and to carry out further analyses, it was deemed necessary that a project or number of collaborative projects should be formed bringing together the relevant stakeholders including financial industry and industrial members in order to follow up on these findings. The full workshop report is available on the European Commission web site under ICT FP7 Security. The workshop was organised and hosted by the European Commission's JRC with support from the European Finance Forum in service for European Commission's INFSO-F5 Unit Security .

A number of projects were submitted to the joint ICT / security call of framework programme 7 and accepted following the workshop, including the PARSIFAL coordination actions project and the CoMiFin project. Both projects are planned to start on September 1, 2008.

References

[Arendt, Haemmerli] Challenges for the Protection of Critical ICT-Based Financial Infrastructures – Workshop Summary ftp://ftp.cordis.europa.eu/pub/fp7/ict/docs/security/2007-09-24-25-report-workshop-financial-industry-frankfur_en.pdf

[Arendt] European CIIP Newsletter, Volume 3, Number 3, 01/2008: Protection of Critical ICT-Based Financial Infrastructures (pdf 1,2 MB) http://www.irriis.org/ecn/ECN%20issue%208%20v1.02.pdf

European Commission's JRC http://ec.europa.eu/dgs/jrc/index.cfm

European Commission's INFSO-F5 Unit Security http://cordis.europa.eu/fp7/ict/security/home_en.html

Joint ICT / security call of Framework Programme 7 FP7-ICT-SEC-2007-1.7. November 2007

Related EU Projects

www.deserec.eu   DEpendability and Security by Enhanced REConfigurability

www.ist-securist.org   ICT Security & Dependability Taskforce

www.serenity-project.org System Engineering for Security & Dependability

Regulations that apply on the financial sector and CFI in Europe

(a) Directive 2004/39/EC of the European Parliament and of the Council of 21 April 2004 on markets in financial instruments (MiFID)

(b) Oversight standards for euro retail payment systems adopted in June 2003 by the governing Council of the European Central Bank (ECB)

(c) Directive 2006/48/EC of the European Parliament and of the Council of 14 June 2006 on the taking up and pursuit of the business of credit institutions

(d) Directive 2006/49/EC of the European Parliament and of the Council of 14 June 2006 on the capital adequacy of investment firms and of credit institutions

(e) Proposal for a Directive on payment services in the internal market amending Directive 97/7/EC, 2000/12/EC and 2002/65/EC (COM(2005) 603)

(f) Directive 2000/46/EC of the European Parliament and of the Council of 18 September 2000 on the taking up, pursuit of and prudential supervision of the business of electronic money institutions

(g) Directive 1998/26/EC of the European Parliament and of the Council of 19 May 1998 on Settlement Finality.

Security for VoIP,
Mobility
and Web

Evaluating Measures and Countermeasures for SPAM over Internet Telephony

Andreas U. Schmidt[1] · Nicolai Kuntze[1] · Rachid El Khayari[2]

[1]Fraunhofer Institute SIT
{andreas.schmidt | nicolai.kuntze}@sit.fraunhofer.de

[2]Technical University Darmstadt
rachid.el.khayari@googlemail.com

Abstract

Nowadays telephony has developed to an omnipresent service. Furthermore the Internet has emerged to an important communication medium. These facts and the raising availability of broadband internet access have led to the fusion of these two services. VoIP is the keyword that describes this combination.

Furthermore it is undeniable that one of the most annoying facets of the Internet nowadays is email spam, which is considered to be 80 to 90 percent of the email traffic produced.

The threat of so called voice spam or Spam over Internet Telephony is even more fatal than the threat that arose with email spam, for the annoyance and disturbance factor is much higher. From the providers point of view both email spam and voice spam produce unwanted traffic and loss of trust of customers into the service.

In this paper we discuss how SPIT attacks can be put into practice, than we point out advantages and disadvantages of state of the art anti voice spam solutions. With the knowledge provided in this paper and with our SPIT producing attack tool, it is possible for an administrator, to find out weak points of VoIP systems and for developers to rethink SPIT blocking techniques.

1 What is SPAM over Internet Telephony?

In order to know how to deal with SPIT, we must at first know what SPIT is and we will find that SPIT is described very similar in different publications and the descriptions can be summarized as 'unwanted', 'bulk' or 'unsolicited' calls. In [2] e.g. SPIT is defined as 'unsolicited advertising calls', which is of course already a special form of SPIT (namely advertising calls). In [3] SPIT is defined as 'transmission of bulk unsolicited messages and calls' which is a more general definition than the first one, as it doesn't characterize the content and includes also messages. Nevertheless the most precise definition is found in [1] where 'Call SPAM' (as the authors call it) is defined as 'a bulk unsolicited set of session initiation attempts (e.g., INVITE requests), attempting to establish a voice, video, instant messaging, or other type of communications session'. The authors of [1] go even one step further and classify that 'if the user should answer, the spammer proceeds to relay their message over the real-time media.' and state that this 'is the classic telemarketer spam, applied to SIP[1]'. We can easily see that the presented definitions so far are very similar, but differ in their deepness.

---

1 The whole discussion is based on the Session Initiation Protocol (SIP, RFC 3261)

N. Pohlmann, H. Reimer, W. Schneider (Editors): Securing Electronic Business Processes, Vieweg (2008), 329-340

1.1 SPIT is not SPAM!

Although SPIT contains the phrase 'SPAM' and has some parallels with email spam, it also has major differences. The similarity of email spam and SPIT is that in both cases senders (or callers) use the Internet to target recipients (or callees) or a group of users, in order to place bulk unsolicited calls [3]. The main difference between email spam and SPIT is that an email arrives at the email server before it is accessed by the user. This means that structure and content of an email can be analyzed at the server before it arrives at the recipient and so SPAM can be detected before it disturbs the recipient. As in VoIP scenarios delays of call establishment are not wished, session establishment messages are forwarded immediately to the recipients. Besides this fact the content of a VoIP call is exchanged not until the session is already established. In other words if the phone rings it is too late for SPIT prevention and the phone rings immediately after session initiation, while an email can be delayed and even, if it is not delayed, the recipient can decide if he wants to read the email immediately or not. In addition to these aspects another main difference between email spam and SPIT is the fact, that the single email itself contains information that can be used for spam detection. The header fields contain information about sender, subject and content of the message. A single SPIT call in contradiction is technically indistinguishable from a call in general. A SPIT call is initiated and answered with the same set of SIP messages as any other call.

1.2 How does a SPIT producing tool work?

The next questions that have to be considered are, how attackers behave and what techniques are used in order to generate SPIT. We can split the SPIT process into three steps:

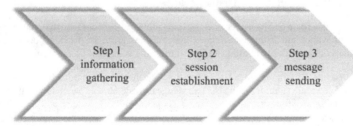

Figure 1: Three steps of SPIT

These three steps can be viewed as fundamental and are fulfilled by any attacker in a systematic manner. The first step the 'Information gathering' is used in order to find out targets for possible future attacks. The second step the 'session establishment' leads to the establishment of a communication session wit the victims. In the last step of SPIT the 'message sending' media is exchanged between attacker and victim.

1.2.1 SIP XML Scenario Maker

Now what we need is a tool that implements the presented SPIT process. Therefore we developed SIP XML Scenario Maker (SXSM), a tool with which it is possible to scan systematically for targets, establish sessions to these targets and exchange pre recorded media. SXSM is based on SIPp [12] developed by HP and expands SIPp with a graphical user interface that allows us to fulfill the requirements stated above. SXSM can be used in order to create any kind of SIP messages, put them into a sequence as XML scenarios, execute created scenarios and evaluate the result of the execution.

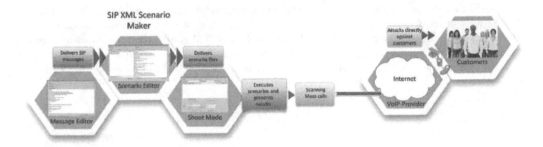

Figure 2: SXSM Workflow

We will now take a look on how SXSM works. First SXSM consists of the following three modes.

1.2.1.1 Message Editor

The message editor can be used to organize and create custom SIP messages that can later be used in the scenario editor. The power of this mode lies within the possibility to create any kind of SIP message and manipulate SIP header fields in any way. SXSM is pre configured with a complete set of standard compliant SIP messages.

1.2.1.2 Scenario Editor

The scenario editor is the core element of SXSM. In this mode the user can create SIP scenarios based on the message bricks created in the message editor mode. Additionally the created scenarios can be organized in different sets.

In order to create a new scenario the user simply needs to select the messages that should be contained in the scenario in the preferred order and then let SXSM create an XML scenario file automatically. The XML file can then be viewed in detail and tweaked manually (if wished).

1.2.1.3 Shoot Mode

Within the shoot mode the user puts the previously generated scenarios into a batch and execute them one after the other. The results of the execution are presented within the process output window. Before execution the user can specify scenario specific settings, such as e.g. how often and in which time intervals the scenario should be executed. Additionally he can adjust and set global parameters such as information about target (targeted username, remote IP, remote port) and about himself (local IP, local Port).

The scenarios are then played with the specified settings and the result is presented as a success rate. If e.g. 5 out of 10 selected scenarios were finished successfully the success rate would be fifty percent. Additionally the user can consult log files that are presented in case of unsuccessful execution.

1.2.2 How can we use SXSM as attack tool?

The goal that we wanted to reach was the creation of a tool with which it is possible to implement a SPIT attack in its fundamental three steps.

With SXSM we can now create scenarios for each of the three steps and execute them against any target. At first we can create a scenario for information gathering which we can call a scan attack scenario. The scan attack scenario can be implemented as follows. As SXSM contains the possibility of injecting values from CSV (Comma Separated Values) files, we would create a CSV file containing all usernames that we want to scan for. Then we would create a scenario with standard SIP messages that works e.g. as follows:

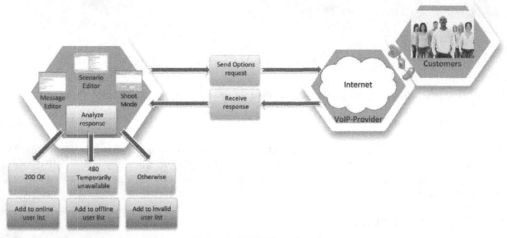

Figure 3: SXSM Scan Attack

With a scenario file that corresponds to the presented sequence of messages and logging methods, an attacker can populate lists of targets for future attacks.

The next steps would be session establishment and media exchange. With SXSM we could create a second scenario that establishes sessions to the targets collected in the first step.

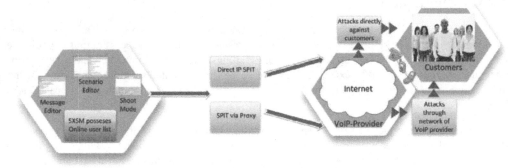

Figure 4: SXSM Session establishment

In Figure 4 we can see, that session establishment can be reached via two ways. SPIT via Proxy uses a valid account from targeted VoIP provider and the provider's network (Proxy, Registrar) in order to establish a session. In Direct IP SPIT context the targeted endpoint (telephone) is contacted directly via his IP and Port.

With these two simple scenarios based on standard SIP messages we implemented the whole SPIT process and are able to execute the attack against any target.

1.3 How can we stop these SPIT attacks

The question that we will answer now is what has been done so far in order to mitigate the threat of SPIT. Therefore we will present a short overview of countermeasures that have crystallized in research.

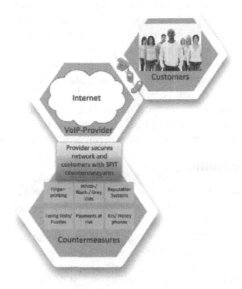

Figure 5: SPIT Countermeasures

1.3.1 Device Fingerprinting

The technique of active and passive device fingerprinting is presented in [4] and is based on the following assumption: Having knowledge about the type of User Agent that initiates a call, helps finding out whether a session initiation attempt can be classified as SPIT or not. So if we can compare the header layout and order or the response behavior of a SIP User Agent with a typical User Agent, we can determine if the initiated session establishment is an attack or a normal call. The authors describe two types of techniques that can be used for that purpose Passive and Active Device Fingerprinting.

1.3.1.1 Passive Fingerprinting

The e.g. INVITE message of a session initiation is compared with the INVITE message of a set of 'standard' SIP clients. If the order or appearance of the header fields does not match any of the standard clients, the call is classified as SPIT. The fingerprint in this case is the appearance and the order of the SIP header fields. The authors of [4] present a list of collected fingerprints of standard hard and soft phones.

1.3.1.2 Active Fingerprinting

User Agents are probed with special SIP messages and the responses are analyzed and compared with the response behavior of standard clients. The fingerprint in this case is the returned response code and the value of certain header fields. If the fingerprint doesn't match any of the standard clients, the call is classified as SPIT. The authors recommend the sending of specially crafted standard compliant and non compliant OPTIONS requests, in order to analyze the response behavior of a client.

1.3.2 White Lists, Black Lists, Grey Lists

The White List technique is presented e.g. in [2] [1] and works as follows: Each user has a list of users that he accepts calls from and any caller who is not present in the list will be blocked. In addition the private White Lists can be distributed to other users. If e.g. a caller is not present in the White List of the callee, White Lists of other trusted users can be consulted and their trusted users (up to a certain level). Black Lists are the contradiction of White Lists and contain only identities that are already known as spammers. Any call from a caller whose identity is present in the callee's Black List is blocked. Even Black Lists can be implemented as distributed Black Lists, where a callee can consult the Black Lists of other users. Grey listing works as follows: On initial request of an unknown user (not in White List) the call is rejected and the identity is put on the Grey List. As stated in [2] in case the caller tries calling back within a short time period, the call will be accepted. An adaption of this technique is described in [1] as Consent Based Communication. In case of Consent Based Communication the call of an unknown caller is initially blocked and put on the Grey List. The callee can consult the Grey List and decide, if he will accept future calls from this identity or block it permanently (e.g. put it on the Black List).

1.3.3 Reputation Systems

Reputation based mechanisms are described in [5] or in [1] and can be summarized as follows: After receiving a call, the callee can set a reputation value for the caller, that marks this caller as spitter or not. This reputation value must be assigned to the identity of the caller and can be used for future session establishment requests. This technique can be used e.g. as attachment to Grey listing [1] in order to provide a better decision basis. The authors of [5] explain that the user feedback can be used additionally for calls that were not detected by other SPIT preventing components. The way the reputation value is generated can differ. The SPIT value can be e.g. an additional SIP header, or included in a special error response code or distributed via SIP event notification mechanism. An adaption of this method can be found in [6] where user feedback is combined with statistical values in order to calculate a reputation value. The reputation value is e.g. composed of a value representing the number of times an identity occurs in other users' Black Lists, call density, call length or similar statistic values. The assumption behind this approach is that the calculated value will differ much between 'normal' users and spitters.

1.3.4 Turing tests, Computational Puzzles

Turing test are tests where the caller is given a challenge that a human can solve easily and that is hard to solve for a machine. Therefore Turing tests or CAPTCHA (Completely Automated Public Turing test to tell Computers and Humans Apart) are tests, that countermeasure Calling Bot attacks in VoIP scenarios and work as follows: On initial call establishment attempt, the caller is transferred to an interactive System where he is challenged with a task e.g. dialing 5 digits that he is hearing (so called Audio CAPT-CHA). While the numbers are read out background music or any other kind of noise is played, so that speech recognition systems can't be used to solve the task. A human caller in contradiction will solve the task without difficulties and only if the task is solved, the call will be forwarded to its destination. Turing tests can be used in combination with white lists, solving the introduction problem as described in [8].

Computational Puzzles seem at first sight very similar to the Turing tests concept. As described in [7] a SIP Proxy or User Agent Server can request from a User Agent Client (caller) to compute the solution to a puzzle. The goal of this method is to raise CPU costs of a call and so reduce the number of undesirable messages that can be sent. Turing test in contradiction have the goal to block non-human callers, as described above.

1.3.5 Payments at risk

Payments at risk mechanisms can be used in order to demand payment from an unknown caller. In [1] this technique is described as follows: If user A wants to call user B, he must first send a small amount of money to user B. When User B accepts the call and confirms that the call is not a SPIT call, the amount will be charged back to user A. With this technique it is possible to raise costs for SPIT callers while keeping 'normal' calls cheap. In [1] it is described as an auxiliary technique that solves the introduction problem of White lists, this means, that payment is only required for callers who are not on the White list of callee. In general the payment could be demanded for every call, but this would make the telephony service more expensive. An adaption of this method is described in [9]. Here the Payment technique is used in combination with a SPIT prediction value that is computed at server side. If the SPIT likelihood is high the call is rejected, if the SPIT likelihood is small the call is forwarded to the callee and if the SPIT likelihood value is in between payment is demanded automatically. Only if the payment is fulfilled the call will be forwarded to its target. The difference between the two approaches is that in the first case the paid amount is only charged back for non SPIT calls and in the second case, callers who reject payment are treated as spitters.

1.3.6 Intrusion Detection Mechanisms, Honey phones

Intrusion Detection Systems are (generally described) systems, that can be used for detection of any kind of abnormal behavior within an e.g. network and so reveal attacks. An implementation of this technique is presented in [10] based on the Bayes inference approach combined with network monitoring of VoIP specific traffic. The Intrusion Detection System is designed as a defense mechanism against different VoIP specific attacks including scan attacks and SPIT attacks. For every attack a conditional probability table (CPT) is defined for variables such as request intensity, error response intensity, parsing error intensity, number of different destinations, maximum number of dialogs in waiting state, number of opened RTP ports, request distribution and response distribution. The concept behind this technique is that the different attacks affect these variables in different ways, e.g. a SPIT attack usually has a higher probability of a higher number of destinations than normal traffic. So a belief of a network trace can be calculated with the aid of likelihood vectors that were defined in the CPT. In the end the trace can be categorized as an attack or normal trace (refer to [10] for detailed description).

Honey phones can be used as part of an Intrusion Detection Systems as described in [2] [11] and can be viewed as VoIP specific Honey pots. A Honey pot represents a part of a network that is not accessible by 'normal' users and therefore any access to the Honey pot can be viewed as an attack. VoIP specific Honey pots can be used in order to detect Scan attacks or SPIT attacks. As described in [11] the Honey pot is implemented as a complete parallel VoIP infrastructure that is logically and physically separated from the normal network and so simulates a whole VoIP network. Let us assume a Scan attack as described earlier. When the attacker sends e requests to valid assigned contact addresses they are forwarded through the normal SIP network (Proxy, UAC), but when the attacker tries to send requests to an unassigned or invalid contact the request will be forwarded to the Honey pot, where the requests can be monitored and treated adequately.

1.4 Are we now secured against SPIT?

The question must be answered wit 'no', because the presented countermeasures inherit weaknesses that can be exploited by attackers. In fact we can expand SXSM with special scenarios that implement exploits of weaknesses of countermeasures, as we can see in the figure below.

Figure 6: SXSM Attacks

1.4.1 Weakness of Device Fingerprinting

The weakness of passive fingerprinting is described by the authors of [4] themselves. As passive finger-printing only analyses the order and existence of the header fields of an INVITE message, an attacker simply needs to order the header fields in the same way as one standard client. In that case the passive fingerprinting mechanism can't detect the attack.

We can state nearly the same for active fingerprinting as an attacker only needs to behave like one stand-ard client when receiving unexpected or non standard compliant SIP messages. It is very simple for an attacker to develop an attacking SIP client that behaves exactly like a standard client, because he can imitate the behavior of a standard client e.g. with SXSM. We can call this attack **Device Spoofing**. As Device Fingerprinting is discussed as a server side anti SPIT mechanism, it is useless against Direct IP Spitting as the clients don't have any chance to verify the fingerprint of the attacking client.

In the end we will take a look on practical issues of Device Fingerprinting. When we take a look at today's VoIP universe, we will find out that there exist a vast variety of hard- and soft phones. Each of these phones has its own SIP header layout and behavior and even within a product family header layouts and behavior differ even between two versions of the same device. The result is, that an ad-ministrator who uses Device Fingerprinting in order to protect his system, must always keep the list of fingerprints up to date. Otherwise it can lead to blocking of calls although the calls are not SPIT. Let us e.g. assume that a caller uses a standard client and that the manufacturer sends out a firmware upgrade, that makes major changes to the SIP Stack. Any calls of this user are blocked or marked as SPIT, until the administrator of the VoIP network updates the fingerprint list and this procedure will repeat any time a new firmware version is rolled out or new clients are released. Taking it even one step further, we can see, that as more and more clients and versions are released, the fingerprint list will become wider and wider and in the end nearly any combination of e.g. header fields will be present in the list. The main problem of device fingerprinting is that it is derived from a HTTP security technique. In that scenario only few clients (web browsers) from few developers exist, in contradiction to the VoIP world.

1.4.2 Weaknesses of White Lists, Black Lists, Grey Lists

Black Lists can not really be viewed as a SPIT countermeasure, because additional methods are needed to classify a caller a spitter. A Black List on server side would require e.g. statistical methods for clas-sifying a caller as spitter. In case of a client side Black List, the user must mark a caller as a Spitter, e.g. after receiving an initial SPIT call from this caller. Both server side and client side Black List are very useless against Direct IP Spitting for different reasons. Server sided Black Lists are bypassed by Direct IP Spitting, because the SIP messages are sent directly to the client. Client sided Black Lists are circumvented by Direct IP Spitting, because the caller can take on any identity in order to place calls. So if one identity is blocked he can simply switch the Identity. We can call this attack **SIP Identity Spoofing** and any attacker, who can spoof SIP identities, can easily bypass Black Lists.

White Lists are at first sight harder to circumvent than Black Lists, because the attacker has no knowledge about the entries of the White List of the victim. So even if he wants to spoof an identity, the attacker doesn't know which identity he must take on, in order to place a successful call. In case of Direct IP Spitting the attacker could simply try out all existing accounts with a brute force attack until he finds out which identities are not blocked. A less exhausting procedure can be performed in case of distributed or imported white lists [2]. In that scenario the attacker needs one valid account. After adding the victim to the attacker's white list, he can now select that he wants to import the white list of the victim. So he can get access to all entries of the victim's white list and can spoof these identities e.g. in a Direct IP Spitting attack.

The Grey List mechanism can be bypassed the same way as White List mechanisms, as it just represents a mechanism that allows first time contact. All in all we can say, that any attacker who is able to perform SIP Identity Spoofing, can bypass Black Lists, White Lists and Grey Lists.

In the end we will take again a look at the practical side of the presented mechanisms. The concepts of Black, White and Grey Listing are derived from the Instant Messaging world, where it is a matter of course, that users first ask for permission, before they are added to another user's buddy list and only buddies can communicate with each other. When a user receives a communication request, he receives the profile of the other user containing e.g. nick name, email address, full name or even profile photo. On basis of this information, the user can decide and is able to decide, if he wants to accept messages in future from that party or not. Taken to the VoIP scenario this mechanism seems very impractical as the introduction problem has to be solved. Let us assume e.g. an employee of a bank wants to call one of his customers. In case of white listing the call can not be successfully routed to its target, as customers usually don't have the phone numbers of employees of their home bank listed in the White List. The decision basis for accepting or rejecting a call is simply the phone number that is sent by the caller. If the call is rejected at first (Grey listing) the callee must decide if he wants to accept future calls and he must base this decision on the phone number. We can easily see that this fact is very impractical.

1.4.3 Weakness of Reputation Systems

Reputation systems that are based on negative reputation can be bypassed in same way as Black Lists [1]. A user with a negative reputation can be viewed as globally blacklisted as his calls are blocked e.g. for any user (this depends on the policy that is used). Nevertheless an attacker that is black listed simply needs to gain access to a new 'clean' account. In case of a SPIT value as SIP header, the SPIT value can be spoofed by the attacker (e.g. with Direct IP Spitting) and we can call this attack **SIP Header Spoofing**. The attacker can simply set or change values of header fields, when he uses Direct IP Spitting. In addition an attacker can create several accounts with the aim of pushing the SPIT value of one account up or down (depending on implementation). This attack can be called Reputation Pushing or Pulling and is also referred as Ballot Stuffing [14].

Again we will also take a closer look at practical issues of the anti SPIT mechanism. At first we must admit, that Reputation systems are more auxiliary features than SPIT blocking mechanisms. The reason for this argumentation is that the user must classify a call as SPIT via a button or by entering a value. This value is used for future decisions on that SIP identity. So initially SPIT is not prevented by this technique. Then the SPIT value of an identity has to be shown to callees, so that they can decide about accepting or rejecting the call. Let us assume a Spitter has achieved a SPIT value or SPIT probability of e.g. thirty percent and then calls a victim. What should happen now? When the call is forwarded to the user and the value is e.g. shown in the display of the callee's phone, he can decide to accept or reject the call on a better decision basis. The problem is that anyhow his phone rings and that is what should be prevented. He could have just picked up the call and listened the first 5 seconds to know that it is SPIT. So the SPIT value didn't just add one percent of benefit. On top of this fact attackers could misuse the scoring system and create enough accounts in order to threaten 'normal' users with collectively giving them negative reputation [1].

1.4.4 Weakness of Turing tests and Computational Puzzles

Turing tests seem at first sight very effective for SPIT prevention in combination with white lists, but nonetheless have weak points. The first approach of bypassing Audio CAPTCHA is relaying the CAPTCHA to human solvers. An attacker could pay cheap workers, who are only hired to solve Audio CAPTCHA. In countries with cheap labor this would raise the costs per call only marginally [1]. In order to reduce the costs, an attacker could even e.g. set up an adult hotline and could dispatch Audio CAPTCHA to the customers of this service. This technique is known from visual CAPTCHA where the images from CAPTCHA protected sites are copied and relayed to a high traffic site owned by the attacker. All in all we can state, that an attacker who can detect CAPTCHA and relay it to human solvers is able to bypass Turing tests and we can call this attack **CAPTCHA Relay Attack**.

Computational Puzzles can not really be viewed as SPIT prevention mechanisms. It is obvious, that attackers usually possess high computational power. So circumventing a system protected by Computational Puzzles, doesn't even demand a special attack. The attacker just needs sufficient CPU power.

In the end again we will take a look at some practical issues of the described techniques. As far as Turing tests are concerned, we can see that this method is very intrusive. User Interaction is forced every time a caller is not present in the White List of a callee. The difficulty with Computational Puzzles is that different VoIP endpoints have different abilities in computational power. So if the task is to hard to solve (consumes too much CPU power), session establishment will be delayed very much for e.g. a low-end cell phone, while attackers with high CPU power PCs won't be concerned much. With this fact Computational Puzzles are very ineffective and contra productive, because they only bother 'normal' users.

1.4.5 Weakness of Payment at risk

In which way Payment at risk can be bypassed depends mainly on the way it is implemented. Demanding payment for each call won't be very realistic, because this would require a high administrative overhead and more costs for service providers. Let us assume Payment at risk combined with White listing, so that payment is only required for callers that are not present in the callee's White List. In this case a caller could simply spoof identity as described in the section about White List. In the second scenario, where Payment at risk is combined with a Reputation system, the attacker just needs to achieve an adequate reputation value, as described in the corresponding section. Let us even assume that Payment at Risk is used for every call. Even In that case an attacker could circumvent it, by impersonating as another user, so that he can establish calls and shift the costs on to 'normal' customers. In which way this kind of **SIP Identity Hijacking** [13] attack is fulfilled is another question and out of scope for now.

Besides the technical aspects, practical issues of Payment at Risk are numerous. At first the relative high costs, that are required for micropayment will must be viewed, the inequities in the value of currency between sender and recipient [1] and the additional interactions that a user must take (e.g. confirming a call from an unknown party as non SPIT).

1.4.6 Weakness of IDS, Honey phones

Intrusion Detection Systems base on the assumption, that the characteristics of attacks differ much from characteristics of normal calls. At first sight this assumption seems logic, as e.g. within a SPIT attack, the attacker calls hundreds or thousands of victims within an hour, while a normal user wouldn't even send out one percent of this amount of calls. Nevertheless the attacker has two possibilities in order to bypass detection by an Intrusion Detection System. The first is to align his behavior with the behavior of normal users, e.g. adjust the call rate to 5 calls per hour. Obviously this technique is hard to fulfill, because this would make an attack very inefficient as it would consume too much time, but on the other hand the goal of a spitter is not to reach as much users as possible within the shortest time period. Reaching e.g. thousand users with a call rate of 5 calls per hour would take approximately 8 days. We can call this technique **Call Rate Adaption**. This means that an attacker is able to adjust his call rate (e.g. number of calls per time slot, number of simultaneous calls). As the call rate is not the only variable that is used in order to detect abnormal behavior an attacker can use a second technique in order to not be detected by Intrusion Detection Systems. The attacker can use different accounts for his attacks, so that statistic values are spread over several accounts. Let us assume that an attacker has one hundred valid user accounts. With this amount of accounts he can partition the targeted user accounts into one hundred groups and use only one account per group. The users from group one are only called with account one and so on. It is harder for a monitoring system to detect attacks that are originated from different sources, as there must be a technique to correlate partial attacks to one complete attack. This attacking technique can be called **Account Switching**, as the attacker switches the used account while he is performing an attack.

Honey pots are very effective against scan attacks as anyone who tries to reach invalid or unassigned identities, will be trapped and so Honey pots are very effective against SPIT. When the Spitter can't scan the network for assigned and unassigned numbers, he is forced to view all numbers as assigned. When he views all numbers as assigned, he will sooner or later step into the trap, because he will establish calls to endpoints that are part of the Honey pot. Nevertheless attackers can trick the Honey pot mechanism with SIP Identity Hijacking. When an attacker impersonates the accounts of normal users and then performs SPIT attacks with these normal accounts, he will access end points in the Honey pot system with normal accounts. So the assumption that accesses to the Honey pot are only established by attackers is lapsed.

In the end we will take again a look at the practical issues of the presented solutions. The practical problem with intrusion detection systems in general is that they base on statistical assumptions that are not verified. The question that has to be solved is: Where is the borderline between normal usage and abnormal usage? The publishers state that statistical values are assumed or derived from attack characteristics, but in order to reduce the rate of false negative and false positive classifications, the knowledge basis must be precise. So we can say that what we lack is knowledge of SPIT characteristics as we nowadays can't really distinguish SPIT from normal traffic unless the SPIT attacks are excessive. Honey pots have the disadvantage, that they only detect access to invalid or unassigned accounts, this means that an attacker who only accesses valid accounts won't be handled by a Honey pot.

2 Conclusion

As a summary we can now say that we learned how SPIT is put into practice, why it is a threat, what mechanisms have already been developed against it and how these mechanisms can be bypassed. The following figure puts the puzzle together and shows how SXSM can be used in order to evaluate SPIT countermeasures:

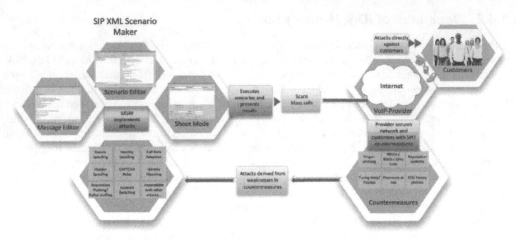

Figure 7: Holistic view on SXSM in SPIT context

The image shows that SXSM can be used by a VoIP network administrator in order to reveal weak points of the system or in order to test the robustness of used countermeasures, by figuring out weak points deriving attacks from these weak points and putting the attacks into practice.

References

[1]   J. Rosenberg, C. Jennings, RFC 5039 – The Session Initiation Protocol (SIP) and Spam, IETF, 2008.

[2]   M. Hansen, M. Hansen, J. Müller, T. Rohwer, C. Tolkmit and H. Waack, Developing a Legally Compliant Reachability Management System as a Countermeasure against SPIT, 2007.

[3]   S. Dritsas, J. Mallios, M. Theoharidou, G.F. Marias and D. Gritzalis, Threat Analysis of the Session Initiation Protocol Regarding Spam, IEEE, 2007.

[4]   H. Yany, K. Sripanidkulchaiz, H. Zhangy, Z. Shaez and D. Saha, Incorporating Active Fingerprinting into SPIT Prevention Systems, 2007.

[5]   M. Stiemerling S. Niccolini, S. Tartarelli, Requirements and methods for SPIT identification using feedbacks in SIP. Internet-draft, 2008.

[6]   F. Wang, Y. Mo, B. Huang, P2P-AVS: P2P Based Cooperative VoIP Spam Filtering, 2007.

[7]   C. Jennings, Computational Puzzles for SPAM Reduction in SIP. Internetdraft, 2008.

[8]   H. Tschofenig, E. Leppanen, S. Niccolini, M. Arumaithurai, Automated Public Turing Test to Tell Computers and Humans Apart (CAPTCHA) based Robot Challenges for SIP. Internet-draft, 2008.

[9]   S. Liske, K. Rebensburg, B. Schnor, SPIT-Erkennung, -Bekanntgabe und -Abwehr in SIP-Netzwerken, 2007.

[10] M. Nassar, R. State, O. Festor, Intrusion detection mechanisms for VoIP applications, 2007.

[11] M. Nassar, S. Niccolini, R. State, T. Ewald, Holistic VoIP Intrusion Detection and Prevention System, 2008.

[12] SIPp at Sourceforge, http://sipp.sourceforge.net/index.html.

[13] Two attacks against VoIP, http://www.securityfocus.com/infocus/1862.

[14] Dellarocas, C., Immunizing Online Reputation Reporting Systems Against Unfair Ratings and Discriminatory Behavior, 2000

Influence of Security Mechanisms on the Quality of Service of VoIP

Peter Backs[1] · Norbert Pohlmann[2]

[1]Sirrix AG
Lise-Meitner-Allee 4, D-44801 Bochum
p.backs@sirrix.com

[2]Institute for Internet Security
University of Applied Sciences Gelsenkirchen
Neidenburger Str. 43, D-45877 Gelsenkirchen
norbert.pohlmann@informatik.fh-gelsenkirchen.de

Abstract

While Voice over IP (VoIP) is advancing rapidly in the telecommunications market, the interest to protect the data transmitted by this new service is also rising. However, in contrast to other internet services such as email or HTTP, VoIP is real-time media, and therefore must meet a special requirement referred to as Quality-of-Service to provide a comfortable flow of speech. Speech quality is worsened when transmitted over the network due to delays in transmission or loss of packets. Often, voice quality is at a level that even prevents comprehensive dialog. Therefore, an administrator who is to setup a VoIP infrastructure might consider avoiding additional decreases in voice quality resulting from security mechanisms, and might leave internet telephony unprotected as a result. The inspiration for this paper is to illustrate that security mechanisms have negligible impact on speech quality and should in fact be encouraged.

1 Introduction

Telephony systems are the most important communication media in modern society[1]. Nonetheless, most users still tolerate the inherent security weaknesses in voice transmission over telephones. Indeed, circuit-switched telephone communication is not encrypted and the call participants are not authenticated. Circuit-switched telephony security is based on physical protection of the telephone line, which leaves communication data completely exposed to an attacker gaining physical access. The same situation applies to VoIP; the attacker must have access to the telephony device of a call participant or the network media carrying the voice data. In comparison to classic telephone technology, however, access to transport media is achieved far more easily. So-called Spoofing Attacks can be used to fake the identification (ID) of a caller, allowing the redirection of VoIP traffic through the system of an attacker to be easily eavesdropped. Another threat is inherent to internet routing technology, as IP packets are not meant to be transported over fixed routes from one host to another. Instead, routes are determined dynamically and beyond the control of communicating peers. In this way, a malicious system could be found along the route of a packet, exposing voice content if not secured properly. Furthermore, the ability to intercept

---

1 A dedicated study ascertained by University of Applied Science Wiesbaden, Clarity Voice Commerce Research Center, Fachverband für Sprachtechnologien, Voice Commerce Application Committee (VASCom) and Technologiestiftung Hessen (TSH) points out, that telephone communication remains the most important communication channel between a company and its customers.

N. Pohlmann, H. Reimer, W. Schneider (Editors): Securing Electronic Business Processes, Vieweg (2008), 341-346

voice data traffic is not dependent on special hardware, as is the case with ISDN, for example. Instead, a standard PC and freely-available software is sufficient for very effective attacks. To sum up, the danger of a successful attack against VoIP is even greater than that inherent to classic telephone technology.

1.1 Securing Voice-over-IP

Towards this end, several solutions have been developed that offer the security required. Typically, there are two approaches applied towards realizing these solutions: the establishment of a Virtual Private Network (VPN) and the employment of VoIP-specific protocols.

The first of these approaches, VPN, protects any kind of IP traffic independently of the communication service employed. There exist a variety of VPN solutions on the market. Most are based on the IPSec standards from IETF [IPSEC_1], [IPSEC_2], while another very popular product is the open, but not standardized, OpenVPN [OVPN].

A VPN normally extends protection from one site to another. The IPSec standards cover end-to-end protection, but the protocol is not so widely used. The advantage of site-to-site protection is that transmitted data is encrypted transparently for the VoIP participants, but connections are only protected between VPN nodes.

On the other hand, VoIP-specific concepts were developed to specifically protect VoIP connections. The Real-time Transport Protocol (RTP) is used to transfer real-time data, such as a voice stream. The Secure RTP (SRTP) standard extends RTP capabilities by encrypting and signing its payload. Similarly, the standard Session Initiation Protocol (SIP), used to signal calls, has been extended to a more secure variant, SIPS. In contrast to a VPN, SRTP offers end-to-end protection of voice data. However, a special client is required to support SIPS and SRTP. As well, a cryptographic key infrastructure must be deployed including all VoIP participants and not only the viewer VPN nodes.

1.2 Quality of Service in Voice over IP

When referring to quality in VoIP, quality of data transmission over the network and quality of speech is important. Quality of transmission refers to the parameters of the network voice media is transmitted over, including end-to-end delay, variation in delay, packet loss and bandwidth. In contrast to quality of speech, quality of transmission way can be objectively characterized by these parameters. Voice quality is the quality of the transmitted audio data in comparison to a face to face dialog. The only way to rate this quality is by personal impression. Voice quality is mainly influenced by the voice codec, the algorithm used to compress the media stream. Both factors are connected, as quality of data transmission directly influences the quality of speech. A high end-to-end delay also impacts on quality of speech, when flow in dialog is disturbed for instance.

2 Impact of Security on Quality of Service

The security aspects of these implementations are based on well known cryptographic procedures and met with general acceptance. However, research has yet to be conducted to ascertain the overall impact when using VoIP with these security implementations. This paper addresses this gap in knowledge by analyzing and comparing common VoIP security implementations as to their effect on VoIP usage. Besides organizational and technical efforts, such as manual keying (if no cryptographic key infrastructure has been deployed), security mechanisms affect the Quality-of-Service (QoS) of a VoIP connection.

Parameters of the QoS that are affected include end-to-end delay, variation of delay (jitter), packet loss and bandwidth consumption.

The impact on QoS is easy to measure across a VPN when specific tools are used. These tools act as VoIP extensions sending test calls to one other. When set in different networks connected by a VPN tunnel, the impact on quality can be determined by comparing against those results obtained when the VPN functionality is disabled (i.e. the reference measurement). Figure 1 shows the testing environment consisting of two separated networks connected by a routing network. Security gateways at the network boundary feature VPN functionality. OpenVPN and OpenSWAN were chosen as a representative selection of most common VPN solutions.

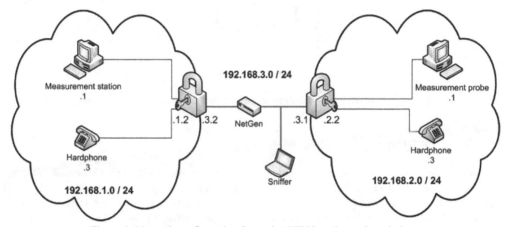

Figure 1: Network configuration for testing VPN based security solutions.

In fact, the above mentioned tools are only useful when analysing transparent security concepts. If the security solution has to be implemented by the VoIP participants, the test tools must implement them as well. As this is not the case, no measurements can be obtained when the VoIP-specific SRTP standard is employed. However, the behaviour of SRTP implementations is more predictable due to its greater simplicity. Firstly, cryptographic calculations are distributed over the VoIP clients as opposed to being concentrated to a single point as in the case of a VPN. Furthermore, stream cipher algorithms encouraged by the SRTP standard are supposed to work fast, even on embedded devices, so as to expect that additional computing would be minimized. Last, but not least, SRTP does not tunnel the entire VoIP packet into a new one, but merely encrypts the voice data and appends a checksum instead. In contrast, VPN tunnelling adds additional headers which can be of even bigger size than the VoIP payload itself, resulting in bandwidth more than double of the unencrypted VoIP stream. The simpler concept of SRTP implies faster processing. As a result, the impact of SRTP implementations should be considered less than that experienced when applying VPN protection.

2.1 Delay, Jitter and Packet Loss

To investigate the validity of these assertions, the influence on the QoS stemming from the various security processes was measured. It was concluded that none of the security implementations tested had a significant impact on the delay, jitter or packet loss. The end-to-end delay increased less than two milliseconds. According to the ITU-T, a delay in a voice connection of 150 milliseconds or less still allows for optimal voice quality. Hence, the delay introduced when protecting the signal is negligible. Jitter and packet loss measurements were essentially equal in protected versus unprotected connections.

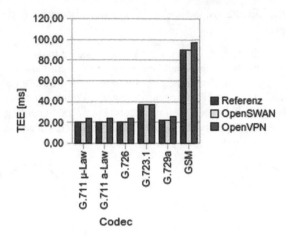

Figure 2: End-to-end delay (TEE) for different voice codecs and security solutions.

2.2 Bandwidth

In contrast to delay, jitter and packet loss, bandwidth requirements increased more substantially. Depending on the voice coding and framing parameters, as well as the security software employed, the bandwidth consumed by a protected VoIP connection is more than double that of an unprotected one. Therefore, if the available bandwidth is limited, protection could be a restricting factor. Two of the factors, the voice transmission settings and the security software, can be tweaked so as to tune down the bandwidth requirements. To begin with, the VoIP software can be set up to submit more than one voice frame per RTP packet, with the effect that packet overhead (and, therefore, security overhead) is reduced. That is, if two frames are sent in one RTP packet, the overhead is halved. This reduces the bandwidth but causes an additional delay due to the accumulation of an extra frame for each transmission. Another option to tune the bandwidth is the choice of the voice codec. This way, the additional bandwidth required for the cryptographic functionality can be compensated by the use of a low-bandwidth codec. In most cases, however, this also has the effect that voice quality decreases and the sensitivity to packet loss increases. The security settings can be adjusted to further reduce the bandwidth of the signal. The most influential of these stems from the security protocol employed. Whereas SRTP merely adds a signature to the RTP packet, VPN solutions encapsulate the entire RTP packet, resulting in more overhead. Furthermore, SRTP encourages the use of stream cipher encryption. Stream ciphers tend to process streamed data more efficiently, as they do not make use of fixed block sizes. The IPSec and OpenVPN protocols both rely on block ciphers, which pad the payload to fit the block size and, therefore, increase the overhead. SRTP is most often the optimal choice to reduce the bandwidth requirements of a secure connection.

Table 1: Bandwidth consumption [Kbps] of voice codecs at different packeting settings, security protocols and security protocol cipher block size (BS).

Codec	Voice stream, Circuit-switched	Segm. / packet	RTP n/a	IPSec BS 16	IPSec BS 8	OpenVPN BS 16	OpenVPN BS 8	SRTP n/a
G.711	64	1	96	147,2	140,8	166,4	153,6	102,4
		2	80	105,6	102,4	115,2	108,8	83,2
G.723.1	5,3	1	16	32	29,867	38,4	34,133	18,133
		2	10,667	20,267	18,133	21,333	20,267	11,733
	6,3	1	17,067	36,267	32	38,4	36,267	19,2
		2	11,733	20,267	19,2	23,467	21,333	12,8
G.726	16	1	48	96	89,6	115,2	102,4	54,4
		2	32	60,8	54,4	64	60,8	35,2
	24	1	56	108,8	102,4	115,2	108,8	62,4
		2	40	67,2	60,8	70,4	67,2	43,2
	32	1	64	121,6	108,8	128	121,6	70,4
		2	48	73,6	70,4	83,2	76,8	51,2
	40	1	72	121,6	115,2	140,8	128	78,4
		2	56	80	76,8	89,6	83,2	59,2
G.729a	8	1	40	96	83,2	102,4	96	46,4
		2	24	48	44,8	57,6	51,2	27,2
GSM (FullRate)	13	1	29,2	54,4	51,2	64	57,6	32,4
		2	21,2	33,6	32	38,4	35,2	22,8
iLBC	13,33	1	24	40,533	38,4	46,933	42,667	26,133
		2	18,667	26,667	25,6	29,867	27,733	19,733
	15,2	1	31,2	60,8	54,4	64	57,6	34,4
		2	23,2	36,8	33,6	38,4	36,8	24,8

As table 1 illustrates, the bandwidth consumed by a protected VoIP stream may be more than double the bandwidth of an unprotected stream even when using the same speech codec. The differences are even more significant when comparing the influence of codecs. In any case, the figure above should allow one to estimate the volume of VoIP traffic to expect and be a useful reference for tweaking it.

3 VPN Gateway Load

Another important fact regarding VoIP and VPN security mechanisms is the load on the VPN gateways. As a central node protecting all passing data, the VPN gateway has to perform encryption and verification for all VoIP clients on the network. Measurements showed that VoIP packets, in particular, stress the gateway more than ordinary IP traffic. This is due to the very small packet size in VoIP streams in comparison to, e.g., FTP or HTTP. Due to the higher average load, gateways tend to be quicker to reach their limit in throughput when VoIP packets are handled. The dramatic decrease in throughput is shown in Figure 3. The lines show the end-to-end delay when raising the data throughput of the gateway. At the point of singularity, the gateway can be considered overloaded and at the point of maximum throughput. The difference in the maximum throughput when sending small packets, as opposed to larger packets, is apparent in the thick and thin lines of each colour. The reference, which implements ordinary routing devices instead of securing VPN stations, performs a maximal throughput of roughly 60 Mbps when routing VoIP packets versus 95 Mbps when sending larger packets. The same situation can be noted when implementing VPN gateways. When using Open VPN, the throughput drops from 40 to 15 Mbps, which is nearly the same when implementing OpenSWAN.

To compensate for this, an administrator might install more powerful gateway hardware or even consider a clustering solution, which also renders failover services.

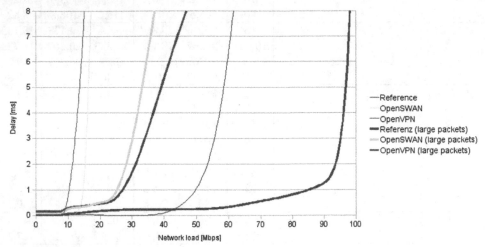

Figure 3: Limit in network load depending on security solution implemented and the network packet size.

4 Conclusion

To sum up, the QoS parameters of a voice stream, including delay, jitter and packet loss, are hardly affected by security measures. Special considerations have to be taken with regard to the consumption of bandwidth by a secure, versus insecure, call. The overhead for protection may have a significant impact on the required bandwidth, but the administrator has several ways to compensate for this. Also, the administrator must consider that a security gateway will overload more easily when processing VoIP as opposed to other internet services; however, this can be resolved easily enough by scaling server capacity. In any case, secure VoIP should not be dismissed due to misgivings of decreased voice quality, but encouraged by the many risks addressed by the protection it provides.

References

[ZDNT03] Fiutak, Martin: Telefon toppt E-Mail, 2003, http://www.zdnet.de/news/tkomm/0,39023151,39118288,00. htm.

[OVPN]   OpenVPN community: OpenVPN website, http://www.openvpn.net

[IPSEC98_1] Kent, Stephen / Atkinson, R., RFC 2401: Security Architecture for the Internet Protocol, IETF, November 1998

[IPSEC98_2] Kent, Stephen / Atkinson, R., RFC 2406: IP Encapsulating Security Payload (ESP), IETF, November 1998

The security of mass transport ticketing systems

Marc Sel · Stefaan Seys · Eric Verheul

PricewaterhouseCoopers Enterprise Advisory Services
{marc.sel | stefaan.seys}@pwc.be
eric.verheul@pwc.nl

Abstract

Mass transport ticketing systems in most developed countries are making a rapid transition from 'traditional' paper or carton-based ticketing systems towards a contactless 'smart card' based approach. This article discusses the main IT security aspects of mass transport ticketing systems (metro, bus, etc).

We introduce the standards that emerged over the years, and we outline the core functionality of the IT aspects of a mass transport ticketing system.

We discuss some examples, and subsequently we address security and anti-fraud aspects. We also put some security breaches related to the use of the Philips/NXP Mifare family in perspective. We describe an alternative approach such as proposed by Calypso, and formulate conclusions and lessons learnt.

1 Introduction

1.1 Setting the scene

Mass transport systems in most developed countries are constantly evolving to offer better services for a better price. Organisations such as the UITP (International Association for Public Transport [UITP]) provide a global forum where operators promote ideas and turn them into reality. Over the last years, many operators are making a rapid transition from 'traditional' paper or carton-based ticketing systems towards a combination of contactless smart cards and cheap disposable tickets. These new technologies allow them to introduce flexible fare systems to better meet their clients' expectations, as well as to fight the increasing level of ticketing fraud. There are significant parallels with the credit card industry where an irreversible migration from magstrip to chip is taking place. This article discusses the security of such new ticketing systems.

1.2 About standards

Obviously, such systems have a long tradition, reflected in a number of existing standards. In 1998 the ISO 14443 Standard for Proximity Cards (13,56 MHz contactless interfacing) was published, including both -A (Mifare) and –B (RATP) variants. Today most readers support both variants, and most contactless systems rely on the standard for their radio interface.

Other influential standards include the EN 1545 Data Model family outlining the major data types, on which the ENV 12896 (Public Transport Data Model – [PTDM]) builds. This is further complemented by the EN 15320 (Interoperable Public Transport Application), and other models such as from the Calypso Network Association [CNA]. In 2004 the CEN TC278 WG3's 'Standard Architecture' was approved, and in 2007 the ISO 24014-1 Standard Architecture (Interoperable Fare Management System) was published.

Furthermore the CEN's CWA 14838 family describes EU policy and user requirements, provides guidance on smart card use, and outlines process requirements.

In some cases, standards may actually be competing, as in the case of the UK where London's Oyster followed another approach than the area outside London, governed by ITSO. Nevertheless, millions of users are served daily by cards such as Navigo (Paris), Mobib (Brussels), Oyster (London), OV-chipkaart (NL) etc. According to Eurosmart, a strong forum of leading smart card providers (see [Eurosmart]), some 170 million transport cards were shipped in 2007.

1.3 Functional aspects

A mass transport system allows people to travel from one place to another for a certain price, often subsidised. Mass transport operators offer a collection of possible fares. More often than not, the government's subsidising the system reflects the importance paid to the 'universal service' aspect of mass transport.

A passenger can purchase a contract in many forms (a single trip, multiple trips, season tickets etc.) at various points of sales. We use the term 'contract' to refer to the travel rights a passenger purchases. This contract can be stored either on a throw-away card or on a reusable, personalised or anonymous card.

When travelling, passengers have to demonstrate they are in possession of a valid contract. Most systems today are already (or are becoming) 'closed', i.e. a passenger needs to use his contract to enter the network. This is referred to as check-in. At the other end of the journey, the passenger has to perform a check-out. Intermediate validation may also be required, for example to calculate the optimal fare when switching transport mode. Individual verification by a controller only happens for a fraction of the passengers.

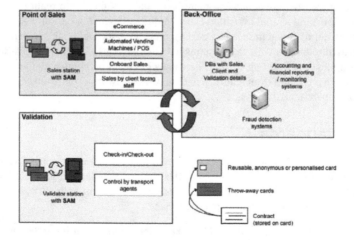

Figure 1: Components of a Mass Transport Ticketing system.

Figure 1 gives an overview of the most important functional components for a single operator system. The degree to which those components are connected on-line is an important feature of such a system. In a truly on-line system, the validator could check over the network whether a particular ticket is valid or not in a central database. However, since target time for performing a validation is 200 to 300 milliseconds, validation is a demanding process. Most systems download significant amounts of information to the validator, to speed-up processing and to cater for potential network problems.

1.4 Card issuance and personalisation

Different types of contactless cards are used. There is an obvious cost/capacity trade-off. Card memory typically ranges from ¼ K to 8K+ bytes. For example a 1K card handles usually maximum five contracts, a 4K card more than ten. What is particularly relevant here is that the card can store a history of previous journeys (but not necessarily a full journey log) which will influence the next fare to pay.

The first type is a cheap throw-away card that can be used for a single trip or for a certain amount of time (for example one day). We refer to these cards as 'tickets'. These tickets are issued with the contract already stored on the ticket. For single trip tickets, the contract on the ticket is flagged as 'used' at check-in (first validation) time, and subsequently cannot be used a second time. Tickets that are valid for a day will simply have an expiration time and will no longer be accepted when trying to validate them after this time. Sample cards include e.g. the Mifare Ultra-Light, which are priced around 0,20 to 0,5 euro for at least 100.000+ quantities.

The second type of cards is more expensive but can be recharged with different contracts. These cards have non-volatile rewritable memory that can be used to store any content that adheres to the data model specified for the card. These cards may be personalised for the passenger and contain the name, age and possibly other personal data, or they may be anonymous. These cards are issued at a point of sales at request of the passenger. If a passenger wishes, he can immediately purchase a contract that will be transmitted to the card (this will typically happen the first time a passenger purchases a monthly or yearly subscription). Sample cards include e.g. the Mifare Classic or DESFire, which may be priced around 1 euro or less for at least 100.000+ quantities. More expensive cards including Java cards typically cost less than around 5 euro.

To conduct his business, it is necessary for an operator to have an overview of all issued cards and tickets. Therefore, the IT system for card issuing has to maintain detailed records of all issued cards. The sales application will provide updates of all issued cards to a central database. The validators will upload details of the actions they performed as well.

1.5 Sales

Four main channels are commonly used to sell contracts to passengers:

1. Points of sales (POS) with client facing staff. Here, passengers can obtain a new card, new contracts, or stored value on their card. The sales application should be able to securely create new tickets or value, transfer it to the card and transfer all relevant transaction details to back office database systems.
2. Automated POS. This functionality is similar to the above, but usually only a subset of contracts can be purchased here (usually no monthly subscriptions). The security requirements are similar to the previous case.

3. eCommerce. Passengers purchase contracts over the Internet. The purchases are logged within the central databases at the back office and transferred to points of sales where the passengers can load their newly purchased contracts onto their cards. This may be possible at the validation points. The security requirements here are different: sales details have to be securely forwarded to all the points of sales (and validation points) and sales details have to be forwarded to the back office databases.

4. Sales onboard the vehicles. Some operators allow passengers to purchase contracts or tickets once they have boarded the vehicle. Usually the types of contracts that can be purchased here is limited. The security requirements are similar to the first two sales channels we discussed.

1.6 Contract validation

There are two main types of validation. The first type is performed by the passenger to ensure his ticket is valid. It is often implemented as the check-in/checkout to get the physical access to the transport network. The validating equipment needs to decide in milliseconds whether a valid contract is present in the list of current contracts, whether it has a new contract ready for download to the card, or whether it should decrease the stored value counter to pay for the check-in. And obviously, the black list needs to be verified as well. At positive outcome, the contract is marked as 'active' to prevent reuse and to allow agents to verify that passengers have actually validated their contract. The second type is validation by an agent. Here, agents will enter vehicles unexpected and verify that every passenger has a validated contract. Passengers without a valid contract will be fined. Usually, details of all validations are transferred to central databases stored within the back office of the operator.

1.7 Communication: Point of Sale to back office and vehicle to back office

Both sales and validation details have to be communicated to the back office databases. This can be straightforward when the points of sales have a fixed line to the back office, but more difficult when the validation happens on moving vehicles.

The technology used is depending on the environment and existing infrastructure. This can be a mix of wireless LAN standards, UMTS solutions, fibre back bones, etc. The transfer may take place in (near) real-time, or in batch.

1.8 Back Office control and monitoring

Back office control and monitoring is an important tool in the prevention of both internal and external fraud in any financial system. In mass transport ticketing systems, the back office will normally try to collect as much information as possible and permitted. This includes:

- Card issuing details: who has obtained which card at what time, who has delivered it, etc.
- Passenger history: all the card related actions (purchase, renewal, lost cards, etc.)
- Sales details: date, contract type, passenger ID, price, point of sales, etc.
- Validation details: date, location of validation, result of validation, etc.

It is obvious that there is a trade-off between the strength of controls and privacy. To respect privacy, it is recommended to at least segregate the databases into a database for basic customer information, another database with more detailed attributes such as full address data, and a third database to log the transactions performed by the customer.

Using this data, the back office can build automated controls. The first type of control is performed by the sales department: reconciling expected income with the actual income. This control should happen on incremental levels: ranging from individual sales agents, over different sales channels, to overall checks.

The second type of controls is more specific to mass transport systems. Here the back office will build a number of checks that will detect 'unusual' behaviour. This can range from suspicious check-in/check-out sequences, suspicious timing of validation, suspicious locations of validations, etc.

As these controls rely on the completeness of the sales and validation details, the back office should also have sufficient controls to monitor the completeness of the related databases. These controls could include checksums on batches of data, verifying the number of transactions, etc.

Obviously these controls should be monitored and a dashboard should indicate potential fraud. Once fraud has been detected, corrective measure should be taken. The required action depends on the type of fraud: internal fraud may lead to discharging personnel, while external fraud will usually lead to black listing the card and possibly prosecuting the fraudster.

For types of fraud with little false positives, automated response could be used. Typical examples include the detection of card cloning. These cards can be automatically added to a black list without human intervention.

2 Two cases

2.1 The London Oyster

The London Oyster card serves as a relevant example of a contactless transport card. It is based on a Philips/NXP Mifare Classic card and allows travel on London transport (TfL – Transport for London), underground, DLR, National Rail and busses. According to the TfL website, the main contract was awarded in 1998 to the TranSys consortium for approximately 1.6 billion US dollar, for 17 years creation and operation of the system. The main card providers are SchlumbergerSema and G&D. The system was launched in 2003 with optional annual and monthly season tickets, and staff cards. Subsequently annual, monthly and weekly tickets were mandatory making use of the Oyster. Furthermore, 'Pay As You Go' was added, with possible auto-loading. The current Oyster allows a complex zone/time/age multi-modal fee structure but is nevertheless quite user friendly, with a daily price cap much appreciated by its users. According to TfL, in 2006, more than a billion (1014 million) journey stages were made via the London Underground. By March 2007, approximately two third of all underground journeys were made with Oyster. By 2009, compliance with ITSO standards (which are used in neighbouring transport systems) is intended. For more information refer to [TfL].

2.2 The Sydney Tcard failure

The Sydney Tcard serves an illustrative purpose of a larger scale failure. After 11 years and 95 million Australian dollars, the government called the program to a halt in January 2008. Sydney's public transport system is overseen by the NSW government, and includes State Transit, Sydney Ferries and CityRail. The main contractors were Integrated Transit Solutions Limited and ERG Group.

Various reasons have contributed to the overall failure, including the government demand to include multiple complex tariff schemes and 120 different CityRail ticket products for busses and ferries. Facing a potential 95 million dollar claim, ERG temporarily suffered a self-imposed trading halt on the Australian Stock Exchange. The project will go back to the drawing board. The NSW is reconsidering their options to revive the project as from the summer of 2008.

3 Security aspects

Basic requirements can be derived from use cases. Figure 2 show the most important use cases of a mass transport ticketing system.

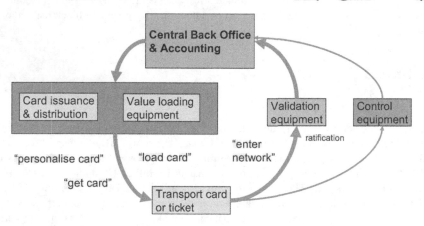

Figure 2: High-level Use Cases

The *first use case* is card personalisation. Depending on the type of personalisation chosen, the card may be anonymous, or may be a one-year season ticket for a particular student, or any other case.

The security properties depend on the type of card. Throw-away cards for single use generally do not have strong security capabilities. The cards may have a unique identity number that cannot be changed. They have 'write once read many' (WORM) memory cells to store the data. And there is a means to irreversibly write to the card, e.g. to indicate that the ticket has been used (e.g. by blowing a fuse on the chip). As there are no protected cryptographic secrets stored on the card, it is possible to clone these cards. This is possible by intercepting the data they transmit and using it to emulate the card and the contract to a transponder.

Real chip cards have stronger security properties. These cards contain non-volatile memory with an authorisation mechanism. The card will only write to memory if the transponder can prove that it knows the correct cryptographic key. In turn, the transponder will only accept cards that can prove that they possess the appropriate key (using a challenge/response based protocol). The cryptographic keys used should not be exportable. If the cryptographic algorithm or its usage has weaknesses then keys can be recovered through cryptanalysis. Also the cryptographic algorithm should employ cryptographic keys of sufficient bitlength (entropy), to withstand brute force kind of attacks. Currently a symmetric keylength of 80 is considered the bare minimum, see [keylenght]. The proprietary Mifare Classic cryptographic algorithm (CRYPTO1) employs a 48 bit keylength which means that this algorithm became susceptible for brute force attacks as soon as the algorithm was known. However, it turned out that CRYPTO1 and its usage actually has weaknesses allowing for far more efficient attacks then brute force attacks.

The *second use case* is loading a contract on a card. This usually happens after the contract has been purchased. The cards will only respond to terminals that can prove knowledge of the correct cryptographic key. Such keys are stored within a Security Authentication Module (SAM). The transponder will use the functionality offered by the SAM to write data to the card. In a model based on symmetric keys, every card will normally have its own personal key that is derived from a master key and the unique identity of the card. The SAMs will all contain this master key, and a number of keys for the specific operations such as loading or validating. During the challenge/response protocol between the SAM and the card, the card will reveal its identity, which allows the SAM to compute the personal key of the card. This key is used for mutual authentication. Access control to the cards memory can be managed in the card data model (e.g., different SAMs can have access to different parts of the memory, some parts can be readable without authentication, etc.). These SAMs will be present in every piece of equipment that needs to write to the card (transponders at points of sales, validation stations, etc.). As these SAMs are dispersed at various public locations, it is important to protect them from theft. Next to physical theft protection, other measures need to be taken to prevent abuse of SAMs. Possible measures are limiting the number of times a SAM can be used. In this case, a 'master SAM' is used to set the ceilings in the other SAMs (using secure authentication). Other means are to store the ID of the SAM in every contract that it creates. This allows validation stations to consult a black list of stolen SAMs before validating a card.

The *third use case* is validating a contract. If the data stored on the card is readable for anyone, this will not require a SAM. The validation terminal will interrogate the card and verify that the contract is valid. If outcome of the validation has to be registered on the card, then a SAM is required to write this information to it.

The back office should be aware of all transactions related to cards and contracts. This means that all points of sales, validation stations and mobile terminals of patrolling agents have to be connected to the back office databases. The solution for these connections will be a composition of rather heterogeneous combinations of wireless connections, wired LAN, fibre back bones, UMTS, etc. As validation stations will be mounted on moving vehicles or carried around by patrolling agents, these connections will not be available at all times. This means that local caches of the gathered data are required. These caches can be pushed to the back office once a connection is available (for example in the bus depots). Obviously network layer security mechanisms have to be put in place to ensure that only authorised components have access to this heterogeneous network. These mechanism will typically be a mix of different technologies including PKI, VPNs, SSL connections and application layer security.

4 Mifare woes

NXP and its licensees market variants of the Mifare product family, for various purposes including mass transport systems. Two particularly relevant examples are the Mifare Ultralight, used as disposable ticket and the Mifare Classic used as anonymous or personalised card. Implementations include the London Oyster, and the Dutch national OV (Openbaar Vervoer = Public Transport) chipcard. Security weaknesses have recently been demonstrated for both the Ultralight and the Classic.

4.1 Mifare Ultralight problems

In the Netherlands, students of the University of Amsterdam evaluated the security of the disposable OV-chipcard, intended for a nation-wide roll-out. This card is based on the Mifare Ultralight. Such a card contains 512 bits of non-volatile storage, organised into a UID, lock bytes, OTP memory and a user area. The UID provides a unique identifier. The lock bytes contain bits that can force other bits into read-only mode. Executing such a lock cannot be reversed. The lock bytes also contain some block-locking bits which can prevent other lock bits from being activated. These bits can be used to prevent that information bits on a card can be locked. The OTP is a One Time Programmable counter, which is irreversible. It is used e.g. to keep track of the number of rides on a ticket. Finally the user area offers 48 bytes that are application specific. Here transaction data such as check-in/check-out as well as general information about the card (holder, issuer, contracts, etc) is stored.

Various attack scenarios were performed on the real system, leading to the conclusion that a single disposable ticket could be used for an almost unlimited number of trips, by backing-up and rewriting ticket data. No cryptographic knowledge or specialised hardware was required for this attack. The Dutch press was made aware of this in July 2007, and the implementer subsequently fixed the problem which was related to the usage made of the OTP counter by the reader. For the detailed report of Pieter Siekerman (from PricewaterhouseCoopers) and Maurits van der Schee refer to [vdS-S].

4.2 Mifare Classic problems

In December 2007, on the CCC '07 conference, weaknesses in the CRYPTO1 proprietary and not disclosed algorithm were presented by Karsten Nohl and Henryk Plötz. They reverse-engineered the algorithm by analysing the physical implementation of the gates on the chip. They claim the algorithm is a linear feedback shift register algorithm with a 48 bit key. Given the current state of the art in computer hardware and crypt-analysis, 48 bits can be considered as too short.

In the Netherlands, TNO was invited to conduct evaluations by TLS, the OV-Chipcard operator. The outcome of these evaluations was subsequently released to the public (see [TNO-P]) and confirmed the problem.

This started further research, leading to the publication in March 2008 by Digital Security group of the Radboud University Nijmegen that they were able to crypt-analyse Mifare Classic keys in seconds. PricewaterhouseCoopers and Radbout University jointly performed an analysis of the use of the Mifare Classic as a nation-wide civil servant card for an EU Member State. While the details of this analysis remain at the discretion of this government, it is fair to state that our analysis confirmed the general line of thought that Mifare Classic can no longer be considered as secure in a number of usage scenarios. For more details please refer to [Radbout].

4.3 Way forward

NXP suggests the use of Mifare DESFire, Mifare Plus and SmartMX. Obviously, there is also a list of vendors with competitive products (Infineon, STM, etc). We recommend to consistently apply risk analysis to drive the overall price/quality decision.

5 An alternative approach

5.1 The Calypso approach

Calypso is proposed as a de-facto standard by the Calypso Network Association. It defines the interface between cards and terminals. The basis of the specification is 'Calypso Specification for Ticketing, Card Specification[1]', complemented by a set of 'Calypso Technical Notes[2]'. It relies on other well-known standards such as ISO 14443 et ISO 7816-1 – 3 for the radio link, ISO 7816-4 for APDU commands, and EN 1545 for the ticket/card data model. The components standardised are a Calypso-compliant smart-card, a disposable ticket, and a SAM (Secure Access Module). Main actors are CNA (Calypso Network Association), Innovatron (patentholder for some ISO 14443 et Calypso application patents (particularly « Session sécurisé et indivisible » and « ratification »), RATP (the Paris –based transport operator), and Spirtech.

The security of Calypso is to a great extend based on the use of diversified keys and MACs (message authentication codes). Cryptographically the security is based on DES, DESX and/or 3DES. Keys are managed in SAM hardware, with different keys being used for different functions (such as loading of a contract versus validation), and individually diversified keys. Apparently the use of AES has not yet been envisaged. The actual detailed security features of Calypso are not publicly available, and as such there is some 'security by obscurity' flavour present.

As Calypso is mainly focused on defining the interface between cards and terminals, various other aspects of a mass transport system such as an overall data model, and the application and back office aspects as well as interoperability with other fare systems still remain to be addressed outside the Calypso model.

5.2 Calypso implementations

There are many different ways of implementing a Calypso based system. Cards can be provided by some of the world's most respected names in smart card manufacturing. Applications and back office functions need to be developed to meet the specific requirements of the market. According to the Calypso Network Association, Calypso-based systems have been implemented in 21 countries, with more than 30 million contactless cards, relying on 300.000 terminals in some of the largest intermodal networks in the world such as Paris. Brussels is also currently migrating from magnetic-based system onto a Calypso implementation.

---

1   Document 010209-MU-CalypsoCardSpec
2   Documents CalypsoTN001 – TN014

6 Conclusion

Mass transport ticketing systems face universal problems with often quite tailor-made solutions that reflect the particular situation where the system operates. Adequate security should be considered a mandatory quality. The 'security by obscurity' approach of Mifare-based solutions can be considered as a thing of the past, and we recommend consistently avoiding this approach.

Good cryptography and security engineering are required as the foundation to build a performing, user-friendly and secure system. Such a system should contain comprehensive controls that span from card to accounting and financial systems, including the back-office.

References

[CCC07]   Mifare Classic hack: Karsten Nohl, Starbug, HenrykPlötz, CCC report CCC '07, http://events.ccc.de/congress/2007/Fahrplan/events/2378.en.html

[CNA]   Calypso Network Association – www.calypsonet-asso.org

[Eurosmart] Eurosmart – 'the voice of the smartcard industry' – www.eurosmart.com

[keylength] Refer to www.keylength.com

[PTDM]   Public Transport Data Model – www.transmodel.org

[Radbout] Radbout University OV-chipcard wiki: https://ovchip.cs.ru.nl

[RFIDIOt] Adam Laurie's www.rfidiot.org library and website

[TfL]   Transport for London, the London Oyster card: tfl.gov.uk

[TNO]   TNO, 'Security Analysis of the Dutch OV-Chipkaart,' TNO report 34643, 2008. http://www.translink.nl/media/bijlagen/nieuws/TNO_ICT_-_Security_Analysis_OV-Chipkaart_-_public_report.pdf

[UITP]   UITP – the International Association of Public Transport – www.uitp.org

[vdS-S]   Mifare Ultralight hack report: http://staff.science.uva.nl/~delaat/sne-2006-2007/p41/report.pdf

Authentication for Web Services with the Internet Smart Card

Walter Hinz

Giesecke & Devrient GmbH
Walter.Hinz@gi-de.com

Abstract

Conventional smart cards according to ISO 7816 exhibit only limited connectivity with IT equipment, as special drivers and special software are required to bridge the gap.

The Internet Smart Card offers a new approach to overcome this gap. By providing a communication stack which is directly compatible with popular interfaces, such as USB and TCP/IP, and by introducing an innovative CardToken form factor the Internet Smart Card enables easy-to-use smart card applications.

Examples are presented where the Internet Smart Card provides authentication solutions for the internet without the need for complicated installation of driver software and without the need for additional hardware.

1 Introduction

For a long time smart cards have been designed for use in a well defined, restricted environment which followed the rules of the ISO 7816 series of international standards. Whereas the high degree of interoperability gave rise to some really vast fields of application, first of all to mention mobile communication, the integration of smart cards into an application in most cases requires the development of specialised interface equipment in order to meet the physical and logical requirements of the ISO standard. Such a device, often referred to as an *interface device* or *IFD* has to be integrated into every mobile phone, every smart card payment terminal, and so on.

In order to connect a smart card to information technology devices like personal computers a *smart card terminal* is required for interconnection. Although there are also smart card terminals with their own display and keyboard, in most cases the purpose of the smart card terminal reduces to the tasks of mechanical interfacing, power supply, and protocol conversion. The smart card terminal occupies a computer interface, some power for its own operation, but makes no real contribution to the functionality of the smart card.

The transition from serially interfaced smart card terminals to USB smart card terminals did not change the situation very much. Although the power for the terminal and the card is now supplied by the USB, getting rid of the extra power supply, the other sources of inconvenience remain. USB power may be even a source of new troubles, as it now makes a difference whether a smart card terminal is connected to an active or passive USB hub. An active hub supplies 500 mA, whereas a passive hub delivers 100 mA maximum which may be insufficient for a terminal and a smart card.

Unless the application software is aware of the specific smart card terminal used, all these terminals require the installation of software drivers which transform the logical terminal and smart card interfaces

N. Pohlmann, H. Reimer, W. Schneider (Editors): Securing Electronic Business Processes, Vieweg (2008), 357-366

into a more or less standardised *application programming interface* or API. Examples of these APIs are PC/SC (personal computer/smart card) and CTAPI (card terminal API). Although the installation of these software drivers is brought about by sophisticated automatic routines there is always the danger of incompatibility with other software already installed on the PC.

The problems encountered with card terminals and their driver software gave rise for the demand for more convenient methods of interfacing personal computers with smart cards. It was the general idea that the future smart card should "speak" the language of IT equipment rather than vice versa. A most promising candidate for such a common interface turned out to be the Universal Serial Bus (USB) which was going to be implemented on smart cards for other reasons.

Meanwhile the mobile communication industry had become dissatisfied with the rather low bandwidth of the legacy ISO 7816 interface on their SIM cards. It was sufficient for the traditional network authentication task in mobile phones, and also for applications such as the phone book. The throughput was, however, considered too low for handling of multimedia content, and therefore the industry demanded a *high speed interface* for SIM cards.

There were two candidates for this high speed interface, both derived from existing standards, but with partially reduced functionality and different contact layout. One candidate was the Multi Media Card (MMC) interface, and the other was USB full speed. It took quite a while until ETSI (the European Telecommunication Standardisation Institute) eventually standardised a variant of the USB interface as the high speed interface for smart cards early in 2007.

This decision was great luck for the class of applications discussed in this paper, as the semiconductor industry now had the opportunity to develop smart card chips which would meet both the requirements for serving as a high-bandwidth SIM card and also for direct interfacing to PCs.

2 The Internet Smart Card

We will present here the concept of the Internet Smart Card which meets in our opinion all the requirements for easy inter-operation with IT equipment. Why it carries its name will be clear at the end of this section.

In the preceding section we discussed mainly the hardware aspects of interfacing smart cards. Although the availability of USB smart card chips is essential, some more steps have to be taken before we arrive at the envisioned solution which requires no additional hardware and no additional software drivers.

2.1 The Card Token Form Factor

The high bandwidth SIM card was standardised with the conventional smart card contact layout in mind. Two of the eight contacts according to ISO 7816 were "reserved for future use", and these contacts, C4 and C8 were chosen for the USB bus signals D+ and D-. Obviously this contact layout does not match with that one of a USB type A socket. Again, some kind of adapter would be needed to connect such a USB smart card to a PC, although it would have only a mechanical, not an electrical function.

A very helpful idea was the design of an alternative chip module as a carrier for the smart card chip. The conventional chip module has the well known appearance with six or eight gold contacts, and we designed a chip module with four stripes which resemble the contact layout of a USB plug. This USB chip module can be placed into a standard sized smart card body just like the conventional one, using the same production equipment. A pierced outline as is known from SIM cards, enables easy removal of a small part which would fit into a USB socket.

Fig. 1: Sample Card Token

Only one problem remains: the thickness of a smart card is 0,8 mm whereas a USB plug should be about 2 mm thick. The smart card plug-in is inserted into a mechanical adapter made of two moulded plastic pieces, and the resulting assembly perfectly fits into the PC's USB socket. A hole in the adapter enables the user to insert the CardToken into his or her key ring or to fasten it to a lanyard etc.

It was mentioned that the card token can be produced with standard smart card manufacturing equipment, this includes also optical and electronic personalisation. The card can be shipped to the end customer by mail, together with the parts for the adapter. The end user removes the plug-in from the card and assembles the CardToken to its final form. Then the CardToken can be plugged into a USB socket of the user's PC and can be used immediately.

2.2 The Communication Stack

One of the main requirements for the Internet Smart Card was the abdication of additional drivers. However, as the relevant operating systems always rely on USB device drivers, this means that only drivers should be used that are already present in standard OS installations. It was another requirement that the "high level language" should be of a kind that is already spoken throughout the IT world.

These requirements brought us to design a communication stack based on the "Internet" and "TCP/IP" paradigms and collect all the necessary "glue" from the protocols already present on PCs. The choice of "Internet" protocols ultimately led to the designation "Internet Smart Card".

As already discussed above the physical communication layer is represented by the USB full speed interface specification, and this layer is widely determined by the chip hardware used. Full speed means that the hardware is capable of transporting 12 Mbits/s half duplex which scales down considerably in the real application.

The choice of a suitable data link layer is very crucial, as it determines the networking properties of the device. After earlier experiments with link layers based on serial communication, such as SLIP (serial line interface protocol) we turned to a more sophisticated ethernet emulation. This has the advantage that the Internet Smart Card appears to the PC as a fully routable network node.

Unfortunately there is a choice between as many as three different ethernet emulation protocols which can be used on PC equipment, and the choice is even dependent on the operating system.

Microsoft Windows supports the proprietary RNDIS (remote network device interface specification) protocol, for which drivers are already present in XP and Vista installations. Even the older Windows 2000 can be retrofit with an RNDIS driver. So, obviously the RNDIS protocol should be implemented on the Internet Smart Card.

Linux and Mac OS, on the other hand, support the more generic CDC-Ethernet protocol. Fortunately the protocol selection mechanism allows for an automatic protocol selection on the side of the Internet Smart Card without excessive overhead, therefore it is quite easy to handle both host operating systems.

The third data link layer protocol, EEM (ethernet emulation model) follows a W3C specification which is tailored exactly to the purpose of an ethernet link over USB, hence the functionality and also the implementation footprint are reduced as compared to the other protocols, However, EEM device drivers would have to be installed for all operation systems, and that violates the basic requirement "no additional drivers".

Based on the ethernet emulation the TCP/IP stack implementation seems conventional. However, the small memory footprint on the Internet Smart Card demands for some reduction in functionality. For example, in order to save buffer space the maximum transmission size is reduced to fit into just one USB message. The TCP/IP stack is accompanied by some little "helpers" that are commonly know, such as DHCP (dynamic host configuration protocol), DNS server (device name system), and a rudimentary ICMP (internet control message protocol) implementation which facilitates to "ping" the Internet Smart Card from the host and thus to check the health of the communication stack.

The whole communication stack of the Internet Smart Card follows a recommendation which has been formulated as a result of the project InspireD which was sponsored by the European Commission under the FP6 framework, and which was already reported on the ISSE 2005 in Budapest [LiMa05]. The objective of InspireD was the specification of a *Trusted Personal Device*, and the Internet Smart Card clearly is example for such a TPD.

2.3 The Application Protocol

A TCP/IP stack in general is capable of transporting quite a lot of application protocols. A by far not exhaustive enumeration yields FTP (file transfer protocol), HTTP (hypertext transfer protocol), SSH (secure shell), and many others. Clearly the choice of application protocol is determined by the application envisaged. A simplified statement might be that the TCP/IP stack on the Internet Smart Card supports any socket oriented application protocol. Considering the Smart Card Web Server discussed below the HTTP protocol was actually implemented.

2.4 The Smart Card Web Server

The Smart Card Web Server (SCWS) is the topmost software level on the Internet Smart Card that is unique for all possible applications. For the user it appears as any web server on the internet: it accepts HTTP GET and POST commands and, possibly after some processing, delivers HTML (hypertext mark-up language) pages as a response. For enhanced security the SCWS supports the protocols SSL 3.0 (secure socket layer) and TLS (transport layer security) which ensure authentic and confidential communication.

The content delivered can be a static HTML file stored on the card, it can also be a graphic file. Apart from the limited storage capacity which restricts the file size for the content and leads to simplified page layout there is practically the same user experience as if he was browsing the real internet. The capabilities of the SCWS can be significantly enhanced by the inclusion of one or more *servlets* which offer the possibility to implement web applications and provide dynamic web pages resulting from calculations and/or internal state changes. A very simple example of such a servlet function is the check of a Personal Identification Number (PIN) as a prerequisite to get access the other capabilities of the Internet Smart Card.

Parameters can be passed to the servlet either through the URL – a mechanisms also referred to as CGI (common gateway interface) – or through the content included in an HTTP POST request. The latter case would normally be used for the PIN check example cited above. The servlet has also access to the parameters passed by the HTTP protocol and can manipulate these in the HTTP response messages.

2.5 The Gateway Function

A very specific servlet function is that of a secure gateway. This servlet would display on a web page a list of links to external web services which can be called indirectly through the gateway. All content received from the external server would be received by the Internet Smart Card and possibly filtered or pre-processed before it would be sent to host browser for display. Any on-site user action would again be passed through the Internet Smart Card to the external server.

The filtering capability of the gateway servlet would allow the replacement or insertion of data in any direction. For example, credentials required to log into a web portal could be stored on the Internet Smart Card (only) and inserted into the data stream when required for user authentication. The user would not even have to know these credentials, and any malware on the PC would have no chance to get knowledge of these credentials and thus no chance to impersonate the user. This is especially true if the connection to the external server is secured by the SSL/TLS protocol. Although the data are passed through the PC's communication stack there is no way to read the confidential content.

As there is not enough memory on the Internet Smart Card to store complete HTTP messages the gateway functionality requires message processing on-the-fly which is best done by concurrent input and output data streams. A suitable operating system based on the microkernel approach allows for both multiple concurrent tasks and multiple threads with each task.

2.6 The Operating System

The following figure gives a coarse overview of the multitasking operating system. The microkernel which runs in system mode contains only those functions requiring global privileges. Primarily these comprise the scheduler, memory management, and inter-task messaging. All the other functions – especially those concerning I/O – are moved into *services* running in user mode with less privileges. Communication between services and application tasks is only possible through inter-task messages.

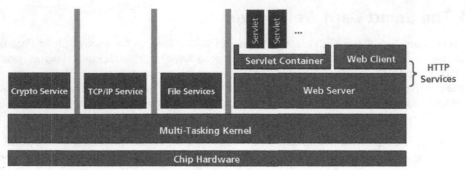

Fig. 2: The ISC multitasking operation system

2.7 Self Configuration

In the discussion about the communication stack it was already mentioned that the Internet Smart Card relies completely on device drivers which are already present in relevant PC operating systems. There remains, however, the task to associate the Internet Smart Card with the driver which is quite normal for USB devices but different from the pre-configured mass storage devices. For the vast majority of users who use Microsoft Windows XP or Vista the Internet Smart Card brings a built-in solution to this problem.

When the CardToken is inserted into the USB socket of a Windows PC, the Internet Smart Card is first identified as a CD-ROM drive. A start-up program is launched through the auto-start facility which tries to detect the status of the PC. If the PC is already configured for the Internet Smart Card, an *ISCservice* is running which takes care of the ISC. Otherwise the configuration program associates the ISC with the RNDIS driver and installs and starts the ISCservice already mentioned.

In any case the ISCservice issues a request to eject the emulated CD-ROM which, in turn, gives rise to the ISC OS to stop the CD-ROM emulation and to start the communication stack. On the PC the CD-ROM drive disappears and the ISC is re-enumerated as a network device which completes the automatic configuration.

Even if the automatic mechanisms should not work properly on a particular PC there is a chance to configure the PC manually. It is possible to start the start-up program manually from the Windows explorer, and it is also possible to eject the CD-ROM drive, e.g. by the context menu.

3 Applications

3.1 Network Configuration

When the Internet Smart Card is present on a PC it forms an additional network branch with its own IP address range which should be distinct from the other networks present. It is possible to provide a configuration page with the ISC where the IP address range can be changed should there be a conflict. Another possibility is to chose public IP addresses (you need just two: one for the ISC and on for the PC interface) which are guaranteed to be unique. In the following figure the choice of free IP addresses is demonstrated.

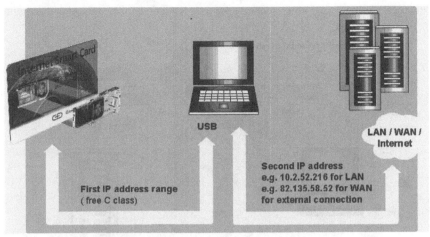

Fig. 3: Network Configuration

The Internet Smart Card can communicate with the external web server by using a feature present on most current PC operating systems which is called *Internet Connection Sharing* and implements NAT routing. If required for the specific application, Internet Connection Sharing is automatically enabled by the automatic configuration.

3.2 Authentication Gateway

Technically the Authentication Gateway is an application proxy which controls all the data traffic between the host and a server out on the Internet. In addition, the proxy plays an active role during the authentication of the user to the server. In the following we will explain how exactly the message flow and what the contribution of the Internet Smart Card is.

The user's first step in using the Authentication Gateway is to enter a URL like https://isc.intern into the request field of his browser where `isc.intern` is the host name of the Internet Smart Card. With this command he establishes a secure SSL connection to the Internet Smart Card web server. Next the Internet Smart Card asks for authentication with a user specific PIN number. After the user has entered the correct PIN number the Authentication Gateway is ready for its genuine function.

The Authentication Gateway displays a web page with several (at least one) links to external servers that are supported by the Authentication Gateway. After the user has clicked on one of these links the Authentication Gateway establishes a (preferably also SSL secured) connection to the external server. From the explanation above it is clear that for the Authentication Gateway Internet Connection Sharing must be enabled during the Self Configuration process.

For the course of the discussion it is assumed that the link to the external server invokes a login page. The Authentication Gateway presents the login page to the user on the host, but with the fields where he would normally enter his credentials disabled. The only action which is left to the user is to click on the "login" button. The login command is, as the first step, sent to the Authentication Gateway which inserts the user credentials which have been stored on the device in advance into the data flow and forwards it to the external server. Upon receiving the correct credentials the external server authenticates the user and proceeds as usual. Every web page from the server is sent to the Authentication Gateway and from there to the user's browser, and every action of the user is securely passed through the Authentication Gateway.

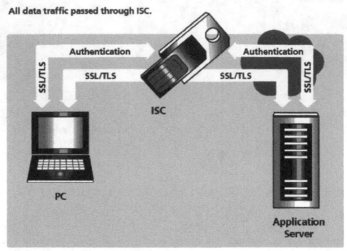

Fig. 4: Authentication Gateway

In order to achieve this message flow the Authentication Gateway has to analyse each web page passed through and to modify all links pointing to the server site into links pointing to itself, thereby preserving the original link in the form of a specific CGI parameter. This enables the Authentication Gateway to reconstruct the original URL when one of such links is activated by the user in the course of his action.

The question how the server list with the stored credentials comes into the Authentication Gateways needs some further consideration. Basically there are two possibilities: either the links and credentials are loaded during a personalisation session when the Authentication Gateway is prepared for a specific user. This would be the case when the Authentication Gateway is issued – like conventional smart cards – by an institution which wants secure access to its own server portal.

The other possibility to build the server list is that the user purchases a "blank" Authentication Gateway and adds servers at will in special training sessions. In such a training session he would enter his credentials by himself, and the Authentication Gateway would store the server link and the user credentials. After this training session the Authentication Gateway would be used exactly as described above.

It should be noted that the external server need not be aware that the credentials are provided by the Authentication Gateway rather than by the user himself, especially in the second case. When the first possibility is chosen it is, in turn, not necessary that the user knows his credentials used for login. This enhances security drastically, because he cannot loose or give away what he actually does not know. Also it is not possible for Trojan horse malware to record credentials that are never typed on the user's keyboard. As all the traffic between the browser and the portal web server is passed through the Internet Smart Card, this mode of operation is also called the *full content protection* mode.

3.3 Transaction Authentication

In this application the Internet Smart Card is used "only" to secure a specific transaction within a web session running in the normal way between a user and an external web server. Most of the web session is not critical, so it is not necessary to divert all traffic through the Internet Smart Card as in the previous example.

The critical transaction – which is essentially a high-level "commit" – is initiated when the user clicks on a specific button. The link on this button points to the Internet Smart Card and contains a session ID and a specifically generated random number from the server. Before the Internet Smart Card continues with the task requested, the user has to self-authenticate by entering his PIN number – just to make sure that someone else is not misusing his Internet Smart Card.

The Internet Smart Card can now proceed in one of two distinct ways. Using the same communication approach as explained in the section about the Authentication Gateway the Internet Smart Card establishes an SSL connection to the server authenticating itself to the server with an SSL client certificate. So the server is sure that a genuine Internet Smart Card is making the request. The Internet Smart Card uses a card specific key to generate a signature of this transaction, this also involves card specific data, such as a card ID number and a card generated random number, thereby ensuring that a captured signature cannot be used in a replay-attack.

The server recognises that the signature from the Internet Smart Card is correct in the context of the transaction and eventually performs the action requested.

The Transaction Authentication protocol requires a mutual authentication between the Internet Smart Card and the server before the transaction signature is actually generated. In the example explained above the mutual authentication is achieved by the exchange of server and client SSL certificates. By re-design of the messages exchanged – employing elements of secure messaging according to ISO 7816-X – it is possible to avoid the overhead of establishing a separate communication channel just for the purpose of mutual authentication.

In this latter communication model HTTP re-direct commands are used to communicate indirectly between browser and server and vice versa for the purpose of mutual authentication. The necessary data exchange is achieved by URL-encoded parameters. The browser executes these re-directs and thus forwards the authentication data. In practice there is a combined message flow comprising both device authentication and transaction authentication in that order.

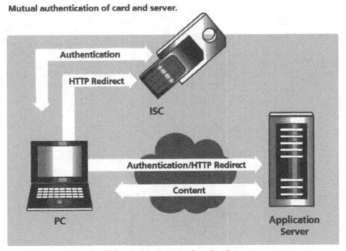

Fig. 5: Mutual Authentication

This operational mode is also designated as *transaction authentication* mode. Because the data exchange between Internet Smart Card and server is on top of HTTP commands, it is not suitable for the transport of bulk data, such as complete web pages. In some cases it is advantageous that the transaction authentication mode of the Internet Smart Card does not require Internet Connection Sharing to be enabled, therefore the two networks, one comprising the PC and the Internet Smart Card, and the other one reaching out to the internet, remain completely separate on networking level. It also makes no difference for messaging whether the PC has immediate internet access or whether an internet access proxy is in between.

4 Conclusion and Outlook

In this paper we have tried to outline the technical considerations that have led to a new form factor and a new generation of smart cards. These Internet Smart Cards combine low costs, compared with conventional smart cards or with token solutions, with ease of use.

In the conference talk we will also present some examples from the real world to demonstrate that the technology is available and can be supplied.

References

[LiMa05]   Linke, Andreas; Manteau, Laurent: Report on the European Research Project Inspired: The Fututre of Smart Cards. In: Paulus, Sachar; Pohlmann, Norbert; Reimer, Helmut (Editors): ISSE 2005 – Securing Electronic Business Processes, Friedr. Vieweg & Sohn Verlagsgesellschaft, 2005, p. 274-281.

Hardened Client Platforms
for Secure Internet Banking

C. Ronchi · S. Zakhidov

EISST Development Laboratories
edl@eisst.com

Abstract

We review the security of e-banking platforms with particular attention to the exploitable attack vectors of three main attack categories: Man-in-the-Middle, Man-in-the-PC and Man-in-the-Browser. It will be shown that the most serious threats come from combination attacks capable of hacking any transaction without the need to control the authentication process. Using this approach, the security of any authentication system can be bypassed, including those using SecureID Tokens, OTP Tokens, Biometric Sensors and Smart Cards. We will describe and compare two recently proposed e-banking platforms, the ZTIC and the USPD, both of which are based on the use of dedicated client devices, but with diverging approaches with respect to the need of hardening the Web client application. It will be shown that the use of a Hardened Browser (or H-Browser) component is critical to force attackers to employ complex and expensive techniques and to reduce the strength and variety of social engineering attacks down to physiological fraud levels.

1 Introduction

The slower penetration and adoption of online banking compared to other Internet transactional activities is a clear indication that both the financial institutions and the end users are aware of the high vulnerability of current e-banking platforms. Recent FFIEC regulations requiring two-factor authentication in financial business are aimed at mitigating the risks associated with the use of such Internet-based applications and services. The rise in the variety and sophistication of cyber fraud and identity theft points, however, to the strong need to provide protection well beyond the simple perimeter level. In fact, the focus of attacks is consistently moving from the authentication/identification steps to the manipulation of the user interface and to sophisticated and powerful social engineering schemes.

A recent comprehensive report [Oecd08] from the OECD warns that: "The past five years have indeed brought a dramatic surge in the use of malware to attack information systems for the purpose of gathering information, stealing money and identities or even denying users access to essential electronic resources." In particular, a new wave of threats has emerged that directly attacks the Web browsers by means of malware capable of monitoring/modifying the user interface elements on-the-fly and of fooling the users in believing that they are carrying out a totally secure transaction. The most serious threats are actually a combination of Man-in-the-PC (MITPC) and Man-in-the-Browser (MITB) attacks with the power to hack any transaction without the need to control the authentication process. Using this approach, the security of basically any authentication system can be bypassed, including those using SecureID Tokens, OTP Tokens, Biometric Sensors and Smart Cards. To grasp the relevance of these threats, it suffices to note that the necessary technology and know-how required to craft a malware capable of carrying out such attacks is currently widely available and affordable to even low budget criminal operations.

N. Pohlmann, H. Reimer, W. Schneider (Editors): Securing Electronic Business Processes, Vieweg (2008), 367-379

To counteract this potentially devastating new generation of attacks, two principal approaches have been recently proposed, both of which are based on the use of dedicated client devices. We will refer to these platforms as the ZTIC and the USPD solutions and have chosen to discuss these in detail mainly because they represent two alternative approaches to secure Internet banking, regardless of the details of their possible future implementations.

The ZTIC position statement on the security of current e-banking platforms can be summarized as follows [Ztic08]: "Firstly, the SSL/TLS connection used to secure the communication between client and server ends on the potentially unsafe client PC. Secondly, the display and keyboard of the client PC is used for all interaction with the user. Consequently, there is no truly reliable way for the user to verify that she does connect to a genuine server nor can she decide whether the information displayed on her screen is genuine or not". The ZTIC solution therefore places prime focus on the parents-of-all-threats, *i.e.* the vulnerabilities of the TLS connection and of the host PC interface elements, and proposes to implement a provably secure TLS channel between the Bank server and a client device, equipped with interface elements (display, buttons, etc.) external and independent from the host PC. The high level architecture of the ZTIC platform can be depicted as follows:

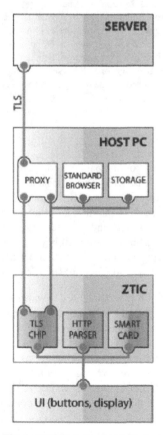

Fig. 1: ZTIC high level architecture

The USPD position statement on the new generation of e-banking platforms can be summarized as follows [Crsz08]: "The attack vectors employed by hackers are determined by a least-effort maximum–gain approach and can exploit very effectively the standard browsers' security vulnerabilities and the e-banking applications' usability flaws. The use of a Hardened Browser (or H-Browser) component is critical to force attackers to employ complex and expensive techniques and to reduce the strength and variety of social engineering attacks down to physiological fraud levels." The USPD platform therefore places prime attention on protecting the client environment in which the customers are operating by hardening the Web browser component and considers this an essential element to achieve higher protection against all type of attacks, even when the TLS channel between the Bank server and the client device can be shown to be provably secure.

The high level architecture of the USPD platform can be depicted as follows:

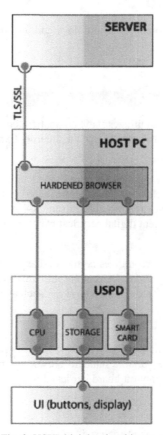

Fig. 2: USPD high level architecture

The distinctive attributes of the two architectures are the employment of an H-Browser and of an encrypted local storage in the USPD case, and the implementation of a provably secure TLS channel and external display/buttons in the ZTIC case. It should be stressed that the external User Interface elements are optional in the UPSD device, while they are fundamental elements of the ZTIC architecture. Finally, while both the ZTIC and USPD employ a provably secure TLS channel to communicate with the server, we will also discuss the security of platforms which implement the server channel using only on-board hardened resources (SSL library and hardware cryptography functions).

In this paper, we will first review the security of current e-banking platforms and then discuss the advantages of hardening the client application domain from the point of view of the attackers' return on investment (ROI). In fact, the ultimate deciding factor directing the target of hacking activities worldwide is mainly the expected financial return weighted against the required efforts. In other words, our analysis will attempt to show that the e-banking Institutions should be first and foremost concerned about achieving *practical* security against realistic attack scenarios, utilizing a variety of protection mechanisms which must force hackers to constantly upgrade and redesign their attacking tools and techniques.

2 Opening Scenario

Let us start by laying a common ground for terminology and understandings, which will allow us then to quickly focus on the core issues.

2.1 Definitions

Definition 1:
A 1G e-banking platform is one which utilizes static authentication credentials and relies totally on pre-installed PC resources (e.g. a standard browser, such as Internet Explorer, and a persistent password).

Definition 2:
A 2G-A e-banking platform is one which utilizes time-limited authentication credentials generated with the use of an external device and relies totally on pre-installed PC resources (e.g. a standard browser, such as Internet Explorer, and a challenge-response or scratch-list system). A 2G-B e-banking platform is a 2G-A system which utilizes a client digital certificate kept in the host PC certificate store.

Definition 3:
A 3G e-banking platform is one which utilizes certificate-based authentication credentials generated/ stored using an external device (e.g. Smart Card or crypto-chip) and avoids as much as possible to use any PC resources, employing a portable standard browser, such as FireFox, pre-installed on the device itself.[1]

Definition 4:
A 4G e-banking platform is a 3G platform with a hardened browser (H-Browser) pre-installed on the external device, which replaces the portable standard browser component of 3G[2]. A 4G platform can implement the TLS channel using only on-board hardened resources (SSL library and hardware cryptography functions).

Definition 5:
An attack is Scalable if it can be launched against a larger number of targets without requiring any new investments or synchronous human intervention. A Scalable attack can also exploit the results and resources employed during the first-hacking efforts – technical, logistic and financial – on all subsequent attacks.

---

1 This platform is currently being deployed by the Swiss bank, Migros to all its existing e-banking customers using Kobil's M-IDentity devices: http://www.prosecurityzone.com/Customisation/News/IT_Security/Finance_and_Banking_Security/USB_based_secure_internet_banking_at_Migros_bank.asp
2 This platform has been selected for deployment by three Swiss Cantonal banks, based on the Crealogix CLX Stick devices: http://www.crealogix.com/de/ResourceImage.aspx?raid=5141

Definition 6:
A confusion attack is a series of attention-catching decoy events caused by malicious software aimed at confusing the end-user with respect to the actual processes occurring in the background. In this sense, just by casting reasonable doubts on the system's security, a confusion attack may also have the only goal of inducing a user to abort a transaction which could've otherwise been successfully and securely completed.

2.2 Objectives

A suitable e-banking platform should provide end users with means for successfully completing secure transactions over Internet. Three principal indicators which could be considered when evaluating the appropriateness of an e-banking platform are:

- T_A (the ratio of the number of aborted transactions over the total number of attempted transactions)
- T_L (the ratio of the number of completed legitimate transactions over the total number of attempted transactions)
- T_F (the ratio of the number of completed fraudulent transactions over the total number of attempted transactions)[3].

It is an established fact that today's standard Web browsers are highly vulnerable to phishing and to attacks on the credentials, the certificate store and the user interface elements. At the same time, social engineering attacks exploit to the maximum extent possible the interface manipulation vector in order to confuse the end-users and to steer them to initiate and complete a fraudulent transaction without realizing it. Indeed, the low cost (few thousand Euros) and skills required for carrying out a successful scalable attack are easily affordable by individual hackers and criminal organizations worldwide, thereby making such threats potentially crippling for the entire e-banking community.

Of course, not only the security, but also the privacy of the e-banking transactions is totally dependent on the confidentiality assurances provided by the host PC interface elements (display, keyboard, etc.). It is a rather widespread opinion within the community of e-banking security experts to consider securing the end-users' PC a lost battle, not worth the investment of any considerable resources. While this may very well be the case, it is important to stress that attacks which require the installation of PC components or modifications to the operating system's core constitute a minority of the current known threats. At any rate, these attacks are generally only partially scalable thanks to the mid-term responsiveness and effectiveness of perimeter defenses (anti-viruses, operating system patches, etc.). As we will show in the next section, these facts suggests that the first line of protection of e-banking platforms should always focus on the target providing the highest ROI for hackers, *i.e.* the Web browser.

2.3 Attacks Metrics

In this section we will profile the landscape of threats against existing e-banking platforms, starting with a description of the main attack vectors exploited in three principal attack categories: Man-in-the-Middle (MITM), Man-in-the-PC (MITPC) and Man-in-the-Browser (MITB). In what follows, we will use the following abbreviations for referring to the different attack vectors:

- BROW-CERT   = Browser Certificate Store Attack
- BROW-DNS   = Browser DNS Library Attack
- BROW-SSL   = Browser SSL Library Attack

---

3   Where, of course: $T_A + T_L + T_F = 1$

- CERT-SPOOF   = Certificate Spoofing
- CH-BREAK   = Channel Breaking
- CODE-BREAK   = Code Breaking
- DNS-SPOOF   = DNS Spoofing/Poisoning
- DOM-CAPTCH   = DOM Data Capturing/Patching
- HFILE-MAN   = Hosts File Manipulation
- INFACE-MAN   = Interface Manipulation
- IP-RROUTE   = IP Rerouting
- KEY-LOG   = Keystroke Logging
- MEM-DUMP   = Memory Dumping
- MEM-PATCH   = Memory Patching
- OS-CERT   = Operating System Certificate Store Attack
- OS-DNS   = Operating System DNS Library Attack
- OS-SSL   = Operating System SSL Library Attack
- SCREEN-C   = Screen Capturing
- SCRIPT   = Script-based Attack
- SOC-ENG   = Social Engineering

Table 1: Taxonomy of Attacks.

	1G	2G-A	2G-B	3G
Man-in-the Middle	CH-BREAK	CH-BREAK	CERT-SPOOF	N/A
	CERT-SPOOF	CERT-SPOOF	DNS-SPOOF	
	DNS-SPOOF	DNS-SPOOF	IP-RROUTE	
	IP-RROUTE	IP-RROUTE	SOC-ENG	
	SOC-ENG	SOC-ENG		
Man-in-the-PC	IP-RROUTE	IP-RROUTE	IP-RROUTE	IP-RROUTE
	HFILE-MAN	HFILE-MAN	HFILE-MAN	HFILE-MAN
	INFACE-MAN	INFACE-MAN	INFACE-MAN	INFACE-MAN
	KEY-LOG	KEY-LOG	KEY-LOG	KEY-LOG
	MEM-DUMP	MEM-DUMP	MEM-DUMP	MEM-DUMP
	MEM-PATCH	MEM-PATCH	MEM-PATCH	MEM-PATCH
	OS-CERT	OS-CERT	OS-CERT	OS-DNS
	OS-DNS	OS-DNS	OS-DNS	SCREEN-C
	OS-SSL	OS-SSL	OS-SSL	SOC-ENG
	SCREEN-C	SCREEN-C	SCREEN-C	
	SOC-ENG	SOC-ENG	SOC-ENG	
Man-in-the-Browser	BROW-CERT	BROW-CERT	BROW-CERT	BROW-CERT
	BROW-DNS	BROW-DNS	BROW-DNS	BROW-DNS
	BROW-SSL	BROW-SSL	BROW-SSL	BROW-SSL
	DOM-CAPTCH	DOM-CAPTCH	DOM-CAPTCH	DOM-CAPTCH
	INFACE-MAN	INFACE-MAN	INFACE-MAN	INFACE-MAN
	KEY-LOG	KEY-LOG	KEY-LOG	KEY-LOG
	SCRIPT	SCRIPT	SCRIPT	SCRIPT
	SOC-ENG	SOC-ENG	SOC-ENG	SOC-ENG

It is interesting to note that although both the 2G-B and 3G platforms can implement a mutually authenticated SSL session, only the 2G-B is vulnerable to Man-in-the-Middle attacks. The reason is that the 3G platform employs a hardware device with a tamper-proof non-exportable certificate store, while the 2G-B platform relies on critical PC resources to store the client certificate and to establish the SSL connection. Therefore, attackers can still implement several techniques to exploit the operating system's vulnerabilities to compromise the SSL client certificate and gain direct control over the TLS channel and then fool the user to believe he's communicating with the Bank server.

It is, however, also fair to say that this type of attack is much less likely to succeed and therefore less frequent than a direct attack to the Web browser, as shown in the next table, where we provide a comparative estimate of the frequency distribution[4] of hacking efforts among the three main classes of attacks:

Table 2: Distribution of Attacks

	1G	2G-A	2G-B	3G
Man-in-the Middle	Very High	High	Very Low	N/A
Man-in-the-PC	Low	Very Low	Low	Very Low
Man-in-the-Browser	Very Low	Low	Very High	Very High

The above frequency distributions are only partially mirrored by the estimated cost[5] of crafting and distributing a successful attack, as shown in the following table:

Table 3: Cost of Attacks

	1G	2G-A	2G-B	3G
Man-in-the Middle	Very Low	Very Low	Low	N/A
Man-in-the-PC	Low	Low	Low	Low
Man-in-the-Browser	Low	Low	Low	Low

As we can see, the price tag of hacking the current e-banking platforms (including those employing the most advanced authentication systems) is beyond doubt quite enticing even for low budget criminal operations. On the other hand, a second critical parameter which strongly influences the targeting decisions of hackers is the possibility to widely distribute an attack to millions of end-user, *i.e.* the ability to achieve global scalability:

Table 4: Scalability of Attacks

	1G	2G-A	2G-B	3G
Man-in-the Middle	Very High	Very High	Low	N/A
Man-in-the-PC	Low-High	Low-High	Low-High	Low-High
Man-in-the-Browser	High	High	High	High

As shown in the above table, all attacks exploiting the Web browser's vulnerabilities enjoy high scalability, while Man-in-the-PC attacks are somewhat less scalable, since they require some form of transaction steering in real-time or exploit operating system's vulnerabilities which can be offset by updates to the PC's perimeter defenses (*e.g.* anti-virus, anti-malware, operating system updates).

All previous considerations contribute to the final table shown below, where we provide an estimate of the Return on Investment for the hacking efforts against each e-banking platform. The main purpose

---

4 Very Low = Below 5%; Low = Between 5% and 45%; High = Between 45% and 75%; Very High = Over 75%
5 Very High = Estimated cost of attack > € 50,000; High = Estimated cost of attack between € 20,000 and € 50,000; Low = Estimated cost of attack between € 5,000 and € 20,000; Very Low = Estimated cost of < € 5,000

here is to help focus the attention and protection efforts on the elements which are the most likely targets of criminal activities, simply based on a least-effort maximum-gain logic:

Table 5: ROI of Attacks

	1G	2G-A	2G-B	3G
Man-in-the Middle	Very High	Very High	Low	N/A
Man-in-the-PC	High	High	Low	Low
Man-in-the-Browser	High	High	High	High

3 Future Scenarios

In the previous section we analyzed the vulnerabilities of the current e-banking platforms and, following a practical ROI approach, we determined that the criminal efforts in most cases will focus on hacking the Web browser. This conclusion *per se* is quite obvious and not particularly original, since the need to secure the Internet banking client application has been the source of intense debating already for several years [Guph06]. However, the novelty emerging from the most recent approaches to securing Internet banking lies in the concept of coupling the client software hardening to a hardened client device and to periodic secure code upgrades. In fact, as we will see, tightly integrating the application and device domains can allow to achieve much higher security against threats coming from all the three main attack categories considered in the previous sections.

3.1 The H-Browser: Chimera or Argos[6]?

The increased sophistication and effectiveness of the attacks against Internet banking platforms must be counteracted by an equal improvement in the protection of all the components which are the likely targets of the attacks. Unfortunately, this should include protecting elements which are also external to the strict domain of the client application which the customers use to carry out their transaction. For example, it can be argued that hardening the interface elements of the Web browser alone is not effective against window overlay attacks[7] which effectively bypass the browser's defenses and exploit instead the vulnerabilities of the operating system interface. In fact, this is the prime reasoning of those who advocate a solution capable of securing the transactions independently from any PC interface or operating system library components, such as the ZTIC platform described in the Introduction. The weak point of this approach, however, lies in the fact that the end-users must still rely on those very interface elements which are considered totally untrustworthy and are most likely compromised. In other words, the instructions to users of a ZTIC-like e-banking platform, would sound something like this:

1. Don't trust your PC and your Web Browser
2. Approve a transaction only if the data shown on the external display are correct
3. If in doubt, abort the transaction by pushing one of the buttons on the device

---

6 In Greek mythology, Argos was known for having a multitude of eyes and with his keen vision was regarded as an almost perfect mythological guard creature. Chimera was instead a fire-breathing she-monster having a lion's head, a goat's body, and a serpent's tail, an imaginary monster compounded of many incongruous parts.

7 In a window overlay attack, malicious interface elements (e.g. an invisible window) are placed on top of the legitimate interaction windows, allowing hackers to obtain sensitive information and to control the transaction.

This procedure requires the end users to trust and rely only on the ZTIC's small external display and buttons, while still carrying out the bulk of the transaction using the standard Web browser and PC interface components. Unfortunately, this mode of operation not only degrades the usability of the overall procedure, but more importantly makes the platform itself vulnerable to malicious confusion attacks which may lead to a massive increase in transaction failures and support calls from concerned customers. Indeed, the lack of any hardening on the side of the client application inevitably exposes the e-banking platform to usability limitations, to confusion attacks and to data sniffing, all of which strongly potentiate the social engineering attack vectors.

All the above considerations suggest the following requirements for an effective hardening of the client component, which we call the H-Browser, needed to safeguard the e-banking platform against an extended set of threats:

A] The H-Browser should be fully shielded against direct Man-in-the-Browser attacks, by employing techniques such as: minimal code build[8], anti-reverse engineering, anti-dumping, anti-debugging, anti-patching, anti-monitoring, anti-attaching, dynamic and polymorphic process memory encryption, as well as session data encryption.

B] The H-Browser should include protection for Man-in-the-PC attacks directed against the PC interface elements, employing techniques such as: anti-key logging, anti-screen capturing, anti-steering, anti-overlay and anti-interface manipulation.

C] The H-Browser should be fully integrated with an external hardware device, equipped with a tamper-proof crypto-chip or Smart Card for the storage of digital certificates, capable of executing on-board all the cryptography functions required to establish and maintain a mutually authenticated SSL session with the Bank server.

D] The H-Browser should implement additional protection against various attacks with the use of an Access Control List (ACL) enforcing the catalog of allowed URLs and the corresponding handling and permission rules.

The figure below summarizes these requirements by showing the protection layers of a specific implementation of the H-Browser built by the EISST Development Laboratory as the core component of a 4G-USPD e-banking platform:

---

8 The minimal build concept incorporates several hardening requirements, among which:
- no extensions (BHO's, Active-X, Java, plug-ins, extensions, etc.)
- stripped and static compilation
- no DOM externally available
- no user scripts
- no disk cache

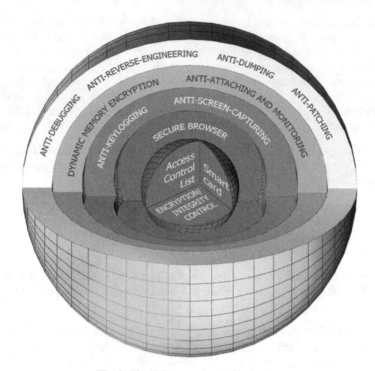

Fig. 3: The H-Browser Protection Layers

It should be stressed that the ultimate goal of such exhaustive hardening and protection activities is realistically that of raising the stakes of the hacking efforts, forcing criminals to invest considerable high-skill resources (*e.g.* several months and over €100,000) on their first-cracking attempt. Furthermore, the use of code obfuscation techniques, which are both polymorphic and virtualized, implies that periodic updates of the executable code will force renewed cracking before a new effective attack code can be exploited. In other words, the regular practice of secure updates can prevent the first-effort hacking patches from being exploited for large scale attacks, which may ultimately become uneconomical.

3.2 New Attack Metrics

Let us now analyze the attack indicators of the 4G, ZTIC and USPD platforms and discuss how the utilization of the H-Browser can modify the attack metrics obtained in Section 2.3. The first impressive improvement is visible in the drastic reduction of the viable attack vectors exploited by the three principal attack categories, as shown in the Table below:

Table 6: Taxonomy of Attacks

	4G	ZTIC	USPD
Man-in-the Middle	N/A	N/A	N/A
Man-in-the-PC	CODE-BREAK	INFACE-MAN	CODE-BREAK
	SOC-ENG	KEY-LOG	SOC-ENG
		MEM-DUMP	
		MEM-PATCH	
		SCREEN-C	
		SOC-ENG	
Man-in-the-Browser	CODE-BREAK	DOM-CAPTCH	CODE-BREAK
	SOC-ENG	INFACE-MAN	SOC-ENG
		KEY-LOG	
		SCRIPT	
		SOC-ENG	

It is important to notice that in order to successfully carry out any attack against a 4G or USPD platform, the Code Breaking vector must first be activated. This is of course not true for the ZTIC platform, which is instead vulnerable to a host of attack vectors, noticeably Interface Manipulation, Key Logging, Screen Capturing and Script-based attacks. All platforms are clearly exposed to Social Engineering, but the lack of any additional protection of the Web browser and PC interface elements strongly potentiates the effectiveness of such vectors against the ZTIC platform. This is reflected in the next Table's entries, where we provide a comparative estimate of the exepected frequency distribution of hacking efforts based on the complexity of the viable attacks vectors:

Table 7: Distribution of Attacks

	4G	ZTIC	USPD
Man-in-the Middle	N/A	N/A	N/A
Man-in-the-PC	Very High	Very Low	Very High
Man-in-the-Browser	Very Low	Very High	Very Low

On the other hand, since higher complexity translates into bigger hacking expenses, it is rather straightforward to obtain the following estimated costs for crafting and distributing a successful attack against the three platforms:

Table 8: Cost of Attacks

	4G	ZTIC	USPD
Man-in-the Middle	N/A	N/A	N/A
Man-in-the-PC	Very High	Low	Very High
Man-in-the-Browser	Very High	Low	Very High

At the same time, the viability of Interface Manipulation and Script-based vectors guarantees High scalability to hacking activities against the ZTIC platform, as shown below:

Table 9: Scalability of Attacks

	4G	ZTIC	USPD
Man-in-the Middle	N/A	N/A	N/A
Man-in-the-PC	Low	Low-High	Low
Man-in-the-Browser	Very Low	High	Very Low

All the indicators above contribute to the final estimate of the Return on Investment for the hacking efforts against each e-banking platform, as shown in Table 3.5:

Table 10: ROI of Attacks

	4G	ZTIC	USPD
Man-in-the Middle	N/A	N/A	N/A
Man-in-the-PC	Very Low	Low	Very Low
Man-in-the-Browser	Very Low	High	Very Low

4 Summary and Conclusions

The Return on Investment (ROI) of the various attacks considered in the previous sections shows clearly that it is much more profitable to launch an attack against a ZTIC e-banking platform than against a 4G or USPD platform. This conclusion holds true despite the fact that the ZTIC architecture can attain provable security on the TLS channel component.

Indeed, based on the above analysis, we believe it is reasonable to conclude that:

- The overall security of a 4G e-banking platform is higher than that of a 3G platform.
- Because of ZTIC's use of an unprotected browser, causing a higher exposure to social engineering attacks, and also because of the inability of the ZTIC platform to protect the privacy of the e-banking transactions:
  $T_F (ZTIC) > T_F (4G) > T_F (USPD)$
- Because of ZTIC's usability limitations and as a possible result of targeted confusion attacks on the ZTIC e-banking users:
  $T_A (ZTIC) > T_A (4G) > T_A (USPD)$
  $T_L (ZTIC) < T_L (4G) < T_L (USPD)$
- The overall security of the USPD e-banking platform is higher than that of a 4G platform, which in turn is higher than that of the ZTIC platform.

Unfortunately, the use of a standard browser exposes any e-banking solution to a multitude of low cost, highly profitable attacks which can be the target of concerted efforts from the hacking community. On the other hand, the 4G platform – which still doesn't establish a provably secure TLS channel with the Bank server, but employs only on-board resources for communicating with the server and, more importantly, integrates the hardened browser component– can raise the stakes of the hacking efforts and lower the malicious activities' overall ROI, discouraging the deployment of massive and scalable attacks.

These conclusions may at first seem theoretically/esthetically disturbing and somewhat counterintuitive. However, consider the following attack scenario on the ZTIC platform:

1. The user plugs the ZTIC device in the PC and establishes a provably secure connection with the Bank server using a standard, unprotected browser;
2. A simple trojan had previously infected the browser and now displays a message to the user saying: "You have received a wire transfer from Mr. So&So, who has later informed us that this wire was sent by mistake. We regret any inconvenience and kindly ask you to acknowledge this communication."
3. The user looks at his "trojan-manipulated" account balance displayed in the browser window and checks that the total amount in his account indeed adds to an extra €50.000!

4. The user clicks on the Acknowledge button. This action starts a legitimate transaction over the provably secure TLS channel for €50.000.

5. The user approves this legitimate transaction by pushing the ZTIC button (after all, it's not his money that he's returning!) and the funds are sent to Mr. Hacker.

Now, this attack is unlikely to be successful in the majority of cases. But it also has a very low cost, it can be launched on a massive scale and has a very large ROI. The hackers just need to count on a few percentage of successful attacks in order to make their efforts worthwhile. There are potentially a multitude of similar social engineering attacks which are made viable by the use of an unprotected Web browser and PC interface.

In conclusion, we believe times are definitely mature for the deployment of a new generation of e-banking portable platforms which can increase today's security by orders of magnitude, while protecting the Bank's infrastructure investments and coexisting with the current authentication and back-end systems. The use of a Hardened Browser component is essential to make MITB and MITPC attacks uneconomical and to reduce the strength and variety of social engineering attacks down to physiological fraud levels (determined basically by the human tendency to trust others).

We believe that the new Smart Card-enabled Smart-USB devices with a portable hardened browser packed with on-board advanced protection features – including a provably secure TLS channel – will soon provide the alternative of choice for all advanced e-banking systems. Employing old generation e-banking technologies will before long expose the slow adopters to increasing levels of attacks as other Banks implement these new generation systems, which enjoy a lower hacking ROI. In fact, as we have shown, the use of an H-Browser has indeed many advantages, including the very unique *practical* advantage of forcing the hackers to follow the (almost-unacceptable for them) canon: "No *new* pain, no *new* gain".

References

[Oecd08]   OECD: Malicious Software (Malware): A Security Threat to the Internet Economy. (http://www.oecd.org/dataoecd/53/34/40724457.pdf).

[Ztic08]   Weigold, Thomas et al: The Zurich Trusted Information Channel: An Efficient Defence against MITM and MS Attacks. IBM Zurich Research Lab – (http://www.zurich.ibm.com/pdf/csc/ZTIC-Trust-2008-final.pdf).

[Crsz08]   Ronchi, Corrado and Zakhidov, Shukhrat: A Road Map Towards a Practically Secure and Portable e-Banking Platform. EISST Development Lab – Technical Report ECS2008-02.

[Guph06]   Gühring, Philipp: Concepts against Man-in-the-Browser Attacks. http://www2.futureware.at/svn/sourcerer/CAcert/SecureClient.pdf

Securing Flash Technology: How Does It Look From Inside?

Helena Handschuh[1] · Elena Trichina[2]

[1] Spansion (EMEA), 105 rue Anatole France
F-92684 Levallois-Perret, France
Helena.Handschuh@spansion.com

[2]Spansion International Inc., Willi-Brandt-Allee 4
D-81829 Munich, Germany
Elena.Trichina@spansion.com

Abstract

In this paper we discuss memories with their basic protection mechanisms and the results of the evaluation of a modern high-density flash memory by an Information Technology Security Evaluation Facility (ITSEF). In a second part, we address the notion of Authenticated Flash and present some authentication methodologies used for existing Flash devices.

1 Introduction

Standard programming devices use two main types of memory: volatile and non-volatile memory. Volatile memory such as SRAM or DRAM typically serves as a scratch pad for storing intermediate computation results or for run-time variables or more generally as a read and write working storage. Volatile memories are very fast in read and write access but loose their contents once the device is powered off. On the other hand, non-volatile memory such as EPROM, EEPROM and Flash is typically used for storing application programs and system code, static application data or user data. Non-volatile memories are able to keep their contents when the power supply is turned off, but once the power is back on, they can also be electrically erased and reprogrammed. This is a major advantage when compared to volatile memory. However, read access and write times are much less efficient and volatility is traded for performance. Exactly which quantities of volatile or non-volatile memory are used in a system is dictated by the system needs. It is a trade-off between speed, density, flexibility, power consumption, reliability, cost and time to market.

In this paper we are interested in studying intrinsic protection mechanisms of a standard Flash memory as compared to other types of non-volatile memories. We first describe basic protection mechanisms on Flash memory sub-systems as they exist today in the market and explain their properties.

Then, we describe the results obtained by submitting a typical high-density Flash memory device to a security evaluation facility and discuss what needs to be done to protect content of such a memory appropriately when it is integrated into a tamper resistant system on chip. Finally, we add a description of more advanced security features of a so-called Secure Authenticated Flash and provide some typical use cases for such memories.

N. Pohlmann, H. Reimer, W. Schneider (Editors): Securing Electronic Business Processes, Vieweg (2008), 380-389

2 Standard Flash Protection Mechanisms

Among the more basic protection mechanisms of Flash memory are those which allow to control or authorize the read and write access to given parts or sectors of the memory array. Such features allow protecting the memory array both against *accidental* and *malicious* read, write and erase operations. Nowadays, we observe a tendency to shift away from hardware implementation of these mechanisms and to move towards more flexibility and thus more software oriented protection features.

The most common security features available on Flash are the following [HTri07]:

1. **Out-of memory map area used for unique device identification or other security purposes**. This area is typically up to 256 bytes and is not directly addressable by any external read, write or erase command. It is located outside the regular addressable memory space and can only be accessed by an internal dedicated finite state machine. It is one-time programmable by a (secret) sequence of commands and can be used to store data such as unique device IDs or the like.

2. **Mechanisms protecting from accidental code and data modification**. These include for example the fact that no write command is accepted on power-on. The complete control over a write operation can be ensured by a special PIN# combination; pins can further be protected and made inaccessible by packaging. In addition, no write cycles are accepted when the power supply on VCC is less than a pre-defined lock-out voltage. To protect against accidental and random voltage glitches, very short pulses (below 5ns) on pins do not initiate any write cycles.

3. **Hardware-based One Time Programmable (OTP) sectors**. These can be implemented in hardware by setting the write enable WE# pin permanently low after the device has been programmed. This typically prevents the entire flash from being erased or re-programmed. In order to add flexibility and prevent only some (e.g., boot code storage) sectors from being erased or written, a special Write Protect Pin (WP#) is used by silicon manufacturers to lock out specific sectors by setting the write enable pin WE# permanently low after programming once.

4. **Flexible low-level software-based OTP**. For even further flexibility, a special OTP (One-Time Programmable) bit is associated with each sector. This bit can only be read by the embedded microcontroller or finite state machine (FSM). The OTP protection bits can only be set once by a special (secret) sequence of commands. Once the bits are set, they cannot be unset. When the bit is set, the sector can only be read; there is no access for write/erase operations.

5. **Firmware or software-based sector protection**. In this case, re-programmable "soft" protection bits are associated with each sector. They can be set and re-set only by specially defined (secret) sequences of commands; they provide a low-level software-based OTP mechanism in the following sense: the chosen combination of soft OTP bits can be changed a number of times according to the requirements of the application; they can also be "locked" by a special long sequence of commands which cannot be undone (this is sometimes called "sealing"). Sealing the configuration of soft OTP bits can be done at any stage in a chip's lifetime, but only once.

6. **Conditional access to locked sectors by password-protected mechanism**. In this case, the previous configuration can be unlocked by presenting a correct 64 to 128-bit password. The password is stored outside the accessible flash memory address space; it is programmed by a special sequence of commands (only once) and itself "locked" by an OTP bit. It can be read and compared only by a special command and cannot be accessed by applications.

3 Evaluating the Robustness of the Protection Mechanisms

In order to assess the intrinsic level of robustness of a high-density Flash memory as compared to other types of non-volatile memories such as EPROM or EEPROM, a high-density Flash memory device has been submitted to a security evaluation facility. In this chapter, we provide an overview of the results obtained from this external evaluation.

3.1 Targets and attack families

When a memory device or a smart card IC is submitted for evaluation, a security laboratory tries to "attack" the system by somehow forcing it into abnormal behaviour using a number of different techniques.

The specific goals the lab is trying to reach are the following:

- Being able to **read or modify executable code, data or secret data** which is stored in the memory or on the device. Secret data can include targets such as cryptographic keys or secret initial values.
- Being able to **modify the device behaviour** somehow in order to exploit this for a subsequent security attack.

The types of techniques used to achieve these goals can be categorized in the following way:

- **Reverse engineering**: this technique typically uses heavy manufacturing and testing equipment and allows learning what the device or memory looks like and how it was built. This equipment is usually found in any silicon manufacturer's factory.
- **Physical modification**: this technique uses standard silicon manufacturing equipment such as focused ion beams (FIBs) or probe stations in order to modify the contents of memory cells or the logic inside the device.
- **Functional stress**: this technique includes applying environmental stress to the memory or device, and trying to inject computation faults.
- **Signal processing**: this technique includes the so-called side-channel attacks which exploit data leakage via measurements on execution time, power consumption or electromagnetic radiation.
- **Software attacks**: this last technique is mostly applied at the application level and exploits weaknesses in protocols, cryptographic algorithms, or software implementation bugs.

3.2 Obtained Results

Unsurprisingly, the results obtained on the submitted device were the following:

1. Depackaging using fuming nitric acid: this step could be performed quite easily.
2. Cross section using a scanning electron microscope (SEM): in this step the evaluator was able to identify the metal layers and the polysilicon layer of the device.
3. Mechanical probing using a FIB and a probe station: this task was achieved on the top level bus lines; this means that very sensitive lines should be buried below a few metal layers so that they cannot be easily reached. Indeed, it was **not possible to probe buried lines due to the tiny technology dimensions** the evaluator had to face.

4. Delayering using wet, dry and/or mechanical etching: successive oxide and metal layers were easily removed and the evaluator was able to identify big logic blocks, some memory cells, and some specific pads. It was however **not easy to analyze the High Density Flash technology and memory design because of the tiny dimensions and glue logic used in the design.**

5. Memory cell qualification for data imaging: this step **could not be done within a reasonable assigned time frame due to tiny technology dimensions.**

The outcome is thus that standard attack techniques seem to work efficiently on this Flash device, but due to very tiny dimensions, it remains more difficult to reverse-engineer and analyse in details.

3.3 Robustness analysis and signal processing

The next step in the evaluation was to analyse the robustness of the submitted Flash to environmental stress and to fault injection. Environmental stress was generated by applying a power supply above or below the specified operating range, temperatures above and below the normal operating range and by exposing the memory to UV light after decapsulation. Fault injection was achieved in the following way: the memory was submitted to power supply glitches in the form of rapid transients, to external clock frequency glitches, white light flashes and a red laser beam. Being able to generate faulty behaviour can typically have interesting consequences on crypto processors executing code or computations; it can change the contents of memory cells or on-chip registers. The final attacks which were applied on the submitted Flash memory were side-channel attacks trying to exploit data leakage using power and electromagnetic attacks.

The obtained results were the following:

1. **Abnormal Voltage**: At low voltage, write and erase operations are impossible. At high voltage, read operations result in occasional bit errors. Write operations result in correct data being written but there may be some side-effects. For example a few more bits may be programmed at the same time. Erase operations are successful but some programmed cells may remain unerased.

2. **Protected Sectors**: Erasing and Programming protected sectors under high voltage results in error messages and is thus impossible to achieve. The sector protection mechanism is robust.

3. **Abnormal Temperature**: The normal operating range given for the device was from -80°C to +200°C. Attempts to execute operations above 200°C result in the Flash memory becoming non-operational. Once the memory cools down, it does not become operational again immediately. This could be used to temporarily block the erase operations on Flash and to use the device without being able to securely erase sensitive data.

4. **Exposing the OTP area to UV radiations:** whatever the tests performed, there is absolutely no reaction. The submitted device is not vulnerable to UV light exposure.

5. **Voltage glitches:** Up to 20ns, glitches have no effect on read operations. Above this, the higher the voltage glitch, the more memory bits are corrupted. Short glitches have no effect on write operations. Long glitches above 100ns result in occasional uncontrolled bit errors. Very long glitches result in aborting the write operation. This could be exploited to prevent raising flags like for IC's in smartcard applications.

6. **Light attacks:** they are more successful on the logic than on the memory cells and can substantially modify the results of a read operation. Write operations are not impacted.

7. **Laser flashes:** laser pulses are able to force the device into reading specific values even though the contents of the memory remains unchanged. Write operations have mixed results; either nothing happens, or some data is written to a nearby (wrong) address. In order to write data in a

slightly more controlled way, one would need to know the exact device configuration, glue logic, addressing scheme, the internal details of the implementation of the write operation and one would have to induce a very long exposure.

8. **SPA and EMA attacks:** on both read and write operations, the strength of the signal seems to follow a bit transition model. One can distinguish between many bit flips and a few bit flips but cannot even recover the Hamming weight of the data. This could lead to template attacks requiring several hundreds of samples, but there is no immediately exploitable vulnerability.

3.4 Conclusions drawn from the evaluation

As a conclusion on the evaluation of the robustness of protection mechanisms of the submitted high-density Flash memory device against classical hardware attacks, one can make the following points:

- Invasive attacks are much more difficult on such small technology. More resources (time, cost of equipment) are required for successful invasive attacks.
- The investigated technology is far less error prone when stressed than other types of non-volatile memory, specifically against fault attacks. There is no identified vulnerability to UV light radiation.
- Unsurprisingly, using such high-density Flash memory device in tamper-resistant applications such as smart cards will require additional hardware protections such as voltage detectors, temperature sensors, glitch detectors and light sensors...

4 From Authenticated Flash to Trusted Execution Environment

Increasingly, embedded and mobile platforms require non-volatile, in-system reprogrammable memories of various densities; Flash provides the means of building such systems from standard, discrete off-the-shelf components. However, for many security-sensitive applications of-the-shelf solutions represent certain dangers – even the systems that were designed to withstand the attacks can be hacked by skillfully exploiting known vulnerabilities of the components [Stei05] or by replacing those with "good" properties with fully compatible components with "bad" properties. Flash manufactures strive to improve their end of system security by enhancing Flash protection mechanisms with cryptographic functionality. In what follows we describe some proposed solutions.

4.1 Enhancing Flash chip with cryptographic functionality

On the hardware level, security requirements for embedded and mobile systems are generally concerned with:

1. Code and data integrity/authenticity, which can be further detailed as:
    a. Protection against any unauthorized code and data modification (integrity);
    b. Protection against unauthorized read and/or copy of code and data (confidentiality);
    c. Protection against attacks involving substitution on board of a "native" component (e.g. Flash chip with authorized software) with another chip (e.g. Flash which has "pirated" software that by-passes conditional access control) as well as protection against inter-chip signal probing attacks or attacks via external physical interfaces.

2. Controlled upgrade of software "in the field" (e.g., activating premium functions in engine control, replacing "buggy" software, etc.)

The initial idea of achieving the first set of objectives had been by introducing a means for authentication between the Flash chip and the host CPU on power-on. Krypto™ Flash developed by ST Microelectronics was the first product enhanced with cryptographic functionality capable of handling device authentication [Secu05], extended later to command authentication [Bert07].

4.1.1 Architecture

The architecture of Flash chips enhanced with cryptographic functionality comprises of the following building blocks:

- Memory array sectors including
  - Top or bottom OTP sectors typically used for storing boot code
- uC (standard flash microcontroller) with the FSM enhanced with
  - Security logic to handle authentication
- Peripherals such as CFI (common flash interface)
- Few hundred bits of OTP area programmed at manufacturing
  - Typically stores unique device identifier but may also be programmed with a random number
- Few hundred bytes of user-programmable OTP area (available for reading only from a special state of the flash uC)
  - Can be used to store user-programmable secret key binding flash to the device
- Hardware key-dependent message authentication code (MAC) function which is either
  - based on a block cipher such as DES; or
  - based on a hash function such as SHA-1
- Monotonic counters that are used for:
  - for nonce (i.e., a non-repeatable value) generation
  - for counting failed authentication attempts
- Hardware random number generator (RNG) to generate random challenges

4.1.2 Authentication between on-board components

The authentication procedure on power-on takes place between the Flash chip and the host CPU; it was designed in order to prevent an unauthorized read access from a parallel processor (which is one scenario often employed, for hacking Set Top boxes). The authentication is done locally, by means, e.g., of a keyed-hash message authentication code (HMAC) cryptographic function and is based on a shared between the host and the Flash secret key; the key must be unique per device.

On power-on, the CPU sends a "Read" access request (as we know, for standard Flash chips, write and erase operations are not available on power-on). As an answer, the Flash sends to the CPU a "Ready to Authenticate" response which includes a nonce (e.g., a value of a specially maintained monotonic counter which is increased after each authentication attempt to exclude replay attacks). The host executes HMAC on this challenge using the shared secret key, and sends the result to the Flash. The Flash executes HMAC on the same nonce using the same shared secret key, compares the result with the received from the CPU value, and if they are equal, the CPU is granted a read access to the Flash chip. From now on, the CPU starts downloading code from a boot sector, as usual.

If the CPU wants to make sure that it is booting from the "legal" Flash chip, a mutual authentication procedure must take place. For this, prior to reading from the Flash, the CPU sends to it an "HW authentication request" which includes a new challenge (i.e., a newly generated by the CPU nonce). The Flash executes HMAC on this challenge using its secret key and sends the result as an answer to the authentication request to the CPU, which also executes HMAC on its challenge with its secret key, compares the results, and if they are the same, the CPU continues booting from the Flash.

Of course, for an authentication scheme to be robust, the host CPU has to have a small amount of embedded immutable memory with BIOS containing HMAC code; this code must be the first to be executed by the CPU. In addition, the CPU must store a unique per device shared key in embedded non-volatile immutable memory; this can be achieved with fuses. For mutual authentication, the host CPU must be able to generate a fresh challenge; this implies that it embeds a RNG.

In [ScTP08] this ability to handle mutual authentication has been used on order to build a very cost-efficient mobile trusted platform, where persistent state information pertinent to secure boot and in particular persistent but updatable information, such as values of monotonic counters, is kept on a discrete Flash chip enhanced with cryptographic functionality.

4.1.3 Authenticated commands

Two problems are apparent. One is that device authentication on power-on does not solve the second objective, namely, secure "over the air" and in the field software downloads/updates from authorized parties. Another, related problem is that if system or application code is buggy, it can be used for example for downloading unauthorized or malicious applications. As Flash is read/written through the standard commands, it is not capable of distinguishing who is executing an operation. The idea of authenticated commands is to add this functionality building on capabilities of Flash device enhanced with cryptographic functionality. The general scheme of an authenticated command is shown in Figure 1 [Bert07]. It works as follows.

The host CPU and the external Flash chip share a secret key. The host requests an access to the Flash chip with an authenticated command. The Flash microcontroller decodes the command and generates a challenge (a freshly generated random number RND can be used as a challenge; if there is no on-board RNG, then a challenge can represent a new value of a monotonic counter which is increased after each authentication attempt) and sends it to the host. The host CPU takes the message m = (CMND|| DATA||RND) comprising the concatenation of the command CMND, the parameters DATA and the received challenge RND and creates message authentication code of this message by computing keyed HMAC function MAC= $HMAC_K(m)$ using a shared secret key K.

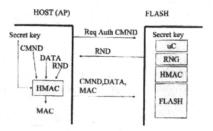

Figure 1: Authenticated Command concept

Then the host CPU sends to the Flash a response in the form [CMND, DATA, MAC]. The Flash micro-controller takes the command and data, concatenates them and computes HMAC of the message using the challenge RND and the shared secret key K. If the resulted MAC is equal to the MAC sent by the host, the Flash chip executes the command.

The principle of local authentication of commands can be extended in such a way that different actors (e.g., device manufactures, telecom operators or other service providers, as well as the device owner) can manage their own memory segments using their own keys. For this, Flash memory can be partitioned into different domains; each domain is associated with a different key, and access to each of the domains may be only granted to an entity which knows the respective key. The command execution flow is similar to the one described above. However, the key provisioning and management problems may soon become too complex.

4.2 Authenticated Flash

A solution which allows solving a problem of key provisioning is based on Public Key cryptography (assuming that there exists a suitable, efficiently maintained public key infrastructure, PKI). Another advantage of PKI is that with the public key digital signature the commands can be authenticated (i.e., their digital signatures verified) remotely. This extension has been addressed by the Authenticated Flash concept announced by Intel [AlvR07].

Authenticated Flash considerably extends the concept of authentication by providing a number of additional hardware and logical components. Instead of performing mutual authentication between the host CPU and the Flash chip locally, it authenticates the individual command requests based on digital signature verification protocols which can be carried out over the network.

The main architectural enhancement is that Authenticated Flash, in addition to SHA-1 based HMAC, also has integrated Public Key Accelerator (PKA) for RSA signature verification. To support generation of random challenges it also has integrated hardware RNG.

This allows for a very versatile usage of Authenticated Flash memory in trusted mobile and embedded platforms. First of all, with the integrated PKA and RNG, Authenticated Flash can fully support all necessary actions required for secure boot, as well as remote attestation and remote authentication. Second of all, Authenticated Flash allows flexible memory partitioning at both, design time and during device operations.

Different blocks of memory may be accessed in different ways: either unconditionally as for "normal" Flash device or with authenticated commands. The system designer can specify at the system design time authenticated and legacy ranges. In other words, the memory space is split (logically) into two different groups. The first (legacy) group comprises the memory blocks which are accessed with standard Flash commands. The second (authenticated range) group comprises blocks access to which is via authenticated commands only. To be able to do so, an RSA public key is associated with the authenticated range at the system design or system personalization time. A private counterpart of this RSA public key must be generated and stored at the host side. If the host possesses embedded or discrete Trusted Computing Module, the private key may be generated and securely stored on such a module. Alternatively, it can be stored on a removable trusted token or even on a remote trusted server.

Every host command to any block within the authenticated range must be signed by the RSA private key. Upon receiving a command request from the host CPU, the Authenticated Flash verifies the command signature, and if valid, executes the command. If the signature is not valid, the operation is terminated.

4.3 "Gatekeeper" chip

The subtle problem with dynamic logical partitioning of a Flash memory array into ranges with different access rules is that it affects mechanisms of Flash File Systems (FFS), in particular, efficiency of handling erase operations and wear-leveling. The problem stems from the fact that erasing in Flash arrays is done by very large sectors, and that an erase operation degrades the quality of memory cells and thus has to be handled by the FFS in such a way that the parts of the Flash device are worn-out "evenly". Just like with hard disc drives, de-fragmentation of sectors occurs naturally during the device life time, with different blocks within the same sector belonging to different files. Thus, when the sector has to be erased (the decision made by a special wear-leveling algorithm) some of its blocks may still have valid data, in which case these data have to be copied into a new location. The reader may guess how it complicates actual implementation of the Authenticated Flash and its FFS.

Spansion offered a different solution: instead of modifying the Flash chip, it modified an access to this chip by providing an additional "secure processor" which acts as a gatekeeper and handles all memory accesses, secure or not, being "sandwiched" with the Flash chip in a multi-chip package [SpSe07]. A secure processor contains its own ARM7-TDMI CPU, cryptographic cores, including RSA accelerators, AES, and RNG. It also has embedded boot ROM, RAM, and it handles both, host (e.g., baseband or application processor) and Flash interfaces. This secure processor provides all cryptographic services (such as computation and verification of digital signatures, integrity checks, mass "on-the-fly" encryption/decryption, authentication protocols...). It also handles "logical" partitioning of flash array into ranges and rich access control policies.

The secure processor provides a trusted execution environment for applications running on the host, which can only access it via carefully designed API.

5 Conclusion

As several other types of memories, Flash memory has advantages and drawbacks both from a technical and security point of view. The evaluation described in this paper was performed on a regular high-density Flash memory which did not include any particular smart-card oriented tamper-resistant mechanisms. This approach allows focusing on the strong and weak points of the technology which in turn allows deciding what kind of additional security features need to be integrated into high-density Flash memory-based smart secure objects.

While Flash devices move beyond basic protection mechanisms, embedding cryptographic functionality and complex access control to memory blocks, robustness of new solutions also needs to be carefully evaluated. This is the objective of future work.

References

[AlvR07]   Alves, Tiago, Rudelic, J.: ARM Security Solutions and Intel Authenticated Flash. White Paper, 2007. http://www.arm.com/pdfs/Intel_ARM_Security_White_Paper.pdf

[Bert07]   Bertoni, Guido: Secure Non-volatile Memory: Is it a New Trend for the Security of Embedded Systems? Presented at the LSEC & IMEC Security Forum 2007. http://www.lsec.be/upload_directories/documents/6STM_Securenonvolatiememory_Bertoni_Guido.pdf

[SpSe07]   Flash Memory Modules Add Security to Handsets. Electronicstalk, 2007. http://www.electronicstalk.com/news/ssi/ssi125.html

[HaTr07]   Handschuh, Helena and Trichina, Elena: Securing Flash Technology. In: Breveglieri, L., Gueron, S., Koren, I., Nacccache, D., Seifert, J.-P. (Eds) 4th Int. Workshop on Fault Diagnosis and Tolerance in Cryptography – FDTC 2007. IEEE CSP, 2007, p. 3-17.

[ScTP08]   Schellekens, Dries, Tuyls, Pim, Preneel, Bart: Embedded Trusted Computing with Authenticated Nonvolatile Memory. In: Lipp, P., Sadeghi, A.-R., and Kock, K.-M. (Eds): TRUST 2008, LNCS 4968, 2008, p.60-74.

[Secu05]   Security Features for NOR Flash Memories. AT Microelectronics, 2005. http://www.st.com/flash

[Stei05]   Steil, Michael: 17 Mistakes Microsoft Made in Xbox Security. Presented at the 22nd Chaos Communication Congress, Berlin, Germany, 2005. http://www.xbox-linux.org/wiki/17_Mistakes_Microsoft_Made_in-the_Xbox_Security_System

German Workshop:
European
Citizen Cards

Deployment of German Electronic Citizen Cards in Banking: Opportunities and Challenges

Matthias Büger

Group Technology & Operations
Deutsche Bank AG
matthias.bueger@db.com

Abstract

The German federal government plans to issue an electronic citizen card (eID) in 2009, replacing the current identity card (Personalausweis). Since the eID should be good for identification in E-government as well as E-business applications, it is aimed to be used in the banking environment. One application would be opening a bank account in the internet. If this was possible, the process would be much easier than today. However, German law still requires a physical ID card. We will discuss the opportunities and the challenges of possible usage of eID in banking.

1 Introduction: authentication & banking

From an IT perspective, a financial transaction consists of receiving data from a customer, processing data and finally giving some notice back. This is the structure of a money transfer, a brokerage order or any other standard transaction in online banking. Hence, the most efficient way to deal with such transactions is to exchange the data electronically.

The challenge is, however, that the data transferred is highly sensitive: Information must not be presented to any unauthorized person. This applies in particular to account information. Data received must be proven authentic before the bank can process a transaction. In case of a legal claim, the bank has to give evidence that the transaction was initiated by the customer. Unfortunately, the Internet itself does not come along with a security layer. There is an old (well known) cartoon, which shows what lies at the heart of the problem.

"On the Internet, nobody knows you're a dog."

Figure 1: Lack of authentication in the Internet

N. Pohlmann, H. Reimer, W. Schneider (Editors): Securing Electronic Business Processes, Vieweg (2008), 393-397

1.1 The PIN-TAN-system

This question of authentication is not new to banks. Ever since banks started online banking, authentication had to be guaranteed. In the 1990s a system named PIN-TAN (personal identification number – transaction number) was established in Germany. Every customer obtains letters with a PIN and a list of TANs. The PIN is needed to log-in to the system, while every transaction is authorized by a TAN. Today, Deutsche Bank (like many other German banks) uses indexed TANs (iTAN), where each TAN in the list has an index and the bank asks to enter a special TAN. This results in a higher level of security. Standard phishing attacks, where an attacker spies out TANs and tries to use them later, do not work with iTAN. There are also other flavours of the PIN-TAN-system. For example, a TAN might be sent on demand as a SMS (sometimes called mobile TAN or mTAN). Overall, PIN-TAN-systems work more or less alike: the user authorises a transaction using a knowledge he had received from the bank before.

Despite academic discussions, in practice the PIN-TAN-system has been working successfully for many years. User acceptance is high: In Germany, there are more than 10 million online banking accounts, and nearly all of them are based on some flavour of the PIN-TAN-system.

There are many reasons for the success of the PIN-TAN-system. The most prominent are: The system is low cost and easy to use. The customer needs only Internet access; neither extra hardware nor software needs to be installed.

1.2 The quest for a nation-wide authentication infrastructure

Though the PIN-TAN-system works successfully, it requires an initial contact when the account is opened. Thus, a nation-wide authentication infrastructure would be helpful. Therefore, most German banks joined the German Signature Alliance (see [Büger, Esslinger, Koy]) founded in 2003 and discussed how a nation-wide authentication infrastructure could be implemented. Such an infrastructure should be based on public key cryptography and work under the legal frame of the European Signature Directive.

Deutsche Bank was one of the fore-runners in the alliance and offered a signature card "dbSignatur-Card" in October 2003, which could be used for online banking as well as other applications or securing Emails.

Figure 2: Usage of dbSignaturCard in online banking

The dbSignaturCard has successfully proved evidence that it is possible to combine bank cards, public key cryptography and online banking. The demand for signature cards, however, is still small. This was not unexpected: There was no killer application for signature cards. Usage of electronic signatures required new hardware (card reader). In online banking, existing systems (PIN-TAN) work quite well. In E-government, the number of use cases is still small. A key finding of the Signature Alliance was to emphasize the importance of the business case. When a document is signed electronically, German signature law states the recipient of a document has the right to ask for the status of the underlying certificate at no cost. In addition, the provider has to store and deliver this information for many years (in some cases up to 30 years). This raises the cost for the provider, which he will charge to the cardholder when issuing the card. The benefit, however, is with the application provider (who can streamline his processes), while the cardholder stays with the cost. No wonder that the demand for signature cards stayed small.

In this situation the introduction of the German electronic citizen card is promising: The card will be issued by the federal government and is mandatory to all citizens. Some questions, however, remain open: How many years will it take before a significant number of citizens are equipped with the new eID? Will there be inexpensive contactless card-readers? Will the identification function of the eID be sufficient to fulfil the legal requirements to open a bank account? If a qualified signature is still needed, how difficult and costly will it be to upgrade the eID?

2 Possible usage of eID in online banking

There are two scenarios in which electronic citizen cards can be used: First, a new customer can be identified with the eID when the account is opened. Today, opening an account online is a difficult and expensive process. The second scenario is to use the eID as an alternative to PIN/TAN in online banking (like the dbSignaturCard). We will have a closer look at both cases:

2.1 Opening an account with an eID

From a bank's perspective, opening an account in the Internet is one of the most interesting use cases for an electronic citizen card. German law[1] states that the bank has to identify the person when opening an account. The money laundering law[2] describes the way the bank has to identify its customers: The identification may either be based on the (physical) ID card, the passport or a qualified electronic signature. For an online account, identification based on a physical ID card or passport is a complicated and expensive process: In this case, banks use the Postident[3] scheme, which means that the customer is identified at the local post office or by the postman. As long as the customer has not shown-up at the post office, the bank is not allowed to open the account. The cost (about 5-8 EUR per identification due to company information[4]) is charged to the bank. In the context of the Internet, this identification scheme is a kind of workaround which is necessary since there is no online authentication.

---

1 [AO] § 154 AO (2) Niemand darf auf einen falschen oder erdichteten Namen für sich oder einen Dritten ein Konto errichten oder Buchungen vornehmen lassen, Wertsachen (Geld, Wertpapiere, Kostbarkeiten) in Verwahrung geben oder verpfänden oder sich ein Schließfach geben lassen.

2 [GwG] § 1 Abs. 5 GwG Identifizieren im Sinne dieses Gesetzes ist das Feststellen des Namens aufgrund eines gültigen Personalausweises oder Reisepasses sowie des Geburtsdatums, des Geburtsortes, der Staatsangehörigkeit und der Anschrift, soweit sie darin enthalten sind, und das Feststellen von Art, Nummer und ausstellender Behörde des amtlichen Ausweises. Die Identifizierung kann auch anhand einer qualifizierten elektronischen Signatur im Sinne von § 2 Nr. 3 des Signaturgesetzes erfolgen.

3 Postident-Verfahren: Identification either at the post office or by the postman when the post is delivered.

4 Based on company data Deutsche Post AG, July 2008

The fact that the qualified electronic signature is explicitly mentioned in the money laundering law shows that the government sees the need to allow opening an account online. As mentioned above, the identification functionality of the electronic citizen card is not a qualified signature. Thus, based on the current legislation, the eID could only be used to identify the customer if it was upgraded with a qualified signature.

The German federal government recently announced that they plan to review the underlying regulations will be reviewed before the eID is enrolled. In particular, an adjustment of the money laundering law is discussed which should allow to open a bank account based on the identity functionality of the eID. Such an adjustment would make sense since the law aims to prevent money laundering by identifying the person – which the identification function does. There seems to be no need for a qualified signature. On the other hand, the regulator does not always treat the electronic channel in the same way as the traditional one. For example, in Germany paper based invoices need not to be signed. But if an invoice is electronically transferred, a qualified signature is mandatory. Today, this rule even prevents banks from delivering electronic account statements to its business clients, because under some circumstances account statements have to be treated as invoices.

Before processes are redesigned, the question has to be answered whether a qualified signature or the identification functionality of the eID is used. In case a qualified signature is still required, the same signature can be used to approve transactions. Thus, there is not much process redesign needed. The problem remains that many customers might not have an upgraded eID.

In case identification based on the eID was sufficient, the process would become more complicated. There would be no signed contract and no kind of specimen signature with the bank, neither a handwritten nor an electronic one. How could the signature on an order be verified? The bank could send a letter with authentication data (like TANs) to the customer's address. This address is known as part of the identification process. The bank could also ask the customer to return a copy of his ID showing the hand-written signature. Alternatively, the bank could ask the customer to visit a retail branch and show his ID before the first transaction is cleared. Since identification by eID requires an adjustment of the existing law, it is academic to discuss how the process would look like. But is clear that using the identification functionality of the eID would require significantly new processes.

2.2 Approval of online banking transactions with an eID

As mentioned above, there are a number of successfully running mechanisms. Customers might, however, wish to use the eID for their convenience. In particular, if a customer has numerous accounts or has already opened the account using the eID, he might ask to use his eID instead of the established banking systems.

As in the last section, we have to distinguish between two scenarios: In case the eID comes along with a qualified signature, it is an (relatively) easy task to use this signature in online banking. Deutsche Bank, for example, has already integrated the dbSignaturCard in its online banking. In order to use the qualified signature on the eID, most part of the existing process could stay unchanged. The bank has only to map the eID to the account before the first usage. This can be done when the account is opened or with the help of the existing authentication schemes.

If the bank can only use the identification functionality of the eID, procedures become more complicated. Clearly, an online banking user could identify himself with the eID when entering the online banking portal. But how can a transaction be approved? Identification is not a signature. Hence, transactions cannot be signed. Due to German jurisdiction, clicking on a button (e.g. "I accept") could be a volition.

In this case the bank has to prove evidence that the customer (and no one else) clicked on the button. One way might be to ask the customer to identify himself directly before the click, but it is not clear if this is sufficient. In any case, such new procedures would be subject to discussion with the regulator.

3 Conclusion

Secure identification and authorisation of transactions are crucial for online banking. Since the Internet itself does not come along with such an infrastructure, the banking industry has set-up their own[5]. This infrastructure, however, requires a first contact and does not work for opening an account in the Internet.

Deutsche Bank welcomes the new German citizen card because it supports the bank in making the Internet a secure place. If well established, such an infrastructure can be used to open accounts or approve online banking transactions.

An important decision is still open to the regulator: Will the identification functionality of the eID be sufficient for banking purposes or will the qualified signature remain the only key to electronic accounts? Clearly, processes would be easier with signatures. The problem is, however, that we would run again into a critical mass problem since the citizen card has to be upgraded with costs, before it can be used.

When the above stated decision is finally made and the legal situation is set, the bank will decide how the new citizen card can be integrated into the processes. Using the eID in banking is an opportunity and can bring online banking forward. This is, however, not an easy task and there are still legal and organizational challenges ahead.

In addition, it would be helpful if the German citizen card fits in an international framework from a technical and legal perspective. On the technology side, this means usage of European standards. On the regulatory side, a legal framework for secure identification in the Internet should be rather European than national. It should be avoided that the legal effect of identification by citizen card differs by country.

References

[AO]   General German Fiscal Law "Abgabenordnung", issued October 1st 2002 (BGBl. I S. 3866; 2003 I S. 61), latest amendment December 21th 2007 (BGBl. I S. 3198).

[GwG]   German Money Laundering Law "Geldwäschegesetz", issued October 25th 1993, Bundesgesetzblatt (BGBl. I S. 1770), latest amendment December 21th 2007 (BGBl. I S. 3089).

[Büger, Esslinger, Koy] Büger, Matthias; Esslinger, Bernhard; Koy, Henrik: Das deutsche Signaturbündnis. In: DuD – Datenschutz und Datensicherheit No. 3, 2004, p. 133-140.

---

5 PIN-TAN and others, as stated above

Security Requirements for One Stop Government

Georg E. Schäfer

Innenministerium Baden-Württemberg
Stabsstelle für Verwaltungsreform
georg.schaefer@im.bwl.de

Abstract

The highest ranking e-government solutions are based on one-window, one-click or one stop govern-ment concepts. For Europe, the EU services directive sets new requirements for e-government, that have to be met till December 2009. Simple, easy to understand and complete information is one requirement. The other requirements are, that the services covered by this directive shall be available electronically and at a distance (which means mostly "by Internet"). Acceptable solutions are digitally signed mails and, as an alternative or supplement, transaction oriented online services. To implement this, a one stop government with document safe is best practice.

Three more architectures are needed for up-to-date and complete e-Government: One is the Internal Mar-ket Information System, another is the Job Card architecture (or "Electronic Income Certificate") [1] and last but not least the model of S.A.F.E (Secure Access to Federated E-Justice / E-Government) for trusted domains.

These architectures require eCard or eID solutions and e-documents. [2] The powerful e-government architectures available today will be of no practical use if citizen and enterprises do not understand and trust in the basic underlying technologies. Pan-European solutions and conformity are the objective of the the European pilot project on eCards, where Germany participates among others with the eCard API of the Bundesamt für Sicherheit in der Informationstechnik and the public service portal www.service-be.de of Baden-Württemberg.

1 Overview on the Services Directive

The official name of the services directive is "DIRECTIVE 2006/123/EC OF THE EUROPEAN PAR-LIAMENT AND OF THE COUNCIL" of 12 December 2006 on services in the internal market, pub-lished in the Official Journal of the European Union on December 27 in 2006. It can be found on http://europa.eu together with the E-Government Action Plan (KOM(2006)173) dating from April 25, 2006.

The services directive uses its own definition of services (Art. 4). So services of the agricultural and industrial sector may be services covered by the services directive regardless of the taxonomy of econo-mists.

N. Pohlmann, H. Reimer, W. Schneider (Editors): Securing Electronic Business Processes, Vieweg (2008), 398-405

The goals and frameworks of the services directive seen from an IT perspective are documented in the following regulations:

- simplification of procedure (Art. 5)
- establishment of points of single contact (Art. 6), i.e. service providers seeking authorisations from several agencies need to address only one point of contact
- provision of services to fulfil the right to information (Art. 7)
- the general requirement that the member states provide administrative procedure especially to grant authorisations by electronic means (Art. 8)
- authorisation procedure (Art. 13)
- assistance for recipients (Art. 21)
- information on providers and their service (Art. 22)
- the regulation of chapter VI on administrative cooperation
- protection on personal data (Art. 43).

These requests lead to the development of three categories of IT applications:

- The European Commission builds and runs the Internal Market Information System (IMI) as a backbone system for the administrative support between member states. It is accessed with Internet browsers and provides no automatic interfaces at present. According to the rules contained in the service directive, service providers are not required to submit original documents when they apply for authorisations to offer their services in member states. So administrations will use after December 29, 2009 the IMI system, in order to check, if the documents submitted are a sufficient basis for the authorisations requested by the service provider. Taking into account that more than 1000 internal market regulations exist, the IMI system may in future be used not only for the currently intended purposes i.e. the professional qualifications directive and the services directive. For security considerations it is relevant, that IMI will contain very sensitive information about service providers. eCard and eID technology is necessary.
- The authorities of the member states responsible for the authorisations needed, and all agencies or authorities that become single points of contact, are obliged to create an internet web site, so that their administrational services covered by the services directive can be accessed via the internet. Surfing this web site is anonymous, or, as in www.service-bw.de with filtering mechanisms like "I inform myself as a service provider" or "I imform myself as an elderly couple". All competent authorities must provide their services "at a distance". This requires that service providers seeking authorisations use a qualified signature with eID or eCard technology.
- The screening of the regulations of the member states, that may have to be simplified or abolished due to the services directive, will be accomplished with the assistance of a database system. This system will contain all relevant regulations for authorisation schemes in the different member states concerning foreign service providers. The access is via the internet, so that service providers, member states and the commission can assess these regulations. This IT-system is not described here in more detail, as it may use a common architecture.

2 Short Description of IMI

The IMI system consists of

- a database of the competent authorities and of the users in these authorities,
- data catalogues for questions concerning the inter-administration communication. They are worded in all languages of the European Union. They can be translated automatically from one language to another.
- A kind of an e-mail system, that allows competent authorities from one member state to send requests to competent authorities of other member states in order e.g. to check the validity of a document that the service provider did not submit as an original or a officially accepted translated copy.
- Processing rules, e.g. for deleting documents after a specific period of time or for setting an alarm if a request is open for a longer time.

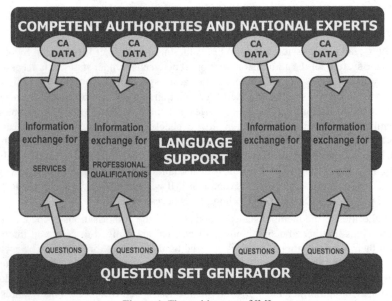

Figure 1: The architecture of IMI

IMI will be expanded according to the requirements of chapter VI "Administrative Cooperation" of the services directive. The current use of user-id and passwords for security is sufficient for exchanging information between administrations but will probably not be possible in the near future e.g. for dealing with alerts according to article 32.

3 Services Directive Requests Simplification and Usability

The services directive stresses the requirement that the relevant administrational procedures and the online systems of the member states become simple and easy to use. The following citations illustrate this concern:

- Where procedures and formalities examined under this paragraph are not sufficiently simple, Member States shall simplify them. (Art. 5 (1))
- Where Member States require a provider or recipient to supply a certificate, attestation or any other document proving that a requirement has been satisfied, they shall accept any document from another Member State which serves an equivalent purpose or from which it is clear that the requirement in question has been satisfied. (Art. 6 (3))
- The information shall be provided in plain and intelligible language. (Art. 7 (2))
- ... in a clear and unambiguous manner, that they are easily accessible at a distance and by electronic means and that they are kept up to date (Art. 7 (3))
- Member States shall ensure that the points of single contact and the competent authorities respond *as quickly as possible* to any request for information or assistance as referred to in paragraphs 1 and 2 and, in cases where the request is faulty or unfounded, inform the applicant accordingly *without delay*. (Art. 7 (4))
- access to a service activity and to the exercise thereof may be easily completed, at a distance and by electronic means (Art. 8 (1))
- schemes shall be based on criteria which preclude the competent authorities from exercising their power of assessment in an arbitrary manner. (Art. 10 (1))
- proportionate to that public interest objective; (d) clear and unambiguous; (e) objective; (f) made public in advance; (g) transparent and accessible. (Art. 10 (2))
- **But:** .... does not require those authorities to provide legal advice in individual cases (Art 7 (6))

The services directive sets new standards for usability. Only the best practices of content presentation, wording and suitability for disabled users shall meet these requirements.

Of great importance is the portal architecture, since simple e-mail or content presentation techniques will not meet the standards. Since the online system will accept scanned documents, as it allows the service providers applying for authorisations to submit their documents electronically and as it will allow the competent authorities to deliver their authorisations electronically, a storage area should be part of the IT architecture. This storage area must comply with the data privacy regulations. Encryption and electronic signature are necessary. The storage area will be like a safe for documents, thus a "document safe", secured by eCard and eID.

One-stop government denotes an infrastructure with a document safe, a storage area for formatted data (like names, birth dates, addresses, insurance numbers, addresses for water and energy supply companies, car registration identifications) and a functionality to start administration processes by "one key stroke". A typical application would be moving a household from one city to another. Well implemented, this can be done by sending specific information to all relevant organisations and displaying all other information according to what is needed. A one-stop government architecture is suitable for much more than only the implementation of the services directive.

This one-stop government or one-window solution gets high ranking in assessments. So much depends on trust and acceptance of citizen and enterprises.

4 Minimum Model for e-Government Citizen Portals

The services directive requests that not only the information and the services shall be provided in the Internet, but it also sets standards on how this shall be done. The interconnection of the information on the competent authorities and all other organizations (directory service), that may be useful to the service provider, the online services and the electronic forms, the explanation of the administrational procedures, the indexes to the whole system etc. shall be implemented within an integrated and secured IT system.

Starting from any competent authority the user can access name, e-mail address and phone number of the officer, the description of all administrative procedures and all forms. The document safe, as explained in chapter 4, is another indispensable component. To allow the service provider to submit his electronic and digitally signed documents for the various authorisations, a workflow engine is needed as well. The workflow engine transmits the formatted data and the relevant e-documents from the document safe to the competent authorities.

Minimum Modell for eGov Citizen Portals

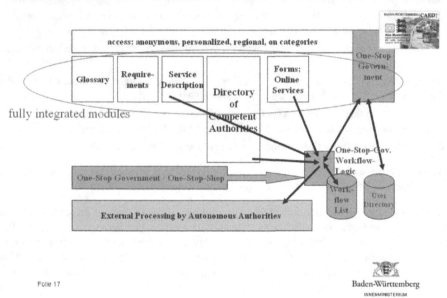

Folie 17

Baden-Württemberg
INNENMINISTERIUM

Figure 2: IT architecture for a citizen portal

What is missing for a full functionality portal is an e-mail server with e-mail boxes for citizens and enterprises.

This architecture is called a minimum model for the implementation of the services directive, as all components have a legal basis. E.g. article 21 requires that the recipient can choose to interact with the administration by the single point of contact or the competent authority. Article 21 Nr. 1 (c) requires that contact details of all organizations shall be given in a simple and easy to understand way. Such requirements lead to the above mentioned interaction between the modules of the minimum model.

A payment functionality will be necessary at least in those countries where, other than in Germany, an automatic direct debiting infrastructure (legal, organizational and technical) is not available. To enable flexible process management between administrations and private companies, a dynamic workflow and collaboration technique is essential, except in countries where powerful service providers bridge the gap between administrations and companies. Archiving is substantial, if the data privacy regulations accept registration of personal data by the one-stop government infrastructure.

E-payment, security of the document safe and the qualified signature for the e-documents require, that one eCard with eID and all functionality will be provided on the market. All Internet applications shall use it. No fraud is acceptable.

5 Job Card Architecture

Usually we think of online services for citizen, when we talk about e-government. But the administrative burden for enterprises requires e-government solutions, too. What enterprises complain mostly about the German bureaucracy is that public administrations demand in many cases employers to confirm the income of their personnel in the form of income certificates. 3 million enterprises print 60 million income certificates per year. To ease that burden a data pool was invented, where employers store income certificates for their employees monthly in encrypted form in a data flow already used for social security insurance means. It does not matter, if these certificates are needed or not. The encryption design allows to read the data records in this data pool only by the employees concerned. No other people or organisation can read the data and retrieve the certificates. The employees need an eCard or eID, to decrypt their personnel certificates.

If someone whose income data is stored in the pool applies for aid or subsidy, the agency responsible for aid and subsidy gets access to the data pool with the personal eCard or eID of the citizen. Thus the agency is able to read the personnel data records through the eCard or eID only at the moment, the citizen gives access explicitly.

Data Pool for Certificates of Employees

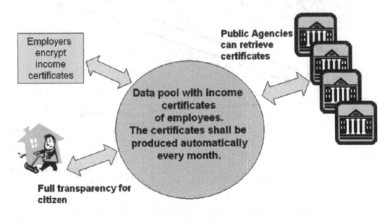

e 3: Job Card Architecture

The architecture is not as simple as the picture makes it look like. Sophisticated data privacy regulation and mechanisms are necessary to implement the architecture. A variety of eID techniques should support this technology to avoid that people needing aid and subsidy should invest money in costly eID cards. Electronic documents with qualified signatures of employers and – depending on the use – of employees and citizen are needed to document the data transferred in a reliable way. Citizen coming with these e-documents in printed form to an agency shall be served in much the same way like citizen using e-documents in electronic form.

Foreign authorities must understand and handle e-documents like a domestic agency at least within Europe. An infrastructure will be built for e-government concepts consisting of IMI, a document safe (with e.g. e-documents) infrastruture (provided e.g. by private Internet providers instead of public administrations) and an eID on signature cards, encryption cards and – hopefully – bankcards and health cards.

6 Secure Access to Federated E-Justice / E-Government (S.A.F.E.)

Having implemented all architectures mentioned above, there is still some functionality needed for e-government missing. Considering that in Europe a large number of distributed registration databases (for commerce, trade, etc.) and other applications are available and legally justified, the trusted, unified and standardised use is a challenge for IT architects. The solution is Distributed Identity Management for a highly secured single sign-on.

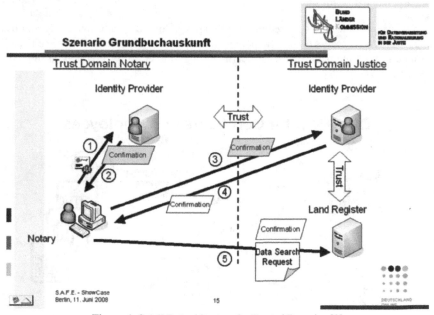

Figure 4: S.A.F.E. Architecture for Trusted Domains [3]

The numbers at the arrows describe the sequence of control flow to obtain the trust of the partner domain. Finally access is given to the target system, which is a land register in this example.

7 Conclusion

The progress of e-government is huge. Reliable, user-friendly and efficient e-government architectures are available. The implementation is begun. What remains uncertain is how citizen and enterprises accept the basic technologies underlying these architectures. Fact is, that only few enterprises use the full functionality of e-procurement. Currently e-signature is not much used, especially in its legally binding form of the qualified digital signature. But without these basic technologies a widespread use of the architectures mentioned above will not happen.

References

[1]   Decision of the Federal Government of Germany on June 25, 2008. To find the draft legislation search for "ELENA" at www.bundesdatenschutzbeauftragter.de

[2]   Kowalski, Bernd; eCard-API-Framework; presentation on the 2. Berliner signaturkonferenz on April 15, 2008.

[3]   Bund-Länder-Kommission für Datenverarbeitung und Rationalisierung in der Justiz; Secure Access to Federated E-Justice / E-Government (S.A.F.E.); Show Case, presentation in the Bundeshaus Berlin on June 11, 2008

Infrastructures and Middleware for the Application of eID Cards in eGovernment

Thomas Walloschke

Fujitsu Siemens Computers GmbH
thomas.walloschke@fujitsu-siemens.com

Abstract

Cross border eID interoperability is one of the main goals to meet the pan-European challenge. At the same time appropriate conformance to any requirements of flexibility, legal certainty as the case may be guaranteed future will be stipulated.

The German approach is based on an eGovernment Middleware concept – the eCard-API-Framework – which complies with these requirements with a maximum level of compliance, technical security and usability. On the other hand a European eID card driven concept has to be built on a European wide certificate service infrastructure as well.

All interoperability aspects of European Citizen Card (ECC) applications should be satisfactoribly including national secrecy obligations.

1 Introduction

European countries face a number of pan-European electronic identity – eID – challenges, which urgently call for cooperative solutions. Interoperability is an integral element of such solutions and a prerequisite for their success. Individual member states continue to be the front-line actors in dealing with eID solutions. However, in today's electronic identity environment, which recognizes no national boundaries, a state can any longer, effectively deal by its own individual efforts only.

On May 30, the European Commission (EC) started the pilot project STORK (Secure idenTity AcrOss BoRders LinKed) [IDABC-STORK] to ensure cross-border recognition of national electronic identity systems and enable easy access to public services in 13 member states (Austria, Belgium, Estonia, France, Germany, Italy, Luxembourg, Netherlands, Portugal, Slovenia, Spain, Sweden and the U.K.) of the European Union (EU) plus Iceland.

The EC project will enable EU citizens to prove their identity and use national eID systems throughout the EU, not just in their home country. The plan is to align and link these systems without replacing existing ones [LSP-STORK]. Recent experiences in several countries need to serve as evidence to the need for a broader-than-ever understanding of a global electronic identity.

The German government developed a set of platform-independent interfaces – the eCard-API-Framework [eCard-TR] – intending to support discretionary smart cards and facilitating their integration into various eID-applications [eCard-ISSE2007]. One of the main goals is provisioning to provide full interoperability of recent and upcoming identity and signatures technologies and to consort the variety of government projects which issue or use smart cards for authentication and signature purposes **[Kowa07]**.

On July 23, the Federal Cabinet started the German eID approach, the electronic Identity Card (Elektronischer Personalausweis or ePA) **[eID-Card]**, which will be introduced in 2010. The plan is to align and link this eID Card to the eCard-API-Framework as a security infrastructure to enable manifold online and offline services.

As there are similar requirements for handling electronic identities in other European countries, the Federal Office for Information Security (Bundesamt für Sicherheit in der Informationstechnik, BSI) decided to introduce the eCard-API-Framework as German STORK technology for cross-border processes as well – to provide a basis for a comprehensive eID-framework for Europe and beyond.

Last but not least there is a need to talk about PKI strategies and deployment. After many years of half-starts, PKI is now in its second implementation phase. Facts concerning recent real life implementation have to be discovered and the chicken and egg problem between technology and services has to be overcome.

2 Interoperability Strategy

As the last years ISSE the eCard-API-Framework report **[eCard-ISSE2007]** pointed out technical and theoretical aspects, this year growing emphasis is being placed on controlling the completely implemented framework itself. Launching the eCard-API-Framework is a significant cornerstone for the European security market.

This chapter insofar provides a brief overview of the global interoperability strategy and in subchapter 2.1 particularly concentrates on the middleware aspects of the global interoperability of the eCard-API-Framework based on its politically started eCard-Strategy-Projects. Subchapter 2.2 provides an overview of infrastructures such as EU-wide PKI strategies and deployments.

2.1 Middleware: eCard-API-Framework

The middleware concept eliminates the need of special knowledge in cryptology, eID or signature technology as it integrates a security layer of the operating system. As the EU showed in 2007 **[IDABC-SIG2007]** the pan-European concept recommended an eSignature framework model (Fig. 1):

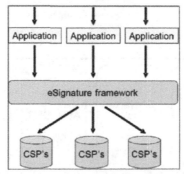

Fig. 1: EU eSignature framework model 2007 **[IDABC-FIG1]**

2.1.1 eCard-API Concept

The model is reflected in an eCard-API-Framework. The different application layer concepts were described in the 2007 eCard-API-report **[eCard-ISSE2007]** and – in short – allow processing every established signature card and card reader.

For the usage of the German eID Card (ePA) and the eHealth Card (eGK) the features were extended.

Fig. 2 shows the context of the eCard physical Card Projects and the logical Integration Projects.

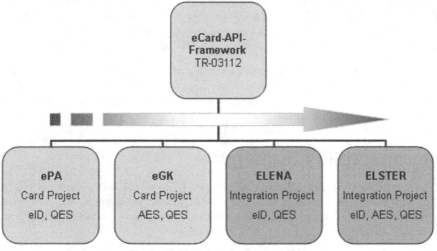

Fig. 2: eCard-Projects in Germany 2008

As the eCard-API-Framework's functionalities will extend constantly over the next years it will look
like in Fig. 3.

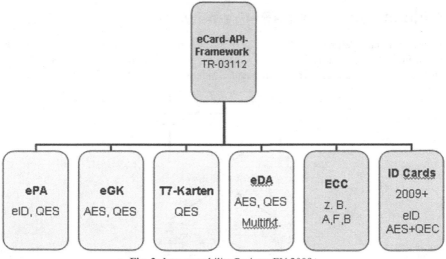

Fig. 3: Interoperability Projects EU 2009+

2.1.2 eCard-API Technology [GER-STORK]

The eCard-API Framework defines a four-layer-architecture that is visualized in Fig. 4:

- Application Layer,
- Identity Layer,
- Service Access Layer,
- Terminal Layer.

The Application Layer may comprise different applications which access the services provided by the eCard-API-Framework in order to access eID-functions, secure electronic documents by means of (advanced) electronic signatures and/or encryption or to obtain access to some electronic service provided by a service provider. For instance, a web page granting access to eGovernment services and requiring a strong authentication operates within the Application-Layer.

The Identity Layer provides functions to establish secure sessions (e.g. using RFC2246) and secure documents in various formats by means of (advanced) electronic signatures (e.g. according to ETSI-101733 or ETSI-101903) and encryption (e.g. using RFC3369 or XML-Enc). The functions for generating and verifying electronic signatures are closely aligned to the recently finalized standard **[OASIS-DSS]**.

The Service Access Layer provides the basic authentication functionality using arbitrary smart cards. The authentication services are accessed using the "Service Access Interface" which is currently standardized in ISO24727-3 and prCEN15480-3. In order to be able to use arbitrary identity tokens – especially tokens which fail to provide a standardized cryptographic information application according to ISO7816-15 – the generic card services will use the XML-based CardInfo-structure introduced in **[HOW-24727]** and currently discussed in CEN TC 224 WG 15.

The Terminal Layer provides a homogeneous interface for arbitrary card terminals, which is currently standardized in prCEN15480-3 and ISO24727-4. While the basic functions of this interface are similar to PC/SC this interface also allows to use more sophisticated interface devices according to SICCT-v1.1 **[SICCT]** for example supporting multiple slots (for contact-based and/or contactless cards) as well as functional units (e.g. display, keypad, biometric sensors).

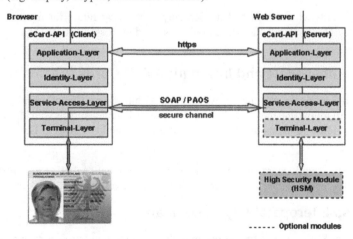

Fig. 4: eCard-API-Framework with ePA scenario **[GER-STORK]**

2.1.3 National eID Card: ePA – Elektronischer Personalausweis

One of the major eID Card projects in Germany is the integration work of the electronic Identity Card into the eCard-API-Framework.

The national security requirements which are described in [EAC-TR] had to be considered and will be evaluated within the scope of the security certification procedure duties, which have been started now in the BSI. This process will be ongoing in 2008.

2.1.4 National eHealth Cards

The German healthcare department is introducing smart card technology [ISO7816-4], [ISO7816-4] for the residents of Germany: the "Elektronische Gesundheitskarte" or eGK. The electronic chip in these cards will contain personal data, insurance details and medical history records.

These smart cards can easily be read and processed with the eCard-API-Framework already.

2.1.5 ELENA (ELektronischer EntgeltNAchweis)

The eCard-API-Middleware supports the electronic remuneration statement application system [ACT-ELENA] as well in accordance with the full set of all established signature cards, the ePA and the eGK.

2.1.6 ELSTER (ELektronische STeuerERklärung)

As the electronic tax declaration transmission system [ACT-ELSTER] needs identification and encryption facility there is a wide field for the eCard-API-Middleware to support most tax applications.

2.1.7 Signature Cards

The eCard-API-Middleware supports all established signature cards and card readers.

2.1.8 eDA Cards (Elektronischer DienstAusweis)

Personal service cards will be launched in Germany in the near future for nearly all employees of Public authorities. These smart cards can easily be read and processed with the eCard-API-Framework already.

2.1.9 EU Member State and International ID Cards

The volume of the European eID market will extend within the next months and years. Further EU Member States will follow and introduce ID Cards with eID-Functionality as well. This flexible middleware approach will help to overcome the obstacle of interoperability efforts in EU and other countries as well.

The eCard-API-Framework coordinates the individual needs of national eID Card workflow specifications as well as the "normal" concurrent signature card challenges as an everyday task.

2.1.10 Cross-Interoperability in Germany

The German eCard-Strategy joins the corresponding technology and project requirements with the – now implemented – eCard-API-Middleware as follows (Fig. 5):

	eID	AES	QES	ELENA	ELSTER
ePA	x		x	x	x
eGK		x	x	x	x
T7-Card		x	x	x	x
eDA		x	x	x	x
ID Cards	x	x	x		

Fig. 5: Examples of eCard-Cross-Interoperability

2.2 Infrastructures

2.2.1 European PKI-Structures

In 2007 the EC identified and analysed the similarities and differences in the use of electronic identities and signatures in eGovernment applications in each member state in both, the legal context and the technical implementation aspects. They prepared conclusions and recommendations on addressing interoperability issues related to the mutual recognition of electronic identities and signatures for eGovernment applications/services **[IDABC-SIG2007]**.

There is a clear need for applications to identify the signatory of a document in order to start a workflow processing the document. Another mean of achieving CA trustworthiness while solving issues raised by the list of supervised CSP, is to implement the European IDA Bridge/Gateway CA (EBGCA) model **[IDABC-EBGCA]** that uses the centralised administrative structure of a bridge and distributes trust using to both, cross-certifications and Certificate Trust Lists.

Indeed the EBGCA project proved that the concept of a Bridge/Gateway CA is the most suited to achieve CA trustworthiness at a European level.

The EU recommendations are shown in Fig 6 and Fig 7.

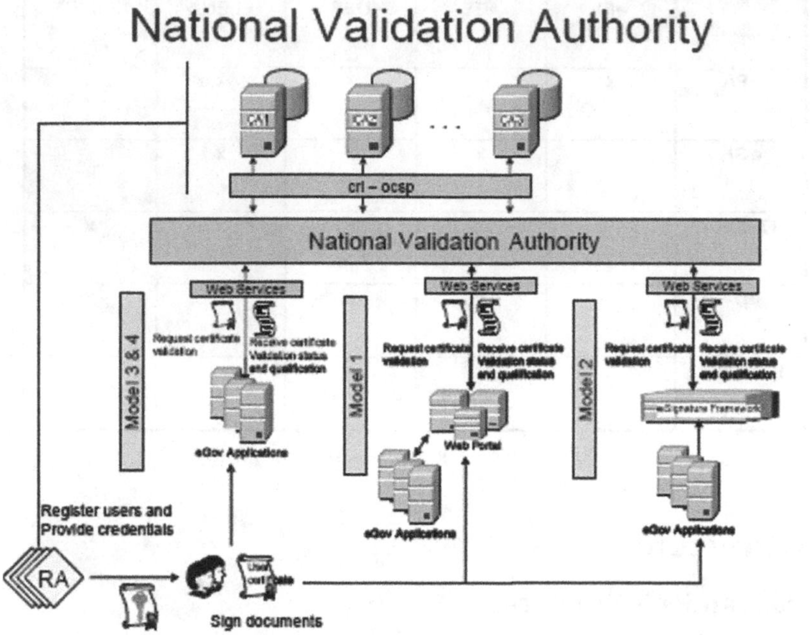

National Validation Authority

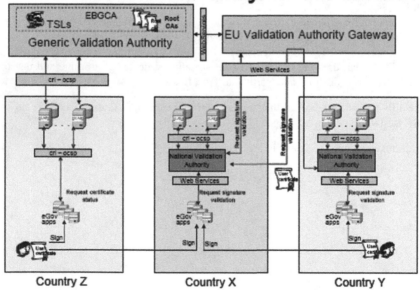

Fig. 6: National Validation Authority **[IDABC-FIG2]**

Validation Authority Federation

Fig. 7: Validation Authority Federation **[IDABC-FIG3]**

2.2.2 eSignature Framework Model

As mentioned in **[IDABC-SIG2007]** very often, eSignature frameworks (Fig. 1) have been introduced in the member states to allow for rapid deployment of eGovernment applications by providing eSignature primitives such as certificate validation, card access. Such framework may results from national legal provisions or national initiatives to support a specific eSociety policy (e.g. introduction of the eID Card or the new eCard-API-Framework).

3 Large-scale Pilot Projects and eGovernment Services – the European Approach

The problem areas of electronic identity – eID – and pan-European online public procurement are tackled at European level by two proposed LSPs supported by the Competitiveness and Innovation Programme (CIP) and particularly by the ICT Policy Support Programme managed by DG INFSO **[IDABC-LSP]**.

Secondly the recent European concept starts the development of eGovernment services and also focuses on the development of the European Interoperability framework and its future direction **[IDABC-EUeGov]**.

3.1 STORK

The STORK LSP consortium is facing the challenge around eID interoperability and works out solutions which provide cross-border recognition of eID and authentication across Europe.

3.1.1 German eID Solution

The eCard strategy of the German Government aims at providing a common strategic framework for a number of eGovernment initiatives in the areas of user identification, social security information and health insurance services. It was devised by the Ministry of Economics and Technology and the Ministry of the Interior and is supported by the Ministries of Health and Finance.

The common strategy coordinates the different federal eCard initiatives (such as the eHealth insurance card, the eID card, ELENA and ELSTER) as well as the access to important databases and services in the areas of social security and tax procedures. Among other things, it defines common standards in order to foster the development and take-up of transactional eGovernment services and to maximise efficiency gains and cost savings. The eCard-API Framework defines a simple and platform-independent interface to provide interoperability between eGovernment services and the various smart cards, such as the eHealth card and eID Card.

The introduction of the German eID Card aims at the enhancement of the traditional German ID card with electronic functionalities in order to face upcoming challenges in eGovernment and eBusiness areas in the 21st century.

The integrated contactless microcontroller provides three main applications (IAS Services):
- Electronic Machine Readable Travel Document (ICAO Application),
- Citizen Identification and Authentication (eID Application),
- Qualified Electronic Signature (eSign Application).

The ICAO Application holds the electronic MRZ data, the facial image and optionally the fingerprint data that are protected by Extended Access Control (EAC) according to TR-03110v2 **[EAC-TR]**. The eID Application provides additional data groups holding for instance family name and given name, academic title, date and place of birth, eye colour, height, place of residence, nationality and artistic name. The data are protected by modular EAC according to prEN14890 and a PIN only known to the card holder. Hence, in order to get access to the data and to identify a citizen, the citizen's consent (PIN) and an appropriate Authorization Certificate is needed. These certificates are issued and distributed in the same way as in the EAC-PKI known from the ICAO Application. The eSign Application implements an electronic signature in accordance to the German Signature Law. It is not part of the core functionality of the ePA and can be loaded onto the card at the citizen's expense.

In summary, beside the already accepted ICAO Application within the EU, the ePA serves as a secure data container granting access to the data after a successful mutual authentication and the establishment of a secure channel. The personal data are not centrally stored due to German privacy regulations. The 1:1 connection between an eService Provider and the ePA is realized by an appropriate middleware installed on both entities according to the eCard-API specification **[eCard-TR]** The realization basically does not take Application or ID Provider into account.

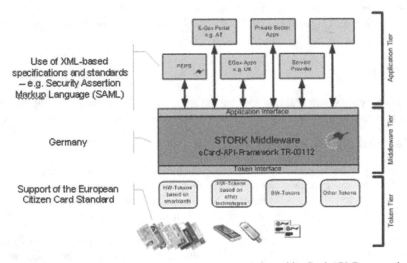

Fig. 8: eCard-Cross-Border-Project – German eID-Solution with eCard-API-Framework
[GER-STORK]

3.1.2 eID Trends across Europe

Currently different trends can be seen across Europe **[IDABC-LSP]**:
- Belgium, Portugal and others favour an eID smart card.
- The Austria and Slovenia approach is based on virtual identification.
- The Anglo-Saxon model is based on other identification tools such as the passport.
- French personal data are centrally stored due to national regulations.

The implementation of an EU wide interoperable system for recognition of eID and authentication will enable business, citizens and government employees to use their national electronic identities in any Member State.

3.2 PEPPOL

A further important CIP large-scale project currently under negotiation with the Commission is PEP-POL [IDABC-LSP] which is focused on pan-European Public Procurement Online. With the participation of Austria, Denmark, Finland, France, Germany, Hungary, Iceland, Italy, Norway and the UK, the PEPPOL consortium has good representation across Europe.

The LSP will focus on eSignatures, Virtual Company Dossier, eCatalog, eOrdering, eInvoicing, Consortium Management, Awareness Training and Consensus building, Solutions Architecture Design and Validation.

3.3 Services Directive

The implementation of the Services Directive [IDABC-EUeGov] was highlighted as a case in point where the various ICT aspects should have been developed sooner. The Directive's three-year implementation period ends in December 2009 and involves a complex series of actions by member states including the creation of points of single contact – the one-stop shop to centralise cross border information and services for users. All member states are currently trying to implement the Directive and are battling with electronic barriers.

The challenge is Article 8 of the Directive which relates to electronic processes for completing formalities and procedures. There is also an obligation to promote administrative simplification (Art. 5) and not impose further barriers for other EU citizens. The preliminary results of a stocktaking study on the implementation of Article 8 show that there has been a low take-up of electronic means in member states.

There are still a number of remaining issues concerning interoperability and there are indeed at lot of elements that have to be put in place before we can use electronic means.

3.4 Formal Relationship

Nevertheless, so far, we observe still missing formal relations between STORK, PEPPOL [IDABC-LSP], the Services Directive [IDABC-EUeGov] and the EBGCA [IDABC-EBGCA]. It would be interesting in analyzing a correlated roadmap for these projects, with clear terms and outputs, with visible relations between them.

The implementation of the eCard-API-Framework in every of these projects could be an opportunity to set up the dedicated technical coordination authority for eID and signature requirements.

4 Conclusion

In conclusion it could be pointed out that the eCard-API-Framework [eCard-TR] is an excellent solution for the pan-European eID interoperability challenge. The eCard-API-Framework technology will help to build and promote a coherent EU eID market. Drawing a parallel with these successes makes very optimistic for the development of a European eID market.

Sooner rather than later opportunities will emerge in the security domain and will lead us to new major national and EU European eID-interoperability programmes.

Acronyms

CSP	Certificate Service Provider
PKI	Public Key Infrastructure
ePA	Elektronischer Personalausweis, electronic ID Card, national ID document, [ACT-ePA]
eGK	Elektronische Gesundheitskarte, electronic Health Card (eHC)
ELENA	Elektronischer Entgeltnachweis, electronic remuneration statement application system [ACT-ELENA]
ELSTER	Die ELektronische STeuerERklärung, electronic tax declaration transmission system [ACT-ELSTER]
eDA	Elektronischer Dienstausweis, Personal service card for nearly all employees of Public authorities
ECC	European Citizen Card [IDABC-STORK]
AES	Advanced Electronic Signature, [ACT-1999/93/EC], [ACT-SigG]
QEC	Qualified Electronic Certificate, [ACT-1999/93/EC]
QES	Qualified Electronic Signature, [ACT-SigG]
eID	Electronic Identity
ICAO	International Civil Aviation Organization
MRZ	Machine Readable Zone

References

[Kowa07] B. Kowalski: A survey of the eCard-Strategy of the German Federal Government, (in German), Proceedings of BIOSIG 2007, GI Lecture Notes in Informatics, 2007

[eCard-TR] Federal Office for Information Security: eCard-API-Framework – Technical Directive BSI-TR-03112, v1.1, 2008

[EAC-TR] Federal Office for Information Security: EAC – Technical Directive BSI-TR-03110, v2.0, 2008

[eCard-ISSE2007] Dr. Detlef Hühnlein, Manuel Bach: From the eCard-API-Framework towards a comprehensive eID-framework for Europe, ISSE 2007

[IDABC-STORK] European eGovernment Services (IDABC): Large Scale Pilots show the way forward, via http://ec.europa.eu/idabc/en/document/7555, 2008

[LSP-STORK] European Commission: Project factsheet : eID – easier access to public services across the EU, via http://ec.europa.eu/information_society/activities/egovernment/implementation/ict_psp/doc/eid_factsheet.pdf, 2008

[GER-STORK] German STORK Consortium: German input to the study on eID so-lutions for WP 5, 2008

[eID-Card] The Federal Ministry of the Interior of the Federal Republic of Germany: Kabinett beschließt neuen Personalausweis mit Internetfunktion, via http://www.bmi.bund.de/cln_012/nn_122688/Internet/Content/Nachrichten/Pressemitteilungen/2008/07/e__Personalausweis.html, 2008

[IDABC-SIG2007] European eGovernment Services (IDABC): Preliminary Study on Mutual Recognition of eSignatures for eGovernment applications, ENTR/05/58-SECURITY/SC1/D2&D3, v3.0, 16-October-2007

[IDABC-EBGCA] European eGovernment Services (IDABC): Bridge/Gateway Certi-fication Authority, via http://europa.eu.int/idabc/en/document/2318, 2004

[IDABC-LSP] European eGovernment Services (IDABC): Large-Scale Pilots show the way forward, SYNeRGY, April 2008, ISSUE 10, http://ec.europa.eu/idabc/servlets/Doc?id=30895, 2008

[IDABC-EUeGov] European eGovernment Services (IDABC): European eGovernment Services many valuable lessons learned through IDABC projects, SYNeRGY, April 2008, ISSUE 10, http://ec.europa.eu/idabc/servlets/Doc?id=30895, 2008

[ISO7816-4] ISO/IEC: Identification cards — Integrated circuit cards — Part 4:Organization, security and commands for interchange, ISO7816-4, Version 2005-01-15

[ISO7816-15] ISO/IEC: Information technology : Identification cards – Integrated circuit(s) cards with contacts, Part 15: Cryptographic information application, ISO/IEC 7816-15, 2003

[OASIS-DSS] OASIS: Digital Signature Service Core Protocols, Elements, and Bindings, Version 1.0, OASIS Standard, via http://docs.oasisopen.org/dss/v1.0/oasis-dss-core-spec-v1.0-os.pdf

[HOW-24727] D. Hühnlein, M. Bach: How to use ISO/IEC 24727-3 with arbitrary Smart Cards, in C. Lambrinoudakis, G. Pernul, A.M. Tjoa (Eds.): TrustBus 2007, LNCS 4657, SS. 280–289, 2007.

[SICCT]   TeleTrusT: SICCT-Spezifikation, Version 1.1.0, 2006-12-19, via http://www.teletrust.de/fileadmin/ files/publikationen/Spezifikationen/SICCT_Spezifikation_1.10.pdf

[IDABC-FIG1] European eGovernment Services (IDABC): Preliminary Study on Mutual Recognition of eSignatures for eGovernment applications, Model 2: common eSigna-ture framework model, p. 51, ENTR/05/58-SECURITY/SC1/D2&D3, v3.0, 16-October-2007

[IDABC-FIG2] European eGovernment Services (IDABC): Preliminary Study on Mutual Recognition of eSignatures for eGovernment applications, National Validation Au-thority, p. 135, ENTR/05/58-SECURITY/ SC1/D2&D3, v3.0, 16-October-2007

[IDABC-FIG3] European eGovernment Services (IDABC): Preliminary Study on Mutual Recognition of eSignatures for eGovernment applications, European Validation Au-thority Gateway, p. 136, ENTR/05/58-SECURITY/SC1/D2&D3, v3.0, 16-October-2007

[ACT-ePA] The Federal Ministry of the Interior of the Federal Republic of Germany: Entwurf eines Gesetzes über Personalausweise und den elektronischen Identitätsnachweis sowie zur Änderung weiterer Vorschriften, via http://www.bmi.bund.de/Internet/Content/Common/Anlagen/Gesetze/Gesetzentwurf__ePersonalaus-weis,templateId=raw,property=publicationFile.pdf/Gesetzentwurf_ePersonalausweis.pdf, 2008

[ACT-ELSTER] Verordnung über die elektronische Übermittlung von für das Be-steuerungsverfahren erforderlichen Daten (Steuerdaten-Übermittlungsverordnung – StDÜV), via http://www.gesetze-im-internet.de/ bundesrecht/std_v/gesamt.pdf, 2003

[ACT-ELENA] The Federal Ministry of Economics and Technology: Gesetz über das Verfahren des elektronischen Entgeltnachweises (ELENA-Verfahrensgesetz), via http://www.bmwi.de/BMWi/Redaktion/PDF/Ges-etz/gesetzentwurf-verfahren-des-elektronischen-entgeltnachweises-elena,property=pdf,bereich=bmwi, sprache=de,rwb=true.pdf , 2008

[ACT-SigG] The Federal Ministry of Economics and Technology: Gesetz über Rahmenbedingungen für elektronische Signaturen (Signaturgesetz – SigG), via http://www.bundesnetzagentur.de/media/archive/2247. pdf , 2001

[ACT-1999/93/EC] European Parliament: Community framework for electronic signa-tures, Directive 1999/93/ EC, via http://europa.eu/scadplus/leg/en/lvb/l24118.htm, 2000

Securing Contactless Chips with PACE

Dennis Kügler

Federal Office for Information Security
Godesberger Allee 185-189
53175 Bonn, Germany
Dennis.Kuegler@bsi.bund.de

Abstract

PACE (Password Authenticated Connection Establishment) is a cryptographic protocol that was developed to provide a secure knowledge-based authentication mechanism for contactless chips. The problems that are inherent to (but not limited to) contactless chips are described and PACE as a solution based on cryptographic tools is sketched. Finally, it is shown how to use PACE together with traditional short PINs of 4-6 digits as access control mechanism for contactless chips withstanding denial-of-service attacks.

1 Introduction

Compared to contact-based chips, contactless chips have certain advantages but also some disadvantages. The durability of contactless chips is clearly the most attractive advantage and their most annoying disadvantage is skimming, due the lack of control as the card holder does not have to insert a card in a reader to make use of the chip. Furthermore, eavesdropping on the communication between chip and reader is also often considered as problematic.

Those disadvantages are however not new at all, they are not even inherent to contactless chips as the same problems are similarly present in contact-based chips:

- While possession of the card is required for contact-based chips, it is not necessary for contactless chips, e.g. chips compliant to ISO14443 may be activated in a distance of approximately 10-20 cm and thus an authentication mechanism is required to prevent skimming. Nevertheless, contact-based chips usually also require authentication of the user to prevent misuse of e.g. a lost card.

- The possibility of eavesdropping on the communication is inherent to the technology used for contactless cards. For contact-based chips however, the problem does similarly exist, but is usually ignored. Moreover, the electromagnetic emission of a contact-based reader often is even higher than the emission of the predominant magnetic component of the field used for communication as defined by ISO 14443.

PACE was designed to advance the contactless technology by evading its disadvantages. This is accomplished by introducing appropriate cryptographic countermeasures. From a user perspective handling a contactless chip should be very similar to handling a contact-based chip using traditional security mechanisms commonly used for contact-based chips. The level of security provided is however much higher.

N. Pohlmann, H. Reimer, W. Schneider (Editors): Securing Electronic Business Processes, Vieweg (2008), 418-423

2 Password Authenticated Connection Establishment

PACE [BSI3110] is a cryptographic protocol to "amplify" a weak password to derive cryptographically strong keys used to establish an encrypted and integrity-protected channel. The protocol is based on an anonymous Diffie-Hellman key exchange authenticated by a password.

2.1 Diffie-Hellman Key Exchange

A Diffie-Hellman key exchange [DiHe76] consists of (at least) two parties, where each party randomly chooses a temporary ephemeral key pair based on pre-agreed domain parameters. The public keys are then exchanged and both parties compute the shared secret from their own private key and the public key of the other party. The shared secret is then used to derive symmetric session keys for encryption and integrity protection of further communication.

2.1.1 Man-in-the-Middle Attacks

While the Diffie-Hellman key exchange is secure against passive attacks, i.e. an attacker eavesdropping on the channel is not able to extract the shared secret and the derived session keys, it is vulnerable to active attack, i.e. man-in-the-middle attacks, where the attacker is in between the communicating parties and pretends to each party to be the other party.

To protect the key exchange against man-in-the-middle attacks, an authentication of the exchanged keys is required and a PKI-based authentication-mechanism is commonly used, i.e. the ephemeral public keys are signed and exchanged together with the corresponding signature certificate. Thus, using the PKI each party is able to determine the identity of it's communication partner and man-in-the-middle attacks are prevented.

2.1.2 Password-based Authentication

In some scenarios PKI-based authentication of ephemeral public keys is however impractical:
- The certificates and thus the identities of the communicating parties are in general exchanged in plaintext. Therefore, an attacker is able to profile users based on their locations and communication partners. Such attacks can be mitigated to a certain extent by postponing the authentication until a secure but unauthenticated channel has been established, e.g. the "Privacy Protocol" [prEN14890] uses this approach. This simple countermeasure however only protects against passive attackers.
- Each party must be able to validate the identity of the other party. This is often impossible as the identity of the communication partner is sometimes completely unknown. Especially in scenarios where chip cards are used, the identity of a reader not in possession of the card holder is usually difficult to find out.

An alternative to PKI-based authentication is password-based authentication, i.e. the exchanged ephemeral keys are authenticated by a pre-shared weak password, which is exchanged on a secure channel, e.g. by reading a barcode optically, by reading a password using OCR, or by entering a password on a keyboard.

Trivial approaches like sending the password in plaintext after securing the channel using an anonymous Diffie-Hellman key exchange, obviously do not work. It is also not advisable to use the password as key for a symmetric authentication mechnanism (MAC), as due to the low entropy of the password, brute-force attacks on the password become easily possible.

The first protocol that solves the problem was EKE [BeMe92]. For this "Encrypted Key Exchange" the password is used as key for a symmetric encryption of exchanged ephemeral public keys. One precondition for the security of this scheme is that the exchanged keys themselves do not contain any redundancy as this would allow brute-force attacks on the password. Unfortunately, for most Diffie-Hellman variants the underlying group structure implies such a redundancy.

Enhanced versions of EKE like SRP [Wu00] and PAK [BoKP00] optimize the usage of the symmetric cipher; instead of using a standard blockcipher, the encryption function is designed to be "compatible" to the used Diffie-Hellman group.

SPEKE [Jabl00] uses a slightly different approach: The password is used as parameter of the Diffie-Hellman group, in more detail, the password is used to derive a new generator of the group. This is in principle a kind of indirect encryption, while the public keys are exchanged in plaintext, the corresponding private keys can only be used if the correct generator is known.

2.2 PACE

The password-based schemes sketched above are patented and are at least in the original variant not suited to be implemented with elliptic curves. For a description of elliptic curve cryptography and the advantages see e.g. [BSI3111].

PACE is a new password-based scheme to authenticate a Diffie-Hellman key exchange, that was developed to be free from patents and suitable for elliptic curves.

The PACE protocol consists of the following steps:

1. The initiator randomly chooses a nonce and encrypts it with a symmetric blockcipher using a key derived from the password.

2. Both parties calculate a random generator based on the random nonce. This may be implemented as follows:

   a. Both parties randomly generate a shared ephemeral generator of the used group. This is usually implemented by a (first) Diffie-Hellman key exchange.

   b. Both parties calculate another generator based on a) the nonce and b) the ephemeral generator.

3. Finally, a (second) Diffie-Hellman key exchange based on the just calculated generator is used to calculate a shared secret, which is in turn used to derive session keys and to perform a mutual authentication.

3 Applications

PACE may be used for contactless but also contact-based chips to establish an authenticated and encrypted communication. In general PACE is intended to be used with a very short password.

3.1 PIN-Concept

Two types of passwords are distinguished for PACE:

- Card Password: The card password is printed/displayed on the card, i.e. it is a Card Access Number (CAN). This number may be machine readable and is only used to simulate the insertion of the card in a reader, i.e. only a reader that knows the CAN may establish a communication with the card.
- User Password: The user password is a secret number, also known as Personal Identification Number (PIN) that should only be known to the card holder.

PINs are commonly used with contact-based chips and are usually associated with a retry counter to prevent brute-force attacks on those very weak passwords (usually 4 to 6 digits). While PACE also associates the PIN with a retry counter, the CAN deliberately remains unprotected. In an optimal implementation the CAN would be a dynamically generated number displayed on the card and changed for every new connection. If a more static CAN is used, it becomes slightly easier for an attacker to succeed with the simulated insertion of the card, but as this does not allow the attacker to perform any further actions, this is only relevant for denial-of-service attacks.

3.2 Denial-of-Service

Not only contactless chips but also contact-based chips suffer from the problem that the PIN may be blocked by an attacker, which leads to a denial-of-service attack as the card holder is at least temporarily unable to use the card, i.e. upon unblocking of the PIN.

To block a PIN in terms of a denial-of-service attack, the attacker only has to get close enough to the chip, approximately 10 cm, and to decrease the retry counter to zero by entering a wrong PIN multiple times.

3.3 Delayed Blocking

To prevent attacks on the availability of the chip, the concept of delayed blocking is introduced by PACE. The retry counter RC is therefore defined as follows:

- RC>1: The PIN is operational and may be used normally.
- RC=1: The PIN is suspended. To resume a suspended PIN, both the CAN and then the PIN must be entered correctly within the same session.
- RC=0: The PIN is blocked. To unblock a blocked PIN, the mechanism provided by the chip must be used, e.g. entering the PUK (PIN unblock key) correctly.

Thus, within the state RC=1 the attacker must guess the CAN in a brute-force attack before blocking the PIN becomes possible. Even a short CAN therefore provides protection against denial-of service attacks when used in combination with a suitable delay in case of an incorrectly entered CAN.

Delayed blocking is shown in Figure 1.

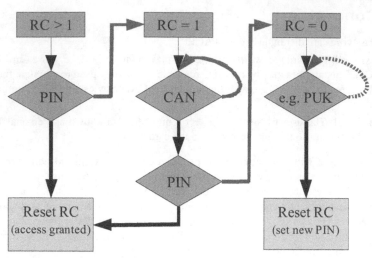

Figure 1: Delayed Blocking

3.4 PACE with CAN

Besides the just described delayed blocking PACE with CAN may also be used to simulate the insertion of the card to separate the actions "Insertion" and "Activation" (e.g. generation of an electronic signature), which requires the holder to submit the PIN over a secured channel established with PACE using the CAN.

Note however that if the CAN is known to the attacker, PACE with CAN allows to mount a man-in-the-middle attack. To prevent such attacks, an additional PKI-based authentication of at least on party over the channel protected by PACE is required.

If e.g. Terminal- and Chip Authentication according to [BSI3110] are used after PACE, both parties know from each other the following:

- The chip knows that it talks to an terminal authorized by the user and by the PKI and what data the terminal is authorized to access.
- The terminal knows that is communicates securely with the correct chip, i.e. with the chip intended by the user.

In [BSI3117] it is described how to use a contactless chip as secure signature creation device for qualified electronic signatures.

4 Conclusion

PACE allows to use traditional PIN-based authentication mechanisms with contactless chips. Compared to those traditional PIN-based mechanisms where the PIN is usually sent in plain over an unsecured channel, PACE provides much more security as the PIN is used to establish a secure channel and it is not required to exchange the PIN itself. Therefore, even contact-based chips may benefit from using PACE instead of the traditional mechanisms.

Literature

[BeMe92] Bellovin, S. M. und Merritt M.: "Encrypted Key Exchange: Password-Based Protocols Secure Against Dictionary Attacks". In Proceedings of the IEEE Symposium on Research in Security and Privacy, 1992.

[BoKP00] Boyko, V.; MacKenzie, P. und Patel, S.: "Provably Secure Password Authenticated Key Exchange Using Diffie Hellman". In Eurocrypt 2000 Proceedings.

[BSI3110] Bundesamt für Sicherheit in der Informationstechnik: "Advanced Security Mechanisms for Machine Readable Travel Documents – Extended Access Control, Version 2.0. BSI Technical Guideline TR-03110.

[BSI3111] Bundesamt für Sicherheit in der Informationstechnik: "Elliptic Curve Cryptography Based on ISO 15946". BSI Technical Guideline TR-03111.

[BSI3117] Bundesamt für Sicherheit in der Informationstechnik: "eCards mit kontaktloser Schnittstelle als sichere Signaturerstellungseinheit". BSI Technische Richtlinie TR-03117.

[DiHe76] Diffie, W. und Hellman, M. E.: "New Directions in Cryptography". In IEEE Transactions on Information Theory (22:6), 1976, Seiten 644-654.

[Jabl96] Jablon, D.: "Strong Password-Only Authenticated Key Exchange". In Computer Communication Review, ACM SIGCOMM, vol. 26, no. 5, Pages 5-26, 1996.

[pr14890] CEN: "Application Interface for Smart Cards used as Secure Signature Creation Devices", prEN14890.

[Wu00] T. Wu: "The Secure Remote Password Protocol". In Proceedings of the 1998 Internet Society Symposium on Network and Distributed Systems Security, 2000, Pages 97-111.

Index

C

D

E

F

G

H

I

Q

R

S

T

IT-Management und -Anwendungen

Ralf Buchsein | Frank Victor | Holger Günther | Volker Machmeier
IT-Management mit ITIL® V3
Strategien, Kennzahlen, Umsetzung
2., akt. und erw. Aufl. 2008. XII, 371 S. mit 93 Abb. und Online-Service Br.
(Edition CIO) EUR 39,90   ISBN 978-3-8348-0526-3

Gernot Dern
Management von IT-Architekturen
Leitlinien für die Ausrichtung, Planung und Gestaltung von Informationssystemen
2. verb. und erw. Aufl. 2006. XVI, 341 S. mit 151 Abb.
(Edition CIO) Br. EUR 49,90   ISBN 978-3-528-15816-3

Knut Hildebrand | Marcus Gebauer | Holger Hinrichs | Michael Mielke (Hrsg.)
Daten- und Informationsqualität
Auf dem Weg zur Information Excellence
2008. X, 415 S. mit 108 Abb.
Br. EUR 39,90   ISBN 978-3-8348-0321-4

Klaus-Rainer Müller | Gerhard Neidhöfer
IT für Manager
Mit geschäftszentrierter IT zu Innovation, Transparenz und Effizienz
2008. X, 187 S. mit 9 Abb. und Online-Service (Edition CIO)
Geb. EUR 49,90   ISBN 978-3-8348-0481-5

**VIEWEG+
TEUBNER**
Abraham-Lincoln-Straße 46
65189 Wiesbaden
Fax 0611.7878-400
www.viewegteubner.de

Stand Juli 2008.
Änderungen vorbehalten.
Erhältlich im Buchhandel oder im Verlag.

Understanding IT

Martin Ruckert
Understanding MP3
Syntax, Semantics, Mathematics, and Algorithms
2005. xiv, 250 pp. Softc. EUR 39,90   ISBN 978-3-528-05905-7

Klaus D. Niemann
From Enterprise Architecture to IT Governance
Elements of Effective IT Management
2006. xii, 232 pp. with 89 figs. and Online-Service. Softc. EUR 56,90
ISBN 978-3-8348-0198-2

Diffenderfer, Paul M.; El-Assal, Samir
Microsoft Dynamics NAV
Jump Start to Optimization
2., rev. Ed. 2008. XII, 304 pp. with 209 fig.
softc. EUR 49,90   ISBN 978-3-8348-0516-4

Heinrich Seidlmeier
Process Modeling with ARIS
A Practical Introduction
2004. XVI, 192 pp. and Online-Service
softc. EUR 49,90   ISBN 978-3-528-05877-7

**VIEWEG+
TEUBNER**

Abraham-Lincoln-Straße 46
65189 Wiesbaden
Fax 0611.7878-400
www.viewegteubner.de

Stand Juli 2008.
Änderungen vorbehalten.
Erhältlich im Buchhandel oder im Verlag.

IT–Sicherheit und Datenschutz

Heinrich Kersten | Gerhard Klett
Der IT Security Manager
Expertenwissen für jeden IT Security Manager - Von namhaften Autoren
praxisnah vermittelt
2., akt. und erw. Aufl. 2008. XII, 252 S. mit 21 Abb. (Edition <kes>)
Br. EUR 49,90   ISBN 978-3-8348-0429-7

Klaus-Rainer Müller
IT-Sicherheit mit System
Sicherheitspyramide - Sicherheits-, Kontinuitäts- und Risikomanagement -
Normen und Practices - SOA und Softwareentwicklung
3., erw. u. akt. Aufl. 2008. XXVI, 506 S. mit 38 Abb. mit Online-Service
Geb. EUR 74,90   ISBN 978-3-8348-00368-9

Norbert Pohlmann | Helmut Reimer (Hrsg.)
Trusted Computing
Ein Weg zu neuen IT-Sicherheitsarchitekturen
2008. VIII, 252 S. mit 49 Abb. Br. EUR 34,90   ISBN 978-3-8348-0309-2

Horst Speichert
Praxis des IT-Rechts
Praktische Rechtsfragen der IT-Sicherheit und Internetnutzung
2., akt. und erw. Aufl. 2007. XVIII, 368 S., mit 12 Abb. mit Online-Service
(Edition <kes>) Br. EUR 49,90   ISBN 978-3-8348-0112-8

**VIEWEG+
TEUBNER**

Abraham-Lincoln-Straße 46
65189 Wiesbaden   Stand Juli 2008.
Fax 0611.7878-400   Änderungen vorbehalten.
www.viewegteubner.de   Erhältlich im Buchhandel oder im Verlag.

Printed in the United States
By Bookmasters